Communication and Emotion

Essays in Honor of Dolf Zillmann

LEA COMMUNICATION SERIES

Jennings Bryant/Dolf Zillmann, General Editors

Selected titles in Communication Theory and Methodology Subseries (Jennings Bryant, series advisor) include:

Berger • *Planning Strategic Interaction: Attaining Goals Through Communicative Action*

Dennis/Wartella • *American Communication Research: The Remembered History*

Ellis • *Crafting Society: Ethnicity, Class and Communication Theory*

Greene • *Message Production: Advances in Communication Theory*

Heath/Bryant • *Human Communication Theory and Research: Concepts, Contexts, and Challenges, Second Edition*

Jensen • *Ethical Issues in the Communication Process*

Reese/Gandy/Grant • *Framing Public Life: Perspectives on Media and Our Understanding of the Social World*

Riffe/Lacy/Fico • *Analyzing Media Messages: Using Quantitative Content Analysis in Research*

Salwen/Stacks • *An Integrated Approach to Communication Theory and Research*

For a complete list of other titles in LEA's Communication Series, please contact Lawrence Erlbaum Associates, Publishers

Communication and Emotion

Essays in Honor of Dolf Zillmann

Edited by

Jennings Bryant
David Roskos-Ewoldsen
University of Alabama

Joanne Cantor
University of Wisconsin–Madison

LONDON AND NEW YORK

Camera ready copy for this book was provided by the editors.

First published 2003 by Lawrence Erlbaum Associates, Inc.

Published 2019 by Routledge
2 Park Square, Milton Park, Abingdon, Oxon OX14 4RN
52 Vanderbilt Avenue, New York, NY 10017

Routledge is an imprint of the Taylor & Francis Group, an informa business

Cover design by Kathryn Houghtaling Lacey

Library of Congress Cataloging-in-Publication Data

Communication and emotion : essays in honor of Dolf Zillmann / edited by Jennings Bryant, David Roskos-Ewoldsen, Joanne Cantor.
p. cm. (LEA communication series)
Includes bibliographical references and index.
ISBN 0-8058-4032-X (cloth : alk. paper)
1. Interpersonal communication. 2. Communication. 3. Emotions. I. Bryant, Jennings. II. Roskos-Ewoldsen, David R. III. Cantor, Joanne. IV. LEA's communication series.
BF637.C45 C6375 2003
302.2—dc21 2002192728
CIP

ISBN 13: 978-0-8058-5783-2 (pbk)
ISBN 13: 978-0-8058-4032-2 (hbk)

Contents

Dolf Zillmann (2000)

To
Valtra

SECTION I:

Introduction

1

A Brief Biography and Intellectual History of Dolf Zillmann

Jennings Bryant
David Roskos-Ewoldsen
University of Alabama

Joanne Cantor
University of Wisconsin—Madison

An abbreviated professional biography of Dolf Zillmann—a *Who's Who* entry, for example—might look something like this:

> **Dolf Zillmann.** *Nee* March 12, 1935, in Meseritz, Mark Brandenburg, Poland (then Germany). *Education:* Diploma, Architecture, Staatliche Werkakademie, Kassel, Germany, 1955; Diploma, Communication and Cybernetics, Hochschule für Gestaltung, Ulm, Germany, 1959; Ph.D., Communication and Social Psychology, University of Pennsylvania, 1969. *Family:* Wife: Valtra Zillmann, nee Riedle, born May 29, 1938; Children: Martin Zillmann, born May 10, 1959; Tomas Zillmann, born February 28, 1964. *Academic Employment:* Assistant Professor, University of Pennsylvania, 1969–1971; Associate Professor, Indiana University, 1971–1975; Professor of Communication and Psychology, Indiana University, 1975–1988; Director, Institute for Communication Research, Indiana University, 1974–1988; Professor of Communication and Psychology and Senior Associate Dean for Graduate Studies and Research, University of Alabama, 1989–2001. *Books: Hostility and Aggression* (1979), *Connections Between Sex and Aggression* (1984), *Selective Exposure to Communication* (1985), *Perspectives on Media Effects* (1986), *Pornography: Research Advances and Policy Considerations* (1989), *Responding to the Screen: Reception and Reaction Processes* (1991), *Media Effects: Advances in Theory and Research* (1994), *Media, Children, and the Family: Social Scientific, Psychodynamic, and Clinical Perspectives* (1994), *Connections Between Sexuality and Aggression, 2nd ed.* (1998), *Media Entertainment: The Psychology of Its Appeal* (2000), *Exemplification in Communication: The Influence of Case Reports on the Perception of Issues* (2000), and *Media Effects: Advances in Theory and Research, 2nd ed.* (2002).

Although accurate, such a synopsis provides no indication of the confluence of forces that helped create one of the most productive and influential scholars in the annals of communication inquiry, nor does it even begin to explain the unique qualities of the individual who undoubtedly generated more "name-brand" theories than anyone in the history of communication research. In this chapter we attempt to identify some of the intellectual streams that contributed to the scholarship of Dolf Zillmann, and we strive to "put a face" on the brilliant scholarship presented and discussed in the remainder of this volume on Communication and Emotion, which is devoted to our mentor and friend.

EARLY FORCES

Dolf Zillmann was born into a banking family in Meseritz, Mark Brandenburg, in what was then Germany but which became part of Poland after World War II. His father was a pacifist and refused to fight in the Hitler regime. Therefore, the senior Zillmann was made a civilian logistical officer and was separated from his family during the war. Toward the end of the war, the father, who never fit in because of his pacifism, was killed.

The remainder of the Zillmann family spent much of the war fleeing the Russians, ending up in the Hessen region of Germany, near Marburg: "It was just my mother, my sister Annemarie, and me. We left home, leaving everything behind, and fled without even a suitcase." Conditions were stark, food was scarce, and life was at peril.

Education during the war years was often an afterthought, because many of the eligible teachers were in combat, and others who allegedly were "teachers" really were Nazi propaganda specialists. In many instances, retirees who were too old for military duty were called on to teach in the primary and secondary schools. You had to want an education badly to receive one; some home schooling was essential, and much learning was self-acquired. Obviously Dolf Zillmann thrived in this challenging educational environment. In fact, by age 12 he had been "drafted" to assist in teaching in a secondary school by a retired teacher who had been brought back from Breslau to serve as school Director.

It is likely that these early educational experiences were critical in helping to create a Renaissance scholar who has consistently refused to accept disciplinary boundaries. To this day, the intellectual life of Dolf Zillmann is typified by independent, continuous learning without walls. So what if one has to delve deeply into psychophysiology or biochemistry to conduct theoretical research on emotion? That's not so different from teaching oneself math or history in order to teach those subjects to one's peers.

INITIAL HIGHER EDUCATION

Dolf Zillmann's initial higher education involved professional study in architecture at the Hochschule für Gestaltung in Ulm, Germany. Perhaps presciently, in light of Zillmann's later extensive research program in media effects, a television program played an important role in getting him to Ulm. In those days, people rarely had television sets in their homes. One day, while with friends in a café in Kassel, Zillmann saw on the café's television set Theodor Heuss, the President of Germany, and Walter Gropius, master of the Bauhaus tradition, dedicating some beautiful new buildings that were designed to house the New Bauhaus architecture school in Ulm. Prior to World War II, right-wing German authorities had closed the original Bauhaus school of design, craft, and architecture founded by Walter Gropius in 1919. After the war, Bauhaus traditions were continued with the founding under Max Bill of the Hochschule für Gestaltung (College for Design) in Ulm. When Zillmann watched the televised opening of this new school, designed to cultivate and spread the New Bauhaus ethos, his interest was captured. He immediately traveled to Ulm, where he had the good fortune of running into Max Bill himself. Professor Bill was excited about the school and told Zillmann, "Oh, this is an elite school, and we need people just like you!" Zillmann was sold, and he received a full fellowship with no obligations, which gave him ample time for diverse intellectual explorations during his architecture study.

Dolf Zillmann, in 1958, as a student of architecture at the Hochschule für Gestaltung in Ulm, Germany. Little did he know where his career would take him.

Zillmann considers this time at the Hochschule für Gestaltung at Ulm to have been a remarkable educational experience. The student body was incredibly cosmopolitan—"full of strange characters"—and the faculty and students were the elite of the New Bauhaus movement, including peers like Ulm design student Ferdinand Porsche. The breadth of scope and the complexity of the New Bauhaus education allowed Zillmann to combine his interests in aesthetics, mathematics, civil engineering, and the like and permitted him to explore many dimensions of his creativity in applied pursuits. For example, he was able to work with Max Bill and enter competitions for the design of major buildings in cities like Zurich. This study and its resultant diploma in architecture led Zillmann to many practical applications, like city planning for Esfahan, then the capital of Persia, and designing public buildings in various European cities. Zillmann specialized in public architecture (especially public libraries), because, as he put it, "with Europe in ruins, architects were in great demand." He also dabbled in residential architecture, but the sorts of compromises required in working with the future homeowners left him somewhat disenchanted with such endeavors.

Putting his architectural training to good use in Lausanne, Switzerland. Apparently for lack of satisfying challenges, he would soon be back at college, studying communication and related fields.

Dolf Zillmann's architectural education also contributed greatly to his future research in communication. Not only did this education enhance his interests and expertise in aesthetics, which ultimately contributed considerably to his research in entertainment theory, it also honed his skills in drafting and photography. As his legions of graduate students know, Zillmann often created and manipulated his own stimulus materials, including cartoons and photographs, and he did this with incredible precision as well as remarkable flair. This ability undoubtedly was facilitated by his early education and experiences in architecture.

As Dolf Zillmann's interest in architecture waned, he utilized his Geschwister-Scholl-Stiftung fellowship at the Hochschule für Gestaltung in Ulm to take additional coursework in industrial design, a specialized form of civil engineering. His graduate students in communication will all recognize the practical value of this degree: In addition to developing his own stimulus materials, Zillmann has also designed and created much of the technical apparatus for his experiments. This specialized instrumentation has lent an exceptional degree of precision and creativity to his research—in ways most of us cannot even begin to approximate.

From this education in design, Dolf Zillmann continued to migrate into cognate areas, beginning his foray into communication. In fact, the focus of the next iteration of his program at Ulm was on Communication and Cybernetics. Although Zillmann's host institution continued to be Ulm, his principal advisor and source of influence during this period was a professor at the University of Stuttgart, Max Bense, founder of what became known as the "Stuttgart School" of aesthetics and semiotics. A highly visible, and on occasion, politically controversial scholar and teacher, Bense had been a visiting professor at Ulm, where Zillmann first met him. Like Zillmann, Bense had delved deeply into a variety of disciplines during his formative years; in his case, physics, mathematics, chemistry, and geology had been major foci. All of these disciplines contributed to Bense's abstract theories of aesthetics, which were extremely mathematical in orientation. Zillmann recognized the value of additional study with Max Bense, and fortunately his fellowship allowed him to travel. Therefore, Zillmann became a special student in Bense's Institut für Wissenschaftstheorie (Institute for Theory of Science) at the University of Stuttgart, where he studied and began a lifelong friendship with Max Bense (who died in 1990). With Bense, Zillmann explored mathematical theories of aesthetics, semiotics, and information theory, among many other areas of inquiry.

During his formative explorations into communication theory, scholars at other universities also interested Zillmann, and he frequently traveled to study with them. For example, he became a special student at the University of Munich, where he took medical courses with Herbert Schober on the physiology of vision. During this period, he also benefited from encounters with Norbert Wiener, the founder of cybernetics, with Andreas Speiser, the founder of structure theory, and with many other leading scholars throughout Germany. Courses in theater, dance, anthropology, biology, sociology, and the like were worked into the smorgasbord that was Zillmann's curriculum in Communication and Cybernetics, which was integrated under the tutelage of Max Bense.

THE COHEN HOLDING GROUP

While Dolf Zillmann was at Ulm working on his diploma thesis in Communication and Cybernetics, one of his professors approached the renowned Swiss industrialist and media mogul Victor N. Cohen, while the Cohens were window-shopping in Zurich's famous Bahnhofstrasse. The professor interrupted Cohen, who owned the largest communications company in Switzerland, with a cold pitch that, as legend has it, went something like this: "Sorry, I am not exactly sober, but I know who you are, and I know what you do. You have to get Zillmann." Soon afterward, Dolf Zillmann got a call from Victor Cohen, inviting him to Zurich, although Zillmann really was not even in the job market. Cohen created a special position for Zillmann, something like an internal consultant, which gave Zillmann access to the entire Cohen Holding Group. His role was to study company initiatives and operations and give weekly lectures on topics that seemed important for Cohen's various undertakings.

Soon Zillmann was serving as scientific advisor to the advertising and marketing groups, to a film company, and to other divisions of the company. However, he was also made leader of a design group, with responsibilities for developing and testing new products and marketing campaigns for companies like General Electric, DuPont, Kodak, Ciba (now Novartis), Hoffmann-LaRoche, and General Motors. The new products were to be ergonomic in design, in adherence to the Bauhaus philosophy. The credo of the group was, "Give us a product, and we'll improve on it. We'll make it serve its function better." The design group conducted operations that ranged from basic product design through marketing and advertising and including evaluation, and Zillmann's group developed and employed a variety of innovative communication research techniques to facilitate the work of

Cohen Holding. During 1959–1965, when Zillmann was with the Cohen Holding Group, he directed teams developing products as diverse as prefabricated houses, vacuum cleaners, watches, kitchen appliances, electric razors, and containers. He also received several international patents for mechanical engineering aspects of these products and garnered international awards for excellence in both product and packaging design.

Zillmann (with bow tie) in the communication business, leading a planning session in the Cohen Holding Group in Zürich, Switzerland, sometime in the early 1960s.

In many ways, through his work with the Cohen Holding Group, Zillmann was pioneering practices in what now is commonly referred to as Integrated Communication. However, in this instance, the comprehensive communication plans included product or idea design, as well as marketing, advertising, and public relations.

A FOOT IN ACADEME

While working with Cohen, Dolf Zillmann continued to pursue academic interests. He taught at Ulm, assuming the paradoxical title of "permanent visiting professor." He also taught advertising and marketing seminars in some of the preeminent business schools in Switzerland. Zillmann often utilized specialized academic research seminars to help bridge gaps between industry and academe. For example, he planned an international campaign against smoking for the Swiss and German Ministries of Public Health in such a seminar, the results of which were presented at an International Conference on Preventive Medicine in Luzern, Switzerland, in 1964. And he developed an international sign system for pharmaceutical products for the Ciba Corporation between 1965 and 1968, also utilizing a research seminar in Experimental Semantics as a critical vehicle for idea development, implementation, and evaluation.

Wanting to have a foot in academe, during his years in the industry Zillmann taught persuasion and public-health campaigns as a visiting professor at his German alma mater. The photograph shows him in 1962 at the very beginning of his college teaching career.

Zillmann regularly received encouragement from scholars like Max Bense to begin a formal doctoral program. However, he found it very difficult to give up the rewarding life he had in Zurich, in which he had a hand in so many different and exciting aspects of the fusion of industry and academe. One aspect of this fusion was the creation of an Institute for Communication Research within the Cohen Holding Group, to which prominent scholars would be invited in for lectures and discussion with the employees.

Reaping the benefits of success in the communication industry, Zillmann in 1964 is setting sail on the Lake of Zürich. Who else sails dressed in a bow tie?! His former colleagues still wonder why he abandoned "the good life" for the austerity of a professorial career.

The first guest of the Institute for Communication Research was Percy Tannenbaum, one of the early facilitators of international communication research initiatives. Osgood, Suci, and Tannenbaum's *The Measurement of Meaning* (1957) had recently been published and was creating a stir in academe and industry alike. Moreover, Zillmann had pioneered a methodology called Aspect Analysis that was quite similar to the semantic differential utilized by Osgood et al. When someone at Cohen learned that Tannenbaum was in Greece, he was invited to Zurich to speak at the Institute for Communication Research.

As might be expected by those who know both Zillmann and Tannenbaum, they had many interests in common, and they found that they loved to argue over all aspects of their commonalities and differences. The offshoot of this intellectual kindredship was that Tannenbaum successfully recruited Zillmann for doctoral study in the United States. According to Zillmann, Tannenbaum was successful, in part, because "he was a very imposing guy, and he could handle me at the time, because my English was not very good then."

DOCTORAL STUDY IN THE STATES

Dolf Zillmann began doctoral study at the University of Wisconsin, where Percy Tannenbaum was on the communication and psychology faculties. Tannenbaum and Zillmann essentially formed what Zillmann called a "mutual catalytic society." As previously mentioned, both were interested in the dimensionality of semantics and had independently developed systems for assessing meaning through the use of scales, relying on factor analysis and related statistical procedures to probe for underlying structures. Another shared interest was in iconic communication. Both Zillmann and Tannenbaum had conducted systematic research on photography, using various aspects of the formal features of "visual language" to examine the impact of iconography, an interest Zillmann would continue throughout his career. Both were fascinated by various aspects of emotionality, a topic that would lead to a seminal jointly authored publication entitled "Emotional Arousal in the Facilitation of Aggression through Communication," published in *Advances in Experimental Social Psychology* in 1975. Moreover, both investigators obviously shared interests in the social and psychological impacts of media. However, Tannenbaum was never truly Zillmann's mentor in the way Bense had been. Instead, this was a collaboration between two mature investigators, although one was a professor and the other a doctoral student.

After the two had spent a year together in Madison, Tannenbaum accepted a faculty position at the University of Pennsylvania, and Zillmann received a Research Fellowship to continue his doctoral education in communication and social psychology at the University of Pennsylvania. It is a common misconception that Zillmann received his training at the Annenberg School; in reality, he did not take courses in that program. Most of his training was in psychology, especially with Albert Pepitone in aggression and Richard Solomon in motivation and emotion, and he studied with Aaron Katcher in the medical school. Katcher had an important influence on Zillmann, because it was from Katcher that Zillmann learned the principles and mechanics of physiological research, which left a prominent stamp on his work in communication and emotion. They also published early research on excitation-transfer theory together, so Katcher's role was pivotal in facilitating the physiological aspects of Zillmann's research program.

While at the University of Pennsylvania, Zillmann also taught courses in animal communication, quantitative semantics, statistics, and research methods. Moreover, much of Zillmann's research at Pennsylvania was on cybernetics and computer applications. One of his early English-language journal publications was entitled "The Sequential Expansion of a Decision Model in a Spatial Context," published in *Environment and Planning* in 1969, which presented the implications of a computer model of emotional "panic" behavior. During this period Zillmann also received a National Science Foundation (NSF) grant to develop advanced statistical computer programs, including various sophisticated analysis of variance routines, as well as to develop unique programs in Chi-Square analysis and other nonparametric statistical techniques. Zillmann's doctoral students from the 1970s are convinced that the elegance and utility of those programs has yet to be matched by statistical packages such as SPSS and SAS.

The dissertation committee that Zillmann pulled together at the University of Pennsylvania was representative of the breadth of his interests. Percy Tannenbaum served as chair, and other members were Albert Pepitone, Aaron Katcher, Larry Gross, and Sol Worth. His 1969 dissertation was entitled

Zillmann started his academic career in communication at his American alma mater, the University of Pennsylvania, in 1969. The photograph shows him in a faculty meeting at the Annenberg School of Communication. From left to right are professors Larry Gross, Klaus Krippendorf, Dolf Zillmann, Percy Tannenbaum, and George Gerbner.

"Emotional Arousal as a Factor in Communication-Mediated Aggressive Behavior," and it led to the first published article on excitation-transfer theory: "Excitation Transfer in Communication-Mediated Aggressive Behavior," published in the *Journal of Experimental Social Psychology* in 1971. With this publication, his American communication career was fully launched.

AN INITIAL PROFESSORIAL APPOINTMENT

Between 1969 and 1971, Zillmann was an Assistant Professor in the Annenberg School for Communication at the University of Pennsylvania. He continued teaching many of the same courses he taught as a graduate student, and he obtained grants from the NSF to support the computer generation of mathematical structures for the advanced analysis of variance, and from the National Institute of Mental Health for the support of research into the effects of exposure to portrayals of aggressive and sexual behaviors.

Dolf Zillmann during his early years at Penn. The blackboard shows that excitation-transfer theory was in the making.

THE BLOOMINGTON YEARS

In 1971, Dolf Zillmann accepted an Associate Professor appointment at Indiana University, and the Zillmann family relocated from the urban East to the heart of the American Midwest—Bloomington, IN. This was to prove to be a long and productive sojourn, as Zillmann remained on the IU faculty as Associate Professor (1971–1975) or Professor (1975–1988) of Communication, Professor of Psychology (1979–1988), and Professor of Semiotics (1981–1988) for a total of 17 years. During that period, Zillmann also served as Founding Director of the Institute for Communication Research (1974–1988), Director of the Interdisciplinary Doctoral Program in Mass Communication (1974–1976), Director of the Graduate Program in Communication (1979–1980), and Department Chair in Telecommunication (1979–1980).

The Indiana years were crammed with prodigious programmatic empirical efforts in various aspects of communication and emotion, including NSF-supported research on diverse aspects of excitation-transfer theory, aggression, pornography, humor, suspense, sports, and so forth. Essentially Zillmann served as research team leader as well as mentor for a revolving cast of eager doctoral students who benefited greatly from his tutelage and from the flexible research facility that was the Institute for Communication Research (ICR). Very few unassuming Tudor houses ever

Zillmann's initial support group at Indiana University, Jennings Bryant and Joanne Cantor, during a most productive research period. Yes, we looked like this in 1973.

hosted and facilitated as much research activity as did this jerry-rigged laboratory facility, whose internal structure was frequently altered to accommodate new research protocols. So productive was his research group during these Indiana years that many of the mass communication doctoral students who worked as ICR Research Assistants with Zillmann graduated with several articles already published in prestigious journals, as well as with numerous other manuscripts "in press." Naturally, other preeminent communication programs often hired these fledgling scholars when they graduated with their C.V.'s engorged by collaboration with their incredibly productive mentor. A number of these students have become leading lights in communication scholarship, and their students—Zillmann's intellectual grandchildren—are now reaching prominence throughout the academy.

Zillmann caricatured by doctoral students as the wizard of excitation transfer. The text on the book he holds is "Violence, Erotica, and You"; that on the plate by the fire is "Arousal for Fun."

In addition to generating a plethora of journal articles, during the Bloomington years, Zillmann crafted a number of distinguished chapters and books that essentially defined several domains of research in communication and emotion: entertainment theory, mood management theory, selective exposure, excitation-transfer theory, disposition theory, anatomy of suspense, misattribution theory of humor, massive-exposure media effects, coition as emotion, sportsfanship, rhetorical questions and persuasion, three-factor theory of emotion, empathy theory, connections between sex and aggression, and others. Remarkably, all of these theories and their attendant research traditions are indelibly associated with the name Dolf Zillmann, and all had their nexus in the hills of Monroe County, Indiana, during the less-than-two-decade period of Zillmann's service to Indiana University.

BAMA BOUND

During 1987–1988, Zillmann was a Visiting Fellow at Wolfson College of Oxford University in England. This was a time of writing and reflection; it also proved to be the prelude to a move to Alabama. In 1989, Zillmann joined the University of Alabama as Professor of Communication and Psychology and Senior Associate Dean for Graduate Studies and Research in what was to become the College of Communication and Information Sciences. His primary administrative assignment was to launch a new

In 1983, with his German mentor, Max Bense (at right), and Bense's wife, Elisabeth Walther (best known for her biography of Charles Sanders Peirce), in Suzette near Avignon in France. In veneration of Peirce, Bense's home was christened Maison Milford (Milford, MA, being Peirce's birth place).

doctoral program in mass communication. Between 1989 and 2001, Zillmann led that program to national prominence, and in 2001 he received the University of Alabama's highest award, the Burnum Distinguished Faculty Award, in recognition of his distinguished and outstanding service.

The Alabama sojourn was also a period of increasing internationalization of the Zillmann research program, as he developed a collaborative venture between Alabama and the University of Klagenfurt in Austria, while serving as a Fulbright Professor in Klagenfurt in 1991–1992. He also served as Visiting Professor at the University of Hannover and at the University of Amsterdam. These international appointments led to productive collaborations with a number of European scholars. Moreover, several European students migrated to Alabama to undertake graduate education under Zillmann's tutelage, and distinguished European professors came to Alabama for postdoctoral study with Zillmann. This was also a period in which Zillmann galvanized his international stature by giving numerous keynote addresses at prestigious international research symposia or conferences.

The Benses on a return visit to the Zillmann's summer home in the mountains of North Carolina, in 1989. At right is Valtra Zillmann.

While at Alabama, Zillmann taught a number of specialized research seminars in topics of interest to him, such as Sports in the Media, Humor and Comedy, Effects of Erotica, Effects of Popular Music, News and the

Perception of Social Reality, and Psychology of Dramatic Exposition. These seminars served as vehicles to extend his programmatic research in these several areas, and the students in these seminars prepared many "Top Rated" convention papers and published articles on these topics. In many instances, during his time at Alabama, Zillmann extended and refined his programmatic research and theory in areas in which he had previously carved out niches. Three major areas of primary research that came of age during the Alabama years were news research, research into music enjoyment and effects, and inquiry into the relationships between communication and pain management. The Zillmann theory that is undoubtedly most closely identified with the Alabama years is exemplification theory. Although his news research began at Indiana, this program reached maturity theoretically and flourished empirically at the University of Alabama.

Zillmann with his American mentor, Percy Tannenbaum, in a friendly exchange of ideas, sometime in 1997. Notwithstanding rumors to the contrary, the discussants actually enjoy the occasional disagreement.

REFLECTIONS ON ADDITIONAL INFLUENCES

We have discussed some of the individuals who have had an impact on Dolf Zillmann, largely through his personal contact with them, either through their teaching or via research collaboration. Other scholars whom Zillmann has never met have had considerable impact on him through their intellectual legacy. One of these individuals was Sigmund Freud. It was during the Ulm years that Zillmann was first exposed to the works of Freud, and throughout his career Freudian ideas have been examined. Zillmann ultimately supported and extended some of Freud's ideas (e.g., misattribution theory of tendentious humor). Other Freudian ideas (e.g., identification) have been modified or refuted in Zillmann's theories and research. Whatever the outcome, Zillmann has almost always found Freud's ideas to be provocative.

Many "classic" Western philosophers have also influenced Zillmann. In particular, the works of Plato, Aristotle, Kant, Locke, Hobbes, Hume, Schopenhauer, and Adam Smith were frequently cited and systematically examined by Zillmann. Early psychologists, such as William James, William McDougall, B. F. Skinner, Walter Cannon, and Daniel Berlyne, were also catalytic forces in Zillmann's work.

The work of Stanley Schachter played a prominent role in Zillmann's theoretical hierarch y. The two-factor theory of emotions was a linchpin of excitation-transfer theory, and Schachter's protocols also impressed Zillmann during his formative years. Likewise, Leon Festinger's social comparison theory has been an important component of Zillmann's theorizing.

On one occasion, Zillmann noted that a childhood experience with a children's puppet show—a street performance of Rumpelstiltskin—was a catalytic event in stimulating his interest in entertainment, especially regarding the role of moral judgment in the enjoyment of various aspects of drama. After seeing a particularly rousing demonstration of this drama, long before television, his young mind was set to wondering about the mechanics of entertainment, generating questions that were addressed many years later in his laboratories.

Zillmann also credits several essentially anonymous students with prompting key ideas via classroom questions that led to theory development or refinement. Issues like dispositional override of empathy and the role of rooting in the enjoyment of sports contest were often refined in classroom discussions, as well as in meetings of the various research teams Zillmann fostered.

THE PLACE OF PERSONAL INTANGIBLES

Tracing some of the intellectual forces that have helped precipitate the corpus of Dolf Zillmann's work, it became obvious that numerous personal characteristics have been as critical to his successes as have been these external forces. Many of these are essentially endogenous variables. For example, you cannot account for the magnitude or quality of Zillmann's theoretical work without taking into account his sheer brilliance. Generations of students have come away from their initial encounter with Zillmann shaking their heads and murmuring, "that's got to be the 'brightest' person I ever met." Without his superior intellect, it is clear that far less would have been possible than what he has accomplished.

Similarly, how can you account for the numerous "fresh" perspectives on old ideas reflected in Zillmann's scholarship without relying on constructs like "originality"? Clearly, Dolf Zillmann is that rare original thinker who turns ideas "on their heads" on a regular basis. This generative factor helps account for the myriad theories of communication and emotion that he has developed.

Zillmann with mentor Tannenbaum during the 2000 annual get-together at the shores of the Pacific in California.

Less obvious factors that have constantly contributed to his incredible productivity are other, even subtler, personal attributes that Zillmann possesses. One such set of attributes is his rare combination of self-discipline and tenacity. External motivation has always seemed less important to Zillmann than self-motivation. This internal drive to better understand and clarify phenomena has resulted in extraordinary discipline, which has exhibited itself in his application to arduous scholarship day in and day out throughout his long and productive career. The tenacity to carry on year after year without significant periods of rest and recuperation in a manner that is almost ascetic in character (although no one would argue that Zillmann has ever denied himself essential creature comforts, like gourmet food or fine wine!) has also been a hallmark of Zillmann's distinguished career. One thing is obvious: Zillmann could never be accused of a tenure surge. Every year of his professional life has been characterized by the maximal level of productivity possible.

THE X-FACTOR

And then, there is the X-factor! One could never account for the inordinate productivity or impact of Dolf Zillmann without taking into account (and thanking!) his lifelong helpmate, research assistant, intellectual partner, co-conspirator, personal trainer, personal chef, and best friend, Valtra Zillmann. The untold number of hours that Valtra Zillmann has spent in the library or at the computer or typewriter, working hand in hand with Dolf Zillmann, has made her the world's second foremost expert in communication and emotion. She's the wizard of his Oz. No one could be a better X-factor!

Zillmann receiving the University of Alabama's Burnum Distinguished Faculty Award. From left to right, Provost Nancy Barrett, Dolf Zillmann, and Mrs. & Dr. John F. Burnum.

A FINAL WORD

When we began this chapter, we thought that we would be inadequate to the task of explaining that which is Dolf Zillmann, and we were right. To our credit, however, we don't think that even Dolf Zillmann is capable of explicating and adequately explaining Dolf Zillmann.

Nevertheless, on behalf of his several generations of inspired and well-educated mentees and collaborators, at least we can sincerely, humbly, and earnestly express to the master our unwavering and heartfelt gratitude. Thank you, Dolf, our dear and faithful mentor and friend.

SECTION II:

Essential Theories and Concepts in Communication and Emotion

2

Excitation-Transfer Theory and Three-Factor Theory of Emotion

Jennings Bryant
Dorina Miron
University of Alabama

Excitation-transfer theory and the more inclusive three-factor theory of emotion might well be regarded as the crown jewels of Dolf Zillmann's abundant contributions to theory construction. Without question, Zillmann developed an invaluable model from this complex fusion of elements from psychophysiology, biochemistry, communication, and cognate disciplines. Today, some 30 years after Zillmann's initial articulation of excitation-transfer theory, we have a cogent, elegant, and extremely comprehensive theory of communication and emotion that explains and predicts a vast array of human communication behaviors. Artfully developed and scrupulously researched by Zillmann and several generations of graduate student mentees, these complex theories provide roadmaps in several uncharted territories of emotionality.

The goal of this chapter is not to rephrase excitation-transfer theory and three-factor theory. Their creator has dutifully updated and refined these theories whenever fresh empirical evidence or emerging conceptual developments warranted. References to these updates are provided throughout this chapter, and it should be noted that Zillmann has continued this tradition in the final chapter of this volume. Space does not allow us to attempt a history of the programmatic development of this theory or the innovative designs and methodologies used to develop them. Rather, what we have attempted to do is showcase the fine threading and lacing of theory construction that produced excitation-transfer theory and then molded it into the three-factor theory of emotion.

A MAJOR RECONCEPTUALIZATION OF EMOTION

Growing concern about the increasingly violent media content in the late 1960s and early 1970s spurred debate over possible effects of such content on the real-life behavior of media consumers. The major initial players in the theoretical arena were the ancient doctrine of catharsis versus the instigational-effect hypothesis derived from stimulus–response models of behaviorism. Feshbach (1955, 1956) borrowed and built on the Aristotelian concept of catharsis and anticipated that vicarious participation in the aggressive behaviors depicted by the media would diminish aggressive inclinations in audience members. The rather tenuous backing for catharsis (Feshbach 1961, 1964) left the academic community in doubt and prompted researchers to examine the alternative possibility of enhancement effects of media violence on human aggression. Berkowitz's (1962, 1965a, 1969, 1970, 1973) cue elicitation model proposed that frustration-motivated aggressive responses were triggered by cues available in the individual's environment, including media content. The experiments conducted by Berkowitz and his associates (e.g., Berkowitz, 1965b; Berkowitz, Corwin, & Hieronimus, 1963; Berkowitz & Geen, 1967; Geen & Berkowitz, 1966, 1967) found that depicted violence, as compared to neutral communication, facilitated subsequent aggressiveness in previously frustrated individuals. Holmes' (1966) research indicated that the performance of retaliatory acts does not necessarily purge the individual of noxious arousal, but that such arousal could linger for some time and was possibly perpetuated by these acts. Walters and his coworkers (e.g., Walters & Thomas, 1963; Walters, Thomas, & Acker 1962), among others, found that exposure to communication-mediated violence could increase aggressiveness even in individuals who were not provoked prior to exposure.

When the negative effects of media violence began to be acknowledged as normative findings with significant social implications, theorists focused increasingly on explanatory mechanisms of how media facilitated hostility and aggression. For example, Bandura and his associates (e.g., Bandura 1962, 1965, 1973; Bandura, Ross, & Ross, 1963) proposed that aggressive responses are imitated and that media violence is an important source of social learning. They set out to determine the conditions under which imitation could take place. Gerbner (e.g., 1968, 1970, 1971) and his associates adopted a broader (societal) and less psychological and more radical perspective, frequently called the *cultivation hypothesis*. Cultivation posited that media, especially television, create a ubiquitous and inescapable symbolic environment that distorts people's view of reality. Because of television's crime-laden content, heavy viewers were thought to perceive the world as more hostile and violent, resulting in an endemic mean-world syndrome.

Toward the end of the 1960s, when research evidence about the facilitating effect of media violence had reached a critical mass, researchers began to gravitate toward detailed psychological phenomena that appeared to have more explanatory potential or be technically more compelling. The major areas of interest were the changes that occur in media consumers during exposure (both cognition and emotion) and the nature of postexposure responses (e.g., aggressive, hostile, and prosocial behaviors). Psychological research and theory were scrutinized for possible applications to communication phenomena. Established theories of emotion that had hypothesized specific visceral changes linked with the induction of particular emotions (e.g., James, 1884) were assiduously challenged. Schachter (1970, 1971; Schachter & Singer, 1962) deemed extant conceptualizations of emotion to be lacking and provided evidence against them. He proposed a two-factor theory of emotion (Schachter, 1964). The first factor he considered was the interoception of nontrivial sympathetic excitation (i.e., that exceeding the baseline level) that served to gauge the intensity of excitation, possibly in combination with exteroception via conditioning (i.e., learning of associations between internal and external body changes, such as redness of cheeks and a burning sensation). As the physiological response (i.e., arousal) was found to be largely nonspecific (i.e., not well differentiated across emotions), a second factor was needed to account for the distinct experience of various emotions. Schachter considered that factor to be the exteroception of the immediate environment, which enabled the individual to attribute a cause to the emotional response being experienced. Such understanding/judgment was presumed to guide response behaviors. Schachter's two-factor theory thus posited a critical interplay between excitation and cognition in emotional processes.

Schachter's argument was congruent with a variety of prior research findings as well as previous conceptualizations. For instance, Cannon (1929) examined the emergency function of emotions and posited that their role was to ready the body for immediate energetic responses dictated by perceptions of imminent danger, independent of action particulars. Hull's (1943, 1952) drive theory predicted that arousal energizes any behavior that requires above-normal deployment of energy. On the cognitive side, Hebb (1955) endorsed Hull's concept of drive as an energizer (i.e., considered arousal to be a general drive state) and stressed the cue function in the guidance of behavior (imported by Berkowitz into the field of communication in the late 1960s). In the late 1950s, attribution theory (e.g., Heider, 1958; Jones & Davis, 1965) proposed that humans seek to comprehend the causal relationships that govern our interactions with the environment, and that such endeavors provide epistemic motivation for our actions. Berlyne (1960) held that such epistemic motivation is most pronounced under conditions of uncertainty. Festinger (1954), Schachter (1959), and Bem (1972) pointed to the role of inferential processes in determining the appropriate response under conditions of ambiguity.

So, bits and pieces of extant theory were beginning to help clarify aspects of emotional behavior, but an articulated and comprehensive model to describe causes, manifestations, and effects was not yet available and was sorely needed. Looking at the landscape of emotion theory in psychology from the field of communication, the most promising candidate for importation appeared to be Shachter's two-factor theory, which was among the most sophisticated models available at the time. The question was how media messages induce or alter emotional states in audience members.

Applying a general model developed in psychology to account for emotional processes affected by mediated communication involved developments that progressed in two stages. In the early stage, the predictions about the roles of the two Schachterian factors were tested in the media environment while trying to account for the then most salient mass communication issue of aggression facilitation and escalation. Zillmann addressed this problem with excitation-transfer theory. Then a hoard of questions that had surfaced during the first stage of exploration forced expansion of the essential conceptualization and modeling if new issues were to be accommodated. Zillmann continued to lead this theoretical quest through a programmatic effort that spanned more than three decades, advancing Schachter's two-factor theory into a new three-factor theory of emotion.

A summary of the dynamics of Zillmann's approach to emotion should probably start with Hullian drive theory. Hull (1943, 1952) posited that the environment successively changes the operating habitat in such a way that the excitational residues, presumably unique to some prior distinctive drive stimulus, may become an element of irrelevant drive for subsequent, unrelated habits. By analogy, residual physiological excitation caused by exposure to media violence could be expected to integrate additively as an irrelevant drive with subsequent excitation generated by other stimuli, elevate the prior level of excitation, and facilitate behavioral responses to those stimuli. Hullian theory contributed the ideas of excitation residuals and their integration in succession. Zillmann collapsed and connected Hull's drive theory and Schachter's two-factor theory, which posited an excitatory and a cognitive component of emotional states. In contrast to Hull's hypothesis that excitatory reactions "lose" their specificity under new stimulation, Schachter claimed that emotional arousal is nonspecific, and the individual cognitively assesses the emotion he is experiencing for the purpose of behavioral guidance and adjustment. Zillmann adopted and modified Schachter's view on this issue.

Zillmann's (1968) crucial addition to this formulation was the observation that the latency and decay of cognitive adjustment and excitational adjustment differ—the latter being sluggish due to the mediation of slow humoral processes. He examined the issues created by this lag and determined that in a rapid succession of stimuli the nonspecific excitation (as posited by Schachter) produced by subsequent stimuli "piggybacks" prior residual excitation that has not had the time to completely decay (as posited by Hull). This is the nexus of excitation-transfer theory. On the other hand, cognitive assessment of the current emotional state (as posited by Schachter) links the current circumstances (i.e., the apparent causes of emotion) and the additive level of intensity of excitation. The linchpin mechanism posited and empirically tested by Zillmann is misattribution on the part of the individual experiencing the emotional state (Tannenbaum & Zillmann, 1975): The individual believes that all the excitation he or she currently feels is entirely due to the current stimulus environment. In other words, the individual fails to recognize the contribution of residual levels of prior excitation. Zillmann further deduced and tested the hypothesis that misattribution results in inappropriate (disproportionate) responses to the current circumstances.

Zillmann placed the notion of enhancement of arousal through excitation transfer within the purview of the general law of initial values (Sernbach 1966; Wilder, 1857). Accordingly, he proposed that excitatory reactions are inversely proportional to prestimulus levels of excitation. Zillmann reasoned that

> such a qualification, which is necessary mainly to prevent the prediction of excitatory intensity above maximally possible levels, gives extreme residues

> little power to influence extreme emotional reactions. In contrast, it projects comparatively strong transfer effects for moderate residues that enter into moderate emotional reactions. (Zillmann, 1983c, p. 228)

The relevance of excitation-transfer theory to the escalation of hostility and aggression in real life as an effect of sequential emotion-eliciting events (either occurring in real life or delivered by mass media) cannot be overstressed. The final section of this chapter addresses some of the most important applications of this imminently generalizable theory.

Over time, Zillmann put together a solid account of physiological phenomena (neural activation and endocrine processes) involved in the excitation-transfer process that was posited by his theory. He pioneered and sensitively perfected appropriate experimental methodologies, identified phases of excitation and conditions of transfer, and developed a rigorous system of propositions—all of which have enhanced the validity and elegance of this theory, as well as trim it toward parsimony and simplicity (Tannenbaum & Zillmann, 1975). In addition to conducting programmatic empirical research, Zillmann has regularly reviewed relevant emerging research in the fields of communication and psychology and has periodically updated his model (e.g., 1983c, 1996b, 1998b). It would take an entire volume to examine the laborious development of the two theories under discussion; therefore, we chose to emphasize a few productive developments that resulted in theoretical advancements.

ESSENTIAL THEORETICAL COMPONENTS AND FORMULATIONS

Excitation

Schachter's (1964) two-factor model helped popularize the idea that arousal is nonspecific. That view fit well within the existing framework of neural activation theory (Lindsley, 1951, 1957), which posited diffuse projections from the reticular formation (Tannenbaum & Zillmann, 1975). Consequently, in excitation-transfer research the assessment of stimuli-producing excitation was conducted in terms of the amount of arousal affected by different types of stimuli. The typology was qualitative, but excitation was measured quantitatively. Given the quantitative focus, experimental manipulation was generally narrowed down to negative stimuli (already known to have stronger excitatory effects than positive stimuli). Moreover, because excitation-transfer research took place in a context of high concern about the role of media in aggression, media violence was the negative stimulus of primary concern. Real-life aggression was added for comparison and seriation purposes. Sexual media content was included in the mix on grounds of Freudian theory—based on propositions advanced by Hartmann, Kris, and Loewenstein (1949)—which hypothesized the fusion between sexual and aggressive drives, together with the possibility of displacement. A stronger reason was the empirical finding that "erotic communications ... are generally associated with greater excitatory potential than are aggressive materials" (Zillmann, Hoyt, & Day, 1974, p. 303). The excitatory potential and effects of violence-plus-sex combinations were examined for consecutive and simultaneous/fused patterns.

In spite of the relatively simple stimulus constellation, these studies of excitation transfer led to a disconcerting conclusion:

> The relationship between arousal and aggression is apparently more complex than many investigators had imagined. Arousal is evidently not a universal energizer of aggression, it does not have appetitive properties. And if it does energize aggression, energization is not necessarily in proportion to prevailing levels of arousal. Rather, arousal is a potential energizer whose operation depends on a set of favorable circumstances. (Zillmann, 1983a, p. 96)

This conclusion practically wiped out the illusion of expeditious predictability of aggression-facilitation effects based on violent content of media material (corresponding to the hypodermic needle or magic bullet view of media effects in general) and shifted research focus toward circumstances and conditions for transfer and the psychological variables of the individual experiencing the excitation.

Time

One of the most critical variables in the phenomenon of excitation transfer is time, which affects both the excitatory levels and the cognitive processes involved in emotions. Time in connection with excitatory processes has been discussed in terms of response latency and excitation decay, the latter being particularly relevant to emotional processes associated with exposure to mediated communication. As noted by Zillmann (1971), "The cognitive adjustment precedes the excitational adjustment" (p. 442) but, in the context of communication effects on postexposure behavior, "the latency of an excitatory response may be considered negligible" (p. 442). However, the decay of excitation is comparatively slow and may be due to homeostatic mechanisms, fatigue or exhaustion, or intervening distractions (Tannenbaum & Zillmann, 1975).

The decay process links time with the quantitative aspect of excitation (its intensity), but it is also affected by seriation, which is crucial for excitation transfer. Seriation has two time-related aspects: item order or position in the series (e.g., contiguous, preceding, subsequent, intervening between two other items, initial, final) and time spacing (distance in time between items). Seriation is also contingent on item distinctiveness, which is a qualitative component. The qualitative distinctions depend on which criteria are relevant to the person who assesses the sequence. Some major distinctions used by investigators of the effects of media violence on audience emotions and behaviors have been the source of stimulation (media vs. personal real-life experience), stimulation intensity, hedonic quality, item role in the causal chain (stimulus, response, mediator), moral values, and absence versus presence and amount of violence in the content. In terms of effects (response components), distinctions have been made between physiological arousal, cognitions, and behaviors.

The time-related effects within the framework of Zillmann's excitation-transfer theory are quite complex. In order to examine possible facilitative effects on aggression and/or hostility, researchers had to consider a wide range of experimental situations, varying the sequencing of stimuli (media and real-life sources), along with other variables, such as stimulus intensity, hedonic quality, aggressive/violent content (vs. neutral content), duration, relative distribution in time (spacing, concomitance). Essentially, the questions were how much excitation can build up through exposure to various sequences, and how much of that excitation can affect audience behavior in terms of level of interpersonal aggression—the major manipulation being timing.

Cognition

Zillmann began this research program by building on Schachter's (1964) assumption that arousal and cognition "operate side by side" (Tannenbaum & Zillmann, 1975, p. 177). According to Schachter's two-factor theory, the role of cognition was hinged on interoception of excitation, exteroception of external/visible body changes, and exteroception of the excitatory environment. Judgments were expected to link symptoms to causes (perform attribution), construct the specific differences between emotions (posited to have nonspecific excitation), assess the appropriateness of excitation level (energy build up for response action), and, generally speaking, mediate response behavior. According to Tannenbaum and Zillmann (1975), the Schachterian model failed to raise important questions such as "how the two ingredients arise, how each plays its respective role, and if and how they interact in determining the final response" (p. 178). Consequently, Zillmann deemed the two-factor model "rudimentary and incomplete rather than faulty. The model fails to address, let alone answer, what is involved in the guiding or channeling of behavior through cues" (p. 75). Very soon after excitation-transfer theory was articulated, Zillmann signaled that the two-factor model was due for expansion in order to accommodate such issues.

Attribution and Misattribution

"Both the two-factor theory of emotional state and the excitation-transfer theory are based on the notion of a misattribution of arousal" (Cantor, Bryant, & Zillmann, 1974, p. 820). Assessing research findings, Cantor, Zillmann, and Bryant (1975) observed that "residual arousal which is properly recognized as such not only does not intensify ongoing responses, but may actually impair them" (p. 74). They interpreted the phenomenon as a demonstration of "the crucial role of misattribution of arousal in the enhancement of emotional responses by residual excitation" (p. 74). Beside that reassurance, they must have read a warning that other cognitions in addition to exteroception were at play in excitation transfer. Because they were talking of "recognition," the scope of their research had to be expanded to include cognitive processes prior to the current excitatory reaction. The Schachterian two-factor bubble was about to burst.

On the other hand, recognition of the centrality of attribution in the model directed research back to the time factor. Cantor et al. (1975) addressed the conditions needed for misattribution. They refined the model adding time phases of excitation decay: the initial phase, when residuals are still accompanied by the perception of apparent cues that affect correct "recognition" of causes and thus prohibit transfer; the second phase, when those cues are no longer perceived (being replaced in the individual's consciousness by cues related to a different, subsequent source of excitation); and the last phase, when the residual excitation has completely decayed and there is no prior excitation left to transfer. Zillmann's revamped theory limited excitation transfer to the second phase (Tannenbaum & Zillmann, 1975).

Attentional Shift

A special situation of arousal decay became apparent from the work on cognitive processes in excitation transfer: the attentional shift. Bandura (1965) had envisaged the possibility that severely provoked (and thereby aroused) persons witnessing communication-mediated aggressive performances might experience pseudo-cathartic phenomena, more precisely a dissipation/reduction of noxious arousal caused by "noninstrumental cognitions that supersede the preoccupying instrumental ones" (Zillmann & Johnson, 1973, p. 264). Zillmann and Johnson (1973) suggested, "Bandura's basic proposition concerning attentional shifts may be modified to accommodate a postulated interaction between motivational state and communication-induced cognitions" (p. 265). Zillmann and Johnson considered the possibility that exposure to communication, in general, might impede or prevent rumination (Bandura, 1973) and thus disrupt the arousal-maintaining perpetuation of disturbance-related cognitions.

Zillmann refined Bandura's attentional shift hypothesis, positing differential effects dependent on the degree of correspondence between the content of the motivational state and the content of the intervening mediated communication (e.g., Bryant & Zillmann, 1977). According to Zillmann and Johnson (1973), "Communications involving contents which relate to the individual's acute emotional state potentially reiterate arousal-maintaining cognitions ... and prevent pronounced decay of arousal" (pp. 265–266), whereas exposure to neutral materials effect a "significant decrease of aggressiveness" (p. 274). Zillmann, Hoyt, and Day (1974) generalized that "the duration of communication effects responsible for initial motivation and energizing of a response is dependent upon the excitation-modifying capacity of any particular post-exposure treatment" (p. 304).

Systematic research on misattribution gave Zillmann grounds to talk about the considerable potential of arousing media messages to affect real-life behaviors, either when consumed in sequences or experienced in conjunction with arousing real-life events. In 1975, Tannebaum and Zillmann offered these reflections:

> Most people probably do not consider arousal from media exposure to be pronounced enough to warrant any attention, and hence they do not expect

> it to affect their behavior. Dismissing such arousal as trivial, the individual will tend to attribute any accumulating residues not to the preceding communication events but to the new stimulus situation in which he finds himself. [The new situation could be either a real-life one or another mediated message.] Moreover, by virtue of their very "unreal" and symbolic (possibly fantasy-encouraging) content, communication messages are generally not related to the person's real and immediate problems and concerns. This should further encourage the misattribution of accruing arousal and hence make the person all the more vulnerable to transfer effects in his postcommunication behavior. (p. 187)

This realization was the decisive puncture that exploded the Schachterian two-factor bubble: It pointed to the possibly overpowering effects of previously developed cognitions.

Hedonic Assimilation

Zillmann, Mody, and Cantor (1974) noted that "both the hedonic tone and the excitatory potential of prior stimuli can modify the individual's response to witnessed displays of emotions" (p. 346), with negligible interaction between the two factors. The authors suggested that the factors were independent and additive. Zillmann et al. found evidence supportive of a hedonic-set mechanism[1] and concluded that "cognitive adjustment to subsequent stimuli is an important prerequisite for excitation transfer" (p. 346). They reasoned that "under conditions in which cognitive adjustment is not achieved," it is likely that "persistent preoccupation with the arousing experience will reduce attention to subsequently presented stimuli" (p. 347). In other words, attention is not uniformly deployed to process incoming stimuli, but it is mediated by personal relevance (i.e., connectivity to the memory store that beats the time barrier and shares semantic meaning with the incoming stimuli). Zillmann et al. (1974) stressed "the importance of taking cognitive adjustment to subsequent stimuli into consideration when predicting effects of residual arousal" (p. 347) and pointed to the theoretical possibility of combining message chunks in distinct ways to "control the intensity of affective states experienced by the audience and, in the final

---

[1]The hedonic-set theory anticipates greater ease in maintaining the hedonic value of one's immediately prior affective state than in adapting to a hedonic state of contrasting value. The lags of neural and especially hormonal activity associated with affects (even small ones) underlie the cognitive parsimony implied by the theory.

analysis, the overall impact of a dramatic sequence" (p. 348). Thus, Zillmann and his associates heralded an era of emotion management and laid a cornerstone for a science of emotion engineering.

From Legitimation to Dispositions

Also in the area of response inertia (consistency), an additional complication surfaced in relation to legitimation processes associated with moral judgment and the individual's general value system. Zillmann and associates conducted experiments with various sequences of real-life and media-induced emotions in order to clarify the mechanism through which media content facilitates aggressive behavior. They resorted to experimental manipulation of variables such as energizing sources (media vs. physical exercise) responsible for the escalation of excitation, levels of aggression in media content, presence or absence of instigation, position of instigation relative to media content (before vs. after), timing of retaliation opportunity that affects excitation decay, as well as intervening messages that affect excitation decay. Overall, Zillmann and his associates found support for excitation transfer independent of excitation source and for the facilitating effect of excitation induced by the media (possibly in combination with real-life sources) on real-life aggression. But in experiments based on the instigation–retaliation paradigm, the researchers faced a dilemma: What exactly prompted retaliation, the motivation effected by the instigational intervention, or the aggression cues possibly picked from intervening aggressive content, as suggested by Berkowitz (1965b, 1970)? Through persistent, meticulous, and ingenious experimentation, Zillmann and associates established that transfer-enhanced aggressive response was contingent on instigation; that is, transfer and escalation of excitation did not automatically enhance behavior aggression, it required a motivation (Tannenbaum & Zillmann, 1975; Zillmann & Johnson, 1973). Such motivation for retaliation surprisingly was found to be resistant in time and to manifest itself whenever the conditions for retaliation exist, even after complete excitation decay (Bryant & Zillmann, 1979). That discovery suggested the possibility of cognitive revival of the original emotion caused by the instigation, including even some excitation. The phenomenon was labeled "predisposition to aggress" (Tannebaum & Zillmann, 1975, p. 185). This element no longer fitted into the Schachterian two-factor theory of emotion.

REFINING THE MODEL

When Zillmann and Bryant (1974) set out to investigate the role of dispositions in excitation transfer, they made the following assumption:

> During the emotional experience of anger, the individual forms an aggressive disposition that (a) may be of considerable duration and (b) can be reinstated and reactivated at later times. The more intensely anger is felt and presumably rehearsed, the more pronounced the aggressive disposition becomes. And, if, for whatever reason, the immediate execution of this disposition is not possible or does not appear opportune, it remains latent until reinstated by spontaneous or stimulus-induced cognitions associated with the provoking circumstances. (p. 783)

Although the three-factor theory of emotion was "officially" launched by Zillmann in 1978, the previous quote demonstrates that the disposition factor, which was the main innovation relative to Schachter's two-factor theory, had come under investigation in the context of emotionality somewhat earlier, and was conceptualized as a separate unit before being integrated into the earlier general model of emotion imported from psychology.

In fact, the idea of predisposition had been employed in earlier research on aggression. Zillmann and Bryant (1974) referred to Berkowitz's (1965a) assumptions that people tend to complete a predisposed aggressive response, and an aggressive predisposition can be reinstated until the consummatory goal response has been made or its objective has been accomplished. Zillmann and Bryant (1974) pointed out that Berkowitz's hypothesis was "not quite in line with the popular view that aggression can be held in check by giving the would-be aggressor a chance to cool off (p. 790). The longevity of aggressive dispositions was tentatively attributed to endocrine changes.

In 1978, Zillmann articulated the advances made by recent experimental research with Schachter's two-factor model, on which he superimposed a behaviorial perspective:

> As in behavior theory, the motor aspects of behavior are considered either unconditional (such as in startle reactions) or acquired through learning (such as in atypical phobias). It is obviously assumed that the ES–ER connection preexists or is established without the involvement of "cognitive operations at higher levels." The motor behavior associated with emotions is thus seen as an unmediated, direct response made without appreciable latency to the presentation of the emotion-inducing stimulus. (Zillmann, 1978, p. 355)

The emotional stimulus–response connections were presented as the third factor, which was labeled *the dispositional component.* Zillmann's reformulation accounted for the occurrence of spontaneous motor responses in emotional states. Schachter's excitatory component was maintained as the energizing mechanism for the motor responses. The experiential component, including conscious experience of both motor and excitatory responses through intero- and exteroception, was defined as the *appraisal function* (Zillmann, 1978, p. 359), that is, a "modifier or a corrective that, within limits, controls the more archaic, basic emotional responsiveness governed by unlearned and learned S–R connections" (p. 357). Zillmann's new three-factor theory viewed the experiential factor as a mediator of both dispositional and excitatory reactions.

As previously mentioned, the three-factor theory has been periodically revisited, polished, and updated with the latest pertinent research findings (Zillmann, 1983c, 1996b). The 1996 version of the theory (Zillmann, 1996b) emphasized the interdependencies between the three components/factors. The function of the experiential component was the "appraisal of emotional reactions and action in the context of circumstances" or the "scrutiny of the utility of the action" (p. 247). "As individuals become aware of their aimless, excited behavior, they are likely to perform an epistemic search directed at the comprehension of the inducement of their state of elevated excitation" (p. 248). According to the new formulation, "All motor elements of emotional behavior are under volitional control" (p. 248), which means that overt action that is considered inappropriate can be immediately inhibited or redirected as soon as noticed.

> In contrast, the theory posits that excitatory responding is not readily controlled by volition. The incipient excitatory reaction may be modified to some degree by incoming information that proves anger, fear, or any other emotional upheaval groundless. However, the counterregulatory response tends to run its course, being primarily controlled by homeostatic regulation.... The three-factor theory allows emotion-controlling response dispositions to be formed on the basis of the contemplation of frequently occurring circumstances that have been associated with emotional experiences in the past. (p. 249)

The 1996 version of the three-factor theory thus provides a compelling argument for the functional unity to the tripartite structure.

NOTHING MORE PRACTICAL THAN GOOD THEORY

Escalating Anger, Impulsive Aggression, and Judgmental Biases

Because excitation-transfer research and theorizing developed in part to address concerns about the impact of media violence on users' hostility and aggression, it is not surprising that the discussion of research findings and theory predictions has focused primarily on such issues.

The enhancement of excitation through transfer gave prominence to the issue of supra-excitation, the resulting deterioration of cognitive processes, and the bias of behavioral responses toward hostile and aggressive actions.

The inverted-U model predicted the relationship between arousal and behavioral efficiency (Freeman, 1940; Hebb, 1955, 1966; Malmo 1959, 1975; Yerkes & Dodson, 1908). Emotion research showed that

> at extreme levels of arousal, the cognitive mediation of behavior is expected to be greatly impaired, and behavior is expected to be controlled by the more basic mechanics of learning.... Hostile and aggressive behaviors are expected to become impulsive—that is, to become behaviors composed of learned reactions associated with great habit strength, conceivably even of unlearned defensive reactions. (Zillmann, 1993, p. 94)

Supra-excitation pairs with cognitive deficit. The twofold phenomenon occurs under conditions of limited cognitive capacity (Zillmann, 1994a) and manifests as "inability of extremely agitated and aroused persons to conceive and execute rational, effective courses of action ... 'blindness' or overinvestment of attention in the emergency at hand" (pp. 58–59; i.e., the here and now), "exaggerated self-concern" (p. 98), "little if any attention ... given to suffering by others, especially by parties who issued threats and continue to pose dangers" (p. 104), and deteriorating empathic sensitivities. Moreover, prolonged experiences of challenge and stress eventually produce the catecholamine rush that is typical of fight-or-flight reactions; this fosters an exaggerated perception of danger, overreaction and belligerent response, illusion of power and invulnerability, and trivialization of risks and costs. As pointed out by Zillmann (1994a),

> the tendency to respond with vigorous action to endangerment undoubtedly has served humans well during the course of evolution.... Temper tantrums, for instance ... intimidate opponents and prompt them to yield, potentially

> making the display of a fit of bad temper an effective coercive strategy.... [But] the utility of archaic vigorous action as a means of coping with endangerment and of conflict resolution has been lost for the most part.... Responding "emotionally" to threats of self-esteem, social status, social power, or economic standing not only tends to lack adaptive utility but also can be counterproductive and maladaptive.... Staying calm and collected in devising strategies for effective action would better serve their welfare and self-interest. (p. 48)

Under excitation-transfer theory, something counterintuitive happens. In arousal-escalating sequences of perceived provocations,

> the excitatory contribution of provocations diminishes as their ordinal position in the escalation sequence increases. Or expressed in terms of time, their contribution is smaller, the later they occur in this sequence. This gives great excitatory starting power to minor disagreements but assigns trivial effect to their placement late in the excitatory sequence. [Also,] disagreements that materialize when excitation is at extremely high levels are extremely intensely experienced. The magnitude of the excitatory contribution from such disagreements may be of little consequence here. It could, nonetheless, eventually be "the straw that breaks the camel's back." (Zillmann, 1994a, p. 52)

The "prolonging of acute agitation, a condition viewed as readiness for violent action (see Heiligenberg, 1974, for a discussion of the ecological significance of aggression readiness)" (Zillmann, 1994a, p. 52), creates a judgment bias. The agitated person develops the impression that nonviolent options fail to resolve the conflict, of which the person becomes less and less tolerant, and the option of envisaged resolution is narrowed down to instantaneous and vigorous relief-providing actions. This process pattern accounts for the aggressive-termination bias inherent in high-arousal situations.

The three-factor theory of emotional state puts this bias in a temporal perspective. "Appraisals and repeated reappraisals of the circumstances in which individuals find themselves are capable of modifying excitatory activity" (Zillmann, 1994a, p. 55), resulting in hostile and aggressive dispositions. As shown by Zillmann, "Humans have the capacity to delay the execution of aggressive activities" (Zillmann & Bryant, 1974, p. 783); they often engage in "unproductive rumination in anger" (Zillmann, 1998a, p. 109) and "save" aggression-patterned memories as dispositions that can later on reinstate readiness for aggressive action, including excitation. Consequently, manifestations of aggression and violence become rather unpredictable in time, and the self-control and social control of violent acts become problematic.

Further aggravating the situation is the fact that cognitive deficit occurs regardless of the hedonic valence of the emotion being experienced and is merely a function of excitation intensity. If we consider entertainment effects, highly exciting activities that people enjoy (e.g., games, dancing) have the potential to jeopardize the appropriateness of their responses to postentertainment situations while the residual arousal is still high, making them prone to violence.

What can be done? The "solution" would be to prevent excitation transfer, so that arousal doesn't reach dangerous levels. Research on conditions for transfer identified the critical points at which intervention can either facilitate or block transfer.

The first factor to consider is time. One solution would be to space out arousing media stimuli to allow for complete decay of excitation induced by each one of them. Another preventive or curative solution would be interspersing arousing with unarousing or calming activities, using distractors to speed up the decay of excitation. But we do not always have control of the stimulus sources. When we do, we can only control our stimulation to some extent, and other people's stimulation even less.

A serious problem that undercuts control strategies is hedonic greed, the natural need and drive for more and more excitation, which makes people spontaneously seek rather than avoid arousal. And when they have reached a level that is too high and dangerous, they lose control and cannot disengage, but tend to consume the pent-up emotions through vigorous (violent) action, without much thought. Education for self-control may help, theoretically at least, train for the ability and habit of accounting for and monitoring one's emotions. This might reduce the incidence of misattribution and consequently of excitation transfer and aggressive action. But probably the most important of all is to deal with inhibited/censored aggressive responses, train the ability to block one's natural anger rumination and hate recycling. That can theoretically be done in various ways: "cooling down," analyzing, reasoning, focusing on logical cause–effect links, working out risk-free and cost-effective solutions, relativizing, changing perspectives, and devising alternative nonaggressive approaches. All these shift processing away from the formation of hostile, aggressive, or violent dispositions toward creativity, which holds more promise in terms of problem-solving effectiveness, emotional balance, and hedonic welfare.

Sex and Aggression

The theories under discussion here also have a modest lesson to teach about sexual arousal. Traditionally, sexual excitedness was not thought of as an emotion, "certainly not as one comparable to the likes of anger and fear" (Zillmann, 1986, p. 174). But, in reality, all three do share high arousal. Fe a r and anger are hedonically negative emotions geared toward self-preservation, whereas "coition" (Zillmann, 1986) is hedonically positive and geared toward species preservation. At the physiological level, the three overlap in the sense that they share sympathetic activation, but they differ because coition has additional parasympathetic arousal. Zillmann (1986) discussed in detail the central, autonomic, endocrine, and behavioral connections among the three emotions and theorized them as the "fight-flight-coition trichotomy" (p. 174). Zillmann argued that their co-elicitation was philogenetically adaptive, linking self-preservation to species preservation, but he reasoned that in the modern society, the linkage ceased to be necessary.

Relevant to our discussion here is the "behavioral facilitation due to sympathetic commonality" (p. 180) and the heightened risk of co-occurrence, misattribution, transfer, and escalation of excitation, potentially leading to violent dénouement. Hedonic theory (as shown in the Enjoyment of Violence chapter in this volume), accounts for the historical development of sexual practices involving simultaneous violence, or alternating sex and violence, for the purpose of maximizing arousal and ultimately enjoyment. But, as shown in that chapter, such practices are not infallible and not without serious costs.

AROUSAL AND ART

Excitation-transfer theory and the three-factor theory of emotions are also illuminating for the realm of entertainment, which is not exactly a trivial component of contemporary life. The major areas of application discussed and theorized by Zillmann are suspense (Zillmann, 1980, 1991b, 1996a; Zillmann, Hay, & Bryant, 1975), empathy (Zillmann, 1991a, 1994b), drama (Zillmann, 1994b, 1996a, 1996b), and humor (Cantor, Bryant, & Zillmann, 1974; Zillmann, 1983b; Zillmann & Bryant, 1991; Zillmann & Cantor, 1972, 1976). The research findings and the theorizing provide guidance for both the creative and the enjoyment aspects of entertainment.

Drama: Suspense and Empathy

The mechanism of suspenseful drama (e.g., Zillmann, 1980, 1996a), in a nutshell, is the following: (1) creating positive and negative dispositions toward characters by engaging them in a conflict; (2) credibly and repeatedly endangering the liked characters for a long time, placing them under high probability of suffering harms or losses (creating fears but not destroying hope through the spectator's certainty of harm or loss); (3) putting the disliked characters in a position of undeserved advantage, gain, and unlikely punishment (creating retaliatory dispositions with the audience); and (4) finishing with a surprising but strongly desired happy ending (the liked characters win and/or the disliked lose). The higher the arousal build-up through skillful excitation transfer, the higher the enjoyment of the final resolution. A "treasure-hunt" form of suspense, involving dangerous pursuits of rewards, is theoretically possible but less popular, probably because of its lower potential and fewer opportunities for arousal escalation. Zillmann (1996a) explained drama series in terms of macrostructure at the show level, with an anticipated happy ending and therefore little suspense, and microstructure at the episode level, with credible dangers and great suspense.

Various authors have tried to account for the enjoyment of suspense. Fenickel (1939, 1945) hypothesized that the mastery of difficulties produces functional pleasure. Berlyne (1960) proposed the arousal-jag model, claiming that the mere reduction or termination of an aversive state is a sufficient condition for the experience of positive affect. Bandura's (1969) behavior modification theory posited that anxious people's heavy consumption of suspenseful drama could be viewed as a self-administrated behavior-modification program. Zuckerman (1974, 1976) defined a biological need for and enjoyment of high stimulation. According to Zillmann (1996a), the enjoyment of suspense (and drama, in general) by the audience is a matter of excitation build-up achieved through the witnessing of successive and combinatory arousing events and culminating with a hedonically positive experience. The processing and enjoyment of suspense are contingent on viewers' (rather than the author's) framework of moral values.

Zillmann's excitation-transfer theory can be applied to optimize the sequencing of scenes for arousal maximization. The method is interspersing arousing and interfering scenes to facilitate misattribution of excitation, but keeping the arousing scenes close enough so that the arousal of a scene can be enhanced by the residual excitation of the previous arousing scene. The hedonic quality of scenes is largely irrelevant to excitation build-up, with one exception: The end must be hedonically positive in order to convert the arousal escalated by prior negative stimuli into enjoyment for the viewer to be satisfied with the solution. The mechanism of disposition formation in Zillmann's (1978) three-factor theory of emotion is relevant to the formation of audience dispositions toward characters, which can be changed in the course of action in order to increase the level of uncertainty, which in turn elicits higher arousal.

A contentious issue related to drama is that of empathy. The concept originated in German aesthetics (Brentano, 1924/1874; Lipps, 1903, 1906, 1907; Prandtl, 1910; Worringer, 1959/1908). Initially, it meant "feeling into" another entity or situation (Zillmann, 1994b). The earlier concept of sympathy defined in England by Smith (1971/1759) had identified important components of that emotional phenomenon such as automatic response, cognitive instigation, and anticipatory nature. Freud (1964a/1923) 1964b/1921) postulated identification as the mechanism of empathy. Zillmann (1994b) challenged the interpretation of identification as ego-confusion and advanced a respondent-as-witness hypothesis, arguing that observers of drama act as third parties "who did succumb to the theatrical, cinematic illusion that social reality unfolded before them" (p. 36) and who "respond most strongly to those portrayals that most closely replicate the stimulus fields that strongly arouse them outside the cinema" (p. 38). This modern approach implies temporary blurring of the distinction between the real and the fictional environment and assumes the co-participation of the audience in the fictional events as observers that are distinct from the fictional characters.

Zillmann (1994b) explained emotional involvement with drama using the notion of dispositionally controlled empathy. His three-factor theory of empathy (Zillmann, 1991) posits three types of empathy: innate/reflexive, acquired/learned, and deliberate cognitive maneuvers (e.g., perspective taking, role taking). This typology points to the significance for empathy of a person's conditioning history concerning the expression of emotions. It predicts that respondents to drama bring to the theatre or cinema "a set of empathic response dispositions, part of which are reflexive, part of which are acquired through a large number of learning trials or a few critical experiences, and part of which derive from deliberate perspective taking. Zillmann's model of empathy anticipates emotional reactions (including excitation) to witnessing situations and/or actions that cause emotions and/or other people/characters expressing emotions. Zillmann (1994b) applied the condition of concordance (hedonic compatibility) pioneered by

Berger (1962), and posited that "affective dispositions toward models allow empathic reactions, whereas negative affective dispositions impair, prevent, or hedonically reverse them" (p. 44). As empathizing is an emotional experience, it involves the responder's moral framework within which he or she makes judgments, takes sides, and chooses to empathize or counterempathize.

The media provide a huge number of dramatic situations that elicit empathic responses. As posited by Gerbner in his cultivation theory (e.g., 1969, 1970, 1972), the situations are similar over time and consistent in space; therefore, they tend to produce consistent emotional dispositions in the audience as well as personal patterns of emotional response to drama and analogous dramatic situations in life. This may become dangerous, because in real-life states of high arousal the individual is likely to disregard reality–fiction differences (because of cognitive deficit under stress) and to resort to dispositions rather than reflections, and those dispositions may have been acquired from fiction and may be inappropriate for resolving real-life situations. The higher the excitation build-up in the drama people watch and learn from, the higher the likelihood of drama-like emotional responses (including empathizing and antiempathizing) in critical, highly arousing, real-life situations.

Comedy: Humor

From an arousal perspective, the problem with humor is whether the hedonic value of the arousing context that theoretically may enhance the enjoyment of humor through transfer really matters or not. We have seen that it is irrelevant to hostility and aggression effects, but it is relevant to empathic responses. Findings that the appreciation of humor is enhanced by prior sexual arousal (e.g., Lamb, 1968; Strickland, 1959) could not clarify the issue because sex and humor are both hedonically positive, so there was no risk of interference. Cantor, Bryant, and Zillmann (1974) examined findings of experimental studies that manipulated sources of negative emotions and found they were mixed. Studies conducted by Schwartz (1972) and Zillmann and his associates (Cantor, Mody, & Zillmann, 1974; Cantor & Zillmann, 1973) found a trend of decreasing humor appreciation with increasing arousal. Limited cognitive capacity was assumed to have caused it. But for the middle level of arousal, the excitation from prior negative emotions appears to enhance the enjoyment of humor. The main theories considered by Zillmann as a possible explanation of that phenomenon were discomfort relief, conversion of empathic grief to amusement (McDougall, 1908, 1922), and excitation transfer. The latter appeared to have more empirical support, but only for midlevel excitation. So, the explanation cannot be simple. Berlyne (1967) postulated that moderate increases in arousal are rewarding, whereas high levels tend to be aversive. This means that arousal itself has hedonic effects. Godkewitsch (1972) and Schwartz (1972) extended the effects of arousal to encompass the enjoyment of subsequent humor, which they postulated to vary as an inverted-U function of arousal. This explanation is compatible with empirical findings at both middle and high levels of arousal (enhancement of enjoyment in the middle range and decrease in the high range). From the perspective of excitation transfer, this means that humor cannot resolve intense negative emotions; it is simply ignored under such conditions. So, there is no hope of catharsis. At the middle level of arousal, the enjoyment of humor is enhanced; therefore management for excitation transfer makes sense (standard interspersing for misattribution and fast-paced sequencing for incomplete decay of residuals).

THE FUTURE

The two Zillmannian theories discussed in this chapter, excitation-transfer and the three-factor theory of emotion, are vigorously anchored in physiology through both theory and experimental research, and they have a perennial object of interest—emotions. As pressure for rationality increases in Western cultures, so does the spontaneous (and market-induced) demand for emotionality through entertainment. This possibly is a balancing effect, a response to the increased need for pleasure. The new media technologies have a huge capacity to facilitate the creation and distribution of entertainment fare, and their interactivity has potential for stepping up arousal, both in isolation and synergistically. At the same time, the mass character of these media suggests the possibility of social-scale emotion-related phenomena that may be affected by arousal escalation. The next big question may be, do Zillmann's theories help account for addictive videogame playing or compulsive web surfing? What are the mechanisms of emotion enhancement that drive the adoption and use of new media?

REFERENCES

Bandura, A. (1962). Social learning through imitation. In M. R. Jones (Ed.), *Nebraska symposium on motivation*. Lincoln: University of Nebraska Press.

Bandura, A. (1965). Vicarious processes: A case of no-trial learning. In L. Berkowitz (Ed.), *Advances in experimental social psychology* (Vol. 2, pp. 1–55). New York: Academic.

Bandura, A. (1969). *Principles of behavior modification*. New York: Holt, Rinehart & Winston.

Bandura, A. (1973). *Aggression: A social learning analysis*. Englewood Cliffs, NJ: Prentice Hall.

Bandura, A., Ross, D., & Ross, S. A. (1963). Imitation of film-mediated aggressive models. *Journal of Abnormal and Social Psychology, 66,* 3–11,

Bem, D. J. (1972). Self-perception theory. In L. Berkowitz (Ed.), *Advances in experimental social psychology* (Vol. 6, pp. 1–62). New York: Academic.

Berger, S. M. (1962). Conditioning through vicarious instigation. *Psychological Review, 29,* 450–466.

Berkowitz, L. (1962). *Aggression: A social psychological analysis*. New York: McGraw-Hill.

Berkowitz, L. (1965a). The concept of aggressive drive: Some additional considerations. In L. Berkowitz (Ed.), *Advances in experimental social psychology* (Vol. 2, pp. 301–329). New York: Academic.

Berkowitz, L. (1965b). Some aspects of observed aggression. *Journal of Personality and Social Psychology, 2,* 359–369.

Berkowitz, L. (1969). The frustration-aggression hypothesis revisited. In L. Berkowitz (Ed.), *Roots of aggression: A re-examination of the frustration-aggression hypothesis* (pp. 1–28). New York: Atherton.

Berkowitz, L. (1970). The contagion of violence. An S–R mediational analysis of some effects of observed aggression. In W. J. Arnold & M. M. Page (Eds.), *Nebraska Symposium on Motivation* (Vol. 18, pp. 95–135). Lincoln: University of Nebraska Press.

Berkowitz, L. (1973). Words and symbols as stimuli to aggressive responses. In J. F. Knutson (Ed.), *The control of aggression: Implications from basic research* (pp. 113–143). Chicago, IL: Aldine.

Berkowitz, L., Corwin, R., & Hieronimus, M. (1963). Film violence and subsequent aggressive tendencies. *Public Opinion Quarterly, 27,* 217–229.

Berkowitz, L., & Geen, R. G. (1967). Stimulus qualities of the target of aggression: A further study. *Journal of Personality and Social Psychology, 5,* 364–368.

Berlyne, D. E. (1960). *Conflict, arousal and curiosity*. New York: McGraw-Hill.

Berlyne, D. E. (1967). Arousal and reinforcement. In D. Levine (Ed.), *Nebraska Symposium on Motivation*. Lincoln: University of Nebraska Press.

Brentano, F. C. (1924). *Psychologie vom empirischen standpunkt* [Psychology of the empirical point of view]. Leipzig: F. Meiner. (Original work published 1874)

Bryant, J., & Zillmann, D. (1977). The mediating effect of the intervention potential of communications on displaced aggressiveness and retaliatory behavior. In B. D. Ruben (Ed.), *Communication Yearbook 1* (pp. 291–306). New Brunswick, NJ: Transaction-ICA Press.

Bryant, J., & Zillmann, D. (1979). Effect of intensification of annoyance through unrelated residual excitation on substantially delayed hostile behavior. *Journal of Experimental Social Psychology, 15,* 470–480.

Cannon, W. B. (1929). *Bodily changes in pain, hunger, fear, and rage: An account of* researches *into the function of emotional excitement* (2nd ed.). New York: Appleton-Century.

Cantor, J. R., Bryant, J., & Zillmann, D. (1974). Enhancement of humor appreciation by transferred excitation. *Journal of Personality and Social Psychology, 30,* 812–821.

Cantor, J. R., Mody, B., & Zillmann, D. (1974). Residual emotional arousal as a distractor in persuasion. *Journal of Social Psychology, 92,* 231–244.

Cantor, J. R., & Zillmann, D. (1973). The effect of affective state and emotional arousal on music appreciation. *Journal of General Psychology, 32,* 97–108.

Cantor, J. R., Zillmann, D., & Bryant, J. (1975). Enhancement of experienced sexual arousal in response to erotic stimuli through misattribution of unrelated residual excitation. *Journal of Personality and Social Psychology, 32,* 69–75.

Fenickel, O. (1939). The counterphobic attitude. *International Journal of Psychoanalysis, 20,* 263–274.

Fenickel, O. (1945). *The psychoanalytic theory of neurosis*. New York: Norton.

Feshbach, S. (1955). The drive-reducing function of fantasy behavior. *Journal of Abnormal and Social Psychology, 50,* 3–12.

Feshbach, S. (1956). The catharsis hypothesis and some consequences of interaction with aggressive and neutral play objects. *Journal of Personality, 24,* 449–462.

Feshbach, S. (1961). The stimulating versus cathartic effects of a vicarious aggressive activity. *Journal of Abnormal and Social Psychology, 63,* 381–385.

Feshbach, S. (1964). The function of aggression and the regulation of aggressive drive. *Psychological Review, 71,* 257–272.

Festinger, L. (1954). A theory of social comparison processes. *Human Relations, 7,* 117–140.

Freeman, G. L. (1940). The relationship between performance level and bodily activity level. *Journal of Experimental Psychology, 26,* 602–608.

Freud, S. (1964a). The ego and the id. In J. Strachey (ed. and trans.), *The standard edition of the complete psychological works of Sigmund Freud* (Vol. 19. pp. 13–66). London: Hogarth. (Original work published 1923)

Freud, S. (1964b). Group psychology and the analysis of the ego. In J. Strachey (ed. and trans.), *The standard edition of the complete psychological works of Sigmund Freud* (Vol. 18, 69–143). London: Hogarth. (Original work published 1921)

Geen, R., & Berkowitz, L. (1966). Name mediated aggressive cue properties. *Journal of Personality, 34,* 456–465.

Geen, R., & Berkowitz, L. (1967). Some conditions facilitating the occurrence of aggression after the observation of violence. *Journal of Personality, 35,* 666–676.

Gerbner, G. (1968). *Dimensions of violence in television drama.* Report to the Mass Media Task Force, National Commission on the Causes and Prevention of Violence.

Gerbner, G. (1969). Toward "Cultural Indicators": The analysis of mass mediated message systems. *AV Communication Review, 17*(2), 137–148.

Gerbner, G. (1970). Cultural indicators: The case of violence in television drama. *Annals of the American Academy of Political and Social Science, 388,* 69–81.

Gerbner, G. (1971). Violence in television drama: Trends and symbolic functions. In G. A. Comstock & E. A. Rubinstein (Eds.), *Television and social behavior. Vol. 1. Content and control* (pp. 28–187). Washington: Government Printing Office.

Gerbner, G. (1972). Communication and social environment. *Scientific American, 227*(3), 152–160.

Hartmann, P. D., Kris, E., & Loewenstein. R.M. (1949). Notes on the theory of aggression. *The Psychoanalytic Study of the Child, 3-4,* 9–36.

Hebb, D. O. (1955). Drives and the C. N. S. (Conceptual Nervous System). *Psychological Review, 62,* 243–254.

Hebb, D. O. (1966). *A textbook of psychology* (2nd ed.). Philadelphia: Saunders.

Heider, F. (1958). *The psychology of interpersonal relations*. New York: Wiley.

Heiligenberg, W. (1974). Processes governing behavioral states of readiness. In D. S. Lehrman, J. S. Rosenblatt, R. A. Hinde, & E. Shaw (Eds.), *Advances in the study of behavior* (Vol. 5, pp. 173–200). New York: Academic.

Holmes, D. S. (1966). Effects of overt aggression on level of physiological arousal. *Journal of Personality and Social Psychology, 4,* 189–194.

Hull, C. L. (1943). *Principles of behavior: An introduction to behavior theory.* New York: Appleton-Century-Crofts.

Hull, C. L. (1952). *A behavior system: An introduction to behavior theory concerning the individual organism.* New York: Wiley.

James, W. (1884). What is emotion? *Mind, 9,* 61–78.

Jones, E. E., & Davis, K. E. (1965). From acts to dispositions: The attribution process in person perception. In L. Berkowitz (Ed.), *Advances in experimental social psychology* (Vol. 2, pp. 219–266). New York: Academic.

Lamb, C. W. (1968). Personality correlates of humor enjoyment following motivational arousal. *Journal of Personality and Social Psychology, 9,* 237–241.

Lindsley, D. B. (1951). Emotion. In S. S. Stevens (Ed.), *Handbook of experimental psychology* (pp. 473–516). New York: Wiley.

Lindsley, D. B. (1957). Psychophysiology and motivation. In M. R. Jones (Ed.), *Nebraska symposium on motivation* (Vol. 5, pp. 44–105). Lincoln: University of Nebraska Press.

Lipps, T. (1903). *Ästhetik: Psychologie des Schönen und der Kunst. Vol. 1: Grundlegung der Ästhetik* [Aesthetics: The psychology of beauty and art. Vol. 1: The foundations of aesthetics]. Hamburg: Voss.

Lipps, T. (1906). *Ästhetik: Psychologie des Schönen und der Kunst. Vol. 2: Die ästhetische Betrachtung und die bildende Kunst* [Aesthetics: The psychology of beauty and art. Vol 2: Aesthetic contemplation and the fine arts]. Hamburg: Voss.

Lipps, T. (1907). Das Wissen von fremden Ichen [Learning about the stranger self]. *Psychologische Untersuchungen 1*(4), 694–722.

Malmo, R. B. (1959). Activation: A neuropsychological dimension. *Psychological Review, 66,* 367–386.

Malmo, R. B. (1975). *On emotions, needs, and our archaic brain.* New York: Holt, Rinehart & Winston.

McDougall, W. (1908). *An introduction to social psychology.* London: Metuhen.

McDougall, W. (1922). A new theory of laughter. *Psyche, 2,* 292–303.

Prandtl, A., (1910). *Die Einfühlung* [Empathy]. Leipzig: J. A. Barth.

Schachter, S. (1959). *The psychology of affiliation: Experimental studies of the sources of gregariousness.* Stanford: Stanford University Press.

Schachter, S. (1970). The assumption of identity and peripheralist-centralist controversies in motivation and emotion. In M. B. Arnold (Ed.), *Feelings and emotions* (pp. 111–124). New York: Academic.

Schachter, S. (1971). *Emotion, obesity, and crime.* New York: Academic.

Schachter, S., & Singer, J. E. (1962). Cognitive, social, and physiological determinants of emotional state. *Psychological Review, 69,* 379–399.

Schwartz, S. (1972). The effects of arousal on appreciation for varying degrees of sex-relevant humor. *Journal of Experimental Research in Personality, 6,* 241–247.

Sernbach, R. (1966). *Principles of psychophysiology.* New York: Academic.

Smith, A. 1971. *The theory of moral sentiments.* New York: Garland. (Original work published 1759).

Strickland, J. F. (1959). The effect of motivation arousal on humor preferences. *Journal of Abnormal and Social Psychology, 59,* 278–281.

Tannenbaum, P. H., & Zillmann, D. (1975). Emotional arousal in the facilitation of aggression through communication. In L. Berkowitz (Ed.), *Advances in experimental social psychology* (Vol. 8, pp. 149–192). New York: Academic.

Walters, R. H., & Thomas, E. (1963). Enhancement of punitiveness by visual and audiovisual displays. *Canadian Journal of Psychology, 17,* 244–255.

Walters, R. H., Thomas, E., & Acker, C. W. (1962). Enhancement of punitive behavior by audio-visual displays. *Science, 136,* 872–873.

Wilder, J. (1957). The law of initial values in neurology and psychiatry: Facts and problems. *Journal of Nervous and Mental Disease, 125,* 73–86.

Worringer, W. (1959). *Abstraktion und Einfühlung: Ein Beitrag zur Stilpsychologie* [Abstraction and empathy: A contribution to the psychology of style]. Munich: Piper.

Yerkes, R. M., & Dodson, J. D. (1908). The relation of strength of stimulus to rapidity of habit formation. *Journal of Comparative Neurology and Psychology, 18,* 459–482.

Zillmann, D. (1968). *A theory of excitation transfer.* Unpublished manuscript.

Zillmann, D. (1971). Excitation transfer in communication-mediated aggressive behavior. *Journal of Experimental Social Psychology, 7,* 419–434.

Zillmann, D. (1978). Attribution and misattribution of excitatory reactions. In J. H. Harvey, W. J. Ickes, & R. F. Kidd (Eds.), *New directions in attribution research* (Vol. 2, pp. 335–368). Hillsdale, NJ: Lawrence Erlbaum Associates.

Zillmann, D. (1980). Anatomy of suspense. In P. Tannenbaum (Ed.), *The entertainment functions of television* (pp. 133–163). Hillsdale, NJ: Lawrence Erlbaum Associates.

Zillmann, D. (1983a). Arousal and aggression. In R. G. Geen & E. I. Donnerstein (Eds.), *Aggression: Theoretical and empirical reviews* (Vol. 1, pp. 75–101). New York: Academic.

Zillmann, D. (1983b). Disparagement humor. In P. E. McGhee, & J. H. Goldstein (Eds.), *Handbook of humor research, Vol 1: Basic issues* (pp. 85–107). New York: Springer.

Zillmann, D. (1983c). Transfer of excitation in emotional behavior. In J. T. Cacioppo & R. E. Petty (Eds.), *Social psychophysiology: A sourcebook* (pp. 215–240). New York: Guilford.

Zillmann, D. (1983d). Unterhaltende Ungewissheit [Entertaining uncertainty]. In E. Walther & U. Bayer (Eds.), *Zeichen von zeichen für zeichen: Festschrift für Max Bense* (pp. 68–75). Baden-Baden: Agis.

Zillmann, D. (1986). Coition as emotion. In D. Byrne & K. Kelley (Eds.), *Alternative approaches to the study of sexual behavior* (pp. 173–199). Hillsdale, NJ: Lawrence Erlbaum Associates.

Zillmann, D. (1991a). Empathy: Affect from bearing witness to the emotions of others. In J. Bryant & D. Zillmann (Eds.) *Responding to the screen: Reception and reaction processes* (pp. 135–167). Hillsdale, NJ: Lawrence Erlbaum Associates.

Zillmann, D. (1991b). The logic of suspense and mystery. In J. Bryant & D. Zillmann (Eds.), *Responding to the screen: Reception and reaction processes* (pp. 281–303). Hillsdale, NJ: Lawrence Erlbaum Associates.

Zillmann, D. (1993). Mental control of angry aggression. In D. M . Wegner & J. W. Pennebaker (Eds.), *Handbook of mental control* (pp. 370–392). Englewood Cliffs, NJ: Prentice Hall.

Zillmann, D. (1994a). Cognition-excitation interdependencies in the escalation of anger and angry aggression. In M. Potegal & J. F. Knutson (Eds.), *The dynamics of aggression: Biological and social processes in dyads and groups* (pp. 45–71). Hillsdale, NJ: Lawrence Erlbaum Associates.

Zillmann, D. (1994b). Mechanisms of emotional involvement with drama. *Poetics, 23,* 33–51.

Zillmann, D. (1996a). The psychology of suspense in dramatic exposition. In P. Vorderer, H. J. Wulf, & M. Friederichsen (Eds.), *Suspense: Conceptualizations, theoretical analyses, and empirical explorations* (pp. 199–231). Mahwah, NJ: Lawrence Erlbaum Associates.

Zillmann, D. (1996b). Sequential dependencies in emotional experience and behavior. In R. D. Kavanaugh, B. Zimmerberg, & S. Bein (Eds.), *Emotion: Interdisciplinary perspectives* (pp. 243–272). Mahwah, NJ: Lawrence Erlbaum Associates.

Zillmann, D. (1998a). Does the tragic drama have redeeming value? *Spiel, 17,* 1, 4–14.

Zillmann, D. (1998b). The psychology of the appeal of portrayals of violence. In J. Goldstein (Ed.), *Why we watch: The attractions of violent entertainment* (pp. 179–211). New York: Oxford University Press.

Zillmann, D., & Bryant, J. (1974). Effect of residual excitation on the emotional response to provocation and delayed aggressive behavior. *Journal of Personality and Social Psychology, 30,* 782–791.

Zillmann, D., & Bryant, J. (1991). Responding to comedy: The sense and nonsense in humor. In J. Bryant & D. Zillmann (Eds.), *Responding to the screen: Reception and reaction processes* (pp. 261–279). Hillsdale, NJ: Lawrence Erlbaum Associates.

Zillmann, D., & Cantor, J. R. (1972). Directionality of transitory dominance as a communication variable affecting humor appreciation. *Journal of Personality and Social Psychology, 24,* 191–198.

Zillmann, D., & Cantor, J. R. (1976). A disposition theory of humor and mirth. In A. J. Chapman & H. C. Foot (Eds.), *Humor and laughter: Theory, research, and applications* (93–115). London: Wiley.

Zillmann, D., & Johnson, R. C. (1973). Motivated aggressiveness perpetuated by exposure to aggressive films and reduced by exposure to nonaggressive films. *Journal of Research in Personality, 7,* 261–276.

Zillmann, D., Hay, T. A., & Bryant, J. (1975). The effect of suspense and its resolution on the appreciation of dramatic presentations. *Journal of Research in Personality, 9,* 307–323.

Zillmann, D., Hoyt, J. L., & Day, K. D. (1974). Strength and duration of the effect of aggressive, violent, and erotic communications on subsequent aggressive behavior. *Communication Research, 1,* 286–306.

Zillmann, D., Mody, B., & Cantor, J. R. (1974). Empathic perception of emotional displays in films as a function of hedonic and excitatory state prior to exposure. *Journal of Research in Personality, 8,* 335–349.

Zuckerman, M. (1974). The sensation seeking motive. In B. A. Maher (Ed.), *Progress in experimental personality research* (Vol. 7, pp. 80–148). New York: Academic.

Zuckerman, M. (1976). Sensation-seeking and anxiety traits and states as determinants of behavior in novel situations. In I. Sarason & C. D. Spielberger (Eds.), *Stress and anxiety* (Vol. 3, pp. 141–170). New York: Halsted.

3

Disposition-Based Theories of Enjoyment

Arthur A. Raney
Florida State University

The appeal and enjoyment of media entertainment have been the subject of much research interest in recent years (see Zillmann & Vorderer, 2000). "Why do we like what we like?" is a question that both content providers and social scientists seek to answer. A leading explanation of enjoyment focuses on the affective dispositions that viewers form toward the characters in those presentations; simply put, enjoyment of some types of entertainment is predicted by what happens with and to the characters that we like and/or dislike. Collectively these explanations are known as *disposition theory*. Although no single collection of statements called "disposition theory" exists to explain and predict enjoyment of all entertainment fare, disposition-based approaches to several types of entertainment have been forwarded.

The purpose of this chapter is to summarize the various theoretical assertions pertaining to the enjoyment of entertainment that are collectively referred to as disposition theory. To accomplish this, we trace the historical development of the theory through the work of Dolf Zillmann and his colleagues in the areas of humor appreciation, drama appreciation, and sports spectatorship. We then analyze the similarities in the application of the theory across these entertainment types, as well as the dissimilarities. The chapter concludes with suggestions for future research and theory development in the area of entertainment studies.

DISPOSITION THEORY AND HUMOR

Finding pleasure in the misfortunes of others is a curious but seemingly universal human phenomenon. Who hasn't experienced a bit of amusement in seeing, for instance, the schoolyard bully trip and fall into a mud puddle? Or chuckled to themselves on seeing a taskmaster of a boss spill a couple of drops of hot coffee on him- or herself? Or even guffawed when our inattentive friend walks headlong into a lamp post? For centuries, philosophers and scholars have attempted to understand and explain the humor derived from witnessing such acts.

Plato acknowledged the tendency for people to laugh at such incidents, suggesting that rejoicing in the misfortune of our enemies is part of human nature and morally justifiable. Humor found at the expense of one's friends, however, was morally impermissible because the response was presumed to be motivated by pride and envy. Centuries later, Thomas Hobbes, in *Leviathan,* made similar observations about the amusement derived from the faults of others. Hobbes argued that laughter at others' imperfections allows imperfect people–out of a need and in an attempt to improve their self-concept–to laugh at those who are a bit more imperfect. The influence of Hobbes is readily apparent on so-called superiority theories of humor that are based on the assumption that an innate need to feel superior drives social comparisons of oneself with weaker or inferior others.

However, the tradition of superiority theories fails to address Plato's problem with laughter at friends versus laughter at enemies. According to superiority theories, as long as the other party is perceived as inferior, we should find humor in their injury regardless of our relationship with him or her. This seems to defy common sense and social custom. Whether we agree with Plato and evaluate the activity in moral terms or not, laughter in the face of a family member's or friend's misfortune does not sit well with most people. Humor that comes from the pain, misery, or weakness of our enemies is much more palatable. Therefore, our relative affiliation with the one experiencing the setback dictates the propriety of our humor response.

Wolff, Smith, and Murray (1934) were the first to acknowledge the importance of relational affiliations in modern humor studies. The researchers distinguished between people and objects that we care for (i.e., affiliated objects) and those that we do not (i.e., unaffiliated objects). Common sense, social customs, and/or moral considerations render laughing at the misfortune of an affiliated object inappropriate or deplorable.

The misfortune of unaffiliated objects–or what Wolff and his associates termed "an unaffiliated object in a disparaging situation" (p. 344)–can lead to amusement-inducing experiences. In these situations, no social or moral sanctions inhibit our laughter response; the (lack of a) relationship between the one experiencing the disparagement and the one witnessing it provides absolution to the response. Therefore, as superiority theories suggest, the witness is free to express the emotion of sudden glory that comes when another person proves to be his or her lessor.

Although this innovative thinking changed forever the direction of humor research, its major limitations soon became apparent as well. As Wolff and his associates began testing their propositions, the researchers chose to operationalize their affiliation dichotomy in terms of group membership (e.g., Jews vs. non-Jews, Blacks vs. Whites, Catholics vs. Protestants). Although group membership and psychological affiliation with that group tend to be highly correlated, the relationship is not guaranteed. For example, a female of the Methodist faith may feel much more aligned with her Protestantism than another person of the same faith; an Hispanic man may feel much less affiliated with his ethnic group than do many of his Hispanic friends. Reliance on de facto group-membership classifications disregards the question of how affiliated (or unaffiliated) an individual feels with those groups.

To avoid problems with such misclassifications, Hyman (1942) introduced the concept of a reference group, that is, a group to which an individual relates or aspires to relate him- or herself as a member. In this way, distinctions can be made between, for instance, an individual who takes pride in his being a Southerner as opposed to another who is a Southerner simply by virtue of his birthplace. The presumption with regard to humor is that a situation or joke that disparages a Southerner should appear less funny to the pro-Southern witness than to the ambivalent-Southern one. Acknowledging the importance of reference groups (slightly altered and termed *identification classes* by La Fave) as an attitudinal construction of group membership has received a fair amount of attention (although with somewhat mixed support) in humor studies (La Fave, 1972; La Fave, Haddad, & Marshall, 1974; La Fave, McCarthy, & Haddad, 1973; Priest, 1966).

The advances in humor studies during the previous four decades seemed significant, in particular with the attention given to affiliations, reference groups, and identification classes. However, even with these advances, several holes in our understanding of humor still remained. The presence of these theoretical holes was first identified by Zillmann and Cantor (1972) and then cogently argued in full by Zillmann and Cantor (1976). The researchers identified three major limitations to then-existing humor theories. First, the authors rejected the dichotomous conceptualization of groups (e.g., affiliated vs. unaffiliated groups) in favor of a "conceptual continuum of affective dispositions ranging from extreme negative affect through a neutral point of indifference to extreme positive affect" (Zillmann & Cantor, 1976, p. 100). They argued that neither Hyman's reference groups nor La Fave's identification classes improved on Wolff et al.'s (1934) notion of simple affiliation. Instead, Hyman and LaFave's work only helped better distinguish who was an affiliated person or group and who was an unaffiliated one; this was seen as a "matter of method and procedure, not their contributions of theory" (p. 98). Furthermore, from a group-classification perspective, humor responses were contingent solely on the presence or absence of a positive disposition toward the group. Reference groups or identification classes do not take into account dislike or hate (i.e., negative affect) for a group. The proposed continuum was sensitive to both: It acknowledged degrees of affect toward the disparaged and/or the one disparaging, as well as positive and negative valences associated with the affect.

Secondly, according to the reference-group construct, a humorous response to a joke is dependent on the ability of the listener (a) to classify each character in the joke in terms of some group membership, and (b) then to determine his/her own reference to or identification with those characters and groups. Such a theory disregards the ability of the listener to respond discriminately to the characters as individuals. To address this problem, Zillmann and Cantor (1972) proposed the vital role of empathy in encoding humorous situations. More specifically, the individual interpreting a joke or witnessing a humorous situation first identifies the roles and activities of the characters and then (a) reacts with empathy toward characters whose roles and activities are associated with positive experiences of the interpreter; (b) reacts with antipathy or counterempathy toward characters whose roles and activities are associated with negative experiences of the interpreter; or (c) does both. Empathic and counterempathic reactions lead us to take sides with one character or set of characters over another. In other words, we align with those in a humorous situation that are more experientially close to us, and we align against those that are more experientially distant.

Such emotional responses, Zillmann and Cantor (1976) argued, are not bound to group classifications. If the interpreter of a humorous situation can understand enough to have an emotional reaction to the characters (as opposed to the more cognitive exercise of reference-group evaluations), then a disposition can be formed. These "gut reactions" are not dependent on typologies, but rather on the roles and activities of individual actors in the situation; thus, reference groups and identification classes are rendered useless. For instance, back to a previous example, the importance of a joke about someone "being reared in the South" is only important in a joke if the listener responds emotionally to issues regarding birthplace (or can identify with the emotionality conveyed in such a reference). Without the emotional response, the proposed humor associated with the reference is lost on the listener. Such a group affiliation is only valid if it is supported by an affective disposition. Because of the apparent supremacy of these dispositions, the researchers suggested that reference-group and identification-class constructions are theoretically subsumed under disposition-oriented ones.

Finally, Zillmann and Cantor argued that these affective gut-responses vary greatly over time.[1] This is a radical departure from the previous humor theories that were based on more stable understandings of affiliation, which had been summarily conceptualized as a manifestation of one's personality. In fact, Wolff et al. (1934) described many affiliations as "permanent" and/or "quite stable." By suggesting that affective dispositions are more contingent on emotional states than personality traits, Zillmann and Cantor (1976) recognized and "accommodate[d] the affective dynamics of individuals" (p. 104). More simply stated, we do not always respond to similar humorous stimuli in a similar manner; our emotional state plays a large role in our responses. This would explain, for example, why we might laugh at the disparagement of our best friend with whom we are temporarily angry or why we might denounce the ridicule of our worst enemy who had just uncharacteristically treated us well. Our transitory emotional state has altered our reactions in these situations.

Similarly, by accommodating affective dynamics, the researchers help explain how we can find humor in a joke that offers little (or no) general description of its characters–for example, the standard "Two men walk into a bar..." construction. According to previous theories, our humorous response would be contingent on our group classification of the joke's characters based on cues in the jokework and the subsequent evaluation of our affiliation to those characters based on those classifications. The only problem is that this type of joke provides no such cues. We cannot find the joke work (see Freud, 1960) humorous because we have not connected with the disparaged actor's group membership(s) more than the disparaging one; we have no way of determining such connections. Rather, Zillmann and

---

[1]Although the authors do not directly identify the role of mood in this process, Zillmann's work in the area–see chapter 4, this volume–might give some indication of its proposed influence on the process of disposition formation.

Cantor (1976) argued that we find the joke work humorous because we react *in situ* with negative emotions toward the provoking act by the one and with mirthful emotions toward the retaliation by the other (presumably because of basal-moralistic considerations of justice). The disparaging actor gets his comeuppance, and we get a nice chuckle as a result.

In an attempt to address these shortcomings, the researchers offered a disposition theory of humor, which characterizes a humorous response to a disparaging joke as a function of affective dispositions situationally formed toward the characters in the joke. The way the theory works is explained in this example: When you hear a joke in which one character disparages another, you immediately and emotionally react to the characters and the behaviors they display in the joke along a continuum of affect. You tend to empathize more with characters with whom you share relevant, positive experiences and less with those with whom you share relevant, negative experiences. As a result, you form affective dispositions toward the characters; you take sides. Who you take sides with/against and how strongly you take those positions is determined by your initial reaction. Consequently, your humor appreciation for the joke will be higher, the more negative your disposition toward the character who is disparaged, and/or the more positive your disposition toward the character responsible for the disparagement. Your humor appreciation for the joke will be lower, the more positive your disposition toward the character who is disparaged, and/or the more negative your disposition toward the character responsible for the disparagement. Or, as Zillmann and Cantor (1976) stated,

> humor appreciation varies inversely with the favorableness of the disposition toward the agent or entity being disparaged, and varies directly with the favorableness of the disposition toward the agent or entity disparaging it. Appreciation should be maximal when our friends humiliate our enemies, and minimal when our enemies manage to get the upper hand over our friends. (pp. 100–101)

Where does this fit in the larger humor-research context? This theory addresses only disparaging situations and, thus, fits squarely in the tradition of superiority theories of humor. The theory acknowledges the traditional importance placed on affiliations to characters in humor appreciation. However, the theory renders useless dichotomous conceptualizations of group and nongroup memberships and accompanying cognitive evaluations–which are thought to be based on stable and unchanging personality traits–in favor of discriminate, empathy-driven affective responses.

The disposition theory of humor's reliance on affective dispositions as a predictor of humor appreciation has been met with much support in the humor literature. For an extensive analysis of this rich research tradition, see chapter 15, this volume. Suffice it to say at this point, the introduction of the disposition theory of humor changed the direction of humor research, as well as the study of all entertainment appreciation.

DISPOSITION THEORY AND DRAMATIC PRESENTATIONS

One key distinction of the disposition theory of humor is that it is only applicable in humorous situations that involve a disparagement. Freud (1960) referred to such humorous situations as *tendentious.* What permits tendentious humor to be funny, stated Freud, is the joke work, or "the construction of the joke" (p. 54), that surrounds the disparaging offense. It is the presence of joke work that gives us the moral sanction to laugh at the misfortune of others; it becomes our excuse for violating existing social standards that prohibit such activity. Dramatic presentations, however, do not contain joke work and, thus, cannot offer us the guilt-free opportunity to enjoy the disparagement, maltreatment, or misfortune of others. How then can we be morally justified in appreciating a nonhumorous, dramatic presentation containing the mistreatment of others?

Zillmann and Cantor (1976) initially addressed this question by differentiating the nature of the appreciation associated with humorous and dramatic presentations.[2] Appreciation (or enjoyment) in general is associated with a feeling of euphoria, or positive affect, in response to any number of stimuli. The way that we express that euphoria is mirth, which can be manifest in a variety of external (e.g., a smile, laughter) and internal (e.g., positive or negative emotions) ways. When we experience mirth, we attempt to appraise or explain its cause.[3] For example, when we experience mirth in conjunction with a humorous situation containing disparagement, we attribute our feeling

---

[2]See chapter 6, this volume, for a more thorough treatment of the various natures of entertainment appreciation.

[3]This process is similar to our empathic responses to stimuli; see chapter 5, this volume, for further explanation of this affective-appraisal process.

of euphoria to the "funny" nature of the stimulus (i.e., the joke work). As a result, we appraise our response in light of the stimulus and call it "humorous." When we experience mirth in conjunction with the same disparagement in a dramatic situation, we do not refer to the feeling as "humor," but rather (generally and less specifically) as "enjoyment." If humorous responses and nonhumorous responses are both characterized as mirthful, and if humorous responses can be predicted by affective dispositions, then certainly nonhumorous responses can likewise be predicted by affective dispositions, if the differences in the presentations are accounted for.

Two major differences in the nature of the presentations are evident. First, dramatic presentations differ from humorous ones in that the former may involve both the debasement and benefaction of characters; as previously stated, humorous situations are only dependent on debasement. For example, it would not be humorous per se for your best friend to win the lottery jackpot. You may react with mirth to such an announcement, but you would not appraise your positive affect as "humor." Drama, on the other hand, allows such a turn of events. In fact, the benefaction (as well as the debasement) of others is a common theme in modern dramatic presentations.[4] Accordingly, any theory attempting to predict dramatic appreciation must address mirthful responses to the good fortune, as well as the misfortune, of characters.

Secondly, as previously discussed, a dramatic presentation involving the misfortune of others differs from tendentious humor in that it lacks joke work. As a result, "drama ... does not offer moral amnesty" (Zillmann & Cantor, 1976, p. 110) in the same manner as humor. That is, our enjoyment of drama depicting loss or misfortune is not readily excusable. Research suggests that if the misfortune or debasement depicted in a drama is perceived as justified, then the situation can (presumably) offer such amnesty and thus be enjoyed without guilt (Raney & Bryant, in press; Zillmann & Bryant, 1975). In other situations, enjoyment tends to be inhibited because of social sanctions against finding joy in the misfortune of others. If, despite these sanctions, an unjustified debasement is enjoyed, it is thought that the individual rationalizes the enjoyment by ascribing joke work-like qualities to other aspects of the presentation (e.g., precision of the dialogue, overall aesthetic quality) that subsequently serve as moral sanctions for the enjoyment.

---

[4]Benefaction in this case is different from a character getting the upper hand in a disparaging situation. The latter is dependent on a debasement of someone or something; the former is not.

As previously suggested, humor appreciation involves considerations of justice and, thus, some level of moral judgment. However, these considerations are kept at a minimum because of the presence of joke work. The stated research in drama enjoyment suggests that more intense considerations of moral propriety will be required. Any theory attempting to predict dramatic appreciation must therefore address this increased role of moral judgment.

With these two key differences in mind, a reasonable starting point for developing a theory of drama enjoyment is considering affective dispositions formed toward characters. As previously mentioned, affective dispositions can serve as a guide to predicting the enjoyment of humorous situations. One could expect that the same is true to some extent for dramatic situations. Applying the principles of affective dispositions from the disposition theory of humor to dramatic situations, we should expect that enjoyment should increase the more negative your disposition is toward the character who experiences misfortune, and that enjoyment should decrease the more positive your disposition is toward the character who experiences misfortune. Furthermore, remembering that dramatic presentations may also include the benefaction of a character, we should expect that enjoyment should increase the more positive your disposition is toward the character who experiences good fortune, and that enjoyment should decrease the more negative your disposition is toward the character who experiences good fortune. Finally, remembering from the disposition theory of humor that affective dispositions may be formed toward both the one who causes the misfortune to occur as well as the one who receives it, we should expect (based on our cultural values[5]) that enjoyment should increase the more positive your disposition is toward the character who causes the misfortune or good fortune, and that enjoyment should decrease the more negative your disposition is toward the character who causes the misfortune or good fortune. In other words, enjoyment increases the more we dislike characters that suffer and/or the more we like characters that prosper or succeed; enjoyment decreases the more we like characters that suffer and/or the more we dislike characters that prosper or succeed. This is

---

[5]Zillmann and Cantor (1976) correctly identified that "in our cultural situation, both benefaction and successful debasement seem equally meritorious. He who successfully disparages someone else enhances himself by doing so.... The glory-through-malevolence phenomenon shows once more the disparagement bias and the pervasiveness of malevolence in humor and drama appreciation" (p. 113).

precisely the disposition theory of mirth put forward by Zillmann and Cantor (1976), with mirth referring to reactions to nonhumorous (and thus dramatic) presentations.

As a proposed comprehensive theory of drama, the model addresses one of the distinctions between humor and drama previously raised: benefaction as a theme in drama. However, the second distinction–the increased role of moral judgment in drama–was not addressed. Again, without joke work as a scapegoat, dramatic presentations require heightened moral scrutiny of the characters and their behaviors to justify enjoyment of misfortune. What is in question here concerns the affective dispositions held toward characters. However, the distinction not only concerns the formation of affective dispositions toward characters, but also the maintenance or monitoring of those dispositions.

With the disposition theory of humor in mind, we have no reason to think that feelings toward characters in a drama are initially created in a manner any different than those in humor: The viewers evaluate the roles and behaviors of the characters in light of the viewers' own experiences. They form positive dispositions for characters who possess or display behaviors associated with positive past experiences and negative dispositions for characters who possess or display behaviors associated with negative past experiences. These affective responses are quickly formed, vary in relative strength or degree, and are dependent on many situational factors. The reliance on stereotypes and archetypes by writers of this genre helps with initial disposition formation. In this way, affective dispositions toward dramatic characters are formed in a similar manner as those in humorous situations.

In drama, however, viewers must constantly justify the moral propriety of their emotional side-taking. To do so, viewers must act as "untiring moral monitors," who continually render verdicts about the rightness or wrongness of a character's actions (Zillmann, 2000). As a result, when viewing a drama, we like characters whose actions we judge as proper or morally correct, whereas we dislike characters whose actions we judge as improper or morally incorrect. The strength of these affective dispositions, again, ranges on a continuum of affect, and because of this our constant moral monitoring is subject to change as the dramatic accounts progress. This intertwining of affective dispositions and moral judgment leads to what many refer to as our emotional involvement in drama, where we react with emotion to the emotional expressions of the characters.

Hoffmann (1987) and Zillmann (1991, 1994, 2000) identified empathy as the crucial mechanism that governs this process of emotional involvement.

For example, we respond with empathy to situations that evoke positive emotions in liked characters; we respond with counterempathy to situations that evoke positive emotions in disliked characters. The intensity of these empathic responses is a function of the magnitude of our positive or negative affect toward the characters, which is governed by our constant moral judgment of their actions. Therefore, the more proper we judge a character's actions, the more positive our affective disposition toward that character. In turn, the more positive our affective disposition, the more intense our empathic response. Conversely, the more improper we judge a character's actions, the more negative our affective disposition toward that character. In turn, the more negative our affective disposition, the more intense our counterempathic response.

Furthermore, the progressive, unfolding nature of drama allows the direction and magnitude of our affective dispositions to create active expectations or anticipatory emotions about characters. For example, not only do we like it when good things happen to characters we like, but we also hope for good things and fear for bad things to happen to those characters. Likewise, we dislike it when good things happen to characters we dislike, so we fear for prosperity and hope for misfortune to befall those characters. Ultimately, the outcomes associated with these anticipatory emotions dictate our enjoyment of or disappointment with a dramatic presentation. More specifically, hoped-for outcomes will lead to enjoyment and positive reactions, and feared-for outcomes will lead to disappointment and negative reactions.

This process of drama appreciation was summarized and presented by Zillmann (2000) as a moral-sanction theory of delight and repugnance. The model (see Fig. 3.1) serves as an extension of the disposition theory of mirth and as a more comprehensive explanation of the nature of drama appreciation. The model addresses both justice (i.e., positive or hoped-for) and injustice (i.e., negative and feared for) outcomes in dramatic presentations. More specifically, in the justice condition of moral-sanction theory (i.e., the top path of the model), witnessing the victimization of a disliked antagonist at the hands of a liked protagonist fosters delight, the experiential intensity of which increases with the liking of the protagonist, the disliking of the antagonist, and the extent to which the antagonist is deemed deserving of a particular victimization. Furthermore, witnessing the benefaction of a liked protagonist fosters delight, the experiential intensity of which increases with the liking of the protagonist and the extent to which the protagonist is deemed deserving of a particular benefaction.

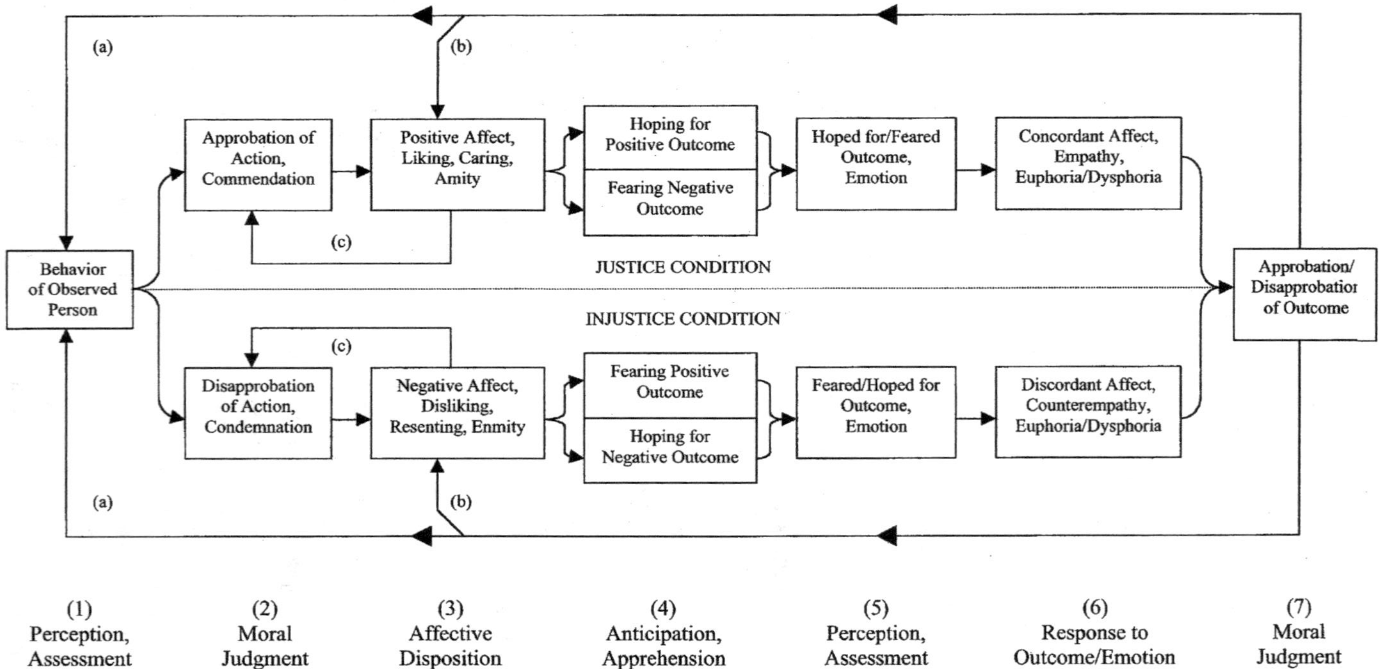

Fig. 3.1. Model of moral-sanction theory of delight and repugnance (adapted from Zillmann, 2000).

In contrast, in the injustice condition of moral-sanction theory (i.e., the bottom path of the model), witnessing the victimization of a liked protagonist at the hands of a disliked antagonist fosters repugnance, the experiential intensity of which increases with the liking of the protagonist, the disliking of the antagonist, and the extent to which the protagonist is deemed undeserving of a particular victimization. Witnessing the benefaction of a disliked antagonist fosters repugnance, the experiential intensity of which increases with the disliking of the antagonist and the extent to which the antagonist is deemed undeserving of a particular benefaction.

Strong support has been found for these disposition-based approaches to drama appreciation; a few key studies are highlighted here. Zillmann and Bryant (1975) first established the role of moral judgment in the formation of affective dispositions in drama. Children at varying levels of moral development (based on Kohlberg, 1981; Piaget, 1948) viewed one of three versions of a fairy tale in which a good king is given an opportunity to enact retribution on an evil king who had previously planned to banish him to the kingdom's wasteland. The three versions differed in the severity of punishment handed out by the good king: under (the evil king was forgiven), equitable (the evil king received the banishment that he had planned for the good king), or excessive (the evil king was publicly beaten and imprisoned for life) retribution. It was predicted that the more morally mature children (7- to 8-year olds) would be free to enjoy the equitable-retribution version, but not the under- or excessive-retribution ones that violated sanctions of moral propriety. In contrast, children at an earlier stage of development (4-year olds) would be unable to make such moral judgment-based distinctions and would, thus, enjoy the condition in which the wrong had been most "appropriately" righted (i.e., the excessive-retribution condition). These predictions were supported in full, and thus the importance of moral-judgment considerations in drama appreciation was also first supported.

To examine the claims regarding a viewer's affective dispositions and emotional reactions to characters, Zillmann and Cantor (1977) exposed elementary school children to a film that contained either a liked or disliked character, and in which the character experienced either a benefiting or victimizing situation. As expected, the students perceived the character as either "good" or "bad" based on the manipulation; and further, they came to like the good character and dislike the bad one. Moreover, when the children's unobtrusively recorded facial expressions were examined, the researchers observed that the children exhibited joy when the good character exhibited joy at his benefaction; they also exhibited pain when the protagonist cringed at his victimization. Similarly, the children cringed when the bad character exhibited joy and reveled when he exhibited pain (presumably because of moral-judgment considerations). These findings are perfectly in line with the general disposition theory of mirth and the more specific moral-sanction theory of delight and repugnance.

Further supp ort for disposition-based approaches to dramatic presentation has been found in examinations of fright-inducing entertainment (Hoffner & Cantor, 1991; Oliver, 1993), action films (King, 2000), reality-based programming (Oliver, 1996), crime-based fiction (Raney & Bryant, in press), and news programming (Zillmann, Taylor, & Lewis, 1998).

DISPOSITION THEORY AND SPORTS SPECTATORSHIP

Disposition-based explanations of enjoyment have also been applied to a third type of situation: sports spectatorship. Most sports enthusiasts know the adage, "It is not whether you win or lose, but how you play the game." When it comes to understanding the enjoyment derived from watching sports contests, nothing could be further from the truth. Although some have observed that the quality of play enhances enjoyment (Bryant, Comisky, & Zillmann, 1981), most acknowledge that in the sports world winning is everything, or more specifically for enjoyment, who wins is everything. Spectators have their favorite players and/or teams; the whole notion of a "sports fan" is based on the truly fanatic attitudes held and behaviors displayed by some in support of these athletes and teams. As a result, viewers find great pleasure in seeing their favorite teams succeed and great disappointment in seeing them fail. In the same manner, many spectators revel in the defeat of a hated team and cringe when the team is victorious.

Given such a dynamic, along with the dramatic qualities of sporting events (Bryant, Brown, Comisky, & Zillmann, 1982; Bryant, Comisky, & Zillmann, 1977), it should be of little surprise that a prominent explanation of sports-spectatorship enjoyment is based on affective dispositions. The disposition theory of sportsfanship was articulated most comprehensively in Zillmann, Bryant, and Sapolsky, 1989–renamed the disposition theory of sports spectatorship in Zillmann and Paulus (1993)–as a derivation of the more general disposition theory of mirth (Zillmann & Cantor, 1976). In delineating the theory, the researchers acknowledged that spectators[6] form various positive dispositions toward or allegiances with teams and players; however, unlike previous disposition-based approaches, the way these dispositions are formed is not readily explained. As before, these dispositions are thought to occur on a continuum of affective dispositions ranging from extreme positive to extreme negative affect. Although not specifically noted by the researchers, it is agreed that these dispositions are generally more stable than in other situations and are predictive of future spectatorship (Zillmann & Paulus, 1993).

Also, as was the case with tendentious humor and dramatic presentations, it is presumed that these emotional connections impact in a predictable manner the enjoyment of contests involving the liked or disliked competitors. More specifically, the disposition theory of sports spectatorship offers two major and three derived propositions. First, enjoyment from witnessing a team or player winning increases with positive affective dispositions toward the competitors and decreases with negative affective dispositions toward the competitors. In other words, fans enjoy seeing their preferred teams win and detest seeing rival teams win. Secondly, enjoyment from witnessing a team or player lose increases with negative affective dispositions toward the competitors and decreases with positive affective dispositions toward the competitors. Or, fans hate seeing their favorite teams lose but find enjoyment in seeing rival teams defeated.

As a result of these two major proposals, we should expect that maximum enjoyment from sports spectatorship is derived from witnessing an intensely liked team defeat an intensely disliked team. Conversely, minimum enjoyment (as well as maximum disappointment or "negative enjoyment"; Zillmann & Paulus, 1993, p. 605) comes from witnessing a loved team fall to a hated one. And finally, the outcome of a contest between similarly liked or disliked competitors will generate an intermediate level of enjoyment.

Numerous studies have found support for the disposition theory of sports spectatorship; see chapter 18, this volume, for a review of this literature.

---

[6]The more inclusive term *spectator* is preferred to *viewer* or *listener* to demonstrate the sufficiency of the theory to address enjoyment of live-attended and mediated sports contests.

CHARACTERIZING DISPOSITION THEORIES

As previously noted, a single explanation of enjoyment that we call *disposition theory* does not really exist. Instead, disposition-based theories of appreciation or enjoyment have been forwarded for three types of media content: tendentious humor, drama, and sports. Various differences between these types of content dictate subtle differences in the application of the theories and, thus, render efforts to forge a single, more general disposition theory of media content futile. However, we can identify the similarities between these theories to better understand how disposition-based theories could be developed with other media contents.

Enjoyment-Oriented Theories

First and foremost, disposition-based theories are concerned with and are predictive of enjoyment or appreciation of content. As such, they fall under the larger rubric of entertainment studies that include selective processes, excitation transfer theory, mood theory, and various uses and gratification approaches; see chapter 6, this volume, as well as Zillmann and Vorderer (2000) for a more thorough overview of this area. Given the increasing presence of and emphasis placed on entertainment today, the importance of these and similar theories will only grow. Although disposition theories cannot ultimately predict whether an individual will like or dislike a specific character, a joke, or a story, they can serve as useful aides in understanding how and why people enjoy these things. And, as in the case of sporting events (Zillmann & Paulus, 1993), they may also be helpful in predicting future exposure to similar media content.

However, many key issues regarding this still nebulous term *enjoyment* remain. To most accurately represent the Zillmann literature, we should note that the term a p p*reciation* is used almost exclusively to refer to one's hedonic response to media fare. Only in the last decade or so have others–this author included–started using the (arguably broader) term *enjoyment*. Are the two terms indeed synonymous? Perhaps that is a question for further study. At a minimum, further explication of enjoyment is needed. Much like the term *entertainment,* scholars have yet to conclusively define *enjoyment*. And although we might suggest one definition–the pleasure experienced from consuming media entertainment–this does little to help our understanding of what leads to this pleasure, how and why it differs between individuals, and how it differs between media content. When we say that we enjoyed the hockey match on Friday night and also the opera on Sunday, we may use the same terms but certainly describe different responses. Furthermore, when we say in one breath that we enjoyed, for instance, the film *The Godfather,* and in the next breath say that we enjoyed the Marx Brother's film *Animal Crackers,* again surely we are describing two entirely different experiences.

With this in mind, Carpentier and her colleagues (Carpentier, Yu, Butner, Chen, Hong, et al., 2001) initially examined the entertainment concept empirically to better understand and eventually offer a reliable and heuristic definition of it. To do so, the researchers had 410 participants view an action, comedy, or horror film and then describe their resulting feelings using descriptive mood adjectives provided in two instruments. The findings verify what has been implied herein: Entertainment (and thus enjoyment) is a multidimensional concept that varies even as it is applied within a single medium (in this case, motion pictures). A look at the 12 most frequently selected mood adjectives for each genre reveals strikingly few similarities: Between the horror and action groups, only four adjectives were found in both lists (*anxious, alert, tense,* and tired); between action and comedy, only 1 (*amused*); and between horror and comedy, none. In light of the findings, the researchers suggested that "because the dimensionality of the entertainment experience of watching different genres of media fare is markedly different among genres, conceptualizations of the enjoyment of different genres will have to proceed rather idiosyncratically" (p. 16).

Disposition-based theories indeed tap into this construct that we collectively, if nonspecifically, label *enjoyment.* To date, researchers have adapted their dependent measures to evaluate the term as it is applied to humor, drama, and sports. Although myriad entertainment forms are yet to be fully explored in a similar fashion, the groundbreaking work of Carpentier et al. should not be overlooked. Exploring the differences in enjoyment between media content should prove to be extremely worthwhile; disposition-based theories will certainly play a large role in those explorations.

Emotional-Response Theories

Secondly, disposition theories involve the role of affective responses to media content as predictors of enjoyment. More specifically–although the limits of this chapter do not allow full exploration of this–empathy has been identified as the chief mechanism guiding these emotional responses. Furthermore, understanding the relationship between affective dispositions and empathic reactions is a key to understanding enjoyment. This emphasis on emotions is in contrast to more cognitive-based proposals like reference-group theories of humor. Theories of affective responses necessarily acknowledge the dynamic and situational nature of those responses; this feature sets disposition theories apart from previous conceptualization.

Recent work has sought to better understand the role of cognition in the disposition-formation process. In particular, Raney and Bryant (in press) further explored the role of moral judgment in the enjoyment of drama. More specifically, a theoretical framework is offered in which subjectively held notions of social justice interact with affective responses to characters and their behaviors as predictors of disposition formation, thus influencing the enjoyment of crime-based dramas. The researchers acknowledged the predictive power of the disposition theory of drama, where affective dispositions toward characters are based on the viewer's moral evaluation of the role and behaviors of characters. However, they seek to expand the perspective by arguing that because moral considerations are at the heart of disposition formation, then subjectively held notions of basal morality must influence how these dispositions are formed in the first place. Furthermore, the statements about justice that results from the crime drama's resolution offer further opportunity for moral judgment that is not necessarily bound to the characters. This meta-judgment of the story's themes and message, and its impact on enjoyment, was first raised by Raney and Bryant (2002).

The researchers offer a rudimentary theoretical model that seeks to address both the affective and cognitive processes inherent in the entertainment experience. The resulting integrated model of enjoyment for crime drama is presented in Fig. 3.2. Audience members bring the cognitive and affective tools (audience inputs) necessary for judgment to the entertainment experience; the crime dramas then offer the viewer a scenario including characters, behaviors, and an overall story in which to utilize those tools (message inputs). What results are judgments of the characters themselves and judgment of the collective resolution of the drama's conflict. Both the judgment of the characters and the judgment of the justice that is rendered are thought to influence the entertainment experience. More specifically, enjoyment is seen as the product of dispositional affiliations (i.e., as predicted by disposition theory) and the judgment of the justice rendered by each viewer. Maximum enjoyment, then, is the perfect intersection (or maximizing) of these two evaluations.

Therefore, Raney and Bryant (2002) seeks to extend disposition-theory research with dramatic presentations by arguing that certain cognitive structures must precede and coexist with affective responses, which are based on moral judgment, and that by evaluating those structures before exposure, we might better predict how dispositions are formed. Understanding better how affective dispositions are formed–not only in drama, but also in many other areas (e.g., sports fandom)–should be a goal of entertainment scholars in the future.

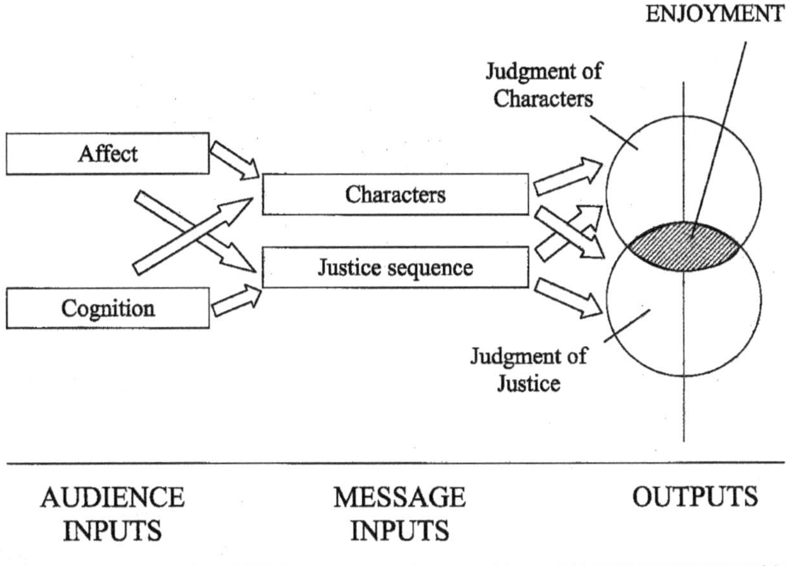

Fig. 3.2. Integrated model of enjoyment for crime drama (from Raney & Bryant, 2002).

Continuum of Dispositional Affiliation

One of the major advances of the disposition theory of humor that carried over to subsequent disposition-based theories was the emphasis on dispositional intensity or magnitude. Previous dichotomous conceptualizations of affiliation prove to be ineffective in consistently predicting enjoyment. This change also allowed for the introduction of negative responses or disliking, which proves crucial in our understanding of both dramatic and sports appreciation. And finally, although not highlighted earlier, this continuum of affective disposition allows a viewer to be ambivalent or neutral toward a character or sports team. These features achieve the level of response sensitivity wished for by La Fave's (1972) identification-class construct.

One area of research that begs for further development is fanship. With little effort, you can probably bring to mind a friend who is such a sports fanatic that he paints his body for the big game, wears the team colors the rest of the year, and mourns openly after a defeat. Or you may know someone that is such a fan of the television series *Star Trek* (and its various spinoffs) that she dresses in full makeup and costume to attend international conferences celebrating the show and its stars. Extreme types of fandom have received some attention from critical and cultural scholars (e.g., Brown, 2001; Sanders, 1994) but relatively little from empirical, social scientists. Exploring this phenomenon will shed further light on the continuum of affective response to characters on which disposition-based theories of enjoyment are dependent.

Character Focused and Driven

The starting place for theories of this kind is the viewer's feelings about the characters. Many features of the media content will influence what the feelings will be and how they will be formed, but the emphasis is still on the characters. Disposition theories do not address formal features of a presentation that may impact enjoyment (e.g., camera movements, sound effects, music); they have not to date addressed the impact of one's viewing environment, age, or moral maturity on entertainment. Disposition-based approaches focus on how characters are liked by viewers; what happens with, to, and between those characters; and how those events lead to increased or decreased enjoyment.

As our entertainment-laden society continues to foster various cults of personality, entertainment scholars may want to explore, especially with fictional content, how a viewer's previous exposure to, and affiliation with, an entertainer influences their subsequent evaluation of that entertainer. Furthermore, with the amount of information concerning an actor's private life that is available on various entertainment shows and Web sites, consumers tend to know more about individual actors than ever before. One might imagine that individuals then use that information to form judgments about entertainers without regard to the stories in which they act or games in which they play. To date, the disposition theory of drama has ignored these prior attitudes; they have relied solely on the dispositions formed as a result of a specific piece of content.

One area of future disposition research will be the role of these a priori judgments and the expectations they create on enjoyment. For instance, it seems reasonable to suggest that individuals may base their expectations for enjoyment on an actor's previous roles or a player's past performance. For example, comedians Robin Williams and Jim Carrey found much early success with their over-the-top, often physical, comedy routines. When the actors began filling dramatic roles, some viewers may have watched the performances with the previous work in mind, expecting humor where none was intended. Such expectations surely have some impact on enjoyment. Similarly, the publicity of celebrity scandals may impact consumers' attitudes toward certain stars, and those attitudes may also influence the moral judgments that viewers make about the characters played by those stars. This intersection of actors and the roles they fill could prove to be fertile ground for entertainment study.

Acknowledgment of Individual Differences

As a result of many of these features, disposition theories openly embrace the differences between individuals in terms of emotional responsiveness, personal experiences, basal morality, and countless other psychological and social-psychological factors. Furthermore, disposition theories acknowledge that humans are undergoing constant change from one mood to the next and from one day to the next. As a result, our responses to media content will likewise be dynamic and often unpredictable across time. The previously cited work of Raney and Bryant (in press) further acknowledged the role of individual differences in enjoyment by attempting to understand the role of subjectively held notions of social justice in the enjoyment of crime dramas.

Dependent on Considerations of Justice

One feature that tendentious humor, drama, and sports all have in common is conflict. In every situation, two or more parties, objects, or even ideas are presented in opposition to one another. If we assume that affective dispositions are formed more positively for one side in a conflict over the other (made possible by the continuum of affective dispositions), then it is apparent that our enjoyment of the situation will be bound to our appraisal of the conflict's resolution. The more we favor the side that comes out on top, the more we enjoy the situation. The less we favor the side that succeeds, the less we enjoy the situation.

As was stated earlier, the way that we morally justify or condemn inequities in this power dynamic is by evaluating the moral propriety of the conflict outcome. Not only do we enjoy our favored party winning because we like them, we like them (and thus enjoy their success) because we think that they *should* win. Those individuals and/or teams toward whom we have a positive disposition are morally "right" in their domination of another; our judgment of their moral makeup is a large part of what our positive disposition is based on in the first place. Their personal conviction, character, roles, and behaviors allow us to morally justify (or decry the injustice of) their supremacy over another. So whether, for example, it is in a joke where the victim turns the tables on his tormentor, or in a drama where the virtuous heroine is vindicated in the final act, or in a sporting event where the hard-playing, tradition-laden team outclasses the over-paid, thuggish prima donnas, the justice (or "justness") or lack thereof that results from their conflict is of ultimate importance to our enjoyment. Moral judgments of justice, equity, and propriety are essential to any disposition-based theory of enjoyment.

THE FUTURE OF DISPOSITION THEORY RESEARCH

The presence of entertainment in our society increases constantly and will surely not fade any time soon. In response, the sophisticated, social-scientific investigation of media entertainment must be continued and expanded. Certainly, disposition-based theories of enjoyment will play a major role in this area for years to come. The principles of the theories should be applied to new media content–the latest wave of reality-based programs, game shows, situation comedies, talk shows, and anything else Hollywood sends our way–to see how the enjoyment process is altered by these different content types.

We will also need to further study the way that dispositions are formed, searching for predictors here as well. For instance, when evaluating a character in terms of our "experiential closeness" to him or her, what matters from our experiences? To what extent do some group memberships (in particular, things like race, ethnicity, and/or citizenship) have an impact on disposition formation? In terms of sports spectatorship, other than geographic proximity and educational affiliations, what might predict team fanship? Furthermore, in this day of rampant free agency in the professional ranks, which is more important for sports enjoyment, dispositions toward teams or toward individual players? The questions are limitless.

And finally, we should also see how dispositions are formed differently across media types. What are the important factors in disposition formation? For dramas, a major one appears to be the perceived morality of the characters. Surely, this is not the case for sports fanship. Sapolsky (1980) found that race membership can predict enjoyment of interracial basketball contests; however these distinctions are not sufficient to predict the appreciation of a tendentious joke. These and other differences should provide entertainment researchers with a constant stream of disposition-related questions for years to come.

REFERENCES

Brown, J. (2001). *Black superheroes, milestone comics, and their fans.* Jackson, MS: University Press of Mississippi.

Bryant, J., Brown, D., Comisky, P., & Zillmann, D. (1982). Sports and spectators: Commentary and appreciation. *Journal of Communication, 32*(1), 109–119.

Bryant, J., Comisky, P., & Zillmann, D. (1977). Drama in sports commentary. *Journal of Communication, 27*(3), 140–149.

Bryant, J., Comisky, P., & Zillmann, D. (1981). The appeal of rough-and-tumble play in televised professional football. *Communication Quarterly, 29,* 256–262.

Carpentier, F. D., Yu, H., Butner, B., Chen, L., Hong, S., Park, D., & Bryant, J. (2001, April). *Dimensions of the entertainment experience: Factors in the enjoyment of action, comedy, and horror films.* Paper presented at the annual meeting of the Broadcast Education Association, Las Vegas, NV.

Freud, S. (1960). *Jokes and their relation to the unconscious.* (James Strachey, Ed. and Trans). New York: W. W. Norton & Company. (Original work published 1905)

Hoffmann, M. L. (1987). The contribution of empathy to justice and moral judgment. In N. Eisenberg & J. Strayer (Eds.), *Empathy and its development* (pp. 47–80). Cambridge: Cambridge University Press.

Hoffner, C., & Cantor, J. (1991). Factors affecting children's enjoyment of a frightening film sequence. *Communication Monographs, 58*(1), 41–62.

Hyman, H. H. (1942). The psychology of status. *Archives of pyschology,* No. 269. New York: Columbia University.

King, C. M. (2000). Effects of humorous heroes and villains in violent action films. *Journal of Communication, 50*(1), 5–24.

Kohlberg, L. (1981). *Essays on moral development.* San Francisco: Harper & Row.

La Fave, L. (1972). Humor judgments as a function of reference groups and identification classes. In J. H. Goldstein & P. E. McGhee (Eds.), *The psychology of humor* (pp. 195–210). New York: Academic.

La Fave, L., Haddad, J., & Marshall, N. (1974). Humor judgments as a function of identification classes. *Sociology & Social Research, 58,* 184–194.

La Fave, L., McCarthy, K., & Haddad, J. (1973). Humor judgments as a function of identification classes: Canadian vs. American. *The Journal of Psychology, 85,* 53–59.

Oliver, M. B. (1993). Adolescents' enjoyment of graphic horror: Effects of attitudes and portrayals of victim. *Communication Research, 20(1),* 30–50.

Oliver, M. B. (1996). Influences of authoritarianism and portrayals of race on Caucasian viewers' responses to reality-based crime dramas. *Communication Reports, 9(2),* 141–150.

Piaget, J. (1948). *The moral judgment of the child.* Glencoe, IL: Free Press.

Priest, R. F. (1966). Election jokes: The effects of reference group membership. *Psychological Reports, 18,* 600–602.

Raney, A. A., & Bryant, J. (2002). Moral judgment and crime drama: An integrated theory of enjoyment. *Journal of Communication, 52*(2), 402–415.

Sanders, J. (1994). *Science fiction fandom*. Westport, CN: Greenwood Press.

Sapolsky, B. S. (1980). The effect of spectator disposition and suspense on the enjoyment of sport contests. *International Journal of Sport Psychology, 11*(1), 1–10.

Wolff, H. A., Smith, C. E., & Murray, H. A. (1934). The psychology of humor. *Journal of Abnormal and Social Psychology, 28,* 341–365.

Zillmann, D. (1991). Empathy: Affect from bearing witness to the emotion of others. In J. Bryant & D. Zillmann (Eds.), *Responding to the screen: Reception and reaction processes* (135–167), Hillsdale, NJ: Lawrence Erlbaum Associates.

Zillmann, D. (1994). Mechanisms of emotional involvement with drama. *Poetics, 23,* 33–51.

Zillmann, D. (2000). Basal morality in drama appreciation. In I. Bondebjerg (Ed.), *Moving images, culture, and the mind* (pp. 53–63). Luton: University of Luton Press.

Zillmann, D., & Bryant, J. (1975). Viewers' moral sanction of retribution in the appreciation of dramatic presentations. *Journal of Experimental Social Psychology, 11,* 572–582.

Zillmann, D., Bryant, J., & Sapolsky, B. S. (1989). Enjoyment from sports spectatorship. In J. H. Goldstein (Ed.), *Sports, games, and play: Social and psychological viewpoints* (2nd ed., pp. 241–278). Hillsdale, NJ: Lawrence Erlbaum Associates.

Zillmann, D., & Cantor, J. (1972). Directionality of transitory dominance as a communication variable affecting humor appreciation. *Journal of Personality and Social Psychology, 24,* 191–198.

Zillmann, D., & Cantor, J. (1976). A disposition theory of humor and mirth. In T. Chapman & H. Foot (Eds.), *Humor and laughter: Theory, research, and application* (pp. 93–115). London: Wiley.

Zillmann, D., & Cantor, J. (1977). Affective responses to the emotions of a protagonist. *Journal of Experimental Social Psychology, 13,* 155–165.

Zillmann, D., & Paulus, P. B. (1993). Spectators: Reactions to sports events and effects on athletic performance. In R. N. Singer, M. Murphey, & L. K. Tennant (Eds.), *Handbook on research in sport psychology* (pp. 600–619). New York: Macmillan.

Zillmann, D., Taylor, K., & Lewis, K. (1998). News as nonfiction theater: How dispositions toward the public cast of characters affect reactions. *Journal of Broadcasting and Electronic Media, 42*(2), 153–169.

Zillmann, D., & Vorderer, P. (2000). *Media entertainment: The psychology of its appeal.* Mahwah, NJ: Lawrence Erlbaum Associates.

4

Mood Management and Selective Exposure

Mary Beth Oliver
Pennsylvania State University

Habits, tastes, and enduring dispositions are obviously important predictors of entertainment choices. Although some viewers have affinities for themes featuring love and romance, other viewers long for the thrills that accompany action adventure or suspense. With these more stable entertainment preferences in mind, it is also apparent that entertainment choices vary within individuals, with any given viewer preferring one type of genre or media offering at one time and opting for a different genre at another. Indeed, one can easily imagine phrases that viewers frequently voice that capture this type of variability, including comments such as, "I feel like a good mystery tonight," or "I'm in the mood for a comedy."

Scholarship on mood management and viewers' selective exposure embraces these variations in entertainment choices, suggesting that much of the variation reflects a basic human drive to enhance or maintain positive states and to diminish or avoid negative ones (Zillmann, 1988a, 1988b; Zillmann & Bryant, 1985). Of course, what is meant by "positive" and "negative" states and the characteristics of media content that may serve these ends is complex and sometimes subtle. As a result, questions about how and when mood management may operate has resulted in a large body of research that not only provides insight into viewers' entertainment choices, but that also examines fundamental questions concerning human needs and desires.

The first section of this chapter outlines the primary assumptions and processes involved in mood management as first articulated by Zillmann and his colleagues (Zillmann, 1988a, 1988b; Zillmann & Bryant, 1985). The second section then examines empirical evidence, both experimental and correlational, that illustrates the operation of mood management as it pertains to a variety of different types of media content. The final section of this chapter examines entertainment genres that are seemingly at odds with the basic assumptions of mood-management theory and touches on Zillmann's (2000b) more recent theorizing that accommodates these genres.

FUNDAMENTAL ASSUMPTIONS AND PROCESSES

The most basic, underlying assumption that mood-management theory makes is that hedonistic motivations govern much of human behavior (Zillmann, 1988a, 1988b; Zillmann & Bryant, 1985). That is, to the extent possible, individuals tend to arrange their environments such that pleasure is maximized or maintained, and pain is diminished or alleviated. The arrangement of environments can take many forms, including physically moving away from or avoiding situations that create negative affect (such as avoiding a stressful traffic jam), or moving toward or selecting situations that result in gratification (such as strolling in a beautiful garden; Zillmann 1988a). However, insofar as entertainment provides its audience with the opportunity to symbolically arrange the environment, mood-management theory posits that viewers' entertainment choices should similarly reflect the motivation to maximize pleasure and minimize pain.

Although mood management suggests that people's behaviors often conform to this hedonic assumption, this theory also makes clear that individuals are not necessarily aware of their motivations. Rather, people are thought to initially arrange their environments (including media environments) in a random fashion, with arrangements that succeed in achieving hedonic ends leaving memory traces and serving as reinforcements, thereby increasing the likelihood of their occurrence in the future (Zillmann, 1988a, 1988b). Given that the resulting pattern of stimulus arrangement is conceptualized as reflecting operant learning, mood-management theory does not assume that individuals will necessarily be aware of their motivations for media selection. That is, although individuals may behave in ways that are consistent with hedonic considerations, it is not necessarily assumed that individuals are cognizant of these considerations or are therefore necessarily able to articulate their motivations (Zillmann 1988a, 1988b, 2000b; Zillmann & Bryant, 1985). One important methodological implication of this assumption is that self-report data that are characteristic of much uses and gratifications research may not be appropriate for testing hypotheses exploring mood-management predictions (Zillmann, 1985; Zillmann & Bryant, 1985). Consequently, experimental studies employing behavioral measures tend to be more typical of mood-management research, although a wide variety of methodologies have contributed to the scholarship in this area.

With these assumptions in place, Zillmann and his colleagues have set forth numerous propositions that detail examples of negative and positive states that likely play important roles in the selective exposure process, and the characteristics of media entertainment that likely serve in the regulation of these states (see Zillmann, 1988a, 1988b; Zillmann & Bryant, 1985). In terms of the states themselves, mood-management theory suggests that one predictor of viewers' entertainment choices is the need to regulate physiological arousal. Specifically, given that both overstimulation (i.e., stress) and understimulation (i.e., boredom) are less than optimal states, mood management proposes that individuals experiencing over- or understimulation will choose to view entertainment that serves to bring levels of arousal back to optimal, comfortable levels. In addition to arousal, mood management also states that affect serves as an important predictor of entertainment selection. Specifically, this theory argues that individuals in negative or dysphoric moods will tend to choose entertainment that will help alleviate or diminish their states, but that individuals in positive or upbeat moods will tend to choose entertainment that will help intensify or prolong their states.

What aspects of media entertainment serve in the regulation of arousal and affect, resulting in the highest levels of gratification? The propositions of mood-management theory outline numerous media characteristics that likely serve these ends, although there are undoubtedly additional characteristics that await future studies. Among the characteristics that have been mentioned, however, are entertainment's excitatory potential, its hedonic valence, its semantic affinity to the viewer's current state, and its absorption potential (Zillmann, 1988b).

Of these characteristics, the excitatory potential of entertainment is clearly most related to the regulation of arousal, with mood-management theory predicting that individuals who are overstimulated or stressed will opt for more soothing, calming fare, whereas individuals who are understimulated or bored will opt for more exciting entertainment. The other three characteristics have the clearest applications for the regulation of mood. Specifically, individuals who are experiencing negative affect should be expected to choose entertainment that has a positive or uplifting valence as a way of breaking out of their bad moods. Additionally, these individuals should also be expected to avoid thoughts that remind them of their current affective states. Consequently, these individuals should be likely to avoid entertainment that has a strong semantic affinity with the circumstances that created their moods, and should opt for media fare that is absorbing so as to disrupt ruminations about their current affective states. In contrast, the maintenance of positive moods should benefit from the continued rumination about one's state, and should therefore lead viewers in good moods to avoid absorbing content, if media is consumed at all, and to select fare featuring positively valenced tones and high levels of semantic affinity (Zillmann 1988a, 1988b).

In addition to these characteristics, there are further narrative elements of media fare that Zillmann and his colleagues have highlighted as important to viewers' gratification. Specifically, disposition theory suggests that viewers' experiences of media entertainment are a function of both their dispositions toward the characters portrayed and the outcomes that the characters experience (Zillmann, 1985, 1991a, 2000a; Zillmann & Cantor, 1977; see chaps. 3 and 5, this volume). Gratifications are thought to be highest when liked or beloved characters are shown experiencing positive outcomes or rewards, or when disliked or hated characters are shown experiencing disappointments or negative outcomes. In contrast, gratification is thought to be lowest when liked characters are shown suffering and when disliked characters are shown prevailing.

Finally, the identification of these affective states and the types of media characteristics that are thought to serve as important regulators should not be understood as ignoring more enduring preferences or as discounting individual differences in the media selection process. In fact, Zillmann (2000b) explicitly acknowledged that individual differences likely play crucial roles in a variety of ways, including influencing individuals' affective reactions to different situations, and moderating the specific strategies that individuals employ in the regulation of their moods. As a result, Zillmann (2000b) suggested that future research would benefit from the exploration of the interaction between state-specific affect and more enduring traits that likely moderate the selective exposure process in a way that optimizes hedonic concerns.

EMPIRICAL EVIDENCE OF MOOD MANAGEMENT IN SELECTIVE EXPOSURE

As mentioned previously, the preponderance of research on mood management has employed experimental procedures to examine how viewers' entertainment choices reflect the hypothesized regulation of affective states. Given that affective states are conceptualized as independent variables, experimental work in this area has typically taken the form of the manipulation of some aspect of affect, and the subsequent measurement of media selection. However, studies that have employed alternative methodologies such as quasi-experimental designs and correlational data also offer evidence for the basic tenets of mood management.

Regulation of Arousal

The idea that media entertainment can elicit physiological arousal is well documented in a long history of research (see Zillmann, 1991c). In addition, research from a uses and gratifications perspective often reports that both relaxation and excitement are frequently mentioned motivations for using television (see Rubin, 1994). Although this type of evidence suggests that media fare may present the opportunity for viewers to regulate their arousal, it does not clearly provide evidence that they make use of entertainment for these ends.

To explore selective exposure to media entertainment as a function of physiological arousal, Bryant and Zillmann (1984) randomly assigned participants to conditions involving the performance of tasks inducing low levels of arousal (boredom) or high levels of arousal (stress). Subsequently, while the participants were ostensibly waiting for a second portion of the study to begin, they were given the opportunity to view television as a way of passing the time. Among the programs available for viewing during this waiting period were materials that had been rated in a pretest as relaxing (e.g., a concert of lullabies) or materials that had been rated as exciting (e.g., a quiz-show "play-off"). Consistent with mood-management predictions, stressed participants watched significantly more relaxing programming than did the bored participants, whereas bored participants watched significantly more exciting programming than did the stressed participants. In addition, physiological indicators of arousal (i.e., heart rate) showed that this pattern of media selection was successful in regulating arousal levels, whereas arousal levels were not regulated among the participants who deviated from this pattern (e.g., bored participants who chose relaxing programming).

Although experimental methods clearly provide the most robust examination of the regulation of arousal via entertainment selection, additional support for mood-management's predictions has also been obtained in more naturalistic, correlational studies. For example, Anderson,

Collins, Schmitt, and Jacobvitz (1996) employed television viewing diaries and observational data recorded via time-lapsed video to explore the relationship between stressful life events and the selection of and attention to television (Studies 2 and 3). Consistent with mood-management predictions, among both male and female participants, stressful life events were associated with greater viewing of comedy and lesser viewing of news or documentary programming. In addition, among females, stressful events were associated with greater viewing overall, and among males, stressful events were associated with greater attention to the screen while viewing.

Relief from Bad Moods

In addition to examining how boredom and stress influence viewers' selection of media content, a considerable body of research has also examined how viewers' mood states predict media choices. As with studies of arousal, research in this area has employed both experimental and correlational methods, with the preponderance of evidence suggesting that viewers behave in ways that are consistent with hedonic considerations assumed by mood management.

In an earlier experimental study on affect and selective exposure, Zillmann, Hezel, and Medoff (1980) randomly assigned participants to one of three conditions in which affect was manipulated via bogus feedback from the experimenter. Specifically, participants were shown 20 photographs of individuals and were asked to identify the ambiguous emotions being expressed in each photograph. Participants in the positive-affect condition were praised for their strong performance on the task, participants in the negative-affect condition were insulted for their poor performance, and participants in the neutral-affect condition were told that their performance was normal. After completing the task, participants were allowed to view television while ostensibly waiting for a second portion of the study to begin. Contrary to predictions, participants in the negative-affect condition were significantly less likely to select comedy programs for viewing. However, a subsequent study described by these authors (Medoff, 1979, as cited in Zillmann et al., 1980) provided insight on these counterintuitive results. Namely, the comedy selections available to participants in the Zillmann et al. (1980) study consisted primarily of humor featuring insults and "put downs." Given that these types of portrayals were arguably reminiscent of the circumstances that elicited negative affect (i.e., high on semantic affinity), it is understandable that this type of fare would be actively avoided. Subsequent research (Medoff, 1979, as cited in Zillmann et al., 1980) confirmed the idea that provoked individuals show considerable avoidance of hostile humor, but do not show such avoidance of humor devoid of hostility or ridicule.

Although mood-management theory has tended to focus on viewers' selection of television entertainment, additional research has applied this theory to viewers' selective exposure to other types of media formats and genres. For example, in a recent study, Knobloch and Zillmann (2002) explored viewers' selective exposure to different types of music as a function of mood state. In their study, moods were induced via bogus feedback procedures analogous to those described earlier, though in this study, feedback was provided by computerized responses. Subsequently, participants were presented with a list of eight songs to listen to during a 10-minute period, with half of the songs pretested as high on energy/joyfulness, and half as low on energy/joyfulness. Consistent with predictions, participants in the bad-mood condition sampled and listened to the high energy/joyful music significantly more than did participants in the good-mood condition.

Biswas, Riffe, and Zillmann (1994) also reported similar effects of positive and negative mood states, but this time in the context of news exposure. In their study, positive and negative affect was manipulated, and participants subsequently selected six news stories they would like to read from a series of 12 good-news and bad-news stories. Among female participants, patterns in news selection were consistent with mood-management predictions, with participants in the negative-affect condition selecting significantly fewer bad-news stories than did participants in the positive-affect condition. In contrast, men showed a slight tendency in the opposite direction, selecting a greater number of bad-news stories in the negative than positive-affect condition (although this difference did not reach statistical significance). Although men's news selection patterns seem decidedly at odds with hedonic considerations, these authors pointed to prior research suggesting that under some circumstances, males may be particularly likely to behave in ways that sustain negative or unpleasant affect when the opportunity to retaliate against the source of antagonism is a possibility. If this interpretation is correct, males' maintenance of their negative mood may actually be consistent with an instrumental goal that could eventually lead to relief from noxious affect.

In addition to exploring the effects of manipulated mood states on selective exposure, additional support for mood management's predictions has also been reported for more naturally occurring mood states. For example, Meadowcroft and Zillmann (1987) reasoned that because premenstrual and menstrual phases of the menstrual cycle are associated with negative affect, women in these stages of their menstrual cycles should be more likely than women not in these stages to opt for cheerful or upbeat entertainment that would help to alleviate feelings of dysphoria. To examine these predictions, female undergraduates (who were neither pregnant nor using oral contraceptives) were asked to imagine that they had an evening free to watch television, and were asked to select 3 hours worth of programming from a series of program descriptions containing comedies, game shows, and dramas. In a later session, these women were also asked to provide information concerning their position in the menstrual cycle. Consistent with predictions, the selection of comedy programs was highest among women in the menstrual and premenstrual phases, whereas selection of game shows and dramas did not significantly vary as a function of menstrual position (see also Helregel & Weaver, 1989).

PARADOXES OF NEGATIVE-AFFECT PRODUCING ENTERTAINMENT

As described previously, numerous studies have reported considerable support for mood management's fundamental assumption that individuals select entertainment in a way that is consistent with the maximization of pleasure and the minimization of pain. Naturally, this makes a great deal of intuitive sense because entertainment, almost by definition, is a pastime that should be pleasurable. Nevertheless, a variety of genres and media content clearly deviate considerably from what would normally be considered "pleasant" or "upbeat"—at least on the face of it. Television shows focusing on the disappointment and humiliation of game-show contestants, movies dwelling on senseless violence, and songs mourning unrequited love are but a few of the many examples of media fare that are puzzling in light of mood management's assumptions of hedonistic motivations. This final section considers three different types of entertainment that are curious in light of hedonic considerations, and in so doing describes how other researchers have attempted to account for their popularity, and how Zillmann's former and recent theorizing on mood management addresses these paradoxical genres.

Crime Dramas

Suffering, pain, and terror are arguably not experiences that most individuals would choose to endure. As a result, the popularity of crime dramas where characters are routinely brutalized and hapless victims are shown suffering devastating losses is curious, at best. Obviously, viewers must experience some gratification in response to these types of media portrayals, although their popularity seems to be at odds with the maintenance of positive or uplifting affective states.

Numerous studies have pointed out that the world of television is a much more violent and dangerous place than actual crime statistics suggest (e.g., Oliver, 1994; Potter et al., 1995). As a result, a variety of studies from a cultivation perspective have reported that heavy viewing of television per se and of crime dramas in particular is associated with higher estimates of crime prevalence and with greater fears of crime and concerns for safety (Gerbner, Gross, Morgan, & Signorielli, 1994). Of course, given that cultivation has typically employed survey techniques, the correlational relationship between media exposure and viewers' responses allows for alternate interpretations of the causal relationship between these variables. That is, although cultivation suggests that media exposure leads to fear and insecurity, another plausible interpretation is that fear and insecurity may lead to greater interest in and exposure to media portrayals of crime (Zillmann & Wakshlag, 1985).

At first glance, the idea that viewers who fear crime would have preferences for entertainment that prominently features their fears seems decidedly at odds with mood-management predictions. However, Zillmann and his colleagues have suggested that these patterns in entertainment selection are consistent with mood management because crime dramas may be comforting to viewers who are anxious or fearful (Zillmann, 2000b; Zillmann & Wakshlag, 1985). Specifically, although crime dramas obviously feature the suffering of individuals who have been wronged in some way, they also typically feature the restoration of justice in which the "wrongdoers" are captured and punished for their transgressions (Zillmann & Wakshlag, 1985). Given that disposition theory predicts the greatest level of enjoyment when liked characters prevail and disliked characters suffer, the plotline of most crime dramas holds great promise of being perceived as gratifying, and particularly among those viewers who are especially concerned about issues of safety. That is, the combination of both disposition theory and mood management would suggest that feelings of anxiety may lead to greater selection of crime-ladened entertainment, but particularly if the drama features justice restoration.

Support for this line of reasoning has been obtained in numerous studies employing a variety of methodologies. For example, Reith (1987) examined Nielsen ratings for television crime programs over a 20-year period, comparing popularity ratings with crime rates. As predicted, after controlling for linear increases in crime rates over the years, rates in a given year were significantly associated with crime-show popularity the following year. Of course, the use of aggregate data means that these results are open to numerous alternative interpretations. However, experimental data provides additional support for the idea that concern about crime may increase interest in entertainment in which criminal justice prevails. For example, Wakshlag, Vial, and Tamborini (1983) induced apprehension about crime by showing participants a documentary about crime that implied a strong likelihood of victimization. Afterward, participants were given the opportunity to select 7 films from a list of 14 for possible viewing in a subsequent task. Although the apprehensive participants selected films that contained significantly lower levels of victimization than did the control participants, the apprehensive participants simultaneously selected films that contained significantly higher levels of restorations of justice.

Violence and Horror

Perhaps even more apparently puzzling than the enjoyment of crime drama is the gratification that many viewers seem to experience from motion picture genres such as horror films or slasher movies that not only feature horrendous acts of violence, but that also provide detailed examinations of characters' terrifying attempts to fend off their attackers, and the bloody and gory ways that many victims meet their final end. Much of the same reasoning applied to viewers' enjoyment of crime dramas has also been applied to viewers' enjoyment of these more extreme forms of violent entertainment. Specifically, Zillmann (1980) pointed out that these genres typically feature at least one character who is undoubtedly shown suffering unimaginable horrors, but who is also typically portrayed as eventually escaping danger or fighting off the crazed tormenter. The idea that multitudes of characters are portrayed as "getting the ax" throughout the course of many films is not inconsequential, however, and may actually serve to enhance viewers' ultimate gratification. Specifically, the application of excitation-transfer theory suggests that the arousal elicited from feelings of anxiety and suspense associated with anticipated and actual screen violence carries over and intensifies feelings of gratification when the protagonist escapes from danger (Zillmann, 1980, 1991b, 1998b; Zillmann, Hay, & Bryant, 1975). Consequently, horror and suspense may actually lay the groundwork for particularly heightened levels of enjoyment.

Of course, because some viewers may experience heightened gratification from viewing "acceptable" resolutions in graphic horror does not clearly imply that viewers select this form of entertainment as a way of managing moods. That is, the aforementioned explanation does not, in an of itself, explain the circumstances under which viewers would opt for this particular type of entertainment over others that could also create enjoyment, or why some viewers express great enthusiasm for these types of films, whereas other viewers find them repulsive, at best.

As with the selection of crime drama, though, some research on viewers' selective exposure to horror suggests that more transitory states of anxiety or fear may increase viewers' interest. For example, Boyanowsky, Newtson, and Walster (1974) reported that attendance at a violent movie about a gruesome murder increased 63% 2 days following the actual murder of a female student in the same town, whereas attendance at a nonviolent motion picture across the street remained stable. Furthermore, these authors also reported that women who lived in the same dorm as the victim (and who, therefore, were presumably particularly frightened by the crime) evidenced more interest in the violent than nonviolent film, whereas women who lived elsewhere showed no such preferences. These authors interpreted these findings as suggesting that individuals in a heightened state of fear or anxiety may choose to expose themselves to representations of their fears in a safe context as a way of coping with or mastering their fears. In a later experimental study, Boyanowsky (1977) offered a comparable explanation, suggesting that fearful individuals may expose themselves to similarly noxious media portrayals as a way of relabeling their anxieties to some external source.

The idea that viewers may take comfort in violent portrayals under some circumstances is also consistent with Fenigstein's (1979) research on aggressive thoughts and behaviors as predictors of selective exposure to media violence. Specifically, Fenigstein (1979) reported that among male participants, those who had been induced to think aggressive thoughts (Study 1) or to behave in an aggressive manner (Study 2) were significant by more likely than other participants to select violent as opposed to nonviolent media entertainment for viewing in a subsequent task. Fenigstein and Heyduk (1985) offered numerous possible interpretations for these findings, including the idea that violent programming may be comforting in some circumstances because it may help to justify one's own level of aggressiveness. If this interpretation is correct, then viewers' attraction to media violence may indeed function in a way that is consistent with more long-term hedonic goals. Of course, whether or not this strategy, if employed, is actually effective awaits further study.

In addition to suggesting that media violence may be comforting to viewers under some circumstances, additional research suggests that individual differences likely play important roles in predicting the types of viewers who should be most likely to employ this particular mood-management strategy (Zillmann, 1985). For example, although prior research suggests that viewers select media in a way that allows stressed viewers to unwind and that provides bored viewers the opportunity to increase their arousal, there are clearly variations in what might be considered the "optimal" level of excitation. Zuckerman's (1979, 1994) research on sensation seeking illustrates the importance of individual differences, showing that individuals who score high on this trait tend to enjoy and seek out experiences and stimuli that provide opportunities to experience high levels of arousal. This trait implies, then, that graphic horror or other extreme forms of suspense should be particularly appealing for people who are chronically in need of arousal and excitement. Of course, these same individuals must be at least minimally tolerant of or willing to endure the portrayed suffering that creates the arousal. Consequently, one would also expect that graphic horror would be appealing to individuals who harbor a certain degree of callousness, aggressiveness, or lack of empathy. Consistent with this line of reasoning, research generally suggests that viewing and enjoyment of a variety of horror films and similarly violent programming is positively associated with both sensation seeking and psychoticism (Aluja-Fabregat & Torrubia-Beltri, 1998; Tamborini & Stiff, 1987; Zuckerman, 1996; Zuckerman & Litle, 1986).

The various perspectives on enjoyment of crime, violence, and horror considered in this chapter provide a variety of possible explanations for why viewers may opt to expose themselves to this form of entertainment in a way that is consistent with mood-management considerations. Nevertheless, considerably less research attention has been directed toward the enjoyment and selection of media violence than has been given to the possible harmful effects that media violence may have on viewers. However, future research would benefit from a greater exploration of viewer enjoyment, as any complete understanding of the effects that media violence may have on its audience must also account for why some viewers find this type of fare particularly gratifying.

Tearjerkers in Movies and Music

Just as violence and horror represent seemingly paradoxical genres given mood-management considerations, tearjerkers and mournful love songs also represent puzzling forms of media fare. After all, tearjerkers are presumably produced with the idea of eliciting sadness, and a tearjerker that jerks no tears represents a poor example of a film in this genre. What possible gratification could viewers find from entertainment that is expressly designed to create negative affect? Although sadness-evoking entertainment has not generated nearly the amount of research as has violent entertainment, various explanations for viewers' enjoyment have been considered. Whereas some of these explanations appear inconsistent with mood-management considerations, other explanations may be subsumed under a more encompassing mood-management model of viewers' selective exposure.

In considering the possible explanations for viewers' enjoyment of tragedy, Zillmann (1998a) discussed how disposition theory and excitation transfer might be applicable to this genre in a similar way to enjoyment of suspense. Namely, Zillmann (1998a) pointed out that although beloved characters are typically shown suffering heartbreaking if not fatal misfortunes in tragedies, this entertainment also often concludes with an uplifting or hopeful resolution or lesson. In this regard, the distress that viewers likely experience when seeing protagonists suffer misfortunes should ultimately serve to heighten the gratification experienced during the hopeful or reassuring conclusions.

If this interpretation for the enjoyment of tragedy is correct, then gratification would appear to be dependent on viewers' experience of grief or sadness during the dramatic portrayal, for without distress, heightened feelings of gratification should not be expected. Consistent with line of reasoning, Oliver (1993) reported that respondents' ratings of enjoyment of tearjerkers they had seen in the past were positively correlated with their ratings of how sad the films had been. The idea that sad responses to tragedy may heighten gratification also implies that individual differences associated with greater emotional responsiveness to others' suffering should be predictive of greater enjoyment of this type of entertainment fare. Numerous studies have reported support for this type of argument, showing that females report greater enjoyment than do males, and that higher levels of trait empathy are associated with greater enjoyment (Oliver, 1993; Oliver, Sargent, & Weaver, 1998; Oliver, Weaver, & Sargent, 2000).

Despite the idea that heightened negative affect appears to be associated with greater gratification, the importance of uplifting or satisfying resolutions to viewers' enjoyment has received somewhat mixed support. On the one hand, Mills (1993) found that participants reported feeling better after viewing sad films featuring less tragic than highly tragic endings. On the other hand, Mills also reported that participants rated sad films featuring highly tragic endings as more appealing (Study 1) or as equally appealing (Study 2) as films featuring less tragic endings. Similarly, Oliver (1993) reported that participants' overall enjoyment of sad films was unrelated to their agreement with one particular item pertaining to resolutions: "I enjoy sad movies provided that they have happy endings." Hayes (2000) reported similar findings, at least among participants who scored high on a scale measuring enjoyment of sad films per se. For these participants, anticipated enjoyment of two specific sad films did not vary as a function of whether the films were described as featuring happy or sad endings. However, Hayes (2000) did report that among participants who scored low on overall enjoyment of sad films, anticipated enjoyment of the two specific films was higher when the films featured happy rather than sad endings. Given the somewhat mixed findings for the importance of happy endings to viewers' enjoyment of sad films or related genres, it is useful to consider other possible explanations that do not necessarily rely on uplifting or hopeful resolutions.

In this regard, some additional explanations for the enjoyment of sad films or tragedies have suggested that, contrary to mood management's assumptions, negative affect may not always be perceived as negative or something necessarily to be alleviated. For example, Oliver (1993) suggested that in understanding viewers' responses, it is important to recognize the distinction between emotional responses (e.g., sadness), and cognitive appraisals of emotional responses (i.e., meta-experiences of moods; Mayer & Gaschke, 1988). Specifically, Oliver (1993) argued that for some viewers, the experience of sadness itself may be gratifying, and particularly among individuals who have been rewarded in the past for showing empathy and concern for others (e.g., women). Mills (1993) made a similar claim, suggesting that for viewers who believe that empathy is a favorable trait, the experience of sad responses to tragic portrayals indicates the presence of the favored characteristic (see also Feagin, 1983). The idea that sadness may be gratifying under some circumstances is consistent with recent theorizing concerning the importance of context in the process of mood regulation. For example, Erber and Erber (2000) argued that individuals may not always engage in pleasure enhancement and pain avoidance when the situation suggests that negative affect is the most appropriate response (e.g., a funeral). Similarly, Martin and Davies' (1998) mood input model suggests that people seek positive outcomes rather than positive moods per se, and that positive outcomes may be indicated by the experience of negative affect under some circumstances. For example, if a person's desired outcome is to feel compassionate, the experience of sadness in response to another's loss may be perceived favorably as an indication of the achievement of the desired outcome. Applied to the enjoyment of tragedy, all of these perspectives imply that gratification may follow hedonic considerations as suggested by mood management. However, these perspectives also imply that the focus of the hedonism may be best shifted from mood per se to cognitive appraisals of the experienced moods. If these perspectives are correct, future research would benefit from greater exploration of the variables that are predictive of cognitive appraisals of emotion (or meta-moods), including situational variables and individual-difference variables, among others.

All of the aforementioned explanations may point to why viewers are able to find sad films or genres gratifying. However, they do not necessarily explain selective exposure to entertainment of this sort. That is, the aforementioned explanations do not address the question, "What affective states are predictive of viewers' selective exposure to sad films or tragic entertainment?" However, a number of additional studies imply that, perhaps paradoxically, tragedy may be most likely to hold appeal among those viewers who are feeling sad or melancholy themselves.

Arguably, one of the most popular accounts for the appeal of tragedy is the notion of catharsis. Aristotle wrote that one effect of tragedy is the arousal of pity and fear, and the "proper purgation of these emotions" (Aristotle, 1961, p. 61). Although evidence of cathartic responses to other genres such as violence have garnered almost no support among social scientific studies, the idea that sad films or tearjerkers can somehow release and therefore diminish negative affect has considerable popular appeal. References to "getting it all out" or "having a good cry" seem to point to viewers' beliefs that the viewing of sad films can result in affective benefits. Although Zillmann's (1998a) review of the literature in this area led him to conclude that social scientific evidence is also lacking for the cathartic benefits of sad films, a variety of studies have offered evidence for the general notion that individuals seem to report preferences for this type of entertainment when they are feeling blue themselves.

Mares and Cantor (1992) examined the selection of and response to negatively and positively valenced media portrayals among lonely and nonlonely elderly viewers. In many respects, the nonlonely viewers in the sample behaved consistently with mood-management considerations. Namely, in selecting entertainment, nonlonely participants preferred programs featuring positive portrayals of characters, and positive portrayals of older characters in particular. In addition, for these participants, viewing a media portrayal featuring the story of a sad, isolated man facing problems associated with old age resulted in significant increases in negative affect. In contrast, the lonely participants preferred negative rather than positive programs, and particularly negative programs featuring older characters. In addition, for lonely participants, viewing the media portrayal featuring a sad, isolated man resulted in significant decreases in negative affect. These authors interpreted the lonely participants' responses as consistent with social comparison theory (Festinger, 1954), suggesting that the comparison of one's self with others who are worse off may result in increases in self esteem.

Gibson, Aust, and Zillmann (2000) also considered the idea that downward social comparison may help account for the popularity of musical genres that bemoan lost loves and that sing of sorrowful situations. However, their study found mixed evidence for the idea that love-sick individuals would prefer these types of songs. Specifically, individuals who scored high on a measure of loneliness did not rate videos featuring love-lamenting themes as any more enjoyable than did individuals scoring low on loneliness. However, lonely males in the sample did rate love-celebrating videos as less enjoyable than did their nonlonely counterparts. In addition, in a second part of the study, participants who had been asked to imagine a hypothetical situation of abandonment by a lover reported greater interest in listening to love-lamenting than love-celebrating music, whereas the opposite musical interests were indicated among participants who had been asked to imagine that their romantic interest was reciprocated. In a later discussion of this study and of the popularity of love-lamenting music per se, Zillmann (2000b) also suggested that viewers' attraction to these types of themes might ultimately prove comforting to listeners by making them feel understood by others who have shared similar fates.

Goldenberg, Pyszczynski, Johnson, Greenberg, and Solomon (1999) also recently highlighted the importance of feelings of connectedness in their account of the appeal of tragedy. Specifically, these authors employed terror management theory to examine viewers' enjoyment and responses to tragic and nontragic literary excerpts. Based on past research, Goldenberg et al. (1999) suggested that when individuals become aware of or are reminded of their own mortality, they become attracted to cultural expressions of tragedy as a way of vicariously expressing their fears in a safe and manageable manner. Consistent with this line of reasoning, participants who had been instructed to think of their own mortality reported greater preferences and emotional responses to tragic over nontragic literary excerpts than did participants in a control condition. Although Goldenberg et al. (1999) applied terror-management theory to tragedy specifically, future research may profitably consider how this theory could help explain viewers' attraction to other media content such as crime or horror that also prominently features characters who endure negative experiences and loss.

Obviously, the idea that sad or tragic media would enjoy any popularity, and particularly among people who are feeling down or blue, appears contradictory to mood management's most basic assumption of hedonistic motivations. Does the selective exposure to and enjoyment of tearjerkers and tragedies represent seemingly illogical attempts to experience and prolong negative affect? Zillmann (2000b) discussed several ways that mood management theory may be expanded to help account for these "counterhedonistic selections." First, Zillmann pointed out the distinction between spontaneous and telic hedonism, with spontaneous hedonism referring to immediate gratification seeking, and telic hedonism referring to putting off immediate gratification for some future (and presumably larger) benefit. Applied to media consumption, Zillmann (2000b) argued that although the majority of entertainment choices are likely governed by immediate hedonic considerations, there might be circumstances where people opt to prolong their negative states for some future, positive outcome. For example, a person feeling blue or melancholy may choose to sustain those feelings because reflection on the state may be more effective in bringing about a satisfactory resolution than would avoidance of the state.

Second, Zillmann (2000b) pointed out that some counterhedonistic selections might reflect information seeking rather than exposure to positively valenced materials. For example, Zillmann suggested that in the Mares and Cantor (1992) study, the lonely viewers' preferences for portrayals featuring other lonely people might have reflected the viewers' interest in gathering information about old age that might ultimately help them improve their situations. However, Zillmann also pointed out that although informational utility may help explain the selection of some counterhedonistic media fare and should be incorporated into considerations of media choices, the selection of most entertainment is likely governed by attempts at immediate mood repair, with hedonic concerns the dominant, driving force (Zillmann, 2000b).

CONCLUDING COMMENTS

Mood management's account of selective exposure to media entertainment answers many questions surrounding the gratifications that viewers derive from what is arguably the most popular pastime. The idea that hedonic motivations play a central role in this regard not only has great intuitive appeal, but has also enjoyed considerable empirical support across a wide variety of genres. Of course, there are numerous questions that await future study and that go to the heart of the nature of human needs and desires. In his recent essay on the value of tragedy, for example, Zillmann (1998a) suggested that the most profitable explorations of this particular genre might move beyond enjoyment, and instead focus on how this genre could serve to make us "cognizant of our vulnerabilities, compassions, and needs for emotional wellness" (p. 12). Of course, this particular function of entertainment may ultimately serve to enhance pleasure, but pleasures of this sort move beyond immediate hedonistic gratifications and touch on the very things that make human life valuable and worthy. Grappling with these sorts of issues is clearly a gargantuan task, and one that is perhaps best left to philosophers rather than media scholars. However, understanding the ways in which cultural expressions, including media entertainment, may play a role in helping individuals contemplate both the comedy and tragedy of human life is a very noble cause, and one that is most deserving of our research attention.

REFERENCES

Aluja-Fabregat, A., & Torrubia-Beltri, R. (1988). Viewing of mass media violence, perception of violence, personality and academic achievement. *Personality and Individual Differences, 25,* 973–989.

Anderson, D. R., Collins, P. A., Schmitt, K. L., & Jacobvitz, R. S. (1996). Stressful life events and television viewing. *Communication Research, 23,* 243–260.

Aristotle. (1961). *Poetics* (S. H. Butcher, Trans.). New York: Hill & Wang.

Biswas, R., Riffe, D., & Zillmann, D. (1994). Mood influence on the appeal of bad news. *Journalism Quarterly, 71,* 689–696.

Boyanowsky, E. O. (1977). Film preferences under conditions of threat: Whetting the appetite for violence, information, or excitement? *Communication Research, 4,* 133–144.

Boyanowsky, E. O., Newtson, D., & Walster, E. (1974). Film preferences following a murder. *Communication Research, 1,* 32–43.

Bryant, J., & Zillmann, D. (1984). Using television to alleviate boredom and stress: Selective exposure as a function of induced excitational states. *Journal of Broadcasting, 28,* 1–20.

Erber, R., & Erber, M. W. (2000). The self-regulation of moods: Second thoughts on the importance of happiness in everyday life. *Psychological Inquiry, 11,* 142–148.

Feagin, S. L. (1983). The pleasures of tragedy. *American Philosophical Quarterly, 20,* 95–104.

Fenigstein, A. (1979). Does aggression cause a preference for viewing media violence? *Journal of Personality and Social Psychology, 37,* 2307–2317.

Fenigstein, A., & Heyduk, R. G. (1985). Thought and action as determinants of media exposure. In D. Zillmann & J. Bryant (Eds.), *Selective exposure to communication* (pp. 113–139). Hillsdale, NJ: Lawrence Erlbaum Associates.

Festinger, L. (1954). A theory of social comparison processes. *Human Relations, 7,* 117–140.

Gerbner, G., Gross, L., Morgan, M., & Signorielli, N. (1994). Growing up with television: The cultivation perspective. In J. Bryant & D. Zillmann (Eds.), *Media effects: Advances in theory and research* (pp. 17–41). Hillsdale, NJ: Lawrence Erlbaum Associates.

Gibson, R., Aust, C. F., & Zillmann, D. (2000). Loneliness of adolescents and their choice and enjoyment of love-celebrating versus love-lamenting popular music. *Empirical Studies of the Arts, 18,* 43–48.

Goldenberg, J. L., Pyszczynski, T., Johnson, K. D., Greenberg, J., & Solomon, S. (1999). The appeal of tragedy: A terror management perspective. *Media Psychology, 1,* 313–329.

Hayes, J. G. (2000, November). *Sad films: An examination of sex, endings, and enjoyment.* Paper presented at the annual meeting of the National Communication Association, Seattle, WA.

Helregel, B. K., & Weaver, J. B. (1989). Mood-management during pregnancy through selective exposure to television. *Journal of Broadcasting & Electronic Media, 33,* 15–33.

Knobloch, S., & Zillmann, D. (2002). Mood management via the digital jukebox. *Journal of Communication, 52*(2), 351–366.

Mares, M. L., & Cantor, J. (1992). Elderly viewers' responses to televised portrayals of old age: Empathy and mood management versus social comparison. *Communication Research, 19,* 459–478.

Martin, L. L., & Davies, B. (1998). Beyond hedonism and associationism: A configural view of the role of affect in evaluation, processing, and self-regulation. *Motivation and Emotion, 22,* 33–51.

Mayer, J. D., & Gaschke, Y. N. (1988). The experience and meta-experience of mood. *Journal of Personality and Social Psychology, 55,* 102–111.

Meadowcroft, J. M., & Zillmann, D. (1987). Women's comedy preferences during the menstrual cycle. *Communication Research, 14,* 204–218.

Mills, J. (1993). The appeal of tragedy: An attitude interpretation. *Basic and Applied Social Psychology, 14,* 255–271.

Oliver, M. B. (1993). Exploring the paradox of the enjoyment of sad films. *Human Communication Research, 19,* 315–342.

Oliver, M. B. (1994). Portrayals of crime, race, and aggression in "reality-based" police shows: A content analysis. *Journal of Broadcasting & Electronic Media, 38,* 179–192.

Oliver, M. B., Sargent, S. L., & Weaver, J. B., III. (1998). The impact of sex and gender role self-perception on affective reactions to different types of film. *Sex Roles, 38,* 45–62.

Oliver, M. B., Weaver, J. B., & Sargent, S. (2000). An examination of factors related to sex differences in enjoyment of sad films. *Journal of Broadcasting & Electronic Media, 44,* 282–300.

Potter, W. J., Vaughan, M., Warren, R., Howley, K., Land, A., & Hagemeyer, J. (1995). How real is the portrayal of aggression in television entertainment programming? *Journal of Broadcasting & Electronic Media, 39,* 496–516.

Reith, M. (1987). Is there a relationship between the popularity of crime series on television and unemployment and crime in society? *European Journal of Communication, 2,* 337–355.

Rubin, A. (1994). Media uses and effects: A uses-and-gratifications perspective. In J. Bryant & D. Zillmann (Eds.), *Media effects: Advances in theory and research* (pp. 417–436). Hillsdale, NJ: Lawrence Erlbaum Associates.

Tamborini, R., & Stiff, J. (1987). Predictors of horror film attendance and appeal: An analysis of the audience for frightening films. *Communication Research, 14,* 415–436.

Wakshlag, J., Vial, V., & Tamborini, R. (1983). Selecting crime drama and apprehension about crime. *Human Communication Research, 10,* 227–242.

Zillmann, D. (1980). Anatomy of suspense. In P. H. Tannenbaum (Ed.), *The entertainment functions of television* (pp. 291–301). Hillsdale, NJ: Lawrence Erlbaum Associates.

Zillmann, D. (1985). The experimental exploration of gratifications from media entertainment. In K. E. Rosengren, L. A. Wenner, & P. Palmgreen (Eds.), *Media gratifications research: Current perspectives* (pp. 225–239). Beverly Hills: Sage.

Zillmann, D. (1988a). Mood management: Using entertainment to full advantage. In L. Donohew, H. E. Sypher, & E. T. Higgins (Eds.), *Communication, social cognition, and affect* (pp. 147–171). Hillsdale, NJ: Lawrence Erlbaum Associates.

Zillmann, D. (1988b). Mood management through communication choices. *American Behavioral Scientist, 31,* 327–340.

Zillmann, D. (1991a). Empathy: Affect from bearing witness to the emotions of others. In J. Bryant & D. Zillmann (Eds.), *Responding to the screen: Reception and reaction processes* (pp. 135–167). Hillsdale, NJ: Lawrence Erlbaum Associates.

Zillmann, D. (1991b). The logic of suspense and mystery. In J. Bryant & D. Zillmann (Eds.), *Responding to the screen: Reception and reaction processes* (pp. 281–303). Hillsdale, NJ: Lawrence Erlbaum Associates.

Zillmann, D. (1991c). Television viewing and physiological arousal. In J. Bryant & D. Zillmann (Eds.), *Responding to the screen: Reception and reaction processes* (pp. 103–133). Hillsdale, NJ: Lawrence Erlbaum Associates.

Zillmann, D. (1998a). Does tragic drama have redeeming value? *Siegener Periodikum für Internationale Literaturwissenschaft, 16,* 1–11.

Zillmann, D. (1998b). The psychology of the appeal of portrayals of violence. In J. H. Goldstein (Ed.), *Why we watch: The attractions of violent entertainment* (pp. 179–211). New York: Oxford University Press.

Zillmann, D. (2000a). Humor and comedy. In D. Zillmann & P. Vorderer (Eds.), *Media entertainment: The psychology of its appeal* (pp. 37–57). Mahwah, NJ: Lawrence Erlbaum Associates.

Zillmann, D. (2000b). Mood management in the context of selective exposure theory. In M. E. Roloff (Ed.), *Communication yearbook 23* (pp. 103–123). Thousand Oaks, CA: Sage.

Zillmann, D., & Bryant, J. (1985). Affect, mood, and emotion as determinants of selective exposure. In D. Zillmann & J. Bryant (Eds.), *Selective exposure to communication* (pp. 157–190). Hillsdale NJ: Lawrence Erlbaum Associates.

Zillmann, D., & Cantor, J. R. (1977). Affective responses to the emotions of a protagonist. *Journal of Experimental Social Psychology, 13,* 155–165.

Zillmann, D., Hay, A., & Bryant, J. (1975). The effect of suspense and its resolution on the appreciation of dramatic presentations. *Journal of Research in Personality, 9,* 307–323.

Zillmann, D., Hezel, R. T., & Medoff, N. J. (1980). The effect of affective states on selective exposure to televised entertainment fare. *Journal of Applied Social Psychology, 10,* 323–339.

Zillmann, D., & Wakshlag, J. (1985). Fear of victimization and the appeal of crime drama. In D. Zillmann & J. Bryant (Eds.), *Selective exposure to communication* (pp. 141–156). Hillsdale, NJ: Lawrence Erlbaum Associates.

Zuckerman, M. (1979). *Sensation seeking: Beyond the optimal level of arousal.* Hillsdale, NJ: Lawrence Erlbaum Associates.

Zuckerman, M. (1994). *Behavioral expressions and psychobiological bases of sensation seeking.* New York: Cambridge University Press.

Zuckerman, M. (1996). Sensation seeking and the taste for vicarious horror. In J. B. Weaver & R. Tamborini (Eds.), *Horror films: Current research on audience preferences and reactions* (pp. 147–160). Mahwah, NJ: Lawrence Erlbaum Associates.

Zuckerman, M., & Litle, P. (1986). Personality and curiosity about morbid and sexual events. *Personality and Individual Differences, 7*, 49–56.

5

Rethinking Empathy

Amy I. Nathanson
Ohio State University

Empathy has become an important construct in mass communication research. It has been used to explain both children's and adults' reactions to films and characters (Wilson & Cantor, 1985; Wilson, Cantor, Gordon, & Zillmann, 1986; Zillmann & Cantor, 1977), enjoyment of films (de Wied, Zillmann, & Ordman, 1994), responses to coviewing others (Tamborini, Salomonson, & Bahk, 1993), and attraction to programs (Cantor, 1998). Perhaps because of its accessibility within everyday language, the scientific meaning of empathy is sometimes taken for granted rather than carefully considered. However, empathy is a complex idea, and some researchers are still struggling to define its conceptual boundaries.

The purpose of this chapter is to rethink the empathy construct. This exercise includes reviewing previous conceptualizations, noting commonalities and discrepancies, and advancing new issues to consider in building our understanding of empathy. Theories and research relating to the development, precursors, and effects of empathy also are considered. Measurement issues are discussed insofar as they speak to empathy's conceptualization. Finally, the implications of these issues for past and future mass communication research are explored.

WHAT IS EMPATHY?

In everyday language, empathy signifies a generally positive or desirable trait. However, empathy often is used in place of more appropriate terms like *sympathy, identification,* or *caring.* Levy (1997) admitted that gaining any precision or common agreement on the term's meaning is probably hopeless when it comes to everyday conversation. He suspected that "empathy will continue to be used in imprecise, emotive ways—in self-help books and books of popular psychology, for example—to mean more or less 'a warm, supportive, non-judgmental fellow-feeling;' a quality to be nurtured in oneself and sought after in a Significant Other" (p. 183).

Although the scientific community has been more careful in explicating empathy and making efforts to develop clear criteria for its identification and use, the construct is still enmeshed in a series of conceptual dilemmas. This is evident in the fact that most researchers who use the empathy construct devote a significant amount of attention to defining how their ideas differ from others who have studied empathy.

Fortunately, some of the conceptual controversies appear to have been resolved via consensus. However, others still linger. Moreover, some complicated issues surrounding this construct have not been adequately considered; as a result, these issues are devoid of controversy but also devoid of clarity. The subsections that follow review and discuss previous and existing controversies, as well as introduce other conceptual issues that should be addressed.

The Components of Empathy

One of the biggest debates surrounding empathy concerns whether it is a cognitive or an affective response (Shantz, 1975). Those who consider empathy in cognitive terms say that empathy occurs when an individual can correctly identify the feelings of another person (Borke, 1971). From this perspective, children who recognize that another child is feeling happy during their birthday celebration are said to exhibit empathy. The cognitive approach to empathy emphasizes the importance of skills, such as role-taking or perspective-taking.

Richardson, Hammock, Smith, Gardner, and Signo (1994) demonstrated the importance of the cognitive elements of empathy in their three-part study of the relationship between empathy and aggression. Although they measured both affective and cognitive elements of empathy, they found that their cognitive measure—perspective-taking—was inversely related to more forms of aggression than was their affective measure (called *empathic concern*). In a follow-up study, they found that participants who had been instructed to engage in perspective-taking administered lower-level shocks to experimental confederates than participants who had not received this training. As a result, it seems as though perspective-taking, conceptualized as cognitive empathy, plays an important role in tempering aggression.

However, if empathy is simply the ability to accurately identify the feelings of others, it is unclear how it is distinct from other constructs, such as social understanding, social cognition, or affective perspective-taking (Barnett, 1984; Feshbach, 1978; Kurdek & Rodgon, 1975). In fact, a separate school of thought argues that empathy involves more than just recognizing others' emotions. Specifically, it claims that empathy occurs when individuals actually feel the same emotions as other individuals they have observed (Feshbach & Roe, 1968). From this perspective, affective elements are the defining characteristics of empathy (Hoffman, 1975).

Measures that reflect this perspective include the Feshbach and Roe Affective Situation Test for Empathy (FASTE), which involves asking children how they feel after seeing other children display a variety of emotions. Empathy is believed to occur when the respondent's self-reported emotion matches the emotion of the child depicted in the observed scenes. Scoring procedures also allow for matching within categories of emotions (Feshbach & Roe, 1968). For example, a child who reports feeling bad in response to seeing a television scene featuring a sad child is still believed to have experienced empathy. If the child reported a hedonically positive emotion, such as happiness, then empathy is not believed to have occurred. This scoring procedure implies, then, that empathy need not involve an exact match in emotions between the observer and the observed, so long as the valence of the emotions does match.

Mehrabian and Epstein's (1972) emotional empathy scale also illustrates the affective approach to empathy. This measure consists of 33 items tapping a variety of emotional responses and tendencies, including susceptibility to emotional contagion, extreme emotional responsiveness, and the tendency to be moved by others' positive and negative emotional experiences.

Integrating the Cognitive and Affective Components of Empathy

Although some researchers emphasize either the cognitive or affective components of empathy, most now recognize that empathy includes both elements. According to Duan and Hill (1996), the idea that there are separate types of empathy—cognitive and affective—suggests a false dichotomy, when in fact both cognitive and affective processes are interdependent. However, disagreement still exists regarding the proper multidimensional conceptualization of empathy and which components are most important.

For example, three-dimensional conceptualizations of empathy have been proposed by both Feshbach (1982) and Levy (1997). Although both conceptualizations approach empathy from a perspective that recognizes both cognitive and affective elements, they define the dimensions in unique ways. Davis (1980, cited in Davis, 1983) offered a four-dimensional conceptualization of empathy, operationalized in the Interpersonal Reactivity Index (IRI). Three of the four components of Davis' approach are affective, including fantasy, or the tendency to become emotionally involved with fictional characters (as explained later, this component is similar to what others call fictional involvement). Later, Davis (1983) empirically validated his multidimensional IRI by demonstrating that the four dimensions constituted unique but related aspects of our reactivity to the observed experiences of others.

Davis' conceptualization of empathy appears to be popular and is endorsed by other researchers. For example, Dillard and Hunter (1989) suggested that empathy research abandon Mehrabian and Epstein's Emotional Empathy Scale and use the Davis scale instead. Thornton and Thornton (1995) also advocated Davis' measure, with some slight modifications. In their factor analysis of both the IRI and Eysenck and Eysenck's (1978) unidimensonal empathy scale, the I_7, they proposed a five-factor solution that included all of Davis' dimensions plus a new facet the authors called emotional response matching. They defined this factor as the sharing of others' negative emotions. Thornton and Thornton's analysis makes it clear that the Davis measure, although comprehensive, does not directly address the sharing of emotions between the observer and the observed.

Summary

Current thinking on empathy acknowledges that both cognitive and affective skills and tendencies are important aspects of this experience. Although the multidimensional conceptualization is popular, a consensus regarding the proper multidimensional conceptualization has not yet been reached. Fortunately, there is often overlap among these various approaches, even if the specific labels used are not identical. However, given the variety of multidimensional approaches, it can be difficult to synthesize the research that emerges from them. Future research should work toward developing a consensus regarding the most appropriate conceptualizations and labels for these components.

WHAT SKILLS DOES EMPATHY REQUIRE?

With a multidimensional conceptualization of empathy in mind, we can now consider the kinds of skills required to produce empathic reactions. In order to experience the cognitive aspects of empathy, the ability to engage in perspective-taking is essential (Hoffman, 1975). This requirement should render young children incapable of experiencing empathy until they develop the ability to see the world from a non-egocentric perspective.

However, children often appear as though they do experience empathy. For example, young children may report feeling sad because they witness another child receiving discipline. How, then, can we explain the fact that young children seem to display empathy when we know that they have not yet achieved the cognitive skills required of empathic responses?

Shantz (1975) offered an answer to this question. She explained that young children's ability to identify the emotions of another child is probably not indicative of their role-taking abilities. Rather, the children are probably reacting to the observed child's situation. Because most of the empathy measures involve very common situations that the respondents have likely experienced in the past (e.g., a birthday party, getting lost), the children who appear to be perspective-taking simply may be reacting to the depicted situation. For example, the child who appears happy when observing another child open birthday presents may be reacting personally to the presents themselves, as if he/she were receiving them. As a result, this child is not considering the observed child's feelings; instead, the child is responding egocentrically. It is important, then, to determine whether seemingly empathic reactions are actually personal responses to specific situations.

Empathy also requires inference skills. When we understand how another is feeling based on similar experiences that we have encountered in the past, we have actually achieved understanding via inference. As a result, it may be impossible for us to empathize with others if we cannot connect their experience with something we have felt before. For example, someone who is childless may find it hard to share in another's joy over their child's first day at school. At an even more basic level, we can infer emotions in others simply by witnessing their facial and postural features. In other words, because we see another person who is teary-eyed and slouching, we infer that they must feel sad. The fact that empathy requires inference skills again limits young children's capacity to experience empathy (Collins, Wellman, Keniston, & Westby, 1978).

According to Roberts and Strayer (1996), emotional insight is another skill that is required to feel empathy. That is, we must be able to recognize our own emotions before we can identify emotions in others. If we cannot, for example, recognize signs of anger in ourselves and label our emotions this way, then we do not have the skills to recognize this emotion in others. Roberts and Strayer explained that a common finding is a mismatch between children's self-reported emotions and those indicated by their facial expressions. This may be caused by the child's misunderstanding of his or her emotions or a denial of those emotions (e.g., a boy who feels sad may deny feeling sad because of perceived social sanctions against boys expressing sadness). Regardless of the reason, it seems that the ability and motivation to identify one's own emotions facilitates empathic responding.

It should be noted that emotional insight only translates into empathic responses by making inferences. Hart (1999) explained that the comparison of one's own emotions experienced in response to previous situations with those of another individual in a different situation must involve inference-making. For example, we conclude that the other person must feel sad in a particular situation because we know that we felt sad when we faced a similar situation.

Hoffman (1975) also suggested that empathy requires a clear awareness on our part that others are distinct beings (a concept called person permanence) who have unique identities (an awareness reflected in personal identity). For example, we must realize not only that others exist independently from us, but also that they have thoughts, feelings, and perspectives that are distinct from us. Although person permanence emerges in the first year of life, personal identity doesn't develop until about 6–9 years of age (Hoffman, 1975). For example, a 6-year-old boy who has just visited the ocean may talk to other children under the assumption that they too have visited the ocean. The 6-year-old may conclude that because he has seen the ocean, every other child has also seen it. This assumption reflects the 6-year-old's inability to recognize that other children have unique circumstances and separate lives. Hart (1999) echoed these ideas, suggesting that we must have a cognitive awareness and representation of others as separate from, rather than extensions of, ourselves. For example, the child who attributes the emotions of others to him or herself, without recognizing the source of these feelings, cannot be said to feel empathy. It is only when children begin to realize that the emotions of others have informed their own emotions can we label their response empathic.

The ability to maintain moderate levels of emotional expressiveness is another skill required of empathic responding (Roberts & Strayer, 1996). Emotional expressiveness refers to the intensity with which individuals express their emotions. According to Roberts and Strayer (1996), very low levels of emotional expressiveness indicate a lack of connection to affect-inducing situations or a tendency to overcontrol emotions. For example, individuals who display few signs of sadness in response to personally devastating situations may be said to be emotionally unexpressive. On the other hand, very high levels of emotional expressiveness reflect an exaggerated focus on the self that is so intense that it can disrupt productive behavior (e.g., individuals who experience extreme highs and lows in response to relatively minor events). Individuals at either extreme should have difficulty experiencing empathy. In the former case, the individual has difficulty engaging in emotional situations and therefore can neither identify nor express the emotions of others. In the latter case, the individual's affective response to another's situation is so extreme and self-oriented that it prevents the individual from recognizing and responding to the emotions of others. In this situation, the individual becomes focused on his/her own emotional responses rather than the target's emotions.

Overall, it seems unlikely that empathy is purely an automatic or innate response to others' emotions. We may be born with the capacity for empathy, but the actual experience of empathy requires certain skills or tendencies that develop over time, including perspective-taking and inference abilities, a sense of person permanence and personal identity, emotional insight, and moderate levels of emotional responsiveness. Although some of these traits may develop with cognitive maturation, others may require exposure to certain experiences.

HOW CAN WE DIFFERENTIATE EMPATHY FROM OTHER AFFECTIVE REACTIONS?

One important issue concerns how we can distinguish empathy from other affective reactions that might resemble empathy. This is a complicated issue, as empathy involves feeling certain emotions; yet, empathy is distinct from the sheer experience of emotions.

It is important to remember that empathy is a response to others. Individuals who feel empathy, then, would not otherwise experience an affective reaction to the observed situation if it were not for their attention to the perspective of another individual. As a result, situations that directly produce in the observer affect that matches the affect in the observed cannot be said to be empathy-inducing situations. Rather, they should be construed as affect-inducing situations. The fact that the observer and the observed share the same affect should be regarded as a coincidence and not evidence of empathy.

Zillmann (1991) provided several examples of situations in which individuals might believe they are experiencing empathy when in fact they are experiencing an independent affective reaction. He described a situation where parents might mistakenly believe they are empathizing with their child's positive feelings when they experience joy upon witnessing the child receive a college diploma. However, their child's graduation day has likely independently produced in them feelings of pride about their own successes in raising the child.

Media effects research should carefully consider the distinction between empathy and other affective reactions that may resemble empathy. If this research proceeds without any awareness that emotional matching between participants and mediated characters may be coincidental, then faulty conclusions about the research may be drawn. For example, when viewing a movie scene depicting a fight between the protagonist and the antagonist, individuals may express fear and anxiety. If these emotions match the emotions the protagonist expresses during the scene, we might conclude that the viewers are experiencing empathy (or, fictional involvement) with the protagonist. However, the viewers' fear and anxiety may stem from the movie scene itself. That is, if the camera work focuses on frightening or grotesque images, such as weapons and bloody bodies, then the viewers' seemingly empathic reactions may reflect their affective responses to seeing these images. In this case, the fear and anxiety produced by the movie is independent of their thinking about the protagonist. Researchers in this area, then, should remind themselves that empathy is an other-oriented response and should incorporate measures that will permit them to assess this response independently from other affective responses.

HOW DOES EMPATHY OCCUR?

A full understanding of empathy cannot be gained without considering how empathy occurs. The major question underlying this issue concerns whether empathy is an innate, automatic response to certain others or conditions or whether empathy is a learned response that develops over time (Levy, 1997). In other words, are we born with empathic tendencies or must we learn to feel empathy through experience? Of course, finding the answer to this question will involve considering some of the issues reviewed earlier, such as the notion that empathy requires certain cognitive skills or life experiences.

Empathy as Innate Predisposition

As Feshbach (1978) explained, some advocates of the empathy as affect position believe that empathic reactions are automatic, primitive, and unlearned. For example, infants who cry at the sound of other infants' cries are said to display empathy. Levy (1997) noted that the original conceptualization of empathy revolved around the idea of motor mimicry.

As Zillmann (1991) explained, many scholars from the early 20th century (e.g., T. Lipps and W. McDougall) advocated this position. Some of these thinkers believed that innate predispositions lead us to imitate the facial, postural, and gestural expressions of others' experience of emotions. By assuming these expressions, the scholars believed, we come to actually feel the emotions associated with them. As a result, we experience empathy as a result of witnessing another's emotional responses. The fact that animals display signs of motor mimicry (e.g., animals who respond in kind to other animals' distress calls) means that empathy, from this perspective, is not a uniquely human response. Of course, if we accept that empathy requires certain skills that develop over time (as was argued earlier), then we cannot conceptualize empathy as such a basic process.

Empathy as Learned

The other dominant explanation for how empathy occurs embraces the idea that empathic reactions are learned over time through experience and conditioning (Berger, 1962). Experience with the modeled emotions becomes essential, from this perspective, to the capacity for empathy. For example, individuals who have lost a pet have likely experienced feelings of sadness and loss. Their past experience then allows them to feel sadness and loss in response to others who have lost a pet. From a classical conditioning paradigm, because sadness and loss were linked with losing a pet, exposure to another situation involving a lost pet (even when it involves another person) elicits feelings of sadness and loss.

This perspective implies that empathy is impossible unless individuals have experienced the very event that an observed other is experiencing. However, common sense suggests that this cannot be true. For example, most of us can probably think back to a situation in which we believed we felt empathy in response to a friend who described a situation that was quite foreign to us. Further, if we accept the notion that empathy is contingent on having experienced the same situation as the observed, then how can we understand the fact that we can empathize with television characters who are being stalked even if we have never been stalked ourselves?

Other scholars in this area (e.g., Humphrey, 1922) accepted the classical conditioning idea in understanding social reactions such as empathy, but also argued that empathy is not contingent on the observer having had an identical experience as the observed. Using the example of the lost pet, it is argued that observers who have never owned a pet will still feel sadness in response to witnessing others lose their pet. The reason empathy can still occur in this situation is that the observed situation elicits related situations that allow the observer to experience empathy. So, seeing another lose a pet evokes memories in the observer of situations of loss that they have experienced, such as losing a loved one. This related experience, then, allows the observer to feel sadness and loss when another individual is enduring a situation with which they have no prior experience.

Zillmann (1991) invoked the concept of stimulus generalization to explain the fact that we can still feel empathy even if our prior experiences are only similar to that of the observed. Stimulus generalization is the notion that, although we may have never experienced a certain stimulus ourselves, we can generalize this stimulus to similar stimuli that we have experienced. For example, if we have never personally encountered a poisonous snake, we can still empathize with a television character's fearful reaction to such a creature because we have personally encountered and been fearful of nonpoisonous snakes in the past. Hence, our emotions can match others' because we have generalized the feared stimulus to similar stimuli that previously have evoked fear in us.

By removing the requirement of identical prior experiences, empathy can be used to understand individuals' emotional responses to a wide variety of situations. This allowance makes the concept more understandable, at least according to common sense. However, on logical grounds, it also calls into question the necessity of prior experiences in the experience of empathy. It seems as though any prior experience that the observer construes as similar to that of the observed will be sufficient to elicit empathy. In fact, the experience may be so remote from the situation observed that an outsider would not be able to associate the two. For example, when we watch a movie such as *Poltergeist* we might say we empathize with the fear the characters express in response to the supernatural forces that have inhabited their home, not because we ourselves have experienced supernatural beings, but because we have felt afraid of unfamiliar situations in the past. It hardly seems, from this example, that prior experience is a necessary component of our experience of empathy.

In fact, Sapolsky and Zillmann (1978) provided evidence that prior experience with a situation—although related to physiological reactions to another experiencing that situation—is unrelated to empathy per se. The goal of their study was to determine whether prior identical or related experience with childbirth would intensify respondents' physiological and emotional responses to a film depicting childbirth. In addition, they assessed whether background characteristics and experience influenced the respondents' tendency to empathize with the pain the woman in the film experienced during childbirth.

They found that participants who had given birth (or who had "primary experience" with childbirth) experienced a faster heart rate during viewing than other participants, including females who had not given birth, and both males and females who either had or had not witnessed another person give birth (either directly or via the mass media). However, prior experience of any kind failed to affect respondents' tendencies to empathize with the film mother's pain during childbirth. These findings indicate that prior experience increases the intensity of physiological reactions but does not necessarily lead to empathy.

These findings also remind us that we need to make a clear conceptual distinction between affective or physiological responses of any kind and true empathic responses. Sapolsky and Zillmann (1978) explained that

> the individual who exhibits an affective reaction might respond not so much to the expression of emotion as to events which in the past have induced affective reactions in her or him. This is to say that the affective reaction may result mainly from a conditioning history which does not involve empathic reactions at all. Conceivably, then, experience may facilitate affective reactions, not empathy per se, because it amounts to a conditioning history. (p. 143)

Perhaps more specifically, by suggesting that empathy is contingent on individuals having experienced only similar or related situations as the objects of empathy, we must specify the boundaries of "similar" or "related." In fact, it seems quite easy to claim we have felt empathy for another if we only need to demonstrate that we have experienced something even vaguely related to the observed's situation. We truly may have experienced empathy in these situations. The question, of course, is whether our prior experience was really an essential component of eliciting empathy.

This is not to say that empathy does not have any learned component whatsoever. For example, it may be impossible for a child to empathize with another's simultaneous experience of both joy and sadness. The child may not yet be cognitively or emotionally mature enough to understand that emotions can be complex and contradictory. Although the child has felt both joy and sadness—independently of one another—he or she may be unable to truly understand another person who is experiencing both. Perhaps prior experience is important, then, at a very basic level. That is, empathy may be contingent on an individual having experienced the observed's emotion in the past. However, empathy may not be contingent on an individual having actually experienced the observed's situation. As Sapolsky and Zillmann (1978) explained, a wide variety of situations can produce the same basic affective responses. It seems, then, that having experience with these basic emotions, rather than experience with the situation or related situations, is the most important element of prior experience. Reducing prior experience to this more basic level implies that all empathic responses are likely once individuals have accumulated enough life experiences to have felt all basic emotions and combinations of them.

Zillmann (1991) also recognized that empathy can occur due to deliberate cognitive efforts, such as perspective-taking. Whereas the previously reviewed perspectives emphasize either innate processes or nondeliberate learning processes in the manifestation of empathy, the perspective-taking approach focuses on individuals' intentional attempts to see the world from another's point of view. That is, this approach recognizes that we can induce empathy in ourselves. This "deliberate empathy" (Zillmann, 1994), however, can ultimately become effortless. As Zillmann (1994) explained, individuals who often use perspective-taking may eventually engage in this cognitive behavior out of habit. In this way, perspective-taking is the cognitive mediator that is responsible for empathy.

Zillmann (1991) suggested that this form of empathy could also have an experiential component, much like the learning approach to empathy discussed earlier. For example, the process of taking another's perspective may call up memories of one's own experiences that are similar to the situation being observed. When this occurs, the resulting affect is partly the result of empathy and partly the result of re-experiencing previously felt emotions. To the extent that perspective-taking leads to the elicitation of powerful emotions associated with one's past, we might question the extent to which the individual is truly experiencing empathy. That is, empathy must be other-oriented; if the primary source of one's emotional output is memories of one's own experiences, then we cannot classify these reactions as empathy.

An Integrative Approach to Empathy

Zillmann (1991) integrated the three major approaches to empathy in his three-factor theory of empathy. This approach is an application of his larger three-factor theory of emotion (see chap. 2, this volume) to the empathy construct. The parent theory suggests that emotions are determined by "dispositional," "excitatory," and "experiential" forces that interact with one another. Dispositional components of emotions include automatic, innate responses (whether conditioned or unconditioned) to situations and stimuli. In the case of empathy, the dispositional component includes the reflexive responses of motor mimicry.

Excitatory components of emotions are also automatic, but they serve to prepare individuals to experience emotions rather than guarantee that they occur. The preparedness comes from physiological changes such as increased arousal. As Zillmann (1991) explained, in the case of empathy, the excitatory component would include automatic or conditioned responses that are also independent of motor responses.

Finally, the experiential component includes individuals' conscious awareness or recognition of emotions, including their appraisals and manipulations of their emotions. In the case of empathy, this refers to perspective-taking or deliberate empathy. One's empathic responses can be evaluated as inappropriate, and individuals can also stop their empathic feelings, in a phenomenon Zillmann (1991) labeled *dispositional override of empathy*. According to this theory, all three components of empathy work together and cannot, independently, account for the manifestation of empathy in every situation.

Summary

Overall, there are many explanations for the occurrence of empathy. However, the majority of them can be classified into one of two perspectives: those that argue that empathy is innate and those that argue that empathy is learned. Other researchers, such as Zillmann, acknowledged both perspectives, as well as additional components, and posited more complex models of empathy. More encompassing perspectives, such as these, appear to have the most potential for understanding the greatest variety of empathy responses.

EMPATHY AND MASS COMMUNICATION

The empathy construct has proven to be useful in understanding individuals' uses of and reactions to television and movies. Ordinally, of course, empathy is used to understand individuals' reactions to other individuals whom they know or can directly observe in real-life situations. However, research indicates that we can also feel empathy for television or movie characters and that these feelings can motivate our viewing and guide our reactions to what we see. The fact that fantasy or fictional involvement has emerged as an important dimension of empathy is evidence that individuals commonly become emotionally involved with mediated characters. As Sapolsky and Zillmann (1978) explained, "In efforts to account for the commonplace notion that movies can move people emotionally, the concept of empathy has been heavily drawn upon for some time" (p. 132). Most of the research in this area can be organized into one of the three major categories discussed below.

Empathy and Responses to Media

One facet of research in this area explores how individual differences in empathy affect responses to the media. For example, Davis, Hull, Young, and Warren (1987) sought to understand the effects of both cognitive and affective components of empathy on individuals' affective reactions to films. In particular, the authors wanted to explore the roles of dispositional empathy (both cognitive and emotional) and cognitively-oriented empathy inducements (i.e., instructions to engage in perspective-taking). Consistent with the more recent trends in the conceptualization of empathy, the authors took a multidimensional approach to empathy so that they could compare the relative and interactive roles of cognitive and emotional elements of empathy in reactions to emotionally arousing films.

They found that the cognitive and emotional elements of empathy were differentially related to participants' affective reactions to the films.

Specifically, individuals' predispositions to feel empathic concern were related to negative affective reactions, whereas perspective-taking was associated with more positive affective reactions. In addition, perspective-taking inducements produced congruent participant–film character emotions among participants who were naturally predisposed to perspective-taking. This suggests that attempts to reduce the harmful effects of media by using perspective-taking training may be more difficult when participants are not accustomed to practicing perspective-taking in everyday life. On a larger, theoretical scale, the Davis et al. (1987) study highlights the advantages of acknowledging both cognitive and affective components of empathy and considering them simultaneously.

Tamborini et al. (1990) also explored both cognitive and affective dimensions of empathy in their study of college students' reactions to viewing graphic horror. The authors sought to understand the role of several dimensions of empathy in individuals' enjoyment of films featuring graphic horror. They measured cognitive or imaginative elements of empathy (e.g., fictional involvement, tendency to have a wandering imagination) and affective elements of empathy (e.g., humanistic orientation, emotional contagion). Overall, they found that enjoyment of graphic horror was related to a lack of empathy. Perhaps the lack of emotional connection to characters allows these viewers to experience pleasant arousal and stimulation from other aspects of the presentation, such as suspenseful music, quick cuts, and so on.

In addition, Tamborini et al.'s (1990) path analysis revealed some evidence of a causal relationship among the dimensions of empathy, with daydreaming predicting fictional involvement, which in turn predicted humanistic orientation, which in turn predicted emotional contagion. In a sense, it seems as though the cognitive elements preceded the affective elements. This finding is consistent with the argument reviewed earlier that cognitive aspects of empathy (e.g., perspective-taking) are necessary but not sufficient conditions for affective responses (Hoffman, 1975).

de Wied, Hoffman, and Roskos-Ewoldsen (1997) focused on a related context when they explored the role of empathy in viewers' reactions to suspenseful drama. The authors made the distinction between empathic distress, which they conceptualized as the fear for a protagonist's well-being, and nonempathic distress, defined as viewers' fear for their own safety. Their distinction reinforces Roberts and Strayer's (1996) point that an exaggerated focus on one's own emotions (i.e., extreme emotional expressiveness) inhibits empathy. de Wied et al. (1997) argued that feelings of suspense may arise from either type of distress or a combination of the two. Although de Wied et al. manipulated levels of nonempathic distress in order to observe the effect of participants' fear for their own safety on feelings of suspense, they also measured participants' trait empathy and explored its relationship with suspense levels.

de Wied et al. (1997) found that participants who earned high empathic sensitivity scores were more likely to experience suspense and distress while viewing suspenseful films than participants with lower empathy scores. In addition, they found that inducing nonempathic distress in participants increased the amount of distress they reported after viewing. Their study should remind us that, although empathy is an important predictor of viewers' reactions to suspenseful films, more self-oriented feelings also contribute to these outcomes.

In an effort to understand why some college students select and enjoy sad films, Oliver (1993) considered the role of empathy. Specifically, she found that enjoyment of sad films held significant relationships with fictional involvement, humanistic orientation, and emotional contagion. This is consistent with research by de Wied et al. (1994), who also found that viewers with high empathic sensitivity scores enjoyed a tragic film better than participants who earned lower empathy scores. Further, Oliver (1993) found that enjoyment of sad films was positively related to having favorable evaluations of the experience of sadness. Oliver explained that some individuals evaluate the experience of feeling sad positively; as a result, this meta-emotion plays an important role in understanding why individuals might purposively subject themselves to sad movies. It is possible that empathic individuals also evaluate the experience of feeling sad positively; if this is the case, then it is understandable why they would enjoy and perhaps seek out sad films. Because the purpose of Oliver's study was not to explore the relationship between empathy and favorable meta-emotions about the experience of sadness, her study did not report any data to confirm this explanation.

Using the empathy construct in a different content context, Aust and Zillmann (1997) argued that the depiction of bad news on television news (which often features victims expressing or displaying negative emotions) should prompt affective, empathic responses among viewers. The strong emotions evoked should then influence viewers' perceptions and judgments on subsequent, related issues they face. They suggested that this kind of effect should be especially strong among individuals who are already high in empathic sensitivity. In fact, they found that individuals with high empathic sensitivity perceived greater danger and personal risk from news stories than did individuals with low empathic sensitivity.

Empathy has also been linked with outcomes that extend beyond the viewing situation. For instance, Tamborini et al. (1993) showed that empathy can influence how individuals respond to one another after viewing films. They found that college students who earned high scores on fictional involvement and empathic concern were more likely to try to comfort a distressed student who coviewed the film. In addition, they found that the hedonic quality of the film they viewed played a role in determining comforting responses. Specifically, participants who viewed a comedy film comforted more than those who viewed a horror film. This finding was consistent with the authors's expectations that comforting is more likely when individuals feel happy themselves. Although the latter finding does not address empathy directly, it suggests that empathic responses (which should precede comforting behaviors) are more likely after viewing comedies, and that horror films may reduce empathic tendencies.

Empathy and Children

Another segment of the research on empathy and mass communication has focused on children as a unique audience. This work reveals that empathy plays an important role in children's uses of and responses to media. For example, Cantor's (1998) review of children's attraction to violent media revealed that children who empathize with aggressive perpetrators are more likely to show interest in violent fare than children who do not. In fact, Johnston (1995) found that adolescents who reported having "gore-watching motivations" for viewing horror were more likely to think about mediated violence from the aggressors' perspectives. By the same token, Cantor (1998) reported that children who empathize with the victims of violence are less interested in violent content. It is likely that empathizing with the victims of violence is simply too upsetting to allow the content to be enjoyable.

Other research in this area has considered the role of empathy in children's reactions to mediated characters. For example, Zillmann and Cantor (1977) examined children's responses to protagonists. From an empathy framework, it was possible that children would adopt the same or similar emotions as the protagonist in a film they viewed. The logic behind this argument is that children will adopt the emotional reactions of others they observe due to either automatic processes or classical conditioning. On the other hand, from a nonempathy perspective, the authors acknowledged that children's reactions to protagonists may be based on their liking of the character or their evaluation of the character's actions. The latter perspective emphasizes the role of cognitions in guiding affective responses to others.

In fact, they found that children did not automatically match the protagonists' emotions. Instead, their affective responses varied according to the protagonist's behaviors. When the protagonist was neutral or positive in his behavior, the children matched their emotions to the emotions he expressed later in the film. However, when the protagonist was malevolent, children experienced counterempathy, or feelings that were hedonically the opposite of the protagonist's likely feelings. As a result, children's liking of characters was an important element in shaping affective responses to those characters. Wilson et al. (1986) later found that the ability to have cognitions mediate affective responses is a cognitive developmental achievement and that automatic empathy (regardless of the character's behaviors) is indicative of less advanced thinking. Given the host of skills that empathy seems to require, perhaps the automatic empathy is not even empathy at all and should be considered a different kind of affective reaction.

Other research on this population has explored the possibility that inducing fictional involvement in children can change their reactions to media. In an experiment with second through sixth graders, Nathanson and Cantor (2000) instructed one group of children to think about the feelings of a victim in cartoon violence while watching the cartoon. Another group of children in the experiment watched the violent cartoon without these instructions. The authors' larger goal was to understand if adults could mediate children's responses to television violence that fails to demonstrate the negative consequences for victims.

They found that children who were instructed to think about the victim's feelings gave less favorable evaluations of the perpetrator of violence, more favorable evaluations of the victim of violence, and perceived the violence committed in the cartoon to be less justified than children who watched the cartoon without any mediation. Further, boys in the mediation condition reported less aggressive tendencies after viewing the cartoon than boys in the no-mediation condition. Other analyses revealed that boys in the mediation condition did, in fact, report more empathy for the victim of violence than boys in the no-mediation condition (Nathanson, 1998). These findings indicate that empathy with characters plays an important role in children's reactions to television. It also suggests that potentially harmful forms of content can be mediated via instructing children to empathize with certain characters.

The Effects of Mass Communication on Empathy

A third segment of the body of research on empathy and mass communication considers empathy as an outcome of the media rather than a predictor. In other words, this research focuses on how our consumption of television and film changes our capacity for experiencing empathy. Zillmann (1991) suggested that the technology involved in the production of television and film can alter our capacities and tendencies for empathic responding. He described situations in which audiovisual media might contribute to greater empathy and also those that might inhibit empathy. For example, television provides us with endless opportunities to witness the emotional reactions of individuals to a variety of situations. The increased exposure to empathy-inducing situations should increase the likelihood that we will experience empathy. This might be particularly true if viewers repeatedly select genres such as soap operas, which not only allow viewers to "get to know" characters on a daily basis, but also feature extreme close-ups of characters' faces that simulate real-life conversations (Perse & Rubin, 1989). Empathic responses, then, might become habitual, and we might apply them in situations that extend beyond the media context.

Zillmann (1991) explained that the empathy-inducing characteristic of audiovisual media has especially profound implications in the case of child viewers. As reviewed earlier, children should acquire the capacity for empathy with development and experience. However, heavy viewers might acquire some affective skills earlier than normal because they have gained experience with the emotions via television. On a very positive note, Zillmann (1991) suggested that television might better prepare children to cope with a variety of affect-laden situations that they would not otherwise know how to handle.

On the other hand, Zillmann (1991) discussed several situations in which television and film may inhibit our empathic tendencies. First, the sheer nature of these presentations may reduce our opportunities for empathic responding. In particular, most television stories progress quickly and do not allow viewers much time to consider the implications of situations for characters' emotions. When potentially empathy-inducing events are depicted, Zillmann (1991) explained that distracting information often is presented soon thereafter. For example, the scene or characters may change so quickly that viewers do not have time to respond to the empathy-inducing situation with empathy.

The rapid storytelling characteristic of television often means that characters also are poorly developed. Zillmann (1991) explained that viewers may develop an "affective indifference" to poorly developed characters; that is, they may never connect with the characters and ultimately become indifferent to their emotional responses. Repeated viewing of poorly developed characters means that viewers will become accustomed to responding to others' emotional situations with affective indifference. The danger in this situation is that viewers will apply their affective indifference to real-world individuals and situations.

Finally, Zillmann (1991) noted that the prevalence of violence in the mass media may inhibit viewers' natural empathic tendencies by encouraging them to focus on aggressive perpetrators rather than victims. Much of the violence on television today is glorified in that attractive perpetrators commit justified, unpunished violence against unattractive victims who appear to suffer few harmful consequences (Smith et al., 1998). Repeated viewing of this kind of fare may train viewers to ignore the emotional conditions of victims. In fact, viewers may develop counter-empathy in response to the victims. As has been suggested before, individuals who continually practice counter-empathy skills (or who learn to ignore victims' suffering) by viewing these kinds of mediated depictions may fail to display appropriate empathic reactions in real-world situations.

In fact, there is some empirical evidence that certain kinds of mediated presentations reduce viewers' capacity for feeling empathy after viewing. Zillmann, Mody, and Cantor (1974) found that highly arousing films, such as those depicting violence or sex, decreased participants' empathic responses to a sad film they viewed subsequently. The authors explained that the viewers likely remained preoccupied with the first film after viewing, which reduced their ability to focus on the feelings of other characters in a different film. If we apply these findings to real-world situations, it is possible that viewers will be less responsive to the emotional states of real-world others after viewing very violent or erotic films.

Summary

Overall, mass communication research has found the empathy idea to be useful. There are theoretical reasons to expect that our exposure to the mass media might enhance and diminish our empathy skills. Although there is some research that shows that both effects can occur, perhaps depending on the content, the majority of work has focused on demonstrating a link between empathy and either our attraction or responses to characters and films.

CONCLUSION

The fact that the definition empathy has been plagued by imprecision and debate does not have to mean that thinking and research involving empathy are inherently problematic. Duan and Hill (1996) said that "the confusion reflects the diversity of the ways in which empathy is conceptualized and suggests that such diversity needs to be understood but not discouraged" (p. 261) so that creative new approaches to empathy can be developed.

In fact, empathy remains an important and useful construct in mass communication research. It can explain our attraction to certain types of content, our reactions to characters, our enjoyment of media, and even the behaviors we perform after exposure has ended. With the emergence and development of interactive forms of mass media, empathy should prove to be an even more important concept. Our likely increasing reliance on empathy makes it even more important for future research to carefully consider the boundaries and applicability of the term. Specifically, researchers should at least consider the following issues: (a) how both cognitive and affective components of empathy relate to outcomes, and which multidimensional conceptualization is most appropriate; (b) whether research participants have sufficient experience or cognitive sophistication to display empathy; and (c) how they will identify empathy as distinct from other affective responses. When research in this area works from a sound and consistent conceptualization, our understanding of a variety of mass communication phenomena should continue to grow.

REFERENCES

Aust, C. F., & Zillmann, D. (1997). Effects of victim exemplification in television news on viewer perception of social issues. *Journalism and Mass Communication Quarterly, 73,* 787–803.

Barnett, M. A. (1984). Perspective taking and empathy in the child's prosocial behavior. In H. E. Sypher & J. L. Applegate (Eds.), *Communication by children and adults: Social-cognitive and strategic processes* (pp. 43–62). Beverly Hills, CA: Sage.

Berger, S. M. (1962). Conditioning through vicarious instigation. *Psychological Review, 69,* 450–466.

Borke, H. (1971). Interpersonal perception of young children: Egocentrism or empathy? *Developmental Psychology, 5,* 263–269.

Cantor, J. (1998). Children's attraction to violent television programming. In J. H. Goldstein (Ed.), *Why we watch: The attractions of violent entertainment* (pp. 88–115). Oxford: Oxford University Press.

Collins, W. A., Wellman, H., Keniston, A. H., & Westby, S. D. (1978). Age-related aspects of comprehension and inference from a televised dramatic narrative. *Child Development, 49,* 389–399.

Davis, M. H. (1983). Measuring individual differences in empathy: Evidence for a multidimensional approach. *Journal of Personality and Social Psychology, 44,* 113–126.

Davis, M. H., Hull, J. G., Young, R. D., & Warren, G. G. (1987). Emotional reactions to dramatic film stimuli: The influence of cognitive and emotional empathy. *Journal of Personality and Social Psychology, 52,* 126–133.

de Wied, M., Hoffman, K., & Roskos-Ewoldsen, D. R. (1997). Forewarning of graphic portrayal of violence and the experience of suspenseful drama. *Cognition and Emotion, 11,* 481–494.

de Wied, M., Zillmann, D., & Ordman, V. (1994). The role of empathic distress in the enjoyment of cinematic tragedy. *Poetics, 23,* 91–106.

Dillard, J. P., & Hunter, J. E. (1989). On the use and interpretation of the emotional empathy scale, the self-consciousness scales, and the self-monitoring scale. *Communication Research, 16,* 104–129.

Duan, C., & Hill, C. E. (1996). The current state of empathy research. *Journal of Counseling Psychology, 43,* 261–274.

Eysenck, S. G. B., & Eysenck, H. J. (1978). Impulsiveness and venturesomeness: Their position in a dimensional system of personality description. *Psychologists Reports, 43,* 1247–1255.

Feshbach, N. D. (1978). Studies of empathic behavior in children. In B. A. Maher (Ed.), *Progress in experimental personality research: Vol. 8* (pp. 1–47). New York: Academic.

Feshbach, N. D. (1982). Sex differences in empathy and social behavior in children. In N. Eisenberg (Ed.), *The development of prosocial behavior* (pp. 315–338). New York: Academic.

Feshbach, N. D., & Roe, K. (1968). Empathy in six- and seven-year olds. *Child Development, 39,* 133–145.

Hart, T. (1999). The refinement of empathy. *Journal of Humanistic Psychology, 39,* 111–125.

Hoffman, M. L. (1975). Developmental synthesis of affect and cognition and its implications for altruistic motivations. *Developmental Psychology, 11,* 607–622.

Humphrey, G. (1922). The conditioned reflex and the elementary social reaction. *The Journal of Abnormal Psychology and Social Psychology, 17,* 113–119.

Johnston, D. D. (1995). Adolescents' motivations for viewing graphic horror. *Human Communication Research, 21,* 522–552.

Kurdek, L. A., & Rodgon, M. (1975). Perceptual, cognitive, and affective perspective taking in Kindergarten through sixth-grade children. *Developmental Psychology, 11,* 643–650.

Levy, J. (1997). A note on empathy. *New Ideas in Psychology, 15,* 179–184.

Mehrabian, A., & Epstein, N. (1972). A measure of emotional empathy. *Journal of Personality, 40,* 525–543.

Nathanson, A. I. (1998). *The immediate and cumulative effects of television mediation on children's aggression.* Unpublished doctoral dissertation, University of Wisconsin, Madison.

Nathanson, A. I., & Cantor, J. (2000). Reducing the aggression-promoting effect of violent cartoons by increasing children's fictional involvement with the victim: A study of active mediation. *Journal of Broadcasting and Electronic Media, 44,* 125–142.

Oliver, M. B. (1993). Exploring the paradox of the enjoyment of sad films. *Human Communication Research, 19,* 315–342.

Perse, E. M., & Rubin, R. A. (1989). Attribution in social and parasocial relationships. *Communication Research, 16,* 59–77.

Richardson, D. R., Hammock, G. S., Smith, S. M., Gardner, W., & Signo, M. (1994). Empathy as a cognitive inhibitor of interpersonal aggression. *Aggressive Behavior, 20,* 275–289.

Roberts, W., & Strayer, J. (1996). Empathy, emotional expressiveness, and prosocial behavior. *Child Development, 67,* 449–470.

Sapolsky, B. S., & Zillmann, D. (1978). Experience and empathy: Affective reactions to witnessing childbirth. *The Journal of Social Psychology, 105,* 131–144.

Shantz, C. U. (1975). The development of social cognition. In E. M. Hetherington (Ed.), *Review of child development research: Vol. 5* (pp. 258–323). Chicago: University of Chicago Press.

Smith, S. L., Wilson, B. J., Kunkel, D., Linz, D., Potter, W. J., Colvin, C. M., & Donnerstein. E., (1998). *Violence in television programming overall.* In Center for Communication & Social Policy (Ed.), National television violence study (Vol. 3, pp. 5–220). Thousand Oaks, CA: Sage.

Tamborini, R., Salomonson, K., & Bahk, C. (1993). The relationship of empathy to comforting behavior following film exposure. *Communication Research, 20,* 723–738.

Tamborini, R., Stiff, J., & Heidel, C. (1990). Reacting to graphic horror: A model of empathy and emotional behavior. *Communication Research, 17,* 616–640.

Thornton, S., & Thornton, D. (1995). Facets of empathy. *Personality and Individual Differences, 19,* 765–767.

Wilson, B. J., & Cantor, J. (1985). Developmental differences in empathy with a television protagonist's fear. *Journal of Experimental Child Psychology, 39,* 284–299.

Wilson, B. J., Cantor, J., Gordon, L., & Zillmann, D. (1986). Affective response of nonretarded and retarded children to the emotions of a protagonist. *Child Study Journal, 16,* 77–93.

Zillmann, D. (1991). Empathy: Affect from bearing witness to the emotions of others. In J. Bryant & D. Zillmann (Eds.), *Responding to the screen: Reception and reaction processes* (pp. 135–167). Hillsdale, NJ: Lawrence Erlbaum Associates.

Zillmann, D. (1994). Mechanisms of emotional involvement with drama. *Poetics, 23,* 33–51.

Zillmann, D., & Cantor, J. R. (1977). Affective responses to the emotions of a protagonist. *Journal of Experimental Social Psychology, 13,* 155–165.

Zillmann, D., Mody, B., & Cantor, J. R. (1974). Empathic perception of emotional displays in films as a function of hedonic and excitatory state prior to exposure. *Journal of Research in Personality, 8,* 335–349.

6

Entertainment Theory

Peter Vorderer
University of Southern California

IS THERE AN ENTERTAINMENT THEORY?

There is no doubt that entertainment plays a prominent role in our everyday lives. More than anything else, it is the media that provide their users with an ever increasing variety of opportunities to be amused, to have fun and pleasure, to be delighted and enlightened, in short, to be entertained. When viewing the changes, both within our economy as well as in our leisure-time activities, it cannot be denied that entertainment has become more indispensable than ever before. As Wolf (1999) claimed, "Entertainment—not autos, not steel, not financial services—is fast becoming the driving wheel of the new world economy" (p. 4). And with respect to our preferred leisure-time activities, researchers not only agree that entertainment is what most people are looking for (Zillmann & Vorderer, 2000, for an overview), some even predict "that entertainment will define, more than ever before, the civilizations to come" (Zillmann, 2000a, p. 18).

Despite this increasing relevance of entertainment, it is astonishing, to the point of being incomprehensible, that the academic effort to deal with this phenomenon has remained rather weak. Admittedly, there have been a number of interesting single case studies demonstrating the relevance of what the media has to offer (e.g., Ang, 1996). And there is, mostly from a critical point of view, research aimed at analyzing and interpreting what entertaining texts, movies, programs, and so forth, may stand for (e.g., Grossberg, 2000). But as an established academic field of study, entertainment research does not yet exist. There has been a certain lack of empirical, that is, systematic research on the uses and effects of entertainment, within the United States as well as in Europe.

There are exceptions, however. In 1980, Tannenbaum brought the scientific community's attention to this topic through his editing of a book that from today's perspective can be seen as the starting point for a systematic effort to establish empirical research on entertainment. One of the contributors to this book was Dolf Zillmann, who at the time had already begun studying entertainment and who since has further developed and refined this initial endeavor (Zillmann, 1978, 1980, 1983, 1985, 1988a, 1988b, 1991, 1994, 1996, 1998, 2000b), either on his own or in collaboration (e.g., Zillmann & Bryant, 1975, 1985, 1986, 1991, 1994; Zillmann & Cantor, 1977). For almost 30 years, Zillmann and his colleagues have developed, proliferated, and finally established a wide range of theoretical assumptions, models, hypotheses, and theories that they have applied to different audiences and to the variety of media offerings. The aim was to specify their pre-understanding and to finally define entertainment with respect to two major academic goals:

- to describe and explain what entertainment is, how it works, what it does to the audience, and

- to answer the question of why the audience is so attracted to it.

Our understanding of entertainment today is based on empirical research and can mainly be attributed to these primarily experimental studies.

Is there a single entertainment theory by Zillmann and his collaborators? I don't think so. Instead there is a research program that is theoretically based and empirically applied, supported, and proved. The theories that are used today to describe and explain specific forms of entertainment (e.g., Bryant & Raney, 2000; Oliver, 2000; Sparks & Sparks, 2000; Vorderer & Knobloch, 2000) were in fact developed by Zillmann and his colleagues. We have mood-management and selective-exposure theory, together with affective-disposition theory, which is based, to a large extent, on Zillmann's theory of empathy. There is excitation-transfer theory, again based on Zillmann's three-factor theory of emotion. All of these theories are described in detail in Part II, this volume, so that I may be brief here. What I am trying to show is that there is no single entertainment theory but a number of different theories that may be and often have been combined in a very useful way.

Based on the notion that entertainment can be described as "any activity designed to delight and, to a smaller degree, enlighten through the exhibition of fortunes and misfortunes of others, but also through the display of special skills by others and/or self" (Zillmann & Bryant, 1994, p. 438), mood-management and selective-exposure theory (chap. 4, this volume) explain why and how the audience seeks entertainment. According to these theories, people's exposure to the media is neither a purely reflexive nor an automatic response to what is offered to the audience, as traditional theories within a stimulus–response paradigm would suggest. Nor is exposure the result of an extensive and reflective investigation of one's own needs, interests, and desires in a certain situation, as the uses-and-gratifications perspective would assume. Based on the general assumption that media users are hedonistically oriented, both theories expect people to maintain and foster their positive moods and to alter their negative moods by selecting those media products on offer that best serve these interests. By using the media "to full advantage" (Zillmann, 1988b, p. 147), users benefit from their own previous experiences with different media products, thereby behaving rationally and, in most cases, unaware of the underlying psychological processes involved.

What the audience is going through while being exposed to the media is best described within affective-disposition theory (chap. 3, this volume). Based on Zillmann's understanding of empathy (chap. 5, this volume), this theory describes how the media users first perceive, assess, and then morally judge the actions of protagonists and antagonists in a narrative. As a consequence of the resulting approbation or disapprobation of a character's behavior, they develop positive or negative affects that again lead to hopes and fears relevant to the outcome of the story. The viewers hope for a positive outcome and fear a negative outcome for their liked, sometimes even beloved protagonist, whereas at the same time fearing a positive outcome and hoping for a negative outcome for their resented antagonist. Thus, affective dispositions lead to anticipatory affects that again result in specific affective reactions, depending on the actual outcome.

A prototypical entertainment experience like suspense, for example, can be seen as a direct consequence of these affective dispositions. The protagonist will be liked due to his or her behavior, leading to fear with respect to the highly probable negative outcome that awaits, so that finally empathic distress for the viewer will ensue as a result (Vorderer, 1996; Vorderer & Knobloch, 2000). From this perspective, affective-disposition theory does not just show what people are going through when they feel entertained but rather specifies the relations between particular narratives, affective dispositions, and the experience of entertainment.

Excitation-transfer theory (cf. chap. 2, this volume), finally, describes the primarily physiological processes that take place at the end of, or even after, exposure and attempts to explain why media users deliberately accept and often even seek disconcerting or burdening experiences during exposure. Using the example of suspense mentioned earlier, given that viewers are empathic with the protagonist and that the protagonist undergoes situations of considerable challenge, danger, despair, and at times even hopelessness, the empathic stress felt by the viewers will be very intensive and sometimes even stronger than they would otherwise prefer. Due to excitation transfer, however, viewers will not only experience immense relief but also gain positive, even euphoric gratifications through the observation of the story's outcome, that is, through the resolution of the distressing situation. Even more important, excitation-transfer theory holds that the more distressing the situation prior to resolution, the more intensive the feelings of relief and gratification after exposure. Hence, when it comes to explaining media users' deliberate and often repeated exposure to at least transitory disconcerting contents, excitation-transfer theory is necessary in order to remain consistent with the hedonistic notion that underlies all of Zillmann's theories.

This, I hope, should demonstrate that "entertainment theory" can only be seen in the specific combination of these three theories. And what we gain from this is more than single theories but rather a research program, due to the manifold applications of the previously mentioned theories; humor and suspense, sports and horror, pornography and music, news and information are only a few of the most prominent examples that show how broad the potential field of application is. Part III, this volume, provides a thorough overview of these fields of study and the influence of Zillmann's research program on entertainment.

Given this bouquet of theories (which are partially intertwined) together with the broad and highly relevant applicability, what else is there to ask for? Are there any shortcomings or desiderata within this research program on entertainment? Are there other fields of application that have been neglected? Not really. Zillmann and his collaborators have developed this theoretical perspective so thoroughly and have backed up their perspective with empirical, mainly experimental, research so thoroughly that any critic would be hard put to point out putative weaknesses. At the same time, it would be unwise to praise a scholar for his richness of ideas and for his impact on the field without even elaborating on his approach. As a researcher in the field of entertainment myself, I have always worked with and had a rapport with Zillmann's approach. At the same time, I have identified three problems that I often feel to be a challenge for both myself and other researchers in the area. In discussing these problems here, I hope to provoke contemplation, discussion, and more empirical work. The three problems referred to are the following:

- the role that negative moods and burdening feelings play within the entertainment experience,
- the diversity of individual users, social and cultural situations, and media products on offer, and
- the new, so-called interactive media and how entertainment can best be conceptualized within them.

I summarize here a few aspects relating to these problems and conclude with some questions and proposals about possible future directions of entertainment research.

DISTRESSING EXPERIENCES DURING EXPOSURE: ARE WE STILL TALKING ENTERTAINMENT?

No one would doubt that feelings like suspense while watching a movie, for example, are part of what we call entertainment, at least if we regard entertainment as a reception phenomenon (Bosshart & Macconi, 1998) rather than as an objective feature of media products (Vorderer, in press). Most media users not only select suspenseful dramas because they expect them to be entertaining, but they even evaluate these dramas more positively after exposure, the more suspense they felt during exposure. If we look closer at what suspense means for the audience, or what kind of experience it provides for the viewers, we will find that it is primarily a feeling of empathic stress (for an overview on the research of suspense, see Vorderer, Wulff, & Friedrichsen, 1996): Based on affective-disposition theory, empathic stress can be described as a mixture of the onlookers' hopes and fears during exposure. They hope for the positive outcome of their beloved protagonist but simply cannot be sure about it. By all means, it looks as if the protagonist will fail, and this is exactly what the audience is urged to anticipate and what makes the viewers suffer. At the same time, the story's villain seems to be well on the way to success, which adds to the viewers' fears about the anticipated outcome (Zillmann, 1996). This may go so far that the audience can hardly bear what it has to witness. Thus, the affective experiences viewers undergo during exposure are sometimes anything but pleasant; they can be distressing, even burdening.

When we take Zillmann's understanding of entertainment as something that delights the audience, these descriptions of suspense (as part of the entertainment experience) seem at odds. It looks like a contradiction to define entertainment with reference to the pleasant aspects underlying media use, while one of the most prototypical dimensions of being entertained, that is, to feel suspense, is often anything but pleasant. I have already mentioned that Zillmann (1996), in order to account for this putative contradiction, refers to the extraordinary relief viewers feel when the suspenseful and thereby distressing drama finally comes to an end, usually in the exact manner that everybody was longing for (Zillmann, 1978, 1983). Due to excitation transfer, the relief felt is so immense and the consequent euphoric feelings so intense, that the onlookers are compensated for what they have just gone through. Some suffering seems to be the price for intense gratification. At first glance, therefore, excitation transfer seems to rescind this contradiction and explain why the audience eagerly accepts distressing experiences during exposure.

The major problem with this "solution," however, has to do with the duration of the various experiences: Why do media users deliberately undergo rather long periods of suffering in order to gain a rather short moment of pleasant, even if intensively delightful, relief (Vorderer, in press)? When it comes to explaining the reading of a suspenseful drama, this problem becomes even more obvious: Why would somebody suffer for days, sometimes for weeks or even for months, when the relief lasts only a few pages, that is, over a period of maybe half an hour or so of reading?

In their study with elderly people, Mares and Cantor (1992) found that participants chose a movie that was said to show a rather sobering picture of the life of an old person over another version that would depict the same person more happily and socially integrated. The authors regarded this alternative as a choice between mood management (when selecting the more positive version) and downward social comparison (when selecting the more sober version) and interpreted their findings as confirmation of social-comparison theory. However, they admitted that even those respondents who selected the relatively depressing version in order to compare themselves with others who were similar to themselves finally felt better, because they could compare themselves with somebody who was worse off. In the end, their selective exposure led to mood management, even if they took a "detour" by way of the version that provided them with a downward comparison (Mares & Cantor, 1992). This looks like a confirmation of Zillmann's perspective on this problem: Media users may seek distress and burdening experiences through the selection of particular media products, because in the long run, they not only feel relief but gain pleasure and manage their moods.

In a more recent study on the selection of music, we have found that most people we interviewed chose a particular kind of music in order to enhance their positive or to alter their negative moods (Schramm & Vorderer, 2001; Vorderer & Schramm, 2001). In particular, when people are confronted with boring routines in their daily life, they often try to use music for mood management. When doing homework, when on long trips in the car, and when feeling angry or exasperated about something, they select music in order to compensate. We also found people who select music to intensify their positive feelings, particularly joy, or when they feel relaxed. This is perfectly in line with mood-management theory and presents no contradiction. But what is of more interest here is the fact that many of our participants also reported selecting music in order to support their less pleasant feelings. When they are sad or melancholic, when they feel abandoned or lovesick, they report choosing sad songs that are capable of intensifying their negative mood. More precisely, from the representative sample of 150 respondents we interviewed in Germany, more than 40% said that they sometimes like to stay in such a mood and that they do so by selecting music that serves this interest best. Particularly adolescents and younger adults, and females more than males, seem to be willing to intensify their sadness. Are they seeking purification? Or do they expect to be better off once they have made their way through an ocean of tears? It appears that they would be motivated by something other than by a simple mood-enhancement mechanism. What could it be? A more complex mechanism, still for mood management, but only after taking a detour, as seems to be the case with the Mares and Cantor study on elderly people? Or is it an additional gratification, something that may at times override mood management? Their basic motive would not be masochistic rather than hedonistic but instead, perhaps, they are willing to accept some suffering as a manifestation of feeling alive, vivid, complex, maybe even a type of companionship with others who suffer the same.

A German saying goes: "Geteiltes Leid ist halbes Leid," which means, "Shared suffering is only half a suffering," pointing to the fact that the understanding and empathy of another person often helps to deal with a burdening situation. Maybe lovesick adolescents really do suffer when they listen to love songs, but at the same time they not only gain some emotional support but also a feeling of togetherness with others having similar feelings. Or is it possible that media users can calculate, when they select a certain media offer, whether the upcoming experience could be useful despite the fact that it won't be easy to handle? Maybe they are willing to accept negative experiences when they provide some potentially relevant information for them, for example, about themselves. And, if the anticipated utility is great enough, they dispense with their search for positive moods. I have proposed elsewhere (Vorderer, 1998) a distinction between "socio-emotions" and "ego-emotions," implying that socio-emotions yield to affective experiences that occur primarily in relation to others as is, for example, the case with empathic feelings. Ego-emotions are meant to refer only to oneself, for example, because a certain story reminds a user of him- or herself. Media users may experience primarily socio-emotions (e.g., empathic stress) or ego-emotions (e.g., unpleasant memories), depending on the specific situation, on the media offer, or on their personality. But they could also experience both dimensions at the same time, because they feel sorry for a protagonist and simultaneously suffer due to the resemblance with their own memories, triggered by the movie. Don't we often find media users who are in fact eager to manage their moods in a way described by affective-disposition theory by relating themselves emotionally to others (protagonists, antagonists), while at the same time often accepting less pleasant entertainment experiences because they get something else out of it?

We do not know very much about the attraction of negative moods and emotions, but it is striking how particularly sad events often are appealing to media users. Why did billions of people all around the globe watch the funeral of the Princess of Wales on TV, and why do so many really enjoy sad movies (Oliver, 1993)? Why is *ER* (on NBC) the most popular and most successful show on American TV, where failure, death, sadness, and hopelessness take place almost every week? Is it merely to serve the media users' wish to reassure themselves about their own situation, or to confirm that they are better off by downward comparison and thereby help to manage their moods? My presumption is that there is more to it than mood management. In respect to this willingness to suffer, I would expect that differences between individuals, social situations, and cultures, as well as the different media products on offer would play a significant role.

THE DIVERSITY OF USERS, SOCIAL SITUATIONS, AND MEDIA PRODUCTS ON OFFER

Zillmann's ideas and theories on entertainment have been repeatedly applied and empirically tested. They have proven to be resistant to falsification attempts, so that any further development and elaboration of his research should instead begin with differentiation rather than with alternatives. I raise a few questions in order to point out possibilities of such a differentiation, that is, with respect to the implied media user, the social situation, and the media products on offer. Zillmann's research program implies

- a rather general, that is, unspecific model of man (as media user);
- a leisure-time situation in the Western world where entertainment may be experienced; and
- prototypical examples for entertainment products on offer.

My questions refer to the diversity that will be found in empirical studies when considering

- different media users who want to entertain themselves;
- different social situations and cultural contexts in which entertainment is possible or apparent; and
- different media products on offer that are capable of entertaining their users.

As far as the users are concerned, research in media psychology in general supports the presumption that individual differences influence not only the actual selection of media products on offer but also the subsequent experience and impact of it. Apparently, males and females do not prefer the same movies (Oliver, 1993, 2000), or talk shows on TV (Bente & Feist, 2000; Trepte, Zapfe, & Sudhoff, in press), and certainly not sexually explicit material (Greenberg & Hofschire, 2000), or the same kind of violence and horror (Sparks & Sparks, 2000). In Germany, an interdisciplinary research group has extensively studied the gender specificity of reading socialization and repeatedly found that differences in reading motivation, interests, and behavior are due to gender-specific conditions (Groeben, 1999).

Even more important than differences in sex and gender are those in personality characteristics (Weaver, 2000). Most media-related behavior also seems to be related to traits (Bommert, Dirksmeier, & Kleyböcker, 2000; Bommert, Weich, & Dirksmeier, 2000). Even the various prerequisites of experiencing entertainment are dependent on the media user's personality: Henning and Vorderer (2001) have recently shown that in addition to gender, media users' need for cognition has a significant impact on their time spent with entertainment television. Also, the readiness to empathize with others is one of the most crucial factors influencing the intensity of emotional distress that is felt by the viewers of a drama and can, therefore, hardly be overestimated in its impact on suspense. Within the context of a research project on interactive television, Vorderer, Knobloch, and Schramm (2001) have developed a short scale to measure this readiness and have found that empathy readiness has the strongest influence on almost every facet of the entertainment experience. In other words, what might be entertaining for those who are able and ready to be empathic with an imperiled protagonist is boring to those who simply can't or won't care for this protagonist at all and, finally, stressful for those who suffer because they empathize too much.

As for the social situation studied in entertainment research, the various theories often imply, and most investigations have in fact been dealing with, a prototypical situation for using the media. Participants are usually regarded as being at leisure where they have a few extra minutes to kill in one way or the other. According to the experimental setting, they usually have the choice of using the media and selecting a particular program (e.g., Zillmann & Bryant, 1994). The idea for this experimental paradigm is striking, the more so as it tells us the media users' interests, intentions, and actions in a way that is less biased and more precise or valid than any questionnaire. By the same token, this is only a standard situation from which many other social situations might deviate. How do users act when they are about to choose between different media instead of between different programs, or between using the media and perhaps going to see a live event? How does watching a TV show compete with reading a book, with contemplating one's own life (Henning & Vorderer, 2001), or with completing a task? Do the same emotional mechanisms take place? Is mood management working across different sorts of activities? We don't really know yet.

The social situation implied in most entertainment research is also one in which the user is regarded as more or less isolated from other people and therefore not considered to be somebody who feels, prefers, decides, selects, and acts as a social being. Media users, however, do belong to different social entities and may be described in terms of social strata, classes, milieus, or life-styles. Their preferences, their choices, and their evaluations of the media are never exclusively a response to the media product itself, but almost always depend on the social group and situation they are part of. Although future research on entertainment could profit primarily from personality psychology when it comes to studying individual differences (see earlier), it should consult social psychology and sociology for a more comprehensive understanding of the situational diversity of media use. From social psychology we can learn a lot about social perception, stereotyping, social comparison (cf. the previously mentioned study by Mares & Cantor, 1992), affiliation, confidence, and social interaction (to name just a few areas), all of which (may) play a role in the relation between media users and media characters, as well as between different users. It's striking how little theoretical input recent research on parasocial interactions and parasocial relations (e.g., Rubin & Step, 2000) has found from these fields of study.

Also, the way people report about their media use and how they assess what they have been exposed to has probably at least as much to do with "impression management" and "self-completion" (Ritterfeld & Vorderer, 1993; Trepte, 2001) as with their individual preferences: Within the cultural context of Western Europe, where the image of entertainment still has some derogatory connotations (Bausinger, 1994) and where social desirability in answering questions about entertainment still seems to play a role, entertaining media use sometimes also has a self-serving function. Among peers, it may be "cool" to listen to a specific kind of music (Hansen & Hansen, 2000), to watch particular TV shows (Trepte et al., 2001), or to be able to face a horror movie (Sparks & Sparks, 2000). Peers might tell each other who they are by evaluating soap operas in a particular way or gain in self-confidence by preferring comedies and thereby demonstrating to themselves and others how "funny" and "easy going" they are. To summarize, when exposed to the media, different people entertain themselves differently, according to their personal characteristics, their membership in different social groups, and various social situations in which entertainment may take place.

Certainly, entertainment has also gone global, and the most successful entertainment programs today are those that are sold and appreciated worldwide.

But despite all the similarities between entertainment programs in the United States, Asia, or in Europe, there is clear evidence that users within these different cultures tend to deal differently with what they see and hear. A most impressive research example on this question was given by Liebes and Katz (1986), who showed how different ethnic groups interpreted the TV show *Dallas*. More than anything else, this shows that an internationally successful entertainment program might be appealing to a very big and diverse group of people all over the world, but for different reasons. Or, to turn this argument around, a program that is considered entertaining and thereby very successful in one country, does not have to be comparatively successful in another, though similar country. To use a specific example, the already mentioned NBC-produced show *ER* is one of the most successful of its type in the United States, although it has failed to attract a large audience in Germany. German TV users are used to American products and often like them immensely, so the argument that this particular show would have come as a surprise to the German audience is not relevant. The private Channel Pro7 that broadcasts *ER* in Germany has repeatedly tried to find an attractive time slot for the show. Why has there been so little success so far? Based on the lack of intercultural entertainment research, I can only speculate: *ER* focuses its stories around human endeavors. A manageable number of primarily sympathetic young medical doctors try to help others and themselves—often in vain. In a way, everybody is on the edge of either a great success or a big failure. That is not unusual for a TV show that tries to entertain the audience. What makes *ER* unique is the depth and development of characters. But still, all of that should make the show as successful in Germany as it is in the United States. However, the characters in *ER* often represent different ethnic groups. Quite regularly, the conflicts arise around ethnic differences, attitudes, and prejudices. Is it possible that these conflicts simply cannot be appreciated in a country like Germany with only one, recently acquired, major immigrant population of Turkish people? That the German audience does not understand the characters because they do not understand ethnic diversity seems to be a possible explanation for the differences in the attractiveness of *ER*. The real reasons, however, can only be discovered with more intercultural research on global entertainment. In summary, we know a lot about how people deal with entertainment in general, but we know little about how different people in different social groups and situations and in different cultures deal with entertainment.

What do we know about how people deal with different media products on offer? The volume on media entertainment that, under Zillmann's leadership, was published last year (Zillmann & Vorderer, 2000) does in fact show that lately very different entertainment programs have come under the consideration of empirical researchers: humor and comedy (Zillmann, 2000b), drama (Vorderer & Knobloch, 2000), violence, mayhem, and horror (Sparks & Sparks, 2000), sex (Greenberg & Hofshire, 2000), affect-talk (Bente & Feist, 2000), children's programs (Valkenburg & Cantor, 2000), sports (Bryant & Raney, 2000), music and music videos (Hansen & Hansen, 2000), and even video games (Grodal, 2000). Why and how people use the media, how they assess them and what kind of impact they have on their audience has also been described by the various theories on entertainment. However, what we do not yet know sufficiently is specifically how these products work or with what differences. Are the affective dispositions that viewers develop toward protagonists of a drama comparable to those they hold in respect to talk show guests? Is fearing for a beloved protagonist in a suspense story similar to fearing the ongoing development and the outcome of a horror movie? Is an adult's feeling empathy with a character the same as a child's wishful identification (Hoffner, 1996) with a hero? Does humor in a comedy show compare to humor in a sports program? Does mood management through music work the same way it does through selecting a funny show? If we look at the diversity of entertainment experiences that result from the uncountable combinations of different users, different social situations and cultures, and different media offers, we get a clue as to what still has to be done if we want to move further on Zillmann's tracks toward a better understanding of entertainment.

INTERACTIVE MEDIA AND ENTERTAINMENT

In addition to the previously mentioned possibilities of further differentiation in the research field of entertainment, there is, probably more than anything else, one single technological development that has completely questioned our theorizing about entertainment. That is the fast proliferation of interactive media that not only changes the media users' potential in dealing with media products on offer but also affects their perception of and expectations about the media. Most entertainment theory has implied a rather passive media user, somebody who is exposed to a program, who can perceive and then cognitively and emotionally respond to it. With the development of interactive media, this situation has changed. Today, young people in particular increasingly expect the media to involve and immerse them not only by the vividness and dramatic art of the exposure but they also want to be engaged in the action. This does not mean that there is no more need for relaxation or being idle in front of the TV set or that the audience only wants to be "hyperactive" (Schoenbach, 1997). But in an increasing number of situations, adolescents are not satisfied with the role of pure observer anymore, they want to be involved and influence the narrative that they are exposed to simultaneously. Today, there is more money spent on computer games than on TV for the younger audience.

The challenge for entertainment theory is not the development of new media per se. The challenge is that the appeal of using these new media in an entertaining way cannot be described and explained as has the use of traditional media. According to affective-disposition theory, for example, entertainment is based on a TV audience's observation and moral judgement of the protagonists' and antagonists' behavior (see earlier, as well as chap. 3, this volume). It is the hopes and fears in reference to what the audience may observe, it is the empathy for all the emotions of the protagonists, for example, empathic stress, and finally it is the resolution of the story that lead to euphoric feelings based on excitation transfer that viewers regard as good entertainment. The situation is quite different for the media user when he or she is playing a computer game (Grodal, 2000; Klimmt, 2001). Certainly, the appeal of the story remains crucial, the protagonists and the antagonists still have to be in conflict with each other, and the player still has to care about the characters in order to be entertained. But in addition to this, and this may be even more important, the players have to respond immediately with an action that is not only cognitive and emotional, they have to decide what to do next. They have to make a move (sometimes very quickly), if they are to achieve something. Based on what the players are doing, they receive feedback appropriate to their achievement. Are they better than their competitors, better than their enemies, or at least better than themselves, when they compare what they do now to what they did last time? There is no way that it can be considered entertaining when the answer to all of these questions is negative. Conversely, they will indeed be well entertained when they succeed, when they make progress, when the feedback tells them that they did well or better than last time. Thus, the situations for "traditional entertainment" and "interactive entertainment" appear to be quite different (Vorderer, 2000).

There is an even more complex alternative being developed, going beyond simple interactivity, in "immersion cinema experiences," a combination of high definition digital cinemas with interactive game play set up in a group-based social environment, where large format screens, high fidelity surround sound, and group-based interactive consoles are combined (Spiegel, 2001). There are three distinct areas of interactive functionality:

- The console's function for personal interactivity allows for the selection of any object or character in the show and the ability to investigate it through the use of images, video and animations from the data base....
- Collaboratively, the console supports interfaces that allow you to have functional control of any aspect of the show's multi-path-narrative....
- Competitively, the console becomes a group game station.... In the competitive mode the console can function to give individual influence on a character in the storyline. (Spiegel, 2001, p. 103)

It is evident, that users of this kind of interactive cinema are simultaneously entertained in different ways. Sure, involvement is still the most prominent method of entertainment here, although it is now labeled *immersion* and brought to a more intensive level than is usually the case with television. But even more important is that there are different strategies that immerse the audience: "We believe that the more we can involve the audience in a role through narrative and interactive participation the more successful an Immersion Cinema Experience will be" (Spiegel, 2001). That is, it is not only the role of the witness but also the role of the participant that attracts the user that adds to his or her entertainment experience (Vorderer, 2000).

However, there also seem to be limitations in how far the user wants to go, or how powerful and influential the audience wants to be. In an experiment with 427 participants, where one third of the sample saw a 30-minute movie in a traditional way, one third had a chance to select the outcome of the movie, and one third had three options to decide how this movie should continue, we found rather weak differences in the respondents' evaluations of the movie, in their feelings of empathy toward the protagonists and suspense throughout the movie (Vorderer, Knobloch, & Schramm, 2001). Only when dividing the sample into those with greater cognitive capacities (operationalized by response times and level of education) and those with lower cognitive capacities did we find that the first group appreciated the movie more when it was interactive, and vice versa. It is too early to draw conclusions but a good time to risk a first thesis:

Media users (particularly younger people who have grown up with the internet and games) want entertainment to be more and more interactive. They want to be included through involvement and immersion; but at the same time, they are not really attracted to making decisions about the plot. Why not? Maybe because the plot, irrelevant of what the audience wants, expects, or can decide, is the major prerequisite for feeling empathic stress, as described by affective disposition theory.

WILL THERE BE AN ENTERTAINMENT THEORY IN THE FUTURE?

Given the success of Zillmann's various theories on entertainment and the more recent technological developments in the area of interactive media, the question arises as to whether we are able to adequately describe and explain interactive entertainment. I have proposed the psychological theory of playful action as a useful frame for such a purpose (Vorderer, 2000). Within that psychological theory (Oerter, 1999), play is considered a particular form of action that is characterized by three major aspects:

1. It is intrinsically motivated and highly attractive;
2. it implies a change in perceived reality, as players construct an additional reality while they are playing; and
3. it is frequently repeated.

In addition to that, games may also be rather suspenseful and sometimes even lead to players' disappointment, as is the case when one of them loses. According to Oerter (2000), games are often played on an intellectual level that doesn't fully challenge the cognitive capacities and the competence of the players. In particular children's playing is considered a form of coping with their own lives, that is, an activity that helps children to compensate for their problems, desires, and social pressures. Early games of make believe even express the children's wish for control and power as well as their desire to overcome their inability to influence their environment. These activities are said to help children come to terms with their own identity and individuation (Oerter, 1999, 2000).

In contrast to Oerter, who considered religion and art, and to a certain degree even labor, as follow-up phenomena of playing that are guided by the same mechanisms and serve the same function as playing does for children, I would suggest extending his theory on adults' entertaining use of the media. We have already seen that the use of the media in general is an activity that is not primarily serving extrinsic but rather intrinsic purposes and that this is particularly true within the context of entertaining media use. As far as the changes in perceived reality are concerned, media psychology is ripe with descriptions of ways media users change their sense of reality by taking on the reality provided by the media while temporarily ignoring the physical and social reality in which they are actually living and of which the media is part (Rothmund, Schreier, & Groeben, 2001). This sense of nonmediation has been labeled with different terms, such as *identification* (Oatley, 1994), *involvement* (Vorderer, 1993), *immersion* (Biocca & Levy, 1995), *absorption* (Wild, Kuiken, & Schopflocher, 1995), or *presence* (Lombard & Ditton, 1997). But despite the variety of terms, they all attempt to describe and explain what media users are going through in terms of their sense of reality.

Like intrinsic motivation and change in perceived reality, repetition is also typical for entertainment, as most media users develop entertainment preferences and return to them in a more or less regular way. Also typical are the games' potential to disappoint the players and the low intellectual level on which they are often played (Salomon, 1979, 1984).

Despite all these similarities, Oerter (2000) argued that playing, which he saw as a coping mechanism, simply becomes superfluous once alternative activities are possible or available for older children and adults. They can serve their needs with pure fantasies, daydreaming, or actions within the social reality. He thereby implied that grown-ups have no more reason to compensate, to cope with the burden of their social reality. In contrast, studies on the motivations of using entertaining media and on the desire to become involved have shown how much (adult) media users are looking for distraction or for alternative, if only temporary, realities to take them away into a dream-like world (Henning & Vorderer, 2001). These journeys into alternative worlds are most often (but not always) pleasant, sometimes more and sometimes less suspenseful, seldom disappointing (although it happens), but in any case almost always compensatory. They seem to serve a psychological function just as games do for kids.

The major advantage of conceptualizing entertainment as playful action lies in the fact that within that frame interactive media use can be described and explained just as sufficiently as the use of noninteractive media. As can be seen within the context of computer games, where users continually influence the unfolding story (Grodal, 2000), the theory of playful action offers an opportunity to describe this experience as an intrinsically motivated action, accompanied by a change in perceived reality that is repeatedly used and highly attractive, and at times both verbal and visually depicting, in that the game itself gives feedback to every single move and action of the player.

Sure, entertainment is more than the competitiveness of a computer game; but it is also more than the emotions that occur in respect to a beloved or resented protagonist or antagonist (Klimmt, 2001). Interactive entertainment can best be described as a combination of the different experiences a user can have at the same time. Without Zillmann's research, we wouldn't have a clue what entertainment means or does to the audience. But given how much he has contributed to our understanding of entertainment, it is almost our obligation to move his work forward.

REFERENCES

Ang, I. (1996). *Watching* Dallas: *Soap opera and the melodramatic imagination*. London: Routledge.

Bausinger, H. (1994). Ist der Ruf erst ruiniert... Zur Karriere der Unterhaltung [Once you've lost your reputation... On the career of entertainment]. In L. Bosshart & W. Hoffmann-Riem (Eds.), *Medienlust und Mediennutz: Unterhaltung als öffentliche Kommunikation* (pp. 15–27). Munich: Ölschläger.

Bente, G., & Feist, A. (2000). Affect-talk and its kin. In D. Zillmann & P. Vorderer (Eds.), *Media entertainment: The psychology of its appeal* (pp. 113–134). Mahwah, NJ: Lawrence Erlbaum Associates.

Biocca, F., & Levy, M. (1995). Communication applications of virtual reality. In F. Biocca & M. Levy (Eds.), *Communication in the age of virtual reality* (pp. 127–157). Hillsdale, NJ: Lawrence Erlbaum Associates.

Bommert, H., Dirksmeier, C., & Kleyböcker, R. (2000). *Differentielle Medienrezeption* [Differential media reception]. Münster: LIT Verlag.

Bommert, H., Weich, K. W., & Dirksmeier, C. (2000). *Rezipientenpersönlichkeit und Medienwirkung: Der persönlichkeits-orientierte Ansatz der Medienwirkungsforschung* [The recipient's personality and media effects: The personality-oriented approach of media effects research] (2nd ed.). Münster: LIT.

Bosshart, L., & Macconi, I. (1998). Defining "entertainment." *Communication Research Trends, 18*(3), 3–6.

Bryant, J., & Raney, A. A. (2000). Sports on the screen. In D. Zillmann & P. Vorderer (Eds.), *Media entertainment: The psychology of its appeal* (pp. 153–174). Mahwah, NJ: Lawrence Erlbaum Associates.

Greenberg, B. S., & Hofschire, L. (2000). Sex on entertainment television. In D. Zillmann & P. Vorderer (Eds.), *Media entertainment: The psychology of its appeal* (pp. 93–111). Mahwah, NJ: Lawrence Erlbaum Associates.

Grodal, T. (2000). Video games and the pleasures of control. In D. Zillmann & P. Vorderer (Eds.), *Media entertainment: The psychology of its appeal* (pp. 197–213). Mahwah, NJ: Lawrence Erlbaum Associates.

Groeben, N. (Ed.). (1999). *Lesesozialisation in der Mediengesellschaft. Ein Schwerpunktprogramm (IASL-Sonderheft)* [Reading socialization in the media society. A focus program (IASL-Special Edition)]. Tübingen: Niemeyer.

Grossberg, L. (2000). *What's going on? Cultural studies und Popularkultur.* Wien: Turia und Kant.

Hansen, C. H., & Hansen, R. D. (2000). Music and music videos. In D. Zillmann & P. Vorderer (Eds.), *Media entertainment: The psychology of its appeal* (pp. 175–196). Mahwah, NJ: Lawrence Erlbaum Associates.

Henning, B., & Vorderer, P. (2001). Psychological escapism: Predicting the amount of television viewing by need for cognition. *Journal of Communication, 51,* 100–120.

Hoffner, C. (1996). Children's wishful identification and parasocial interaction with favorite television characters. *Journal of Broadcasting & Electronic Media, 40,* 389–402.

Klimmt, C. (2001). Computer-Spiel: Interaktive Unterhaltungsangebote als Synthese aus Medium und Spielzeug [Computer games: Interactive entertainment offers as synthesis of medium and toys]. *Zeitschrift für Medienpsychologie, 12*(1), 22–32.

Liebes, T., & Katz, E. (1986). Patterns of involvement in television fiction: A comparative analysis. *European Journal of Communication, 1*(2), 151–171.

Lombard, M., & Ditton, T. (1997). At the heart of it all: The concept of presence. *Journal of Computer Mediated Communication, 3*(2). Retrieved May 18, 2000, from http://209.130.1.169/jcmc/vol3/issue2/lombard.html

Mares, M.-L., & Cantor, J. (1992). Elderly viewers' responses to televised portrayals of old age: Empathy and mood management versus social comparison. *Communication Research, 19,* 459–478.

Oatley, K. (1994). A taxonomy of the emotions of literary response and a theory of identification in fictional narrative. *Poetics, 23,* 53–74.

Oerter, R. (1999). *Psychologie des Spiels. Ein handlungstheoretischer Ansatz* [The psychology of play. A theoretical approach to implementation]. Weinheim: Beltz.

Oerter, R. (2000). Spiel als Lebensbewältigung [Coping with life through play]. In S. Hoppe-Graff & R. Oerter (Eds.), *Spielen und Fernsehen. Über die Zusammenhänge von Spiel und Medien in der Welt des Kindes* (pp. 47–58). Weinheim: Juventa Verlag.

Oliver, M. B. (1993). Exploring the paradox of the enjoyment of sad films. *Human Communication Research, 3,* 315–342.

Oliver, M. B. (2000). The respondent gender gap. In D. Zillmann & P. Vorderer (Eds.), *Media entertainment: The psychology of its appeal* (pp. 215–234). Mahwah, NJ: Lawrence Erlbaum Associates.

Ritterfeld, U., & Vorderer, P. (1993). Literatur als identitätsstiftendes Moment? Zum Einfluß sozialer Kontexte auf den Leser [Does literature bring about identity? On the impact of social contexts on the reader]. *Siegener Periodicum zur Internationalen Empirischen Literaturwissenschaft, 2,* 217–229.

Rothmund, J., Schreier, M., & Groeben, N. (2001). Fernsehen und erlebte Wirklichkeit I: Ein kritischer Überblick über die Perceived Reality-Forschung [Television and perceived reality I: A critical review of research on perceived reality]. *Zeitschrift für Medienpsychologie, 12*(1), 33–44.

Rubin, A. M., & Step, M. M. (2000). Impact of motivation, attraction, and parasocial interaction on talk-radio listening. *Journal of Broadcasting and Electronic Media, 44,* 635–654.

Salomon, G. (1979). *Interaction of media, cognition, and learning.* San Francisco, CA: Jossey-Bass.

Salomon, G. (1984). Television is "easy" and print is "tough": The differential investment of mental effort in learning as a function of perceptions and attributions. *Journal of Educational Psychology, 76,* 647–658.

Schoenbach, K. (1997). Das hyperaktive Publikum: Essay über eine Illusion [The hyperactive audience: Essay on an illusion]. *Publizistik, 42,* 279–286.

Schramm, H., & Vorderer, P. (2001, September). *Das Unterstützen und Kompensieren positiver und negativer Stimmungen und Emotionen durch Musik: Ein differenzierter Blick auf die Moodmanagement-Theorie anhand empirischer Ergebnisse* [Supporting and compensating of positive and negative moods and emotions by music: A differentiated look on the mood-management theory with empirical results]. Paper presented at the second conference of the expert group Media Psychology in the Germany Society of Psychology (Deutsche Gesellschaft für Psychologie, DGPs), Landau.

Sparks, G. G., & Sparks, C. W. (2000). Violence, mayhem, and horror. In D. Zillmann & P. Vorderer (Eds.), *Media entertainment: The psychology of its appeal* (pp. 73–91). Mahwah, NJ: Lawrence Erlbaum Associates.

Spiegel, S. (2001). Interview with Stacey Spiegel, Chief Executive Officer, Immersion Studios, Inc., Toronto. *Zeitschrift für Medienpsychologie, 12,* 103-105.

Tannenbaum, P. H. (Ed.). (1980). *The entertainment functions of television.* Hillsdale, NJ: Lawrence Erlbaum Associates.

Trepte, S. (2001, September). *Die Fernsehnutzung zur Konstruktion des Selbst* [TV use as a construction of one's self]. Paper presented at the second conference of the expert group Media Psychology in the German Society of Psychology (Deutsche Gesellschaft für Psychologie, DGPs), Landau.

Trepte, S., Zapfe, S., & Sudhoff, W. (2001). Talkshows nicht nur zur Unterhaltung: Empirische Ergebnisse und Erklärungsansätze für die Nutzungsmotive Orientierung und Problembewältigung [Talk shows not only-entertainment: Empirical results and an approach at understanding the usage motives, orientation and problem solving involved]. *Zeitschrift für Medienpsychologie, 12*(2), 73–84.

Valkenburg, P. M., & Cantor, J. (2000). Children's likes and disklikes of entertainment programs. In D. Zillmann & P. Vorderer (Eds.), *Media entertainment: The psychology of* its appeal (pp. 135–152). Mahwah, NJ: Lawrence Erlbaum Associates.

Vorderer, P. (1993). Audience involvement and program loyalty. *Poetics. Journal of Empirical Research on Literature, Media and the Arts, 22,* 89–98.

Vorderer, P. (1996). Toward a psychological theory of suspense. In P. Vorderer, H. J. Wulff, & M. Friedrichsen (Eds.), *Suspense: Conceptualizations, theoretical analyses, and empirical explorations* (pp. 233–254). Mahwah, NJ: Lawrence Erlbaum Associates.

Vorderer, P. (1998). Unterhaltung durch Fernsehen: Welche Rolle spielen parasoziale Beziehungen zwischen Zuschauern und Fernsehakteuren? [Entertainment through television: How important are parasocial relationships between viewers and personae]. In G. Roters, W. Klingler, & O. Zöllner (Eds.), *Fernsehforschung in Deutschland: Themen, Akteure, Methoden* (pp. 689–708). Baden-Baden: Nomos.

Vorderer, P. (2000). Interactive entertainment and beyond. In D. Zillmann & P. Vorderer (Eds.), *Media entertainment: The psychology of its appeal* (pp. 21–36). Mahwah, NJ: Lawrence Erlbaum Associates.

Vorderer, P. (2001). It's all entertainment—sure. But what exactly is entertainment? Communication research, media psychology, and the explanation of entertainment experiences. *Poetics, 29,* 247–261.

Vorderer, P., & Knobloch, S. (2000). Conflict and suspense in drama. In D. Zillmann & P. Vorderer (Eds.), *Media entertainment: The psychology of its appeal* (pp. 59–72). Mahwah, NJ: Lawrence Erlbaum Associates.

Vorderer, P., Knobloch, S., & Schramm, H. (2001). Does entertainment suffer from interactivity? The impact of watching an interactive TV movie on viewers' experience of entertainment. *Media Psychology, 3,* 343–363.

Vorderer, P., & Schramm, H. (2001, September). *Wer nutzt wann warum welche Musik? Empirische Ergebnisse einer repräsentativen Telefonumfrage* [Who uses when why which music? Empirical results of a representative telephone survey]. Paper presented at the International Annual Conference of the German Society of Music Psychology (Deutsche Gesellschaft für Musikpsychologie, DGM), Hildesheim.

Vorderer, P., Wulff, H. J., & Friedrichsen, M. (Eds.). (1996). *Suspense: Conceptualizations, theoretical analyses, and empirical explorations.* Mahwah, NJ: Lawrence Erlbaum Associates.

Weaver, J. B., III., (2000). Personality and entertainment preferences. In D. Zillmann & P. Vorderer (Eds.), *Media entertainment: The psychology of its appeal* (pp. 235–248). Mahwah, NJ: Lawrence Erlbaum Associates.

Wild, T. C., Kuiken, D., & Schopflocher, D. (1995). The role of absorption in experiential involvement. *Journal of Personality and Social Psychology, 69,* 569–579.

Wolf, M. J. (1999). *The entertainment economy. The mega-media forces that are re-shaping our lives.* London: Penguin Books.

Zillmann, D. (1978). Attribution and misattribution of excitatory reactions. In J. H. Harvey, W. J. Ickes, & R. F. Kidd (Eds.), *New directions in attribution research* (Vol. 2, pp. 335–368). Hillsdale, NJ: Lawrence Erlbaum Associates.

Zillmann, D. (1980). Anatomy of suspense. In P. H. Tannenbaum (Ed.), *The entertainment functions of television* (pp. 133–163). Hillsdale, NJ: Lawrence Erlbaum Associates.

Zillmann, D. (1983). Disparagement humor. In P. E. McGhee & J. H. Goldstein (Eds.), *Handbook of humor research: Vol. 1. Basic issues* (pp. 85–107). New York: Springer-Verlag.

Zillmann, D. (1985). The experimental exploration of gratifications from media entertainment. In K. E. Rosengren, L. A. Wenner, & P. Palmgreen (Eds.), *Media gratifications research: Current perspectives* (pp. 225–239). Beverly Hills, CA: Sage.

Zillmann, D. (1988a). Mood management through communication choices. *American Behavioral Scientist, 31,* 327–340.

Zillmann, D. (1988b). Mood Management: Using entertainment to full advantage. In L. Donohew, H. E. Sypher, & E. T. Higgins (Eds.), *Communication, social cognition, and affect* (pp. 147–171). Hillsdale, NJ: Lawrence Erlbaum Associates.

Zillmann, D. (1991). Empathy: Affect from bearing witness to the emotions of others. In J. Bryant & D. Zillmann (Eds.), *Responding to the screen: Reception and reaction processes* (pp. 135–167). Hillsdale, NJ: Lawrence Erlbaum Associates.

Zillmann, D. (1994). Mechanisms of emotional involvement with drama. *Poetics, 23,* 33–51.

Zillmann, D. (1996). The psychology of suspense in dramatic exposition. In P. Vorderer, H. J. Wulff, & M. Friedrichsen (Eds.), *Suspense: Conceptualizations, theoretical analyses, and empirical explorations* (pp. 199–231). Mahwah, NJ: Lawrence Erlbaum Associates.

Zillmann, D. (1998). The psychology of the appeal of portrayals of violence. In J. H. Goldstein (Ed.), *Why we watch: The attractions of violent entertainment* (pp. 179–211). New York: Oxford University Press.

Zillmann, D. (2000a). The coming of media entertainment. In D. Zillmann & P. Vorderer (Eds.), *Media entertainment: The psychology of its appeal* (pp. 1–20). Mahwah, NJ: Lawrence Erlbaum Associates.

Zillmann, D. (2000b). Humor and comedy. In D. Zillmann & P. Vorderer (Eds.), *Media entertainment: The psychology of its appeal* (pp. 37–57). Mahwah, NJ: Lawrence Erlbaum Associates.

Zillmann, D., & Bryant, J. (1975). Viewer's moral sanction of retribution in the appreciation of dramatic presentations. *Journal of Experimental Social Psychology, 11,* 572–582.

Zillmann, D., & Bryant, J. (1985). Affect, mood, and emotion as determinants of selective exposure. In D. Zillmann & J. Bryant (Eds.), *Selective exposure to communication* (pp. 157–190). Hillsdale, NJ: Lawrences Erlbaum Associates.

Zillmann, D., & Bryant, J. (1986). Exploring the entertainment experience. In J. Bryant & D. Zillmann (Eds.), *Perspectives on media effects* (pp. 303–324). Hillsdale, NJ: Lawrence Erlbaum Associates.

Zillmann, D., & Bryant, J. (1991). Responding to comedy: The sense and nonsense in humor. In J. Bryant & D. Zillmann (Eds.), *Responding to the screen: Reception and reaction processes* (pp. 261–279). Hillsdale, NJ: Lawrence Erlbaum Associates.

Zillmann, D., & Bryant, J. (1994). Entertainment as media effect. In J. Bryant & D. Zillmann (Eds.), *Media effects: Advances in theory and research* (pp. 437–461). Hillsdale, NJ: Lawrence Erlbaum Associates.

Zillmann, D., & Cantor, J. R. (1977). Affective responses to the emotions of a protagonist. *Journal of Experimental Social Psychology, 13,* 155–165.

Zillmann, D., & Vorderer, P. (Eds.). (2000). *Media entertainment. The psychology of its appeal.* Mahwah, NJ: Lawrence Erlaum Associates.

7

Gender Socialization of Horror

Norbert Mundorf
Joanne Mundorf
University of Rhode Island

Dolf Zillmann's work is characterized by a continuous exploration of new frontiers in the emotional impact of and exposure to entertainment media. Although the genres explored are often considered superficial, of little cultural value, even "sleazy," they are typically the ones that get the ratings, box office revenues, video rental receipts, and tremendous profits. For instance, according to Perkins (2001), HBO claims that the sexually explicit reality-based program *Real Sex* subsidizes quality programs like Spike Lee's *4 Little Girls* (which generated only one third the audience of the former in a given week). Similarly, viewers have been drawn to horror films since the first ghastly images appeared on the big screen. The horror genre has continued to fascinate audiences through the combination of frightening plots with nonverbal elements. Horror films seem to tap an inner vein that is subliminal and emotional in nature. Increasingly they also have incorporated the ever-popular ingredients of violence and sex. Nevertheless, as Dolf Zillmann and his colleagues have shown, they also fulfill important social and psychological functions.

EARLY HORROR IMAGERY

Roots of Gothic Horror

Early horror films were rooted in the increasing popularity and profitability of 19th century English Gothic novels and their stage adaptations (Tamborini & Weaver, 1996). The first half of that century saw the publication of horror novels such as Mary Shelley's F *rankenstein* (1818), Edgar Allen Poe's tales of terror like *The Fall of the House of Usher* (1839) and *The Raven* (1845).

These developments in 19th-century literature followed the tradition of the macabre. Similarly, the considerable popularity of the writings of the Marquis de Sade (1740–1814) in postrevolutionary France drew on explicit details of violent and sexually explicit scenes. Although William Hogarth, the Marquis de Sade, and others dwelled on violence, they lacked the ghostly and supernatural elements of the Romantic period during the latter part of the 19th century.

The connection of 19th-century Romantic horror novels to the 12th century term *Gothic* alludes to their medieval settings. Ironically, medieval advances in print technology by way of Johannes Gutenberg's use of moveable type for his 1455 Bible also led to the first publication of a book about Vlad Tepes (Vlad the Impaler), also known as Dracula (son of the dragon/devil/vampire) detailing his barbarism against the Germans. This book, entitled *The History of Voivode Dracula* (Geschichte Dracole Waide), was published in 1463. In 1897, Bram Stoker used the legend of Dracula as inspiration for his book.

Horror on Stage

The Théâtre du Grand Guignol, a theatre in Paris that featured bloodshed and gore for entertainment, opened in Paris in 1897. This small and popular theatre shocked audiences with realistic representations of life through illusions of gore that were successfully conveyed by using real animal body parts and a variety of fake blood consistencies.

From 1901 until 1926 the playwright André de Lorde, nicknamed "The Prince of Terror," wrote an average of four plays a year whose themes focused on the grotesque and horrific. The Grand Guignol became "a place of international pilgrimage" during his tenure (Lester, 1997).

Attractive women flocked to each performance in great numbers. A doctor was always in attendance to assist swooning spectators. Interestingly, it was mainly male playgoers who succumbed, probably because, unlike their female escorts, the men refrained from covering their eyes during the most horrifying moments (Lester, 1997).

Horror in Real Life

The renown of the Grand Guignol in Europe during the early part of the 20th century reflected pervasive media coverage of horrendous crimes, such as the 1888 Jack the Ripper murders in London. Gruesome crime was featured in the *Yellow Pre* s.s Many experienced real bloodshed and mutilation during WWI and in its aftermath of veterans returning from this bloody war with severed limbs and mental anguish.

Horror in Early Film

Horror films have attracted viewers since the invention of the film projector late in the 19th century. The improvement of film technology brought increasingly sophisticated means of filmic expression within the horror film genre. Public interest in the grisly subject matter fueled the production of early films focusing on horrific content, such as Thomas Edison's 1893 *Execution of Mary, Queen of Scots.* It "treated" the audience to a public decapitation and included details like the falling of the ax followed by the head rolling in the dust. The invention of the projector by the Lumiere brothers in 1895 allowed them to make a series of film shorts. The shot of a train speeding toward the viewer had a terrifying impact. People jumped back from the screen in fear of being run over by the train (Dashiell, 2000).

The first experiments in horror film were initiated by a French magician, George Melies. In *Terrible Turkish Executioner,* images made their screen debut that forecast many of the images of horror seen in later films. Heads are chopped off, and bodies are cut in half, albeit with an element of comedy. A dancing skeletal apparition scares a young woman in *The Monster* (1903). Melies pioneered many of the special effects used in today's films: fade-in, fade-out, dissolve. Melies made over 500 films between 1902–1913 (Kaminsky, 1996).

EVOLUTION OF THE HORROR FILM

Tamborini and Weaver (1996) reviewed numerous attempts at defining horror and arrived at three main categories: (1) supernatural, Gothic, or demonic horror; (2) quasi-science fiction, science fiction, and Armageddon; and (3) nonsupernatural, psychological (or maybe realistic) horror. A review of the history of horror films will illustrate the roots and influences pertaining to these categories of horror.

In 1910 Edison filmed one of the first monster depictions on film, F *ankenstein,* and in 1911 the first American film studio opened in Hollywood. Initially "movies were considered a vulgar form of entertainment, at least in America" (Wiseman, 1964, p. 6). Only after famous stage actors began to appear on film was movie going seen as a culturally acceptable pastime. DW Griffith's filmic techniques became standard in the ensuing decades. The dramatic use of close-ups and special lighting effects to create certain moods made Griffith a forerunner of future horror films.

Expressionism and Surrealism

The post-WWI era in Europe produced the artistic trends of expressionism and later surrealism, which were stimulated by political, economic, and social upheaval. Anxiety and fear found a sense of immediacy in expressionist film. Spectator involvement enhanced the emotional impact. Two well-known horror films from this era are *The Cabinet of Dr. Caligari* (director: Robert Wiene, 1919) and *Nosferatu* (director: Murnau, 1921).

The Cabinet of Dr. Caligari uses interiors with sharp and distorted angles to agitate viewers. "The film's conscious detachment from reality" made "significant contributions to the technique of film itself, such as careful use of light and shadow, mirrors, camera movement, and acting geared primarily to the camera" (Schrader & Schebera, 1988, p. 90). Early on Krakauer claimed that these films created a "mood of horror" (Schrader & Schebera, 1988, p. 90). Kracauer (1947) even suggested that the story of Caligari is a premonition of Hitler's real-life terror.

Murnau's Gothic *Nosferatu* employs mist and shadows to create an eerie sense of dread. The monster's lifeless, hypnotic stare, sharp teeth, and large hands with sharp, pointed fingernails terrified viewers. This film engendered a tradition of movies with the vampire theme, which was standard horror fare up until the recent filming of Bram Stoker's novel by director Francis Ford Coppola.

The release of films like these in the 1920s caused the first outcry among parents about the dangers of movies to their children. The Payne Fund Studies were the first to document the effects of frightening media on children.

THE HORROR FILM INDUSTRY

While Europe was experimenting, horror film was commercialized in the United States. From fairly innocuous beginnings during the 1930s, each decade of horror movies is characterized by an escalating level of terror and gore.

During the early 1930s horror films attracted sizeable audiences and were initially deemed a worthwhile endeavor for the *Big Five*. But profits were slight compared to other films, and these larger corporations left the horror film genre to the smaller Universal Pictures. Universal was successful in developing a profitable and low-cost production formula that recycled sets, used the same actors in a variety of horror films, and found sources for film content in noncontemporary and noncopyrighted fiction to avoid writer costs. These stories had drawn audiences to theatres in the past, so success was predictable, and risk was minimal (Gomery, 1996).

Universal's repertoire of horror films was based on supernatural myths, which the studio adapted to the 1930s censorship code. The main characters consisted of vampires, werewolves, Frankenstein monsters, zombies, or mummies, sometimes with a mad scientist. The setting was often foreign and murky (Gomery, 1996). These films were mild in tone compared with the earlier tradition of horror established in the theatre: There was little or no bloodshed, and shock effect was more often implied than revealed.

Universal's release of *Dracula,* starring Bela Lugosi, in 1931 typified the standard horror film. Unlike Murnau's *Nosferatu,* the Lugosi Dracula is a charming, well-groomed, somewhat handsome "man about town." He is a swarthy, exotically foreign, wealthy prince from a distant castle in the Carpathian Mountains. His female victims are captivated by his alluring smile and Slavic accent. It is left to the men to identify Dracula as the vampire, sucking the life's blood from their female companions. The sexual undertones between Dracula and his female victims are reminiscent of Nosferatu's fate when Mina lured him into her boudoir until sunrise to finally destroy him (and herself).

These low-cost popular films firmly established the horror genre in the 1930s. They allowed for original screenplays with the same, recycled characters and themes. Horror films were distributed worldwide, and their success ensured the filming of sequels (Gomery, 1996).

The early 1940s witnessed a shift from the supernatural/Gothic to psychological horror. The 1942 release of *Cat People,* directed by Val Lewton, heralded a series of films that introduced a psychological element into the horror genre. Unlike earlier films, a female is the perpetrator in *Cat People.* She is driven by unconscious fears, which ultimately prove true. The presence of a psychologist in the film signifies the popularity of Freudian psychology during the 1940s. Unable to accept the supernatural explanation, the psychologist kisses his patient (a taboo), thereby arousing the beast (sexual desire) inside her. The woman transforms into a panther, and she destroys the doctor. In the end, she is destroyed by this release of her own passions.

Post-World War II

These "tepid horror films" (Tamborini & Weaver, 1996) peaked by the mid-1940s. The end of World War II brought about a sociological shift in the United States with the move to suburbia and the advent of television. With the advent of television the government focused censorship attention on the new medium (TV) and relaxed film codes; this gave the film industry creative choice of content. Studios now had free rein to include more explicit material in horror films.

One form of entertainment established in the 1920s was pulp fiction, which became increasingly violent and graphic by the 1940s. These "bloody pulps" were popular with adolescent boys. Comic books included graphic scenes of horror in bright colors. By the mid-1950s comic books had become wildly popular. "The bright colors added a vividness to the gore that black-and-white film could not match" (Tamborini & Weaver, p. 11).

One result of post-WWII prosperity and the baby boom was a large population of affluent teenagers. With the growth in automobile ownership, the number of drive-in theaters increased from 155 in 1946 to 5000 by 1958. During this same time span, 5000 indoor theaters closed nationwide ("Welcome," n.d.). Movies at the drive-ins were typically black-and-white "B" movies, often of the SciFi or horror genres, "All the better for teenage snuggling, of course.... In the 1950's and '60's, the most popular place to take your date was to the drive-in theater" (Moe, 2001).

The horror genre during the late 1950s was geared toward that teenage audience. A phenomenon known as the "teenpic" emerged as studios marketed vintage Gothic horror films to youthful viewers. "Chiller theater" (Sapolsky & Molitor, 1996, p. 34) encouraged the production of a new generation of horror films and directors.

The British studio Hammer Films recycled old supernatural Gothic horror stories to capitalize on American teenage audiences. During the late 1950s they released a series of "horror teenpics" (Sapolsky & Molitor, 1996, p. 34). The Hammer *Dracula* and *Frankenstein* films were different from their predecessors: The addition of color introduced a new level of gore to the film content as cameras zoomed in for close-ups of gruesome, bloody scenes. Viewers responded with screams of enjoyment. In the United States, films like *Teenage Werewolf* and *Teenage Frankenstein* wrote teenagers right into the story.

Science Fiction Horror

Growing anxiety about technology and the threat of nuclear disaster set the stage for a new type of film: science fiction horror. Although Frankenstein was probably the first science fiction horror movie, the genre did not become popular until the 1950s. *The Thing* (1951) and *Invasion of the Body Snatchers* (1956) represent a "more distopian outlook" (Cook & Bernink, 1999, p. 192), as the public became more concerned about "the subjection of the human to the powers of science and technology" (p. 193).

Hitchcock

1960 brought a turning point in the horror film genre. Hitchcock's *Psycho* forever changed the direction of horror films. Psycho combined psychological and realistic horror. Bloodshed now became more explicit and graphic.

The psycho-maniac introduced by Hitchcock launched the graphic horror movie; *Psycho* may be the first slasher film. Sapolsky and Molitor (1996) explained that the interest in the horror genre by a famed director "legitimized blood and gore" (p. 35) and thus opened the door for imitators of explicit violence and bloodshed.

The New Gore

The success of *Psycho* and the Hammer productions attracted the attention of producer Roger Corman. His series of black-and-white, cheaply made horror films used unknown actors and combined all types of horror to increase box office income (Cook & Bernink, 1999, p. 263). Throughout the early 1960s, Corman produced several movies based on Edgar Allen Poe stories like *The Fall of the House of Usher* and *The Raven*. *The Haunted Palace* incorporated many horror elements: "The theme of black magic which undermines and is opposed by the community; the rational man of science who believes himself able to explain everything; the 'good' woman as victim; and the themes of psychic possession and physical deformity" (Cook & Bernink, 1999, p. 263).

Raising the "gore" bar to new levels was George Romero's 1968 film *Night of the Living Dead*. Appealing to the growing campus community, it depicts some of the most memorable, horrific scenes in film history. The fact that the film is in black and white does not lessen the impact of zombies devouring human entrails and limbs. Crane views this film as "the supreme expression of contemporary nihilism" (Cook & Bernink, 1999 p. 204), where the only survivor, a Black man, is mistaken for a zombie and shot by the "redneck posse" (Cook & Bernink, 1999, p. 204).

The Slasher

Films like *The Texas Chainsaw Massacre* (1974) continued to cater to movie going college students. But what sets this film apart is the reality-based drama. The "man-beast" is motivated purely by his madness to massacre others. The bar rose another notch with a series of "slasher" films. Special effects technology and the new high-speed film brought more exciting scenes of bloodshed and brutality. The VCR also created a demand for a larger number of films.

The popularity of slasher films, especially among teenagers and college students, encouraged studios to recycle the basic ingredients of the storyline: Extreme violence often involves killing and mutilation with sharp objects (hence the term "slasher"), attractive girls are either sexually promiscuous or virginal (bad girl/good girl), and a psychopathic killer systematically kills off victim after victim. Finally, only a handful of virtuous characters are left, and sometimes the killer is caught. But maybe not, the sequel is on its way!

Films that worked well in this type of horror genre were the *Halloween* series first filmed in 1978, the *Friday the 13th* cycle first filmed in 1980, and *Nightmare on Elm Street*. Having won over the campus culture with previous films, studios began targeting the teenage population with these films to increase their profits.

The "era of the blockbuster" (Gomery, 1996, p. 60) successfully introduced films like *Jaws* (1975), which were marketed on a grandiose scale. When studios realized billions could be earned from blockbuster releases, the low-cost sequel was written into the script.

The *Alien* (begun 1979) cycle of films added a new dimension to science fiction horror: angst. One of the most terrifying aliens ever brought to the screen, the monster in *Alien* can be found anywhere out there, or inside us.

Recent Trends

During the 1990s a new type of horror film made its way into horror fan's hearts. These films were a prelude to the popular 2001 reality-based television shows like *Survivor. The Blair Witch Project* (1994) was a low-cost (filmed in black and white with a video camera) horror film, reminiscent of

The Texas Chainsaw Massacre in that it "manages to blur the lines between reality and fiction" (Saravia, n.d.). The lack of gore and bloodshed and the implied horror hark back to the earlier Gothic horror films of the 1930s and 1940s (Saravia, n.d.).

Crossover films, which fall into the horror film variety, also made their debut in the 1990s. *Silence of the Lambs* (1991) was a high-end production featuring world-class actors, that attracted audiences of all ages and a variety of socioeconomic backgrounds. The film combined the nonsupernatural, psychological horror, and a touch of Gothic (Hannibal's prison cell is both eerie and compelling). The mutilation scenes remind us of slasher films when a "sacrificial lamb" (the prison guard) obliviously wanders around the prisoner's cell unaware of the malignant intent brewing in the mind of Dr. Lector. The film forces us to confront (on a silver platter) the concept of cannibalism, a sociological taboo to most of "civilized" humanity. The trend of crossover horror has also continued to draw viewers of all ages. *Hannibal* (whose main character is fondly known as "Hannibal the Cannibal"), the sequel to *Silence of the Lambs,* came out in theaters during Spring 2001. *American Psycho* (2000) also draws on the slasher formula, but this time with a touch of social criticism. The obvious reference to Hitchcock's *Psycho* is recognizable throughout the film. Based on the book with the same title, the film is a social satire of the excesses of the 1980s; it "captures the insanity of that period like nothing else" (Universal Studies, 2000).

The horror film genre has carried on the tradition of a teenage dating vehicle, catering to even younger audiences along with the teen and campus cultures. Films like the 1997 *I Know What You Did Last Summer* and the horror parody *Scream* have continued to rely on the slasher modus operandi (sequels and all). Most of the social psychological research related to horror has focused on slasher films.

EFFECTS OF HORROR

The remainder of this chapter focuses on effects and enjoyment of horror movies. There is obvious concern about the effects of exposure to this genre. However, much of the research on effects of horror is confounded with effects of violent or sexual media content. Research on media violence includes other violent genres, from crime drama to action-adventure and reality-based material, but also the type of fare featured in many horror movies since the 1960s.

Data on the effects of horrific violence per se are difficult to isolate. One may assume comparable effects of horror and other violence exposure, even though the graphic nature of horror may lead to priming effects (Tamborini & Salomonson, 1996) that can result even from brief viewing episodes.

Much media effects research has followed the modeling or conditioning paradigms. One implication is that, given appropriate contingencies, the more extensive the exposure to model behavior the greater the modeling effect. Modeling may have considerable influence, in particular because antagonists in horror often survive and even resurface in the sequel. Teenager viewers might take behavioral cues from the often unpunished violence in horror, which is then reinforced through arousal.

Social cognition theory has espoused priming, which can explain effects based on brief, even one-time exposure. Cognitive and emotional components are seen as nodes in a network of associative pathways. These nodes are activated and may trigger other nodes along these pathways through spreading activation (Collins & Loftus, 1975). For instance, males primed to have aggressive thoughts "subsequently delivered the most intense electric shock to a fellow student whenever that person made a mistake" (Berkowitz & Rogers, 1988, p. 88). Priming can explain possible horror effects in that violent behavior scripts are activated and energized via the high levels of arousal prevalent in horror movies (Tamborini & Salomonson, 1996).

Priming effects can be extended and can also be reactivated when participants encounter stimuli that remind them of prior primes (Jo & Berkowitz, 1994). A number of variables tend to facilitate priming effects, such as the interpretation of messages, relationship to characters on screen, and nature of the target of aggression. Limited research on the priming effects of horror is available, however.

Differences in the effects of horrific violence compared to other types of violence, if any, might result from exposure patterns and demographic audience characteristics: Horror seems to appeal primarily to young males, and most horror is typically limited to feature films, whereas other violence is often found in weekly or daily series.

Donnerstein, Linz, and Penrod (see 1987 for a summary) have focused on slasher films, which tend to spice up graphic horror with sexual imagery. Interpreting their effects has been controversial and has lead to an extended debate across opposing viewpoints. Negative effects on attitudes toward woman were found. A key point of contention is if these effects are due to violent victimization of females in the slasher film, as suggested by

Donnerstein and his colleagues, or if they are due to the promiscuity and indiscriminate sexual behaviors of the females in the movies.

Weaver (1986) demonstrated greater attitudinal impact of a video featuring female promiscuity compared to a slasher film. He attributed this impact to the priming of a promiscuity schema, which is generalized from the female protagonist to women in general. He explained the findings resulting from nonviolent as well as violent sexual fare from a social cognition perspective: Social categories (schemata) simplify perception of complex relationships and facilitate processing of new information. New information is then put into existing categories based on perceived similarities. When a category is repeatedly activated, category differences and social judgments are "exaggerated and distorted" (p. 31). Such social judgments are typically not subject to extensive search and reflection. Instead, they often follow a rule of thumb, based on recently activated categories (Sherman & Corty, 1984). One of these categories is female sexual promiscuity, the tendency to categorize women as "good girls/bad girls," permissive/restrictive, and so on. Exposure to sexual fare not only activates this category, but it also appears to exaggerate perceptions of female permissiveness.

Weaver found by far the strongest reduction in recommended incarceration in a mock rape trial after exposure to sexual material featuring insatiable, indiscriminate women (37%), more so than "rape and terror," (28%) and far more than "lovers' sex" (11%). It should be noted that the effect was strongest for nonviolent pornography. Apparently, the portrayal of women as nymphomaniacs, rather typical for this genre, leads viewers to a generalized view of women as sexually nondiscriminating, which makes rape a more excuseable offense. Terrorization of women as found in slasher films such as *Toolbox Murders* also had a strong impact.

The type of portrayal in nonviolent erotica contributed a sizeable difference: The nymphomaniac condition is more likely to trigger perceptions associated with promiscuity and related social judgments. Socially cognitive reasoning can also explain the impact of sexual fare on attitudes toward relationships, marriage, and the desire to have children. Research also has shown that exposure to graphic horror tends to reduce the level of comforting (Tamborini & Salomonson, 1996).

Another, rather speculative effect of viewing horror would be affective cleansing as proposed in catharsis, as espoused by Freud and his followers, as well as by Andre de Lorde of the Grand Guignol. One implication of the extended Aristotelian concept of catharsis is that viewers of violent and sexual content can use it to overcome pent-up aggression or sexual repression and insecurities. Studies have failed to support catharsis, the assumption that exposure to "bad" emotions leads to a cleansing of these or similar undesirable states. Zillmann and Gibson (1996) in particular have demonstrated the limited usefulness of catharsis theory in explaining effects of exposure to horror.

ENJOYMENT OF HORROR FILMS

Excitement and mass appeal derived from witnessing displays of graphic violence have been prevalent since the gladiators of ancient times, medieval witch hunts, and the public executions during the French Revolution. One may construe under some circumstances that the victims of ancient violent displays "deserved it," because they were criminals, debauched aristocrats, or witches, and that the display served a deterrent function. In that sense the public violence would result in a "satisfying resolution." However, we can safely assume that many spectators came for the thrills and entertainment in itself. Even though it is fictional, the graphic horror of modern film and video has recaptured the terror and gore of these events in vivid colors and sounds.

Quite a number of armchair speculations have been applied to the enjoyment of horror (Zillmann & Weaver, 1996). Compared to other media content, explaining enjoyment of horror involves numerous complications. Most importantly, there is typically no happy ending. In some horror movies, the protagonist narrowly escapes, and the monster is seemingly destroyed. However, often we see a final scene that implies that something is still out there, that Jason is still alive, that the dead are still walking the earth, and that the crazed killer just escaped from the insane asylum again. Even a minimally satisfying resolution (Zillmann, 1994), when protagonists get away with dear life, may not sufficiently explain the popularity of horror movies.

In order to explain the appeal of horror to the viewing public and particular audience segments, we briefly delineate horror versus suspense, discuss the role of individual differences in horror enjoyment, and finally analyze horror in the context of gender-role socialization.

Viewer Disposition, Empathy, Victimization: Horror Versus Suspense

Horror movies are typically considered prime examples of fear-inducing media content. However, related genres also involve significant "scary" scenarios. Notable examples are mystery, and in particular suspense (see chap. 16, this volume). Increasingly, we see films that represent crossover phenomena and largely defy attempts at clearly defining the genres. Zillmann's excitation transfer theory has provided a concise explanation of the enjoyment of suspenseful movies based on arousal and dispositional characteristics. In a typical suspenseful movie—as in a horror movie—the liked protagonist(s) experiences a series of increasingly dangerous and fear-inducing situations. Protagonists ("good guys") and antagonists ("bad guys") are clearly established through moral choices and behavior (Zillmann, 1994). Antagonists are usually male and typically portrayed as mean, vicious, and violent.

Contrary to the lunatics and undead of horror, protagonists in suspense tend to have a particular agenda or a set of motivations: greed, power, lust, the other deadly sins (cf. the movie *Seven*), politics, and drug trafficking. Peripheral characters are victimized first. The hero is often less vulnerable initially, but will face death several times in the course of the movie, leading to the predictable hero-in-peril scenario (Zillmann, 1980).

This typical pattern is maintained throughout suspense and horror movies. Likeable characters are continuously assaulted, threatened by knives, guns, and bombs, shot at, or thrown off a cliff, whereas antagonists have the upper hand. From a dispositional and arousal perspective, the viewer will experience negative affect, even disphoria, while he/she vicariously fears for the lives of heroes and victims on the screen.

The negative affect experienced throughout the suspense and horror movie will lead to ever-increasing arousal levels in the viewers. Zillmann (1994) has pointed out this paradox of the enjoyment of suspense: "The heroes are tormented and about to be overpowered and destroyed by evil forces or extraordinary dangers.... How can anybody, under these circumstances, enjoy drama?" (p. 451) The majority of viewers like to be on the edge of their seats, but with the expectation that they will finally find relief by a happy ending of sorts. A series of ever-increasing dangerous situations will often peak with a near disaster, such as an airliner with 300 passengers (almost) exploding (*Die Hard III*), or a meteorite (almost) hitting the earth (*Armageddon*).

Excitation-transfer theory implies that residual arousal from the preceding distress situation will intensify the enjoyment of the satisfying resolutions. Critical differences between suspense and horror are the personalities and motivations of the antagonists and, perhaps more importantly, the plot developments, and in particular the ending. Horror enjoyment is typically not based on a happy ending. Needless to say, horror also tends to dwell more on blood and gore, as well as the expression of terror by the (predominantly female) victims (Sapolski & Molitor, 1996).

A number of researchers have attempted alternative explanations for the enjoyment of horror. We will discuss several of these.

Arousal and Individual Differences

Fear-based arousal from horror may have great enjoyment value for viewers who are seeking excitement for its own sake. Zillmann (1994) pointed out that people who are insufficiently stimulated and bored will appreciate any shake-up of their excitatory state. A number of researchers have identified individual difference variables that correlate with the enjoyment of horror.

Tamborini and Salomonson (1996) pointed to the intense affective reaction triggered by aversive stimuli, sound, music, and special effects (p. 189). Although attraction to such events and media portrayals may not be considered pathological (Zuckerman, 1996), there is considerable variation in the enjoyment of fear-inducing events. Zuckerman identified a relationship between sensation seeking and interest in both morbid and sexual events. Zaleski (1984) found a preference for negatively arousing pictures related to high sensation seeking, especially among men. For men in particular, horror film and X-rated movie attendance correlated significantly. Sensation seeking correlated highly with self-reported viewing of horror films. Similar correlations were found by Edwards (1991) and Tamborini and Stiff (1987). Tamborini, Stiff, and Zillmann (1987) found that boredom susceptibility and enjoyment of pornography, among other variables, correlated with preference for graphic violence only when the victim was female. Interestingly, males liked horror movies because of their destructiveness, whereas females enjoyed the presence of a just ending.

Several researchers have explored the relationship between arousal needs and horror exposure. Lawrence and Palmgreen (1991) showed that arousal needs play a critical role in movie-going motives. This impact tends to vary by age, in that young adult movie-goers looked to other audience members' reactions to increase their enjoyment of a film. This age group was guided "by needs for risk taking, internal cognition, and internal sensation" (Lawrence & Palmgreen, 1996, p. 165). However, even within this age group, individual differences affect movie preferences. Johnston and Dumerauf (1990) found thrill and adventure seeking to be related to graphic horror preference among teenagers, along with a low level of empathy. An additional variable was rebelliousness. Edwards (1991) also found correlations between all sensation-seeking scales and interest in horror.

Lawrence and Palmgreen (1996) compared horror movie fans and nonfans on a series of dimensions. Horror fans seem to be drawn more than nonfans to erotic films, science fiction, suspense/mystery, action/adventure, and comedy, whereas musical and historical films, as well as those dealing with social issues, appeal significantly more to nonfans. As far as individual differences between these groups, horror fans in this study were considerably younger ($m = 24.1$ years) than nonfans ($m = 40.9$ years); they go to movies more, often spontaneously, but rarely alone. Particularly interesting for the explanation of horror consumption behavior is the observation that fans "use other audience members' reactions to facilitate their own enjoyment of theatrical films" (p. 172). Compared to other movie types females rank their liking for horror movies lower than males do; one of the reasons may be that females are more easily offended by graphic nudity, sex, and violence. Clearly, needs for psychological arousal correlate with horror film preference (p. 175).

Gender-Role Socialization Model of Affect

The approaches previously discussed generated numerous partial explanations for the enjoyment of horror. However, none of them has produced a comprehensive model that is comparable in scope to the theory of suspense, for instance. Zillmann, Weaver, and their colleagues have developed a model that explains exposure to and enjoyment of horror in the context of gender-specific role expectations and behaviors. They emphasized the social uses of horror based on gender socialization differences. The basic premise of this work is that, traditionally males were raised to face the numerous dangers in their environment and to show courage under pressure. By contrast, the traditional female gender model implies the need for comfort and protection by the male companion. Zillmann and Gibson (1996) produced ample evidence for this gender-role pattern across cultures and throughout history. They traced the origins to the gender-role segregation in hunter–gatherer societies. In many primitive societies initiation rites for prepubescent males were severe. Young males were expected to show callousness toward bloodshed. This had obvious adaptive utility for hunting, for defense of family and property, as well as for warfare. Early civilizations, such as the Greeks and Romans, featured blood sports as mass entertainment and as means of controlling social upheaval. The Roman philosopher Ovid was one of the first to point out the social function of fear: The more terrified women are of mayhem, the more they seek comfort from male companions.

Mythologies of cultures are laden with products of human imagination driven by fear. Fairytales were often full of danger and fear-inducing details. The content of these fairytales gave the teller opportunity to comfort children early on and establish social bonds. They capitalized on children's anxieties and fostered their emotional dependency on caretakers.

Opportunity for gender-specific mastery of threat has vanished with the contemporary industrial society; however, most men are still socialized along "traditional" gender-role models. The horror film has become a forum for gender-specific socialization of fear and its mastery in modern times. It permits a rite of passage at a minimum of skill, cost, and risk. The gender-role socialization model of horror thus implies that young males use horror to show off their courage and mastery in the face of danger, whereas it permits females to show their need for comfort and protection by a male companion. Following these gender-role expectations, by implication, should enhance the enjoyment of the horror movie as well as the mutual liking of the couple viewing the movie.

Content of horror movies dwells on female victimization and tends to foster female anxieties and fears. Sapolsky and Molitor (1996) analyzed the premise that women in horror films are portrayed as victims of extreme violence: "Females are victims of slashers as often as males, and sex and violence are not commonly linked" (1993, p. 41). They found that women were more than twice as likely to be seen in fear than men in seven out of ten films released in 1989. Although horror movies typically separate sexual and violent content, they employ some degree of sexual titillation prior to victimization. Maslin (1982) asserted that "the carnage is usually preceded by some sort of erotic prelude: footage of pretty young bodies in the shower, or teens changing into nighties for a slumber party, or anything that otherwise lulls the audience into a mildly sensual mood" (Weaver, 1996, p. 37).

Zillmann and Weaver (1996) discussed a set of propositions pertaining to the model that ascertains that horror is a convenient way for males and females to display gender-specific behaviors in modern society. Males may, in fact misattribute their ability to display fearlessness and courage to their enjoyment of the horror movie. Notably behavioral displays along gender lines may maximize not only liking of the movie but also the appeal of the opposite-gender companion. Specifically, males are expected to display courage and fearlessness, in contrast to female exhibition of distress and need for comfort. Witnessing situational control may coincide with increased respect for and compliance with the peer.

In an elaborate study, Zillmann, Weaver, Mundorf, and Aust (1986) tested a number of propositions related to the model. Male and female participants viewed segments from a horror movie together with an opposite-gender companion who they thought was a fellow participant; he or she was actually a confederate of the experimenters. Participants in this simulated "blind date" viewed a particularly gory segment from *Friday the 13th Part III*. Although several males were killed and maimed by Jason, the maniac with the hockey mask, during this segment, the primary target was the female protagonist who almost succeeded in killing Jason, only to see him rise again shortly before the end of the segment.

To test the impact of gender-typed behavior patterns, the opposite-gender companions were instructed to act in one of three modes: mastery, indifference, and distress. For instance, in the distress condition a female (male) confederate would display fear while watching the horror segment in the company of the male (female) participant. Respondents then filled out a number of instruments assessing their liking of the movie, appeal of companion, willingness to cooperate with the companion. They also participated in a second part of the study where they were to respond when the confederate gave an obviously exaggerated age estimate. The goal of this part of the study was to measure compliance based on confederate behaviors.

The findings of this study confirmed a number of Zillmann and Weaver's (1996) propositions and lent considerable support to the overall model. Although females overall enjoyed horror less compared to males, enjoyment ratings for the companion conditions were along expected gender lines. Males liked the movie segment twice as much if their female companion appeared fearful, compared to mastery or indifference. By contrast, females liked the movie much more when their male companion showed courage or indifference compared to fear. In fact, female enjoyment was virtually nonexistent when "he" was scared.

Although impact of behavior on perceived physical appeal ratings was less clearcut than movie ratings, an interesting interaction emerged. The study employed two male and two female confederates; attractiveness ratings were established *a posteriori* from members of the participant pool. There was no significant impact of behavior on appeal for those confederates who received high attractiveness ratings. However, the male companion, who had received considerably lower independent attractiveness ratings, was judged to be much less attractive when exhibiting distress. However, his appeal ratings rivaled his more attractive colleague when he exhibited mastery or indifference in the face of horror. The corresponding (reversed) effect was nonsignificant, even though in the expected direction, for the female confederates, presumably because the gap in their appeal was less pronounced (confederate attractiveness was not one of the original variables). However, the strong effect for female assessment of a "not so handsome" male's attractiveness lends considerable support to several propositions and to the model as a whole. Presumably, females seek comfort in males during fearful situations; the male who provides this comfort is considered attractive, even if his physical appearance is lacking.

Regardless of gender or appeal, respondents preferred confederates who exhibited mastery for a (fictitious) collaboration task. Apparently, courage in the face of terror generalizes to the ability to face other challenges. Finally, the estimation task conformed to expectations for female respondents, whereas males tended to become more resistant, the more self-confidence the female companion displayed. In spite of this unexpected twist, the study showed that fear-inducing stimuli such as horror serve as a vicarious testing ground for male courage and mastery of challenges. Although it is expected that gender typing by and large concurs with biological sex, there is a wide range of masculinity or femininity within males and females.

Mundorf, Weaver, and Zillmann (1989) demonstrated gender-role related distortions. Males overestimated female fright responses to horror, and females underestimated male fright compared to self-assessment of the genders and same-gender assessment. Corresponding gender-based distortions were found for boredom (essentially a measure of callousness) and enjoyment. Mundorf et al. also explored gender typing based on the Bem (1985) Sex Role Inventory. They assessed femininity and masculinity across biological gender and found that distortions based on biological gender were exaggerated for sex-typed individuals (feminine females and masculine males) compared to their cross-sex-typed counterparts. Assessments were most accurate for undifferentiated females. Apparently males, even if undifferentiated, are still subject to gender-role distortions, indicating that "at least for men, the impact of gender role socialization on judgments of affective dispositions and emotional conduct may be more pervasive than previously thought" (Mundorf, Weaver, & Zillmann, p. 671).

Similarly, Harris et al. (2000) found that biological sex was a better predictor of gender-specific behaviors and attitudes than psychological gender. They concluded that "it may be that social norms involved with dating are so powerful that they override gender attitudes" (p. 263). They tested the gender-role model in an ecologically valid way, using autobiographical memory of watching a scary movie. Their findings corroborated assumptions from the model: A majority of the scary movie viewing took place in a dating situation (for 57% of males and 48% of females) alone on a date or with another couple. Both genders were involved in choosing the movie. Females, more than males, reported emotional effects after viewing, such as anxiety, fear, and sleeping with the light on. Reactions during viewing revealed interesting gender differentiation, which again supports the model: Males were significantly more frequently amused and entertained, were surprised at the date's reaction, as well as sexually aroused compared to females. By contrast, females reported being very jumpy, holding onto their date, as well as yelling and screaming significantly more often than did males. Finally, twice as many males than females wanted their dates to think that they weren't scared.

A Look into the Future: Interactive Horror

Video, computer, and Internet games are often highly violent, sometimes gory, and contain a number of features found in horror films. Many contain some sexual fare. Compared to the usual horror viewing situation, interactive play typically entails a higher degree of emotional and cognitive involvement. Players are drawn into the game. Content can be modified, the player can take on the identity of different participants in a story, and different levels of difficulty can be selected. Some games also provide tactile feedback in addition to the traditional video and audio. Steuer (1992) pointed to speed (response time to input), range (the extent to which attributes can be manipulated), and mapping (match with the real environment) as key factors in interactivity. Tamborini et al. (2000) utilized the concept telepresence, the (perceived) ability to alter the form and content of the environment which leads to greater involvement. Tamborini (2000) pointed out that video games are higher not only in interactivity and vividness but also that users need to pay careful attention, make mental maps for future use, and coordinate visual attention with motor behavior. The user needs to act in order for the game to proceed, leading to "a strong sense of involvement" (p. 12). Moreover, many games involve vicarious aggressive action, priming aggressive scripts (Anderson & Dill, 2000) and suggesting aggressive environments and violent problem-solving strategies.

Experimental research exploring the emotional impact of violence and horror in interactive media is still in its infancy. Tamborini and his coworkers have addressed some of the key issues in a series of studies dealing with violent video games. Although not all violent games can be characterized as horror (Doom may be an example for both), audience responses to violent video games may permit some generalizations to the future of horror consumption.

Tamborini et al. (2000) tested the impact of different game conditions on players' hostile thoughts and surprisingly found that level of hostile thought was highest when participants *observed* a violent game being played. The authors attributed this unexpected finding either to the high level of frustration among those excluded from playing themselves or to the involvement of those learning to play the game, which may then distract them from hostile thoughts. Further analysis showed that in the standard (violent, non-VR) game condition those participants high on presence unexpectedly had a much lower level of hostile thought compared to those low on presence. Immersive tendencies in general were also associated with lower hostile thought. These findings also may indicate that being involved in the game may serve to deflect hostile thought, or lead to greater enjoyment and thus reduced hostility.

Although the video game situation tends to be solitary, increasingly games via the Internet permit multiple players. Also, conceivably "Teleimmersion" (Lanier, 2001) will permit players in the future to virtually become a part of the story. One may expect that greater explicitness and three-dimensional features will enhance the impact of interactive horror versus its traditional varieties. Moreover, similar to Internet pornography, control over access is lessened compared to other media, and children and teenagers gain access to more explicit content at ever younger ages.

CONCLUSION

Coping with fear is one of the most basic human emotions. Horror triggers vicarious fears. Not only can (mostly adolescent) viewers derive enjoyment from the thrill that horror provides, horror also gives them a chance to "act out" deep-seated gender-based emotions. Although traditionally males had the opportunity to display their manliness in various situations, in modern times they have limited opportunity to do so. Males use it as a vehicle to display their mastery of fear and danger. Females, on the other hand, use horror-viewing situations as an opportunity to seek comfort from their male companion.

Interestingly, the development of the depiction of women in horror films seems to coincide with changing gender roles since the 1950s. Although women have gradually made significant advances in most areas of society, horror movies and their promotional materials increasingly emphasize female victimization. The 1960s and 1970s revealed major steps in women's equality and workforce participation. At the same time, horror movies grew both in quantity and intensity of violent targeting of females. Although horror films are fictitious, we should be concerned about their impact on impressionable teenage viewers, both males and females. Children and teens are exposed and habituate to violent content at an early age. Often there is little corrective information being provided by schools, parents, or the media themselves.

Although to some horror is yet another form of cheap entertainment, to others it might be a vehicle to live out emotions that otherwise may not find an acceptable venue. Dolf Zillmann has helped us understand this complex relationship.

REFERENCES

Anderson, C. A., & Dill, K. E. (2000). Video games and aggressive thoughts, feelings, and behavior in the laboratory and in life. *Journal of Personality and Social Psychology, 78,* 772–790.

Bem, S. L. (1985). Androgyny and gender schema theory: A conceptual and empirical investigation. In T. B. Sonderegger (Ed.), *Nebraska Symposium on Motivation: Readings towards a psychology of androgyny* (pp. 48–62). Boston: Little, Brown.

Berkowitz, L., & Rogers, K. H. (1988). A priming analysis of media influences. In J. Bryant & D. Zillmann (Eds.), *Perspectives on media effects* (pp. 57–82). Hillsdale, NJ: Lawrence Erlbaum Associates.

Collins, A., & Loftus, E. (1975). A spreading activation theory of semantic memory. *Psychological Review, 82,* 407–428

Cook, P., & Bernink, M. (1999). *The cinema book*. London: British Film Institute.

Dashiell, C. (2000). *The oldest movies.* Retrieved January 20, 2002, from http://www.cinescene.com/dash/lumiere.html

Donnerstein, E. (1984). Pornography: Its effect on violence against women. In N. Malamuth & E. Donnerstein (Eds.), *Pornography and sexual aggression* (pp. 53–82). Orlando, FL: Academic.

Edwards, E. (1991). The ecstasy of horrible expectations: Morbid curiosity, sensation seeking, and interest in horror movies. In B. Austin (Ed.), *Current research in film: Audience, economics, and law* (Vol. 5 pp., 19–38). Norwood, NJ: Ablex.

Gomery, D. (1996). The economics of the horror film. In J. B. Weaver & R. Tamborini (Eds.), *Horror films: Current research on audience preferences and reactions* (pp. 49–62). Mahwah, NJ: Lawrence Erlbaum Associates.

Harris, R. J., Hoekstra, S. J., Scott, C. L., Sanborn, F. W., Karafa, J. A., & Brandenburg, J. D. (2000). Young men's and women's different autobiographical memories of the experience of seeing frightening movies on a date. *Media Psychology, 2,* 245–268.

Jo, E., & Berkowitz, L. (1994). A priming analysis of media influences: An update. In J. Bryant & D. Zillmann, *Media effects: Advances in theory and research* (pp. 43–60). Hillsdale, NJ: Lawrence Erlbaum Associates.

Johnston, D., & Dumerauf, J. (1990, November). *Why is Freddie a hero? Adolescents' uses and gratifications for watching slasher films.* Paper presented at the Speech Communication Association, Chicago, IL.

Kaminsky, M. (1996). *Smoke and mirrors.* Retrieved January 20, 2002, from http://www.victorian.fortunecity.com/tollington/94/aug98/Melies.htm

Kracauer, S. (1947). *From Caligari to Hitler: A psychological history of the German film.* London: Princeton University Press.

Lanier, J. (2001, April). *Virtually there: Three-dimensional tele-immersion may eventually bring the world to your desk* [Electronic version]. *Scientific American.* Retrieved June 5, 2001, from http://www.sciam.com/2001/0401issue/0401lanier.html

Lawrence, P. A., & Palmgreen, P. C. (1991, May). *Arousal needs and gratifications sought from theatrical films.* Paper presented at the meeting of the International Communication Association, Chicago.

Lawrence, P. A., & Palmgreen, P. C. (1996). A uses and gratifications analysis of horror film preferences. In J. B. Weaver & R. Tamborini (Eds.), *Horror films: Current research on audience preferences and reactions* (pp. 161–178). Mahwah, NJ: Lawrence Erlbaum Associates.

Lester, G. (1997, January). *Reign of terror: The peculiar charms of the Grand Guignol.* Retrieved January 20, 2002, from http://www.fas.harvard.edu/~art/caligari1.html

Maslin, J. (1982, November 21). Bloodbaths debase movies and audiences. *The New York Times, 2,* 1, 13.

Moe. (2001). *Moe's bommerabilia: Pop culture 50s to 70s.* Retrieved January 28, 2002, from www.wtv-zone.com/moe/moesboomerabilia

Mundorf, N., Weaver, J. B., & Zillmann, D. (1989). Effects of gender roles and self perceptions on affective reactions to horror films. *Sex Roles, 20,* 655–673.

Perkins, K. P. (2001, May 29). HBO says Real Sex subsidizes quality shows. *Providence Journal,* F5.

Sapolsky, B., & Molitor, F. (1996). Content trends in contemporary horror films. In J. B. Weaver & R. Tamborini (Eds.), *Horror films: Current research on audience preferences and reactions* (pp. 33–48). Mahwah, NJ: Lawrence Erlbaum Associates.

Saravia, J. (n.d.). *The Blair Witch Project: An introspective analysis of the scariest horror films since The Exorcist.* Retrieved January 20, 20 02, from http://www.moviething.com/members/movies/faust/index3.shtml

Schrader, B., & Schebera, J. (1988). *The "golden" twenties.* New Haven: Yale University Press.

Sherman, S. J., & Corty, E. (1984). Cognitive heuristics. In R. S. Wyer & T. K. Srull (Eds.), *Handbook of social cognition* (Vol. 1, pp. 189–286). Hillsdale, NJ: Lawrence Erlbaum Associates.

Steuer, J. (1992). Defining virtual reality: Dimensions determining telepresence. *Journal of Communication, 42*(4), 73–93.

Tamborini, R. (2000, November). *The experience of telepresence in violent video games.* Paper presented at the National Communication Association, Seattle, WA.

Tamborini, R., Eastin, M., Lachlan, K., Fediuk, T., Brady, R., & Skalski, P. (2000, November). *The effects of violent virtual video games on aggressive thoughts and behaviors.* Paper presented at the National Communication Association, Seattle, WA.

Tamborini, R., & Salomonson, K. (1996). Horror's effect on social perceptions and behaviors. In J. B. Weaver & R. Tamborini (Eds.), *Horror films: Current research on audience preferences and reactions* (pp. 179–198). Mahwah, NJ: Lawrence Erlbaum Associates.

Tamborini, R., Stiff, J., & Zillmann, D. (1987). Preference for graphic horror featuring male versus female victimization: Individual differences associated with personality characteristics and past film viewing experiences. *Human Communication Research, 13,* 529–552.

Tamborini, R., & Weaver, J. B. (1996). Frightening entertainment: A historical perspective of fictional horror. In J. B. Weaver & R. Tamborini (Eds.), *Horror films: Current research on audience preferences and reactions* (pp. 1–14). Mahwah, NJ: Lawrence Erlbaum Associates.

Universal Studios. (2000). *American psycho: The vision.* Retrieved January 20, 2002, from http://www.americanpsycho.com/film/index.html

Welcome to the drive-in theater. (n.d.). Retrieved January 23, 2002, from www.driveintheater.com

Weaver, J. B. (1986). *Effects of portrayals of female sexuality and violence against women on perceptions of women.* Unpublished doctoral dissertation, Indiana University, Bloomington.

Wiseman, T. (1964). *Cinema.* New York: A. S. Barnes & Company.

Zaleski, Z. (1984). Sensation seeking and preference for emotional visual stimuli. *Personality and Individual Differences, 5,* 607–608.

Zillmann, D. (1980). Anatomy of suspense. In P. H. Tannenbaum (Ed.), *The entertainment functions of television* (pp. 133–163). Hillsdale, NJ: Lawrence Erlbaum Associates.

Zillmann, D. (1994). Entertainment as media effect. In J. Bryant & D. Zillmann (Eds.), *Media effects* (pp. 437–462). Hillsdale, NJ: Lawrence Erlbaum Associates.

Zillmann, D., & Gibson, R. (1996). Evolution of the horror genre. In J. B. Weaver & R. Tamborini (Eds.), *Horror films: Current research on audience preferences and reactions* (pp. 15–31). Mahwah, NJ: Lawrence Erlbaum Associates.

Zillmann, D., & Weaver, J. B. (1996). Gender-socialization theory of reactions to horror. In J. B. Weaver & R. Tamborini (Eds.), *Horror films: Current research on audience preferences and reactions* (pp. 81–101). Mahwah, NJ: Lawrence Erlbaum Associates.

Zillmann, D., Weaver, J. B., Mundorf, N., & Aust, C. F. (1986). Effects of an opposite-gender companion's affect to horror on distress, delight, and attraction. *Journal of Personality and Social Psychology, 51,* 586–594.

Zuckerman, M. (1996). Sensation seeking and the taste for vicarious horror. In J. B. Weaver & R. Tamborini (Eds.), *Horror films: Current research on audience preferences and reactions* (pp. 147–160). Mahwah, NJ: Lawrence Erlbaum Associates.

8

Exemplars in the News: A Theory of the Effects of Political Communication

Hans-Bernd Brosius
Ludwig Maximilians-Universität

Press articles and broadcast news shows or magazines frequently incorporate different types of information to describe a problem. Summary-type descriptions of reality are based on a broad set of data and are, therefore, usually valid, but frequently not graphic or vivid. On the other hand exemplars, that is, personal descriptions by people who are concerned or interested in an issue, are vivid, but often not very valid, because in selecting exemplars, a journalist doesn't necessarily care about representativeness. Journalists frequently use exemplars as a device to illustrate particular assertions about the state or the urgency of particular social problems. Exemplars depict people concerned about a problem who speak their mind about it, or who repeat the opinions of people who are involved in a problem, or of the "man in the street." Journalism manuals (e.g., Brendel & Grobe, 1976; Haller, 1987) recommend using exemplars to make a report authentic and vivid and, at the same time, make a complex and abstract issue interesting and comprehensible for the recipients. Aside from exemplars, news reports often also mention figures and facts that quantify the importance of a problem. Case-type illustrations are thus presented along with summary-type descriptions of reality.

Although both types of information (exemplars and summary-type descriptions of reality) relate to the same problem and may even have similar content, they differ in validity, comprehensibility, vividness, and persuasive power. Summary-type descriptions of reality usually comprise a larger number of cases. They are representative and systematic, and they quantify a problem. They are usually made available by reliable sources (e.g., government authorities, universities). Exemplars, on the other hand, show individual cases that may or may not be representative of the problem addressed. Their selection is guided by the subjective sentiment of a journalist. Exemplars usually emphasize particular aspects of the problem, and sometimes it isn't feasible to generalize from the sample of exemplars to the specific problem. In spite of this, it can be assumed that, owing to their greater vividness, exemplars influence recipients' opinions and judgments more strongly than summary-type descriptions based on systematic surveys. In other words, although a summary-type description of reality using statistical or representative information is of higher validity for making judgments about problems, the perception of problems is more strongly influenced by singular, less valid exemplars that possess more vividness and emotional proximity.

EMPIRICAL EVIDENCE

Results from social psychology (see Baesler & Burgoon, 1994; Bar-Hillel, 1980; Hamill, Wilson, & Nisbett, 1980; Wilson, Northcraft, & Neale, 1989) show that people do not rely on summary-type descriptions (or baserate information) when making judgments about an issue. They even seem to have difficulties processing this kind of information correctly. More recently some results from communication studies of the effectiveness of exemplars in media reports have been published. Zillmann, Perkins, and Sundar (1992) wrote several versions of a magazine report on the success of various diets. The experimental report was specifically concerned with gaining weight after a diet. A summary-type description of the problem (it was said explicitly a third of the people regained weight after having been on the respective diet) was combined with exemplars. In the first condition (labeled *selective* by the authors) the report presented as exemplars only those people who corresponded to the problem described, that is, those who had gained considerable weight. In the second condition, exemplars were selected representatively: Two thirds of the persons had not gained weight, and one third had. In the third condition both types of exemplars were mixed evenly.

Directly after the presentation, readers of the different versions of the articles were asked to estimate the percentage of people who had gained weight after the diet. Results show that participants in the selective condition (in relation to both others) widely overestimated the percentage of those who had gained weight. Although the correct number (one third) was mentioned in the text, these respondents estimated that three fourths of the people who had been on the diet regained weight after it was over. One can conclude that participants relied more heavily on the less valid but vivid exemplars. This result, however, did not show 2 weeks later, when the estimates were influenced neither by the distribution of exemplars in the text nor by the statistical information, but by the respondents' preconception of the issue of dieting.

Gibson and Zillmann (1994) replicated these results for television reports. Their study also found that the extremity of the exemplars affected judgment. The more extreme the exemplars presented, the more recipients overestimated the frequency of particular events, in this case robbery against car drivers.[1] Further studies have been conducted by Gibson and Zillmann (1998), Gan, Hill, Pschernig, and Zillmann (1996), Zillmann, Gibson, Sundar, and Perkins (1996) and Perry and Gonzenbach (1997). Although results varied in detail and according to additional variables under study, the basic gist of all the studies was that exemplars, their distribution, and there extremity have a strong impact on people's beliefs and perceptions.

Brosius and Bathelt (1994, see also Brosius, 1995) studied the effects of exemplars in a series of five experiments trying to identify conditions under which the exemplification effects did or did not occur. Participants were given four reports that varied the distribution of the exemplars while the summary-type description of reality remained the same. The reports dealt with the issues of the implementation of card telephones, the quality of dining hall meals, the quality of Frankfurt cider, and obligatory computer courses for students. Each report contained, in the introduction, a summary of the issue that defined the position of the majority. It was stated, for instance, that a clear majority of Frankfurt citizens considered the quality of the traditional cider as poor. Percentage figures were not given in order to

---

[1]In the studies mentioned, judgments on the facts themselves were ascertained. The effect of the exemplars consisted in their stronger influence (as compared to other types of information) on the judgment of a problem. A different effect of exemplars was shown by Iyengar (1991). Broadening his studies on agenda setting and priming, Iyengar investigated the influence of exemplars on the attribution of blame. In his opinion, exemplars give an episodic frame to a problem, whereas the presentation of statements and other devices set up a thematic frame. Iyengar, for example, showed that the presentation of homelessness with exemplars led to attributing more blame for their fate to the homeless people themselves, as compared to presenting the issue with statistics and statements.

avoid measuring mere recall effects. After this summary-type description of reality, a number of exemplars were presented; that is, in the cider example several Frankfurt citizens' opinions were quoted. In the first experiment, two versions were used: In the first version (labeled *representative*) four of five exemplars were in line with what the summary said was the majority, and one exemplar was at odds with it. In the other version (labeled *discrepant*) it was exactly the opposite: four exemplars were at odds with the purported majority, and one was in line with it.

In all four issues, the distribution of the exemplars affected the way recipients perceived the population's opinions (e.g., the Frankfurt citizens' opinions on cider). For two issues (dining hall meals and cider, that is to say issues that involve one's taste) the participants' own opinions also were influenced significantly. For the other two issues, there was a similar tendency which failed to reach significance. That is to say, recipients joined the majority of the people whose opinions they had heard or read. For instance, the participants who had listened to a majority of opponents of card telephones were more opposed to these telephones than those respondents who had listened to a majority of adherents. The influence of exemplars on opinions was weaker than on perceptions of the population's opinion. This can be explained by the participants' preconception, which weakened the persuasive power of the exemplars and impeded attitude change.

In four additional experiments, Brosius and Bathelt (1994) replicated these results (a strong effect of exemplars on the perceived opinion of the populations and a weaker, but often significant, effect on one's own opinion) under different conditions. In the second experiment, it was shown that the way the summary-type information described reality did not modify the results. Independent of whether the summary was formulated in absolute—speaking of a "vast majority"—or in relative terms ("more and more citizens..."), the effect of the exemplars was always there. In the third experiment, participants were given different distributions of exemplars. Some versions presented only one point of view, others contained a balanced share of both points, and still others contained only the opposite of the first point of view. Results show that recipients almost perfectly "calculated" the population's opinion from the distribution of the exemplars. The perception of who is in the majority and in the minority was determined by the distribution of exemplars. In a fourth experiment, reports were given to the

---

[2]Gibson and Zillmann (1994) used television material and were able to demonstrate a strong effect of exemplars for television also.

respondents in a radio version for one group and as a newspaper article for the other. The effect of the exemplars was equally strong for both media.[2] In addition, the effect was measured a week after the experiment (long-term effect). After a week, there were only traces of effects on personal opinion, but the effects on the perception of the population's opinion were as strong as before. That is to say, exemplars are capable of influencing the perceived opinion of the population on a long-term basis, even if the effect on one's own opinion is mostly leveled out by preconceptions. In the fifth experiment the exemplars were construed in a way that they all contained the same argument using different language rather than in a way that presented several arguments. This was done in order to meet the objection that the exemplars provide argumentative assistance to recipients, which is the cause of their effect. In other versions, the summary-type description of reality was repeated at the end of the report in order to give equal space to both summary and exemplars. The strong effect of the exemplars, however, remained almost unchanged under all these impeding conditions. Even when the summary-type description was repeated at the end and when the respondents read only exemplars with weak arguments, the exemplars still had a strong influence.

At this point it can be stated, by summarizing research on exemplification effects, that exemplars and their distribution in terms of pro and con statements exert a clear influence on the way recipients think about facts and issues and on the judgments they make. All attempts to trace back the effect of exemplars to other causes have failed thus far. It is obviously an inherent quality of exemplars that makes recipients' judgments so strongly influenced by their distribution.

Experimental studies discussed so far used students for the most part or other young people in the exemplars. This creates a high level of similarity between the sociodemographic features of the exemplars and the respondents in the studies (students as well). Numerous empirical studies show that the behavior of models who are similar to the recipient with respect to gender, age, and social status is more likely to be imitated than the behavior of other models (for an overview, see Bandura, 1994). The results of an experiment (Brosius, 1999) show, however, that exemplar effects occur independent of the similarity between exemplars and recipients. The author presented his respondents with four issues. As in previous experiments, one version presented four exemplars in accordance with the news story's baserate information, another version four exemplars inconsistent with baserate information. In addition, two more independent variables were used. In one condition exemplars were presented as being students (similar to the participants in the study), and in the other condition they were presented as being pensioners. Half of the participants saw pictures of the respective exemplars, the other half did not. The results repeated the main effect of exemplar distribution. Neither visualization nor attributed role of the exemplars had an intervening effect on recipients' judgments.

A recent study by Brosius, Schweiger, and Rossmann (2000) again demonstrated the stability of the exemplification effect. The authors conducted two experiments (with 307 participants) that varied the number and the type of sources of exemplars. In the first experiment, newspaper articles were presented in four versions. In the first two versions, the distribution of exemplars was representative of the summary-type description in the article. In the other two versions, exemplars contradicted it. A further distinction between the versions was based on the source of exemplars. In one version, exemplar information came from five different people; in the other version all information was provided by one person only. The second experiment also varied the representativeness of exemplars. In addition, one version presented identifiable individuals as sources, the other referred to vague groups ("the citizens think..."). Again, no influence of the intervening variables (number or type of exemplar sources) could be found. In other words, the exemplification effect was equally strong across all experimental variations of the exemplar source.

Daschmann (2001) conducted nine experiment with a total of more than 1,300 participants. His studies yield an additional and impressive body of evidence for the strong effect of exemplars compared to the effect of summary-type descriptions of reality. His results show that (a) exemplification effects also occur when exemplars (compared to the baserate information) cover only a minor space in an article; (b) exemplars attributed to an anonymous individual have a similar effect as personalized exemplars; (c) exemplification effects are independent of prior opinions and involvement of recipients; and (d) exemplification effects cannot be explained by the vivid character of exemplars. In two of his experiments, Daschmann also presented exemplar information without attribution to a single individual. The exemplification effect vanished under these conditions.

Taken together, the empirical evidence shows the following: (a) exemplars have a strong impact, and baserate information has a weak impact on recipients' judgments; (b) one-sided selection of exemplars leads to one-sided judgments; (c) the more extreme the selectiveness, the more extreme are the corresponding judgments; (d) dramatic and extreme exemplars have stronger effects; (e) exemplification effects are stable over time; and (f) recipients are not aware of the effect (cf. Daschmann, 2001; Zillmann & Brosius, 2000).

CONSEQUENCES FOR JOURNALISM

The strong effect of vivid but less valid exemplars, as compared to less vivid but valid summary-type descriptions of reality, was confirmed by all of the experimental studies done so far. It was shown that the distribution of exemplars had a decisive influence on the perception of majority and minority opinions. Recipients perceived the population's opinion on a controversial issue in a way suggested by the selection of exemplars.

Exemplars not only affect the perception of the population's opinion but also—in part—the recipients' own opinions. This, however, is only true for issues involving one's taste, not for attitudinal issues. The difference is supposedly based on the fact that because of existing preconceptions, opinions on attitudinal issues (for example, attitudes toward card telephones traffic banning) are more resistant to change than opinions on matters of taste (quality of cafeteria food or quality of apple wine).[3]

Not only do exemplars have a strong effect, they are also used frequently in mass media reporting (cf. Daschmann & Brosius, 1999). This is to say, they are an important subject of media effects research, as well as of journalism research. Journalists might endurably affect the perception of an issue and the population's (or concerned people's) opinions about it by a particular structure of exemplars. This might not appear to be significant for issues such as the quality of Frankfurt cider. However, for issues in the field of political communication, such as AIDS, biogenetic engineering, nuclear power, unemployment, or election campaigns, the importance of exemplars can hardly be underestimated. When for instance, several persons with AIDS are shown in a news broadcast, this might lead to overestimating the risk of infection or the spread of the disease. Or, when the "man in the street" is asked his opinion on biogenetic engineering, the selection of exemplars can affect the way recipients perceive the population's opinion, and maybe how they think about it themselves. As to the concept of "precision journalism"

[3]Another explanation would be that recipients find the exemplars' opinions on matters of taste more credible. Taste is not subject to logical reasoning. Opinions on attitudinal issues can probably be thought about with more sophistication.

(cf. McCombs, Cole, Stevenson, & Shaw, 1981; Meyer, 1973), journalists are called on to consider our results so far when they select and put together exemplars in an effort to relate social problems adequately.

Bearing in mind how accurately recipients reflect the distribution of exemplars in their perception of the population's opinion (cf. the third experiment, Brosius & Bathelt, 1994), the conclusion of this research for journalists whose aim is objective reporting is this: Exemplars should be presented only when reliable figures about the relevant population are available, or when they can be reasonably estimated. Exemplars should then reflect the distribution of opinions as they are known. However, two cases have to be distinguished. If the subject at hand is one that requires the description of certain persons' opinions, as was the case in this study, then a representative selection of exemplars meets the standards of objective and precise reporting.[4] If it is, however, intended to draw attention to a particular problem, a journalist runs into a dilemma. This becomes apparent when the experimental issue of Zillmann et al. (1992) is considered. Even though the probability of regaining weight after a particular diet might be small, news stories reporting such cases could mislead readers. Even if journalists present a mixed sample of exemplars (some who regained weight, some who did not), recipients might still overestimate the danger of regaining weight after the diet. This refers to an inherent problem; Journalism seeks the extreme, the unusual, the unlikely. Although the likelihood of events or occurrences might be extremely low, journalists will seek exemplars that can support their arguments. Considering this, the combination of exemplar use and journalists' tendency to seek unlikely and extreme events and occurrences might lead recipients to overestimate the number of people affected by a social or political problem, thus overestimating its importance and urgency.

Aside from the (quantitative) distribution of exemplars, their quality supposedly also has an effect. Looking at news coverage, it can be seen that journalists tend to present extreme exemplars, that is, the people who suffer most from a problem, the dirtiest sewer, the people with the most extreme views (cf. Gibson & Zillmann, 1994; Shoemaker, Chang, & Brendlinger, 1987). Assumedly, extreme exemplars such as these have a stronger effect by making the problem appear more severe than it probably actually is.

---

[4]News reports might appear to be correct in terms of accuracy and objectivity, because they supply the reader or viewer with a summary-type description of reality. In terms of effect, however, they can be tendentious at the same time, because they present a selection of exemplars that is not representative.

EXEMPLARS IN THEORIES OF MEDIA EFFECTS

How can exemplification effects be incorporated into existing theories of media effects? Given their ubiquity, it is very likely that older theories have come across this type of effect. First, recipients' ability to transform perceived distributions of exemplars almost exactly into notions of the population's opinions was interpreted by Noelle-Neumann (1984) as quasi-statistical perception. Based on a re-analysis of survey results, she claims that people permanently watch their environment in order to be able to estimate majorities and minorities for a given issue. The mass media play an important part in her theory of the spiral of silence: They relate perceptions of one's environment. If media information is at odds with information from one's own environment, one is likely to rely more on one's direct observations. In many areas relevant to modern society, however, recipients hardly have a chance to gain direct information about facts, problems, or people. In these cases, they are easily deceived into taking the exemplars selected by journalists as typical or representative.

In their third experiment, Brosius and Bathelt (1994) showed that the ratio of pro and con exemplars was strongly related to the extent recipients regard one or the other view as dominant. The ease with which a small number of exemplars affects the perception of majorities and minorities can be regarded as a cause of the process that is implied in the theory of the spiral of silence (Noelle-Neumann, 1984, 1991). Recipients' ability to form an impression of the population's opinion from the distribution of exemplars confirms the existence of a quasi-statistical sense postulated by Noelle-Neumann. The major vehicle that sets a spiral of silence in motion is, according to Noelle-Neumann, a distorted perception of majority and minority opinion, which can be created by a story that uses exemplars. As journalists frequently look for new trends and new problems, and cover them, they offer minorities a forum for presenting their views and opinions. If this is done in the form of exemplars, the minority view will appear to recipients as more important than it actually is. This might set in motion a spiral of silence. Even if issues involving one's taste are not important in political communication, and attitudes on other issues are evidently less likely to be affected, it can be assumed that consonant news coverage with a biased selection of exemplars may, in the long run, lead to opinion change in political issues.[5]

[5]For instance, street interviews on voting intentions should have a stronger influence on the perception of majority opinions than summaries of survey results. In a relatively unobtrusive way, a certain opinion distribution can thus be suggested to recipients, without explicit statements on factual distributions being able to change that impression.

Second, exemplification theory can be related to the cultivation hypothesis of Gerbner and his colleagues and thus to entertainment rather than informational material. Cultivation theory claims that heavy viewers derive their picture of the world (i.e., their reality perceptions) from the presentation of reality in entertainment programs of television rather than from real-world cues. The authors argued, for example, that recipients who often watch crime on television overestimate the probability of crime in reality. If individual crimes are seen as exemplars, Gerbner's results can be interpreted as effects of exemplars: Recipients overestimate crime rates and are more afraid of falling victim to crime, because they have watched more exemplars of crime and because they have seen more protagonists becoming crime victims. In general, entertainment programs on television with their fictional content can be seen as abundantly providing exemplars. The characteristics of these exemplars, their behavior and opinions, can shape recipients' perception of reality, according to the results of the experiments described earlier. Thus, exemplification can be seen as a vehicle of effects in both spiral-of-silence theory and cultivation theory.

WHY ARE EXEMPLARS SO POWERFUL?

The question still remains as to why exemplars are such powerful means of influencing people's beliefs and perceptions. Several theories in cognitive and social psychology could help to answer this question.

First, Paivio's dual coding theory (1971, 1986) would claim that, in terms of exemplification theory, exemplars consist of concrete imaginable stimuli that evoke both a visual and a verbal representation in memory, whereas summary-type descriptions of reality would only leave a verbal memory trace because of their abstract contents. Although such an explanation cannot be rejected immediately, it seems to be far-fetched. Paivio's dual coding theory was mostly tested using simplistic stimulus materials. For example, pictures of animals were remembered better than printed words describing these animals. The question remains as to whether complex stimuli like exemplars pertain to mere pictures or mere texts. At least, additional assumptions would be necessary. Also, the exemplification effect is certainly not a mere memory effect.

---

[6]See Gerbner, Gross, Morgan, and Signorielli (1982), Gerbner, Gross, Signorielli, and Morgan (1980), and more recent results by Potter (1991a, 1991b), and Potter and Chang (1990).

Second, vividness could be a theoretical concept for the explanation of exemplification effects. According to Nisbett and Ross (1980), vivid stimuli are more easily recalled and influence subsequent judgments more than pallid stimuli. Consequently, more vivid exemplars have to be stronger in terms of effects compared to summary-type descriptions of reality. We do not think that the effectiveness of exemplars is completely based on their vivid nature. Brosius and Bathelt (1994, first experiment) showed that vivid exemplars did not have stronger effects on judgments compared to nonvivid ones. If exemplification were based on vividness alone, one would have expected a linear relationship between the degree of vividness in exemplars and their effectiveness. In addition, empirical data on the vividness effect is poor. Taylor and Thompson (1982) conducted a meta-analysis of studies with vivid and pallid stimuli. They concluded that only a few studies could find a vividness effect, whereas the majority failed to show such an effect. Also, vividness effects would need further explanation. Vividness is not a measurable aspect of a stimulus. The vivid character could lie in the type of language, the imagery value of the stimulus, the emotional components, and so on. Therefore, vividness effects often come as post-hoc explanations of identified differences.

Third, the salience concept (McArthur, 1981) can also be applied. This concept would claim that exemplars are more salient than summary-type descriptions, thus having a greater impact on judgments. Salient stimuli are those that "stick out" and draw more attention than other stimuli. In most experimental studies a stimulus is made salient by giving it unusual characteristics. For example, in a discussion group of eight people, one male of seven female discussants would be regarded as salient. His contributions would influence viewers' judgments more strongly than those of any other person. Applying these thoughts to exemplification studies, one concludes that one exemplar would have stronger effects than several. This would also mean that minority exemplars would have a stronger impact on judgment than the majority. This is clearly contradicted by the experimental results presented earlier.

Fourth, the observed effects can possibly be explained by the fact that studies so far used students, for the most part, or other young people in the exemplars (Brosius, 1999). This creates a high level of similarity between the sociodemographic features of the exemplars and the participants in the studies (students as well). Social learning theory (e.g., Bandura, 1994) has primarily been applied to the reception and imitation of aggressive behavior, although it has a more general range. This study purports that learning from a model might play a role in the presentation and reception of exemplars. The argument is that recipients might consider the exemplars model persons and adopt their attitudes and behavior to their own repertory. For the application of Bandura's theory to exemplars, primarily two conditions are important. First, the conspicuousness and the exceptionality of the model plays a part. People learn from a model mostly when the model draws attention to him- or herself. Exemplars could draw the recipients' attention by merely standing out of the usual flow of news stories. Second, the similarity between model person and recipient affects learning from the model. The (perceived) similarity between model and recipient is among the most effective variables in the imitation of model behavior. Numerous empirical studies show that the behavior of models who are similar to the recipient with respect to gender, age, and social status is more likely to be imitated than behavior of other models. The results of one of the experiments previously described (Brosius, 1999) clearly exclude social learning theory as a theoretical explanation for strong exemplar effects.

The reason why exemplars are the effective persuasive devices they are can probably be deduced from the way news stories are received. To know the meaning of the summary-type description of reality and to contrast it with the exemplars requires that the recipient follow the news attentively and carefully think through it. In the age of information overload, this probably is neither feasible nor reasonable. Recipients process a large share of media content in a state of limited attention. A rational recipient carefully comparing different pieces of information to one another, applying logical and rational criteria of judgment, would finally conclude that the summary-type description is the more reliable source of information. Recipients instead follow a representativeness heuristic (Tversky & Kahneman, 1973). They draw conclusions from the sample of exemplars presented by journalists on the population at large.

In mass communication, applying a representativeness heuristic is only reasonable if the recipients can rely on journalists to select a representative sample of exemplars. In contrast to mass media reception, everyday communication usually does not provide anything but exemplars for coming to a judgment. Our acquaintances' opinions, our friends' adventures, our neighbors' experiences are our major source for information. Summary-type descriptions of reality, if looked on in terms of human history, are a relatively new source. Assumedly people are therefore unaccustomed to them, whereas being guided by exemplars can be considered as normal. The direct and practicable reality of the exemplars creates in the recipient (because of his everyday experience) the illusion of having ascertained for himself that others think about a problem in a certain way. The impression of reality as "seen with one's own eyes" appears to be more reliable and more useful than summary-type descriptions of reality from journalists who possibly cannot even be trusted.

This reasoning corresponds to the assumption that recipients apply a kind of everyday rationality when they use the news media (Brosius, 1995). Especially when they are not much involved, recipients make use of heuristics when they process news content (see Chaiken, 1980; Chaiken & Stangor, 1987; Petty & Cacioppo, 1986). They do that in ways similar to everyday situations. For instance, they rely on the observation of individual cases in order to form an impression of a general tendency. This type of behavior appears to be irrational at first glance. From the perspective of the recipients, however, it might well be rational (thence the notion of everyday rationality): A complete processing of the information, if balanced against its importance and against the information gain to be obtained, might well be too expensive.

One possible reason for the strong and consistent exemplification effect might lie in human nature and the phylogenetic roots of our information system. In everyday communication situations (other than in mass communication) people can rely only on case information to form a judgment about a certain issue or person. Opinions of neighbors, experiences of friends, and reports of visitors make up our main information source. For thousands of years this type of information was the only kind available. Statistical data and summary descriptions based on a mass of experiences that are beyond our experiential horizon have been available for only a few years. Survey research and collection of statistical data are recent phenomena compared to the history of human nature. Human beings have been dependent on information provided by their fellow citizens. Few people will base their decision on which dentist to choose on a representative survey or statistical data. They will ask their acquaintances although their information might be inadequate. The friend highly recommending a certain dentist might be the only one satisfied with this doctor. This is not very likely though. The friend serves as an exemplar. We are accustomed to basing our judgments on such exemplars. If two people tell us that a certain district in town is dangerous and that they had nasty experiences there, we will believe them. Collecting such kinds of information might be misleading. But in terms of human history, it has long been the only way to form a judgment. Also, in everyday situations, lacking statistical data, basing one's judgments on exemplar information is, strictly speaking, rational behavior. In terms of probability, a sample of one exemplar makes a better judgment compared to a condition when no information is available. In everyday communication, this is the normal situation; no other information is available.

REFERENCES

Baesler, E. J., & Burgoon, J. K. (1994). The temporal effects of story and statistical evidence on belief change. *Communication Research, 21,* 582–602.

Bandura, A. (1994). Social cognitive theory of mass communication. In J. Bryant & D. Zillmann (Eds.), *Media effects: Advances in theory and research* (pp. 61–90). Hillsdale: Lawrence Erlbaum Associates.

Bar-Hillel, M. (1980). The base-rate fallacy in probability judgments. *Acta Psychologica, 44,* 211–233.

Brendel, D., & Grobe, B. E. (1976). *Journalistisches Grund-wissen: Darstellung der Formen und Mittel journalisti-scher Arbeit und Einführung in die Anwendung empiri-scher Daten in den Massenme-dien* [The basics of journalism: Formats and tools of journalistic work]. München: Saur.

Brosius, H.-B. (1995). *Alltagsrationalität in der Nachrichtenrezeption: Ein Modell der Wahrnehmung und Verarbeitung von Nach-richteninhalten* [Everday rationality in news reception: A model of information processing of news content].Opladen: Westdeutscher Verlag.

Brosius, H.-B. (1999). The influence of exemplars on recipients' judgments: The part played by similarity between exemplar and recipient. *European Journal of Communication, 14,* 213–224

Brosius, H.-B., & Bathelt, A. (1994). The utility of exemplars in persuasive communications. *Communication Research, 21,* 48–78.

Brosius, H.-B., Schweiger, W., & Rossmann, C. (2000). Auf der Suche nach den Ursachen des Fallbeispieleffekts: Der Einfluß von Anzahl und Art der Urheber von Fallbeispielinformation [In search of the causes of exemplification effects: Impact of number of exemplars and type of source]. *Medienpsychologie, 12,* 153–175.

Chaiken, S. (1980). Heuristic versus systematic information processing and the use of source versus message cues in persuasion. *Journal of Personality and Social Psychology, 39,* 752–766.

Chaiken, S., & Stangor, C. (1987). Attitudes and attitude change. *Annual Review of Psychology, 38,* 575–630.

Daschmann, G. (2001). *Der Einfluß von Fallbeispielen auf Leserurteile: Experimentelle Untersuchungen zur Medienwirkung* [The impact of exemplars on readers' judgments: Experimental studies on media effects]. Konstanz: UVK Medien.

Daschmann, G., & Brosius, H.-B. (1999). Can a single event create an issue? *Journalism and Mass Communication Quarterly, 76,* 35–51.

Gan, S., Hill, J. R., Pschernig, E., & Zillmann, D. (1996). The Hebron massacre, selective reports of Jewish reactions, and perceptions of volatility in Israel. *Journal of Broadcasting & Electronic Media, 40,* 122–131.

Gerbner, G. L., Gross, L., Morgan, M., & Signorielli, N. (1982). Charting the mainstream: Television's contributions to political orientations. *Journal of Communication, 32*(2), 100–127.

Gerbner, G. L., Gross, L., Signorielli, N., & Morgan, M. (1980). Aging with television: Images on television drama and conceptions of social reality. *Journal of Communication, 30*(1), 37–49.

Gibson, R., & Zillmann, D. (1994). Exaggerated versus representative exemplification in news reports: Perception of issues and personal consequences. *Communication Research, 21,* 603–624.

Gibson, R., & Zillmann, D. (1998). Effects of citation in exemplifying testimony on issue perception. *Journalism and Mass Communication Quarterly, 75,* 167–176.

Haller, M. (1987). *Die Reportage. Ein Handbuch für Journalisten* [Reporting: A handbook for journalists]. München: Ölschläger.

Hamill, R., Wilson, T. D., & Nisbett, R. E. (1980). Insensitivity to sample bias: Generalizing from atypical cases. *Journal of Personality and Social Psychology, 39,* 578–589.

Iyengar, S. (1991). *Is anyone responsible? How television frames political issues.* Chicago: University of Chicago Press.

McArthur, L. Z. (1981). What grabs you? The role of attention in impression formation and causal attribution. In E. T. Higgins, C. P. Herman, & M. P. Zanna (Eds.), *Social cognition. The Ontario symposium, Vol. 1* (pp. 201–246). Hillsdale, NJ: Lawrence Erlbaum Associates.

McCombs, M. E., Cole, R. R., Stevenson, R. L., & Shaw, D. L. (1981). Precision journalism: An emerging theory and technique of news reporting. *Gazette, 27, 21–34.*

Meyer, P. (1973). *Precision journalism: A reporter's introduction to social science methods.* Bloomington: Indiana University Press.

Nisbett, R. E., & Ross, L. (1980). *Human inference: Strategies and shortcomings of social judgment.* Englewood Cliffs: Prentice Hall.

Noelle-Neumann, E. (1984). *The spiral of silence: Public opinion, our social skin.* Chicago: University of Chicago Press.

Noelle-Neumann, E. (1991). *Öffentliche Meinung: Die Entdeckung der Schweigespirale* [Public opinion: The discovery of the spiral of silence]. Berlin: Ullstein.

Paivio, A. (1971). *Imagery and verbal processes.* New York: Holt, Rinehart & Winston.

Paivio, A. (1986). *Mental representations: A dual coding approach.* New York: Oxford University Press.

Perry, S. D., & Gonzenbach, W. J. (1997). Effects of news exemplification extended: Considerations of controversiality and perceived future opinion. *Journal of Broadcasting & Electronic Media, 41,* 229–244.

Petty, R. E., & Cacioppo, J. T. (1986). *Communication and persuasion.* New York: Springer.

Potter, W. J. (1991a). The linearity assumption in cultivation research. *Human Communication Research, 17,* 562–583.

Potter, W. J. (1991b). The relationships between first- and second-order measures of cultivation. *Human Communication Research, 18,* 92–113.

Potter, W. J., & Chang, I. C. (1990). Television exposure measures and the cultivation hypothesis. *Journal of Broadcasting & Electronic Media, 34,* 313–333.

Shoemaker, P. J., Chang, T., & Brendlinger, N. (1987). Deviance as a predictor of newsworthiness: Coverage of international events in the U.S. media. In M. L. McLaughlin (Ed.), *Communication yearbook* (pp. 348–365). Beverly Hills: Sage.

Taylor, S. E., & Thompson, S. C. (1982). Stalking the elusive "vividness" effect. *Psychological Review, 89,* 155–181.

Tversky, A., & Kahneman, D. (1973). Availability: A heuristic for judging frequency and probability. *Cognitive Psychology, 5,* 207–232.

Wilson, M. G., Northcraft, G. B., & Neale, M. A. (1989). Information competition and vividness effects in on-line judgments. *Organizational Behavior and Human Decision Processes, 4,* 132–139.

Zillmann, D., & Brosius, H.-B. (2000). *Exemplification in communication. The influence of case reports on issue perception*. Mahwah, NJ: Lawrence Erlbaum Associates.

Zillmann, D., Gibson, R. Sundar, S. S., & Perkins, J. W. (1996). Effects of exemplification in news reports on the perception of social issues. *Journalism and Mass Communication Quarterly, 73,* 427–444.

Zillmann, D., Perkins, J. W., & Sundar, S. S. (1992). Impression-formation effects of printed news varying in descriptive precision and exemplifications. *Medienpsychologie, 4,* 168–185.

SECTION III: Empirical Advances in Media Effects

9

Media Violence Effects and Interventions: The Roles of Communication and Emotion

Joanne Cantor
University of Wisconsin–Madison

Media violence is unquestionably the most thoroughly studied and hotly debated media effects topic. Public controversy over the issue waxed and waned in salience over the second half of the 20th century, reemerging in full force during the 1990s. Renewed interest in the problem was due in part to the apparent escalation of violence in both media entertainment and news outlets, and in part to the furor over the increasing number of prominently publicized school shootings in the United States.

This chapter discusses the effects of media violence and the emotional and communicative processes involved in producing them. It also explores means of intervening in these effects through the use of both media-based strategies and interpersonal influences.

CONTENT ANALYSES OF MEDIA VIOLENCE

Starting in 1967, Gerbner and his associates (Gerbner, Gross, Morgan, Signorielli & Shanahan, 2002) produced the annual Cultural Indicators Project, which content analyzed one week of programming on the three major U.S. television networks, ABC, CBS, and NBC, during prime time and on Saturday mornings. Gerbner's definition of *violence* included the threat or occurrence of physical force or harm by intentional means, as well as harm caused by accidents and natural disasters. Gerbner's analyses confirmed that violence was a major component of network television. According to some of his most prominent findings, approximately 80% of programs contained violence. Moreover, Saturday morning children's programs were much more violent than prime-time programming. Furthermore, although male characters were much more likely than female characters to be involved in violence, when involved in violence, females were more likely to be victims than perpetrators. As his inclusion of accidents and natural disasters suggests, Gerbner's research was not motivated by a concern that media violence makes viewers more aggressive. Rather, its focus was on whether television makes viewers believe that violence is pervasive and that the world is more dangerous than it really is.

The 1990s produced a different sort of content analysis, inspired by concerns about the link between media violence and youth violence. The National Television Violence Study (NTVS, 1996, 1997, 1998) analyzed the violence in a large random sample of television programming for three television seasons (1994–1995, 1995–1996, and 1996–1997). Each year, the researchers randomly sampled programs over a 9-month period, producing a composite week of programing (17 hours per day) from each of 23 network and cable channels. The NTVS defined *violence* more narrowly than Gerbner had. It focused on intentional interpersonal harm and eliminated natural disasters and accidents from the definition. The analysis reported a variety of contextual features that research has identified as influencing the impact of a violent presentation on viewers.

According to the NTVS reports, approximately 60% of programs overall contained violence. This percentage cannot be meaningfully compared to Gerbner's, however, because of the NTVS's more narrow definition and broader sampling of programs. More important than the sheer amount of television violence are the findings on the contextual features commonly associated with depicted violence. For example, the content analysis reported that violence on television frequently minimizes the risks of violence, that is, approximately one third of the violent interactions show unrealistically low levels of harm. Morever, television violence is rarely punished: In approximately three fourths of violent scenes, there is no criticism, penalty, or remorse for committing violence, and in more than one third of programs, the violent villains are never punished. The NTVS also concluded that violence on television is often trivialized. For example, approximately 40% of violent scenes occur in a humorous context. As we see later, these prevalent context features make it more likely that child and adolescent viewers will imitate the violence they see or adopt attitudes accepting of violence.

The content of video games has come under increasing scrutiny, especially because many perpetrators of school shootings have reportedly been devotees of violent video games. Although no content analyses of violence in video games have yet appeared, many observers report that the violence in video games continues to escalate (e.g., Anderson & Bushman, 2001), and there is evidence that violent games are the most popular (Lynch, Gentile, Olson, & van Brederode, 2001).

A recent report from UNESCO (Carlsson & von Feilitzen, 1998) revealed that media violence is of worldwide concern and that violent programs and movies from the United States are popular around the world. Moreover, the UNESCO volume includes an interesting chapter on research from Japan (Kodaira, 1998) that asserts that the context features of violence in Japanese television differ from those that are prominent in the United States. Specifically, Japanese television has a much stronger focus on the suffering of the victims of violence and on the arousal of sympathy for them than is typical of western entertainment violence.

META-ANALYSES OF MEDIA VIOLENCE AND AGGRESSION

The hundreds of studies of the relationship between media violence and aggression that have been conducted over the years have been subjected to meta-analysis to determine the degree to which a consensus exists. The most widely quoted of these meta-analyses was conducted by Paik and Comstock (1994). This meta-analysis combined the results of 217 studies appearing between 1957 and 1990, and it included both published and unpublished empirical studies that reported on the relationship between viewing television and a variety of types of antisocial behavior. Using the correlation coefficient (r) as a measure of association, Paik and Comstock reported an overall r of .31. The correlation was .37 for experimental designs and .19 for surveys. Moreover, the strength of the association exhibited a wide range, depending on a variety of factors, including the nature of the dependent measure (from .10 for criminal violence to .52 for playing with aggressive toys), the age of the viewer (from .18 for adults to .46 for preschoolers), and the genre of program (from .19 for Westerns to .52 for cartoons). The authors' conclusions involved the following statement: "The findings strengthen the evidence that television violence increases aggressive and antisocial behavior, this to a varying degree, depending on the choice of variables considered" (p. 538).

A more recent meta-analysis, by Bushman and Anderson (2001), confirms and updates Paik and Comstock's conclusions. Bushman and Anderson's analysis includes studies published between 1956 and 2000. Their criteria for the inclusion of studies were more limited than those of Paik and Comstock. Because they were interested in how published research was related to news reports of media violence effects, they eliminated unpublished studies from their analysis (although they reported that the results were virtually identical when unpublished results were included). Also, they included only studies of aggressive behavior, which means they eliminated measures of self-report of aggressive intent and nonviolent antisocial effects, such as burglary and grand theft. Their meta-analysis, which included 202 independent samples, was cumulative, that is, they showed how the observed effect size changed between 1975 and 2000 as additional studies were published. Overall, the cumulative effect size was found to increase over the years. By 2000, the overall effect size was .20, with .23 for laboratory experiments and .18 for correlational studies. At every stage in their analysis, the lower limit of the confidence interval of the effect size for both correlational and experimental studies was significantly greater than zero. Bushman and Anderson offered the following conclusion: "The cumulative evidence is [now] even more overwhelming in showing that short- and long-term exposure to media violence causes significant increases in aggression" (p. 486).

Anderson and Bushman (2001) have recently conducted a meta-analysis of the relationship between the playing of violent video games and aggressive behavior. They reported a significant positive association and an effect size similar to that for TV and films ($r = .19$, based on 33 independent tests).

In response to critics who argue that the meta-analysis effects are small, Bushman and his associates have compared the media violence results to those of other meta-analyses of well-documented relationships. Bushman and Huesmann (2001) compared Paik and Comstock's results to effects in nine other domains and reported that the media violence effect was second only to the association between smoking and lung cancer. Even using the smaller effect sizes associated with Bushman's two recent meta-analyses (Anderson & Bushman, 2001; Bushman & Anderson, 2001), the media violence effect sizes are still the second largest, larger than, for example, the relationship between condom use and the prevention of sexually transmitted HIV, and stronger than the relationship between exposure to lead and low IQ in children.

For individuals desiring to understand the nature of media violence effects and to intervene in unhealthy and antisocial outcomes, the effect-size issue is less important than an understanding of the psychological mechanisms that are responsible for the effects. Many criticisms of media violence research (e.g., Freedman, 1984) stem from the fact that controlled, experimental studies cannot use dependent variables that impress the skeptics. It is ethically indefensible to create laboratory conditions that promote (and then measure) the perpetration of criminal violence. Valuable experimental studies explore the mechanisms underlying media violence effects and use dependent variables that suggest a predisposition to become violent should the occasion arise, and that constitute unhealthy outcomes in and of themselves. These outcomes include desensitization to violence, increased acceptance of violence, and the willingness to inflict nonviolent negative consequences on another person. In this context, it is instructive to note Zillmann's (1979) distinction between aggressive and hostile behavior. Zillmann calls "aggressive" behavior those activities "by which a person seeks to inflict bodily damage or physical pain" and "hostile" behavior activities "by which a person seeks to inflict harm other than bodily damage and physical pain" (p. 33).

MECHANISMS UNDERLYING MEDIA VIOLENCE EFFECTS ON AGGRESSION AND HOSTILITY

Social Learning and Imitation

The most straightforward mechanism of media violence effects is social learning or social cognitive theory (see Bandura, 1986). Social cognitive theory explicates the ways in which individuals learn not only from direct experience, but from exposure to behavior modeled by others. In addition to occurring in interpersonal contexts, this modeling frequently happens through exposure to the media. Bandura's earliest studies, involving the imitation of filmed models punching Bobo dolls (e.g., Bandura, 1965), are often cited by critics of the media violence literature as evidence that the effects are trivial and not generalizable to real, interpersonal violence. However, there are many studies that demonstrate that the imitation or social learning of media violence produces a wide array of effects, many of which have potentially harmful or actually destructive consequences.

Impressive evidence of the social learning of televised violence comes from a survey of elementary school principals conducted in Israel shortly after television's World Wrestling Federation (WWF) became available there in 1994 (Lemish, 1997). More than half of the principals responding to the survey reported that WWF-type fighting had created problems in their schools. The imitative behavior was easily distinguished from the martial-arts type behaviors that had occurred prior to the arrival of WWF programs. The new behaviors attributed to the program included banging heads, throwing opponents to the floor and jumping onto them from furniture, poking their eyes with fingers, pulling their hair, and grabbing their genital areas. Almost half of the principals reported that such behavior had necessitated first aid within the school, and almost one fourth reported injuries (including broken bones, loss of consciousness, and concussions) that required emergency room visits or professional medical care.

Social cognitive theory also includes the notion of vicarious reinforcement, by which the depicted consequences of witnessed behavior affect the probability that imitation will occur. Research shows that both punishment and depicted pain and suffering lower the tendency to imitate aggression (e.g., Bandura, 1965; Baron, 1971). Recall that content analyses of U.S. television report that violence is frequently shown in a humorous context, that punishment is rare, and that the harmful consequences of violence are often understated. In contrast, the UNESCO volume reports that intense negative consequences of violence are far more common on Japanese television. This suggests that viewers of American television are more likely to imitate TV violence than are their Japanese counterparts.

A longitudinal, developmental model of the acquisition of violent behavior over time via exposure to the mass media has been proposed by Huesmann (1988). This model posits that as a result of repeated exposure to media violence, children acquire cognitive scripts for violent behavior that are later enacted in situations similar to those depicted in the media.

The Aggression-Catharsis Myth

Catharsis theory dates back to the Greek philosopher Aristotle, who argued that by witnessing tragic events in drama, viewers could purge themselves of negative feelings. Freud brought this notion into contemporary use by arguing that angry feelings could be harmlessly "vented" by witnessing other people engage in violence. The notion of catharsis is often cited by producers of violent media to deflect criticism and to claim that violent television shows, movies, and sports actually have a therapeutic effect and reduce societal violence. As appealing and popular as the theory may be, it has not received empirical support. The meta-analyses consistently show that people generally behave more, rather than less aggressively after viewing violence. The rare cases in which individuals behave less aggressively have usually been attributable to other factors, such as when the depiction of severe negative consequences of violence leads to the inhibition of aggression, rather than to the purging of hostile feelings (e.g., Baron, 1971).

Excitation Transfer

Early theories of media violence effects focused mainly on the violent content of such programs. In addition to Bandura's social learning theory, Berkowitz's (e.g., 1965) eliciting-cue explanation posited that media violence provides aggressive cues that "trigger" aggressive responses in individuals who are aggressively aroused. Berkowitz published a series of studies in which participants who were angered and then viewed filmed violence were more aggressive in retaliation than those who were similarly angered but viewed nonviolent films.

Zillmann's approach to these effects was to focus on the physiological arousal produced by exposure to violent media rather than on the presentation of the violent content itself. He developed a theory of excitation transfer (1971b), which is based on a series of assumptions about emotional responding in general. First, the theory notes that most emotions, especially those that Zillmann (1989) termed the *emergency* emotions of anger, fear, and sexual arousal, involve a substantial increase in sympathetic activation. Second, it asserts that the physiological arousal that occurs as the result of an emotion decays relatively slowly and often lingers on for some time after the reason for experiencing the emotion is no longer present and the individual has adjusted cognitively to a different situation. Third, drawing on Schachter's (1964) two-factor theory of emotional state, the intensity with which an emotion is experienced is in part determined by the level of arousal existing at the time. Fourth, even if there may be some difference in the physiological patterns of different emotions, there is great similarity between them in terms of peripheral indices of arousal (e.g., elevated heart rate and blood pressure). Fifth, individuals have relatively poor interoception of their physiological arousal. Therefore, if an individual experiences a second emotion before residues of the previous emotion have subsided, he or she is likely to confuse the residual arousal with the experience of the subsequent emotion. This misattribution (or failure of correct attribution) of the excitatory residues should lead the individual to feel the subsequent emotion more intensely than in the absence of the residues.

Applying the theory to the media violence situation, Zillmann argued that because viewing media violence is physiologically arousing and the media-produced arousal often lingers, people who are angered are likely to feel their anger more intensely after viewing violence, and they therefore may react more violently if provided the opportunity to retaliate against their provoker.

Zillmann has produced a great deal of evidence supporting the role of excitation transfer in media violence effects. In an initial study (Zillmann,

1971a), male college students who were angered and saw a moderately arousing violent film clip delivered more intense shocks to their provoker than did those who were angered and saw a nonviolent, nonarousing film clip. However, angered students who saw a nonviolent, sexual film clip that was more arousing than the violent clip retaliated even more strongly than those who had seen the violence. The level of retaliation was simply a function of the arousal produced by the film clip and independent of the presence of violent content. A subsequent study (Zillmann, Hoyt, & Day, 1974) showed that the intensification of aggressive behavior through film-induced arousal occurs only as long as the duration of the film-induced residual excitation. In this study, male college students were angered and then exposed to one of four movie clips: a prize fight, a brutal massacre, an erotic scene, or a neutral, historical film. All four film clips were followed by a minute of an uninvolving, nonaggressive documentary that was provided to promote the decay of excitation. Physiological measures taken after the uninvolving clip revealed that sympathetic activation from the prize fight and the massacre had returned to the same level as that produced by the neutral, historical clip. Arousal from the erotic film was still elevated. As expected from excitation-transfer theory, retaliatory aggression was enhanced only in the erotic-film condition; it was not significantly different in the two violent film conditions from that in the neutral film condition.

Zillmann, Katcher, and Milavsky (1972) demonstrated that excitation transfer operates through the intensification of emotions rather than simply by intensifying any behavior. Moreover, it showed that physiological arousal even from exercise can intensify aggressive behavior in angry individuals. In their experiment, male college students were either provoked or not and then engaged in strenuous exercise or a nonarousing manual task before being given the opportunity to retaliate against their provoker. As expected, among participants who were provoked, those who had engaged in strenuous exercise (and were therefore experiencing residual arousal) retaliated more strongly than those who had not; among those who were not provoked and were therefore not experiencing anger, there was no difference between the two exercise groups in their subsequent aggressive behavior.

Zillmann and his associates (Cantor, Zillmann, & Einsiedel, 1978) further demonstrated that excitation transfer can predict the retaliatory behavior of females as well as males. In this study, female college students saw a neutral, an aggressive, or an erotic film before either being provoked or not and being given a chance to retaliate. For these women, the erotic film, but not the aggressive film raised sympathetic activation significantly, and consistent with excitation transfer, provoked women in the erotic film condition retaliated more intensely than those who had seen either the neutral or the aggressive film. In addition, in the absence of provocation, the films had no effect on the women's aggressive behavior.

Paik and Comstock's (1994) meta-analysis provides further support for excitation-transfer theory. Their analyses by program characteristics show that the effect size for erotic materials is as large or larger than the effect size for violent presentations. Moreover, the effect size for violent erotica is the largest. Furthermore, the meta-analysis revealed that programs leaving the viewer in "a state of unresolved excitement" produced a stronger effect size than those that did not.

Accessibility of Aggressive and Hostile Cognitions

Taken alone, excitation-transfer theory suggests that sex films, exciting sports events, and even working out at the gym are as likely as media violence to promote aggressive behavior. But excitation-transfer theory cannot account for all effects of media violence. Many studies show that imitation effects can occur in the absence of elevated arousal, and many others show that aggression often increases in the absence of specific provocation. More recent research has explored other mechanisms, beyond social learning and excitation transfer, that can account for effects under such conditions.

Berkowitz has modified his eliciting-cue theory to reflect a more cognitive view of media-violence processes, referred to as a "cognitive-neoassociationistic" model of media influences (e.g., Jo & Berkowitz, 1994). The theory suggests that witnessing violence (either in real life or via the media) activates (or makes immediately accessible) thoughts and concepts related to violence that activate or prime related emotions and action tendencies through associated neural networks in the brain. (See Roskos-Ewoldsen, 2002, for a more recent conceptualization of priming processes.) Viewing violence, then, briefly increases the likelihood that the viewer will have hostile thoughts and be predisposed to choose a violent course of action. Consistent with this reasoning, Anderson and Bushman's (2001) recent meta-analysis of the impact of video games shows that video game violence promotes both aggressive cognition ($r = .27$; 20 independent tests) and aggressive affect ($r = .18$; 17 independent tests) in addition to aggressive behavior. For both cognition and affect, the relationship held true for both males and females, for children and adults, and in experimental and nonexperimental designs.

In an attempt to account for longer term effects of repeated exposure to media violence, Zillmann (Zillmann & Weaver, 1999) has suggested that the frequent, consistent, and repeated activation of particular concepts results in their becoming chronically accessible. According to Zillmann, then, an individual's repeated exposure to media violence may make aggressive and hostile constructs and scripts chronically available and easily primed in a variety of situations. This chronic accessibility of hostile cognitions renders such an individual more likely to engage in hostile, coercive, or aggressive actions than individuals without a history of heavy exposure to media violence.

Zillmann and Weaver (1999) tested this chronic accessibility notion in a delayed-testing situation so that neither a short-term priming effect nor an excitation-transfer effect would be pertinent to any outcome. First, they randomly assigned both male and female college students to view either intensely violent or nonviolent feature films for 4 days in a row. On the 5th day, in a purportedly unrelated study, the participants were put in a position to help or hinder another person's chances of future employment. The results indicated that both men and women who had received the heavy doses of film violence that had ended a day earlier were more harmful to that person's prospects. The surprising finding was that the participants behaved in a more hostile fashion toward her whether she had treated them well or had behaved in an insulting fashion. The repeated violence viewing apparently provided an "enduring hostile mental framework" that affected interactions that were affectively neutral as well as those that involved provocation. These findings indicate that the effects of media violence are not just short lived, and they suggest that children and adolescents who habitually immerse themselves in media violence may have greater difficulty getting along with others in a variety of situations far removed from their media experiences.

Desensitization

Desensitization is another well-documented emotional effect of viewing violence. Desensitization is a process by which an emotional response is repeatedly elicited in situations in which the action tendency that arises out of the emotion proves irrelevant. Desensitization is sometimes used to treat phobias, by gradually and repeatedly presenting the frightening stimulus under nonthreatening conditions. Over time, when desensitization works, the phobic response becomes less and less intense. Analogously, exposure to media violence, particularly that which entails intense hostilities or the graphic display of injuries, initially induces an intense emotional reaction in viewers. With repeated exposure, however, many viewers exhibit decreasingly intense emotional responses to the depiction of violence and injury. Desensitization to violence has been documented in a variety of outcomes. For example, it has been observed as reduced arousal and emotional disturbance while witnessing violence (e.g., Cline, Croft, & Courrier, 1973); as lower readiness to call an adult to intervene in a witnessed physical altercation (e.g., Molitor & Hirsch, 1994); and as less sympathy for the victims of domestic abuse (e.g., Mullin & Linz, 1995).

The Attractions of Violence and the Bidirectional Relationship

It is sometimes argued that the media violence—aggressive behavior connection may be explained by the fact that people who are already violent prefer to watch violence. There is a small but growing body of research on why people are attracted to media violence, and on individual differences in violence-viewing preferences (see Goldstein, 1998). This research confirms that media violence is more popular among aggressive than nonaggressive viewers. However, the many experiments that have randomly assigned participants to view or not to view violence show that the media violence–aggression relationship cannot be explained by selective exposure alone. Moreover, a field investigation by Black and Bevan (1992) demonstrated the bidirectional nature of the relationship between viewing violence and viewers' aggressiveness in a single study. These investigators went to a theater and asked moviegoers to fill out a hostility inventory either before or after they watch e d a movie that they themselves had selected. The findings showed that both the male and female viewers who had chosen a violent film were initially more hostile than the viewers who had selected a nonviolent movie. Moreover, levels of hostility were even higher after the violent movie, but remained low after the nonviolent movie.

INTERVENING IN VIOLENCE

An understanding of the role of emotions in the effects of media violence on aggression is also helpful in developing means of intervening in violence. Zillmann (1979) made an important distinction between incentive-motivated and annoyance-motivated aggression. According to this distinction, the primary function of incentive-motivated aggression is to acquire extrinsic incentives. This type of aggression is usually not associated with strong emotions and is sometimes referred to as aggression that is performed "in cold blood." Research on the social learning of aggression seems most relevant to this type of aggression, and changing the perceived and actual reinforcement contingencies for behaving aggressively could be expected to reduce it. In contrast, the primary function of annoyance-motivated aggression is to reduce or terminate a noxious state. This is aggression that often occurs during acute states of hostility and anger, and it relates to much of the research dealing with the impact of media violence on the retaliatory responses of angry individuals.

Zillmann's (1979) three-factor theory of emotion is helpful in understanding the difficulties of intervening in annoyance-motivated aggression. The three-factor theory contends that emotional experience and emotional behavior are the result of dispositional, excitatory, and experiential components. The dispositional component, or motor responses, and the excitatory component, or arousal responses, are conceived of as more or less immediate responses to an emotion-inducing stimulus. The experiential component, in contrast, often occurs with greater latency and involves the conscious experience of the dispositional and excitatory components of the response. The experiential component produces a so-called feeling state, which may result in the appraisal of the emotional reaction and in some cases serves as a modifier of both the behavioral and affective components of the response. In other words, the third factor serves a response-guiding function that may alter the hedonic valence and intensity of the initial response. For example, an individual may initially respond with anger and make moves toward accosting his "provoker" after having his car rear-ended at a stop sign. However, upon hearing that the accident occurred because the driver of the offending car had a heart attack at the wheel, the individual should soon discover that his anger at the driver is inappropriate, and both his emotional state and his subsequent behavior would likely be altered considerably.

Interpersonal Interventions

Interpersonal communication is one source of information that may foster emotional reappraisal and serve as a means of intervening in a hostile or potentially aggressive encounter. An offending person may provide an explanation that may prompt the angry person to reevaluate the situation and reduce his or her hostility, to inhibit his or her hostile actions, or even to experience an entirely different emotion. The communication of mitigating circumstances is a frequently used form of information intended to reduce the consequences of an offending action, and it has been shown to reduce feelings of hostility and the tendency to retaliate under some conditions (e.g., Burnstein & Worchel, 1962).

The three-factor theory also posits, however, that the dispositional, excitational, and experiential components of an emotion may interact in determining the individual's response. One important way in which these factors interact is that under high levels of physiological arousal, the response-guiding function of the experiential component is severely diminished. More specifically in the aggression context, under extreme levels of anger the individual experiences a reduced ability to modify his emotions and behavior through cognitive reappraisal.

A series of studies by Zillmann and his associates demonstrates the power of mitigating circumstances to reduce anger and retaliation under conditions of low to moderate excitation. Moreover, they show that this method of intervening in hostility and aggression is likely to fail when the provoked individual is experiencing high levels of arousal. In one study (Zillmann, Bryant, Cantor, & Day, 1975), undergraduate males were insulted by an experimenter regarding their performance on a test. They then either performed strenuous physical exercise or engaged in a non-arousing manual task. After the arousal manipulation, a third person either told them or did not tell them about mitigating circumstances underlying their provoker's behavior. Finally, the participants were provided an opportunity to retaliate by filling out an evaluation of the experimenter that would purportedly be used to determine whether his research appointment should be renewed for the upcoming year. The results revealed that for those participants who had performed the manual task and were therefore experiencing only moderate arousal, the mitigating information substantially attenuated their negative evaluations of the experimenter. However, for participants who had engaged in strenuous exercise, the mitigating information had no appreciable effect. The evaluations of the experimenter given by these students were similarly harsh, whether or not they had heard about the mitigating circumstances.

In a second experiment (Zillmann & Cantor, 1976), male undergraduates were given information about mitigating circumstances either before or after being provoked by a rude experimenter, or they were similarly provoked without receiving any mitigating information. Their physiological responses were monitored over the course of the experiment, and at the end of the session, they were given the opportunity to retaliate by a similar evaluation of the rude experimenter. The results revealed that the prior mitigation had powerful effects. Not only did it significantly reduce participants' complaints about the rude experimenter's behavior; it significantly intervened in their emotional response to the provocation. Knowing about the mitigation in advance prevented them from becoming intensely angry in the first place. In contrast, the mitigating information received after provocation was much less effective. Although it did promote the decay of excitation, compared to that of participants who never heard the mitigating information, it did not significantly reduce their complaints about the experimenter. Apparently, these participants had already experienced such intense anger that the mitigation was seen as insufficient to deter the retaliatory action they had become motivated to perform. The conclusion from these two studies is that the interpersonal communication of mitigating information can be a powerful strategy to reduce hostility and aggression. However, an understanding of the interactive components of emotional responding is crucial to designing interventions that use it effectively.

Using Media to Intervene in Aggression

Although there are hundreds of studies that test the media's aggression-promoting capacities, there are relatively few that demonstrate the media's ability to be part of the remedy. It has been documented, however, that the media have a great capacity to distract people from their problems and to help them unwind after confronting their daily problems (see Zillmann, 1991). Zillmann and Johnson (1974) tested the notion that exposure to films can intervene in an angry person's aggressive responses. Undergraduate males interacted with a confederate, who either severly provoked them by administering many shocks, or provoked them only trivially, by delivering only two. All participants were subsequently put in a position to deliver shocks to the confederate. One group did so immediately. The others saw short film clips that were either highly violent (a brutal massacre) or neutral (a historical film) before delivering the shocks. Consistent with earlier research on excitation transfer, when participants were minimally provoked, neither of the films had any effect on the level of shocks they delivered. Under conditions of strong provocation, however, the neutral film produced a significant diminution in arousal and reduced shock delivery to the level that occurred in the low-provocation condition. The violent film reduced arousal somewhat, but not to a significant degree. Moreover, provoked participants who viewed the violent film delivered shock levels as high as did those who retaliated immediately after provocation. The researchers argued that the neutral film diverted attention away from thoughts of the provoking encounter and facilitated recovery from anger. In contrast, the violent film was considered too closely related to the participants' emotional state to effectively intervene in their anger.

Bryant and Zillmann (1977) further studied the ability of media to intervene in hostility and aggression by pretesting a series of film clips to determine their intervention potential. Intervention potential, or the degree to which the clips were mentally absorbing, was tested by presenting them to viewers while they were simultaneously attempting a tactile pattern-recognition task. The more mistakes made while viewing, the higher the intervention potential of a program. In the main experiment, male undergraduates were provoked and then watched one of six video clips with measured intervention potential—a monotonous stimulus, a nature film, a comedy show, a nonaggressive sport, a quiz show, or a highly aggressive contact sport. The results indicated that with the exception of the violent sport, the higher the pretested intervention potential of the program, the more it facilitated the reduction of arousal, and the lower the level of retaliation against the provoker. The violent film, in contrast, in spite of showing the greatest intervention potential during the pretest on unprovoked viewers, resulted in a minimal reduction in arousal and produced a level of retaliation equal to that in the condition of the nonabsorbing, monotonous stimulus.

In summary, then, absorbing programs and films can be useful in calming an angry person's hostility and reducing his or her tendency to aggress. However, programs involving hostility and aggression, even if they are absorbing, are unlikely to perform this function because they tend to reiterate and perpetuate the individual's hostile feelings and retaliatory predispositions.

Reducing Exposure to Media Violence

Given the well-documented relationship between viewing violence and aggressive behavior, a logical approach to the reduction of aggression is to reduce exposure to violent media. A number of studies have reported promising results in this regard. Waite, Hillbrand, and Foster (1992) conducted research in a maximum security forensic hospital based on the observation of patients' increased belligerence and hostility toward staff after watching music television (MTV), a popular channel in all wards. These investigators performed an interrupted time-series analysis on measures of aggression for 33 weeks before eliminating MTV as an option, and for the 22 weeks immediately thereafter. They reported significant reductions in the number of weekly incidents of verbal aggression, of aggression against objects, and of aggression against others as a function of their intervention.

A quite different intervention was reported by Robinson and his associates (Robinson, Wilde, Navracruz, Haydel, & Varady, 2001), involving third- and fourth-grade students at two elementary schools in the same school district. One school was randomly assigned to participate in the experimental intervention, and the other served as the control group. The intervention involved 18 lessons over a 6-month period aimed at convincing the children to reduce their time spent with television, videos, and video games. Children were first asked to keep track of the time they spent with media. Second, they were encouraged to go without these media for 10 days. Finally, they were asked to limit their media use to 7 hours per week or less, and to become more selective in their media choices. At the end of the intervention, children in the experimental group had reduced their television viewing by about one third, and their level of aggression (as measured by peer nomination) was approximately 25% lower than that in the control school.

Promoting Empathy With the Victim

Although reducing exposure to media in general or to media violence specifically is undoubtedly a healthy option, the fact that media violence is so prevalent and so popular (especially among more aggressive children) suggests that many attempts to restrict exposure may fail or may actually increase interest in viewing the prohibited material (see Cantor, 1998b). Another option for reducing media-violence effects is to urge children to view the violence in a different light, in order to modify the effect it would otherwise have. As suggested earlier, one problem with the way violence is usually portrayed on television is that it minimizes the apparent harmful consequences to the victim and thereby encourages the adoption of violent attitudes and behaviors. To determine whether the aggression-promoting impact of viewing violence could be reduced, Nathanson and Cantor (2000) tested an intervention that encouraged children to focus on the feelings of the victim. Their study employed a "classic" cartoon, a genre of media violence that especially trivializes the consequences to the victim.

In Nathanson and Cantor's (2000) experiment, second- through sixth-grade boys were randomly assigned to one of three conditions: a no-mediation group, who watched a Woody Woodpecker cartoon without instructions; a mediation group, who were asked before viewing, to keep in mind the feelings of the man in the cartoon (this was the tree surgeon who was the target of Woody's repeated physical attacks); and a control group, who did not see a cartoon. Consistent with social learning theory, the children who had just seen the violent cartoon without instructions scored higher on proviolence attitudes than the children in the control condition (showing stronger agreement with statements such as, "sometimes fighting is a good way to get what you want"). However, the children who were asked to think about the victim's feelings showed no such increase in proviolence attitudes. As a side effect, this empathy-promoting intervention reduced the degree to which the children found the cartoon funny. An empathy-promoting intervention may therefore not only intervene in the direct effect of viewing violence, it may also interfere with the enjoyment of violence and perhaps ultimately reduce selective exposure to such fare in the future.

MEDIA VIOLENCE AND FEAR

Although the most prominent concerns about media violence have focused on its tendency to promote aggressive and hostile behavior, there is a growing body of research suggesting that media violence promotes feelings of insecurity, fear, and even terror in some viewers. Recent research shows that amount of television viewing is significantly associated with children's levels of anxiety (Singer, Slovak, Frierson, & York, 1998) and with the frequency that they experience sleep disturbances (Owens et al., 1999). Retrospective reports reveal that media-induced fear is a common experience and that it often has long-lasting effects (Harrison & Cantor, 1999; Hoekstra, Harris, & Helmick, 1999). Content analyses of such reports affirm that violence is one of the most prominent themes in fear-evoking programs and movies. Indeed, most media-induced fright responses involve a perceived or imagined threat of violence or harm (Cantor & Wilson, 1988).

Developmental Differences in Frightening Stimuli and Intervention Effectiveness

Research shows that both age and gender are strongly associated with the impact of media on fear (see Cantor, 1998a, 2002, for review). For example, research in cognitive development shows that preschool children are more perceptually dependent than older children, responding to stimuli and events in terms of how they appear rather than in light of their more conceptual aspects (e.g., Bruner, 1966). Studies show that children in this age group are more responsive than older children and adults to the physical appearance of characters and less responsive to their intentions, motivations, or their potential to produce harm (e.g., Hoffner & Cantor, 1985). Developmental research also shows that the acquisition of an understanding of the distinction between fantasy and reality is a competence that develops only gradually throughout childhood (e.g., Flavell, 1963). Consistent with this developmental trend, research shows that the tendency to mention fantasy offerings, depicting threatening events that could not possibly occur in the real world, as sources of fear, decreases as the child's age increases, whereas the tendency to mention fictional offerings, depicting events that could possibly occur, increases (e.g., Cantor & Sparks, 1984). Similarly, the tendency to be frightened by threatening news stories increases with age (Cantor & Nathanson, 1996). Finally, because the ability to think abstractly emerges relatively late in cognitive development (Flavell, 1963), the tendency to be frightened by media depicting abstract threats (e.g., nuclear holocaust) also increases with age (e.g., Cantor, Wilson, & Hoffner, 1986).

Developmental differences have also been observed in the effectiveness of intervention strategies for media-induced fear (see Cantor, 1998a; Cantor & Wilson, 1988). In general, younger children (up to approximately 7 years) benefit more from noncognitive strategies, such as desensitization (e.g., Wilson & Cantor, 1987), than from cognitive strategies. Cognitive strategies, which involve the utilization of information that casts the threat in a less dangerous light, are more effective in reducing the fear of older than younger children (e.g., Wilson & Weiss, 1991).

Gender Differences in Fear Intensity and Choice of Coping Strategies

Gender differences are also common in media-induced fright. A meta-analysis by Peck (1999) reported a moderate gender-difference effect size ($g = .41$), with females exhibiting more fear than males. Females' responses were more intense than those of males for all dependent measures. However, the effect sizes were largest for self-report and behavioral measures (those that are under the most conscious control) and smallest for heart rate and facial expressions. In addition, the effect size for gender differences increased with age. Although more research is needed to explore the extent of gender differences in media-induced fear and the factors that contribute to them, these findings suggest that the size of the gender difference may be partially a function of social pressures to conform to gender-appropriate behavior.

There is some evidence of gender differences in the coping strategies used to counteract media-induced fear, and these gender differences may also reflect gender-role socialization pressures. In studies of adolescents (Hoffner, 1995), and elementary school children (Valkenburg, Cantor, & Peeters, 2000), girls reported using more noncognitive coping strategies than boys did, but there were no gender differences in the use of cognitive strategies. Hoffner (1995) suggested that because boys are less willing than girls to show their emotions, they avoid noncognitive strategies, that are usually apparent to others. In contrast, the two genders employ cognitive strategies with equal frequency because these strategies are less readily observable.

CONCLUSIONS

To summarize, there is ample evidence that violence is a staple of mass media entertainment and that it contributes to viewers' hostility levels and aggressive behaviors via a variety of psychological processes. An understanding of these processes is helpful in making more accurate predictions of viewers' responses and in designing intervention strategies for reducing antisocial effects. Fear is also a common result of exposure to media violence, and research has identified important age and gender differences in both fear responses and effective coping strategies.

REFERENCES

Anderson, C. A., & Bushman, B. J. (2001). Effects of violent video games on aggressive behavior, aggressive cognition, aggressive affect, physiological arousal, and prosocial behavior: A meta-analytic review of the scientific literature. *Psychological Science, 12,* 353–359.

Bandura, A. (1965). Influence of models' reinforcement contingencies on the acquisition of imitative responses. *Journal of Personality and Social Psychology, 1,* 389–595.

Bandura, A. (1986). *Social foundations of thought and action: A social cognitive theory.* Englewood Cliffs, NJ: Prentice-Hall.

Baron, R. A. (1971). Aggression as a function of magnitude of victim's pain cues, level of prior anger arousal, and aggressor–victim similarity. *Journal of Personality and Social Psychology, 18,* 48–54.

Berkowitz, L. (1965). The concept of aggressive drive: Some additional considerations. In L. Berkowitz (Ed.), *Advances in experimental social psychology. Vol 2.* (pp. 301–329). New York: Academic.

Black S. L., & Bevan, S. (1992). At the movies with Buss and Durkee: A natural experiment on film violence. *Aggressive Behavior, 18,* 37–45.

Bryant, J., & Zillmann, D. (1977). The mediating effect of the intervention potential of communications on displaced aggressiveness and retaliatory behavior. In B. D. Ruben (Ed.), *Communication yearbook 1* (pp. 291–306). New Brunswick, NJ: ICA-Transaction Press.

Bruner, J. S. (1966). On cognitive growth I & II. In J. S. Bruner, R. R. Oliver, & P. M. Greenfield (Eds.), *Studies in cognitive growth* (pp. 1–67). New York: Wiley.

Burnstein, E., & Worchel, P. (1962). Arbitrariness of frustration and its consequences for aggression in a social situation. *Journal of Personality, 30,* 528–540.

Bushman, B. J., & Anderson, C. A. (2001). Media violence and the American public: Scientific fact versus media misinformation. *American Psychologist, 56,* 477–489.

Bushman, B., & Huesmann, L. R. (2001). Effects of televised violence on aggression. In D. G. Singer & J. L. Singer (Eds.), *Handbook of children and the media* (pp. 223–254). Thousand Oaks, CA: Sage.

Cantor, J. (1998a). *"Mommy, I'm scared": How TV and movies frighten children and what we can do to protect them*. San Diego, CA: Harcourt.

Cantor, J. (1998b). Ratings for program content: The role of research findings. *Annals of the American Academy of Political and Social Science, 557,* 54–69.

Cantor, J. (2002). Fright reactions to mass media. In J. Bryant & D. Zillmann (Eds.), *Media effects: Advances in theory and research* (2nd ed.). (pp. 287–306). Mahwah, NJ: Lawrence Erlbaum Associates.

Cantor, J., & Nathanson, A. (1996). Children's fright reactions to television news. *Journal of Communication, 46,* 139–152.

Cantor, J., & Sparks, G. G. (1984). Children's fear responses to mass media: Testing some Piagetian predictions. *Journal of Communication, 34*(2), 90–103.

Cantor, J., & Wilson, B. J. (1988). Helping children cope with frightening media presentations. *Current Psychology: Research & Reviews, 7,* 58–75.

Cantor, J., Wilson, B. J., & Hoffner, C. (1986). Emotional responses to a televised nuclear holocaust film. *Communication Research, 13,* 257–277.

Cantor, J., Zillmann, D., & Einsiedel, E. (1978). Female responses to provocation after exposure to aggressive and erotic films. *Communication Research, 5,* 395–412.

Carlsson, U., & von Feilitzen, C. (1998). *Children and media violence: Yearbook from the UNESCO International Clearinghouse on Children and Violence on the Screen*. Göteborg, Sweden: Nordicom.

Cline, V. B., Croft, R. G., & Courrier, S. (1973). Desensitization of children to television violence. *Journal of Personality and Social Psychology, 27,* 360–365.

Flavell, J. (1963). *The developmental psychology of Jean Piaget*. New York: Van Nostrand.

Freedman, J. L. (1984). Effects of television violence on aggressiveness. *Psychological Bulletin, 96,* 227–246.

Gerbner, G., Gross, L., Morgan, M., Signorielli, N. & Shanahan, J (2002). Growing up with television: Cultivation processes. In J. Bryant & D. Zillmann (Eds.), *Media effects: Advances in theory and research.* (2nd. ed., pp. 43–67). Hillsdale, NJ: Lawrence Erlbaum Associates.

Goldstein, J. (Ed.). (1998). *Why we watch: The attractions of violent entertainment.* New York: Oxford.

Harrison, K., & Cantor, J. (1999). Tales from the screen: Enduring fright reactions to scary media. *Media Psychology, 1,* 97–116.

Hoekstra, S. J., Harris, R. J., & Helmick, A. L. (1999). Autobiographical memories about the experience of seeing frightening movies in childhood. *Media Psychology, 1,* 117–140.

Hoffner, C. (1995). Adolescents' coping with frightening mass media. *Communication Research, 22,* 325–346.

Hoffner, C., & Cantor, J. (1985). Developmental differences in responses to a television character's appearance and behavior. *Developmental Psychology, 21,* 1065–1074.

Huesmann, L. R. (1988). An information processing model for the development of aggression. *Aggressive Behavior, 14,* 13–24.

Jo, E., & Berkowitz, L. (1994). A priming effect analysis of media influences: An update. In J. Bryant & D. Zillmann (Eds.), *Media effects: Advances in theory and research.* (pp. 43–60). Hillsdale, NJ: Lawrence Erlbaum Associates.

Kodaira, S. I. (1998). A review of research on media violence in Japan. In U. Carlsson & C. von Feilitzen (Eds.), *Children and media violence: Yearbook from the UNESCO International Clearinghouse on Children and Violence on the Screen* (pp. 81–105). Göteborg, Sweden: Nordicom.

Lemish, D. (1997). The school as a wrestling arena: The modeling of a television series. *Communication, 22,* 395–418.

Lynch. P. J., Gentile, D. A., Olson, A. A., & van Brederode, T. M. (2001, April). *The effects of violent video game habits on adolescent aggressive attitudes and behaviors.* Paper presented at the biennial conference of the Society for Research in Child Development, Minneapolis, MN.

Molitor, F., & Hirsch, K. W. (1994). Children's toleration of real-life aggression after exposure to media violence: A replication of the Drabman and Thomas studies. *Child Study Journal, 24,* 191–207.

Mullin, C. R., & Linz, D. (1995). Desensitization and resensitization to violence against women: Effects of exposure to sexually violent films on judgments of domestic violence victims. *Journal of Personality and Social Psychology, 69,* 449–459.

Nathanson A. I., & Cantor, J. (2000). Reducing the aggression-promoting effect of violent cartoons by increasing children's fictional involvement with the victim. *Journal of Broadcasting & Electronic Media, 44,* 125–142.

National Television Violence Study, Vols. 1–3. (1996–1998). Thousand Oaks, CA: Sage.

Owens, J., Maxim, R., McGuinn, M., Nobile, C., Msall, M., & Alario, A. (1999). Television-viewing habits and sleep disturbance in school children [Abstract]. *Pediatrics, 104,* 552.

Paik, H., & Comstock, G. (1994). The effects of television violence on antisocial behavior: A meta-analysis. *Communication Research, 21,* 516–546.

Peck, E. Y. (1999). *Gender differences in film-induced fear as a function of type of emotion measure and stimulus content: A meta-analysis and a laboratory study.* Unpublished doctoral dissertation, University of Wisconsin–Madison.

Robinson, T. N., Wilde, M. L., Navracruz, L. C., Haydel, K. F., & Varady, A. (2001). Effects of reducing children's television and video game use on aggressive behavior: A randomized controlled trial. *Archives of Pediatrics and Adolescent Medicine, 155*(1), 17–23.

Roskos-Ewoldsen, D. R., Roskos-Ewoldsen, B., & Carpentier, F. D. (2002). Media Priming: A Synthesis. In J. Bryant & D. Zillmann (Eds.), *Media effects: Advances in theory and research* (2nd ed., pp. 97–120). Mahwah, NJ: Lawrence Erlbaum Associates.

Schachter, S. (1964). The interaction of cognitive and physiological determinants of emotional state. In L. Berkowitz (Ed.), *Advances in experimental social psychology* (Vol. 1. pp. 49–80). New York: Academic.

Singer, M. I., Slovak, K., Frierson, T., & York, P. (1998). Viewing preferences, symptoms of psychological trauma, and violent behaviors among children who watch television. *Journal of the American Academy of Child and Adolescent Psychiatry, 37,* 1041–1048.

Valkenburg, P. M., Cantor, J., & Peeters, A. L. (2000). Fright reactions to television: A child survey. *Communication Research, 27,* 82–99.

Waite, B. M., Hillbrand, M., & Foster, H. G. (1992). Reduction of aggressive behavior after removal of music television. *Hospital and Community Psychiatry, 43,* 173–175.

Wilson, B. J., & Cantor, J. (1987). Reducing children's fear reactions to mass media: Effects of visual exposure and verbal explanation. In M. McLaughlin (Ed.), *Communication Yearbook 10* (pp. 553–573). Beverly Hills, CA: Sage.

Wilson, B. J., & Weiss, A. J. (1991). The effects of two reality explanations on children's reactions to a frightening movie scene. *Communication Monographs, 58,* 307–326.

Zillmann, D. (1971a). Excitation transfer in communication-mediated aggressive behavior. *Journal of Experimental Social Psychology, 7,* 419–434.

Zillmann, D. (1971b). The role of excitation in aggressive behavior. In *Proceedings of the Seventeenth International Congress of Applied Psychology* (pp. 925–936). Brussels: Editest.

Zillmann, D. (1979). *Hostility and aggression.* Hillsdale, NJ: Lawrence Erlbaum Associates.

Zillmann, D. (1989). Aggression and sex: Independent and joint operations. In H. Wagner & A. Manstead (Eds.), *Handbook of social psychophysiology* (pp. 229–259). New York: Wiley.

Zillmann, D. (1991). Television viewing and physiological arousal. In J. Bryant & D. Zillmann (Eds.), *Responding to the screen: Reception and reaction processes* (pp. 103–133). Hillsdale, NJ: Lawrence Erlbaum Associates.

Zillmann, D., Bryant, J., Cantor, J., & Day, K. L. (1975). Irrelevance of mitigating circumstances in retaliatory behavior at high levels of excitation. *Journal of Research in Personality, 9,* 282–293.

Zillmann, D., & Cantor, J. (1976). Effect of timing of information about mitigating circumstances on emotional responses to provocation and retaliatory behavior. *Journal of Experimental Social Psychology, 12,* 38–55.

Zillmann, D., Hoyt, J., & Day, K. D. (1974). Strength and duration of the effect of aggressive, violent, and erotic communications on subsequent aggressive behavior. *Communication Research, 1,* 286–306.

Zillmann, D., & Johnson, R. C. (1974). Motivated aggressiveness perpetuated by exposure to aggressive films and reduced by exposure to nonaggressive films. *Journal of Research in Personality, 7,* 261–276.

Zillmann, D., Katcher, A. H., & Milavsky, B. (1972). Excitation transfer from physical exercise to subsequent aggressive behavior. *Journal of Experimental Social Psychology, 8,* 247–259.

Zillmann, D., & Weaver, J. B., III. (1999). Effects of prolonged exposure to gratuitous media violence on provoked and unprovoked hostile behavior. *Journal of Applied Social Psychology, 29,* 145–165.

10

Pornography and Erotica

Dan Brown
East Tennessee State University

Kinsey, Pomeroy, and Martin (1948) noted that no aspect of human behavior has received more thought and discussion than human sexuality, and modern media own no claim to originating public fascination with sexually explicit material. *Venus of Willendorf*, a statue of a female with enlarged sexual organs dates to 30,000 BC (Webb, 1982). Anal intercourse appears frequently on Peruvian ceramics dating to 1500 BC (Brewer, 1982). "In every modern language the amount of deliberately pornographic material that has been produced is beyond ready calculation" (Kinsey, Pomeroy, Martin, & Gebhard, 1953, p. 672).

Pornography engenders a huge commercial interest (Attorney General's Commission on Pornography, 1986) in catering to the demands of a large and diverse population of its consumers. During the 1950s and earlier, such material typically was sold from the back rooms of magazine vendors' shops disguised as mere newsstands (Brown & Bryant, 1989). By the late 1980s, pornography had "gone truly public. . . . Thanks to the new communication technology, pornography has become an affordable form of entertainment for all" (Zillmann & Bryant, 1989, p. xii). Nielsen NetRatings reported that 17.5 million World Wide Web surfers accessed pornographic web sites from their homes in January 2000, a 40% increase in web viewing of pornography in a 4-month period (Koerner, 2000).

Despite its popularity, pornography engenders strong negative reactions. "Concerned citizens and community groups crossing every line of socioeconomic status, race, religion, and political philosophy are frustrated, outraged, and hostile to many of the acts of pornographers in our society" (Sears, 1989, pp. 324–325). Gross (1983) "can hardly believe one needs to provide evidence of the overwhelming preponderance of antipornography sentiments on the part of public figures in this society" (p. 109), but the popularity of such content extends far beyond limited minorities to the general population (Bryant & Brown, 1989).

Bryant and Zillmann (2001) identified the following consistent survey findings about pornography use. First exposure to pornography is occurring at younger ages than in previous generations, and most high school students have seen pornography, although the rate of exposure is greater among males than among females. So prevalent is this exposure that a strong majority of teenagers and adults confirm that they have seen pornography. This exposure usually occurs in collaboration with peers in social settings as opposed to a solitary activity.

Several studies (e.g., Attorney General's Commission on Pornography, 1986; Slade, 1984; Smith, 1976) documented increased presence of pornography in media content, and two government commissions (Attorney General's Commission on Pornography, 1986; Commission on Obscenity and Pornography, 1970;) conducted inquiries into pornography in American society.

For such a controversial topic, the existence of a considerable body of research is hardly surprising. This chapter summarizes some important findings regarding definitions used in identifying pornographic material, research models for studying effects of such material, sexual arousal effects, cognitive and attitudinal effects, behavioral effects of sexually explicit materials, and public policy issues involving pornography.

DEFINITION OF PORNOGRAPHY AND EROTICA

The word *pornography* comes from the Greek *porno* denoting prostitutes and *graphos* for writing.

> Although there is no widely accepted modern definition, the common element in all definitions is that the material is sexually explicit. Controversy revolves around whether specific depictions are art or smut, good or bad, innocuous or harmful. People often label as pornographic material that violates their own moral standards and use the terms artistic or erotic for sexual materials they find acceptable. (Davis & McCormick, 1997)

Although *Black's Law Dictionary* (Black, 1990) makes no distinction between pornographic and obscene materials, American courts have not defined pornography. Legal actions against sexually explicit materials hinge on whether the pornographic material is obscene. After struggling for many years to define *obscenity,* the U.S. Supreme Court specified in *Miller v. California* (1973) which materials are obscene. Such materials are those that an average person, applying contemporary community standards to evaluate the whole works, would find as appealing to the prurient interest by portraying in a patently offensive way some sexual behavior that is proscribed by a state law. The work must be found to lack serious literary, artistic, or scientific value. Although obscene works lack legal protection under the First Amendment to the U.S. Constitution, law enforcement officials must follow several due process requirements (see Rimm, 1995) to complete a successful legal action against obscenity. For example, they must obtain a court determination of obscenity before removing a publication from circulation (Fort Wayne Books, Inc. v. Indiana, 1989). However, all adult pornographic material is presumed under law as not obscene, and only child pornography is generally legally proscribed. Therefore, legal action against pornographic media content requires a court determination that the material is obscene.

The feminist perspective often blends interpretive characteristics with descriptive components to produce more detailed definitions of pornography. For example, Russell (1994) defined *pornography* as "material that combines sex and/or the exposure of genitals with abuse or degradation in a manner that appears to endorse, condone, or encourage such behavior."

Feminist activists Andrea Dworkin (1981) and Catherine MacKinnon (1987) coauthored a failed antipornography Minneapolis ordinance that was later adopted in Indianapolis in 1984. The ordinance defined *pornography* as "the graphic sexually explicit subordination of women, whether in pictures or in words" (Indianapolis Code, 1984). The ordinance listed specific examples of such subordination in the form of portrayals of women as sexual objects or victims of abuse or degradation. This definition proved to be the undoing of the ordinance (Sears, 1989), which was found to be unconstitutional by the U.S. Supreme Court (American Booksellers v. Hudnut, 1986).

Many social science researchers (e.g., Linz, Malamuth, & Beckett, 1992; Malamuth & Ceniti, 1986) have made no attempt to define *pornography,* using words such as "sexually explicit materials" or "erotica" to "avoid the negative connotations associated with the term 'pornography'" (Perse, 1994, p. 509). References to sexually explicit content could conceivably become controversial, as when public figures explain whether their actions constituted sexual behavior. Zillmann (1984a) defined sexual behavior as "copulatory behavior and as any and every activity that simulates such behavior and that produces the physiological concomitants of copulation in full or in part" (p. 19). Rimm's (1995) survey of pornography on the Internet defined pornography as including "the depiction of actual sexual contact [hereinafter 'hard-core'] and depiction of mere nudity or lascivious exhibition [hereinafter 'soft-core']" (pp. 1849–1850).

The *Final Report* of the Attorney General's Commission on Pornography (1986) listed five classes of pornographic material.

1. Sexually violent materials (e.g., rape or other physical harm in a sexual context);

2. Nonviolent portrayals depicting degradation, domination, subordination, or humiliation;

3. Nonviolent and nondegrading portrayal of intercourse without signs of violence or coercion;

4. Nudity outside the context of sexual activity; and

5. Child pornography.

Zillmann (1984b) described "standard fare" pornography as content that typically involves strangers meeting and being overwhelmed by sexual desire, which they consummate by mutual consent.

> What then follows is really the theme of standard pornography: fellatio, cunnilingus, intercourse in all conceivable positions, including anal intercourse (at least in the newer pornographic movies, this is the standard). What one finds, in addition, is that in less than half of all these cases "one on one" heterosexual intercourse is depicted. More than half of all cases feature a third party. Either that or it is group sex that goes beyond a third party to fourth and fifth parties. So that is standard.... They are eager to please one another. In fact, women tend to over-respond in serving the male interest. (p. 96)

Not all sexual material is automatically pornographic. Zillmann (1984b) distinguished *pornography* from *erotica,* which "features sex devoid of coercion and violence" (p. 95). As with definitions of *pornography,* those of *erotica* (as used by writers opposing pornography) tend to offer both descriptive and interpretive elements. For example, Russell (1994) defined *erotica* as media content that "refers to sexually suggestive or arousing material that is free of sexism, racism, and homophobia, and respectful of all human beings and animals portrayed." Perceived distinctions between the two terms derive importance from differences of opinion about whether pornography and erotic differ in their impact on consumers, a question that is examined later in this chapter.

In resolving such differences of opinion, research findings are hardly unanimous. The structure of the research investigation should be considered in evaluating differences in findings.

THE RESEARCH MODEL

Among researchers who study the impact of pornography on individuals, an important distinction exists between models that focus on short-term experimental results and those that deal with the long-term effects of exposure to pornography. The following description addresses the methods used in studies of effects of violent pornography.

> In the typical study focusing on short term or relatively immediate effects on aggressive behavior, male subjects were first exposed to depictions showing the female victim enjoying or reacting in a positive fashion to sexual aggression or similar mistreatment. Then subjects were given the opportunity to administer electric shocks or other forms of punishment to a female victim. (Linz, Malamuth, & Beckett, 1992, p. 152)

This "one shot" (Zillmann, 1994b, p. 98) paradigm is the most commonly used research paradigm for experimentally studying the effects of exposure to media content (cf. Donnerstein, 1984b; Malamuth, 1984; Sapolsky, 1984; Zillmann, 1989a). The model evaluates a single exposure to the content by measuring effects that might occur immediately after the consumption of the content. Zillmann (1994b) questioned this model as "a means of establishing perceptual, attitudinal, and behavioral changes, especially lasting ones" (p. 123). An alternative research protocol involves repeated exposure to media content in which the exposures resemble actual viewing patterns by having the evaluation of impact of exposure occur after the elapse of time following the exposure.

Two studies (Howard, Reifler, & Liptzin, 1971; Mann, Sidman, & Starr, 1971) from the *Technical Report of the Commission on Obscenity and Pornography*

(1970) pioneered this research paradigm (Zillmann, 1986, 1994b). The results of these studies are reported later under the section of this chapter on behavioral effects of exposure to pornography.

Zillmann and Bryant (1982, 1984) studied the effects of massive exposure of pornography to males and females over 6 weeks. The stimuli depicted only consenting adults who engaged in voluntary, noncoercive sexual behavior. After an interval of a week following the last exposure, respondents viewed three additional films, and both physiological and evaluative assessments were measured from the participants. These measurements also occurred 2 weeks after the end of the initial 6-week period, and new measurements were introduced in the 3rd week.

The 3rd week provided an opportunity for the respondents to recommend a fair sentence in a rape case. Other activities asked the respondents to rate the popularity of various sex practices among sexually active American adults and express their concerns about pornography. Results of these studies follow. This model of studying prolonged exposure results in reports of significant negative effects of exposure to pornography.

COGNITIVE EFFECTS OF SEXUALLY EXPLICIT MATERIALS

Zillmann (1989a) described a list of 17 experimentally demonstrated effects of prolonged consumption of pornography. Cognitive effects of exposure to erotica and pornography include those effects that are associated with perceptions, attitudes, and values. Prolonged exposure to sexually explicit materials tends to reduce attitudinal restrictions against sexually explicit media content. Such exposure produces changes in "sexual callousness, rape proclivity, moral values, family values, perception of normalcy in sexual behavior, attitudes toward censorship, general attitudes toward women, and many other cognitive effects" (Bryant & Zillmann, 1996, p. 202).

Enjoyment and Evaluation of Pornography

Zillmann and Bryant's (1982, 1984) research using the model featuring repeated exposure to pornography with delays between exposure and feedback reveals a strong habituation of excitatory responses to pornography. These responses include physiological measurements, including blood pressure and other ratings of sympathetic activity. However, Zillmann (1989a) found the lack of generalization of habituation to explicit films depicting uncommon sexual activities surprising.

Early feelings of repulsion by the respondents diminished after prolonged viewing of common sexual behaviors, and enjoyment of viewing such material did not appear to increase. Although more favorable evaluations of uncommon sexual activities followed the exposure, the same was not true of common sexual behavior.

Zillmann (1984a) demonstrated that intense enjoyment depends on increased sympathetic activity, a finding that was consistent with the results reported by Howard et al. (1971). This finding drew support from Zillmann and Bryant (1982, 1984), whose respondents reported level or reduced enjoyment of pornography after prolonged exposure. Two weeks after the end of the massive exposure, excitatory habituation and the reported evaluations endured.

Pornography and Attitudes Related to Sexual Behavior, Morality, and Family Values

Zillmann and Bryant (1988a, 1988c) used the prolonged exposure research paradigm in extending their study of the impact of pornography consumption on perceptions and attitudes, marriage and family as social institutions, sexual relationships, sexual satisfaction, and changes in preferences in pornography consumption. Again, 6 weeks of exposure to pornography preceded assessments, but nonstudents as well as students participated in the research that used color and sound videotapes instead of the previously used pornography on film. Again, nonviolent, noncoercive, sexual behavior involving consenting adults constituted the type of explicit sexual activity viewed by the respondents. The findings produced interpretations relevant to public health regarding the consumption of pornography (Zillmann, 1994a).

The values of pornography undermine "traditional values that favor marriage, family and children" (Zillmann, 1994b p. 133). Pornography values focus on short-term personal sexual gratification at the expense of "emotional attachment, of kindness, of caring, and especially not of continuance of the relationship, as such continuance would translate into responsibilities, curtailments, and costs (p. 133).

Prolonged exposure to pornography affected the "perception of the very nature of sexuality" (p. 134), and most of the findings applied equally for males and females as well as for students and nonstudents. "The findings show that repeated consumption of pornography is capable of inducing dissatisfaction with numerous aspects of sexuality" (Zillmann & Bryant, 1988c, p. 449). Regarding the idea that sexual dissatisfaction may prompt many pornography consumers to turn to pornography in the first place, "Pornography seems likely to exacerbate the situation by projecting partners and performances that are out of reach for many. A vicious circle of dissatisfaction seems to be the result" (Zillmann & Bryant, 1988c p. 451). Zillmann and Bryant conceded that explicit sexual display has no monopoly on the ability to present models that enjoy physical superiority over one's sexual partner; common media fare from soap operas to advertisements certainly offer the same potential.

However, by definition, only pornography's explicit graphic display of physical and sexual prowess appears to specifically affect sexual dissatisfaction. The results of the Indiana Inventory of Personal Happiness clearly revealed that items without connections to sexuality remained unaffected, although all items related to sexuality were affected (Zillmann & Bryant, 1988a).

After prolonged pornography exposure, respondents expressed less support for the essential nature of marriage and less desire to have children. The latter result displayed gender specificity, although all subgroups wanted fewer children. The desire for male children dropped by 31%, the desire for female children fell by 61%, and the desire for female children by males practically disappeared. The desire to have female children dropped to one third of its normal level among females who saw prolonged pornography, "supportive of the allegations of feminists (e.g., Lederer, 1980) that most pornography debases women" (Zillmann & Bryant, 1988a, pp. 541–542).

The respondents who experienced prolonged exposure considered both male and female promiscuity more natural than did people who had not seen such material. They also expressed less satisfaction with mates, even within established relationships (cf. Weaver, Masland, & Zillmann, 1984). Mates appeared less physically appealing, their sexual performance less satisfying, their sexual innovativeness less favorable, and their degree of affection less satisfactory.

After prolonged exposure, participants felt less confidence in the sexual fidelity of their partners and greater acceptance of sexual affairs before and outside marriage for both themselves and for their partners. This acceptance included activity by themselves and their partners with third parties. Prolonged exposure brought greater acceptance of the false belief about the risks of sexual repression. Such respondents increased their rating of the importance of recreational sexual behavior lacking in emotional attachment.

Although the prolonged exposure to pornography did not affect attitudes toward nonsexual behavior, viewers did display reduced reluctance to sanction sexually reprehensible behavior. Viewers exposed to prolonged pornography showed no differences in attitudes from respondents who did not see pornography on drunken driving and shoplifting. However, the exposure did show relaxed inhibitions against self-advancement through sexual favors and cover-up of homosexual relations to a heterosexual lover (Zillmann, 1994b). "Presumably because the perception of greater prevalence of particular sexual behaviors grants them greater moral legitimacy, the morality manifest in pornography eventually enters into the moral judgment of sexual conduct generally" (p. 139).

Pornography and Attitudes Toward Women, Sexual Callousness, and Rape Proclivity

Feminists (e.g., Baldwin, 1984; Dworkin, 1979, 1981; Hommel, 1979; Jacobs, 1984; MacKinnon, 1984) charge that pornography teaches women to think of themselves as victims, increasing their tendencies toward submissiveness and powerlessness (Krafka, Linz, Donnerstein, & Penrod, 1997). Others see pornography as a powerful factor in socializing sex roles (Brownmiller, 1975; Malamuth & Briere, 1986). "This general collection of ideas concerning increased female submissiveness and fearfulness has come to be termed the 'cultural climate hypothesis'" (Krafka et al., 1997, p. 153).

This hypothesis draws support from several studies that have exposed males to images of aggressive pornography (Donnerstein, Linz, & Penrod, 1987; Linz, 1989; Linz, Donnerstein, & Penrod, 1984, 1988; Linz & Malamuth, 1993; Malamuth & Billings, 1986, Malamuth & Briere, 1986; Malamuth & Check, 1981; Weisz, & Earls, 1995) and partial support from research with females (Krafka, Linz, Donnerstein, & Penrod, 1997).

Wyer, Bodenhausen, and Gorman (1985) reported variable results by sex of respondents who saw slides of women posing in sexually enticing ways before reacting to a rape trial. Men gave less credibility to the claims of a rape victim and held her more accountable than did the members of a control group. Women who saw the slides found higher credibility and less accountability in a rape victim as compared with the ratings of the controls. These results suggest that even mild pornography promotes the acceptance of the rape myth that women provoke sexual assaults and are responsible for men's sexual aggression.

Zillmann and Bryant (1982) assessed the disposition toward rape through the measurements of recommendations of sentences for a convicted rapist. These recommendations were taken in the 3rd week after the completion of 6 weeks of prolonged exposure to pornography.

Massive exposure to pornography produced shorter prison term recommendations from the respondents, reducing perceptions of the seriousness of the crime of rape. "The number of students who recommended minimal sentences was markedly higher under conditions of massive exposure than in the other conditions. Surprisingly, this trivialization of rape was evident in women as well as in men" (p. 17). However, women did levy more severe penalties than did men.

Zillmann and Bryant (1982) concluded that their findings suggest that "the apparent loss of compassion for women as rape victims ... generalizes to a loss of compassion for women per se, thus undermining supportive dispositions for women's causes" (p. 17). The authors elaborated that the findings "clearly (promote) sexual callousness toward women" (p. 18), but they conceded the possibility that the increased favorable evaluation and acceptance of pornography could have occurred if the participants inferred that the stimulus materials were harmless. Such an inference might have occurred if the participants believed that the researchers would not subject them to potentially harmful consequences. However, Zillmann and Bryant argued that even the participant inference of acceptance of pornography by the experimenters could not have accounted for the observed sexual callousness toward women that resulted from the prolonged exposure.

Although the effect of diminished support for gender equality after prolonged exposure to nonviolent pornography appeared for all groups, males and students favored egalitarianism less than did females and nonstudents (Zillmann & Bryant, 1988c). Buchman (1988) found no differences in such exposure on attitudes toward nonsexual indiscretions. However, consistent with the findings that prolonged exposure trivializes rape, he found that exposure reduced willingness to punish low levels of nonviolent child abuse but not brutality.

Check (1985) conducted the first study directly comparing the effects of violent versus nonviolent pornography on attitudes toward rape. Prolonged exposure to nonviolent pornography increased the likelihood of male respondents' self reports that they would be willing to force a woman into sexual acts against her will and that they would be willing to commit rape. Violent pornography similarly increased the men's reported willingness to commit rape.

Donnerstein (1984a) summarized findings from studies of men who were screened to eliminate those who might be predisposed to violent behavior or who might already be angered in some way before exposure to sexual violence. These men saw films depicting violence against women in a context that promoted sexual arousal, and the results clarified "the mediation of men's callousness toward women" (Zillmann, 1989a, p. 136). The males rated female victims of violent rape as having suffered less injury and being less worthy in general than did men who did not see the films (Linz, 1985). Donnerstein and Linz (1986) reported that experimental data show that young adults are more likely to display sexually callous attitudes about rape and sexual coercion after prolonged exposure to violent pornography. They further contended that the violence, and not the sex, produces the effects. Other studies (Linz, Donnerstein, & Adams, 1989; Linz, Donnerstein, & Penrod, 1984, 1988; Mullin & Linz, 1995) demonstrate that males become desensitized to media portrayals of sexualized violence against women.

Males experience levels of arousal from exposure to scenes portraying female victims who become sexually aroused by the assault that approach those produced by exposure to content that portrays consenting sexual behavior. However, content that depicts more realistic negative victim responses produces significantly less sexual arousal in male viewers (Linz & Donnerstein, 1989; Malamuth & Check, 1980a, 1980b, 1983; Malamuth, Heim, & Feshbach, 1980).

Weaver (1987) displayed sexual, aggressive-sexual, or neutral film segments to both male and female college students. The sexual film group was divided into consensual sex and female-instigated sex. The aggressive-sexual group contained subdivisions of male-coerced sex and eroticized violence. In pretests of the stimulus films, both men and women rated the rape depictions as most intensely sexual and the eroticized violence the least. Men saw some aggressiveness in consenting sex, but women did not. "The men judged rape to be about half as violent as murder, whereas the women considered rape to be about as brutal a crime as murder" (Zillmann & Weaver, 1989, p. 115).

To establish baselines against which to measure responses to stimulus materials, participants evaluated narrative descriptions of females one week before seeing the stimulus materials. The researchers prompted descriptions of women who were assertive or permissive, sexually discriminating or promiscuous.

After seeing a film, the participants responded to portraits of females on color slides. The slides included groups called peers and nonpeers, according to whether they portrayed females who were about the same age or older than the participants. Based on the pretest data, the slides were also divided into subgroups portraying sexually discriminating and promiscuous women.

Exposure to sexually explicit film content strongly influenced the participants' perceptions of portraits of females. Men who saw films of consensual and female-instigated sex perceived the women in the slides as more permissive than did participants who saw other film content. This effect did not emerge among men who saw male-coerced sex or erotic violence. "Men thus generalized, to some degree, the witnessed sexual actions of sexually initiative women and projected traits of these women onto female peers who had been considered nonpermissive by others" (Zillmann & Weaver, 1989, p. 116). Women, however, projected this permissiveness only after seeing filmed scenes of rape and not after viewing other film content types. Seeing erotica, both violent and nonviolent, influenced perceptions of women in portraits who were previously judged as "nice girls" to be more like the perceptions of sexually permissive and promiscuous stereotypes.

Asked to role play in sentencing clearly guilty male offenders in cases including physical victimization of women, including rape, women who saw any erotic film content perceived less innocence in female peers. "In contrast, men deemed sexually discriminating women to be less innocent after exposure to rape and eroticized violence, but not after exposure to consensual and female-instigated sex" (Zillmann & Weaver, 1989, p. 117). Except with aggressive-sexual film content, exposure to erotica "trivialized rape" for both men and women (Zillmann & Weaver, 1989, p. 118).

> Exposure to pornography influences the perception of women in sexual terms, making them appear more promiscuous than they actually are; greater presumed sexual permissiveness and promiscuity then mediates callous dispositions toward the sexual victimization of women, as well as leniency toward the perpetrators of callous and coercive sexual actions against them. (Zillmann & Weaver, 1989, p. 119)

Zillmann and Weaver (1989) contended that these findings contradict the contention (Donnerstein, 1990; Donnerstein et al., 1987) that the violence in sexually aggressive media content is what matters in producing sexually callous and coercive effects. "Sexual themes desensitize men toward rape victims just as strongly as do violent themes with sexual undercurrents. In fact, the findings show that the desensitization effect was the strongest for nonviolent pornography" (Zillmann, 1989a, pp. 236–237).

A meta-analysis of television violence (Paik & Comstock, 1994) found stronger effects in programs containing erotica (both violent and nonviolent) than for programs containing only violence. Paik and Comstock concluded that the evidence supported the sexual callousness model rather than the notion that negative effects in sexually violent media content stem from the violence and not from the sexual materials.

Jansma, Linz, Mulac, and Imrich (1997) identified four factors that "prevent firm conclusions concerning the effects of viewing nonviolent degrading pornography" (p. 2). These factors include a lack of consistency in operationalizing research definitions of what counts as pornography that is degrading or not, determinations by researchers rather than by viewers of what counts as degrading content, study of sexually aggressive outcomes rather than more typical behaviors, and the dispositions toward sexual materials of respective study participants. Jansma et al.'s study measures interactions between men and women after their viewing of sexually violent degrading pornography, a strategy that the authors contend would improve on the attempts by Zillmann and Weaver (1989) to predict men's attitudes toward women.

Jansma et al. (1997) reported that the men's sex-role orientation influences their evaluations of their female partners and called for more research on the interaction between content and individual dispositional variables. However, they conceded that the laboratory setting of their study may have inhibited men's responses, producing a weaker effect that could emerge from evaluating pornography use in natural settings. Jansma et al. noted Perse's (1994) finding that some reasons for using pornography are associated with the acceptance of rape myths that incorporate a group of stereotypical and factually incorrect beliefs about rape.

BEHAVIORAL EFFECTS OF SEXUALLY EXPLICIT MATERIALS

Kelly, Dawson, and Musialowski (1989) identified some prosocial and educational effects of exposure to sexually explicit content. "The problems associated with the various forms of sexually explicit material used in sex therapy are greatly outweighed by its many benefits in a wide variety of different treatment approaches" (p. 85). These authors included in these benefits assessment and treatment of sexual deviance and dysfunction, but they also mentioned the benefits to people who suffer no abnormality of sexual behavior. Such benefits take in enhancement of fantasy that promotes positive outcomes involving "sexual arousal, sexual behavior, affective responses, and perceptions of others" (p. 85).

Zillmann (1989a; 1994a, 1994b; 2000) identified behavioral effects of sexually explicit materials as including shifting preferences for pornographic content, disinhibition, imitation of conduct witnessed in sexually explicit media, aggression, and criminal sexual behavior. Research findings involving these effects are summarized under the following headings dealing with preferences, aggression, and criminal behavior.

Imitation, Disinhibition, and Shifting Preferences for Pornography

In one of the first studies to examine repeated exposure to pornography, Mann et al. (1971) reported that use of pornography by couples who had been married for at least 10 years stimulated sexual behavior for only a short time and in nonspecific ways. The respondents apparently did not expand their sexual repertoire after viewing four sexually explicit films in four successive weekly sessions.

This lack of modeling behavior has more recently been challenged regarding less sexually experienced people than the married couples who participated in the 1971 study (e.g., Bryant, 1985; Wishnoff, 1978). Because of the general belief that stimulation of sexual desire and expansion of sexual repertoires are either unimportant or positive outcomes in the context of public health, the results of this study produced little impact on public health policy making (Zillmann, 1994b).

Howard et al. (1971) pioneered the research paradigm of prolonged exposure with measurement of effects after an interval following that exposure (Zillmann, 1986, 1994b). This investigation examined male college students' responses to fifteen 90-minute sessions with pornographic films over a 3-week period. Eight weeks after the end of the initial exposure period, respondents saw a sexually explicit film. Sexual arousal was measured during and after the viewing, and the participants completed a group of self-perception and attitudinal measurement instruments.

The respondents' strong initial interest in pornography diminished rapidly as the repeated showings progressed. Even new explicit materials failed to restore the initial levels of interest, and boredom was the most frequent description of their reactions, a state that was confirmed by the physiological measurements. The results mostly demonstrated that the respondents tired of seeing the same materials.

Zillmann and Bryant (1986b) unobtrusively monitored choices from a variety of videotaped materials in sessions conducted 2 weeks after an experimental treatment. Respondents who experienced prolonged exposure to pornography displayed a lack of interest in common pornography. Both males and females in the prolonged exposure group preferred pornography depicting less common practices, such as bondage, sadomasochism, and bestiality. However, the males chose this fare with greater frequency than the females. The authors reported that "generally available, nonviolent pornography that exclusively features heterosexual behavior among consenting adults arouses an interest in and creates a taste for pornography that portrays less commonly practiced sexual activities, including those involving the infliction of pain" (Zillmann & Bryant, 1986b, p. 574). The results parallel interviews with managers of adult book and video stores, who reported that "many repeat customers move from the consumption of depictions of common sexual activities to that of pornography showing uncommon and unusual sexual practices" (pp. 576–577).

In other words, pornography consumers progress to harder stuff, more extreme forms of pornography. "The research thus projects that, as a rule, consumers will advance to extreme material before, perhaps, reaching dead end and returning to whatever erotica in their recollection fostered the most gratifying sensations" (Zillmann, 1994b, p. 138). Satisfied curiosity and excitatory habituation provide explanations for this change.

Zillmann (1994b) speculated that younger consumers of pornography may be more motivated by curiosity than by habituation. He expected a shift among older consumers to pornographic content that includes violence. This prediction drew on evidence (Zillmann & Bryant, 1984) that viewers of violence experience increased sympathetic arousal that is "well suited to supplement fading excitement (owing to habituation) with pure erotica" (Zillmann, 1994b, p. 138).

Zillmann (1984a) outlined a convincing summary of theoretical suggestions mixed with the findings of research about habituation and sexual excitation. His summary offers clues about the prospects for modern societies that strive to cope with changing conditions concerning sexual behavior, beginning with the observation that exposure to portrayals of sexual behavior produces high levels of arousal, including feelings of sexual enticement and sympathetic nervous system responses. However, repeated exposure reduces these responses. Zillmann conjectured on the tendency of frequent public availability of sexual cues to lose potency as sexual stimuli with their nonspecific use. "If exposure also occurs while respondents dine in restaurants, drink in bars, loaf at beaches, and shave in bathrooms, conditioning theory projects a deterioration of stimulus control" (p. 196). So, habituation seems likely when sexual cues abound in nonsexual environments, explaining in part the prevalence of evidence in clinical literature that habituation occurs frequently in monogamous relationships.

Research on nonprimate mammals and nonhuman primates reveals that long relationships reduce females' abilities to produce males' sexual arousal. "The males respond with considerably stronger sexual motivation and sexual performance to females outside these consort relationships. Analogous response tendencies are likely to exist in humans, but have not been reliably demonstrated" (p. 199).

> As life . . . is turned into a continual jiggle show, . . . one ought not to expect a burst of sexual excitedness in response to visual manifestations of sexual partners.... Societies such as ours . . . seem to violate the standards of good excitatory housekeeping in the sexual domain. (Zillmann, 1984a, pp. 209–210)

Pornography and Aggression

Exposure to sexually explicit materials can reduce aggression in both males (Zillmann, Bryant, Comisky, & Medoff, 1981; Zillmann & Saplosky, 1977) and females (Baron, 1979; Cantor, Zillmann, & Einsiedel, 1978). Zillmann (1984a) attributed the reduction of aggression to the pleasantness of the content instead of to the use of sexual themes, noting that such materials might be pleasant "but they need not be, for whatever intrinsic or subjective reason. And when they are not, exposure to such themes is likely to annoy already annoyed persons further and thereby increase the propensity for hostile and aggressive action" (Zillmann, 1984a, p. 130).

Other factors identified by researchers as potentially influencing effects of sexually explicit media content include whether the individuals portrayed in the content are "demeaned or dehumanized, whether the viewer becomes disgusted or sexually excited by [the content], and many other elements associated with media message features and individual features and individual differences in users" (Bryant & Zillmann, 1996, p. 203).

Zillmann, Bryant, Comisky, and Medoff (1981) demonstrated that reduced aggression followed viewing of sexually explicit content stemmed from hedonic incompatibility rather than from conflict between sexual and aggressive drives. Zillmann (1984a) summarized the connection between sexual drive and aggressive behavior as lacking uniform effects supported by research.

Zillmann, Bryant, Comisky, and Medoff (1981) "proved the effects of transfer and of annoyance summation to be independent and additive" (Zillmann, 1984a, p. 169). See Cantor's chap. 9, this volume, for the details of excitation transfer. However, Zillmann, Bryant, and Carveth (1981) eliminated from the explanation the contention that the aggression facilitation grew from the presence of aggressive behavior in the stimulus content. Aggressiveness per se had little impact on the effects of viewing erotica (Zillmann, 1984a).

Sapolsky & Zillmann (1981) applied the provocation, exposure, retaliation model to include both males and females, reasoning that females view erotica less frequently and are, therefore, less desensitized to explicit sexual material. The findings reveal that females, but especially males, enjoy watching others engage in sexual intercourse and other sexual behavior. Although the result of viewing such content stimulates sexual desire, the research revealed no evidence that the viewing produced sexual frustration. This result dispelled the notion that aggressive behavior following exposure to sexually explicit fare stems from the cessation of the exposure and consequent sexual frustration. However, increases in motivated aggressive behavior have occurred immediately after pleasant reactions (e.g., Ramirez, Bryant, & Zillmann, 1982). "Frustration, especially sexual frustration, thus can be regarded as a contributing factor, but it should not be considered a necessary or sufficient condition for facilitation of aggression" (Zillmann, 1984a, p. 170).

Zillmann's (1984a) review of the research findings "corroborate the proposal that sex-aggression transfer is not the result of uniquely sexual excitedness, but rather derives from the sympathetic concomitants of this excitedness" (p. 171). Although males may respond to sexually explicit content that promotes callousness toward females with increased aggression toward women, other sexually explicit content apparently does not increase the likelihood of aggression toward people of either sex.

Malamuth and Ceniti (1986) did not find long-term effects of laboratory aggression against women after repeated exposure to either violent or nonviolent pornography. This finding contradicts the results of other investigations that found significant effects of repeated exposure to violent pornography on laboratory aggression against women (Donnerstein, 1980a,

1980b; Donnerstein & Berkowitz, 1981; Malamuth, 1978). Other studies (Linz, Donnerstein, & Adams, 1989; Linz, Donnerstein, & Penrod, 1984) report that the connection between aggression and the use of these materials requires content portraying sexual aggression rather than mere sexual content. However, some research concludes that use of nonviolent sexual materials also promotes aggression but perhaps not to the degree of that encouraged by sexually violent media fare (e.g., Attorney General's Commission on Pornography, 1986; Lyons, Anderson, & Larson, 1994). The logical question that follows is whether the promoted aggression can escalate to the level of criminal behavior.

Pornography and Criminal Behavior. Bryant and Zillmann (1996) noted that the *Final Report of the Surgeon General's Commission on Pornography* (Attorney General's Commission on Pornography, 1986) offers a number of anecdotal examples of the connections between viewing pornography and imitating violent sexually explicit media content. Russell (1988, 1994) contended that pornography causes rape. Clear research evidence regarding such imitation is lacking because of the inability of researchers to study the phenomena experimentally. Both ethical and legal issues constrain such approaches, and the frequency of incidence of imitation has not been systematically studied (Harris, 1994).

Check and Guloien (1989) reported that college men were more likely, after viewing portrayals of rape, to say that they might commit rape if they were certain of getting away with the crime. Bryant and Zillmann (2001) considered the admission of a hypothetical willingness to act as an indication of sexual callousness, which is strengthened by frequent exposure to both coercive and noncoercive pornography. They cited Marshall (1988) as reporting that "rapists who seek inspiration for their actions tend to consume nonviolent rather than violent pornography" (Bryant & Zillmann, 2001, p. 243).

Although the effects of violent pornography are often assumed to generate stronger effects than nonviolent pornography, research remains unavailable to confirm the assumption (Zillmann, 2000). Studies of the rape myth have used pornographic portrayals as stimulus material. Zillmann found studies unconvincing when the researchers used pornographic stimulus material portraying women being forced to have sexual relations and eventually enjoying the experience. Instead, he preferred that approach used by Check (1985) that portrayed genuine suffering by rape victims. This research reports no greater tendency from materials including such suffering than noncoercive pornography to produce statements of willingness to commit rape.

As with studying imitation, ethical and legal constraints prevent the performance of definitive experimental research that would connect actual criminal behavior with exposure to sexually explicit media content. The body of knowledge about the connection stems from interviews with criminals and case studies of crimes.

Bryant and Zillmann (1996) found the results of efforts to explain the connection "more confusing than informative" (p. 202) and unable to provide conclusive evidence. For example, conflicting conclusions emerge from reports of trends in rates of sex crimes and the availability of sexually explicit media content. In Denmark and Japan, the rates of criminal sexual behavior declined with more availability of pornography, but the opposite trends were charted in Australia and the United States. Variations in cultural values and a variety of other factors appear to mediate the effects of using sexually explicit media content on sexual criminal behavior.

PUBLIC POLICY AND POTENTIAL HARM FROM PORNOGRAPHY

Among the staunchest opponents of pornography are feminists who describe pornography as dehumanizing and degrading of women and promoting of hostility among men toward women (Brownmiller, 1975; Burt, 1980; Clark & Lewis, 1977; Dworkin, 1981; Steinem, 1980). MacKinnon (1991), coauthor with Dworkin of the Indianapolis antipornography ordinance, extended the harm of pornography far beyond being offended to the realm of civil rights of women. She calls for the regulation of pornography on the grounds that it plays a central role in the subordination of women.

Zillmann (1994b) wrote that "harm to the consumer can be anything from the compulsive, unmanageable consumption of erotica to the erroneous, self-serving perception of others' willingness to partake in specific sexual ventures and the adoption of callous attitudes about coercive sexual practices" (pp. 119–120). He added social harm of victimization that may stem from pornography consumption, mainly dealing with coercive sexual behaviors. However, the exposure early in life to pornography has not been shown to increase the likelihood of becoming a sex offender (Davis & McCormick, 1997).

Regardless of the identification of potential harm from pornography, First Amendment advocates include pornographic media content as protected speech. "Being offended by pornography, irrespective of the emotional intensity of this reaction, is thus considered trivial and immaterial" (Zillmann, 1994b, p. 118). He elaborated that the restraint of free speech is "deemed censorship, the perpetration of which is something akin to a crime against culture" (p. 118). Although pornography is legally distinct from obscenity, sexually explicit media content enjoys the fervent defense of the academic community and such legal entities as the American Civil Liberties Union.

Given the need to avoid First Amendment conflicts with policy development, Zillmann observed that policy related to pornography can avoid the pitfall of censorship efforts by focusing on education aimed "at correcting inappropriate sex-related perceptions and dispositions" (p. 120). Although violence and coercion seem to be the focus of public debate about the harm of pornography to the exclusion of more subtle effects, Bryant and Zillmann (2001) questioned such a limited view of the potential damage. They recommended that the list of concerns include increasing sexual callousness among adolescents and the weakening of commitment to intimate partners.

However, despite clear evidence of various forms of harm from exposure to pornography, "policy makers and social scientists, as well as their critics from various camps, have been rather confused about the relationship between facts and policy" (Zillmann, 1989b, p. 392). Many academicians and attorneys do not accept the conclusion that consumption of pornography produces negative social effects.

Even feminist spokesperson Gloria Steinem (1980) contended that erotica that depicts egalitarian heterosexual activity does not lead to sexual callousness, "a contention that clashes with metanalyses of pornography effects (e.g., Allen, D'Alessio, & Brezgel, 1995; Allen, Emmers, & Giery, 1995) that show the nonviolent erotic formats to be nearly as potent as the violent formats in fostering sexually callous dispositions toward women" (Bryant & Zillmann, 2001, p. 243).

Despite these difficulties, Zillmann (1989b, 1994b) contended that social science research about the effects of pornography offers the best foundation for formation of public policy concerning its use and availability. He noted that even the advocates of censorship depend on social science research to establish their claims of the harms of pornography. Even so, he admitted that the research on effects of pornography consumption has been so eclectic that its value to policy makers has been limited. Individual researchers remain free to select their research topics and may opt to avoid issues that engender great controversy. Existing research has tended to focus on "the least objectionable research item, the effect of 'the worst kind' of pornography (i.e., sexually violent material) on 'the worst kind' of sexual behavior (i.e., rape)" (Zillmann, 1989b, p. 399).

These shortcomings in the formation of a consistent body of research have contributed to the lack of understanding of results and provided critics with evidence used to attack research findings. Zillmann (1994b) described two strategies that are used to counter the weight of the research evidence. First, critics claimed that the mere existence of some studies that show inconsistent results casts doubt on the antipornography findings. Zillmann (1994b) found the inconsistencies explainable and insufficient to overturn the bulk of the research evidence.

This strategy figured prominently in the aftermath of two major American governmental commissions that studied pornography and its impact. The Commission on Obscenity and Pornography began in 1970 and concluded that insufficient evidence existed to support pornography as the cause of asocial effects. Conservatives criticized the conclusions as being too liberal (Neff, 2001).

The Attorney General's Commission on Pornography was formed in 1985. Although the public reactions tended to find its conclusions too conservative (Neff, 2001), Zillmann (1994b) observed "the fact that most commissioners were ill-prepared to evaluate the merits of particular demonstrations led to conclusions that had little, if anything, to do with the available research" (p. 121). He argued that the Commission's generalization that violent pornography differs from nonviolent pornography in generating negative consequences for society is inconsistent with research findings.

The second strategy for undermining research findings as the basis for policies against pornography hinges on the lack of conclusive proof that pornography causes sexual crimes. Zillmann observed that ethical researchers could never establish such proof. "No experimenter can consider setting up conditions that would place women at risk of being raped—not to mention, that would allow rape to occur" (1994b, p. 144). Therefore, Zillmann conceded that policy decisions will never rest on a foundation with the certainty of proof. He added that society lacks an attitude of consistent opposition to pornography that would surely bring about legislative action against ready availability of such media content.

The prospect of changing attitudes seems unlikely, given the research evidence about the effects of consumption of pornography on habituation and changing preferences for erotica. Modern young people who encounter easily available erotic entertainment seem unlikely to press for its restraint in the market place. If more people were offended by the "pornographic brutalization of human sexuality" (p. 144), education about the negative impact of pornography on society might produce resistance to its availability.

Zillmann (1989b) proposed a strategy for improving the ability of social science research to assist in policy formation. He called for a policy-exploring committee to assess grievances, specify problems, and project policies. Following the reports from the first group, a social science committee would assess the research findings, ignoring policy implications of the findings. Finally, a policy-recommending group would consider the available research in proposing new policies. "The outlined procedure would generate results, however, that should be superior to recommending public policy on the basis of fickle public opinion or the views of a handful of politicians and lawyers" (p. 401).

CONCLUSION

Pornography, loosely defined as sexually explicit material, is generally legal for adult use unless it portrays children. If censorship were legal, such efforts would single out the most offensive materials and create a myriad of constitutional problems. Consequently, most sexual scientists oppose censorship of pornography (Davis & McCormick, 1997).

Research documents increased presence and increased explicitness of sexual content in movies and on television (prime time, soaps, and music videos) during the 1980s and 1990s (Huston, Wartella, & Donnerstein, 1998), as well as the rapid growth in accessing of pornography on the Internet (Koerner, 2000). Barron and Kimmel (2000) reported different levels and amounts of violence across magazines, videos, and Internet newsgroups, with the Internet content showing the most sexually violent content. In the sexually violent Internet content, males typically acted as victimizers of females.

Because of ethical constraints, research about the effects of exposure to pornography for children and teenagers is unavailable. Zillmann (2000) summarized research conclusions regarding the effects of pornography consumption. Young people, usually in their first year of college, after frequently seeing noncoercive but sexually explicit content that is readily obtainable in the market place, quickly overcome negative reactions and come to enjoy the material. However, after prolonged experiences, habituation occurs, reducing enjoyment and requiring the viewing of more unusual sexually explicit content to produce the previous levels of arousal and pleasure. This habituation fits typical paradigms of understanding sexual deviancy. People who have experienced prolonged exposure to sexually explicit content give exaggerated estimates of the frequency of occurrence in the general population of sexual activity, including such atypical sexual behavior as sadomasochism and group sex. Other effects of prolonged exposure include reduced trust in mates, increased perceptions of promiscuity as natural behavior, and tendency to believe that abstention from sexual activity endangers health. The perception of the importance of love in sexual relationships diminishes with the rise of beliefs that the best sex is attained in the absence of emotional involvement with sex partners. Prolonged exposure to sexually explicit fare leads to reduced attractiveness of marriage, family life, and having children.

Zillmann (2000) recommended additional research regarding formation of adolescents' dispositions toward sexuality, especially coercive sexuality. He called for measuring adolescents' exposure to sources of information about sexuality, such as prime time network television, cable television, and Internet sites. This exposure should be correlated with

> perceptions of and dispositions toward relevant sex-related behaviors in prepubertal children and postpubertal adolescents (e.g., sexual curiosity, perceptions and evaluations of sexuality, sexual readiness, sexual callousness, knowledge of heterosexual and homosexual orientations, conceptions of sexual pleasure, notions of gender differences in pleasure seeking, coercive inclinations to achieve sexual access) using repeated measures in yearly intervals for cross-lagged comparisons. (Zillmann, 2000, p. 44)

Zillmann elaborated that these measurements should involve personality traits, "neuroendocrine and related psychological characteristics" (p. 44), and social factors such as peer groups, subcultural groups, and family and school relationships. He also called for experimental measurement of the impact of viewing specific programs on "perceptions of, and dispositions toward, relevant sex-related behaviors in postpubertal adolescents" (p. 44). Finally, Zillmann called for measurement of selective exposure to themes with sexual orientation from a variety of types of sexually oriented media content.

Bryant and Zillmann (2001) acknowledged the difficulty, if not impossibility, of reaching consensus about sexual orientations and preferences. Instead of focusing on those ephemeral concepts, they assumed that a consensus exists about the harm of sexual coercion. They observed that the mistaken focus on sexual coercion plays into the hands of purveyors of pornography by calling for evidence that cannot be proved. Ethical and practical constraints render experimental demonstration of such harm as impossible to deliver, leaving policy decisions no alternative to drawing inferences from a relatively miniscule number of actual cases involving adolescents and children who became victims of sexual coercion.

Bryant and Zillmann assumed that sexual coercion is mediated by dispositions of sexual callousness, and they called for new approaches to defining harm from consumption of pornography, as well as to pornography per se. They questioned the emphasis of legislation on depictions of male genitalia and actual sexual penetrations. Instead, Bryant and Zillmann recommended focus on conditions under which sexual access occurs and their consequences. They were more concerned about the consequences of sexual portrayals in R- and PG13-rated movies and television shows than about the portrayals in hard core pornography. This concern stems from the greater availability to young people of these types of media content (cf. Strasburger & Donnerstein, 1999) than more explicit forms of pornography as sources of knowledge about sex and sexuality.

One inhibiting factor in whether this research will be performed involves potential negative consequences for researchers. Opposition surfaced within the academic community to the findings reported by Zillmann and Bryant (1982) regarding negative effects of prolonged exposure to nonviolent pornography. This opposition was exemplified by a series of attacks (Brannigan, 1987; Christensen, 1986, 1987; Gross, 1983; Linz & Donnerstein, 1988), not merely on the research but also on the methods and motives of the researchers. The attacks charged that the researchers were biased in interpreting their findings (Christensen, 1986; Gross, 1983), that their materials were suspect (Christensen, 1986, 1987), that they failed to compare recommended sentences for rape to actual cases (Brannigan, 1987), that they failed to report attrition rates (Brannigan, 1987), and that their findings were not replicated in subsequent research efforts (Linz & Donnerstein, 1988).

Zillmann and Bryant (1983, 1986a, 1986b, 1987a, 1987b, 1988b) aggressively responded to each of these challenges. They provided additional details of the original research, referred readers to more detailed publications about research on human sexuality, refuted charges about their being biased, answered challenges to their interpretations, defended the need for research involving human participants, and attacked the claim of null findings in other studies to be considered as disproof of actual findings. They also cited benefits to the challenges to the merits of pornography research as having "revealed weaknesses in research procedures (Byrne & Kelly, 1989; Williams, 1979), prompted clarifications, and corrected erroneous accusations" (Brannigan, 1987; Zillmann & Bryant, 1987a).

Although Zillmann and Bryant weathered the attacks on their work and their motives, such controversies could dissuade some investigators from similar risks. Zillmann (2000) pointed out that research that remains to be conducted on the effects of pornography would enable an informed exchange about issues of sexuality that are important to parents and to society. This research should be encouraged.

REFERENCES

Allen, M., D'Alessio, D., & Brezgel, K. (1995). A meta-analysis summarizing the effects of pornography. II: Aggression after exposure. *Human Communication Research, 22,* 258–283.

Allen, M., Emmers, T., & Giery, M. A. (1995). Exposure to pornography and acceptance of the rape myths. *Journal of Communication, 45,* 5–26.

American Booksellers v. Hudnut, 771 F.2d 323, 239 (7th Cir. 1986), aff'd 475 U.S. 1001 (1986).

Attorney General's Commission on Pornography. (1986, July). *Final report.* Department of Justice. Washington, DC: U.S. Government Printing Office.

Baldwin, M. (1984). The sexuality of inequality: The Minneapolis pornography ordinance. *Law and inequality, 2,* 629–653,

Baron, R. A. (1979). Heightened sexual arousal and physical aggression: An extension to females. *Journal of Research in Personality, 13,* 91–102.

Barron, M., & Kimmel, M. (2000). Sexual violence in three pornographic media: Toward a sociological explanation. *Journal of Sex Research, 37*(2), 161–168.

Black, H. C. (1990). *Black's law dictionary.* St. Paul, MN: West.

Brannigan, A. (1987). Pornography and behavior: Alternative explanations. *Journal of Communication, 37*(3), 185–189.

Brewer, J. S. (1982). A history of erotic art as illustrated in the collections of the Institute for Sex Research (The "Kinsey Institute"). In A. Hoch & H. I. Lief (Eds.), *Sexology: Sexual biology, behavior and therapy* (pp. 318–321). Amsterdam, The Netherlands: Exerpta Medica.

Brown, D., & Bryant, J. (1989). The manifest content of pornography. In D. Zillmann & J. Bryant (Eds.), *Pornography: Research advances and policy considerations* (pp. 3–24). Hillsdale, NJ: Lawrence Erlbaum Associates.

Brownmiller, S. (1975). *Against our will: Men, women, and rape.* New York: Simon & Schuster.

Bryant, J. (1985) Effects of pornography: Research findings. *Testimony to the U.S. Attorney General's Commission on Pornography.* Houston, TX.

Bryant, J., & Brown, D. (1989). Uses of pornography. In D. Zillmann & J. Bryant (Eds.), *Pornography: Research advances and policy considerations* (pp. 25–55). Hillsdale, NJ: Lawrence Erlbaum Associates.

Bryant, J., & Zillmann, D. (1996). Violence and sex in the media. In D. W. Stacks & M. B. Salwen (Eds.), *An integrated approach to communication theory and research.* Mahwah, NJ: Lawrence Erlbaum Associates.

Bryant, J., & Zillmann, D. (2001). Pornography: Models of effects on sexual deviancy. In C. D. Bryant (Ed.), *Encyclopedia of criminology and deviant behavior* (pp. 241–244). Philadelphia, PA: Brunner-Routledge.

Buchman, J. G. (1988). *Effects of repeated exposure to nonviolent erotica on attitudes toward sexual child abuse.* Unpublished doctoral dissertation, Indiana University, Bloomington, Indiana.

Burt, M. R. (1980). Cultural myths and supports for rape. *Journal of Personality and Social Psychology, 38,* 217–230.

Byrne, D., & Kelly, K. (1989). Basing legislative action on research data: Prejudice, prudence, and empirical limitations. In D. Zillmann & J. Bryant (Eds.), *Pornography: Research advances and policy considerations* (pp. 363–385). Hillsdale, NJ: Lawrence Erlbaum Associates.

Cantor, J. R., Zillmann, D., & Einsiedel, E. F. (1978). Female responses to provocation after exposure to aggressive and erotic films. *Communication Research, 5,* 395–411.

Check, J. V. P. (1985). *The effects of violent and nonviolent pornography.* Ottawa: Department of Justice of Canada.

Check, J. V. P., & Guloien, T. H. (1989). Reported proclivity for coercive sex following repeated exposure to sexually violent pornography, nonviolent dehumanizing pornography, and erotica. In D. Zillmann & J. Bryant (Eds.), *Pornography: Research advances and policy considerations* (pp. 159–184). Hillsdale, NJ: Lawrence Erlbaum Associates.

Christensen, F. (1986). Sexual callousness reexamined. *Journal of Communication, 36*(1), 174–184.

Christensen, F. (1987). Effects of pornography: The debate continues. *Journal of Communication, 37*(1), 186–187.

Clark, L., & Lewis, D. (1977). *Rape: The price of coercive sexuality.* Toronto, Canada: The Women's Press.

Commission on Obscenity and Pornography. (1970). *The report of the Commission on Obscenity and Pornography.* New York: Bantam.

Davis, C. M., & McCormick, N. B. (1997). *What sexual scientists know about ... pornography, 3*(1) [Brochure]. Society for the Scientific Study of Sexuality. Allentown, PA. Retrieved May 15, 2001, from http://www.ssc.wisc.edu/ssss/wssk_prn.htm

Donnerstein, E. (1980a). Aggressive-erotica and violence against women. *Journal of Personality and Social Psychology, 39,* 269–277.

Donnerstein, E. (1980b). Pornography and violence against women. *Annals of the New York Academy of Sciences, 347,* 277–288.

Donnerstein, E. (1984a). Effects of pornography. In D. Scott (Ed.), *Symposium on media violence and pornography: Proceedings and resource book* (pp. 78–94). Toronto, Ontario: Media Action Group.

Donnerstein, E. (1984b). Pornography: Its effect on violence against women. In N. M. Malamuth & E. Donnerstein (Eds.), *Pornography and sexual aggression* (pp. 53–81). Orlando, FL: Academic.

Donnerstein, E. (1990, April–May). Sexual violence in the media. *World Health,* 26–27.

Donnerstein, E., & Berkowitz, L. (1981). Victim reactions in aggressive erotic films as a factor in violence against women. *Journal of Personality and Social Psychology, 41,* 710–724.

Donnerstein, E., & Linz, D. (1986). Mass media sexual violence and male viewers: Current theory and research. *American Behavioral Scientist, 29,* 601–618.

Donnerstein, E., Linz, D., & Penrod, S. (1987). *The question of pornography: Research findings and policy implications.* New York: Free Press.

Dworkin, A. (1979). Pornography: The new terrorism. *New York University Review of Law and Social Change, 8,* 215–218.

Dworkin, A. (1981). *Pornography: Men possessing women.* New York: Perigee.

Fort Wayne Books, Inc. v. Indiana, 489 U.S. 62 (1989).

Gross, L. (1983). Pornography and social science research: Serious questions. *Journal of Communication, 33*(4), 107–111.

Harris, R. J. (1994). The impact of sexually explicit media. In J. Bryant & D. Zillmann (Eds.), *Media effects: Advances in theory and research* (pp. 163–211). Hillsdale, NJ: Lawrence Erlbaum Associates.

Hommel, T. (1979). Images of women in pornography and media. *New York University Review of Law and Social Change, 8,* 207–214.

Howard, J. L., Reifler, C. B., & Liptzin, M. B. (1971). Effects of exposure to pornography. In *Technical report of the commission on obscenity and pornography* (Vol. 8, pp. 97–169). Washington, DC: U.S. Government Printing Office.

Huston, A. C., Wartella, E., & Donnerstein, E. (1998, April 30). *Measuring the effects of sexual content in the media: A report to The Kaiser Family Foundation.* Retrieved May 15, 20 01, from http://www.kff.org/content/archive/1389/content.pdf

Indianapolis Code § 16-3 (q) (1984).

Jacobs, C. (1984). Patterns of violence: A feminist perspective on the regulation of pornography. *Harvard Women's Law Journal, 7,* 5–55.

Jansma, L. L., Linz, D. G., Mulac, A., & Imrich, D. J. (1997). Men's interactions with women after viewing sexually explicit films: Does degradation make a difference? *Communication Monographs, 64,* 1–24.

Kelly, K., Dawson, L., & Musialowski, D. M. (1989). Three faces of sexual explicitness: The good, the bad, and the useful. In D. Zillmann & J. Bryant (Eds.), *Pornography: Research advances and policy considerations* (pp. 57–91). Hillsdale, NJ: Lawrence Erlbaum Associates.

Kinsey, A. C., Pomeroy, W. B., & Martin, C. E. (1948). *Sexual behavior in the human male.* Philadelphia: W. B. Saunders.

Kinsey, A. C., Pomeroy, W. B., Martin, C. E., & Gebhard, P. H. (1953). *Sexual behavior in the human female.* Philadelphia: Saunders.

Koerner, B. I. (2000, March 27). AdultDex online adult-entertainment exhibition thrives. *U.S. News & World Report, 128*(12), 36.

Krafka, C., Linz, D., Donnerstein, E., & Penrod, S. (1997). Women's reactions to sexually aggressive mass media depictions. *Violence Against Women, 3*(2), 149–181.

Lederer, L. (1980). *Take back the night: Women on pornography.* New York: Morrow.

Linz, D. (1985). *Sexual violence in the media: Effects on male viewers and implications for society.* Unpublished doctoral dissertation, University of Wisconsin, Madison.

Linz, D. (1989). Exposure to sexually explicit materials and attitudes toward rape: A comparison of study results. *Journal of Sex Research, 26*(1), 50–84.

Linz, D., & Donnerstein, E. (1988). The methods and merits of pornography research. *Journal of Communication, 38*(2), 180–184.

Linz, D., & Donnerstein, E. (1989). Effects of counterinformation on rape myths. In D. Zillmann & J. Bryant (Eds.), *Pornography: Research advances and policy considerations* (pp. 259–288). Hillsdale, NJ: Lawrence Erlbaum Associates.

Linz, D., Donnerstein, E., & Adams, S. M. (1989). Physiological desensitization and judgments about female victims of violence. *Human Communication Research, 15,* 509–522.

Linz, D., Donnerstein, E., & Penrod, S. (1984). The effects of multiple exposures to filmed violence against women. *Journal of Communication, 34*(3), 130–147.

Linz, D., Donnerstein, E., & Penrod, S. (1988). Effects of long-term exposure to violent and sexually degrading depictions of women. *Journal of Personality & Social Psychology, 55,* 758–768.

Linz, D., & Malamuth, N. M. (1993). *Communication concepts 5: Pornography.* Newbury Park, CA: Sage.

Linz, D., Malamuth, N. M., & Beckett, K. (1992). Civil liberties and research on the effects of pornography. In P. Suedfeld & P. E. Tetlock (Eds.), *Psychology and social policy* (pp. 149–164). New York: Hemisphere.

Lyons, J. S., Anderson, R. L., & Larson, D. B. (1994). A systematic review of the effects of aggressive and nonaggressive pornography. In D. Zillmann, J. Bryant, & A. C. Huston, (Eds.), *Media, children, and the family: Social scientific, psychodynamic, and clinical perspectives* (pp. 271–310). Hillsdale, NJ: Lawrence Erlbaum Associates.

MacKinnon, C. (1984). Not a moral issue. *Yale Law and Policy Review, 2,* 321–345.

MacKinnon, C. (1987). *Feminism unmodified: Discourses on life and law.* Cambridge, MA & London: Harvard University Press.

MacKinnon, C. (1991). Pornography as defamation and discrimination. *Boston University Law Review, 71,* 795–802.

Malamuth, N. M. (1978, September). *Erotica, aggression and perceived appropriateness.* Paper presented at the 86th annual convention of the American Psychological Association, Toronto.

Malamuth, N. M. (1984). Aggression against women: Cultural and individual causes. In N. M. Malamuth & E. Donnerstein (Eds.), *Pornography and sexual aggression* (pp. 19–52). Orlando, FL: Academic.

Malamuth, N. M., & Billings, V. (1986). The functions and effects of pornography: Sexual communication versus feminist models in light of research findings. In J. Bryant & D. Zillmann (Eds.), *Perspectives on media effects* (pp. 83–108). Hillsdale, NJ: Lawrence Erlbaum Associates.

Malamuth, N. M., & Briere, J. (1986). Sexual violence in the media: Indirect effects on aggression against women. *Journal of Social Issues, 42,* 75–92.

Malamuth, N. M., & Ceniti, J. (1986). Repeated exposure to violent and nonviolent pornography: Likelihood of raping ratings and laboratory aggression against women. *Aggressive Behavior, 12,* 129–137.

Malamuth, N. M., & Check, J. V. P. (1980a). Penile tumescence and perceptual responses to rape as a function of victim's perceived reactions. *Journal of Applied Social Psychology, 10,* 528–547.

Malamuth, N. M., & Check, J. V. P. (1980b). Sexual arousal to rape and consenting depictions: The importance of the woman's arousal. *Journal of Abnormal Psychology, 89*(6), 763–766.

Malamuth, N. M., & Check, J. V. P. (1981). The effects of mass media exposure on acceptance of violence against women: A field experiment. *Journal of Research in Personality, 15,* 436–446.

Malamuth, N. M., & Check, J. V. P. (1983). Sexual arousal to rape depictions: Individual differences. *Journal of Abnormal Psychology, 92*(1), 55–67.

Malamuth, N. M., Heim, M., & Feshbach, S. (1980). Sexual responsiveness of college students to rape depictions: Inhibitory and disinhibitory effects. *Journal of Personality and Social Psychology, 38,* 399–408.

Mann, J., Sidman, J., & Starr, S. (1971). Effects of erotic films on sexual behavior of married couples. In *Technical report of The Commission on Obscenity and Pornography* (Vol. 8, pp. 170–254). Washington, DC: U.S. Government Printing Office.

Marshall, W. L. (1988). The use of explicit sexual stimuli by rapists, child molesters, and nonoffender males. *Journal of Sex Research, 25,* 267–288.

Miller v. California, 413 U.S. 15 (1973).

Mullin, C. R., & Linz, D. (1995). Desensitization and resensitization to violence against women: Effects of exposure to sexually violent films on judgments of domestic violence victims. *Journal of Personality and Social Psychology, 69,* 449–459.

Neff, J. (2001). Pornography: Second presidential commission report. In C. D. Bryant (Ed.), *Encyclopedia of criminology and deviant behavior* (pp. 245–247). Philadelphia, PA: Brunner-Routledge.

Paik, H., & Comstock, G. (1994). The effects of television violence on antisocial behavior: A meta-analysis. *Communication Research, 21,* 516–546.

Perse, E. M. (1994). Uses of erotica and acceptance of rape myths. *Communication Research, 21,* 488–518.

Ramirez, J., Bryant, J., & Zillmann, D. (1982). Effects of erotica on retaliatory behavior as a function of level of prior provocation. *Journal of Personality and Social Psychology, 43,* 971–978.

Rimm, M. (1995). Marketing pornography on the information superhighway: A survey of 917,410 images, descriptions, short stories, and animations downloaded 8.5 million times by consumers in over 2000 cities in forty countries, provinces, and territories. *Georgetown Law Journal,* 1849–1934.

Russell, D. E. H. (1988). Pornography and rape: A causal model. *Political Psychology, 9*(1), 41–73.

Russell, D. E. H. (1994). *Against pornography: The evidence of harm.* Berkeley, California: Russell Publications. Retrieved May 16, 20 01, from http://www.dianarussell.com/pornintro.html

Sapolsky, B. S. (1984). Arousal, affect, and the aggression-moderating effect of erotica. In N. M. Malamuth & E. Donnerstein (Eds.), *Pornography and sexual aggression* (pp. 53–81). Orlando, FL: Academic.

Sapolsky, B. S., & Zillmann, D. (1981). The effect of soft-core and hard-core erotica on provoked and unprovoked hostile behavior. *Journal of Sex Research, 17,* 319–343.

Sears, A. E. (1989). The legal case for restricting pornography. In D. Zillmann & J. Bryant (Eds.), *Pornography: Research advances and policy considerations* (pp. 323–342). Hillsdale, NJ: Lawrence Erlbaum Associates.

Slade, J. W. (1984, Summer). Violence in the hard-core pornographic film. *Journal of Communication, 34*(3), 148–163.

Smith, D. D. (1976). The social content of pornography. *Journal of Communication, 26*(1), 16–24.

Steinem, G. (1980). Erotica and pornography: A clear and present difference. In L. Lederer (Ed.), *Take back the night: Women on pornography* (pp. 35–39). New York: William Morrow.

Strasburger, V. C., & Donnerstein, E. (1999). Children, adolescents, and the media: Issues and solutions. *Pediatrics, 103,* 129–139.

Weaver, J. B. (1987). *Effects of portrayals of female sexuality and violence against women on perceptions of women.* Unpublished doctoral dissertation, University of Indiana, Bloomington.

Weaver, J. B., Masland, J. L., & Zillmann, D. (1984). Effect of erotica on young men's aesthetic perception of their female sexual partners. *Perceptual and Motor Skills, 58,* 929–930.

Webb, P. (1982). Erotic art and pornography. In M. Yaffe & E. C. Nelson (Eds.), *The influence of pornography on behavior* (pp. 80–90). London: Academic.

Weisz, M. G., & Earls, C. M. (1995). The effects of exposure to filmed sexual violence on attitudes toward rape. *Journal of Interpersonal Violence, 10*(1), 71–84.

Williams, B. (1979). *Report of the Committee on Obscenity and Film Censorship.* London: Her Majesty's Stationery Office.

Wishnoff, R. (1978). Modeling effects of explicit and nonexplicit sexual stimuli on the sexual anxiety and behavior of women. *Archives of Sexual Behavior, 7,* 455–461.

Wyer, R., Bodenhausen, G. V., & Gorman, T. F. (1985). Cognitive mediators of reactions to rape. *Journal of Personality and Social Psychology, 48,* 324–338.

Zillmann, D. (1984a). *Connections between sex and aggression.* Hillsdale, NJ: Lawrence Erlbaum Associates.

Zillmann, D. (1984b). Effects of nonviolent pornography. In D. Scott (Ed.), *Symposium on media violence and pornography: Proceedings and resource book* (pp. 95–115). Toronto, Ontario: Media Action Group.

Zillmann, D. (1986). Effects of prolonged consumption of pornography. In E. P. Mulvey & J. L. Haugaard (Eds.), *Report of the Surgeon General's workshop on pornography and public health* (pp. 98–135). Washington, DC: U.S. Public Health Service & U.S. Department of Health and Human Services.

Zillmann, D. (1989a). Effects of prolonged consumption of pornography. In D. Zillmann & J. Bryant (Eds.), *Pornography: Research advances and policy considerations* (pp. 127–157). Hillsdale, NJ: Lawrence Erlbaum Associates.

Zillmann, D. (1989b). Pornography research and public policy. In D. Zillmann & J. Bryant (Eds.), *Pornography: Research advances and policy considerations* (pp. 387–403). Hillsdale, NJ: Lawrence Erlbaum Associates.

Zillmann, D. (1994a). Erotica and family values. In D. Zillmann, J. Bryant, & A. C. Huston (Eds.), *Media, children, and the family: Social scientific, psychodynamic, and clinical perspectives* (pp. 199–213). Hillsdale, NJ: Lawrence Erlbaum Associates.

Zillmann, D. (1994b). The regulatory dilemma concerning pornography. In J. E. Wood, Jr. & D. Davis (Eds.), *Problems and conflicts between law and morality in a free society* (pp. 117–148). Waco, TX: Baylor University.

Zillmann, D. (2000). Influence of unrestrained access to erotica on adolescents' and young adults' dispositions toward sexuality. *Journal of Adolescent Health, 27*(2, Supplement 1), 41–44.

Zillmann, D., & Bryant, J. (1982). Pornography, sexual callousness, and the trivialization of rape. *Journal of Communication, 32*(4), 10–21.

Zillmann, D., & Bryant, J. (1983). Pornography and social science research: Higher moralities. *Journal of Communication, 33*(4), 111–114.

Zillmann, D., & Bryant, J. (1984). Effects of massive exposure to pornography. In N. M. Malamuth & E. Donnerstein (Eds.), *Pornography and sexual aggression* (pp. 115–138). Orlando, FL: Academic.

Zillmann, D., & Bryant, J. (1986a). Sexual callousness reexamined. *Journal of Communication, 36*(1), 184–188.

Zillmann, D., & Bryant, J. (1986b). Shifting preferences in pornography consumption. *Communication Research, 13,* 560–578.

Zillmann, D., & Bryant, J. (1987a). Effects of pornography: The debate continues. *Journal of Communication, 37*(1), 187–188.

Zillmann, D., & Bryant, J. (1987b). Pornography and behavior: Alternative explanations. *Journal of Communication, 37*(3), 185–189.

Zillmann, D., & Bryant, J. (1988a). Effect of prolonged consumption of pornography on family values. *Journal of Family Issues, 9,* 518–544.

Zillmann, D., & Bryant, J. (1988b). The methods and merits of pornography research. *Journal of Communication, 38*(2), 185–192.

Zillmann, D., & Bryant, J. (1988c). Pornography's impact on sexual satisfaction. *Journal of Applied Social Psychology, 18,* 438–453.

Zillmann, D., & Bryant, J. (Eds.). (1989). *Pornography: Research advances and policy considerations.* Hillsdale, NJ: Lawrence Erlbaum Associates.

Zillmann, D., Bryant, J., & Carveth, R. A. (1981). The effect of erotica featuring sadomasochism and bestiality on motivated intermale aggression. *Personality and Social Psychology Bulletin, 7,* 153–159.

Zillmann, D., Bryant, J., Comisky, P. W., & Medoff, N. J. (1981). Excitation and hedonic valence in the effect of erotica on motivated intermale aggression. *European Journal of Social Psychology, 11*(3), 233–252.

Zillmann, D., & Sapolsky, B. S. (1977). What mediates the effect of mild erotica on annoyance and hostile behavior in males? *Journal of Personality and Social Psychology, 35,* 587–596.

Zillmann, D., & Weaver, J. B. (1989). Pornography and men's sexual callousness toward women. In D. Zillmann & J. Bryant (Eds.), *Pornography: Research advances and policy considerations* (pp. 95–125). Hillsdale, NJ: Lawrence Erlbaum Associates.

11

Humor and Learning

Patrice A. Oppliger
LaSalle University

Education has historically been approached as a serious, almost solemn undertaking. However, trends have shifted more recently to embrace a more relaxed, informal learning environment. In the early 20th century trade journals and books began publishing anecdotal evidence on the benefits of classroom humor. It was not until the 1970s that serious psychological studies on humor's effect on learning gained prominence in academic publications. The airing of *Sesame Street* in the late 1960s was one factor that intensified academics', educators', and parents' interest in the effects of humor on learning and sparked investigations into the possible educational uses of humor in television programming.

Bryant and Zillmann (1989) reported that classroom teachers writing in professional journals "laud [humor's] pedagogical benefits and tout it as a highly useful and extremely effective teaching tool for numerous and varied learning tasks and in almost every conceivable classroom context" (p. 49). Powell and Andresen (1985) reported that by the mid-1980s over 50 papers had been published praising the value of humor in teaching. Results of empirical studies on humor and information acquisition, however, are mixed, even indicating potentially detrimental effects (for reviews see Bryant & Zillmann, 1989; Zillmann & Bryant, 1983, 1989). Zillmann pointed out important distinctions between professional trade literature (the "art") and scholarly research literature (the "science") such as the style of reporting and standards of evidence. Bryant and Zillmann (1989) expressed skepticism toward professional publications that do not undergo the scrutiny of peer review. They suggested that many popularizers of humor's benefits in the classroom overtly deny or ignore evidence contrary to their intuition or personal experiences.

The theoretical rigor of research in the area of humor and learning has improved over the years, in large part through Zillmann's work. Zillmann and various colleagues conducted a vast array of studies throughout the last three decades, investigating primary, or direct effects of humor on learning and information acquisition; secondary, or indirect effects such as classroom environment and perception of teachers, and successes and limitations of mediated educational message delivery involving humor. Using a variety of research methods, such as content analysis and experiments, Zillmann looked at humor and learning across contexts such as classrooms, textbooks, and television. This chapter is a summary of general academic and empirical research in the field. The works are organized into three sections: the general psychology behind humor's effect on learning, the specific use of humor in the classroom, and the impact on the audience of children's educational television.

PSYCHOLOGICAL STUDIES

In their investigation into the direct effects of humor on learning, Bryant and Zillmann (1989) proposed the following questions: Does teaching with humor enhance students' attention; does using humor in the classroom help children learn; and does using humor in testing lower students' anxiety? This section looks at many of the answers to questions of vigilance, cognitive processing, and relief theories found in the research.

Vigilance

Zillmann and Bryant (1989) insisted that the first objective in learning must be the attention and retention of the audience, followed by the primary objective, their acquisition of the information. Teachers often use humor in classes to alleviate boredom and to keep students alert. Although students in a classroom are captive, television viewers have the option of watching the program, changing the channel, or even turning off the set. Zillmann and Bryant argued therefore that getting and keeping attention is more important in educational television than with a live teacher.

In learning studies, vigilance is likely to be a better measurement than simple attention. Miron, Bryant, and Zillmann (2001) defined *vigilance* as sustained attention, a steady state of alertness and wakefulness. Vigilance, therefore, means more than exposure; not only is the educational program on the television or the student physically in the classroom, but eyes are on the screen or attention is focused on the teacher or teaching materials. Miron et al. (2001) analyzed the relationship between vigilance and children's learning from television programs in great detail. They concluded that producers of educational programs should construct "viewing-acting-learning" situations and include intermittent salient cues to hook back viewers whose attention has been lost.

Zillmann, Williams, Bryant, Boynton, and Wolf (1980) developed the alerting function premise, a theoretical rationale based on physiological states of attention and vigilance. The premise assumes that attention cannot be at a maximum at all times. Humor is likely to serve an alerting function, regardless of whether the humor is semantically related to the material covered. The premise predicts that the respondent will remain vigilant and alert for some time after a humor reaction, long enough to attend to an educational message that follows. Zillmann and Bryant (1983), however, concluded that not just any kind of attention-getting device will be effective. Content-free audiovisual gimmicks or displays with little meaning are unlikely to attract and sustain selective exposure as effectively as related humorous materials.

Cognitive Processing

Early evidence of a link between humor and learning was presented in a study by Duncer (1945), who found that students did significantly better on a problem-solving task after viewing a humorous clip than after viewing a neutral film or no film. Subsequent investigations, however, varied in their findings. Ziv (1988) found significantly higher objective exam scores at the end of the semester for a group that learned with humor than for a group that learned without it. Although Kaplan and Pascoe (1977) found superior recall for humorous examples in lectures, total test performance was not significantly improved by humor inclusion. Curran (1973) and Hauck and Thomas (1972) found that inclusion of humor did not help in the learning of central content. However, the latter study found that humor did facilitate the recall of incidental content. These inconsistencies in research findings may have emerged because the researchers failed to take into account possible mediating factors. The impact of humor on recall and learning may be mediated by receiver characteristics, the type of humor used, and environmental conditions.

One factor found to influence the impact of humor on learning and recall is the age of the targeted audience. Chapman and Crompton (1978) found superior information acquisition from humorous than from serious versions of educational messages for 5- and 6-year-olds. In an unpublished dissertation by Davies (1978), 8- to 11-year-olds who saw humorous versions of education programs retained more information than those who saw nonhumorous versions. In an experiment testing slightly older children, sixth and ninth graders, Curran (1973) failed to show that humorous cartoons improved retention of verbal material to a greater degree than nonhumorous visual aids or no visual aids. Terry and Woods (1975) found that third graders who took tests with humorously worded problems scored lower in math and equally as well on verbal questions as third graders who took tests without humor embellishment. They also found that humor did not significantly affect fifth graders' math performance and had mixed effects on their verbal performance. That these findings do not lead to consistent conclusions about age differences in humor's effect on learning may signify that age interacts with additional variables such as subject matter and task (e.g., recall vs. problem solving).

Zillmann and Bryant tested not only main effects of humor by age, but also investigated interaction effects between age and relatedness of humor to educational messages. They argued that "the issue of humor that is related versus humor that is unrelated to educational messages is significant: It seems to define a turning point in the effects of the involvement of humor in educational television programs for children versus for adult audiences" (Zillmann & Bryant, 1983, p. 185). In fact, they reported that selective exposure increases for child audiences, whether or not humor was semantically related to the educational material. Children are very accepting of humor that has little or no relationship to the educational material it embellishes. Adults, on the other hand, appear to attend only to well-integrated humor. Beyond simple attention, the beneficial involvement of unrelated humor also seems to be inversely related to age. Vance (1987) found that unrelated humor improved learning for children in early grades. Other research, however, demonstrates that adults are offended by unrelated humor, and therefore, unlikely to learn from it. College students, for example, are apparently not accepting of what they see as arbitrary digressions from the subject matter on the part of their teachers (Zillmann & Bryant, 1983).

Because some research studies find that humorous stimuli are more likely to be recalled than educational information when the two are presented together, it follows that unrelated humor, in particular, may be distracting and thus counterproductive to learning. Kaplan and Pascoe (1977) concluded that attention in their study was likely focused on the humorous examples, which may have distracted listeners from information presented in a nonhumorous manner. The enjoyable humorous parts were believed to preoccupy respondents, who persisted in rehearsal of the humorous information. Humor was seen as actually drawing attention away from the educational parts of the lecture, particularly when the humor is not related to the educational message. This distraction factor is of great concern to critics of educational programming such as *Sesame Street,* which integrates humor quite liberally into its lessons.

Related, or integrated humor often involves exaggeration, irony, or other distortions to make an educational point. Zillmann et al. (1984) found that humorous distortions created confusion in students in kindergarten, first grade, and fourth grade. High funniness ratings suggested that the children recognized and enjoyed the exaggerations as humor; however, instead of resolving the exaggerations, the children took the distortions as fact and answered questions accordingly. Cantor and Reilly (1979) found that well-integrated, ironic humor produced a strong learning impairment for sixth, seventh, and eighth graders.

As a follow-up, Weaver, Zillmann, and Bryant (1988) tested fourth and eighth graders to see if irony with correction would affect learning. They found that adding statements that identified and corrected the irony was not sufficient to overcome the distortion effects. Weaver et al. concluded that the vividness of the ironic images was recalled and not the verbal correction. Some scholars have set the age at which full comprehension and appreciation of irony is achieved at as high as 18 (see Bryant & Zillmann, 1989).

Relief and Arousal

According to Freudian perspective, humor serves a physiological function, helping to alleviate tension and anxiety. Klein (1992) argued that humor plays a role in alleviating stress in early childhood, which then aids in children's emotional, social, and cognitive development. Humor playfully distorts or exaggerates reality, sending a message that life is not overwhelming, and as an added bonus, that learning can be fun.

Research on humor's ability to relieve test anxiety has produced mixed results. Eighth-grade students, in a study by McMorris, Urbach, and Connor (1985), not only rated humorous items on an exam as easier than nonhumorous items, they strongly favored their inclusion on tests. Smith, Ascough, Ettinger, and Nelson (1971) reported that, although inclusion of humor increased the test scores of anxious students, the humor reduced the scores of less anxious students. Townsend and Mahoney (1981) found that humor was detrimental to highly test-anxious college students, who scored significantly lower on exams that included humor than on exams with no humor. Because of these contradictions in the research findings, Zillmann and Bryant (1983) advised educators to proceed with extreme caution: Humor is likely to hurt the performance of some, help others, and have little or no impact on the test scores of the remainder.

The notion of anxiety relief may be just a part of a larger issue of arousal level (either pleasant or unpleasant) influencing learning. Terry and Woods (1975) argued that it is the momentary arousal levels of the students that mediate the effects of humor on test performance. The pleasant feelings generated by humor can alleviate negative emotions such as anxiety. An unpublished study Bryant and Zillmann (cited in Zillmann & Bryant, 1981) found that pleasant mood states have a positive effect on learning. Those pleasant feelings, however, can also become a distraction if they are experienced at high levels. Too much arousal from humor can make it difficult for students to process information, and it becomes distracting. According to McGhee (1980), it may be only after some threshold is reached that viewers stop taking aspects of the presentation of material seriously. He explained the process in terms of a curvilinear relationship where a positive relationship between arousal and learning should exist up to a point. After this point, the effect either gradually levels off or drops quickly and becomes incompatible with learning.

On the other hand, humor may relieve so much anxiety that students become too relaxed and do not perform well. This may explain Smith et al.'s (1971) finding that students with lower anxiety tended to do poorly on humorous tests than nonhumorous tests. They concluded that the humor relieved the anxiety of the highly anxious students to a manageable level, whereas for less anxious students it reduced their anxiety to below optimal level so they were too relaxed.

Cognate Literature

In his reviews on humor and learning, Zillmann looked to cognate literature on informative speaking and persuasion to supplement the scarce research in the field. Gruner (1978) found little support for humor's facilitation of attention and learning in a review of literature on informative speeches. In one of the first investigations in the area, Taylor (1964) found no difference in learning from informative speeches with and without humor. Taylor (1971) later found that participants actually learned more from a nonhumorous than a humorous version. Other studies have likewise found no difference in learning between humorous and serious speeches (Gruner, 1967, 1970; Kennedy, 1972). The one study that did find more learning in the humorous condition (Gibb, 1964) has been criticized for employing inconsistent research methods (e.g., varying times of day). Beyond information acquisition, Gruner (1967) found no difference between speakers who did or did not use humor on evaluations of the degree to which they were expert, knowledgeable, or interesting. However, he did find higher ratings of character and likeability for humorous speakers. When humor was added to a dull speech, listeners rated the speech as more interesting and the speaker as more authoritative (Gruner, 1970).

Theorists have proposed several links between humor and persuasion. Because attention and comprehension are the first two steps in Hovland, Janis, and Kelley's (1953) sequential cognitive processing of persuasion, humor that increases attention and aids in learning can, therefore, affect attitude change. Markiewicz (1974) further argued that humor may be influential in persuasive situations by operating as a reward, with the pleasant feeling induced by humor becoming associated with the message in a classical conditioning sense. Or, he argued, it may serve as a distraction, which would prevent the formation of arguments counter to the message. A majority of studies, however, have yielded nonsignificant results. Gruner (1978) reported that studies found no differences in attitude change between humorous or satirical messages and serious ones (Gruner & Lampton, 1972; Kennedy, 1972; Kilpela, 1961; Lull, 1939; Welford, 1971). Research on advertising is excluded in the analysis.

HUMOR USE IN THE CLASSROOM

Principal cognitive elements, such as learning, have received significantly more attention than the affective dimensions of the learning process (Bryant & Zillmann, 1989). The affective, secondary, or indirect effects studied include the following: improving the classroom environment and making learning more enjoyable, enhancing teacher–student rapport, and affecting perceptions of teachers' competence and credibility. Professional educational publications praise the use of humor in the classroom; however, these conclusions often lack empirical evidence. This section reviews some of the studies on indirect effects on learning, classroom environment, and teacher evaluations. The second part of this section looks at the effects of humor in textbooks.

Teachers' Use of Humor

Rejecting classic notions of serious and formal presentations, a number of educators now advocate more lighthearted and humorous educational approaches. Bryant, Comisky, and Zillmann (1979) found that "the bulk of today's college professors have departed from a stern and strict mode of lesson presentation and have moved toward establishing new norms for pedagogy that include the incorporation of a great deal of humor in the instructional format" (p. 114). Neuliep (1991) reported that most high school teachers indicated that they use humor as a way of "putting students at ease, as an attention-getter, as a way of showing that the teacher is human, as a way to keep the class less formal, and to make learning more fun—and not as a pedagogical strategy for increasing student comprehension or learning" (p. 354).

In one of the first studies of its kind, Bryant, Comisky, et al. (1979) conducted a content analysis of lectures transcribed from seventy randomly selected college courses (seminars were excluded). They found that on average several attempts at humor were made in a 50-minute class. Only 20 percent of the teachers employed no humor whatsoever. In an unpublished follow-up study using the same methodology and coding, Bryant and Hunter (cited in Bryant & Zillmann, 1989) reported that the lectures of 80 junior high teachers used humor slightly less often than the college professors studied. Wells (1974), who observed 10 elementary school teachers and interviewed the teachers plus 60 randomly selected students, found that the teachers used humor more often in a 50-minute time period than the number of humor attempts reported in either of the Bryant and his colleagues' studies. A later examination by Neuliep (1991) reported that high school teachers used humor far fewer times than the previous research indicated. Neuliep's results, however, may not be comparable to the other findings because the teachers' self-reports were used to measure humor use.

Effects on Classroom Environment

Researchers have found a variety of indirect effects of teachers' use of humor in a classroom environment. Evidence consistently supports the assertion that the judicious use of humor in the classroom increases the students' enjoyment of learning, students' perceptions of how much they learn, and how positive they feel about the course content, the instructor, and the behaviors recommended by the course (Gorham, 1988; McGhee, 1980; Zillmann & Bryant, 1989).

According to Bryant and Zillmann (1989), many teachers define a positive classroom environment as "a setting or situation in which communication is free and open, children are stimulated and do not feel threatened, strong empathic bonds are established between teacher and student and among students, and feelings of happiness, goodwill, and the joy of learning prevail" (p. 61). It is generally believed that humor can enhance and create this positive classroom environment. Although most anecdotal evidence supports the use of humor in the classroom, Darling and Civikly (1984) warned that humor that is not judged to be open, honest, and spontaneous might be more destructive to the communicative climate than teaching without any humor. Jacobson (1984) also cautioned that the use of humor by college professors may even be met with suspicion and hostility.

Teacher–student rapport and perceived teacher immediacy have a significant influence on the classroom environment and learning. For example, a large sample of students' self-reports of teacher behavior in a study by Gorham and Christophel (1990) revealed that the number of humorous incidents recorded correlated with the frequency of the teacher's immediacy behavior such as smiling and willingness to engage in conversations outside of class. In addition, teachers' overall immediacy highly correlated with students' perceived learning outcomes. A survey of college students by Wanzer and Frymier (1999) supported a more direct connection between humor and learning. Students' perception of learning was associated with students' perception of teachers' immediacy and perceived humor use by the teachers. Students indicated that they learned more from instructors who use humor frequently and effectively.

Zillmann also investigated the types of humor that influenced teacher–student rapport and under what circumstances. He argued that classroom teachers generally agree that they can improve their rapport with a class by reducing the "personal distance" presumed to exist between "their level" and that of the students (Zillmann, 1977). Therefore, it would seem to follow that self-disparaging humor would help reduce that distance. An experimental study by Stocking and Zillmann (1976), however, found that both females and males who used self-disparaging humor scored lower on person perception scales, such as intelligence, than those who told the same story at someone else's expense. Perhaps joking about a mutually disliked victim brought student and teacher even closer together.

Students generally perceive that their teachers' use of humor is an important factor in the educational process. In a study of open-ended responses of students' considerations of teacher effectiveness, humor consistently ranked in the top 10 (see Bryant, Crane, Comisky, & Zillmann, 1980). An unpublished study by Hezel, Bryant, and Harris (reported in Zillmann & Bryant, 1983) that presented college students with lectures containing no humor, unrelated humor, related humor, or relevant humor found that being "witty" (i.e. using integrated, related, and relevant humor) appears to be a highly valued trait of teachers. Hezel et al. also reported that although teachers who use unrelated humor may be perceived as funny and likable, "only the highly witty professor was deemed motivating" (Zillmann & Bryant, 1983, p. 187). In addition, use of unrelated humor had a devastating effect on the perception of the teachers' intelligence.

Bryant, Crane, and associates (1980) and Darling and Civikly (1984) investigated students' perceptions of male and female teachers' use of humor. Bryant, Crane, et al. (1980) had undergraduates tape-record a teacher's lecture and evaluate the teacher on items such as intelligence and confidence. Analysis revealed a positive correlation between teachers' use of humor and students' evaluation of the teachers; however, findings differed for male and female professors. Although no definite conclusions were drawn, male professors who frequently used humor were rated as being more appealing, better at presenting the material, and better teachers in general than female teachers who used humor. Although students may expect joking from a male professor, Bryant, Crane, et al. reasoned that females' use of humor may have violated sex-stereotyped expectations. An experiment by Darling and Civikly (1984), in which students heard a tape-recording of either a male or female professor using either aggressive or playful humor, likewise found that students held sex-typed expectations of teachers. The researchers argued that female teachers, traditionally seen as nurturing, were penalized for breaking social norms and using aggressive or hostile humor. Male teachers, who are expected to behave in a domineering manner, were rated higher when they used aggressive humor than when they used playful or silly humor. In sharp opposition, the Bryant, Crane and associates study found that female teachers actually benefited from using hostile humor. They reasoned that the use of hostile humor granted females a sense of assertiveness and authority, whereas the use of nonhostile humor by female teachers may have reinforced the stereotype of women as timid and unsure of themselves. Clearly more research needs to be done in the area of teachers' sex and use of humor.

Davies and Apter (1980) argued that beyond immediate information recall, humor may have more long-term, indirect effects such as motivating children to work harder and longer. Ware and Williams (1974) found that teacher qualities such as being humorous were especially effective in stimulating students' desire to learn more about the subject matter. In a survey of students' perception of their teachers' use of humor, Wanzer and Frymier (1999) found self-report attitudes of students toward course content and instructor correlated with their behavioral intent to take another related course or another course with that instructor.

Humor in Textbooks

Innovations in education in the 1960s lead to "open" classrooms and student power. However, the mid-1970s reverted to a back-to-basics movement. Critics called for academic accountability and an assessment of the "education by entertainment" trend (Bryant, Gula, & Zillmann, 1980). One strategy to accomplish these ends was to investigate the practice of including cartoons and other humorous material in textbooks. Not only is humor prevalent in lectures and classroom interactions between teachers and students, but it appears frequently in mediated forms such as textbooks. In a content analysis of 90 randomly selected basic communication textbooks, Bryant, Gula, et al. (1980) found a great deal of humor, which they judged to be used to teach rather than merely to attract the reader. Most humor was harmless, innocent, or nonsense humor.

In an experiment by Bryant, Brown, Silberberg, and Elliot (1981), students read textbooks with no humor, moderate humor, or extensive humor and were then tested over the material. The researchers found there was no significant improvement in test performance in either humor text condition over the no-humor condition. The inclusion of cartoons likewise had no appreciable effect on information acquisition. The most pronounced effect of the use of humorous illustrations was on measures of book appeal, but only when the educational material was easy. When humorous illustrations are employed with more difficult material, increased humor has a less pronounced effect on appeal. In addition, students who read textbooks that contained humor rated the authority, credibility, and believability of the textbook author lower than those who read the no-humor text. In another study, Klein, Bryant, and Zillmann (1982) recruited students to evaluate random textbook chapters on a variety of scales such as interest level, enjoyableness, credibility, and potential to encourage more reading. Results were then compared to the amount and types of humor utilized in the chapter. A regression analysis revealed that although humor was possibly related to enjoyment, there was no association between humor and interest, persuasiveness, and the capacity to motivate students. These findings seem to be in conflict with the general belief of publishers. Klein et al. (1982) concluded that although including humor makes the text more enjoyable and potentially more marketable, it suffers by reducing credibility, while adding no positive effects on learning, persuasion, interest, or motivation to read more.

HUMOR USE IN EDUCATIONAL TELEVISION

Interest in humor's effect on learning intensified with the development of educational television programming. The inclusion of humor in programs such as *Sesame Street* sparked a great deal of interest and controversy (discussed later in this section). Zillmann and his colleagues began their investigation into educational television by conducting content analyses of four popular children's programs that included a general education theme: public television's *Mister Rogers, Sesame Street,* and *The Electric Company,* and commercial television's program *Captain Kangaroo* (Bryant, Hezel, & Zillmann, 1979). They found a great deal of humor in these programs. For *Sesame Street,* nearly one third of the video and one fourth of the audio contained humor. *The Electric Company* contained an even larger proportion. Most of the humor was related somehow to the educational message.

Attention and Information Acquisition

In free-choice situations, nonentertaining educational television is likely to compete very poorly (Bryant, Zillmann, & Brown, 1983). Producers need to catch, focus, and sustain the children's attention, given the other competing choices today such as other programs, the Internet, and video games. Zillmann stressed the major differences between classroom teaching and educational television is that schools provide a captive audience. With educational television, it is much more critical to be able to attract and hold an audience who is free to choose, while still being concerned with the acquisition of educational information and a relaxed and joyful learning environment. Zillmann et al. (1980) claimed that humor can help those not-so-eager students who, if humor were not offered, would turn to another program. When humor is offered, these students are likely to process educational messages while waiting for another episode of fun and laughter to appear.

Wakshlag, Day, and Zillmann (1981) studied selective exposure to educational programs containing either no humor, humor slow pace, humor intermediate pace, or humor fast pace. The results indicated that educational programs without humor are likely to do very poorly in competition with similar educational programs with humor. Distribution of humorous episodes had a strong influence on program selection. The findings revealed a linear increase in attention with the pace of humorous insets. Rapid fire of short bursts of humorous stimuli appears to be the most effective. Wakshlag et al. (1981) argued that "as long as exposure alone is the objective, there seems to be no limit to the projected relationship" (p. 32).

Conflict Over Humor Inclusion

Whereas step one of humorous educational television's effects on learning, attracting an audience, is well established, step two, getting the message across is quite controversial. Critics claim that children will tune into programs that provide a high degree of immediate gratification, and therefore heavy use of humor will produce long-term motivational consequences (Zillmann & Bryant, 1981). In other words, viewers will become spoiled and expect all educational material to be entertaining. Educational programs without humor become "unrewarding" and, even if they stay tuned, viewers may attend less to the educational portions. The distraction rationale predicts that humor will interfere not only with attention, but more directly with concentration.

Critics also claim that the rapid-fire tempo of television programs like *Sesame Street* even shortens the attention span of young children. Singer and Singer (1979) argued that psychologists who have been investigating television have become concerned about the ways in which television's rapid-fire delivery may be affecting young children's capacities for imagination and reflective thought. The development of young children's imaginative skills, according to the Singers, requires that they periodically shift their attention away from a rich visual environment such as television and assimilate new information slowly. Zillmann et al. (1980) explained that humor may interfere with learning because instead of rehearsing the educational information, viewers are preoccupied with the pleasant rehearsal of humorous stimuli.

Two other features of shows like *Sesame Street* that are considered drawbacks to some critics are the playful nature of the program and the passive nature of the medium. McGhee (1980) argued that an individual must be in a more serious frame of mind for permanent cognitive change to occur. The creation of a playful frame of mind might interfere with the acquisition of novel information mainly because it would make any rehearsal requiring effort seem like work and, therefore, undesirable. Salomon (1984) proposed that because television is perceived as easier to process than other media, subject matter is consequently processed more superficially. This superficial processing leads to poorer learning because of this passive attention.

In response to the criticism of programs such as *Sesame Street,* several scholars defend humor use in educational television. Zillmann et al. (1980) strongly supported the view that humor in educational programs for children, even if the humorous stimuli are rather arbitrarily interspersed, increases attention and learning. They claimed that attention elevated to higher levels through the use of humor will remain elevated for at least a portion of the subsequent educational message and thus facilitate learning. Evidence countering distraction concerns, that humor will prevent vital rehearsal processes needed to process new information, can be found in studies discussed early in this chapter by Davies and Apter (1980) and Chapman and Crompton (1978). Not only did these studies find that the inclusion of humor did not impair learning, but information acquisition from the humorous version was actually superior to the nonhumorous version. Even more to the point, Bryant and Zillmann (1989) found that the use of humor significantly increased recall only for those test items based on humorous examples.

Wakshlag and associates (1981) argued that as long as humor is used reasonably, there are no ill effects on learning. If humor is uncritically dispensed or takes up too much of the program, however, it is likely to nullify any beneficial effects on learning and eventually interfere to the detriment of learning. In addition, McGhee (1980) argued that if other aspects of the program begin to become too mentally taxing, humor might provide a period of rest before returning one's attention to the more substantive content of the program.

Aside from the conflict, early studies of *Sesame Street* (see Lesser, 1974) revealed that among disadvantaged children who watched educational television at home, those who gained the most had mothers who often watched *Sesame Street* with them and talked about it with them. One benefit of adding humor to educational television, more than helping with the attention and retention of information, may be that parents and older siblings will be motivated to watch with the child, thus increasing the likelihood that serious learning will take place.

LIMITATIONS AND CONCERNS

Drawing conclusions from the past literature on humor and learning is a challenging task. Experimental studies that use audio or video taped presentations to control for extraneous variables sacrifice external validity in favor of internal validity, whereas more realistic, uncontrolled studies lack the ability to support causal links. Legitimate comparisons of results from studies that use different methods and measurement instruments is another difficulty. Researchers struggle to quantify and evaluate "learning," and many do not differentiate between comprehension and simple recall. The range of measurement used from study to study is also problematic. For example, Gorham and Christophel (1990) and Wanzer and Frymier (1999) employed self-report measures of how much the students thought they learned, whereas other researchers used final exams from actual courses, standardized achievement tests, or tests constructed specifically for the experiment.

CONCLUSIONS

The body of empirical research on humor and learning offers sound advice for educators, with the goal of making teaching with humor more successful and more enjoyable. Although research results on the direct effect of humor on learning are mixed, humor use appears to be beneficial in the classroom. As long as it is somewhat related to the educational material and is not deemed offensive by students, humor is instrumental in creating a positive teacher–student rapport and creating a positive learning environment. Humor can also be an effective attention-getting device in educational television programs when used judiciously. As Zillmann and Bryant repeatedly advised, successful use depends on employing the proper type of humor, under the proper conditions, at the proper time, and with properly motivated and receptive students.

REFERENCES

Bryant, J., Brown, D., Silberberg, A. R., & Elliot, S. M. (1981). Effects of humorous illustration in college textbooks. *Human Communication Research, 8*(1), 43–57.

Bryant, J., Comisky, P., & Zillmann, D. (1979). Teachers' humor in the college classroom. *Communication Education, 28,* 110–118.

Bryant, J., Crane, J. S., Comisky, P. W., & Zillmann, D. (1980). Relationship between college teachers' use of humor in the classroom and students' evaluations of their teachers. *Journal of Educational Psychology, 72,* 511–519.

Bryant, J., Gula, J., & Zillmann, D. (1980). Humor in communication textbooks. *Communication Education, 29,* 125–134.

Bryant, J., Hezel, R., & Zillmann, D. (1979). Humor in children's educational television. *Communication Education, 28,* 49–59.

Bryant, J., & Zillmann, D. (1989). Using humor to promote learning in the classroom. In P. E. McGhee (Ed.), *Humor and children's development: A guide to practical applications* (pp. 49–78). New York, NY: Haworth Press.

Bryant, J., Zillmann, D., & Brown, D. (1983). Entertainment features in children's educational television: Effects on attention and information acquisition. In J. Bryant & D. R. Anderson (Eds.), *Children's understanding of television: Research on attention and comprehension* (pp. 221–240). New York: Academic.

Cantor, J., & Reilly, S. (1979, August). *Jocular language style and relevant humor in educational messages*. Paper presented at the Second International Conference on Humor, Los Angeles.

Chapman, A. J., & Crompton, P. (1978). Humorous presentations of materials and presentations of humorous materials. In M. M. Gruneberg, P. E. Morris, & R. N. Sykes (Eds.), *Practical aspects of memory* (pp. 84–92). London: Academic.

Curran, F. W. (1973). *A developmental study of cartoon humor appreciation and its use in facilitating learning.* Unpublished doctoral dissertation, Catholic University of America.

Darling, A., & Civikly, J. M. (1984). The effect of teacher humor on classroom climate. *Proceedings of the Tenth International Conference on Improving University Teaching* (pp. 788–806). College Park, MD: University of Maryland.

Davies, A. P. (1978). *The importance of humour in childhood learning.* Unpublished Doctoral Dissertation, University of Wales.

Davies, A. P., & Apter, M. J. (1980). Humour and it's effect on learning in children. In P. E. McGhee & A. J. Chapman (Eds.), *Children's humour* (pp. 237–253). Chichester, England: Wiley.

Duncker, K. (1945). On problem solving. *Psychological Monographs, 58.*

Gibb, J. D. (1964). *An experimental comparison of the humorous lecture and nonhumorous lecture in informative speaking.* Unpublished master's thesis, University of Utah.

Gorham, J. (1988). The relationship between verbal teacher immediacy behavior and student learning. *Communication Education, 37,* 40–53.

Gorham, J., & Christophel, D. M. (1990). The relationship of teacher's use of humor in the classroom to immediacy and student learning. *Communication Education, 39*(1), 46–62.

Gruner, C. R. (1967). Effect of humor on speaker ethos and audience information gain. *Journal of Communication, 17,* 228–233.

Gruner, C. R. (1970). The effect of humor in dull and interesting informative speeches. *Central States Speech Journal, 21,* 160–166.

Gruner, C. R. (1978). *Understanding laughter: The workings of wit & humor.* Chicago: Nelson-Hall.

Gruner, C. R., & Lampton, W. E. (1972). Effects of including humorous material in a persuasive sermon. *Southern Speech Communication Journal, 38,* 188–196.

Hauck, W. E., & Thomas, J. W. (1972). The relationship of humor to intelligence, creativity, and intentional and incidental learning. *Journal of Experimental Education, 40*(4), 52–55.

Hovland, C. I., Janis, I. L., & Kelley, H. H. (1953). *Communication and persuasion.* New Haven, CT: Yale University Press.

Jacobson, R. L. (1984, July 11). Use of humor by college teachers found to stir suspicion and hostility. *The Chronicle of Higher Education,* p. 25.

Kaplan, R., & Pascoe, G. (1977). Humorous lectures and humorous examples. *Journal of Educational Psychology, 69,* 61–65.

Kennedy, A. J. (1972). *An experimental study of the effect of humorous message content upon ethos and persuasiveness.* Unpublished doctoral dissertation, University of Michigan.

Kilpela, D. E. (1961). *An experimental study of the effects of humor on persuasion.* Unpublished master's thesis, Wayne State University.

Klein, A. (1992). Storybook humor and early development. *Childhood Education, 68,* 213–217.

Klein, D. M., Bryant, J., & Zillmann, D. (1982). Relationship between humor in introductory textbooks and students' evaluations of the texts' appeal and effectiveness. *Psychological Reports, 50,* 235–241.

Lesser, G. (1974). *Children and television: Lessons from Sesame Street.* New York: Random House.

Lull, P. E. (1939). The effects of humor in persuasive speech. *Speech Monographs, 7,* 36–40.

Markiewicz, D. (1974). Effects of humor on persuasion. *Sociometry, 37,* 407–422.

McGhee, P. E. (1980). Toward the integration of entertainment and educational functions of television: The role of humor. In P. H. Tannenbaum (Ed.), *The entertainment functions of television* (pp. 183–208). Hillsdale, NJ: Lawrence Erlbaum Associates.

McMorris, R. F., Urbach, S. L., & Connor, M. C. (1985). Effects of incorporating humor in test items. *Journal of Educational Measurement, 22,* 147–155.

Miron, D., Bryant, J., & Zillmann, D. (2001). Creating vigilance for better learning from television. In D. G. Singer & J. L. Singer (Eds.), *Handbook of children and the media* (pp. 153–181). Thousand Oaks, CA: Sage.

Neuliep, J. W. (1991). An examination of the content of high school teachers' humor in the classroom and the development of an inductively derived taxonomy of classroom humor. *Communication Education, 40,* 343–355.

Powell, J. P., & Andresen, L. W. (1985). Humour and teaching in higher education. *Studies in Higher Education, 10*(1), 79–90.

Salomon, G. (1984). Television is "easy" and print is "tough:" The differential investment of mental effort in learning as a function of perceptions and attributions. *Journal of Educational Psychology, 76,* 647–658.

Singer, J. L., & Singer, D. G. (1979, March). Come back, Mister Rogers, come back. *Psychology Today,* pp. 56, 59–60.

Smith, R. E., Ascough, J. C., Ettinger, R. F., & Nelson, D. A. (1971). Humor, anxiety, and task performance. *Journal of Personality and Social Psychology, 19,* 243–246.

Stocking, H., & Zillmann, D. (1976). Effects of humorous disparagement of self, friend, and enemy. *Psychological Reports, 39,* 445–461.

Taylor, P. M. (1964). Research reports: The effectiveness of humor in informative speaking. *Central States Speech Journal, 15,* 295–296.

Taylor, P. M. (1971). *The role of listener-defined supportive humor in speeches of information.* Unpublished doctoral dissertation, University of Indiana.

Terry, R. L., & Woods, M. E. (1975). Effects of humor on the test performance of elementary school children. *Psychology in the Schools, 12,* 182–185.

Townsend, M. A. R., & Mahoney, P. (1981). Humor and anxiety: Effects on class test performance. *Psychology in the Schools, 12,* 182–185.

Vance, C. M. (1987). A comparative study on the use of humor in the design of instruction. *Instructional Science, 16*(1), 79–100.

Wakshlag, J. J., Day, K. D., & Zillmann, D. (1981). Selective exposure to educational television programs as a function of differently paced humorous inserts. *Journal of Educational Psychology, 73,* 27–32.

Wanzer, M. B., & Frymier, A. B. (1999). The relationship between student perceptions of instructor humor and students' reports of learning. *Communication Education, 48,* 48–62.

Ware, J., & Williams, R. (1974). Studies on the effects of content and manner of lecture presentations. *Behavior Today, 5,* 120.

Weaver, J., Zillmann, D., & Bryant, J. (1988). Effects of humorous distortions on children's learning from educational television: Further evidence. *Communication Education, 37,* 181–187.

Welford, T. W. (1971). *An experimental study of the effectiveness of humor used as a refutational device.* Unpublished doctoral disseration, Louisiana State University.

Wells, D. A. (1974). *The relationship between the humor of elementary school teachers and the perception of students.* Unpublished doctoral dissertation, United States International University.

Zillmann, D. (1977). Humour and communication: Introduction to symposium. In A. J. Chapman & H. C. Foot (Eds.), *It's a funny thing, humour* (pp. 291–301). Oxford, England: Pergmon.

Zillmann, D., & Bryant, J. (1981). Uses and effects of humor in educational television. In J. Baggaley (Ed.), *Proceedings of the Third International Conference on Experimental Research in Televised Instruction* (pp. 81–103). St. John's: Memorial University of Newfoundland.

Zillmann, D., & Bryant, J. (1983). Uses and effects of humor in educational ventures. In P. E. McGhee & J. H. Goldstein (Eds.), *Handbook of humor research: Vol. 2. Applied* studies(pp. 173–193). New York: Springer-Verlag.

Zillmann, D., & Bryant, J. (1989). Guidelines for the effective use of humor in children's educational television programs. In P. E. McGhee (Ed.), *Humor and children's development: A guide to practical applications* (pp. 201–221). New York, NY: Haworth.

Zillmann, D., Masland, J. L., Weaver, J. B., Lacey, L. A., Jacobs, N. E., Dow, J. H., Klein, C. A., & Banker, S. R. (1984). Effects of humorous distortions on children's learning from educational television. *Journal of Educational Psychology, 76,* 802–812.

Zillmann, D., Williams, B. R., Bryant, J., Boynton, K. R., & Wolf, M. A. (1980). Acquisition of information from educational television programs as a function of differently paced humorous inserts. *Journal of Educational Psychology, 72,* 170–180.

Ziv, A. (1988). Teaching and learning with humor: Experiment and replication. *Journal of Experimental Education, 57,* 5–15.

12

News Features and Learning

S. Shyam Sundar
Pennsylvania State University

We do not often think of news in emotional terms. As a media genre, news is conceptualized primarily as a vehicle for information transmission. Therefore, much of journalism and communication research has focused on the cognitive consequences of news presentations, with very little attention paid to affective considerations. Dolf Zillmann was among the first to problematize the involvement of emotion in processing news stimuli from the media. He has brought to the fore the mediating role played by emotion in profoundly shaping how, and even what, we learn from the news.

Certain features of news presentation lend themselves to clear-cut examination of the emotional potential of news information and its consequent impact on memory and impression formation. Chief among them is the journalistic practice of exemplification. News writing, especially in the last 30 years, has tended toward illustrating, rather than merely stating, positions and circumstances in the news. In order to embed their stories with "human interest," reporters routinely go out of their way to seek personal testimonials that give voice to the raw facts and numbers in their stories. So much so that many, if not most, hard-news stories these days prominently feature case-history information, much like feature stories of yore. Practitioners assume that exemplification is inherently appealing to the consumer and therefore a necessary part of journalistic storytelling, especially in this age of rampant tabloidization and other competitive forces in the media marketplace. What they seem to overlook in the process, however, are the potential consequence of this practice on news receivers' understanding of the story.

Zillmann recognized early on that exemplars (or people's experiences, often within direct quotes) have a strong emotional appeal with the reader, especially in comparison to baserates (i.e., hard facts and numerical/statistical information) in the story. Clearly, news receivers can better relate to information conveyed through stories of other people rather than information conveyed via broad statements about the population. This bias in processing would not be much of an issue if news stories always featured exemplars that accurately reflected the baserates. But the definition of news is such that exemplars more often than not represent the fringes instead of the center of the population distribution. The man-bites-dog paradigm of news dictates that stories dwell on that which is unique and unusual. For example, if a news story is written around a new statistical finding that as much as 20% of marriages end in divorce within 5 years, the reporter would cite this numerical information (i.e., the baserate) but go on to illustrate this story with predominantly, if not exclusively, those cases wherein the marriage was terminated within 5 years (i.e., exemplars), because that is the *raison d'etre* of the story. (The 80% represents the typical; the 20% is the atypical case, hence it's news). Given the relatively greater emotional appeal of exemplifying information, news receivers are likely to ignore or forget the baserate and end up with an exaggerated sense of failed marriages. This is because most, if not all, of the exemplars that come to their mind are of divorce cases, vividly illustrated by the reporter. If the reporter had balanced the exemplar distribution better and included some cases of couples whose marriages worked fine beyond the 5-year mark, then the story might contribute to greater perceptual accuracy in the minds of news receivers (i.e., closer to the 20:80 baserate). This is the central argument made by exemplification theory (Zillmann, 1999).

Empirical research on exemplification and related news features has concentrated on three areas of exemplar presentation: (1) the relative distribution of majority and minority exemplars in a news story; (2) the atypicality of exemplar selection; and (3) the vividness of exemplar descriptions. Each of these species of independent variables has been shown to affect learning from news reports via distinct, yet closely related, theoretical mechanisms (as detailed later). Unlike traditional research on cognitive aspects of news, the body of work on exemplar effects does not operationalize "learning" simply in terms of recall and recognition memory for details in stimulus news stories, but in terms of accuracy of receivers' perceptions of the issues presented in those stories.

EXEMPLAR DISTRIBUTION

At the time Zillmann began his program of research on exemplification, there was only a smattering of psychological research on the powerful influence of exemplar descriptions on impression formation. Much of this research was preoccupied with readers' seemingly curious tendency to ignore or overlook baserate information in favor of colorful exemplifications (e.g., Bar-Hillel & Fischhoff, 1981; Manis, Dovalina, Avis, & Cardoze, 1980) Almost all these experiments used a single exemplar to illustrate an issue. However, we all know that news reports often include multiple exemplars, and given the increased awareness of fairness and social responsibility in professional practice, editors frequently call on reporters to "balance" their stories by including exemplars that tell the "other side" of the story, as well. Therefore, the informational competition in news reports was no longer between baserates and exemplars (that battle was won by exemplars a long time ago) but between exemplars that represented different sides of an issue. This gave rise to a new experimental paradigm that involved presenting news reports on two-sided (rather than one-sided) issues to study participants, and ascertaining their impressions about the real-world prevalence of these two sides. The news reports contained baserate information (about population distribution of the two sides) as well as exemplars, with some exemplars representing one side and some representing the other side of the issue. This procedure not only allowed for exploration of the relative perceptual effects of baserates and exemplars, but also helped assess the relative standing of the two sides in the minds of news receivers as a function of manipulations in the distribution of exemplars depicting the two sides.

The first study that used this paradigm (Zillmann, Perkins, & Sundar, 1992) featured the issue of regaining weight after losing it in a diet program. The baserate provided was that 32.4% of all dieters who lose weight during a diet program regain it all back within a year of losing weight. This baserate information was either precise (i.e., 32.4%) or imprecise (some dieters regained all their weight back within a year) depending on the condition. However, the more important manipulation in the study pertained to distribution of exemplars in the news story. Three different versions of the story were created.

In one version, called selective exemplars, all the people cited in the story were weight-regainers. This is consistent with the journalistic practice of illustrating only the focal point of the story (which, in this case, is the fact that a vast number—nearly a third—of successful dieters regain their original weight within a year after losing it). Although 32.4% is technically a minority (by implication, the majority of successful dieters (67.6%) manage to keep their weight off past the 1-year mark), the newsworthiness of the story lies in the fact that as many as 32.4% of weight-losers regain all their weight back within a year. Therefore, reporters are likely to seek out only those dieters who regained weight and present their individual stories as part of the report.

The second version of the same news story, called *representative exemplars,* featured exemplification that was consistent with population distribution of both sides. That is, three out of nine people quoted in the story regained their weight back within a year, in keeping with the 32.4% baserate. The remaining six exemplars represented the technical majority, namely weight controllers, that is, people who managed to lose weight and keep it off beyond a year. Therefore, the exemplar distribution truly reflected the reported population proportion.

The third version of the story, mixed exemplars, flipped the exemplar distribution in the previous version and featured six exemplars who regained weight and three that managed to keep it off. Here, the focal minority is overrepresented, whereas the technical majority is underrepresented. This sometimes happens in news stories, especially when reporters attempt to pay lip-service to the "other side" by including exemplars that feature the nonfocal aspect of the story. Although this is practiced in order to give a semblance of "balance" to the story, it severely underrepresents the majority side.

Of the three versions, the dominant script in mass media is the one operationalized by selective exemplification. Losing weight by participating in a diet program is the expected norm. Regaining it all back within a year is a violation of this norm. Hence, that is the focal point of interest in the story. What selective exemplification does is not only reiterate this deviation from the expected norm but also entrench the dominant media script in the minds of readers. The redundancy engendered in presenting one exemplar after another talking about regaining their weight is therefore likely to activate the familiar construct of "things don't always work out the way they're supposed to" (or variations thereof) that is repeated over and over again in news stories. Therefore, presenting readers with numerous exemplars of weight-regaining will prime this construct, which in turn will have an undue influence on later impressions and judgments (Srull & Wyer, 1979, 1980).

This whole notion of construct accessibility was used to predict that selective aggregation of exemplars would likely result in exaggerated perceptions of incidence in weight-regaining compared to the other two types of aggregation. Moreover, it was expected that precision in baserate information, by availing itself in short-term memory, would moderate this effect in the immediate aftermath of reading the news story. However, given psychological evidence of poor retention of baserates in the long run, the exemplification effect would be stronger after a period of time.

In a 2 × 3 × 2 between-participants experiment, all respondents ($N=213$) read one of the six aforementioned versions of the diet story and were asked to provide, either immediately or 2 weeks later, their personal estimation of the percentage of weight regainers. Results supported the basic hypothesis: Those who read the selective exemplification version of the news story significantly overestimated the percentage of weight regainers, when asked to provide their estimates immediately after reading the story. Study participants in this condition thought that, on average, as many as 75% of dieters who lost weight regained it within a year (see row corresponding to "Immediate," i.e. first row, in Table 12.1).

TABLE 12.1

Percentage Estimates of Weight Regainers as a Function of Three types of Exemplar Distribution and Time of Assessment of Respondents' Issue Perceptions

	Exemplar Distribution Conditions[1]			Exemplar Combined
Time of Assessment	Selective	Mixed	Representative	
Immediate	75.0^{aA}	62.3^{bA}	58.5^{bA}	65.2^{A}
Delayed[2]	70.2^{aA}	69.2^{aA}	73.8^{aB}	71.2^{B}
Time Combined	73.1^{a}	65.1^{b}	65.2^{b}	

Note. Smaller scores indicate greater accuracy of estimates. Comparisons between means are orthogonal only. Comparisons across exemplar distributions (horizontal) are specified by lowercase superscripts. Comparisons across time of assessment (vertical) are specified by uppercase superscripts. Means having different superscripts differ at $p < 0.05$ by mutliple t or F test. Data, first published in "Impression-Formation Effects of Printed News Varying in Descriptive Precision and Exemplifications" by D. Zillmann, J. W. Perkins, and S. S. Sundar, 1992, *Medienpsychologie: Zeitschrift für Individual- und Massenkommunikation, 4,* 168–185, 239–240. Reprinted with permission.

[1]Selective refers to an exemplar distribution that is entirely consistent with the minority of cases that define the focal point of a news story. Representative refers to an exemplar distribution that correctly represents the proportions of minority and majority cases in the population. Mixed refers to an exemplar distribution that addresses both minority and majority cases, but does so in a selective, nonrepresentative fashion.

[2]Delayed estimates were made 14 days after news exposure.

The greatest perceptual accuracy was achieved by respondents exposed to representative exemplification, with those in the mixed condition reporting percentages in between. However, there was no significant interaction between the exemplification variable and the baserate precision variable, although study participants given the precise baserate were significantly more accurate than those given the imprecise baserate information. Also, contrary to expectation, the exemplification effect did not become stronger over time. Instead, it grew weaker, and a posttest suggested that respondents may have regressed to initially held beliefs (when the dependent measure was administered to respondents from the same population who had not taken part in the experiment, the average estimate was 72%). Therefore, the exemplification effect appeared to be a short-term effect, at least with issues about which news recipients have previously held beliefs (Zillmann, Perkins, & Sundar, 1992). Brosius and Bathelt (1994) reported much the same findings in their experiments with print and radio news stories, but found that when the issue presented in the news story was not a topic on which respondents had prior beliefs, the over-time effect was one of maintenance or regression toward guessing (50%).

Zillmann, Gibson, Sundar, and Perkins (1996) replicated the first study with two experiments, this time using a topic about which study participants would have little or no prior knowledge: the economics of family farms. All respondents read a news story that had two baserates embedded in it: One-third of all family farms in America lose money; in 70% of the cases the banks were largely responsible for the farmers' financial woes. The exemplar distributions were the same as before: In the selective condition, all nine exemplars were farmers who lost money and blamed the banks for it. The representative condition featured exemplar distribution consistent with baserate (i.e., three out of nine farmers losing money and six of them making money), whereas the mixed condition, labeled *blended exemplification,* featured six family farmers who were losing money and three who were making a profit.

The results supported the initial hypothesis about selective exemplification leading to gross exaggeration of the number of family farms losing money (as well as the degree of bankers' culpability in the loss), with representative exemplification contributing to the most accurate perceptions, and blended exemplification falling in between the two. Moreover, these differences as a function of exemplification were maintained over time, thus lending some support to the notion of chronic accessibility. The construct accessed here is one of news value: It wouldn't make news if there weren't a considerable number of family farms losing money. (After all, the majority of family farms making money wouldn't be news because that's what farms—or for that matter all businesses—are expected to do). The redundancy of case histories pertaining to family farms losing money can therefore be said to aid chronic accessibility of the previously mentioned construct (Zillmann & Brosius, 2000). When presented with the dependent measure asking them to estimate the percentage of failing farms, study participants are more likely to have remembered reading numerous cases of farmers losing money than of farmers making money (given the exaggerated exemplification of the former), and therefore overestimated the prevalence of failing farms.

Thus, the effect of exemplar distribution on news receivers' perception of frequency distribution of the two sides of an issue may best be explained in terms of cognitive mechanisms related to priming and accessibility, particularly chronic accessibility. The evidence gathered so far has clear implications for journalistic practice, especially in terms of sourcing patterns in news reports. It's not enough any more to simply feature different viewpoints about an issue in a news story. It's critically important to represent the various sides of the issues proportionally by devoting the appropriate number of exemplars to represent each side, in keeping with baserate information. As a result, this research serves to redefine fundamental notions of balance and fairness in journalistic practice.

EXEMPLAR ATYPICALITY

A related line of research on exemplification effects makes us question an even more fundamental aspect of journalism, namely the definition of news value. As we all know, news value is determined by the unusualness of a case or occurrence. Therefore, by definition, normal cases do not make news. News reports are full of nonroutine, out-of-the-ordinary exemplars. A normal day in India would not make news in the U.S. media, but a series of earthquakes or a major hijacking situation would. Therefore, the only information about India that American news media users get would be about nonnormal events occurring in that country. The big question is whether everyday consumers of news recognize that these occurrences have made it to the news because they are unusual, and that if a riot happened every day, it wouldn't make the news. In other words, do news receivers factor in the atypicality of events and people portrayed in the news while making inferences about social issues in particular and while perceiving reality in general?

If early social-psychology research is any indication, the answer would have to be resoundingly negative. The issue outlined earlier is one of sampling, specifically the ability to recognize the limitations associated with the small size and unrepresentativeness of the kinds of samples (of exemplars) presented in news reports. Tversky and Kahneman (1971) have clearly demonstrated people's lack of sensitivity to sample-size considerations. Empirical evidence indicates that people tend not to seek out larger samples even when additional information is readily available (Borgida & Nisbett, 1977). They are also insufficiently sensitive to the possibility of sample bias (Ross, Amabile, & Steinmetz, 1977) and to the superiority of random samples over samples for which the basis of selection is unspecified (Nisbett & Borgida, 1975). More importantly, they are known to let their sense of frequency estimation be thrown off by extreme examples or misled by irrelevant characteristics of the sample (Rothbart, Fulero, Jensen, Howard, & Birrell, 1978).

Even when given information about a sample's typicality or atypicality, people will often fail to use it. For example, Hamill, Wilson, and Nisbett (1980) conducted a study wherein they exposed study participants to a colorful account of a woman who was a classic case of welfare abuse, in that she was on welfare for many years without ever trying to improve her situation, instead worsening it by marrying many men and giving birth to children every other year. This case history was given to respondents either with a warning that it was not typical of welfare recipients, (whose average stay on welfare lasted only two years, or that this particular case was highly typical of the population of welfare recipients, or without any information about the typicality of the case. Across conditions, it was found that respondents disregarded baserate information (about sample typicality) and let their judgment be overwhelmingly swayed by this single woman's tale, and proceeded to generalize her case to the rest of the population of welfare recipients.

This has obvious implications for learning from news stories. Given that news stories are full of atypical exemplars, recipients of these stories are likely to have a skewed perception of issues presented in them. For example, if a magazine report featured an exemplar of a carjacking victim who died as a result of the crime, this particular victim's circumstance (including the tragic outcome) would bear heavily on readers' later estimates of the prevalence of violent carjackings, regardless of the nature of baserate information accompanying the report. This prediction was borne out by Gibson and Zillmann (1993). They exposed study participants to a news magazine story with baserate information about the percentages of carjacking victims who experienced minimal, minor, severe and extreme outcomes (75%, 21%, 3.8%, and 0.2% respectively) and exemplified it with two exemplars representing one of the four outcome categories. Study participants who read about the extreme-outcome exemplars (i.e., death of carjacking victim) gave significantly higher estimates of the prevalence of carjackings with a deadly outcome and significantly lower estimates of injury-free carjackings compared to their counterparts in the other three conditions. This effect was even more pronounced after a week. Respondents exposed to exemplars portraying deadly carjackings, compared to respondents in the other three conditions, were even more likely to exaggerate their estimates of carjacking after a period of time, showing a kind of sleeper effect. This may be explained by the strong memory trace left by the sensational exemplars, concomitant with the gradually weakening over time of the already minimal effect of baserate information (Zillmann & Brosius, 2000).

The powerful effect of atypical exemplars has been shown to extend even to moral assessment of social realities. The emotional testimony of one miscreant detailing the mitigating circumstances that led to his/her transgression may have the effect of swaying people, especially jurors, toward leniency for the criminal act. American talk-show host Oprah Winfrey is renowned for featuring delinquents in her television program and lending a sympathetic ear to their tales about how their abusive childhood experiences predisposed them to commit crimes in their adult life. The psychological effects of listening to this so-called "abuse excuse" (Dershowitz, 1994) was empirically tested by Hill and Zillmann (1999), who showed study participants an episode of *Oprah* involving emotional testimony from either a mother who murdered her 6-year-old son's alleged molester or a father who stopped making child support payments due to alleged difficulties with his ex-wife. Respondents were then asked by purportedly independent researcher to recommend incarceration sentences for a variety of unrelated crimes. Compared to those in the no-exposure control condition, these respondents gave significantly lower jail sentences, perhaps triggered by the leniency they felt for the criminal in the *Oprah* program they witnessed. In other words, they seemed to have generalized the circumstances surrounding the crime committed by the person they saw on *Oprah* to other criminals as well.

News receivers' tendency to generalize from small samples of exemplars was demonstrated dramatically in an experiment conducted by Gan, Hill,

Pschernig, and Zillmann (1996). Participants were exposed to a television news report about the 1994 massacre in which an Israeli settler gunned down Islamic worshippers in a Hebron mosque, either without any exemplification (None), or with five exemplars hailing the act (Endorse), or with quotes from Israelis condemning the act (Condemn), or with a combination of endorsing and condemning exemplars. The participants were then asked to estimate the percentage of Israelis who, in their opinion, favor the pursuit of peace and the percentage who favor a violent resolution to the Middle-East crisis. As can be seen in Fig. 12.1, the five endorsers (in the Endorse condition) seemed to have completely swayed viewers' perception of Israeli public opinion.

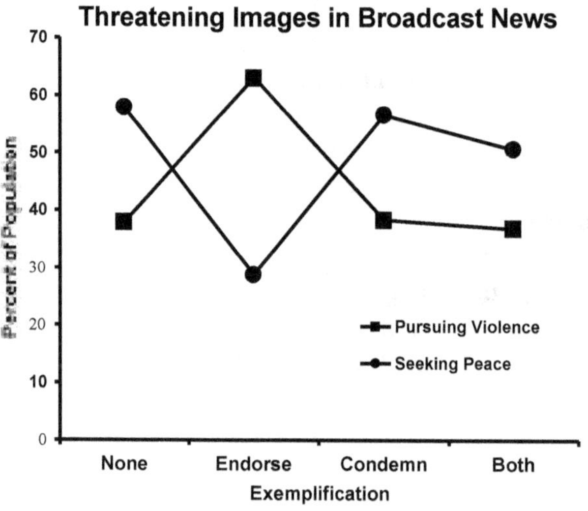

Fig. 12.1. Estimates of Israelis seeking peace with the Palestinians versus those pursuing oppression by violent means as a function of newscasts featuring interviews with Israeli extremists celebrating the Hebron massacre of Palestinian worshippers in a mosque (Endorse), with Israelis deploring the massacre as a heinous crime against humanity (Condemn), or with exemplars of both sides (Both).

Note. Data first published in "The Hebron Massacre, Selective Reports of Jewish Reactions, and Perceptions of Volatility in Israel" by S. Gan, J. R. Hill, E. Pschernig, and D. Zillmann, 1996, *Journal of Broadcasting and Electronic Media, 40,* 122–131. Copyright 1996 by the Broadcast Education Association. Figure from *Exemplification in communication: The influence of case reports on the perception of issues* (p. 103), by D. Zillmann and H.-B. Brosius, 2000, Mahwah, NJ. Copyright © 2000 by Lawrence Erlbaum Associates. Reprinted with permission.

The normative 60–40 distribution in the None condition (i.e., 60% favor peace while 40% favor violence) was maintained when the report featured exemplars that condemned the act (a typical response under the circumstances, at least as far as American news audiences go) or a combination of both types of exemplars. However, when all five exemplars used in the story endorsed the killing, the distribution changed to approximately 30–70. Clearly, the respondents did not consider the typicality (or lack of it) of the small number of exemplars featured in the story and proceeded to generalize from this obviously inadequate sample.

Similar results have been noted with research on image effects (Gibson, chap. 14, this volume). For example, Zillmann, Gibson, and Sargent (1999) found that when a news story about the safety of amusement parks was accompanied by a photograph depicting an injured person on a stretcher being moved into an ambulance in front of a roller coaster, readers' estimations of the safety of coaster rides was markedly lower (and their concern for personal safety significantly higher) than when they read the same story without a photograph or with a picture showing ecstatic children having fun riding a coaster, or with both photographs.

In all these experiments, baserate information was provided to study participants in one form or another, but it was uniformly ignored in favor of clearly unrepresentative exemplars. This tendency to generalize from small, atypical samples of case history information may be due to the operation of the so-called representativeness heuristic, which is basically a relevancy judgment that, under uncertainty, produces a short-cut estimate for the question of the form, "How probable is it that A belongs to category B?" (Kahneman & Tversky, 1973). This heuristic neglects key factors that determine the actual probability of occurrence, such as prior probability of outcomes, sample size, predictive value of the available information, and the element of chance (Fiske & Taylor, 1984). Instead, it relies on the degree of resemblance between the object A and the stereotype associated with category B (Tversky & Kahneman, 1974). Therefore, the welfare recipient in the Hamill et al. (1980) study was generalized by study participants as belonging to the broader class of all welfare recipients. Therefore, the details associated with this one exemplar will be assumed to be characteristic of the entire class of welfare recipients, even if baserate information directly states that this one case is uncharacteristic of the population. Similarly, the tale of the atypical victim of a deadly carjacking influences news receivers' perceptions about the prevalence of fatalities in carjacking incidents. Likewise, they are quick to lump all criminals in the same category as the one exemplar they saw on *Oprah*, portrayed as having been driven to crime due to understandable mitigating circumstances. Even the perception of public opinion can be profoundly influenced by a handful of quotes in a news story, as is evident from the Gan et al. (1996) study.

Such a stable reliance on the representativeness heuristic would be acceptable, even reasonable, in the absence of any baserates pertaining to the topic. But, as mentioned earlier, baserates were made available to study participants in the experiments cited earlier. However, participants' perceptions were clearly more influenced by exemplifying information than baserate information. This inability on the part of news consumers to factor in the potential atypicality of exemplars in news reports puts an enormous onus on journalists. Not only do reporters have to assemble enough exemplars to truly represent the baserates involved, they also have to make sure that the exemplars in their report are typical in most respects to the broad class that they represent. In other words, the story cannot be told through exceptions, but needs to be predominantly exemplified by normal people.

The research pertaining to effects of atypical exemplification lends new meaning to the accuracy and comprehensiveness criteria for a socially responsible press, set forth by the Hutchins Commission on Freedom of Press in 1947 (Commission on Freedom of the Press, 1947; see also Peterson, 1963). Accuracy does not end with getting the quotes right. It now includes the additional responsibility of making sure that the quote is representative. Moreover, in reporting the exemplar, journalists have to be careful not to include too many extraneous details about the person being described and/or quoted in order to add color, or for the sake of human interest. These details are part of exemplifying information, and therefore run the risk of being generalized to all other cases of the population that the exemplar supposedly represents. At a broader level, the research evidence outlined here prompts the news media to rethink their conceptualization of news value, especially in terms of presenting information via examples rather than mere data. Although exemplars have the advantage of attracting and retaining audiences, they also have enormous psychological impact, particularly in shaping audience perceptions of the events and situations reported in the news. Therefore, it is critical for exemplars to be chosen carefully, with a keen eye toward ensuring that they truly represent the population.

EXEMPLAR VIVIDNESS

The primary reason why news receivers remember exemplars better than baserates is the clearly higher vividness of the exemplifying information. Case histories are inherently more colorful, engaging, emotional, and interesting. Baserate information, by contrast, is dull, terse, boring, and, for most people, difficult to picture in their minds. This difference between the two types of information is at the heart of the attentional bias favoring exemplification over baserate information. Not only are vivid parts of a news story more attractive to attend to, they are also easier to remember. Therefore, perceptual decisions based on news information are likely to be influenced more by vivid, rather than pallid, information.

Although psychologists have enthusiastically theorized about the positive cognitive effects of vivid stimuli (e.g., Nisbett & Ross, 1980), a systematic headcount of vividness studies yielded counterintuitive results (Taylor & Thompson, 1982), including the surprising fact that for every study that showed a superior effect for vividness, there was another that showed a significant effect in the other direction (i.e., pallid stronger than vivid in affecting memory). However, no studies had been done comparing vivid and pallid parts in a news report.

Many of the studies from the exemplification effects literature reviewed so far lend indirect support to vividness effects in the news context. In addition, Zillmann and colleagues have directly tested the vividness proposition by adopting operationalizations peculiar to the news domain. In one early study, Gibson and Zillmann (1993) exposed study participants to a news story about amusement parks wherein one-sided personal testimony challenging park safety was presented either within direct quotes or in paraphrased form. In terms of concreteness and perceived proximity criteria of vividness, the quotation version may be considered more vivid than the paraphrased version. As would be hypothesized under the vividness proposition, respondents in the quotation condition gave significantly lower safety ratings to amusement parks than respondents in the paraphrased condition. In a follow-up study, Gibson and Zillmann (1998) examined a two-sided issue in a newsmagazine report, wherein both sides (rich farmers, poor farmers) were represented by exemplars who were either directly cited or paraphrased. The dependent variable in this 2 × 2 factorial experiment was issue perception, measured in terms of respondents' assessment of the plight of farmers as well as their impressions about the actions of government and banks in the matter. Results showed a main effect for quotation, thereby replicating the earlier s t u d yMoreover, the combination effects revealed some interesting patterns. When poor farmers were directly quoted, they managed to sway issue perception in their favor, regardless of whether the opposing side (i.e., rich farmers) was quoted or paraphrased. However, if they were paraphrased while the rich farmers were directly quoted, then the reverse was true: Respondents were much more likely to endorse the rich farmers' views on the issue. It must be noted that the superior effect of quoted testimony (compared to paraphrased testimony) is not simply an effect attributable solely to perceived authenticity. If that were true, then the same results should have been obtained with nonprint media as well, but Gibson and Zillmann (1993) failed to find a significant difference between the two conditions when they presented the story as a radio news report to their respondents. Therefore, vividness appears to be a more likely explanation than authenticity for their results. The quotation manipulation would be more obvious to study participants in print form because it lets them read the descriptions, notice the direct quotes, and let their imagination play a role. Whereas in radio, the lack of self-pacing may have inhibited elaboration of the details embedded in the quotation. Moreover, the vividness of a radio report would depend on how dramatic the delivery of direct testimony is, especially as contrasted with the delivery style of the reporter narrating the main story.

The importance of delivery style in determining vividness was brought home in a study conducted by Aust and Zillmann (1996). They used a television news story to manipulate different degrees of emotional displays by exemplars. The reports pertained to the risk of either encountering food poisoning or being victimized by random handgun violence. The stories either had no live interviews with exemplars (None) or featured testimony ostensibly from actual victims' friends and relatives, delivered either unemotionally (Calm) or with a great deal of emotion (Upset). After viewing the news stories, study participants were asked about their perceptions of the severity of food poisoning and random handgun violence as national problems. They were also asked to assess their own perceived risk of being a victim.

As can be seen in Fig. 12.2, respondents' ratings of risk perception were clearly influenced by the degree of emotionality in exemplar testimony. Those exposed to upset exemplars perceived significantly higher risk compared to those exposed to calm exemplars and those not exposed to exemplars at all. This result may be interpreted in vividness terms. The exemplars in the Upset condition were clearly more vivid than those in the Calm condition, and therefore their testimony was more available to viewers when it came time for assessing risk.

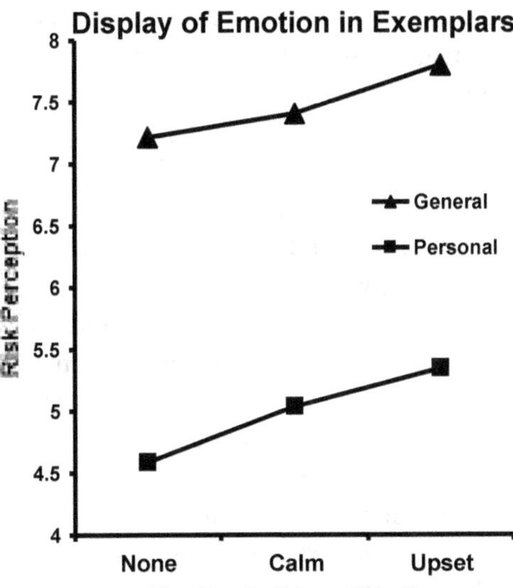

Fig. 12.2. The effect of unemotional (Calm) and emotional (Upset) exemplification of victimization by salmonella food poisoning and random handgun violence (combined). Emotional testimony by relatives and by friends of victims increased assessments of danger to the nation (General) and the likelihood of personal victimization (Personal). Data first published in "Effects of Victim Exemplification in Television News on Viewer Perception of Social Issues" by C. F. Aust and D. Zillmann, 1996, *Journalism & Mass Communication Quarterly, 73*, 787–803. Copyright © 1996. Figure from *Exemplification in communication: The influence of case reports on the perception of issues* (p. 95), by D. Zillmann and H.-B. Brosius, 2000. Copyright © 2000 by Lawrence Erlbaum Associates. Reprinted with permission.

The mechanism governing vividness effects involves the availability heuristic, which is a cognitive shortcut used to evaluate the frequency or likelihood of an event on the basis of how easily and quickly instances or associations come to mind (Tversky & Kahneman, 1973). Naturally, this method is skewed by storage, search, and retrieval biases. Vivid exemplar testimony is likely to have a stronger impression on memory than pallid testimony because vivid stimuli make a stronger impression and therefore are retrieved more easily. Moreover, this effect is likely to be stronger over time because the relative availability of vivid information is likely to become more pronounced, given the diminishing influence of moderating baserate information.

This over-time effect of vividness was noticed by Zillmann and Gan (1996) in a study about image effects in broadcast news. They showed respondents a news report about skin cancer that featured either a threatening or sanitized image of skin cancer. When risk perceptions were assessed immediately after exposure, the difference between respondents in the threatening and sanitized conditions was not significant. However, after a 2-week delay, the difference was palpable: Whereas the effect of the threatening image grew slightly over time, the effect of the sanitized image declined dramatically. It's as if the sanitized image was almost forgotten in a period of 2 weeks. Therefore, when asked about their perceived risk of contracting skin cancer, respondents in the sanitized condition gave significantly lower estimates compared to their counterparts in the threatening condition, for whom the threatening image was presumably still available in memory. Therefore, vividness seems to directly equate to memorability of portrayals, especially over time.

The strong vividness effects noticed in the aforementioned studies carry an important message for practitioners. The journalistic principle of "if-it-bleeds-it-leads" could have impression-formation effects that go well beyond the immediate effect of increased sales or ratings. The vivid exemplar portrayed on the front page or at the beginning of a newscast can have a lasting impact on news consumers. Regardless of the exemplar's typicality, one vivid portrayal is likely to influence audience perceptions in a way that will determine future decisions. Therefore, it is incumbent on journalists, especially those working in broadcast media, to use vivid exemplification with a great deal of caution. A vivid exemplar may make a news story engaging in the short term, but it can also contribute to misconceptions about people, places, and things in the long run.

CENTRALITY OF EMOTION IN NEWS PROCESSING

The cognitive effects of vivid exemplification—any exemplification for that matter—provide converging evidence for the centrality of the role played by receiver emotions in processing news information. There is something about exemplars that evokes a strong emotional response from news receivers. It's not simply exemplar distribution, atypicality, or vividness. It's all these and more, because dressing up baserates (i.e., making them more vivid) does not prove to be enough of a competition to exemplars. Efforts to counter the powerful effect of exemplars by making baserate information more vivid to news receivers have met with spotty success. An early attempt by Sundar (1991) to boost the vividness of baserate information by presenting it in the form of informational graphics (such as pie-charts) failed to yield noticeable effects. A reanalysis of the data using only those respondents who said the stimulus news magazine article was very easy to read showed a positive effect of infographics on recall, but this effect was short-lived (Sundar, Perkins, & Zillmann, 1991). More recently, Chang (2001) found that vivid presentation of baserate information in the form of infographics served to enhance immediate recall of baserate information but failed to influence its utilization in the process of issue perception. Therefore, it's not merely the presentation of exemplars that dictates the demonstrated effects on issue perception, but rather the emotional quality of exemplars. This is especially evident from research that shows that receiver emotions play a role in determining the magnitude of exemplar effects. Aust and Zillmann (1996), for example, showed that the effect of emotional exemplification was especially strong for highly empathic individuals.

Some research conducted prior to exploration of exemplification effects also supports the emotional power of news stories, especially in influencing cognitive activity. Participants who were presented with an emotionally charged, disturbing television news story, compared to those who were exposed to an innocuous, affectively neutral story, were significantly poorer in their ability to recall information from news stories (Mundorf, Drew, Zillmann, & Weaver, 1990) as well as commercials (Mundorf, Zillmann, & Drew, 1991) presented during the 3 minutes immediately following the stimulus news story. Therefore, emotional news stories, especially of a disturbing nature, result in temporary cognitive deficit among viewers, something that has been known to happen during reception of a wide variety of arousing entertainment programming, such as pornography and suspense (Zillmann, 1983, 1991).

In fact, Zillmann and Knobloch (in press) have likened news reception to a theatrical experience and demonstrated that news receivers' affective dispositions toward people and groups in the news determine the intensity and valence of their emotional reactions to the news report, as would be predicted by drama appreciation theory (Zillmann, 1996, 2000). That is, if you like a public figure (say, Bill Clinton), and that person is reported in the news as having faced a misfortune (e.g., impeachment from office), the intensity of the emotion you experience, as well as the degree of your negative affect, will be directly proportional to the extent to which you like the public figure. On the other hand, if you dislike a public figure and they face a similar bad situation as revealed in a news report, you will show positive affect in proportion to your level of disliking of that person. Likewise, news reports of good fortunes for liked and disliked persons will foster positive and negative affect in proportion to your degree of liking and disliking, respectively, for those persons. All this has been shown to be true not only for public persons but also for public groups or agenda coalitions, such as democrats and anti-abortion activists (Zillmann, Taylor, & Lewis, 1998, 1999).

Therefore, contrary to conventional wisdom, attending to news appears to be an intensely emotional affair. The emotion generated by news features can in turn have cognitive consequences, especially in the realms of comprehension, impression formation, and issue perception. More generally, it implies an active, ongoing trade-off between emotional reactivity and cognitive performance while attending to modern media. As Zillmann (1994) pointed out, in ancient times, emotional reactions ran their course, by engaging the cortex for a considerable period of time in preparation for coping responses (flight vs. flight) whereas current-day media force the (essentially emotional) individual to constantly emote as well as acquire and process information. As emerging communication technologies become increasingly iconic, news presentations tend to be concrete and emotional rather than abstract and rational, thereby celebrating the dominance of affect over cognition in influencing information processing, as well as in shaping our perceptions of reality. Zillmann (1994) went so far as to say that human beings are so chronically preoccupied with mood management that vivid media presentations (mostly entertainment) will overshadow pallid ones (such as news) in influencing our consumption patterns in the short term and our cultural future in the long run.

Such a prognostication has important implications for new and forthcoming media vehicles. To begin with, it calls for a serious consideration of the emotional quotient (i.e., the degree to which emotions can be conveyed) of emergent communication technologies in predicting their success. For the future of new media, specifically their effects, lies in the degree to which they permit "emotionalization" of content. To the extent a brand new technology (let's say, virtual reality) achieves a greater emotional bandwidth so to speak, compared to existing technologies, then the processing of information delivered through this new medium will be quite unlike any other technology. There are two primary ways in which this is likely to happen: (1) The new technology will facilitate/allow greater exchange of emotionally significant information (i.e., content and/or formal features that might stir emotions more easily); and (2) certain structural and formal features of the technology will render the medium invisible by focusing receivers' psychological orientation toward sources, rather than the channels, of communication (Sundar & Nass, 2000), thereby encouraging a greater degree of emotional communication with mediated others, such as parasocial interaction (Zillmann & Knobloch, in press).

The research outlined thus far also has implications for theory and practice pertaining to online news via the Internet. By highlighting the powerful emotional appeal of exemplars, research on news features showcases the psychological importance of journalistic sources (Isom, Johnson, McCollum, & Zillmann, 1995; Sundar, 1998) as well as gatekeepers (Sundar & Nass, 2001). Moreover, the explication of psychological mechanisms underlying news processing helps us generate testable predictions regarding cognitive effects of vivid presentations, such as multimedia (e.g., Sundar, 2000), emotionally charged chatroom exchanges with news sources (e.g., Carlson, 1999), and other common practices of modern-day news dissemination. How, what, and how much people learn as a function of these and other news features of new media will depend to a large degree on the extent to which these features evoke and/or convey emotions.

REFERENCES

Aust, C. F., & Zillmann, D. (1996). Effects of victim exemplification in television news on viewer perception of social issues. *Journalism & Mass Communication Quarterly, 73,* 787–803.

Bar-Hillel, M., & Fischhoff, B. (1981). When do base rates affect predictions? *Journal of Personality and Social Psychology, 41,* 671–680.

Borgida, E., & Nisbett, R. E. (1977). The differential impact of abstract vs. concrete information on decisions. *Journal of Applied Social Psychology, 36,* 477–482.

Brosius, H.-B., & Bathelt, A. (1994). The utility of exemplars in persuasive communications. *Communication Research, 21,* 48–78.

Carlson, D. (1999, September). Media giants create Web gateways: "Portals" provide local news, shopping, chat rooms and more. *American Journalism Review, 21*(7), 88.

Chang, H.-C. (2001, August). *Counteracting the biasing effect of unrepresentative exemplification on news readers' issue perception.* Paper presented to the Communication Theory & Methodology Division at the annual convention of the Association for Education in Journalism and Mass Communication, Boston, MA.

Commission on Freedom of the Press. (1947). *A free and responsible press.* Chicago: University of Chicago Press.

Dershowitz, A. M. (1994). *The abuse excuse and other cop-outs, sob stories, and evasions of responsibility.* Boston: Little, Brown.

Fiske, S., & Taylor, S. E. (1984). *Social cognition*. Reading, MA: Addison-Wesley.

Gan, S., Hill, J. R., Pschernig, E., & Zillmann, D. (1996). The Hebron massacre, selective reports of Jewish reactions, and perceptions of volatility in Israel. *Journal of Broadcasting and Electronic Media, 40,* 122–131.

Gibson, R., & Zillmann, D. (1993). The impact of quotation in news reports on issue perception. *Journalism Quarterly, 70,* 793–800.

Gibson, R., & Zillmann, D. (1998). Effects of citation in exemplifying testimony on issue perception. *Journalism & Mass Communication Quarterly, 75,* 167–176.

Hamill, R., Wilson, T. D., & Nisbett, R. E. (1980). Insensitivity to sample bias: Generalizing from atypical cases. *Journal of Personality and Social Psychology, 39,* 578–589.

Hill, J. R., & Zillmann, D. (1999). The Oprahization of America: Sympathetic crime talk and leniency. *Journal of Broadcasting and Electronic Media, 43,* 67–82.

Isom, P., Johnson, D., McCollum, J., & Zillmann, D. (1995). Perception of interviewees with less-than-perfect English: Implications for newspaper citations. *Journalism & Mass Communication Quarterly, 72,* 874–882.

Kahneman, D., & Tversky, A. (1973). On the psychology of prediction. *Psychological Review, 80,* 237–251.

Manis, M., Dovalina, I., Avis, N. E., & Cardoze, S. (1980). Base rates can affect individual predictions. *Journal of Personality and Social Psychology, 35,* 63–78.

Mundorf, N., Drew, D., Zillmann, D., & Weaver, J. (1990). Effects of disturbing news on recall of subsequently presented news. *Communication Research, 17,* 601–615.

Mundorf, N., Zillmann, D., & Drew, D. (1991). Effects of disturbing televised events on the acquisition of information from subsequently presented commercials. *Journal of Advertising, 20*(1), 46–53.

Nisbett, R. E., & Borgida, E. (1975). Attribution and the psychology of prediction. *Journal of Personality and Social Psychology, 32,* 932–943.

Nisbett, R. E., & Ross, L. (1980). *Human inference: Strategies and shortcomings of social judgment.* Englewood Cliffs, NJ: Prentice-Hall.

Peterson, T. (1963). The social responsibility theory of the press. In F. S. Siebert, T. Peterson, & W. Schramm (Eds.), *Four theories of the press* (pp. 87–92). Urbana, IL: Guilford.

Ross, L. D., Amabile, T. M., & Steinmetz, J. L. (1977). Social roles, social control, and biases in social perception processes. *Journal of Personality and Social Psychology, 35,* 485–494.

Rothbart, M., Fulero, S., Jensen, C., Howard, J., & Birrell, B. (1978). From individuals to group impressions: Availability heuristics in stereotype formation. *Journal of Experimental Social Psychology, 14,* 237–255.

Srull, T. K., & Wyer, R. S., Jr. (1979). The role of category accessibility in the interpretation of information about persons: Some determinants and implications. *Journal of Personality and Social Psychology, 37,* 1660–1672.

Srull, T. K., & Wyer, R. S., Jr. (1980). Category accessibility and social perception: Some implications for the study of person memory and interpersonal judgments. *Journal of Personality and Social Psychology, 38,* 841–856.

Sundar, S. S. (1991). *Visual baserate vs. visual exemplar: Perception of an issue as a function of text, infographics and blurbs.* Unpublished master's thesis, University of Alabama, Tuscaloosa.

Sundar, S. S. (1998). Effect of source attribution on perception of online news stories. *Journalism & Mass Communication Quarterly, 75,* 55–68.

Sundar, S. S. (2000). Multimedia effects on processing and perception of online news: A study of picture, audio, and video downloads. *Journalism & Mass Communication Quarterly, 77,* 480–499.

Sundar, S. S., & Nass, C. (2000). Source orientation in human–computer interaction: Programmer, networker, or independent social actor? *Communication Research, 27,* 683–703.

Sundar, S. S., & Nass, C. (2001). Conceptualizing sources in online news. *Journal of Communication, 51*(1), 52–72.

Sundar, S. S., Perkins, J. W., & Zillmann, D. (1991, August). *Perception of an issue as a function of infographics.* Paper presented to the Visual Communication Division at the annual convention of the Association for Education in Journalism and Mass Communication, Boston, MA.

Taylor, S. E., & Thompson, S. C. (1982). Stalking the elusive "vividness" effect. *Psychological Review, 2,* 155–181.

Tversky, A., & Kahneman, D. (1971). Belief in the law of small numbers. *Psychological Bulletin, 76,* 105–110.

Tversky, A., & Kahneman, D. (1973). Availability: A heuristic for judging frequency and probability. *Cognitive Psychology, 5,* 207–232.

Tversky, A., & Kahneman, D. (1974). Judgment under uncertainty: Heuristics and biases. *Science, 185,* 1124–1131.

Zillmann, D. (1983). Transfer of excitation in emotional behavior. In J. T. Cacioppo & R. E. Petty (Eds.), *Social psychophysiology: A sourcebook* (pp. 215–240). New York: Guilford.

Zillmann, D. (1991). Television viewing and physiological arousal. In J. Bryant & D. Zillmann (Eds.), *Responding to the screen: Reception and reaction processes* (pp. 103–133). Hillsdale, NJ: Lawrence Erlbaum Associates.

Zillmann, D. (1994). Cognitive and affective adaptation to advancing communication technology. In P. Zoche (Ed.), *Herausforderungen für die Informationstechnik* (pp. 416–428). Heidelberg: Physica-Verlag.

Zillmann, D. (1996). The psychology of suspense in dramatic exposition. In P. Vorderer, H. J. Wulff, & M. Friedrichsen (Eds.), *Suspense: Conceptualizations, theoretical analyses, and empirical explorations* (pp. 199–231). Hillsdale, NJ: Lawrence Erlbaum Associates.

Zillmann, D. (1999). Exemplification theory: Judging the whole by some of its parts. *Media Psychology, 1,* 69–94.

Zillmann, D. (2000). Basal morality in drama appreciation. In I. Bondebjerg (Ed.), *Moving images, culture and the mind* (pp. 53–63). Luton, UK: University of Luton Press.

Zillmann, D., & Brosius, H.-B. (2000). *Exemplification in communication: The influence of case reports on the perception of issues.* Mahwah, NJ: Lawrence Erlbaum Associates.

Zillmann, D., & Gan, S. (1996). Effects of threatening images in news programs on the perception of risk to others and self. *Medienpsychologie: Zeitschrift für Individual- und Massenkommunikation, 8,* 288–305, 317–318.

Zillmann, D., Gibson, R., & Sargent, S. L. (1999). Effects of photographs in news-magazine reports on issue perception. *Media Psychology, 3,* 207–228.

Zillmann, D., Gibson, R., Sundar, S. S., & Perkins, J. W. (1996). Effects of exemplification in news reports on the perception of social issues. *Journalism & Mass Communication Quarterly, 73,* 427–444.

Zillmann, D., & Knobloch, S. (in press). Emotional reactions to narratives about the fortunes of personae in the news theater. *Poetics.*

Zillmann, D., Perkins, J. W., & Sundar, S. S. (1992). Impression-formation effects of printed news varying in descriptive precision and exemplifications. *Medienpsychologie: Zeitschrift für Individual- und Massenkommunikation, 4,* 168–185, 239–240.

Zillmann, D., Taylor, K., & Lewis, K. (1998). News as nonfiction theater: How dispositions toward the public cast of characters affect reactions. *Journal of Broadcasting and Electronic Media, 42,* 153–169.

Zillmann, D., Taylor, K., & Lewis, K. (1999). Dispositions toward public issues as determinants of reactions to bad and good news. *Medienpsychologie: Zeitschrift für Individual- und Massenkommunikation, 11,* 231–243, 287.

13

What is the Role of Rhetorical Questions in Persuasion?

David R. Roskos-Ewoldsen
University of Alabama

Posing rhetorical questions—questions that the audience is not expected to answer or for which only one answer can be made—has been advocated as a technique of persuasion for several millennia. Indeed, in *The Art of Rhetoric* (circa 330 B.C.; trans. 1926), Aristotle addressed the utility of using rhetorical questions in the conclusion of a speech to challenge the validity of an opponent's arguments. Aristotle's advice concerning rhetorical questions appears literally in the last paragraph. Interestingly, social scientists have paid about as much attention to the persuasive impact of rhetorical questions as Aristotle did. Zillmann's (1972) is the first published experimental study of the persuasiveness of rhetorical questions. Since Zillmann's original publication, only a handful of experiments have been published on the persuasive impact of rhetorical questions.

Despite the scarcity of research on them, rhetorical questions remain a popular tool of persuasion. Howard (1989) found that over 20% of the print advertisements appearing in top consumer magazines over a 3-year period contained a question. The most prevalent form of question was a rhetorical question. This chapter is a review of the findings of the empirical research on rhetorical questions; it explores how well the proposed theoretical explanations of rhetorical questions account for the existing findings, and discusses future directions for research on rhetorical questions.

WHAT ARE THE EFFECTS OF RHETORICAL QUESTIONS?

Persuasion

Whereas Aristotle advocated the use of rhetorical questions as a way to attack or belittle an opponent's arguments, many textbooks on public speaking and persuasion advocate the use of rhetorical questions as a persuasive technique. Indeed, numerous empirical studies have found that rhetorical questions can increase the impact of a persuasive message (Burkrant & Howard, 1984; Enzle & Harvey, 1982; Howard, 1990; Howard & Kerin, 1994; Petty, Cacioppo, & Heesaker, 1981; Swasy & Munch, 1985; Zillmann, 1972; Zillmann & Cantor, 1974). On the other hand, numerous studies have been published suggesting that rhetorical questions are not particularly effective rhetorical tools in some situations (Cantor, 1979; Munch, Boller, & Swasy, 1993; Munch & Swasy, 1988; Pentony, 1990). Indeed, a recent meta-analysis of the research on rhetorical questions concluded that rhetorical questions have no appreciable influence on persuasion (Gayle, Preiss, & Allen, 1998). The answer to the apparent inconsistency between these lines of research lies with examining the limiting conditions on when rhetorical questions influence persuasion.

One factor that may limit the effectiveness of rhetorical questions is the prior attitude of the message recipient. Zillmann (1972) found that rhetorical questions that focus on soliciting agreement (e.g., "Soccer certainly is becoming more popular in the U.S., isn't it?") increased persuasion regardless of the message recipient's prior attitude toward to topic. However, Zillmann and Cantor (1973) demonstrated that prior attitude did influence the effect of rhetorical questions aimed at gaining concessions from the audience (e.g., "How can anybody believe that soccer is less exciting than American football?"). For message recipients with already favorable attitudes toward the advocated position, concession-oriented rhetorical questions increased persuasion. However, when the message was counterattitudinal, concession-oriented rhetorical questions resulted in less persuasion than the same message that contained declarative statements. Unfortunately, these are the only two studies that have explored the effect of prior attitude on the effectiveness of rhetorical questions, so it is difficult to know exactly when prior attitude is an important moderator of the persuasiveness of rhetorical questions.

A second limiting condition on the effectiveness of rhetorical questions involves how motivated message recipients are to process the message. Petty, Cacioppo, and Heesaker (1981) found that when message recipients were not motivated to process a message, rhetorical questions improved persuasion when the message contained strong arguments. On the other hand, when the message recipients were motivated to process the message, rhetorical questions inhibited persuasion when the message contained strong arguments. However, some studies have found that rhetorical questions improve the effectiveness of messages containing strong arguments regardless of the motivation level of the audience (Burnkrant & Howard, 1984; Swasy & Munch, 1985). This limiting condition is addressed in more detail in the next section on rhetorical questions and distraction.

Finally, the placement of rhetorical questions within a message may play an important role in the persuasive effects of the question. In the majority of studies on the persuasive impact of rhetorical questions, an argument is presented and then a rhetorical question related to that argument is asked (Petty et al., 1981; Zillmann, 1972; Zillmann & Cantor, 1973). Indeed, Howard (1990) found that placing rhetorical questions prior to the related argument disrupted persuasion, but placing the question after the argument enhanced persuasion. On the other hand, Burnkrant and Howard (1984) demonstrated that when rhetorical questions were placed in the introduction to a message, they improved the effectiveness of messages containing strong arguments regardless of how motivated message recipients were to process the message.

Distraction and Message Elaboration

Much of the research on rhetorical questions is framed within dual processing models of persuasion such as Petty and Cacioppo's (1986) elaboration likelihood model (ELM).[1] The ELM assumes that there are two general categories of message processing: central and peripheral. Central processing is characterized by the effortful elaboration of the message's content. The nature of the message elaborations (e.g., cognitive responses) influence whether persuasion occurs. If the elaborations are predominately positive, persuasion should occur. If the elaborations are predominately negative, the person's original attitude should be maintained or

[1]There are several dual process models of persuasion including Petty and Cacioppo's elaboration likelihood model and Chaiken, Liberman, and Eagly's (1989) heuristic systematic model (HSM). However, the research on rhetorical questions has been framed specifically within ELM, so I will continue this tradition in this chapter.

strengthened (a boomerang effect). If the elaborations are mixed or primarily neutral, the person will look for peripheral cues to aid in deciding how to react to the message. Thus, when message recipients are centrally processing a message, they are more sensitive to the strength of the arguments contained in the message. Peripheral processing is characterized by the use of simple peripheral cues to determine whether the message recipient agrees with the message. Peripheral cues include such things as source cues (e.g., expertise or attractiveness), cues to the number of arguments presented in a message, the audience's reaction to the message (e.g., applause vs. heckling), and consensus cues (Chaiken, Liberman, & Eagly, 1989; Eagly & Chaiken, 1993; Petty & Cacioppo, 1986). If the peripheral cues are judged to be positive, attitude change should occur. However, if the peripheral cues are judged to be either neutral or negative, then the person's original attitude should be maintained.

Research within the ELM tradition has found that rhetorical questions can distract people from the text they are listening to or reading (Leonard & Lowery, 1984; Munch et al., 1993; Munch & Swasy, 1988; Petty et al., 1981; Swasy & Munch, 1985). For example, Petty et al. (1981) argued that the ELM predicted that when people are highly motivated to process a message, rhetorical questions could interfere with their ability to elaborate on the arguments presented within the message. The idea is that people stop listening to the text and instead try to answer the question that is posed to them. If rhetorical questions distract people, they may decrease the amount of persuasion that occurs. For example, if the rhetorical question distracts people from listening to particularly strong arguments, they will be less persuaded by the message. However, if the rhetorical question distracts people from listening to weak arguments, it may actually improve persuasion (Petty et al., 1981). On the other hand, Petty et al. (1981) maintained that the ELM predicted that under conditions of low motivation to process a message, rhetorical questions could actually increase the likelihood that people centrally process a message. Consequently, they should be more sensitive to manipulations of argument strength.

Petty et al. (1981) conducted a study to test the ELM's predictions concerning when rhetorical questions will enhance or detract from persuasion. In the experiment, they manipulated how involving the topic of the message was (a message advocating senior comprehensive exams at the research participants' university or at a distant university), argument quality, and whether rhetorical questions or summary statements appeared after critical arguments. Petty et al.'s (1981) attitudinal data are consistent with the

ELM's predictions that participants would be more sensitive to manipulations of argument strength when the message was low involving and contained rhetorical questions. However, when the message was highly involving and contained rhetorical questions, participants were less sensitive to manipulations of argument strength, which Petty et al. (1981) interpreted as evidence that rhetorical questions distracted them from centrally processing the arguments.

Within dual process models of persuasion, participants' elaborations of the message (e.g., their cognitive responses) provide additional tests of the theory. The number of cognitive responses that a person produces in reaction to a message is one measure of how much message elaboration is occurring (Petty & Cacioppo, 1986). If participants are centrally processing the message, they should produce more cognitive responses in reaction to the message than if they are peripherally processing the message. In Petty et al.'s (1981) test of the effects of rhetorical questions on persuasion, the cognitive response data—perhaps the more critical data for testing whether rhetorical questions disrupted processing—were not consistent with their hypothesis. Specifically, although Petty et al. (1981) predicted that rhetorical questions should increase central processing for low involving topics, participants in the low topic involvement condition produced more cognitive responses when the message did not contain rhetorical questions ($M \approx 7.1$) than when it contained rhetorical questions ($M \approx 6.4$). In addition, Petty et al. predicted that under conditions of high involvement rhetorical questions should distract message recipients, thereby decreasing central processing. However, participants in the high topic involvement condition produced slightly more cognitive responses when rhetorical questions were included in the message ($M \approx 8.3$) than when they were not included ($M \approx 8.0$).[2] The cognitive response data from Petty et al.'s experiment are not consistent with the distraction hypothesis.

Additional research on the distracting effects of rhetorical questions is somewhat mixed. Research consistently finds that participants rate rhetorical questions as distracting (Leonard & Lowery, 1984; Munch & Swasy, 1988; Petty et al., 1981; Swasy & Munch, 1985). However, there are questions as to the validity of these self-report measures of distraction. Swasy and Munch (1985) found that participants rated messages containing

[2]These means were extracted from Petty, Cacioppo, and Heesacker's (1981) Table 1. They are approximate means because the exact *ns* for each cell are not provided in the table or text. Burnkrant and Howard (1984) also made the point that Petty et al.'s (1981) cognitive response data do not match the predictions from the ELM.

rhetorical questions as more distracting, but there was no effect of rhetorical questions on the number of cognitive responses that they produced in response to the message.

However, further support for the distracting effect of rhetorical questions was found in an experiment by Munch and Swasy (1988). First, Munch and Swasy demonstrated that as the number of rhetorical questions contained in a message increased, recall of the message arguments decreased. This result suggests that participants were paying less attention to the content of the message when it included rhetorical questions. Second, Munch and Swasy found that when the message contained strong arguments, rhetorical questions increased the number of source relevant cognitive responses and decreased the number of message-oriented cognitive responses (see also Swasy & Munch, 1985). Thus, rhetorical questions may decrease the number of message-oriented cognitive responses—a sign of decreased central processing. Interestingly, the total number of cognitive responses produced in reaction to the message stayed the same because of the increase in the number of source-relevant cognitive responses—a sign of increased peripheral processing. These data may explain why the cognitive response data in Petty et al.'s experiment were not consistent with the predictions of the ELM. In that study, rhetorical questions did not decrease the total number of cognitive responses in the high-involvement condition. However, Petty et al. only looked at the total number of cognitive responses. The rhetorical questions may have increased the number of source relevant cognitive responses in the high involvement condition, but unfortunately, Petty et al. did not analyze the target of the cognitive responses (e.g., response to the message or the source).

In a further attempt to understand how the distraction effect of rhetorical questions might influence persuasion, Munch et al. (1993) suggested that rhetorical questions interrupt the processing of the evidence in support of a persuasive claim so that participants who heard rhetorical questions judged the claims advanced in a message to be weaker than did participants who were presented the same information in statement form. In an experimental test of this hypothesis, Munch et al. (1993) demonstrated that this weakening of the claims in a persuasive message mediated the influence of rhetorical questions on persuasion.

An important point concerning the research on the distracting effect of rhetorical questions is that this line of research started with the assumption that under certain conditions rhetorical questions would increase people's motivation to process a message. Recall that Petty et al. (1981) originally proposed that when motivation to process a message was low because the topic was not personally relevant, rhetorical questions could motivate people to process a message to a greater extent. Consistent with the idea that rhetorical questions can increase message recipients' motivation to process a message, Swasy and Munch (1985) failed to replicate Petty et al.'s finding that rhetorical questions made participants less sensitive to manipulations of argument strength under conditions of high involvement. Instead, Swasy and Munch's (1985) results indicate that across levels of involvement, rhetorical questions increased sensitivity to manipulations of argument strength, suggesting that in conditions of both high and low involvement, rhetorical questions increased participants' motivation to critically process the message. In a related study, Howard and Kerin (1994) found that rhetorical questions did increase persuasion with a topic that was presumably minimally involving for most college students (taking daily vitamins). More importantly, using a thought-listing technique, they found that rhetorical questions motivated participants to generate more questions about the topic, which suggests that participants were motivated to more critically process the message. Furthermore, using mediational analysis, they found evidence that the influence of rhetorical questions on attitude change was mediated by participants' generation of further questions about the topic of the message. Certainly, participants' generation of questions about the topic is an indication that they were more critically processing the message.[3] Finally, Burnkrant and Howard (1984) demonstrated that when the introduction to a message contained rhetorical questions, participants produced more cognitive responses than when the introduction contained declarative statements. This effect was particularly pronounced when participants were not initially motivated to process the message. These results suggest that rhetorical questions can increase the intensity of message processing under conditions of low initial involvement.

A final point concerning the potential motivating and distracting effects of rhetorical questions concerns the use of *you* in rhetorical questions. Many of the studies on rhetorical questions used rhetorical questions that contained you (e.g., "Do you believe soccer will ever replace football as the most popular sport in the United States?"). However, research has demonstrated

---

[3]Chaiken, Liberman, and Eagly's (1989) HSM hypothesizes that people are motivated to critically process a persuasive message because their judgmental sufficiency threshold has not been met. Participants having questions concerning a topic is one indication that their judgmental sufficiency threshold has not been reached. Consequently, they are more likely to critically process the message's content in an attempt to answer their questions.

that using second-person pronouns increases participants' motivation to process a message relative to the same message containing third-person pronouns (Burnkrant & Unnava, 1989). The effect of rhetorical questions on message processing may potentially be an artifact of the personal nature of the questions used in these studies instead of the question itself. Unfortunately, no research has been conducted looking at the influence of personal versus impersonal rhetorical questions in a persuasion context. Tamborini and Zillmann (1985) did find that rhetorical questions containing you within a children's educational television program enhanced children's memory for the content of the program more than rhetorical questions not containing you.

Source Perception

Zillmann (1972) proposed that rhetorical questions might result in negative perceptions of the message source because the questions could be perceived as the source using a rhetorical "trick" to try to pressure the audience into accepting the advocated position. Although Zillmann did not find any effects of rhetorical questions on perceptions of the message source, later research did find that the use of rhetorical questions can result in more negative perceptions of the source. Several studies have found that sources were rated as exerting greater pressure on the audience when the source used rhetorical questions (Munch & Swasy, 1988; Swasy & Munch, 1985; Zillmann & Cantor, 1974). In addition, rhetorical questions can result in more negative attitudes toward the message source and in the source being perceived as less of an expert (Swasy & Munch, 1985). As discussed earlier, rhetorical questions increase source-related message elaborations under conditions of high and low topic involvement (Munch & Swasy, 1988; Swasy & Munch, 1985). Furthermore, source derogation increased particularly when sources used weak arguments (Swasy & Munch, 1985). However, it is important to note that in most of this research, the message has either been counterattitudinal or involved a "hard sell."

In a related line of research focusing on interpersonal communication and person perception, Lakoff (1975) argued that tag questions (e.g., "Soccer is an exciting sport, don't you agree?") can be interpreted as indicating that the message source lacks confidence in his or her statement. In an empirical test of Lakoff's hypothesis, Newcombe and Arnkoff (1979) found that tag questions can communicate uncertainty on the part of the message source or condescension to the message recipient by the source. In additional research on rhetorical questions in interpersonal discourse, Leggitt and

Gibbs (2000) found that when people use rhetorical questions as a form of irony, they tend to be perceived as less warm and more angry. A study conducted in a persuasion context also found that sources who use rhetorical questions are perceived as having less confidence in their position (Burnkrant & Howard, 1984).

Knowledge Acquisition

In general, rhetorical questions have been found to improve learning (Gibson, Yi, & Zillmann, 1994; MacLachlan & Jalan, 1985; Tamborini & Zillmann, 1985; Zillmann & Cantor, 1973; however, see Leonard & Lowery, 1984). Basically, the idea is that rhetorical questions arouse curiosity (Berlyne, 1954; Tamborini & Zillmann, 1985; Zillmann, 1972). By arousing curiosity, rhetorical questions motivate people to try to answer the question that is posed. Consequently, people pay closer attention to information relevant to the rhetorical question. For example, Zillmann and Cantor (1973) demonstrated that when participants were in a situation where they could easily be distracted, rhetorical questions improved their retention of information from an educational message. However, when participants were not distracted, the presence of rhetorical questions had no effect on participants' retention of the message's content. In persuasive contexts, questions also appear to improve memory. For example, the presence of questions in a print advertisement heightened memory for the brand names in the advertisement (MacLachlan & Jalan, 1985). Likewise, in another experiment, participants were asked to sit in a waiting room until the "real" experiment was ready to be conducted. While participants waited, a local radio program was played (actually a tape). During the wait, several commercials were played during the radio program. Participants recalled more information from the commercials when they contained rhetorical questions instead of declarative statements (Gibson et al., 1994).

This set of results suggests that rhetorical questions improved learning by inducing curiosity in the research participants. Consistent with this curiosity hypothesis, Tamborini and Zillmann (1985) found that rhetorical questions that were personalized by adding a second person pronoun (e.g., "What do you think the children saw?" vs. "What did the children see?") improved children's retention of information from a children's television program. As discussed earlier, research has found that the inclusion of second-person pronouns in a message increases people's motivation to attend to a message (Burnkrant & Unnava, 1989).

A final point about the impact of rhetorical questions on memory is that although rhetorical questions can influence how well we remember information presented in a message, rhetorical questions may also play a role in memory distortions. Numerous studies have demonstrated that questions can change participants' memory for previous events they have observed (Loftus, 1996). For example, Loftus and Palmer (1974) exposed research participants to a film of a car wreck. Half of the participants were later asked how fast the cars were going when they *smashed* into each other and half were asked how fast the cars were going when they hit each other. Of course the word *smash* implies a more violent wreck than does the word hit. Consistent with the implication of the question, participants in the "smash" condition provided much higher estimates of the speed of the two cars in the accident than did participants in the "hit" condition. Furthermore, after a week's delay, participants were asked whether there was any broken glass in the wreck (there was not). Participants in the "smash" condition were much more likely to erroneously remember seeing broken glass than were participants in the "hit" condition. This, and numerous other studies, have demonstrated that questions can result in distortions in people's memory. However, no research has been conducted on whether rhetorical questions in a persuasive context could have the same, or similar, effects on people's memories.

What Do We Know About the Effects of Rhetorical Questions?

At this point, the research on rhetorical questions suggests that rhetorical questions can, under certain circumstances, enhance persuasion. Specifically, whether the message is counterattitudinal, the placement of the rhetorical question and the strength of the arguments in the message are all potential moderators of the persuasive effectiveness of rhetorical questions. Second, when motivation to process a message is low, rhetorical questions can motivate people to more critically process a message regardless of the placement of the question. However, when motivation to process a message is high, placing a rhetorical question after an argument can at times distract people from processing the message. Further, research suggests that part of the distraction effect may be due to an increased focus on the source of the message. Third, rhetorical questions appear to hurt the credibility and likability of the source of the message. Fourth, rhetorical questions can improve message recipients' memory for the message. An important note, though, is that for all of these identified effects of rhetorical questions, further research is needed to more clearly delineate the conditions under which these effects occur.

CAN EXISTING THEORIES EXPLAIN THE IMPACT OF RHETORICAL QUESTIONS?

In the original experimental study of rhetorical questions, Zillmann (1972) proposed three theoretical explanations of the persuasive impact of rhetorical questions: operant conditioning, the awareness hypothesis, and reactance (see also Zillmann & Cantor, 1974). Since Zillmann's original article, two additional theoretical explanations have been offered: Petty and Cacioppo's (1986; Petty et al., 1981) ELM and Howard's (1990) judgmental model of rhetorical questions.

Operant Conditioning

Presumably, people use rhetorical questions when they wish to highlight a particularly strong argument. If people did pair rhetorical questions with weak arguments, the rhetorical question would draw attention to the weak argument with the concurrent negative reactions to the argument on the part of the message recipient. Consequently, rhetorical questions should be paired primarily with strong arguments. Thus, the pairing of rhetorical questions with strong arguments should be commonplace in everyday discourse. Zillmann (1972) hypothesized that if rhetorical questions were paired with strong arguments repeatedly, people might be operantly conditioned to expect strong arguments when they hear a rhetorical question. In other words, when we hear a rhetorical question, the question is typically paired with a strong argument that serves as a "reward" for the question. Likewise, when we use rhetorical questions, we typically pair them with strong arguments that elicit agreement. This agreement response will also act as a "reward" for our use of rhetorical questions.

This reinforcement history should create the expectation that the arguments paired with rhetorical questions are strong. Consequently, rhetorical questions should gain a persuasive power independent of the actual argument that is used or the audience's attitude toward the topic of the message. Accordingly, the operant condition explanation of rhetorical questions predicts that rhetorical questions should always be persuasive. In addition, Zillmann (1972) argued that the use of rhetorical questions should increase resistance to later counterpersuasion.

As Zillmann (1972) noted, the results of his original experiment on rhetorical questions were consistent with the operant condition explanation. In that research, participants responded favorably to the rhetorical questions regardless of whether the message was pro- or counterattitudinal (he also noted that the results were consistent with the awareness hypothesis, see later). However, subsequent research has cast serious doubt on the ability of the operant conditioning explanation to account for the persuasive impact of rhetorical questions. Clearly, there are instances when rhetorical questions are not persuasive (Cantor, 1979; Munch et al., 1993; Munch & Swasy, 1988; Pentony, 1990). In addition, the operant conditioning explanation has difficulty accounting for (a) the situations when rhetorical questions appear to distract message recipients from processing a message (Leonard & Lowery, 1984; Munch et al., 1993; Munch & Swasy, 1988; Petty et al., 1981; Swasy & Munch, 1985) or (b) the negative effects of rhetorical questions on perceptions of a source using rhetorical questions (Munch & Swasy, 1988; Swasy & Munch, 1985; Zillmann & Cantor, 1974). Although operant conditioning might be able to account for people's positive attitudes toward rhetorical questions, operant conditioning is unable to explain the totality of the effects of rhetorical questions.

Awareness Hypothesis

Although we know that we're not supposed to respond to rhetorical questions with an overt response, questions tend to create a sense of what Berlyne (1954) referred to as "epistemic curiosity." We want to know the answer to the question. Consequently, when we hear a rhetorical question, we access information that is relevant to the rhetorical question in an attempt to provide an implicit answer to the question. However, when we hear a statement, our curiosity is not aroused in the same way. Thus, according to the awareness hypothesis, rhetorical questions serve to heighten our curiosity and increase how much we think about the argument and message topic. Using the terminology of dual process theories of persuasion (Chaiken et al., 1989; Petty & Cacioppo, 1986), rhetorical questions will motivate the message recipient to more systematically process the message. Consistent with the ELM, Zillmann (1972) argued when he originally proposed this idea that the impact of the rhetorical question depends on how the message recipient responds to the information that is highlighted by the question. If the recipient has a positive response to the highlighted information, persuasion will be enhanced. If the recipient has a negative response to the highlighted information, persuasion will be reduced (see also Zillmann & Cantor, 1974).

Consistent with the awareness hypothesis, Enzle and Harvey (1982) found that rhetorical questions can serve as a marker that this is an important issue. In their study, participants were asked to help with an upcoming study. They found that participants perceived a request as more urgent when it was phrased as a rhetorical question than as a statement. Likewise, the research demonstrating that rhetorical questions can motivate participants to more critically process messages is consistent with the awareness hypothesis (Burnkrant & Howard, 1984; Howard & Kerin, 1994; Swasy & Munch, 1985).

The distracting effect of rhetorical questions when participants are already motivated to process a message would appear to be counter to the awareness hypothesis (Leonard & Lowery, 1984; Munch & Swasy, 1988; Petty et al., 1981; Swasy & Munch, 1985). However, the research on the distraction effects of rhetorical questions may not be as inconsistent with the awareness hypothesis as it initially seems. Clearly, how much attention a person pays to a persuasive message can be placed on a continuum. At the low attention end of the continuum would be the situation where the message recipient pays very little attention to the message itself and more attention is given to the cues surrounding the persuasive message—what is referred to as peripheral processing by the ELM. As one moves along the continuum, greater attention is paid to the content of the message. Finally, at the high attention end of the continuum would be the situation where the message recipient pays greater attention to a particular element of the persuasive message such as a specific argument within the message or the source's motivations for delivering the message. Attending to a specific argument or the source of the message could inhibit persuasion because the message recipient is not attending to the message in its entirety. Another way to think about the continuum is that as one moves along the continuum, there is a narrowing of attention from the context of the persuasive message, to the persuasive message itself, and finally to some particular element of the message or context. The awareness hypothesis simply suggests that rhetorical questions narrow message recipients' attention or move message recipients toward the high attention end of the continuum. If the message recipient is at the low end of the continuum (e.g., peripherally processing the message), the rhetorical question would move the message recipients toward the middle of the continuum where they would more centrally process the message. If the message recipient is already at the middle of the continuum (e.g., they are centrally processing the message), the rhetorical question could move them to the point of the continuum where they would pay particular attention to a specific argument or the source of the message. Although the awareness hypothesis and ELM are extremely similar, the difference is that ELM assumes that there are two ways in which a message is processed—central and peripheral—and rhetorical questions influence which type of processing is occurring. The awareness hypothesis, on the other hand, assumes a single type of processing, much like Kruglanski, Thompson, and Spiegel's (1999) unimodel of persuasion, whereby rhetorical questions influence persuasion by narrowing the message recipient's focus of attention rather than switching message recipients between two processing modes.

The awareness hypothesis is able to explain many of the findings concerning rhetorical questions. Obviously, rhetorical questions are persuasive according to this explanation because rhetorical questions motivate message recipients to focus their attention on the message. As Zillmann (1972) originally proposed, if their response to the message is primarily positive, they will be persuaded by the message, and if their response is primarily negative, they will not be persuaded by the message (see also Zillmann & Cantor, 1974). Likewise, this narrowing of attention also explains the influence of rhetorical questions on retention of educational materials because the questions motivate message recipients to attend to the message in more detail. Conversely, rhetorical questions can impair message processing if the question results in the message recipient focusing their attention on a specific part of the message or the surrounding context (e.g., the message source).

Perceptions of the Message Source

A final explanation of the impact of rhetorical questions that Zillmann (1972) proposed involved the impact of rhetorical questions on perceptions of the source and the message recipients' reactions to these perceptions of the source. Because rhetorical questions are a well known rhetorical device, their use should make salient that the speaker is attempting to persuade the audience. In this situation, the audience may respond by forming negative impressions of the speaker because the speaker is perceived as trying to pressure them. In addition, the audience may react negatively to the explicit persuasion attempt in order to protect themselves in a manner similar to psychological reactance. Consequently, rhetorical questions should result in more negative impressions of the speaker and less effective persuasive messages.

Consistent with this proposal, Swasy and Munch (1985) argued that under conditions of low message involvement, rhetorical questions may polarize attitudes because of reactions to the speaker and the perception that the speaker is attempting to "force" message recipients to change their attitudes. Indeed, as discussed earlier, rhetorical questions can result in several different negative reactions to the message source including disliking the source (Swasy & Munch, 1985), perceiving the source as pressuring them (Munch & Swasy, 1988; Swasy & Munch, 1985; Zillmann & Cantor, 1974), and judging the source as less of an expert (Swasy & Munch, 1988) and having less confidence (Burnkrant & Howard, 1984; Newcombe & Arnkoff, 1979).

Although there is clear support for the idea that rhetorical questions have negative effects on perceptions of the message source, there are several unanswered questions in this area of research. For example, under what conditions does this effect occur? As mentioned earlier, the majority of studies finding that rhetorical questions negatively influenced perceptions of the message source involved counterattitudinal messages. Studies using proattitudinal messages have not found negative effects of rhetorical questions on perceptions of the source (e.g., Zillmann, 1972). A second unanswered question concerns how negative perceptions of the source impact the persuasiveness of the message. One could argue that negative perceptions will have little effect because the rhetorical questions are motivating participants to more centrally process the message, which means that peripheral cues will have less impact on the persuasiveness of the message (Petty & Cacioppo, 1986). However, even when a message is being centrally processed, source cues can bias how a message is processed (Chaiken et al., 1989; Petty & Cacioppo, 1986) or operate to disambiguate the message (Chaiken et al., 1989). Research is needed to test the various ways in which rhetorical questions impact perceptions of the source and how these perceptions of the source influence the persuasiveness of the message.

Elaboration Likelihood Model and Message Scrutiny

In reaction to Zillmann's (1972) initial research on rhetorical questions, Petty et al. (1981) proposed that rhetorical questions could influence persuasion in one of two ways: by increasing participants' motivation to process a message or distracting participants from processing the message (see also Petty & Cacioppo, 1986). In an explanation that is very similar to Zillmann's (1972) awareness hypothesis, Petty et al. (1981) argued that when motivation to process the message is low, rhetorical questions could elicit curiosity, which could heighten participants' motivation to centrally process the message. On the other hand, if participants are already centrally processing a message and message recipients covertly answer rhetorical questions, the covert answering of the rhetorical question could disrupt participants' processing of the persuasive messages.

Later, Petty and Cacioppo (1986) also argued that rhetorical questions could operate as a peripheral cue that influences message scrutiny. If rhetorical questions create the impression that the speaker is trying to pressure people, rhetorical questions can influence the perceptions of the speaker and this can influence persuasion if speaker cues are operating as peripheral cues.

Generally, the research on rhetorical questions is consistent with the predictions of the ELM (Leonard & Lowery, 1984; Munch et al., 1993; Munch & Swasy, 1988; Petty et al., 1981; Swasy & Munch, 1985). However, there are exceptions to this general support. For example, Swasy and Munch (1985) failed to replicate Petty et al.'s (1981) distraction effect of rhetorical questions when motivation to process the message is high. Likewise, the ELM explanation has difficulty explaining Zillmann's (1972) original research on rhetorical questions. Participants in Zillmann's study were acting as a jury in a simulated court case. Generally, this is a situation that would evoke central processing on the part of research participants. Yet, despite the fact that the research participants were likely to be centrally processing the message, messages containing rhetorical questions were more persuasive then messages containing declarative statements.

The ELM does a good job of explaining many of the findings concerning rhetorical questions. According to the ELM, if rhetorical questions are paired with strong arguments and the message recipient is not motivated to process a message, rhetorical questions should improve persuasion. However, under conditions of high involvement, rhetorical questions should disrupt persuasion, especially if the message contains strong arguments. In addition, if rhetorical questions result in negative impressions of a source, they may influence persuasion by acting as a peripheral cue. However, the ELM cannot explain how rhetorical questions aid retention of educational materials. Likewise, the ELM is silent as to why rhetorical questions can disrupt message processing.

Judgmental Model of Rhetorical Questions

Howard (1990) argued that rhetorical questions influenced persuasion by motivating people to answer the rhetorical question. However, unlike

Zillmann's (1972) awareness hypothesis where rhetorical questions motivate an information search to find sufficient information to answer the question, Howard maintained that rhetorical questions motivate people to make immediate judgments based on the information that they already have rather than searching for information to make a judgment.

The basic difference in the predictions of the judgmental model and the awareness hypothesis concern the impact of where the rhetorical question is placed relative to the critical argument. If the rhetorical question appears after the critical argument, both the awareness hypothesis and the judgmental model predict that rhetorical questions will enhance persuasion. According to the awareness hypothesis, the rhetorical question will motivate message recipients to consider the arguments they have just heard in more detail, which should enhance persuasion. The judgmental model predicts that the rhetorical question will result in the recipient answering the question while the relevant argument is salient, so the judgment should be easily made and consistent with the accessible arguments (see Roskos-Ewoldsen & Fazio, 1997). However, the awareness hypothesis and the judgmental model make different predictions if the rhetorical question precedes the critical argument. According to the awareness hypothesis, participants will be motivated to find relevant information and will pay particular attention to the subsequent argument. Thus, the rhetorical question should enhance persuasion. However, according to the judgmental model, the rhetorical question will motivate the recipient to answer the question, but there is no salient information available to answer the question because the argument has not yet been presented. Consequently, the judgmental model predicts that if the rhetorical question precedes the critical argument, the rhetorical question will not enhance persuasion. Across four experiments, Howard (1990) found that rhetorical questions presented after the critical argument were more persuasive than rhetorical questions presented prior to the critical argument or conditions where the rhetorical question appeared both before and after the critical argument.

Clearly, Howard's (1990) research supports the predictions of the judgmental model of rhetorical questions. Rhetorical questions appear to generate a strong motivation for an immediate answer to the question. On the other hand, Munch et al. (1993) found that rhetorical questions that appeared after the critical argument disrupted the processing of the argument—a result that runs contrary to the judgmental model. Clearly, whether rhetorical questions motivate people to immediately answer the question or to search for more information or whether they disrupt the processing of the argument is a more complex process than set forth by the judgmental model. In addition, the judgmental model does not do an adequate job of explaining the other findings concerning rhetorical questions, such as the influence of rhetorical questions on perceptions of the message source or on how a message is processed. Of course, the model was not proposed to explain these effects. More to the point, it is unclear whether the judgmental model is really an explanation of how rhetorical questions operate to persuade people, or whether the model simply further delineates the processes by which rhetorical questions work.

THERE IS A NEED FOR FUTURE RESEARCH ON RHETORICAL QUESTIONS, DON'T YOU AGREE?

Irony

One of the common uses of rhetorical questions in day-to-day discourse is to express irony (Gibbs, 2000; Leggitt & Gibbs, 2000; Roberts & Kreuz, 1994). Rhetorical questions are also used to express irony in persuasive settings such as political debates. Despite the fact that rhetorical questions are often used to express irony, none of the research on rhetorical questions and persuasion has focused on rhetorical questions and irony. Indeed, there is scant research on irony and persuasion. However, research has shown that in interpersonal contexts, rhetorical questions used to express irony tend to evoke anger, irritation, disgust, and repulsion (Leggitt & Gibbs, 2000). Thus, one would expect that rhetorical questions as irony might influence perceptions of the speaker, the message, and possibly the target of the message.

Attitude Consolidation and Accessibility

One unexplored consequence of the persuasiveness of rhetorical questions involves the influence of rhetorical questions on attitude consolidation and accessibility. Attitude consolidation involves the initial formation of an attitude (Roskos-Ewoldsen & Fazio, 1997). Persuasion researchers are often criticized because standard attitude measures are insensitive to whether the measured attitude is "real" or is simply expressed as a response to an attitude query (Larson & Sanders, 1975). For example, when listening to low involving persuasive messages, research participants may not form an attitude toward the topic of the message until completing the dependent measures of the experiment that explicitly ask for an attitudinal response. Rhetorical questions should aid in attitude consolidation because the rhetorical question calls for an implicit response from the message recipient. To date, the research on rhetorical questions does suggest that they do invite a response from the audience, either in the form of greater message processing or distraction from message processing while the rhetorical question is answered. The implicit response to the rhetorical question should facilitate attitude consolidation. Understanding when attitudes are spontaneously formed would aid in our understanding of when attitudes are actually stored in memory versus when they are responses to a measurement scale. It would also help in determining what type of persuasive strategies will be most effective at changing the attitude (Roskos-Ewoldsen & Fazio, 1997).

Rhetorical questions may also increase the accessibility of attitudes in memory. Attitude accessibility refers to the ease of activating an attitude from memory. Accessible attitudes are easier to access from memory and are more likely to be spontaneously activated upon the mere presentation of the attitude object than are less accessible attitudes (Fazio, Sanbonmatsu, Powell, & Kardes, 1986; Roskos-Ewoldsen & Fazio, 1992). Accessible attitudes are highly functional and influence whether future persuasive messages relevant to that attitude are attended to and whether the message is processed in a biased manner. In addition, accessible attitudes influence subsequent decisions and behavioral responses to the messages (for reviews see Fazio, 1989, 2000; Fazio & Roskos-Ewoldsen, 1994; Fazio, Roskos-Ewoldsen, & Powell, 1994; Roskos-Ewoldsen, 1997; Roskos-Ewoldsen, Arpin-Ralstin, & St. Pierre, 2002). Rhetorical questions might be particularly effective at increasing the accessibility of attitudes from memory because they motivate the message recipient to make a judgment (Howard, 1990; Zillmann, 1972). A common finding of the research on attitude accessibility is that repeated attitude judgments increase the accessibility of an attitude (Downing, Judd, & Brauer, 1992; Fazio et al., 1986; Houston & Fazio, 1989; Powell & Fazio, 1984; Roskos-Ewoldsen & Fazio, 1992). For example, repeatedly viewing a commercial about a candy bar resulted in more accessible attitudes toward that candy bar than viewing the commercial only once (Berger & Mitchell, 1989). Likewise, in a study where research participants were required to make short speeches about their feelings on a topic, the more times participants were asked to express their attitudes, the more accessible their attitudes were from memory (Downing et al., 1992).[4]

Classification of Rhetorical Questions

At this point, I think it is important to note that the fundamental problem in the study of rhetorical questions is the lack of focus on the persuasive effectiveness of different types of rhetorical questions. Clearly, an ironical rhetorical question is going to have a different effect on an audience than an agreement rhetorical question. Unfortunately, little research has been conducted on how different types of rhetorical questions operate in a persuasive context. Zillmann's original research on rhetorical questions did focus on the differential patterns of effectiveness of different types of rhetorical questions. Zillmann (1972) demonstrated that prior attitude did not influence the effectiveness of agreement rhetorical questions, but Zillmann and Cantor (1974) found that concession questions were effective when the message was congruent with message recipients' prior attitude, but backfired when it was incongruent.

Despite this early demonstration of the differential effectiveness of distinct types of rhetorical questions, few studies have directly explored the effectiveness of different types of rhetorical questions by manipulating type of rhetorical question within a single study. The few experiments that have manipulated the type of rhetorical question have had mixed results. For example, Cantor (1979) found that direct rhetorical questions (operationalized as "Won't you contribute to our fund?") were no more successful at soliciting help (donations for the local chapter of the American Cancer Society) than were polite imperatives (operationalized as "Please Contribute to our fund.") or information questions (operationalized as "Would you like to contribute to our fund?"). However, in a later study, Enzle and Harvey (1982) found that rhetorical questions did result in higher

[4]Downing, Judd, and Brauer (1992) argued that repeated attitude expression results in more extreme attitudes, which are also more accessible from memory. If this is the case, there is a potential confounding of attitude accessibility and attitude extremity. A number of studies have found a moderate correlation between attitude accessibility and attitude extremity (Fazio & Williams, 1986; Houston & Fazio, 1989; Roskos-Ewoldsen & Fazio, 1992). However, a number of other studies have found no effect of repeated expression on attitude extremity (Fazio, 1995; Houston & Fazio, 1989; Powell & Fazio, 1984; Roskos-Ewoldsen & Fazio, 1992). In addition, all of these studies found that attitude accessibility and attitude extremity have independent effects on behavior, perception, and attention.

levels of helping behavior (asking participants in one study to stay after and provide examples of positive social interactions for a future study). Enzle and Harvey hypothesized that the differences in the results of their study and Cantor's (1979) study might be due to the form of the rhetorical question. Specifically, Enzle and Harvey had used indirect rhetorical questions (e.g., "You will help me with my experimental project, won't you?") in their study and Cantor had used direct rhetorical questions (e.g., "Won't you help me with my experimental project?"). In a follow-up study, they found that indirect rhetorical questions were more effective at soliciting help than direct rhetorical questions.

In his tests of the judgmental model of rhetorical questions, Howard (1990) explored whether what he called "doubt" versus "agreement" questions had divergent effects on the persuasiveness of rhetorical questions. The stimulus materials in Howard's study focused on the need to take supplemental vitamins. Doubt questions are designed to motivate the person to consider the relevant information (e.g., "Does your daily intake of vitamins really meet your daily needs?"). On the other hand, agreement questions are designed to elicit a predetermined agreement response (e.g., "Shouldn't your daily intake of vitamins really meet your daily needs?"). Howard (1990) found no difference in the persuasiveness of these two types of rhetorical questions.

I would argue that prior to any meaningful program of research on the effectiveness of various types of rhetorical questions, a useful typology of rhetorical questions must be developed. From a psychological standpoint, a fruitful approach to the categorization of rhetorical questions would focus on the function that the question serves. For example, in research on interpersonal discourse, Roberts and Kreuz (1994) found that rhetorical questions are used to emphasize a point (see also Leggitt & Gibbs, 2000), to provoke thought (see also Howard, 1989), to clarify an issue (see also Howard, 1989), to show positive or negative emotion, and to manage discourse. In a persuasion context, rhetorical questions serve similar functions (e.g., emphasizing a point, provoking thought, clarification, and managing discourse), though some of the functions may be slightly different. In addition, rhetorical questions might function to challenge another person's behavior or statements (Aristotle, 1926; Howard, 1989; Leggitt & Gibbs, 2000) or elicit agreement (Howard, 1989; Zillmann, 1972). Finally, as argued earlier, rhetorical questions can function as a type of irony.

Clearly, these different types of rhetorical questions will have different types of consequences. For example, rhetorical questions that challenge another person's behavior are more likely to result in negative perceptions of the message source than do rhetorical questions that are used to clarify a point or to manage discourse. Likewise, rhetorical questions that emphasize a point or are used to provoke thought are more likely to aid in the retention of the message's content than a rhetorical question designed to elicit agreement.

CONCLUDING COMMENTS

Zillmann's (1972) original study of rhetorical questions started an interesting line of research that has expanded our understanding of rhetorical questions. Rhetorical questions can both aid and hinder persuasion. Likewise, rhetorical questions can increase how much we focus on the content of the message or, conversely, the source of the message. However, as the cliché goes, much more research is needed before we begin to understand the nuances of how rhetorical questions function.

REFERENCES

Aristotle. (1926). *The art of rhetoric* (J. H. Freese, Trans.). Cambridge, MA: Harvard University Press.

Berlyne, D. E. (1954). A theory of human curiosity. *British Journal of Psychology, 45,* 180–191.

Berger, I. E., & Mitchell, A. A. (1989). The effect of advertising on attitude accessibility, attitude confidence, and the attitude–behavior relationship. *Journal of Consumer Research, 16,* 269–279.

Burnkrant, R. E., & Howard, D. J. (1984). Effects of the use of introductory rhetorical questions versus statements on information processing. *Journal of Personality and Social Psychology, 47,* 1218–1230.

Burnkrant, R. E., & Unnava, H. R. (1989). Self-referencing: A strategy for increasing processing of message content. *Personality and Social Psychology Bulletin, 15,* 628–638.

Cantor, J. R., (1979). Grammatical variations in persuasion: Effectiveness of four forms of request in door-to-door solicitations for funds. *Communication Monographs, 46,* 296–305.

Chaiken, S., Liberman, A., & Eagly, A. H. (1989). Heuristic and systematic information processing within and beyond the persuasion context. In J. S. Uleman & J. A. Bargh (Eds.), *Unintended thought* (pp. 212–252). New York: Guilford.

Downing, J. W., Judd, C. M., & Brauer, M. (1992). Effects of repeated expressions on attitude extremity. *Journal of Personality and Social Psychology, 63,* 17–29.

Eagly, A. H., & Chaiken, S. (1993). *The psychology of attitudes.* Fort Worth, TX: Harcourt Brace Jovanovich.

Enzle, M. E., & Harvey, M. D. (1982). Rhetorical requests for help. *Social Psychology Quarterly, 45,* 172–176.

Fazio, R. H. (1989). On the power and functionality of attitudes: The role of attitude accessibility. In A. R. Pratkanis, S. J. Breckler, & A. G. Greenwald (Eds.), *Attitude structure and function* (pp. 153–179). Hillsdale, NJ: Lawrence Erlbaum Associates.

Fazio, R. H. (1995). Attitudes as object–evaluation associations: Determinants, consequences, and correlates of attitude accessibility. In R. E. Petty & J. A. Krosnick (Eds.), *Attitude strength: Antecedents and consequences* (pp. 247–282). Mahwah, NJ: Lawrence Erlbaum Associates.

Fazio, R. H. (2000). Accessible attitudes as tools for object appraisal: Their costs and benefits. In G. Maio & J. Olson (Eds.), *Why we evaluate: Functions of attitudes* (pp. 1–36). Mahwah, NJ: Lawrence Erlbaum Associates.

Fazio, R. H., & Roskos-Ewoldsen, D. R. (1994). Acting as we feel: When and how attitudes guide behavior. In T. C. Brock & S. Shavitt (Eds.), *Psychology of persuasion* (pp. 71–94). Boston: Allyn & Bacon.

Fazio, R. H., Roskos-Ewoldsen, D. R., & Powell, M. C. (1994). Attitudes, perception, and attention. In P. M. Niedenthal & S. Kitayama (Eds.), *The heart's eye: Emotional influences in perception and attention* (pp. 197–216). Orlando, FL: Academic.

Fazio, R. H., Sanbonmatsu, D. M., Powell, M. C., & Kardes, F. F. (1986). On the automatic activation of attitudes. *Journal of Personality and Social Psychology, 50,* 229–238.

Fazio, R. H., & Williams, C. J. (1986). Attitude accessibility as a moderator of the attitude-perception and attitude-behavior relations: An investigation of the 1984 presidential election. *Journal of Personality and Social Psychology, 51,* 505–514.

Gayle, B. M., Preiss, R. W., & Allen, M. (1998). Another look at the use of rhetorical question. In M. Allen & R. W. Preiss (Eds.), *Persuasion: Advances through meta-analysis* (pp. 189–202). Cresskill, NJ: Hampton Press.

Gibbs, R. W., Jr. (2000). Irony in talk among friends. *Metaphor and Symbol, 15,* 5–27.

Gibson, R., Yi, H., & Zillmann, D. (1994). Incidental learning from radio advertisements with and without curiosity-arousing questions. *Advances in Consumer Research, 21,* 282–285.

Houston, D. A., & Fazio, R. H. (1989). Biased processing as a function of attitude accessibility: Making objective judgments subjectively. *Social Cognition, 7,* 51–66.

Howard, D. J. (1989). The prevalence of question use and question strategies in print advertising. *Current Issues and Research in Advertising, 11,* 89–112.

Howard, D. J. (1990). Rhetorical question effects on message processing and persuasion: The role of information availability and the elicitation of judgment. *Journal of Experimental Social Psychology, 26,* 217–239.

Howard, D. J., & Kerin, R. A., (1994). Question effects and question generation and the mediation of attitude change. *Psychological Reports, 75,* 209–210.

Kruglanski, A. W., Thompson, E. P., & Spiegel, S. (1999). Separate or equal? Bimodal notions of persuasion and a single-process "unimodel." In S. Chaiken & Y. Trope (Eds.), *Dual-process theories in social psychology* (pp. 293–313). New York: Guilford.

Lakoff, R. T. (1975). *Language and woman's place.* New York: Harper & Row.

Larson, C., & Sanders, R. (1975). Faith, mystery, and data: An analysis of "scientific" studies of persuasion. *Quarterly Journal of Speech, 61,* 178–194.

Leggitt, J. S., & Gibbs, R. W., Jr. (2000). Emotional reactions to verbal irony. *Discourse Processes, 29,* 1–24.

Leonard, W. H., & Lowery, L. F. (1984). The effects of question types in textual reading upon retention of biology concepts. *Journal of Research in Science Teaching, 21,* 377–384.

Loftus, E. F. (1996). *Eyewitness testimony.* Cambridge, MA: Harvard University Press.

Loftus, E. F., & Palmer, J. C. (1974). Reconstruction of automobile destruction: An example of the interaction between language and memory. *Journal of Verbal Learning and Verbal Behavior, 13,* 585–589.

MacLachlan, J., & Jalan, P. (1985). The effect of pre-question on advertising recall. *Journal of Advertising, 14,* 18–22, 49.

Munch, J. M., Boller, G. W., & Swasy, J. L. (1993). The effects of argument structure and affective tagging on product attitude formation. *Journal of Consumer Research, 20,* 294–302.

Munch, J. M., & Swasy, J. L. (1988). Rhetorical question, summarization frequency, and argument strength effects on recall. *Journal of Consumer Research, 15,* 69–76.

Newcombe, N., & Arnkoff, D. B. (1979). Effects of speech style and sex of speaker on person perception. *Journal of Personality and Social Psychology, 37,* 1293–1303.

Pentony, J. F. (1990). Effect of response involvement, quality of arguments, number of arguments, and style of introduction on persuasion. *Psychological Reports, 67,* 345–346.

Petty, R. E., & Cacioppo, J. T. (1986). *Communication and persuasion: Central and peripheral routes to attitude change.* New York: Springer-Verlag.

Petty, R. E., Cacioppo, J. T., & Heesacker, M. (1981). Effects of rhetorical questions on persuasion: A cognitive response analysis. *Journal of Personality and Social Psychology, 40,* 432–440.

Powell, M. C., & Fazio, R. H. (1984). Attitude accessibility as a function of repeated attitude expression. *Personality and Social Psychology Bulletin, 10,* 139–148.

Roberts, R. M., & Kreuz, R. J. (1994). Why do people use figurative language? *Psychological Science, 5,* 159–163.

Roskos-Ewoldsen, D. R. (1997). Attitude accessibility and persuasion: Review and a transactive model. In B. Burleson's (Ed.), *Communication Yearbook 20* (pp. 185–225). Beverly Hills, CA: Sage.

Roskos-Ewoldsen, D. R., Arpin-Ralstin, L. A., & St. Pierre, J. (2002). The quick and the strong: Implications of attitude accessibility for persuasion. In J. P. Dillard & M. Pfau (Eds.), *Persuasion: Developments in theory and practice* (pp. 39–61). Thousand Oaks, CA: Sage.

Roskos-Ewoldsen, D. R., & Fazio, R. H. (1992). On the orienting value of attitudes: Attitude accessibility as a determinant of an object's attraction of visual attention. *Journal of Personality and Social Psychology, 63,* 198–211.

Roskos-Ewoldsen, D. R., & Fazio, R. H. (1997). The role of belief accessibility in attitude formation. *Southern Communication Journal, 62,* 107–116.

Swasy, J. L., & Munch, J. M. (1985). Examining the target of receiver elaborations: Rhetorical question effects on source processing and persuasion. *Journal of Consumer Research, 11,* 877–886.

Tamborini, R., & Zillmann, D. (1985). Effects of questions, personalized communication style, and pauses for reflection in children's educational programs. *Journal of Educational Research, 79,* 19–26.

Zillmann, D. (1972). Rhetorical elicitation of agreement in persuasion. *Journal of Personality and Social Psychology, 21,* 159–165.

Zillmann, D., & Cantor, J. R. (1973). Induction of curiosity via rhetorical questions and its effect on the learning of factual materials. *British Journal of Educational Psychology, 43,* 172–180.

Zillmann, D., & Cantor, J. R. (1974). Rhetorical elicitation of concession in persuasion. *Journal of Social Psychology, 94,* 223–236.

14

Effects of Photography on Issue Perception

Rhonda Gibson
University of North Carolina

The role of photographic images in the acquisition and retention of information has received considerable research attention, primarily in the area of news. Attempting to determine whether a picture is indeed worth a thousand words, studies have examined ways in which images are capable of enhancing information transmission, focusing on the information processing capabilities of the human brain. Only recently, however, has interest turned to what may be considered a more socially significant effect of photography: its influence on issue perception. Throughout the past decade, Dolf Zillmann has been the leading force behind research efforts to examine the effects of news images on how individuals perceive social phenomena. This chapter briefly summarizes the effects of visuals on information acquisition and retention and then examines in more detail what scholars have learned in recent studies of the effects of photography on issue perception.

EFFECTS OF IMAGES ON INFORMATION ACQUISITION

Cognitive psychologists have learned that the brain is more adept at extracting and retaining information from audiovisual stimuli than from purely verbal information (Anderson & Paulson, 1978; Gehring, Toglias, & Kimble, 1976; Paivio, 1971). Numerous empirical studies have investigated the mnemonic power of images mixed with text in relation to acquisition and retention of information. Studies by Katz, Adoni, and Pnina (1977), Graber (1990, 1996), Brosius (1993), Wanta and Roark (1993), and Brosius,

Donsbach, and Birk (1996), as well as numerous others, suggest that text-consistent images enhance text-defined news recall. Redundancy in the presentation of relevant information is particularly effective in facilitating the recall of this information (Drew & Grimes, 1987; Findahl, 1981; Nugent, 1982; Reese, 1984; Wember, 1976). Graber (1996), likewise, noted that combining pictures with words makes messages more memorable than purely verbal texts, particularly when the pictures contain substantial amounts of dramatic information previously unknown to the viewer and not mentioned verbally.

Grimes (1990) discovered that in television news, information presented in text–image combinations tends to fuse with the passage of time. He refered to this as the translation phenomenon, in which words are remembered as pictures, and vice versa. His study featured a news report on dating services in which the text stated that daters often do not reveal all of their vices. The simultaneously presented footage showed a student with a gin bottle in his back pocket. After a 2-day delay, respondents recalled the text as essentially stating that daters do not reveal their alcoholism, among other vices.

The impact of photography on recall has been shown to vary, however. Several studies have found exceptions to the memory-enhancement capabilities of visual images, especially in television news (Furnham & Gunter, 1985; Gunter, 1987). Gunter (1980) argued that information presented with visuals in broadcast news may actually inhibit the learning of items presented without visuals. Likewise, memory can suffer when audio and video messages offer discrepant information (Warshaw, 1978).

Specific types of visuals, such as emotional images, may interfere with accurate storage of factual verbal information in a news story (Gunter, 1987), and visuals that enhance memory for negative emotional messages may fail to do so for positive ones (A. Lang & Friestad, 1993). In a study of compelling negative images in television news, Newhagen and Reeves (1992) found that such images retroactively inhibit memory for material that precedes them, whereas they proactively enhance memory for material that follows them. Scott and Goff (1988) focused on information acquisition from news reports presented after exposure to unpleasantly or pleasantly arousing images. Counter to the findings of Newhagen and Reeves, these investigators observed a period of impaired information acquisition after exposure to compelling images. After 2 minutes, this effect actually reversed to proactive facilitation. No such effects were observed after exposure to noncompelling images.

Emotion-evoking images in general may be effective in facilitating recall only to the extent that the images portray pivotal events. The involvement of emotional imagery portraying nonfocal events has actually been shown to be counterproductive (Brosius, 1993; Mundorf, Drew, Zillmann, & Weaver, 1990) because it draws attention to itself at the expense of attention to the focal information.

PHOTOGRAPHY EFFECTS ON ISSUE PERCEPTION

Although most image and photography effects research has focused on information acquisition and comprehension, a few studies have looked at other types of effects. Scholars in political science have noted that news reports, by their very nature, often present a distorted view of reality (Donsbach, Brosius, & Mattenklott, 1993; Philo, 1990). A now-classic study designed to examine the distortions that result from routine news editing practices was conducted by G. E. Lang and K. Lang (1953). In order to be able to compare the record of a full event with subsequent television coverage, the Langs filmed a 1951 parade in Chicago honoring Gen. Douglas MacArthur, who had recently been relieved of his duties by the president. Observers stationed by the Langs along the parade route reported relatively small crowds and limited enthusiasm for the embattled general. The television version of the parade was in stark contrast, however, relying on selected images and portraying the parade as a triumphant march. In this coverage, MacArthur appeared to be a celebrated hero welcomed by cheering crowds. The researchers concluded that the footage had been edited to make the story more dramatic and crowd pleasing. They noted that the images were accurate individually, but the overall viewer perception of the event was not.

Other political scientists have noted a democratizing impact of political images in television (Crowley & Mitchell, 1994; Meyrowitz, 1985). By showing close-ups focusing on personal appearance, body language, and signs of emotion, audiovisuals can actually demystify world leaders. Their personal and emotional dimensions become so important that they overshadow other elements of their character and public performance. Political science scholar Hart (1994) charged that television pictures, which bring images of the world's leaders into everyone's living rooms, are seducing Americans into falsely believing that they are sharing power when, in reality, passive television viewing saps their will to physically engage in political action.

Wanta applied the agenda-setting research focus to images in a 1988 study that addressed the ability of dominant photographs in news reports to consciously or subconsciously influence the salience of an issue for a reader. He hypothesized that a story with dominant art (i.e., a photograph much larger than other art on the page) would increase issue salience more than a story without dominant art and that a story with balanced art would increase salience more than a story with no art. The hypotheses were based on the agenda-setting premise that if a newspaper devotes a great deal of space to an issue by running a large photograph, the reader should perceive that issue to be of great importance and should raise it above other issues on his or her agenda. The study presented participants with news stories on three issues: outdated equipment used by the U.S. Department of Defense, an activist group blocking entrances to a Texan's farm to prevent foreclosure by a bank, and a U.S. Department of Health report predicting dangerous consequences for major cities if air pollution standards were not strictly enforced. The story texts were identical across conditions; the manipulation occurred only with images. One story featured a dominant photograph, one story had a photograph balanced in size with other photos on the page, and one story had no photograph. Results showed that differences in ratings of topic importance were significant for only one of the three issues: the pollution story. Wanta noted that pollution was the issue for which one group of respondents received dominant art on the final day of the study, thus the difference could be explained by the recency effect. But he also noted that although neither of the other two issues produced significant results, the mean change scores on national defense did show the expected trend. He argued that his findings have major implications for editors, specifically that they have the power to raise their readers' salience on certain issues over a short period of time merely by increasing the size of photographs, a gate-keeping function that may often be unintended.

The ability of photographs to make a news report appear biased was examined by Culbertson (1974). In this study, the researcher prepared two articles, each defining a controversial proposal and then discussing arguments for and against the proposal under separate subheads. Arguments against were entirely verbal throughout all conditions. Some pro arguments were verbal in a control version but were supplemented with line drawings and photographs in experimental manipulations. In addition, the sensationalism of the messages and images was varied (high, low). Culbertson hypothesized that using photos and drawings to help present pro-arguments would make the articles appear more pro than con. Two news articles were used, with the topics being President Richard Nixon's guaranteed annual income plan and a proposed federal family planning agency. Results showed that for the less sensational of each of the reports, the photographic version was rated more pro than the outline drawing version, which was considered more pro than the version without art. In the highly sensational reports, the use of line drawings and photographs both made the article appear more pro than the verbal-only version.

Zillmann and his colleagues, primarily over the past decade, have looked at the impact of images beyond the subgenre of political news. They have also altered the focus of their investigations from the traditional one of information acquisition and retention to that of issue perception, addressing the role that visual images, primarily in print and broadcast news reports, play in issue perception. The rest of this chapter covers their research into the specific effects of emotional, threatening, innocuous, and incidental images in news on issue perception.

EFFECTS OF EMOTIONAL AND THREATENING IMAGES IN THE NEWS ON ISSUE PERCEPTION

Graber (1996) noted that audiovisuals in the news are uniquely successful in creating a sense of reality, and a sense of actually witnessing an event makes these images powerful tools for manipulating media audiences. Highly vivid emotional and threatening images, in particular, are considered potent journalistic tools with potentially significant political power. Such images have long been believed capable of stirring emotions and fostering public outcry, much more so than news reports without vivid photographs (Perlmutter, 1999; Sharkey, 1993). For instance, images of the impromptu execution of a Viet Cong prisoner in the streets of Saigon by Brig. Gen. Nguyen Ngoc Loan are thought to have severely shocked the American public and fueled sentiment against U.S. involvement in Vietnam (see Fig. 14.1). More recently, the 1992 television footage showing White policemen brutally beating Rodney King, a Black man, enraged millions and led to deadly rioting in Los Angeles. Likewise, news images appear to have dictated U.S. foreign policy concerning Somalia (Sharkey, 1993). An onslaught of images of starving Somali children and adults prompted Americans to pressure government officials to intervene in Somalia. When the U.S. intervention failed, however, and as the U.S. public was then confronted with pictures of jeering Somalis dragging the body of a dead U.S.

soldier through the streets of Mogadishu, kicking it and spitting on it, public sentiment was reversed. Public pressure switched to calls for immediate withdrawal from Somalia, calls that were heeded. Other instances of similarly powerful image effects have been documented (Gerbner, 1992; Johnson-Cartee & Copeland, 1991; Messaris, 1997; Perlmutter, 1999), suggesting that such effects could not have been created by even the strongest verbal account of the pictured event.

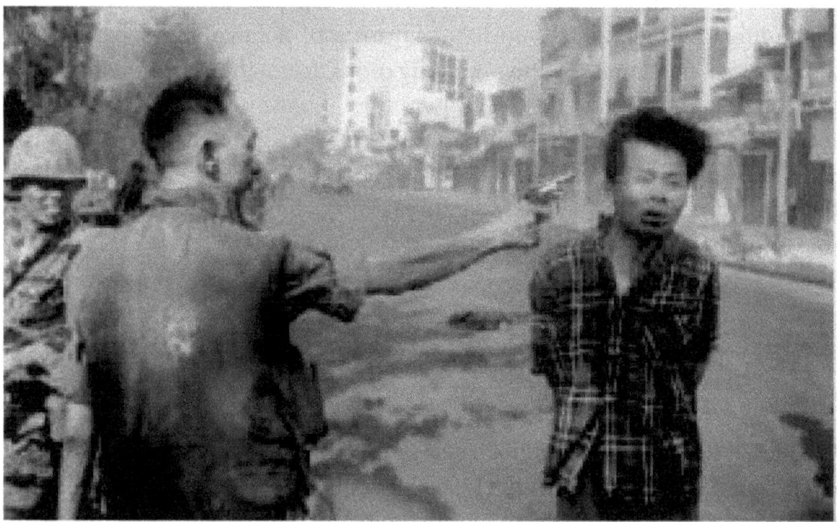

Fig. 14.1. Eddie Adam's Pulitzer Prize-winning photograph of a Saigon execution fueled public sentiment against the Vietnam War.

Brosius (1993) first addressed the influence of images specifically on issue perception in a study of the effects of emotional pictures in television news. The study was designed to examine the effects of viewing emotional images on viewers' recall of items from a news report. Three broadcast news reports were manipulated in amount of visual illustration (none, partly, and fully illustrated) and the type of illustrations (neutral and emotional). The topics of the manipulated reports were (a) a demonstration against the housing shortage and rents in German cities; (b) a report on the problems caused by the heavy traffic in the inner cities; and (c) the pollution of the Baltic Sea and actions undertaken by four nations to solve the problem. Brosius determined that the effects of emotional visuals are reflected not in the exact recall of the text, but instead through specific kinds of errors in recall. The author argued that these errors occur because emotional visuals focus attention on specific parts of a news item and that recall of the overall news report is actually reconstructed from perceptual judgments that are generalized from the individual emotional images. Specifically, Brosius's results revealed that emotional pictures led to more overestimations of the severity of the issue covered in the news report and fewer underestimations compared to the version with the neutral pictures. Thus, variations in the emotional content of images contained in a news report led to differences in perception of the issue involved in the report.

A series of studies by Zillmann and his colleagues examined the effects of threatening images on issue perception in both print and broadcast news. Overall, the findings suggest that images conveying threat and danger appear to exert an especially strong influence on judgment and on the assessment of personal and public risk in particular. These effects tend to persist over time. In addition, the unopposed use of threatening images can lead to serious misassessments of threatening conditions.

The short-term effects of threatening images in broadcast news on issue perception were investigated by Aust and Zillmann (1996). Three versions of two newscasts were created. One report concerned the risk of salmonella poisoning from eating in fast-food establishments, the other the danger of becoming a victim of random violence. The report versions presented either just the narrated issue events proper without interviews of victims and close relatives; the events with added interviews in which victims and close relatives calmly detailed their suffering; or the events with these interviews that were verbatim, but that featured the interviewees in serious emotional distress. Issue perception was clearly influenced by this manipulation. Specifically, the addressed dangers to the public were rated higher after exposure to the emotionally arousing reports than after exposure to either of the nonemotional control versions. Similar effects were observed for the assessment of risk to self.

Short-term plus prolonged effects of threatening images in broadcast news were examined by Zillmann and Gan (1996). The study manipulated a CNN health broadcast about the danger of contracting skin cancer for sunbathers. The broadcast was aired prior to the beginning of summer vacation and targeted young people headed for the beaches. It opened with beach scenes of sunbathers and then addressed the risks associated with extended sun exposure. The etiology of melanoma was explained by several dermatologists. The risks of excessive sunbathing were explained, and the benefits of protective measures such as the use of sunscreen were discussed. Testimony from skin cancer victims was interspersed. In the original broadcast, the sunburned shoulder of one victim was shown, along with a small melanoma on the arm. Although death risks from melanoma were discussed in the news report, the described imagery was rather sanitized and nonthreatening. It allowed the investigators to easily manipulate images without altering the text in any way. A condition of threatening imagery was thus created by replacing the described nonthreatening scene with footage depicting a victim's shoulder largely covered by melanoma skin cancer and a demonstration of the surgical removal of basal cell carcinoma. The newscast closed with a caution against sunbathing and a recommendation to use sunscreen.

Respondents read the melanoma news report along with three other reports for disguise. They evaluated the newsworthiness of the newscast and their emotional reactions to the report. Half of the respondents were immediately given a General Health Survey that included questions about the risk of various activities. Respondents also rated the usefulness of particular precautions in preventing injury. Embedded in the questionnaire were questions about melanoma risk to the public and to self from excessive sun exposure. In addition, questions were asked about the need for protection against melanoma by use of sunscreen. In the condition of delayed assessment, the survey was administered after 2 weeks.

The findings suggest that over time, compellingly threatening images in news reports are capable of exerting a disproportionately strong influence on public perceptions of risk, on the acceptance of protection against it, and on the assessment of personal risk. The involvement of compelling images, compared to that of sanitized images, failed to appreciably affect assessments shortly after the newscast. However, for assessments of melanoma as a threat to public health, the threatening images exerted themselves in the delayed assessment (see Fig. 14.2). Two weeks after exposure to the news reports, the version featuring threatening images yielded risk estimates that markedly exceeded those of the version with sanitized images. This absolute sleeper effect is consistent with the proposal that threatening images continue to impose themselves in memory, whereas the accessibility of other information, such as that found in the text of a report, diminishes over time.

For the assessments of personal risk and perceived need for protection, there was no significant difference between threatening-image and nonthreatening-image conditions immediately after exposure. The sleeper effect of delayed exposure differed, however, from that concerning the assessment of danger to the public. The relative sleeper effect was found:

Instead of a growing effect of public-risk perception after exposure to threatening images, the effect of exposure to sanitized images diminished with time. Thus the newscast featuring threatening images retained its effect over time, presumably because the imagery imposed itself at later times and continued to reinforce the consequences of excessive sun exposure. The newscast featuring sanitized images, however, lost its influence on issue perception, presumably because accessibility of these images deteriorated along with that of the other health information.

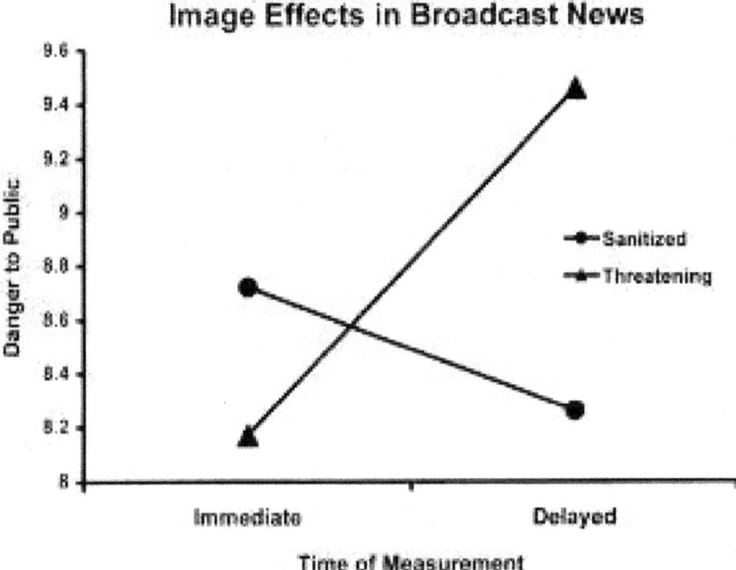

Fig. 14.2. Perception of danger to the public from excessive sunbathing as a function of exposure to a broadcast news story featuring sanitized or threatening images of melanoma and of time of assessment (immediate vs. 2-week delay). The sleeper effect of exposure to the threatening image is evident in the diverging gradients. Authors' data first published in "Effects of threatening images in news programs on the perception of risk to others and self," by D. Zillmann and S. Gan, 1996, *Medienpsychologie: Zeitschrift fur Individual-und Massenkommunikation, 8*(4), 288–305, 317–318.

A different type of threatening image was studied by Gan, Hill, Pschernig, and Zillmann (1996). The study (explained in more detail in Sundar, chap. 12; this volume) investigated the effects of images expressing deep hatred and intent to harm. A broadcast news report about the 1994 Hebron massacre in which an extremist Israeli settler gunned down Islamic worshippers in a mosque varied in the reaction of individuals to the massacre. Versions were created with no reaction images, with images of individuals endorsing the killings as "a good beginning," with images of individuals condemning the killings, and a version including both endorsing and condemning images. Respondents indicated their perceptions of the peace process in the Middle East. Findings indicate that the use of these strong emotional images did indeed influence issue perception. The aggregation of highly favorable reactions to the massacre in a television news report did, as expected, shift perceptions toward greater blame of Israelis for the violence in the Middle East, toward their lesser embrace of peace, and toward a higher likelihood of further violence.

The effects of threatening images in print news reports on reader issue perception were one subject of a 1999 study by Zillmann, Gibson, and Sargent. A news article on the safety of amusement parks, specifically the risks of roller coasters, was presented in four versions: (1) without photographs in a control condition; (2) with a threatening photograph showing an accident victim on a stretcher going into an ambulance in front of a roller coaster; (3) with a nonthreatening photograph showing children having lots of fun on a roller coaster ride; or (4) with both of these photographs (see Fig. 14.3). The report text, which included interviews with accident victims in addition to statistics indicating that rides are safer than ever, was identical across conditions. Respondents indicated their perceptions of amusement park safety and of their personal safety at amusement parks either immediately or after a 10-day delay.

Findings indicate that the threatening image strongly influenced the perception of general and personal safety. Specifically, respondents in the condition with just the threatening image produced assessments of lesser safety and greater personal concerns, an effect that was stable over time (see Fig. 14.4). Although it was expected that the photograph of children having fun on the roller coaster by itself would diminish concerns about the safety of rides, this effect was not detected. The authors suggest this was because the image signaled a mood of carefree joy rather than the presence of amusement park safety.

A study by Gibson and Zillmann (1999), designed primarily to investigate the influence of incidental pictorial exemplification, also found threatening images to affect issue perception in print news reports. In the experiment, a print news-magazine report was created about a fictitious new tick-borne disease that was moving down the Appalachian Mountains into North

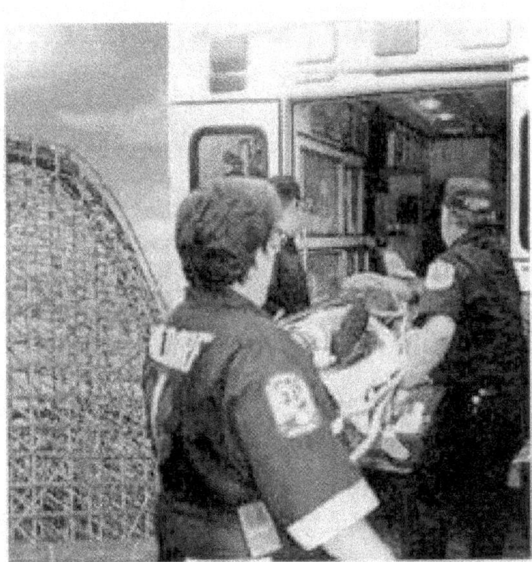

Fig. 14.3. The study featured threatening images (bottom) and nonthreatening images (top) in an attempt to determine the effects of threatening images in print news reports on reader issue perception.

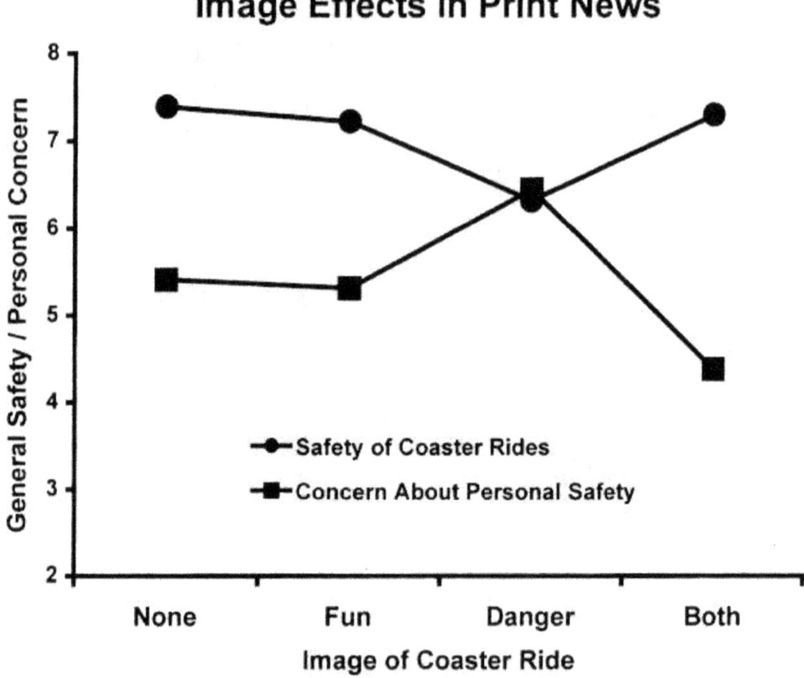

Fig. 14.4. Threatening images in print news reports can influence reader issue perception. The threatening image (Danger condition) depicted an injured person on a stretcher being moved into an ambulance in front of a roller coaster. The nonthreatening image (Fun condition) showed happy children riding a roller coaster. Authors' data first published in "Effects of photographs in news-magazine reports on issue perception" by D. Zillmann, R. Gibson, and S. L. Sargent, 1999, *Media Psychology, 3,* 207–228.

Carolina and other states. The story indicated that children were the main victims of the new disease. The report was presented with or without detailed photographs of two threatening-looking ticks (see Fig. 14.5).

Respondents estimated the risk of contracting the new disease for children of various ethnic groups in the infested areas. The estimates were significantly higher after exposure to the version with the image of the ticks. In addition, the tick images also apparently fostered more careful reading of the text. In an information-acquisition test on the symptoms of the fictitious new disease, respondents in the condition with the tick images performed significantly better than those who had been exposed to the story without the tick images. These finding indicate that threatening images not only influence judgments of risk but also suggest a higher level of salience that can lead to greater attention and information acquisition.

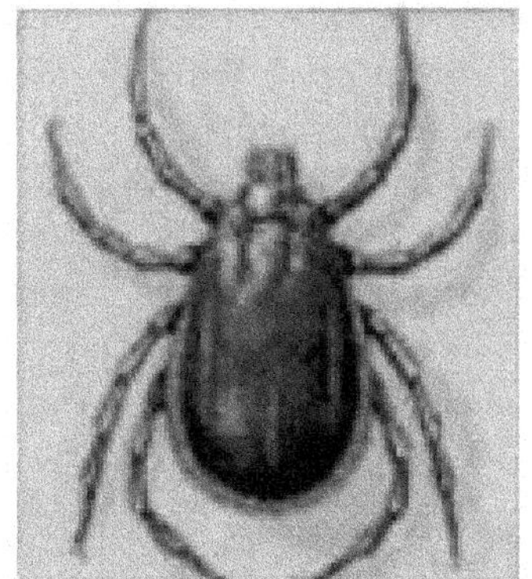

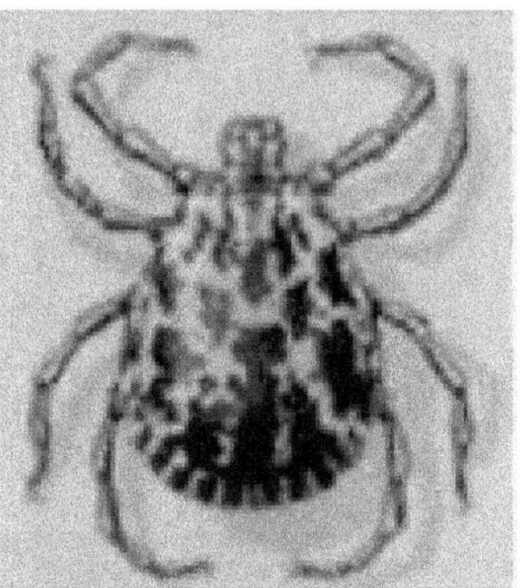

Fig. 14.5. Photographs of threatening-looking ticks in a news report about a fictitious new tick-borne disease influenced judgments of risk and improved information acquisition from the text of the news report.

EFFECTS OF INNOCUOUS IMAGES

Previous studies by Grimes (1990) and Grimes and Drechsel (1996) have shown that the combination of text and images in news, especially broadcast news, is by no means inconsequential for issue perception. They caution against the careless combination of image and text solely for the purpose of creating more interesting news presentations.

Work by Zillmann and his colleagues in three studies further examined the effects of innocuous image content in print and broadcast news on issue perception. Overall, the researchers found that using photographs with nonthreatening content to accompany print news reports may have little effect on issue perception as long as recipients remain aware of much of the information in the actual text report. Over time, however, such awareness diminishes, thereby allowing the retained image to influence the reader's issue perception. In addition, the researchers determined that issue perception can be influenced by the number of visually innocuous sources of information in broadcast news. Incidence estimates and estimates of issue salience tend to increase with the number of visual sources, independent of the information that these sources provide.

Zillmann, Gibson, and Sargent (1999) specifically investigated the influence of innocuous images in print news on issue perception. A story on the economics of family farming was created featuring a balance of exemplars from both poor and rich farmers. The report was titled "New American Farmers Telling Tales of Poverty and Riches." With the text remaining identical, four different image versions were created: (1) a control condition with no photographs, (2) a version with a photograph of a rich farmer, (3) a version with a photograph of a poor farmer, and (4) a version with both of these photographs. The poor-farmer photo showed a thin farmer walking behind an old horsedrawn plow-like device. The rich-farmer photo featured a more portly farmer proudly standing in front of his shiny new truck and private airplane (see Fig. 14.6).

New American Farmers
Telling Tales of Poverty and Riches

Fig. 14.6. A study of the influence of innocuous images in print news on issue perception featured a report titled "New American Farmers Telling Tales of Poverty and Riches." One version of the report (above) featured balanced exemplification with photos of both rich and poor farmers.

Respondents read the farming story along with other articles for disguise. Either immediately or after a 10-day delay, they reported their perceptions of farming economics. Specifically, they estimated the percentages of poor farmers losing money and going into bankruptcy and the percentage of rich farmers making a lot of money and getting rich. Results indicate the images failed to exert any significant influence in the immediate-assessment condition. The balanced text of the news report was apparently remembered at this time, which prevented any distorting image effects. In the delayed condition, however, the images exerted more influence and shifted perception in the direction of their content. The rich-farmer image fostered an overestimation of the prevalence of wealthy farmers, whereas the poor-farmer image led to an overestimation of farmers threatened with bankruptcy. In addition, the poor-farmer condition fostered an absolute sleeper effect. The two balanced photographic conditions did not lead to distorted issue perception: Means of the conditions with either no photographs or photographs of both poor and rich farmers were not significantly different.

Innocuous image effects in broadcast news were the subject of an investigation by Perkins (1999), who looked specifically at the effects of aggregating different numbers of such images in connection with text case studies in reports on various threatening issues. Perkins created two broadcast news reports, one on homeowners' concerns about the presence of dangerous radon gas in their homes, and the other about mothers' protests of the distribution by public libraries of horror-type videos for children, based on the highly successful *Goosebumps* children's book series. In both news packages, the anchor introduced the report, and several visually innocuous sources expressed their opinions. Then the opposing position was taken by an official source, and the anchor closed the report. The radon story featured eight reasons that radon gas is undesirable, focusing on health issues and financial problems caused by the gas. In this report, either two, four, or eight homeowners expressed their concerns about the gas in their homes. The arguments were kept constant across conditions; the only manipulation concerned the number of persons asserting these arguments. All of the "innocuous" speakers had been pretested to ensure they were similar in appeal, credibility, and intelligence.

Likewise, the report on horror videos for children featured eight arguments for removing the videos from the libraries, including ill effects on children such as sleeplessness, nightmares, hyperactivity, and roughhousing. Again, the points were kept constant; only the number of sources asserting them varied.

It was expected that the more innocuous sources presenting arguments in a news report, the more respondents would perceive the issue to be a social problem of concern to many. Results were as expected. In the *Goosebumps* report, the version featuring eight mothers protesting the videos led to perceptions of harm to greater numbers of children and stronger support for the removal of the videos from libraries than did the presentation by four mothers, which in turn produced higher estimates than the report featuring only two mothers.

The radon gas report produced similar differences between the two- and eight-source conditions. However, there was no significant difference between the four-source and eight-source conditions for estimates of the danger and importance of the problem. For incidence estimation, the means of the two-source and four-source conditions were also comparable.

Overall, the results indicate that the number of visible sources, even innocuous ones, presenting their views does influence issue perception. Estimates of the importance and incidence of an issue increase with the number of exemplifying sources.

INCIDENTAL PICTORIAL EXEMPLIFICATION

Grimes (1990) and Grimes and Drechsel (1996) have noted that broadcast newsmakers sometimes face legal difficulties stemming from the use of background footage, or b-roll, designed to enhance the text of a current news report. This video is often pulled from station archives and may not be specifically related to the report with which it is used. Although this incidental placement of images often has no harmful effects, it may occasionally lead to an unintended, often defamatory, "guilt by association" and a resulting libel suit. In one such case, Detroit resident Ruby Clark sued ABC News, alleging that a story on prostitution left viewers with the false impression that she was a prostitute rather than an innocent resident of a neighborhood that had become the center of prostitution problems. She claimed that video showing her walking down the street of her neighborhood immediately after prostitutes were mentioned in an accompanying voice-over could have caused viewers to think she was a prostitute, even though she was identified in the story as a neighborhood resident.

Grimes and Drechsel (1996) utilized this news report and another one cited in a libel suit as the basis for their investigation of the cognitive processes that might lead people to associate defamatory information in news text with nondefamatory accompanying pictures. They predicted that much of this tendency can be explained by schema theory, which states that individuals' perceptions are guided in part by cognitive structures, called *schema,* that help them construct meaning out of the otherwise overwhelming number of external stimuli to which they are exposed. The researchers focused specifically on gender and race schemata, because in many libel cases stemming from incidental image placement, gender and race issues are involved. They explained, for example, that in the Detroit case mentioned earlier, Ruby Clark's legal argument that she would be mistaken for a prostitute seems more plausible because she is Black, because the narration in the news report asserted that most of the prostitutes in the neighborhood were Black, and because there exists a common race schemata that Blacks are more likely to be criminals than victims.

In their study using the prostitution story, they added a second story based on an actual case that involved a Chicago gynecologist, Dr. Victoria Maclin, who sued a television station for libel after the station broadcast a story about a newly filed medical negligence suit and used file footage showing her performing a gynecological procedure. The negligence suit, however, did not involve Dr. Maclin. The suit had actually been brought against a hospital where personnel allegedly treated a patient with a cotton swab that had previously been used on a patient with AIDS. Maclin's suit alleged that the voice–video juxtaposition essentially identified her as a physician guilty of malpractice.

Grimes and Drechsel conducted two experiments using versions of these two broadcast news reports that were manipulated in terms of "schema consistency" of images. In the schema-consistent versions of the two news reports, the doctor in the malpractice story was depicted as a man, and the neighborhood resident in the prostitution story was depicted as White. In the schema-inconsistent version, the doctor was a woman and the neighborhood resident was Black. Then, in the second experiment, two new versions of the stories were produced. In version one of the prostitution story, all actresses were Black. In version one of the malpractice story, all actors were male. In version two, the prostitution story featured all White actresses, and the malpractice story featured all females. Data from the two experiments were merged so the authors could compare all possible versions of the stories.

In a free-recall test, respondents were asked to describe in detail as many of the physical characteristics they could recall for the prostitute, the neighborhood resident, and the doctors. Then in a cued recall test, respondents were given multiple-choice questions about the characters in the stories. The authors had predicted that when the physician in the malpractice report is portrayed as a woman, viewers are more likely to confuse her with the malpractitioner than when the physician is portrayed as a man. Likewise, they predicted, for the prostitution story, that when the neighborhood resident is portrayed as Black, viewers are more likely to confuse her with the prostitute than when the neighborhood resident is portrayed as White. Results were mixed. The cued-recall data provided support for these hypotheses, but the free-recall data did not. The authors argued that their overall findings suggest that in contexts where race and gender can play a role in audience members' construction of meaning, the conditions may be conducive to the creation of libel. In both of their experimental scenarios, they pointed out, nothing literally defamatory was communicated—nothing was said to explicitly link the innocent physician to malpractice or the neighborhood resident to prostitution. Yet many of the study's respondents made just such linkages, both immediately and 3 days later. Overall, Grimes and Drechsel determined that the passage of time can enhance the likelihood that previously developed schemata will shape viewers' recollection of what they saw and heard in news reports.

Gibson and Zillmann (1999) expanded the research on incidental placement of image exemplars to address the effects on issue perception. As described previously in the section on threatening image effects, a print news report was created about a fictitious new disease spread by ticks that was moving down the Appalachian Mountains into North Carolina and other areas. The disease was said to have severe symptoms, even worse than those of Lyme disease. The story indicated that children were the primary victims of the new disease, but it did not mention race or ethnicity in any way, and it masked the gender of the exemplars included in the text of the report. The report, in news-magazine layout, was presented with or without detailed photographs of two threatening-looking ticks. In addition, some versions of the report contained innocuous images of children, the main victims of the disease. Specifically, five versions were created. The first was a control condition with no images, and the second was a condition containing only an image of two "threatening-looking" ticks, as mentioned previously. In addition, three conditions presenting three child victims, along with images of the ticks, were created. The photographs featured obviously healthy young children in school or playing at home, prior to their contracting the new tick-borne disease. The incidental information contained in the photographs was simply the children's race or ethnicity. As shown in Fig. 14.7, the photographs of the children featured either three White children, three Black children, or two White and one Black, an attempt to approximate the ethnic proportion of the actual population. It is important to state again that the text of the news-magazine report did not mention race or ethnicity at all.

Fig. 14.7. The study on the effects of incidental pictorial information on issue perception featured a news report with one version containing photographs of White children and one version containing photographs of Black children. The text of the report did not mention the children's ethnicity at all.

Respondents estimated the risk of contracting the new disease for children of various ethnic groups in the infested areas, by region, and by age group. They also estimated their perception of the danger of the disease. The main concern of the study, of course, was the risk estimation for different ethnic groups, specifically Whites, Blacks, Hispanic Americans, and Asian Americans. The researchers did not expect estimates of Hispanic Americans and Asian Americans to be influenced by the incidental image information; these groups were included in the dependent measures primarily to disguise the main research interest.

Results indicate that incidental image exemplification in print news reports have strong effects. First of all, as mentioned previously, the threatening image of the two ticks fostered higher estimates of risk, irrespective of the ethnicity of victims. Most importantly, selective photographic exemplification of an ethnic group was found to foster higher estimates of risk for that group, as illustrated in Fig. 8. This occurred in spite of the fact that the news report itself made no mention whatsoever of the ethnicity of victims of the disease or the likelihood of a member of any ethnic group contracting the disease. The effects patterns for Hispanic Americans and Asian Americans, who were not pictorially represented in the news report, were relatively similar to that of Blacks, suggesting that respondents grouped people of color together in estimating their risk, regardless of whether that particular minority group was pictorially represented. Balanced visual representation of ethnic groups produced similar estimates of risk for Whites and Blacks and lower estimates of risk for Hispanics and Asians. Overall, the findings of this study suggest considerable influence of photographic information, however incidental to the main focus of the report.

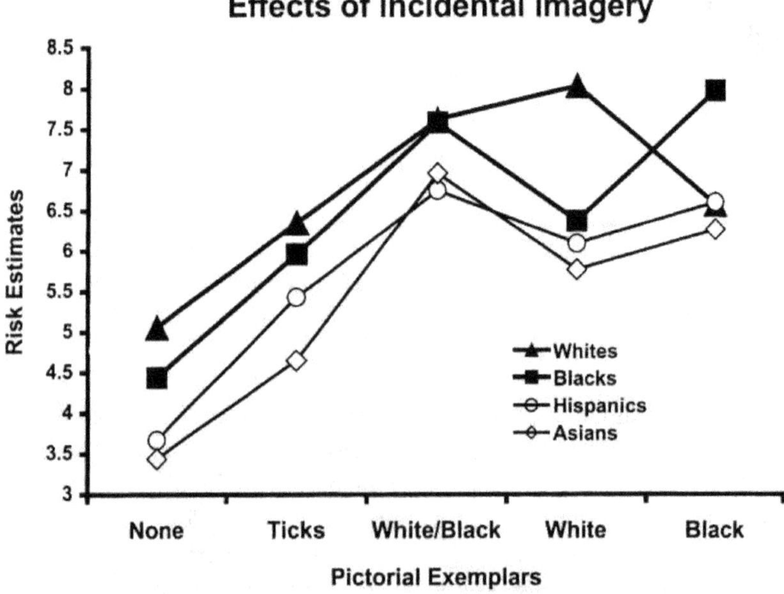

Fig. 14.8. Perception of the risk of tick-borne disease for different ethnic groups as a function of ethnicity-specific pictorial exemplification. Results indicate incidental pictorial exemplification of race had marked effects on reader issue perception. Authors' data originally published in "Reading between the photographs: The influence of incidental pictorial information on issue perception," by R. Gibson and D. Zillmann, *Journalism & Mass Communication Quarterly,* 77(2), 355–366.

Findings from the 10 years of photography effects research previously outlined earlier lead to an overall conclusion that should be of considerable interest to the journalism community: The employment of images—whether they be emotional, threatening, innocuous, or incidental—may amount to additional storytelling that journalists may not be aware of when they select photographs for use with news stories. Such images may be chosen simply to add interest, appeal, or credibility to a news report, but they have been shown to exert a strong psychological impact on readers and viewers, particularly in shaping these audience members' perceptions of the events and phenomena reported in the news. For journalists who strive for a socially responsible press, this is an issue that needs to be addressed. The authors of these studies urge news reporting and layout personnel, whose goal it is to produce accurate news reports, to become aware of the power of visual storytelling on news consumers' perceptions of the issues contained in those reports.

REFERENCES

Anderson, J. R., & Paulson, R. (1978). Interference in memory for pictorial information. *Cognitive Psychology, 10,* 178–202.

Aust, C. F., & Zillmann, D. (1996). Effects of victim exemplification in television news on viewer perception of social issues. *Journalism & Mass Communication Quarterly, 74,* 787–803.

Brosius, H.-B. (1993). The effects of emotional pictures in television news. *Communication Research, 20*(1), 105–124.

Brosius, H.-B., Donsbach, W., & Birk, M. (1996). How do text-picture relations affect the effectivenss of television newscasts? *Journal of Broadcasting & Electronic Media, 40,* 180–195.

Crowley, D., & Mitchell, D. (Eds.). (1994). *Communication theory today.* New York: Polity.

Culbertson, H. (1974). Visual detail, sensationalism and perceived writer stand. *Journalism Quarterly, 51,* 79–86.

Donsbach, W., Brosius, H.-B., & Mattenklott, A. (1993). How unique is the perspective of television? A field experiment on the perception of a campaign event by participants and television viewers. *Political Communication, 10,* 37–53.

Drew, D. G., & Grimes, T. (1987). Audio-visual redundancy and TV news recall. *Communication Research, 14,* 452–461.

Findahl, O. (1981). The effect of visual illustrations upon perception and retention of news programmes. *Communications, 7,* 151–167.

Furnham, A. F., & Gunter, B. (1985). Sex, presentation mode, and memory for violent and non-violent news. *Journal of Educational Television, 11*(2), 99–105.

Gan, S., Hill, J. R., Pschernig, E., & Zillmann, D. (1996). The Hebron massacre, selective reports of Jewish reactions, and perceptions of volatility in Israel. *Journal of Broadcasting & Electronic Media, 40,* 122–131.

Gehring, R. E., Toglias, M. P., & Kimble, G. A. (1976). Recognition memory for words and pictures at short and long-term retention intervals. *Memory & Cognition, 4,* 256–260.

Gerbner, G. (1992). Persian Gulf war, the movie. In H. Mowlana, G. Gerbner, & H. I. Schiller (Eds.), *Triumph of the image: The media's war in the Persian Gulf–A global perspective* (pp. 243–265). Boulder, CO: Westview.

Gibson, R., & Zillmann, D. (1999). Reading between the photographs: The influence of incidental pictorial information on issue perception. *Journalism & Mass Communication Quarterly, 77,* 355–366.

Graber, D. A. (1990). Seeing is remembering: How visuals contribute to learning from television news. *Journal of Communication, 40*(3), 134–155.

Graber, D. A. (1996). Say it with pictures. *Annals of the American Academy of Political Science Scholars, 546,* 85–96.

Grimes, T. (1990). Encoding TV news messages into memory. *Journalism Quarterly, 67,* 757–766.

Grimes, T., & Drechsel, R. (1996). Word–picture juxtaposition, schemata, and defamation in television news. *Journalism & Mass Communication Quarterly, 73,* 169–180.

Gunter, B. (1980). Remembering television news: Effects of picture content. *Journal of General Psychology, 102,* 127–133.

Gunter, B. (1987). *Poor reception: Misunderstanding and forgetting broadcast news.* Hillsdale, NJ: Lawrence Erlbaum Associates.

Hart, R. P. (1994). *How television charms the modern voter.* New York: Oxford University Press.

Johnson-Cartee, K. S., & Copeland, G. A. (1991). *Negative political advertising: Coming of age.* Hillsdale, NJ: Lawrence Erlbaum Associates.

Katz, E., Adoni, H., & Pnina, P. (1977). Remembering the news: What pictures add to recall. *Journalism Quarterly, 54,* 231–239.

Lang, A., & Friestad, M. (1993). Emotion, hemispheric specialization, and visual and verbal memory for television messages. *Commmunication Research, 20,* 647–670.

Lang, G. E., & Lang, K. (1953). The unique perspective of television and its effects: A pilot study. *American Sociological Review, 18,* 3–12.

Messaris, P. (1997). *Visual persuasion.* Thousand Oaks, CA: Sage.

Meyrowitz, J. (1985). *No sense of place: The impact of electronic media on social behavior.* New York: Oxford University Press.

Mundorf, N., Drew, D., Zillmann, D., & Weaver, J. B. (1990). Effects of disturbing news on recall of subsequently presented news. *Communication Research, 17,* 601–615.

Newhagen, J. E., & Reeves, B. (1992). The evening's bad news: Effects of compelling negative television news images on memory. *Journal of Communication, 42*(2), 25–41.

Nugent, G. C. (1982). Pictures, audio, and print: Symbolic representation and effect on learning. *Educational Communication and Technology Journal, 30,* 163–174.

Paivio, A. (1971). *Imagery and verbal processes.* New York: Holt, Rinehart & Winston.

Perkins, J. W., Jr. (1999). *Effects of information source quantity and personal experience in issue exemplification.* Unpublished doctoral dissertation, University of Alabama, Tuscaloosa.

Perlmutter, D. D. (1999). *Visions of war: Picturing warfare from the Stone Age to the Cyberage.* New York: St. Martin's.

Philo, G. (1990). *Seeing and believing: The influence of television.* London: Routledge.

Reese, S. D. (1984). Visual–verbal redundancy effects on TV news learning. *Journal of Broadcasting, 28,* 79–87.

Scott, R. K., & Goff, D. H. (1988). How excitation from prior programming affects television news recall. *Journalism Quarterly, 65,* 615–620.

Sharkey, J. (1993, December). When pictures drive foreign policy: Somalia raises serious questions about media influence. *American Journalism Review,* 14–19.

Wanta, W. (1988). The effects of dominant photographs: An agenda-setting experiment. *Journalism Quarterly, 65,* 107–111.

Wanta, W., & Roark, V. (1993, August). *Cognitive and affective responses to newspaper photographs.* Paper presented to the visual communication division of the annual conference at the Association for Education in Journalism and Mass Communication, Kansas City, MO.

Warshaw, P. R. (1978). Application of selective attention theory to television advertising displays. *Journal of Applied Psychology, 63,* 366–372.

Zillmann, D., & Gan, S. (1996). Effects of threatening images in news programs on the perception of risk to others and self. *Medienpsychologie: Zeitschrift fur Individual- und Massenkommunikation, 8,* 288–305, 317–318.

Zillmann, D., Gibson, R., & Sargent, S. L. (1999). Effects of photographs in news-magazine reports on issue perception. *Media Psychology, 3,* 207–228.

SECTION IV:

Empirical Advances in Research on Media Entertainment

15

Humor and Mirth

Cynthia M. King
California State University, Fullerton

Tragedy is when I cut my finger. Comedy is when you fall down an open manhole cover and die.

–Mel Brooks

The appeal and impact of humor and mirth have been popular research topics for Dolf Zillmann and his associates. In studying the appeal of humor, researchers have explored what makes us laugh—the necessary and sufficient conditions for humor and mirth reactions to occur. In examining the impact of humor and mirth, researchers have explored what happens when we laugh—the emotional, psychological, and physiological impacts of the mirth reactions that humor generates. These researchers are not alone in their interest in humor and mirth. Media audiences appear to share this fascination with the absurd as they exhibit a seemingly insatiable demand for humor and comedy.

Humor figures prominently in virtually all forms of media entertainment. Zillmann and Bryant (1991) noted that comedic elements are found in some of the earliest motion picture productions. For example, in Louis Lumiére's 1895 *L'Arroseur arrosé* a boy steps on a garden hose stopping the water flow only to remove his foot so that the water sprays into the face of the unsuspecting gardener who is inspecting the nozzle. Film historian Mast (1981) credited this film with containing "many elements of a comic art that would one day mature" (p. 21). Today, comedies account for almost one half of the all-time top 100 films in box office sales (see Fig. 15.1). Comedy enjoys similar success on the small screen, accounting for more than one half of the top 100 television shows of all time (see Fig. 15.2).

Humor also permeates genres other than comedy. Cantor (1977) reported that humor is found in virtually all television programming including news,

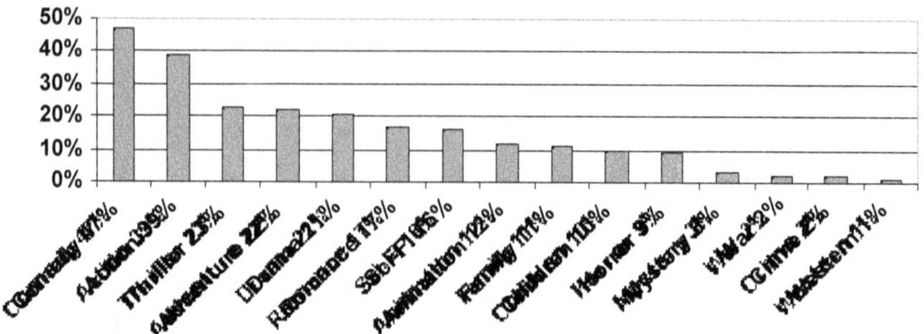

Fig. 15.1. Genre classifications for the top 100 films of all time. Statistics based on North American Box Office Gross Sales as of April, 20 01, from list posted at http://www.the-movie-times.com/thrsdir/Top10ever.html. Because films could be cross-referenced as multiple genres, total percentage exceeds 100%.

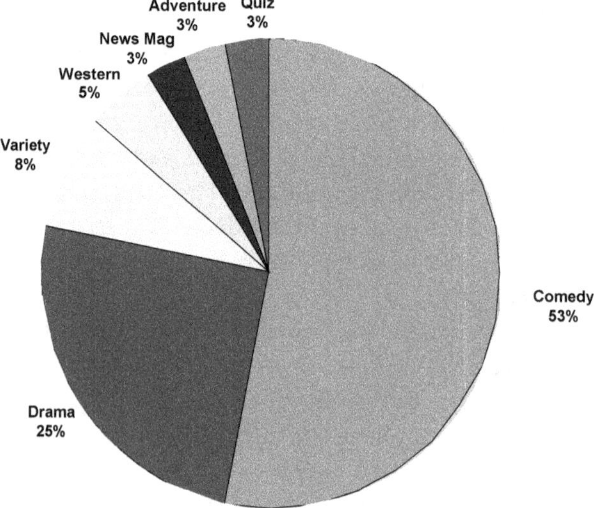

Fig. 15.2. Top 100 television shows of all time by genre. The list of shows and their genre assignments were taken from Brooks and Marsh (1999). The shows are all prime-time network television series. For the figure, genres were collapsed so that comedy also includes shows categorized as situation comedy, comedy/variety, humor and comedy adventure. Drama also includes police drama, drama anthology, detective drama, legal drama, medical drama and fantasy. Variety also includes musical variety, music, anthology, talent and talk, and adventure also includes adventure drama.

sports, soap operas and religious programs. And, interestingly, a little over 75% (36 out of 47) of the top 100 films categorized as comedy are cross-listed under other film genres.[1] Moreover, advertisers also use liberal doses of humor. Researchers found humor in 30% of radio ads and in more than 24% of television ads (Weinberger, Spotts, Campbell, & Parsons, 1995). Recent research has also focused on how humor has invaded action thrillers and horror films with the emergence of wise-cracking action heroes and villains as well as tongue-in-cheek action and horror spoofs (Jablonski & Sutherland, 1999; King, 2000a, 2000b; King-Jablonski & Zillmann 1995).

Humor's prominence in popular culture, however, did not begin with the rise of the mass media. Indeed, Zillmann and Bryant (1991) noted that "humor seems to be a primordial phenomenon. It has been found in all recorded human cultures; not in deficient quantity but in conspicuous abundance" (p. 268). It should not be surprising, therefore, to find that the study of humor and its appeal has also enjoyed a long and rich history.

THEORETICAL ORIGINS

Zillmann and Bryant (1991) provided a succinct review of the origins of humor theory. Some of the earliest theories of humor and comedy are traced back to Greek philosophers Plato (Philebus), Aristotle (Poetics) and Cicero (Oratore). Collectively, they contended that humor exhibits a negativity bias dwelling on the exhibition of baseness and deformities. Their work focused little on why these exhibitions caused mirthful reactions, but instead concentrated on condemning these reactions as inappropriate and immoral (Zillmann & Cantor, 1976). Nonetheless, their ideas, along with early works of British philosophers Hobbes (1651/1968) and Spencer (1888) and German philosopher Kant (1788/1922) provide the foundation for contemporary humor theories.

Humor theorists agree that many forms of humor rely on hostile elements. In fact, humor is often quite aggressive. Zillmann and Bryant (1991) explained that much comedy "can be construed as an aggregation of miniature plots in which some persons or groups triumph over others, and in which these others are debased, demeaned, disparaged, ridiculed, humiliated, or otherwise subjected to undesirable experiences" (p. 270).

[1]Calculations based on North American Box Office Gross Sales as of April, 20 01, from ranked list and genre classifications posted at http://www.the-movie-times.com/thrsdir/Top10ever.html.

Researchers have noted the prevalence of this type of humor in television programs (Stocking, Sapolsky, & Zillmann, 1977). Hobbes (1651/1968), like the early Greek philosophers, condemned hostile humor. According to Hobbes, "Those grimaces called laughter" express the passion of self-glorification, which is brought about "by the apprehension of some deformed thing in another, by comparison whereof they (the glorifiers) suddenly applaud themselves" (p. 125). And he noted that this practice was "incident most to them, that are conscious of the fewest abilites in themselves; who are forced to keep themselves in their own favor, by observing the imperfections of other men" (p. 125). Hobbes (1968) argued that the recognition of these imperfections would prompt a comparison in which the observer can feel superior. Thus, individuals find the disparagement of others amusing because it allows them to feel better about themselves.

Consistent with this sentiment, early psychological research by Wolff, Smith, and Murray (1934) focused on disparagement as the major theme of humor and comedy. Their formula stipulated two conditions, necessary, although not necessarily sufficient for mirth reactions: First, the disposition toward the targeted entity must not be positive (i.e., the individual cannot like or care about the party targeted by the humor); and second, some form of disparagement must be directed at the disliked party. These premises became the basis of what is now called superiority theory (Keith-Spiegel, 1972), which emphasizes how humor makes individuals feel superior to those being ridiculed, and disparagement and disposition theories of humor (Zillmann, 1983a; Zillmann & Cantor, 1976), which emphasize the importance of the relationship between victor and victim in a humorous exchange.

DISPOSITION THEORY

This formula is perhaps most clearly articulated in Zillmann's disposition theory (see chap. 3, this volume; Zillmann, 1980, 1983a, 1996; Zillmann & Cantor, 1976), which, when applied to media entertainment, focuses on audience dispositions toward dramatic characters. In simplified form, this theory suggests that audiences are pleased when good things happen to good characters and when bad things happen to bad characters. Thus, audiences are expected to enjoy humor that teases or ridicules a villainous character, particularly when the barbs are delivered by a likeable, heroic character.

Interestingly, however, audiences appear to find little amusement when "good things" happen to characters no matter how "good" or deserving those characters might be. As Zillmann (2000) noted, "Humor and comedy seem exceedingly partial to dishing out put-downs, mishaps, insults and outright humiliations" (p. 39). The focus is on misfortune rather than triumph, with amusement determined by who "dishes out" and who receives this misfortune. Thus, for humor and comedy, Zillmann has modified disposition theory as follows:

Disposition Toward Victim

1. The more intense the negative affective disposition toward the disparaged agent or entity, the greater the magnitude of mirth.

2. The more intense the positive affective disposition toward the disparaging agent or entity, the smaller the magnitude of mirth.

Disposition Toward the Victor

3. The more intense the negative affective disposition toward the disparaging agent or entity, the smaller the magnitude of mirth.

4. The more intense the positive affective disposition toward the disparaging agent or entity, the greater the magnitude of mirth.

According to these propositions, amusement should be greatest when an extremely disliked victim is disparaged or ridiculed by an extremely well-liked victor. Amusement should be weakest when a liked victim is disparaged by a disliked victor, and other victor–victim combinations should yield intermediate results.

A large number of investigations lend support to the disposition theory of humor and comedy, including studies conducted long before the theory was formally introduced. In studies of ethnic humor involving Jews and Gentiles, Wolff et al. (1934) manipulated the ethnicity of the characters delivering the punch line and of those being victimized by it. Consistent with expectations, they found that Jews found it funnier to see a Jew deliver a punch line victimizing a Gentile, and Gentiles found it funnier to see a Gentile deliver a punch line victimizing a Jew. This same experimental design was used to explore the ethnic humor of Blacks and Whites (Middleton, 1959) and reactions to humor by White, Black, and Hispanic children (McGhee & Duffey, 1983a, 1983b; McGhee & Lloyd, 1981). In each case individuals were more amused by humor delivered by someone of their own ethnicity that victimized individuals of a different ethnicity. This design was also used to investigate gender differences in humor appreciation (Cantor, 1976; Losco & Epstein, 1975; Love & Deckers, 1989; Mundorf, Bhatia, Zillmann, Lester, & Robertson, 1988; Wicker, Barron, & Willis, 1980).

Rather than simply making assumptions about disposition based on demographic differences such as ethnicity or gender, the research design was also expanded to measure dispositions toward both the deliverer and victim of the jokework. For example, Zillmann and Cantor (1972) examined the dispositional relationships between employers and employees and between professors and students and found that the more resentment individuals felt toward the other party, the more they were amused by humor that humiliated the other party. More recently, Zillmann, Taylor, and Lewis (1998) found that resentment toward specific politicians intensified amusement reactions to press release assertions that the politician had contracted a venereal disease. Interestingly, research has also found that disparaging humor can influence perceptions of the individuals involved in the humorous exchange. For example, Stocking and Zillmann (1976) found that individuals who disparaged themselves were perceived as less intelligent, less confident, and less witty. Although these investigations have not explored the appreciation of comedy in media entertainment per se, disposition theory has predicted reactions to other forms of entertainment including the enjoyment of drama (Zillmann, 1980) and sports events (Zillmann, Bryant, & Sapolsky, 1989).

Thus, although comedy is a uniquely popular form of media entertainment, Zillmann's disposition-based explanation for its appeal is based more on its similarity to other dramatic genres than on its differences. Zillmann (2000) emphasized comedy as a form of drama "not only because it also dwells on conflict and its resolution, but mostly because it entails the essential plots for enlightenment that characterize drama" (p. 37). In fact, he emphasized that even humor in its most simple forms reflects basic dramatic principles:

> Joke-telling may, of course, be construed as merely another form of miniature plot presentation. In fact, any kind of humorous expression can be thought of as a miniaturized comic plot—if need be, as a miniaturized miniature plot. All humor, no matter how condensed or reduced, must make a statement or amount to a comment about circumstances. (Zillmann, 2000, p. 42)

Of course, audiences do not laugh at every disparaging comment or act, even when the target is disliked. In some instances, it may be a case of too much of a bad thing. Aristotle (trans. 1966) suggested that the display of serious harm, especially death, evokes pity that would overpower any inclination to laugh. Zillmann (1996) maintained that the enjoyment of drama is greatly influenced by considerations of justice. Similarly, research has found that amusement is influenced by perceptions of justice and retaliatory equity (Cantor & Zillmann, 1973; Zillmann & Bryant, 1974; Zillmann, Bryant, & Cantor, 1974). Audience appreciation of the victimization found in both drama and comedy is thought to be fueled by perceptions that victims are somehow deserving of the treatment they receive. Therefore, disparagement or brutality that is particularly severe may be perceived as unjustified and, thus, less enjoyable. Yet extreme brutality is the focus of much comedy. Consider the slapstick, physical humor of classic shows such as *The Three Stooges* or *Road Runner* cartoons where audiences roll with laughter as characters are hit with frying pans and flattened by dropped anvils. On the other hand, althugh audiences may smile and sometimes even cheer when a villain is killed in a suspenseful action film, such killings usually do not inspire belly laughter. Why is it, then, that regardless of one's disposition toward the victim, audiences laugh at some instances of brutality but not others?

THE COMIC FRAME OF MIND

Zillmann (2000) maintained that such amusement requires a "comic frame of mind." According to Olson (1968), comedy, by its nature, signals "contrariety to the serious" (p. 13). The audience must be "inclined to take nothing seriously and to be gay about everything" (p. 25). Freud (1905/1958) argued that audiences rely on cues that signal the play context of humor and comedy, and he outlined features of Witzarbeit (jokework) that can serve as these cues. Freud (1905/1958) differentiated between nontendentious and tendentious humor. Nontendentious humor relies on jokework including innocuous plays on words, irony and exaggeration that does not victimize, humiliate, or disparage. This is the humor of innocent "Knock, Knock" jokes and "Why did the chicken cross the road" riddles. In contrast, tendentious humor emphasizes the victimization of one party by another. According to Freud, however, although nontendentious jokes and riddles may produce a few smiles and polite giggles, they are rarely capable of producing the intense amusement that tendentious humor elicits with ease. He further maintained that very little of what we label as humor is truly innocent. Instead, much of even the most simple wordplay and jokework include tendentious undercurrents of hostility and taboo topics.

Nonetheless, it is argued that even tendentious humor relies on nontendentious elements—jokework such as plays on words, irony, and exaggeration—to serve as the cues that allow audiences to laugh. It was Freud's contention that audiences do not truly understand what it is about tendentious humor that makes them laugh. He argued that although audiences may believe that they laugh at the jokework and wordplay, the fact that innocent jokework does not create the same level of mirth suggests it is the tendentious elements, the hostility, and taboo topics that truly inspire amusement. The logic is that it is not considered socially acceptable to laugh at others' misfortune. Thus, although deep down audiences might be intrigued, even amused by blatant hostility, they are not free to admit or express that enjoyment due to fear of social censure. In comedy, however, the nontendentious humorous cues that accompany hostility may unconsciously provide audiences with the justification they need to laugh openly. As Zillmann (2000) stated, these cues "set us free to enjoy what we otherwise could not" (p. 48).

These speculations inspired the formulation of a misattribution theory of humor (Zillmann, 1983; Zillmann & Bryant, 1980). As the name suggests, this theory postulates that individuals misattribute their enjoyment of hostile humor to the innocent, nontendentious humorous cues. Following Freud's logic, this theory predicts greater amusement for a combination of nontendentious and tendentious elements than for either element alone. This theory further incorporates the concept of disposition, in maintaining that amusement will be greatest when audiences dislike the victim targeted by both elements. To test this theory, Zillmann and Bryant (1980) manipulated a comic situation containing both nontendentious and tendentious elements. These elements were isolated and experimentally manipulated so that, in one condition only the nontendentious elements were shown (the innocuous "funny" component), in another condition only the tendentious elements were presented (i.e., a mishap befalls the targeted "victim"), and in a third the components were combined (the mishap was associated with the funny element). In each case, respondents were either resentful or indifferent toward the victim. It was found that when audiences were indifferent toward the victim, the combination of jokework and victimization produced amusement approximately equal to the sum of the mirth for victimization and jokework alone. However, for the resented victim, the victimization plus jokework resulted in mirth significantly greater than the additive impact of each element alone. Zillmann (2000) emphasized the implications of these findings:

> Amusement was exceedingly high when all the ingredients of good comedy were present: despised protagonists, their victimization, and the humorous cues that set the audience free to enjoy these characters' demise...the mere presences of an exceedingly innocuous humor cue ... more than doubled amusement in response to the observed misfortune. It allowed onlookers to be malicious with dignity, indeed. (p. 49)

Thus, it would seem that it is these lighthearted cues that differentiate drama from comedy. Although both drama and comedy are governed by disposition theory, the victimization and demise of a villain in a dramatic presentation might produce feelings of exhilaration, even triumph, but laughter would be inappropriate. Comedy, however, is defined by inclusion of humorous cues that create a lighthearted context for this victimization, informing audiences that laughter is not only tolerated, but encouraged. For example, Leslie Nielsen is famous for his parodies of popular action films such as *Wrongfully Accused* (1998), a spoof on *The Fugitive* film and series and *Spy Hard* (1996), which mocks James Bond films. These action-comedies often follow a similar storyline of characters and events as their dramatic counterparts; however, there is additional jokework and exaggeration that signal to audiences that they should not take these events too seriously. Thus, although audiences may have held their breath in suspense and sighed in relief in the original thriller, in the parody the same storyline may have audiences holding their sides and hooting with laughter.

Many other theorists have acknowledged this "signaling function" of humor. Humorous cues are said to signal that the events toward which the humor is directed should not be taken overly seriously (Giles, Bourhis, Gadfield, Davies, & Davies, 1976; Kane, Suls, & Tedeschi, 1977). Kane et al. (1977) contended that "laughter can be used to initiate a cognitive transformation of a situation into a non-serious one" (p. 16). This reasoning is also reflected in Gruner's (1976) explanation of "kidding": "So, most of us learn to kid and be kidded. We recognize the smile of the kidder, we notice his playful demeanor as he warms up on us. And we know that we need to 'play along,' to remain 'good sports,' not to take offense" (p. 65). McGhee (1972) similarly argued that humor can function as a "play cue" that indicates that the events at hand should not be taken too seriously. He further suggested that these cues must be present for audience expectations to shift from those appropriate for drama reception to those appropriate for the reception of humor and comedy. Zillmann (1994) echoed this sentiment in his claim that the "realistic" nature of drama forces audiences to retain their “empathetic sensitivities.” Humor and comedy, however, “encourage lightheartedness, if not outright trivialization of addressed issues” (Zillmann, 2000, p. 42).

INCONGRUITY RESOLUTION

Although many theories of humor reflect a cynical view of human nature that emphasizes the capacity to find amusement in the misfortune of others, there are also more neutral theories of humor appreciation. One popular postulation is the notion of incongruity resolution. Zillmann (2000) characterized incongruity-based humor as humor that “requires the deciphering of ambiguities, a process that can be likened to problem solving” (p. 47). Consider the verbal joke “What is black and white and red all over?” “A newspaper!” The incongruity of how something can be black and white and red all over simultaneously is resolved when the punch line “A newspaper” triggers recognition of the wordplay on red and read.

Several researchers have explored aspects of incongruity in humor (Berlyne, 1969; Nerhardt, 1976; Rothbart, 1976; Schultz, 1976; Suls, 1972). Some theorists even argue that all humor requires the resolution of some form of incongruity (Wyer & Collins, 1992). Speculations regarding why audiences would respond to incongruity resolution with laughter can be traced back to Kant (1788/1922), who proposed that laughter is “an affective reaction that is evoked by the sudden transformation of a strained expectation into nothing” (p. 409, translated in Zillmann, 2000, p. 46). His thinking is interpreted to mean that people would respond in a joyful or amused fashion when what seemed to be a problem suddenly resolved itself (Zillmann, 2000). Spencer (1888) reformulated this conception, claiming that laughter results when an effort suddenly encounters a void. He coined the term *descending incongruity* to describe the transition from problematic to laughable.

Zillmann (2000) speculated that Kant and Spencer had in mind the numerous stressful and potentially threatening situations in everyday life that turn out to be less than anticipated. The thinking is that individuals perceive incongruities as problems, perhaps even threats, that must be eliminated. Cognitively, and perhaps even physiologically, individuals begin to build up and focus their energy on this problem, but when the problem is readily resolved, this apprehension and energy is released in the form of laughter. Such is the case with simple riddles including the newspaper joke related earlier. Although Kant is interpreted as favoring a purely cognitive explanation for the amusement this resolution creates, Spencer favors a more physiological interpretation where the incongruity stimulates actual physiological arousal for use in resolving the incongruity. And, when the incongruity is quickly resolved, laughter becomes a mechanism for depleting this unused energy. This logic works even for unintentional events that trigger laughter. Consider a scenario where two friends are walking along and one stumbles over a curb, but quickly regains balance. The unexpected and thus incongruous stumble may cause apprehension, even fear that the victim might be hurt, but once it is clear that no one has been hurt and no action is necessary, the incongruity is resolved, and both begin laughing, unconsciously releasing the unneeded anxious energy.

A MASTERFUL COPING MECHANISM

Echoing the more cynical sentiments of superiority theories, however, some theorists suggest that incongruity-based humor simply provides individuals with another opportunity to establish mastery and superiority. In noting the similarity between incongruity-based humor and problem solving, Zillmann (2000) suggested that humor is not merely the result of a problem having gone away. He argued that "the process of making it go away, of getting the point of it all ... can be considered an achievement—not one that calls for bringing out champagne, but one that can contribute to the amusement reaction." Again, the amusement is thought to emerge from these feelings of mastery over the jokework, and perhaps, even superiority over those who have not resolved or mastered the joke. According to Freud (1928), humor is a reflection of a sense of ease and confidence in the ability to reduce stressors to manageable challenges. Hayworth (1928) stated that

> those who are obsessed by fears or who suffer from inferiority complexes do not laugh easily ... [Conversely,] if the organism is in an aggressive, conquering attitude it will exult with a feeling of safety over threatened obstructions; it will communicate this to the rest of the group through the conditioned response of laughter. (p. 373)

Similarly, May (1953) argued the following about humor:

> It is an expression of our uniquely human capacity to experience ourselves as subjects who are not swallowed up in the objective situation. It is the healthy

> way of feeling a "distance" between oneself and the problem, a way of standing off and looking at one's problem with perspective. One cannot laugh when in an anxiety panic, for then one is swallowed up, one has lost the distinction between himself as subject and the objective world around him. (p. 54)

Numerous psychological theorists have regarded humor as an adaptive coping mechanism. One of the major characteristics of humor is that it appears to work as a defense against fear, enabling people to gain control over perceived or actual uncontrollable events (Thorson, 1985). According to McDougall (1922), one of the primary roles of humor is to aid in the defense against the grim realities of life. It has been suggested that jokes are often made about those things most feared, and that laughter allows distancing, a release of tension and relief (Leiber, 1986). Indeed, research suggests that humor is expressed when children consider recently threatening challenges that they have to some degree mastered, or material that they have only recently become able to comprehend (Harter, 1974; Harter, Shultz, & Blum, 1971; Pien & Rothbart, 1976; Watson 1972; Wolfenstein, 1954; Zigler, Levine, & Gould, (1967). Martin and Lefcourt (1983) reported similar findings for young adults. As Kris (1940) aptly noted, "What was feared yesterday and mastered is laughed at today" (p. 321).

MOOD MANAGEMENT

The idea that humor can help individuals master their fears and that amusement can relieve tension created by incongruities or other stressors is also consistent with Zillmann's research on mood management (see chap. 4, this volume; Zillmann, 1988; Zillmann & Bryant, 1985). These investigations examine how individuals manage their moods through their entertainment choices. The theory postulates that individuals learn that different genres such as comedy, tragedy, or horror evoke different emotions, and their media selections are then based on a genre's ability to change or enhance their mood states. When distressed, individuals may consciously and unconsciously turn to programming that will lighten their moods. In this case, comedy, with its capacity for easing fears and relieving stress, would seem to be a likely choice. And, because life is invariably filled with sundry stressors, comedy proves to be "a winning formula for media entertainment" (Zillmann, 2000, p. 51).

Indeed, it has been observed that frustrated men and angry women, when given the choice, tend to select comedy over drama, and they pick comedy more frequently than men and women in a neutral state (Medoff, 1979). Disgruntled men and women also showed a preference for humorous game shows (Zillmann, Hezel, & Medoff, 1980). Research also suggests that women may use comedy to manage hormonally induced depressive moods. Premenstral and menstrual women were found to select comedy programs more frequently than women in any other phase of the cycle (Meadowcroft & Zillmann, 1987), and comedy preferences were also found to vary with depressive moods during pregnancy (Helregel & Weaver, 1989).

Although both theory and research suggest that humor can help relieve negative moods, there are times when distressed individuals appear to avoid comedy. When provoked to anger, some individuals, particularly some men, tend to avoid comedy and instead seek exposure to less lighthearted genres (Medoff, 1979; Zillmann, Hezel, & Medoff, 1980). Consistent with mood-management principles, there is some evidence that individuals tend to avoid comedy either when they want to keep the negative emotions alive for some reason (O'Neal & Taylor, 1989) or when negative emotions are particularly strong (Christ & Medoff, 1984). The implication is that there are times when people do not want to be "cheered up." For example, individuals may want to maintain their fervor when preparing for a confrontation with an adversary. Or, individuals in mourning may want to continue grieving for a period. In these situations, individuals might prefer more serious, even hostile or tragic media selections. "But when the daily humdrum with all its little aggravations takes a hold of people, comedy appears to offer pleasant distraction with a high potential for mood repair" (Zillmann, 2000, p. 52).

COMIC RELIEF

Humor's stress-relieving capability is reflected in the dramatic device of comic relief. *Oxford's Companion to the English Language* (1992) defines comic relief as "an amusing scene, incident, or speech introduced into serious, tragic, or suspenseful drama to provide temporary relief from tension." Thus, it is thought that humor is injected into many dramatic productions to provide temporary relief from the tension created by serious, tragic, or suspenseful events in the story. Sorell (1972), a theater historian, noted that comic relief has been used to varying degrees by most dramatists, including Shakespeare. Today, the prevalence of humor in more serious drama is evidenced by the number of popular films of various genres that are cross-listed under comedy. Indeed, of the 47 top-grossing films of all time listed as comedy, 40% (19) were cross-listed with more serious or suspenseful genres including action, adventure, drama, crime, thriller, mystery, and/or horror.[2]

In his treatise *Poetics,* the Greek philosopher Aristotle suggested that humor might facilitate the release of strong emotions, such as those induced by exposure to tragedy or other negative events. Restoration and 18th-century English drama theorists John Dryden and Samuel Johnson argued for the merit of comic relief as a dramatic tool. Dryden (1668) contended the following:

> A continued gravity keeps the spirit too much bent; we must refresh it sometimes as we bait in a journey, that we may go on with greater ease. A scene of mirth, mixed with tragedy, has the same effect upon us which our music has betwixt the acts; which we find relief to us from the best plots and language of the stage, if the discourses have been long. (excerpted in Dukore, 1974, pp. 328–329)

Shurcliff (1968) reasoned that humor appears to function as a means of relief from the heightened arousal associated with the anticipation of a negative experience. Lucas (1958) similarly argued that "an audience may concentrate better on crises if it has relaxed at moments in between. Anyone who has watched a chick struggling out of its shell realizes how often Nature's way is—'Strain—rest—strain—rest'" (p. 175). Consequently, it is thought that humor can help relieve distress created by tense and tragic moments witnessed in dramatic productions much as it does in real life.

Thus, comic relief might appear to serve as a break in serious drama, providing audiences an opportunity to physically relax and settle down after tense or tragic scenes. Excitation-transfer theory (see chap. 2, this volume; Zillmann, 1978, 1983b, 1984, 1993), however, might suggest a somewhat different interpretation of the relationship between serious and comedic elements in drama. According to this theory, the physiological arousal associated with cognitive and emotional reactions decays more slowly than do the cognitive and emotional reactions themselves. It is further postulated that the residual arousal from one reaction can be transferred onto the next, intensifying subsequent emotional reactions. And, because arousal is nonspecific, arousal originally associated with positive experiences and emotions can be transferred onto negative experiences and emotions and

[2]Calculations based on North American Box Office Gross Sales as of April, 2001, from ranked list and genre classifications posted at http://www.the-movie-times.com/thrsdir/Top10ever.html.

vice versa. For example, when individuals receive a scare, their heart rates increase and their blood pressure begins to rise. If the scare turns out to be a false alarm, the fear will probably quickly subside; however, even when a person begins to feel calmer, heart rate and blood pressure may remain elevated. If, during that period, something comes along and triggers another emotional reaction, whether it is more fear, anger, or amusement, the reaction may be intensified by residual arousal from the original scare.

This theory has been used to explain the role of conflict in typical dramatic formulas. It is reasoned that intense conflict in drama generates arousal that intensifies enjoyment of the successful resolution. Following this logic, it would seem reasonable that if humorous scenes follow episodes of intense conflict, amusement reactions might also be intensified. Although this postulation has not been tested with dramatically induced excitation, Cantor, Bryant, and Zillmann (1974) did find that residual excitation from arousing written communication increased appreciation of subsequent cartoons and jokes.

It would seem, then, that a winning dramatic formula would be one that creates a continuous process where arousal is seamlessly transferred from one reaction to the next. Yet, if this is true, it would appear counterproductive to use humor to encourage the audience to relax, and potentially decrease arousal, before the conflict is fully resolved. However, what if humor fails to lower physiological arousal? Indeed, some arousal theories suggest that humor can actually increase arousal levels (Apter, 1982; Apter & Smith, 1977; Averill, 1969; Chapman, 1973; Godkewitsch, 1976; Langevin & Day, 1972). If this is the case, humor may provide affective and cognitive relief from dramatic distress, but may still serve to sustain, if not further increase excitation levels. Distress reactions may thus intensify amusement reactions, which intensify subsequent distress reactions, and so on until the ultimate resolution is reached.

Although drama theorists have embraced the notion of comic relief for centuries, its use as a dramatic device has received little empirical scrutiny. Recent investigations, however, do provide some evidence that comic elements in dramatic genres may at least affectively relieve drama-induced distress (King, 2000a, King-Jablonski & Zillmann, 1995). In these studies, individuals who saw action and horror films containing disparaging humorous dialogue found the films less distressing than did individuals who saw the same films when this humor was edited out. Thus, although humor plays a leading role in comedy, it may also play a significant supporting role in many other dramatic genres. Yet, further research is necessary if these roles are to be truly understood.

LAUGHTER IS THE BEST MEDICINE

Folk wisdom suggests that humor cannot only relieve stress, but also relieve pain, ward off illness, and aid in healing. These speculations have led to a growing body of research on the health benefits associated with mirth reactions to humor. The discipline of humor physiology, known scientifically as *gelotology,* includes the study of "those events occurring in our bodies in association with humorous experiences" (Fry, 1986, p. 81). Although researchers have examined emotional and cognitive reactions, most of this research has focused on physiological changes that occur during mirthful experiences.

Early studies investigated the effects of laughter on muscle tone (Paskind, 1932) and the respiratory mechanism of laughter (Lloyd, 1938). Researchers have continued to examine physiological reactions to humor involving the muscular, respiratory, cardiovascular, endocrine, immune, and central nervous systems. In most instances, mirthful responses are positive and beneficial (Fry, 1986, 1992). Based on the premise that humor can relieve anxiety by making light of otherwise serious situations, humor is approached as a stress reliever in both cognitive and endocrinological terms (Dixon, 1980; Goldstein, 1987; Haig, 1988; V. M. Robinson, 1983). Prolonged negative experiences have been found to increase the release of stress hormones like cortisol and also to impair immunological functions, making individuals more vulnerable to disease. By encouraging a more lighthearted response to life problems, humor may help mitigate these health threats.

Zillmann (2000) differentiated between the health benefits of "state" and "trait" forms of lightheartedness. Lightheartedness can be explored as a transitory state in the form of amusement and laughter induced by exposure to humor and comedy such as that found in entertainment media. And, lightheartedness can be explored as a more stable personality trait, based on the premise that some individuals are more inclined than others are to find humor in a situation or to respond in a lighthearted fashion. Research suggests many benefits of lightheartedness as a personality trait, colloquially, the benefits of possessing a good sense of humor. Sense of humor and humorous coping strategies have been associated with higher morale among seniors (Simon, 1990), greater pain tolerance during dental surgery (Trice & Price-Greathouse, 1986), lower stress reactions to depressive experiences (Nezu, Nezu, & Blissett, 1988), and less impairment of immune functions (measured by concentration of immunoglobulin A in saliva) when faced with imagined daily hassles (Martin & Dobbin, 1988).

Although this research reveals encouraging evidence of health benefits for good humor as a personality trait, of greater interest for media scholars is whether or not amusement induced as a "state" by humorous material such as film or television comedies can produce the same benefits. Humorous material does appear to enhance positive affective states including feelings of relaxation (Prerost & Ruma, 1987), as long as the humor is in "good taste" and is dispositionally appropriate. Analogous to "trait" findings, increases in salivary immunoglobulin A were observed after exposure to comedy as compared to alternatives (Dillon, Minchoff, & Baker, 1985–1986; Labott, Ahleman, Wolever, & Martin, 1990). Similarly, mirthful laughter was found to decrease levels of stress-linked hormones including cortisol and dopac (Berk, Tan, Fry, et al., 1989). Other studies found that the increases in heart rate and blood pressure that occur during laughter can exercise the myocardium and increase arterial and venous circulation, causing an increased movement of oxygen and nutrients to tissues (Fry & Savin, 1988) and promoting the movement of immune elements and phagocytes throughout the system, helping the body fight infections (Dillon, Minchoff, & Baker, 1985). Laughter also appeared to elevate natural killer cell activity (Berk, Tan, Napier, & Eby, 1989). In another study, however, the elevation of killer cell activity appeared more partial to negative emotions than to merriment (Knapp et al., 1992).

Exposure to comedy was also found to increase pain tolerance more than exposure to various nonhumorous stimuli (Cogan, Cogan, Waltz, & McCue, 1987; Nevo, Keinan, & Teshimovsky-Arditi, 1993; Weaver & Zillmann, 1994; Zillmann, Rockwell, Schweitzer, & Sundar, 1993). In these studies, pain tolerance was measured by requests for analgesics, excessive pressure to limbs, or hand submersion in ice water. Compared with serious drama, comedy was found to reduce the number of requests for analgesics at bedtime for older adults (Adams & McGuire, 1986), although a more recent study on postsurgical self-medication (Rotton & Shats, 1996) found exposure to comedy, when compared with serious drama, reduced the number of requests for minor medication, but increased requests for stronger analgesics. In several studies, however, elevated pain tolerance has been associated with positive emotions generally, including but not limited to amusement (Zillmann, Howland, Nichols, & Cleeland, 1991; Zillmann, de Wied, King-Jablonski, & Jenzowsky, 1996). In fact, increased pain tolerance was also observed for exposure to tragedy and crying (Weaver & Zillmann, 1994; Zillmann et al., 1993). However, given that measurements were taken after the conclusion of the film, after the tragic resolution, it is argued that even the impact of tragedy may be the result of positive feelings evoked by the film.

It is unclear why some forms of media entertainment, including comedy, appear to increase pain thresholds, although several explanations have been offered. One thought is that the positive emotions stimulated by media entertainment simply serve to counteract the negative perceptions of the pain. A similar notion, based on the distraction principle, is that any engaging stimulus serves to distract individuals from their pain to the point where they may even continue to cognitively reflect on stimulus (such as a film), and thus remain distracted from the pain, even after the film or other stimuli has ended. Others postulate that the physiological arousal generated by engaging material, whether positive or negative, serves to increase one's pain threshold directly or through the release of special hormones, although research has failed to confirm this relationship.

Still another possibility is that engaging stimuli, such as entertainment, through either excitation-transfer or a more cognitive process, encourage individuals to transfer and misattribute arousal or perceptions associated with the pain to emotional reactions regarding the entertainment. This explanation might help reconcile some of the conflicting research findings, in that, in some cases pain-generated arousal may be misattributed to the film, thus reducing cognitive perceptions of pain and requests for analgesics while increasing emotional reactions to the film. In other cases, however, such as when pain is more salient or acute, reactions to the entertainment might be transferred onto perceptions of the pain, thus increasing perceptions of pain and requests for analgesics. Although some research has failed to find a relationship between arousal and pain tolerance (Zillmann et al., 1996), it is still conceivable that some sort of transfer, physiologically, emotionally, and/or cognitively may occur.

Inconsistencies in methodology and findings make it difficult to draw any conclusions about the health impacts of comedy as transitory state-induced amusement. Clearly, more research is needed to help reconcile these inconsistencies. Nonetheless, given the overwhelming concerns about negative media effects, it is encouraging to see even limited evidence for positive effects of comedy and other forms of media entertainment.

DIFFERENCES IN HUMOR APPRECIATION

Reflecting the state/trait distinctions of humor, some research has examined transitory conditions affecting humor appreciation, whereas other studies have examined the influence of more stable factors. For example, Weaver, Masland, Kharazmi, and Zillmann (1985) studied the more transitory impact of alcohol intoxication on humor appreciation. They found that intoxication increased appreciation of blunt humor, but it decreased appreciation of more subtle humor. Oppliger and Zillmann (1997) explored personality differences in humor appreciation operating under the premise that individuals' humor preferences may reflect their more stable personality traits. Specifically, they found that highly disgust-sensitive individuals were less amused by "disgusting" humor than were individuals exhibiting less trait disgust-sensitivity, whereas highly rebellious individuals were more amused by this humor than were their less rebellious counterparts.

Much research has examined gender differences in humor appreciation. Joking and humor appreciation have traditionally been considered an essentially masculine preserve in Western culture, particularly in the realms of sexual and aggressive humor (Fine, 1976; Freud, 1905/1958; Grotjahn, 1957). Indeed, several studies support the notion of gender differences in preference of these forms of humor (Brodzinsky, Barnet, & Aiello; 1981; Cantor, 1976; Chapman & Gadfield, 1976; Hassett & Houlihan, 1979; Losco & Epstein, 1975; Mundorf, Bhatia, Zillmann, Lester, & Robertson, 1988; O'Connell, 1960; Stocking & Zillmann, 1988; Wilson & Molleston, 1981). However, not all of these studies find that men enjoy hostile humor more than women do. In fact, Wilson and Molleston (1981) found that, for males, greater ratings of hostility were associated with lower funniness ratings. Females were not as affected as males by variations in sexuality, exploitation, and hostility. Relative to males, however, females did give greater ratings of hostility to various types of cartoons and rated them less positively. Several studies report no gender differences for the appreciation of hostile humor. These studies include Zillmann and Bryant (1974) with regard to retaliatory aggression; Leak (1974) with hostile wit and racial wit; Zillmann and Cantor (1972) and Terry and Ertel (1974) with hostile wit; and Gutman and Priest (1969) with aggressive humor. Although it is unclear why these inconsistencies emerge, it has been suggested that gender differences in humor appreciation only emerge when the content of the humor contains material relevant to sex differences in general, in terms of different motives, attitudes, and interests (Wilson & Molleston, 1981).

EFFECTS RESEARCH

Much research has examined the impact of humor on learning (see chap. 12, this volume) and persuasion (see Perloff, 1993), although studies show mixed results. It appears that under some conditions humor can serve to increase attention, which in turn increases message comprehension and message adoption, whereas in other cases humor may produce distraction, thus decreasing attention, comprehension, and message adoption. Numerous studies suggest that humor can influence the persuasiveness of advertisements and commercials. In these studies, humor is often found to increase attention, but results for message comprehension and message adoption vary widely (see Weinberger & Gulas, 1992, for review). Nonetheless, advertising executives endorse the use of humor in advertising (E. A. Robinson, 1997). In defending the use of humor, Lee Clow, chief creative officer of TBWA Chiat/Day in Venice, California, and father of the Energizer bunny said, “They are going to call you on any b.s. you throw at them. Today we have to entertain and not just sell, because if you try to sell directly and come off as boring or obnoxious, people are going to press the remote on you” (cited in E. A. Robinson, 1997, p. 154). Audiences expect media to entertain, and comedy entertains. Interestingly, studies have also found that a humorous program context can influence perceptions of the commercials aired during the show (Murphy, Cunningham, & Wilcox, 1979; Perry, Jenzowsky, King, Yi, Hester, & Gartenchlaeger, 1997), and perhaps even more notably, that humorous commercials can influence perceptions of the programs during which the commercials are aired (Perry, Jenzowsky, King, Yi, & Hester, 1997).

Studies have also examined the impact of humor in entertainment genres other than comedy. For instance, Zillmann, Gibson, Ordman, and Aust (1994) found that closing a newscast with humorous items caused audiences to feel less apprehensive about stories in the news. King-Jablonski and Zillmann (1995) and King (2000a) found that the humorous quips directly associated with the violence in action and horror films influenced not only perceptions of the films themselves, but also perceptions of subsequent depictions of nonhumorous violence, including real, nonfictional violence. In some cases, exposure to film humor served to make real violence appear more intense and distressing, whereas in other cases, film humor appeared to trivialize subsequent depictions of real violence making them appear less intense and distressing. As with other effects of humor, authors speculated that these differences may be dispositionally and contextually mediated. Although additional investigation is needed, these studies suggest potentially significant societal implications for use of humorous cues in news broadcasts and violent, fictional films.

HUMOR AND NEW MEDIA

There is good reason to believe that humor will maintain a pervasive presence in media entertainment. New technology is providing new media and new challenges that are creating an environment in which comedy thrives. Many new media such as the Internet and handheld devices such as cellular phones and palm organizers are thought to be better suited to shorter, less complex entertainment content (Deans, 2000). Although many other dramatic genres require time for character and story development, comedy can be developed quickly and easily. Consider cartoons in which a single still image, often without any text can convey an entire comic plot. As noted earlier, Zillmann (2000) maintained that “any kind of humorous expression can be thought of as a miniature plot—if need be, as a miniaturized miniature plot” (p. 42). Thus, comedy becomes a natural choice for new media.

People need only check their own e-mail in boxes to recognize the proliferation of humor and comedy on the Internet. And it is reported that organizations such as Shockwave.com are enjoying success with so-called “performance animation” including Flash-generated cartoons often lasting just a few seconds that can be downloaded and emailed to friends, and feature recurring characters such as a disco-dancing alien, jiggling to “I Will Survive,” who gets flattened by a falling disco-ball (Deans, 2000). According to Errol Gerson, a senior agent in the new media department of the Los Angeles-based agency Creative Artists Association (CAA), “This interactive programming is going to be a new entertainment format.... It fits the web audience profile, giving people a short laugh every now and then” (cited in Deans, 2000 para. 9, p. 6). Deans (2000) also noted that other popular web formats include short films spoofing TV shows or movies.

Although current technology restricts the length and complexity of the material that can be transmitted through new media devices, it is thought that even if and when these obstacles are overcome, brevity will still rule the day for many of these new media. It is reasoned that when individuals have time for more involved entertainment, they would prefer viewing a big screen from a couch or a theater seat than sitting at a desk squinting at their computer or PalmPilot. Thus, it would appear that humor and comedy are well-positioned to continue their reign in the media entertainment kingdom.

CONCLUSIONS

Research and theory on humor and mirth span an impressive scope of topics. Zillmann and his colleagues have provided compelling theoretical explanations and empirical evidence not only for when and why different audiences are amused, but also for the emotional, cognitive, and physiological impacts this amusement may have on these audiences. The research reviewed here offers valuable insight into how humor and mirth may function in different media contexts. However, the investigations conducted by Zillmann and others also pose perhaps as many questions as they answer, providing rich opportunities for further investigations of humor and comedy in both traditional and new media entertainment environments.

REFERENCES

Adams, E. R., & McGuire, F. A. (1986). Is laughter the best medicine? A study of the effects of humor on perceived pain and affect. *Activities, Adaptation, and Aging, 8,* 157–175.

Apter, M. J. (1982). *The experience of motivation*. London: Academic.

Apter, M. J., & Smith, K. C. P. (1977). Humour and the theory of psychological reversals. In A. J. Chapman & H. Foot (Eds.), *It's a funny thing, humour* (pp. 95–100). Oxford: Pergamon.

Aristotle. (1966). De poetica (I. Bywater, Trans.). In *The works of Aristotle* (Vol. 11, Chapter 2). Oxford, England: Clarendon.

Averill, J. R. (1969). Autonomic response patterns during sadness and mirth. *Psychophysiology, 5,* 399–414.

Berk, L. S., Tan, S. A., Fry, W. F., Napier, B. J., Lee, J. W., Hubbard, R. W., Lewis, J. E., & Eby, W. C. (1989). Neuroendocrine and stress hormone changes during mirthful laughter. *American Journal of the Medical Sciences, 298,* 390–396.

Berk, L. S., Tan, S. A., Napier, B. J., & Eby, W. C. (1989). Eustress of mirthful laughter modifies natural killer cell activity. *Clinical Research, 37,* 115A.

Berlyne, D. E. (1969). Laughter, humor, and play. In G. Lindzey & E. Aronson (Eds.), *Handbook of social psychology* (2nd ed., Vol. 3, pp. 795–852). Reading, MA: Addison-Wesley.

Brodzinsky, D. M., Barnet, K. & Aiello, J. R. (1981). Sex of subject and gender identification as factors in humor appreciation. *Sex Roles, 7,* 561–573.

Brooks, T., & Marsh, E. (1999). *The complete directory to prime time network and cable TV shows, 1946–present.* New York: Ballantine Books.

Cantor, J. R. (1976). What is funny to whom: The role of gender. *Journal of Communication, 26*(3), 164–172.

Cantor, J. R. (1977). Tendentious humour in the mass media. In A. J. Chapman & H. C. Foot (Eds.), *It's a funny thing, humour* (pp. 303–310). Oxford: Pergamon.

Cantor, J. R., Bryant, J., & Zillmann, D. (1974). Enhancement of humor appreciation by transferred excitation. *Journal of Personality and Social Psychology, 30,* 812–821.

Cantor, J. R., & Zillmann, D. (1973). Resentment toward victimized protagonists and severity of misfortunes they suffer as factors in humor appreciation. *Journal of Experimental Research in Personality, 6,* 321–329.

Chapman, A. J. (1973). Funniness of jokes, canned laughter and recall performance. *Sociometry, 36,* 569–578.

Chapman, A. J., & Gadfield, N. J. (1976). Is sexual humor sexist? *Journal of Communication, 26*(3), 141–153.

Christ, W. G., & Medoff, N. J. (1984). Affective state and selective exposure to and use of television. *Journal of Broadcasting, 28*(1), 51–63.

Cogan, R., Cogan, D., Waltz, W., & McCue, M. (1987). Effects of laughter and relaxation on discomfort threshold. *Journal of Behavioral Medicine, 10*(2), 139–144.

Deans, J. (2000, May 22). New media: Gagging to get on the net: TV comedy producers are investing in new entertainment ideas designed to make the City take them seriously. *The Guardian,* p. 6.

Dillon, K. M., Minchoff, B., & Baker, K .H. (1985–1986). Positive emotional states and enhancement of the immune system. *International Journal of Psychiatry in Medicine, 15,* 13–18.

Dixon, N. F. (1980). Humor: A cognitive alternative to stress? In I. G. Sarason & C. D. Spielgerger (Eds.), *Stress and anxiety* (Vol. 7, pp. 281–289). Washington, DC: Hemisphere.

Dukore, F. (1974). *Dramatic theory and criticism: Greeks to Grotowski.* New York: Holt, Rinehart & Winston.

Fine, G. A. (1976). Obscene joking across cultures. *Journal of Communication, 26*(3), 134–140.

Freud, S. (1928). Humor. *International Journal of Psychoanalysis, 9,* 1–6.

Freud, S. (1958). *Der Witz und seine Beziehung zum Unbewussten* [Jokes and their relation to the unconscious]. Frankfort: Fischer Bücherei. (Original work published 1905)

Fry, W. F. (1986). Humor, physiology, and the aging process. In L. Nahemow, K. A. McCluskey-Fawcett, & P. E. McGhee (Eds), *Humor and aging* (pp. 81–98). Orlando, FL: Academic.

Fry, W. F. (1992). The physiologic effects of humor, mirth, and laughter. *The Journal of the American Medical Association, 26,* 1857–1858.

Fry, W. F., & Savin, M. (1988). *Mirthful laughter and blood pressure. Humor, 1,* 49–62.

Giles, H., Bourhis, R. Y., Gadfield, N. J., Davies, G. J., & Davies, A. P. (1976). Cognitive aspects of humour in social interaction: A model and some linguistic data. In A. J. Chapman & H. C. Foot (Eds.), *Humour and laughter: Theory, research, and application* (pp. 139–154). London: Wiley.

Godkewitsch, M. (1976). Physiological and verbal indices of arousal in rated humour. In J. H. Goldstein & H. C. Foot (Eds.), *Humour and laughter: Theory, research, and application* (pp. 117–138). London: Wiley

Goldstein, J. H. (1987). Therapeutic effects of laughter. In W. F. Fry & W. A. Salameth (Eds.), *Handbook of humor and pyschotherapy: Advances in the clinical use of humor* (pp. 1–19). Sarasota, FL: Professional Resource Exchange.

Grotjahn, M. (1957). *Beyond laughter.* New York: McGraw-Hill.

Gruner, C. R. (1976). Wit and humor in mass communications. In A. J. Chapman & H. C. Foot (Eds.), *Humor and laughter: Theory, research, and applications* (pp. 287–311). London: Wiley.

Gutman, J., & Priest, R. F. (1969). When is aggression funny? *Journal of Personality and Social Psychology, 12,* 60–65.

Haig, R. A. (1988). *The anatomy of humor. Biopsychosocial and therapeutic perspectives.* Springfiled IL: Thomas.

Harter, S. (1974). Pleasure derived from cognitive challenge and mastery. *Child Development, 45,* 661–669.

Harter, S., Shultz, T., & Blum, B. (1971). Smiling in children as a function of their sense of mastery. *Journal of Experimental Child Psychology, 12,* 396–404.

Hassett, J., & Houlihan, J. (1979). Different jokes for different folks: Report on PTS humor survey. *Psychology Today, 12*(8), 64–71.

Hayworth, D. (1928). The social origin and function of laughter. *Psychological Review, 35,* 367–384.

Helregel, B. K., & Weaver, J. B (1989). Mood-management during pregnancy through elective exposure to television. *Journal of Broadcasting & Electronic Media, 33*(1), 15–33.

Hobbes, T. (1968). *Leviathan.* Harmondsworth: Penguin. (Original work published 1651)

Jablonski, P. M., & Sutherland, T. (1999). It is so scary it is funny: A content analysis of the use of humor in horror films. *The Journal of Communication Studies, 18,* 26–35.

Kane, T. R., Suls, J. M., & Tedeschi, J. (1977). Humour as a tool of social interaction. In A. J. Chapman & H. C. Foot (Eds.), *It's a funny thing, humour* (pp. 13–16) Oxford: Pergamon.

Kant, I. (1922). Kritik der praktischen Vernunft: Zweites Buch. Analytik des Erhabenen [Critique of practical reason: Second book. Analysis of the revered]. In E. Cassirer (Ed.), *Immanuel Kants Werke* (Vol. 5, pp. 315–412). Berlin: B. Cassirer. (Original work published 1788)

Keith-Spiegel, P. (1972). Early conceptions of humor: Varieties and issues. In J. H. Goldstein & P. E. McGhee (Eds.), *The psychology of humor* (pp. 3–39). New York: Academic.

King, C. M. (2000a). Effects of humorous heroes and villains in violent action films. *Journal of Communication, 50*(1), 5–24.

King, C. M. (2000b, June/July,). What's so funny? Humor in horror films. *Creative Screenwriting,* Vol. 4.

King-Jablonski, C., & Zillmann, D. (1995). Humor's role in the trivialization of violence. *Medienpsychologie: Zeitschrift für Individual- und Massenkommunikation, 7*(2), 122–133, 162.

Knapp, P. H., Levy, E. M., Giorgi, R. G., Black P. H., Fox, B. H., & Heeren, T. C. (1992). Short-term immunological effects of induced emotion. *Psychosomatic Medicine, 54,* 133–148.

Kris, E. (1940). Laughter as an expressive process. *International Journal of Psychoanalysis, 21,* 314–341.

Labott, S. M., Ahleman, S., Wolever, M. E., & Martin, R. B. (1990). The physical and psychological effects of the expression and inhibition of emotion. *Behavioral Medicine, 16,* 182–189.

Langevin, R., & Day, H. I. (1972). Physiological correlates of humor. In J. H. Goldstein & P. E. McGhee (Eds.), *The psychology of humor* (pp. 129–142). New York: Academic.

Leak, G. K. (1974). Effects of hostility arousal and aggressive humor on catharsis and humor preference. *Journal of Personality and Social Psychology, 30,* 736–740.

Leiber, D. B. (1986). Laughter and humor in critical care. *Dimensions of critical care nursing, 5,* 162–170.

Lloyd, E. L (1938). The respiratory mechanism in laughter. *Journal of General Psychology, 10,* 179–189.

Losco, J., & Epstein, S. (1975). Humor preference as a subtle measure of attitude toward the same and the opposite sex. *Journal of Personality, 43,* 321–334.

Love, A. M., & Deckers, L. H. (1989). Humor appreciation as a function of sexual, aggressive, and sexist content. *Sex Roles, 20,* 649–654.

Lucas, F. L. (1958). *Tragedy: Serious drama in relation to Aristotle's poetics.* NY: MacMillan.

Martin, R. A., & Dobbin, J. P. (1988). Sense of humor, hassles, and immunoglobulin A: Evidence for a stress-moderating effect of humor. *International Journal of Psychiatry in Medicine, 18*(2), 93–105.

Martin, R. A., & Lefcourt, H. M. (1983). Sense of humor as a moderator of the relation between stressors and moods. *Journal of Personality and Social Psychology, 45,* 1313–1324.

Mast, G., (1981). *A short history of the movies* (3rd ed.). Indianapolis: Bobbs-Merrill.

May, R. (1953). *Man's search for himself.* New York: Random House.

McDougall, W. (1922). A new theory of laughter. *Psyche, 2,* 292–303.

McGhee, P. E. (1972). On the cognitive origins of incongruity humor: Fantasy assimilation versus reality assimilation. In J. H. Goldstein & P. E. McGhee (Eds.), *The psychology of humor* (pp. 61–80). New York: Academic.

McGhee, P. E., & Duffey, N. S. (1983a). Children's appreciation of humor victimizing different racial-ethnic groups: Racial-ethnic differences. *Journal of Cross-Cultural Psychology, 14*(1), 29–40.

McGhee, P. E., & Duffey, N. S. (1983b). The role of identity of the victim in the development of disparagement humor. *Journal of General Psychology, 108,* 257–270.

McGhee, P. E., & Lloyd, S. A. (1981). A development test of the disposition theory of humor. *Child Development, 52,* 925–931.

Meadowcroft, L. M., & Zillmann, D. (1987). Women's comedy preferences during the menstrual cycle. *Communications Research, 14,* 204–218.

Medoff, N. J. (1979). *The avoidance of comedy by persons in a negative afffective state? Further study in selective exposure.* Unpublished doctoral dissertation, Indiana University.

Middleton, R. (1959). Negro and White reactions to racial humor. *Sociometry, 22,* 175–183.

Mundorf, N., Bhatia, A., Zillmann, D., Lester, P., & Robertson, S. (1988). Gender differences in humor appreciation. *Humor: International Journal of Humor Research, 1–3,* 231–243.

Murphy, J. H., Cunningham, I. C., & Wilcox, G. (1979). The impact of program environment on recall of humorous television commercials. *Journal of Advertising Research, 8*(2): 17–21.

Nerhardt, G. (1976). Incongruity and funniness: Toward a new descriptive model. In A. J. Chapman & H. C. Foot (Eds.), *Humour and laughter: Theory, research and applications* (pp. 55–91). London: Wiley.

Nevo, O., Keinan, G., & Teshimovsky-Arditi, M. (1993). Humor and pain tolerance. *Humor, 6*(1), 71–88.

Nezu, A. M., Nezu, C. M., & Blissett, S. W. (1988). Sense of humor as a moderator of the relation between stressful events and psychological distress: A prospective analysis. *Journal of Personality and Social Psychology, 54,* 520–525.

O'Connell, W. E. (1960). The adaptive function of wit and humor. *Journal of Abnormal and Social Psychology, 61,* 263–270.

Olson, E. (1968). *The theory of comedy.* Bloomington: Indiana University Press.

O'Neal, E. C., & Taylor, S. L. (1989). Status of the provoker, opportunity to retaliate, and interest in video violence. *Aggressive Behavior, 15,* 171–180.

Oppliger, P. A., & Zillmann, D. (1997). Disgust in humor: Its appeal to adolescents. *Humor: International Journal of Humor Research, 10,* 421–437.

Oxford's companion to the English language (1992). Reference obtained through xrefer on line search engine. Retrieved January 19, 2000, from *http://www.xrefer.com/entry.jsp?xrefid=441535&secid=.-*

Paskind, H. A. (1932). Effects of laughter on muscle tone. *Arch Neurological Psychiatry, 28,* 623–628.

Perloff, R. M. (1993). *Dynamics of persuasion.* Hillsdale, NJ: Lawrence Erlbaum Associates.

Perry, S. D., Jenzowsky, S. A., King, C. M., Yi, H., & Hester, J. B. (1997). The influence of commercial humor on program enjoyment and evaluation. *Journalism & Mass Communication Quarterly, 74,* 388–399,

Perry, S. D., Jenzowsky, S. A., King, C. M., Yi, H., Hester, J. B., & Gartenchlaeger, J. (1997). Using humorous programs as a vehicle for humorous commercials. *Journal of Communication, 47*(1), 20–39.

Pien, D., & Rothbart, M. K. (1976). Incongruity and resolution in children's humor: A reexamination. *Child Development, 47,* 966–971.

Prerost, F. J., & Ruma, C. (1987). Exposure to humorous stimuli as an adjunct to muscle training. *Psychology: A Quarterly Journal of Human Behavior, 24*(4), 70–74.

Robinson, E. A. (1997). Frogs, bears, and orgasms. *Fortune, 135*(11) 153–156.

Robinson, V. M. (1983). Humor and health. In P. E. McGhee & J. H. Goldstein (Eds.), *Handbook of humor research, Vol. II. Applied studies* (pp. 109–128). New York: Springer-Verlag.

Rothbart, M. K. (1976). Incongruity, problem-solving and laughter. In A. J. Chapman & H. C. Foot (Eds.), *Humour and laughter: Theory, research and applications* (pp. 37–54). London: Wiley.

Rotton, J., & Shats, M. (1996). Effects of state humor, expectancies, and choice on postsurgical mood and self-medication: A field experiment. *Journal of Applied Social Psychology, 26,* 1775–1794.

Schultz, T. R. (1976). A cognitive-developmental analysis of humor. In A. J. Chapman & H. C. Foot (Eds.), *Humor and laughter: Theory, research and applications* (pp. 11–36). London: Wiley

Shurcliff, A. (1968). Judged humor, arousal, and the relief theory. *Journal of Personality and Social Psychology, 8,* 360–363.

Simon, J. M. (1990). Humor and its relationship to perceived health, life satisfaction, and morale in older adults. *Issues in Mental Health Nursing, 11,* 17–31.

Sorell, W. (1972). *Facets of comedy.* New York: Grosset & Dunlap.

Spencer, H. (1888). *The physiology of laughter in illustrations of universal progress: A series of discussions* (pp. 194–209). New York: D. Appleton.

Stocking, S. H., Sapolsky, B. S., & Zillmann, D. (1977). Sex discrimination in prime time humor. *Journal of Broadcasting, 21,* 447–457.

Stocking, S. H., & Zillmann, D. (1976). Effects of humorous disparagement of self, friend, and enemy. *Psychological Reports, 39,* 455–461.

Stocking, H., & Zillmann, D. (1988). Humor von Frauen und Maennern: Einige kleine Unterschiede. [Humor of men and women: Some small differences] In H. Kotthoff (Ed.), *Das Gelaechter der Geschlecter: Humor und Macht in Gespraechen von Frauen und Maennern* (pp. 210–231). Frankfurt, Germany: Fischer.

Suls, J. M. (1972). A two-stage model for the appreciation of jokes and cartoons: An information-processing analysis. In J. H. Goldstein & P. E. McGhee (Eds.), *The psychology of humor: Theoretical perspectives and empirical issues* (pp. 81–100). New York: Academic.

Terry, R., & Ertel, S. L. (1974). Explorations of individual differences in preferences for humor. *Psychological Reports, 34,* 1031.

Thorson, J. A. (1985). A funny thing happened on the way to the morgue: Some thoughts on humor and death, and a taxonomy of the humor associated with death. *Death Studies, 9,* 201–216.

Trice, A. D., & Price-Greathouse, J. (1986). Joking under the drill: A validity study of the coping humor scale. *Journal of Social Behavior and Personality, 1,* 265–266.

Watson, J. S. (1972). Smiling, cooing, and the "game." *Merill-Palmer Quarterly, 18,* 323–339.

Weaver, J. B., Masland, J. L., Kharazmi, S., & Zillmann, D. (1985). Effect of alcoholic intoxication on the appreciation of different types of humor. *Journal of Personality and Social Psychology, 49,* 781–787.

Weaver, J. B., & Zillmann, D. (1994). Effect of humor and tragedy on discomfort tolerance on discomfort tolerance. *Motor skills, 78,* 632–634.

Weinberger, M. G., & Gulas, C. S. (1992). The impact of humor in advertising: A review. *Journal of Advertising, 21*(4) 35–60.

Weinberger, M. G., Spotts, H., Campbell, L., & Parsons, A. L. (1995). The use and effect of humor in different advertising media. *Journal of Advertising Research, 35*(3) 44–57.

Wicker, F. W., Barron, W. L., & Willis, A. C. (1980). Disparagement humor: Dispositions and resolutions. *Journal of Personality and Social Psychology, 39,* 701–709.

Wilson, D. W., & Molleston, J. L. (1981). Effects of sex and type of humor on humor appreciation. *Journal of Personality Assessment, 45*(1), 90–96.

Wolfenstein, M. (1954). *Children's humor.* Glencoe, IL: Free Press.

Wolff, H. A., Smith, C. E., & Murray, H. A. (1934). The psychology of humor: I. A study of responses to race-disparagement jokes. *Journal of Abnormal and Social Psychology, 28,* 341–365.

Wyer, R. S, & Collins, J. E., II. (1992). A theory of humor elicitation. *Psychological Review, 99,* 663–689.

Zigler, E., Levine, J., & Gould, L. (1967). Cognitive challenge as a factor in children's humor appreciation. *Journal of Personality and Social Psychology, 6,* 332–336.

Zillmann, D. (1978). Attribution and misattribution of excitatory reactions. In J. H. Harvey, W. J. Ickes, & R. F. Kidd (Eds.), *New directions in attribution research* (Vol. 2, pp. 335–368). Hillsdale, NJ: Lawrence Erlbaum Associates.

Zillmann, D. (1980). Anatomy of suspense. In P. H. Tannenbaum (Ed.), *The entertainment functions of television* (pp. 135–167). Hillsdale, NJ: Lawrence Erlbaum Associates.

Zillmann, D. (1983a). Disparagement humor. In P. E. McGhee & J. H. Goldstein (Eds.), *Handbook of humor research: Vol. 1. Basic issues* (pp. 85–107). New York: Springer-Verlag.

Zillmann, D. (1983b). Transfer of excitation in emotional behavior. In J. T. Cacioppo & R. E. Petty (Eds.), *Social psychophysiology: A sourcebook* (pp. 215–240). New York: Guilford.

Zillmann, D. (1984). *Connections between sex and aggression.* Hillsdale, NJ: Lawrence Erlbaum Associates.

Zillmann, D. (1988). Mood management: Using entertainment to full advantage. In L. Donohew, H. E. Sypher, & E. T. Higgins (Eds.), *Communication, social cognition, and affect* (pp. 147–171). Hillsdale, NJ: Lawrence Erlbaum Associates.

Zillmann, D. (1993). Sequential dependencies in emotional experience and behavior. In R. D. Kavanaugh, B. Z. Glick, & S. Fein (Eds.), *The G. Stanley Hall symposium on emotion* (pp. 44–68). New York: Springer-Verlag.

Zillmann, D. (1994). Mechanisms of emotional involvement with drama. *Poetics, 23,* 33–51.

Zillmann, D. (1996). The psychology of suspense in dramatic exposition. In P. Vorderer, H. J. Wulff, & M. Friedrichsen (Eds.), *Suspense: Conceptualizations, theoretical analyses, and empirical explorations* (pp. 199–231). Mahwah, NJ: Lawrence Erlbaum Associates.

Zillmann, D. (2000). Humor and comedy. In D. Zillmann & P. Vorderer (Eds.), *Media entertainment: The psychology of its appeal* (pp. 37–57). Mahwah, NJ: Lawrence Erlbaum Associates.

Zillmann, D., & Bryant, J. (1974). Retaliatory equity as a factor in humor appreciation. *Journal of Experimental Psychology, 10,* 480–488.

Zillmann, D., & Bryant, J. (1980). Misattribution theory of tendentious humor. *Journal of Experimental Social Psychology, 16,* 146–160.

Zillmann, D., & Bryant, J. (1985). Affect, mood, and emotion as determinants of selective experience. In D. Zillmann & J. Bryant (Eds.), *Selective exposure to communication* (pp. 157–190). Hillsdale, NJ: Lawence Erlbaum Associates.

Zillmann, D., & Bryant, J. (1991). Responding to comedy: The sense and nonsense in humor. In J. Bryant & D. Zillmann (Eds.), *Responding to the screen: Reception and reaction processes* (pp. 261–279). Hillsdale, NJ: Lawrence Erlbaum Associates.

Zillmann, D., Bryant, J., & Cantor, J. R. (1974). Brutality of assault in political cartoons affecting humor appreciation. *Journal of Research in Personality, 7,* 334–345.

Zillmann, D., Bryant, J., & Sapolsky, B. S. (1989). Enjoyment from sports spectatorship. In J. H. Goldstein (Ed.), *Sports, games, and play: Social and psychological viewpoints* (2nd ed., pp. 241–278). Hillsdale, NJ: Lawrence Erlbaum Associates.

Zillmann, D., & Cantor, J. R. (1972). Directionality of transitory dominance as a communication variable affecting humor appreciation. *Journal of Personality and Social Psychology, 24,* 191–198.

Zillmann, D., & Cantor, J. R. (1976). A disposition theory of humour and mirth. In A. J. Chapman & H. C. Foot (Eds.), *Humour and laughter: Theory, research, and applications* (pp. 93–115). London: Wiley.

Zillmann, D., de Wied, M., King Jablonski, C., & Jenzowsky, S. (1996, November). Drama-induced affect and pain sensitivity. *Psychosomatic Medicine, 58,* 333–341.

Zillmann, D., Gibson, R., Ordman, V. L., & Aust, C. F. (1994). Effects of upbeat stories in broadcast news. *Journal of Broadcasting & Electronic Media, 38,* 65–78.

Zillmann, D., Hezel, R. T., & Medoff, N. J. (1980). The effect of affective states on selective exposure to televised entertainment fare. *Journal of Applied Social Psychology, 10,* 323–339.

Zillmann, D., Howland, E. W., Nichols, S. N., & Cleeland, C. S. (1991). The effects of induced mood on laboratory pain. *Pain, 46,* 105–111.

Zillmann, D., Rockwell, S. C., Schweitzer, K., & Sundar, S. S. (1993). Does humor facilitate coping with physical discomfort? *Motivation and Emotion, 17*(1), 1–21.

Zillmann, D., Taylor, K., & Lewis, K. (1998). News as nonfiction theater: How dispositions toward the public cast of characters affect reactions. *Journal of Broadcasting & Electronic Media. 42,* 153–169.

16

Suspense and Mystery

Silvia Knobloch
Dresden University of Technology

Considerable portions of media entertainment, consisting of tragedy, horror, suspense, and mystery, concentrate on the negative side of human existence. Conflict and menace are at the very heart of drama (Marx, 1940; Vorderer & Knobloch, 2000). Tragedy, however, tends to appeal more to women and horror to men. In contrast, suspense and mystery widely fascinate the general audience, with very few exceptions. In innumerous novels and movies, protagonists struggle against upcoming threats, and sleuths investigate to solve criminal riddles. Suspense and mystery as genres attain with regularity substantial interest and provide undoubtedly well-established recipes to entertain readers and viewers over and over again.

Beyond these very basic commonalities of broad audience appeal and a negative outlook by focusing on threat and crime, various differences divide the two genres in question. The state of knowledge is reviewed in the following, although any appreciation of suspense and mystery as pieces of art, literature, and/or popular culture will be excluded from consideration. This overview covers theoretical approaches and empirical substantiation for the case of suspense. Unfortunately, so far mystery reception has been investigated on theoretical grounds only.

A BRIEF SYNOPSIS OF SUSPENSE THEORIES SUBSTANTIATED BY EMPIRICAL EVIDENCE

Outlook for Suspense Research

Vorderer, Wulff, and Friedrichsen (1996) have compiled approaches to suspense in an edited book. This volume of the Lawrence Erlbaum series illustrates vividly the variety of perspectives taken to shed light on the phenomenon, although empirically validated concepts are favored here. Gerrig's (1996) view that "a theory [of suspense] will no doubt make references both to readers and to narrative structures: Suspense will arise when readers possessing some particular range of cognitive processes interact with a particular range of narrative features" (p. 93) is shared by other authors. Evidently, more importance has been attached to cognitive processes during experiencing suspense. An essentially cognitive approach, however, does not explain the motivation to turn to suspense-generating entertainment, because cognitions solely do not clarify fascination. If we consider self-exposure to entertainment to be motivated by mood-management intentions, then emotions must be involved. Interestingly enough, the only approach that considers emotions (and cognitions) as components of suspense was proposed by Zillmann (e.g., 1996) and is thereby described in greatest detail.

Gerrig: Suspense as Problem Solving

Gerrig (1996) attached particular importance to contrasting alternatives of further story developments that represent different solutions to a conflict. Thus suspense results from the readers' uncertainty, while they follow the plot, about a protagonist's prospective success in overcoming obstacles. The more likely they think a positive outcome is due to many possible ways out, the less suspense evoked. According to his model, readers experience more suspense when some potential escape route is eliminated, because one possible solution to the problem is crossed out. Gerrig and Bernardo (1994) demonstrated a correlation between suspense and problem-solving processes in a series of meticulous experiments. According to their results, suspense in fact increases when a possible solution to a conflict or problem is ruled out.

Brewer: Structural-Affect Theory

Brewer and colleagues (Brewer, 1996; Brewer & Lichtenstein, 1981, 1982; Brewer & Ohtsuka, 1988) have postulated the structural-affect theory, pertaining also to suspense, and presented several related empirical investigations. An emphasis is set on the first part of the theory's name, because it is more concerned with the sequence in which narrative information is presented to readers (or viewers, respectively, although evidence so far is based on studies of novels). Although affects are seen as results of these text structures, the emotions proper remain vague. Nonetheless, the structural-affect theory is of great interest here, because it suggests a typology of suspense, mystery, and, surprise texts. Although suspense and mystery are the focus of this chapter, surprise (although in a slightly different meaning) will also play a role in the consideration of mystery solutions.

For all three text types, the plot is said to span from an "initiating event" to an "outcome event." The combination and completeness of two structural levels result in specific text genres. Suspense texts feature the simplest constellation thereof, because the sequence of fictional events (event structure) equals the sequence in which the events are presented to the audience (discourse structure). In the story, an intiating event evokes an expectation about the outcome (what *will* happen?). Thus suspense is evoked by following the events that lead toward the outcome and that are presented parallel to their occurrence within the fiction. Surprise texts differ in the regard that essential information on the event level is omitted in the narration and only presented at the end of the story, leading to surprise and reinterpretation of the story events. Hence, this difference between event structure and discourse structure creates surprise in reaction to the text. Finally, readers of a so-called mystery text according to Brewer and his co-workers know about their lack of essential information. In this case fictional incidences are indicated but only depicted toward the end of the story. For this text type, a shift between event structure and discourse structure makes the readers wonder what has happened (e.g., who has murdered the victim). The crucial information completing the picture is presented only late in the discourse structure, although the event is placed early in the event structure. The instigated feeling during mystery reading, then, is curiosity.

Zillmann: A Theory of Suspense and its Components

Zillmann has also compared mystery and suspense (1991b), but has dedicated more interest to suspense (e.g., 1980, 1996; Zillmann, Hay, & Bryant, 1975) relating it to other components of his work such as research on empathy with protagonists (Zillmann, 1991a, 1994, 1996; Zillmann & Cantor, 1977), affective disposition theory, and excitation-transfer theory (1983). He defined the experience of suspense in drama as follows: "(a) Drama must preoccupy itself with negative outcomes, (b) liked protagonists must be selected as targets for negative outcomes so as to make these outcomes feared and dreaded, and (c) for the occurrence of outcomes that threaten liked protagonists, high degrees of subjective certainty (not uncertainty!) must be created" (Zillmann, 1991b, p. 282).

The starting point of a plot that is to evoke suspense in the readers or viewers is clashing interests of good and evil. As well as other drama genres, suspense involves conflict, obviously exploiting the potential of negative depictions to develop stronger emotional impact. This basic feature of drama corresponds well to the "law of hedonic asymmetry" as one of Frijda's (1988) law of emotions. But the solution in the end of the story line is characteristic for suspense. The conceptualizations by Zillmann and Brewer go well together in this point. Suspense results from fearing a bad, but still open ending that is not resolved until the very end of a narrative. Tragedy, for instance, contrasts because therein a bad ending is a given and often already indicated in the beginning of the narrative.

The social constellation within the story and the approach of the viewer toward fictional characters is crucial in Zillmann's suspense theory. For an intense entertaining experience, both need to be clear-cut in the first place. The narrative centers on likable protagonists typically in conflict with repulsive antagonists. It is a rare case that catastrophic forces resulting from nature or technology take the place of the personified evil. Hence, on the fictional level the "good guy" struggles against the villain, and this cast is introduced early in the story and unequivocally portrayed. This scheme allows the audience to quickly develop what Zillmann called *affective dispositions* toward the story's characters. Even at the very beginning, cues help the audience to develop such a disposition. For instance, in the opening scenes a cop as the likeable protagonist saves a colleague's life during a foray and nonchalantly states his good deed as a matter of course. In contrast, the scene introducing the antagonist shows this character tormenting somebody for plain amusement. These very simple descriptions suffice for a partial perception on the audience's side, namely liking the protagonist and condemning the antagonist. Accordingly, the viewers of a suspense film quickly assess the characters and thereby evolve dispositions.

The theory of affective dispositions postulates that witnesses' reactions to events vary along with the events' meaning for those who are truly affected and with the witnesses' partiality regarding those directly involved. Seeing liked individuals blown by fate results as a rule in distress, conveyed by empathic processes. Likewise, observing liked individuals favored by a stroke of luck will foster sympathetic delight. Antipathy toward a person reverses this pattern of empathy into counterempathy. Watching the happiness of a resented individual entails grief and annoyance, whereas a setback or failure of the disliked person causes pleasure and satisfaction.

This emphasis on sociopsychological processes as precondition for suspense distinguishes Zillmann's theory from other—cognitive—approaches. In his model, hedonic valences resulting from social perceptions explain that cognitive processes during the experience of suspense entail considerable emotional involvement. By taking emotions into account, self-exposure to suspense films appears reasonable, because this form of entertainment in the sense of mood management must involve feelings.

Nonetheless, certain cognitive processes are a precondition for suspense. In this regard, Zillmann's (1991b, 1996) view matches Gerrig's (1996) approach inasmuch as the perceived likelihood of a desired outcome is negatively correlated with the level of suspense. Yet Zillmann additionally pointed out that the audience's certainty about the negative outcome, although raising suspense as it increases, should not be absolute. Once the audience is absolutely confident that the protagonist has succumbed and that the desired outcome is ultimately out of reach, suspense will no longer persist, but sadness and disappointment will occur. On the other hand, suspense is also not experienced when the onlookers are positive that the desired outcome is a given. We will return to the issue of uncertainty and certainty of the outcome regarding mystery.

Yet the prevalence of threat and danger in suspense narratives leads to the question of why viewers should care to expose themselves to distressing content. Zillmann offered two explanations to this paradox. From the theory of affective dispositions explained earlier it is easily deduced that positive emotional experiences result from the narrative as long as antagonists get a raw deal. Nonetheless, much of the typical suspense plot is concerned with obstacles in the way of the liked protagonist and is thereby nerve-racking for viewers favoring the hero in peril. Even if the solution at the end of a suspense narrative removes empathic distress, viewers would experience relief only to return to the arousal state they had before. The assumption that the motivation to seek suspense experiences lies only in the relief of stress is not compelling. Hence, a more complex explanation is needed to clarify the paradoxical enjoyment of suspense.

Similarly with Brewer's conceptualization, Zillmann also took a dynamic approach by explaining suspense with his excitation-transfer theory. Very different to Brewer, though, his focus is the development of emotional states along with exposure to the plot. It is readily assumed that distress caused by watching the liked protagonist struggling is followed by relief once a favored outcome is depicted. This contrast between stressful apprehensions ensued by alleviating resolutions is, according to Zillmann, accompanied by specific emotional and psychophysiological processes.

Zillmann's general model of excitation transfer (1971, 1983) lends itself to the explanation of the paradox of suspense, because it postulates that the solution of suspense provides more than just stress relief. He argued that emotions result from arousal on the one hand and cognitive interpretation of this arousal on the other. Although the intensity of an emotion has its origins in the arousal level, the valence of an emotion results from the appraisal. By the same token, the excitation changes comparatively slowly, whereas the cognition adapts quickly to new stimuli. Recipients of suspense narratives go through considerable excitation as they watch or read about the liked protagonist's battle against antagonistic forces. These strongly negative depictions evoke intense arousal more easily than positive messages according to bioevolutionary explanations stressing the need to protect the organism from dangers, not from benefits. This excitation lingers on even if the fictional hero has overcome the disliked opponent, whereas the cognition adapts quickly to the now positive situation. In other words, the excitation is transferred to the now upbeat stimulus. The result is high arousal positively appraised and experienced. Hence, the exposure to a suspenseful plot is very hedonically rewarding in the end, because the recipients are placed in a very intense positive state.

Tan and Diteweg: Suspense and Predictive Inference

The contribution of Tan and Diteweg (1996) is mentioned here, because they have connected Brewer's and Zillmann's approaches. Yet they focused on cognitive processes of predictive inferences during exposure to suspense narratives. Their theoretical approach is very complex and will not be reported in detail, as this chapter concentrates on theories with empirical evidence. The material used in their empirical study was too ambiguous to be considered a suspense movie, as the authors pointed out themselves.

Conclusion on Suspense Research

Before turning to mystery, one of the essential contrasts to suspense can serve as a final note for this section. The experience of suspense has been investigated in great detail, also including the publication of the compendium mentioned earlier (Vorderer, Wulff, & Friedrichsen, 1996).

Empirical studies have been conducted on the development of suspense referring to empathy during film exposure (Vorderer & Knobloch, 1998), its resilience during repeated viewing (Seeger, 1998), the importance of the outcome proper (Gärtner, 1999; Vorderer & Bube, 1996), and the effect of interactivity on the suspense experience (Vorderer, Knobloch, & Schramm, 2001). It is astonishing to compare this body of literature incorporating empirical evidence with what we know about the enjoyment of mystery fiction—which is next to nothing.

DESCRIPTIONS AND SPECULATIONS ON MYSTERY

Conventions of the Genre

Although research has by and large neglected the question of why readers and viewers turn to mystery fiction, analyses of typical structures in this genre are certainly at hand. Before we come to the characteristics of the genre, it should be clarified that the term *mystery* in the context of this chapter does not allude to depictions of forces, technologies, or instances that appear as magic, paranormal, or futuristic. Such interest is very common in science-fiction and horror movies. In contrast, mystery as a literary genre centers on resolving an enigma typically consisting in a crime where the culprit is initially unknown. In difference to horror and science fiction, where problems are supernatural or technological, mystery evolves from crime being a social problem.

A common explanation for the motivation to read mystery novels is that readers enjoy toying with possible solutions of a brainteaser wrapped in a story. It is obvious that the involvement of paranormal forces, then, opens the door to an unlimited number of solutions. Hence, "mystical" aspects would make it impossible for the reader to foresee the outcome and are thereby almost forbidden in the mystery genre including detective stories and the like. In his "Twenty Rules for Writing Detective Stories," Van Dine (1928) in fact excluded paranormal phenomena from mystery writing.

A number of books have assembled ingredients to mystery narratives (as early as 1952: Rodell; recently, Herbert, Aird, Reilly, & Oleksiw, 1999). In the *Companion to Crime and Mystery Writing,* Reilly (1999d) stated that mystery "comes to denominate stories about identification of criminals" (p. 303). Indeed detective stories provide, then, typical examples of the mystery.

> The plots of detective novels follow the pattern of the investigation, not the enactment of the crime itself. The sleuth's application of theory or reason to the details of the crime provides the dramatic action of the narrative.... When readers receive the final, true identity of the culprit and a satisfactory explanation of the motive and means of the crime, the information arrives as a demonstration of the sleuth's ability to uncover knowledge that has been deliberately concealed in mystery by the mechanics of the text. (Reilly, 1999b, p. 116)

The cast of a mystery is by far more complex than one in a suspense narrative. Beyond the central character, usually the sleuth, the victim is a constant but naturally inactive component. A sidekick very often appears as an assistant of the sleuth. Details of the investigation or of the sleuth's reasoning are frequently depicted in dialogs between sleuth and assistant (Sherlock Holmes and Dr. Watson in Arthur Conan Doyle's mysteries form a classic example). A circle of suspects is introduced along the plot. "Characteristically, a small number of persons who had some relationship or business with, or are related to, the victimized party is introduced in a way that gives all persons motive, opportunity, and means for the commission of the unexplained crime.... Typically, just one person is found to be the perpetrator" (Zillmann, 1991a, p. 296). The plot develops with the investigation of the crime, with clues (Reilly, 1999a) marking turning points for the anticipated resolution. The occurrence of both suspects and clues is an issue of the "Twenty Rules for Writing Detective Stories" (Van Dine, 1928), because fairness toward readers requires that the unknown culprit be introduced early in the plot and essential information not be withheld from the audience. Furthermore, detective fiction is said to demand a closed-world setting in order to establish a limited set of suspects and to clarify the social constellation (Hayne, 1999).

Types of Mystery Plots

A synonym for mystery is the term *whodunit,* alluding to the focus on the question of who committed the crime. But as the quote mentions, the detective novel also incorporates the "howdunit" pattern that applies when the criminal act proper is more ambiguous than the culprit. A common example for this subtype that includes locked-room mysteries is Edgar Allan Poe's *The Murders in the Rue Morgue.* Information on the comparative significance of these two types is provided by a content analysis of top-selling mystery books, covering a dozen per decade from the 1920s to the 1990 s (Bryant, Mullikin Parcell, Bryant, & Kwon, 2000). Victimizations occurred in all mystery books with murder accounting for almost three fourths. The expression *whodunit* clearly deserves to be almost synonymous with mystery, because as a matter of fact four fifths of the books focused on the question of *who* committed the crime. In the remaining fifth, the primary mystery was how the crime was committed. Hence, the "howdunit" type also holds its rank within mystery plots. Both subtypes—"whodunit" and "howdunit"—meet the criteria that Brewer has suggested for mysteries. Crucial information is indicated but not revealed until the end of the plot. This shift between event structure and discourse structure evokes curiosity according to Brewer's structural-affect theory (see earlier).

Beyond the two most typical mystery plots, fine differentiations have been suggested for additional schemes. The "whydunit" and the "Had-I-But-Known" differ with regard to the character of central interest. In contrast to plots that put the sleuth in the center of the action (the investigation), these plot schemes attach more importance to persons directly involved in the scenery of the criminal act.

The "whydunit" (see Conley Jones, 1999) is primarily concerned with the question of the motive instead of establishing the identity of the culprit. The psychological motivation of victimization, then, forms the enigma, whereas the perpetrator can even be revealed in the story beginning. The main interest lies in understanding the psychological processes resulting in murder. Some deviance from Brewer's understanding of mystery can be seen in that the "whydunit" is "more likely to move differently through time and to reveal more points of view, utilizing flashbacks and the inner thoughts of a variety of characters" (Conley Jones, 1999, p. 498). The emphasis on subjective viewpoints goes well together, with crime *novel* being the other label attached to the "whydunit." Novels are concerned with feelings and inner processes of characters, whereas narratives focus on actions and are thereby more plot oriented.

The "Had-I-But-Known" mystery pattern typically centers on a young naive female and her amateur efforts to piece together evidence on obscure circumstances in her close environment. The social milieu (usually upper-class) is crucial in this pattern, because family conflicts resulting from criminal secrets in the past stress the importance of the enigma. The conflict resolution clarifies not only secrets of family members but often leads the female narrator to true love (Freier, 1999, p. 197). Examples are *Rebecca* by Daphne du Maurier or, more recently, *Before I Say Goodbye* by Mary Higgins Clark.[1]

---

[1]For other subgenre distinctions, mainly referring to milieu or to procedural features, see, for example *www.mysteryguide.com*

Explanations for the Enjoyment of Mystery

Empirical investigations of mystery enjoyment are not easily found. Although a comprehensive body of literary treatises, essays, and content descriptions exists, there is an obvious gap when it comes to research on the uses and effects of mystery fiction. Although mystery novels exploit common (pseudo-)knowledge on psychology as a source of cues and hints (Krasner, 1983), psychological examinations of mystery enjoyment are rare. But many authors have expressed speculative ideas about the appeal of mystery of which many can be collated to one of the categories discussed later that Zillmann has suggested. Remaining ideas are, for instance, that the "detective novel, thus, is constructed to represent a triumph of detective will and intellectual methodology" (Reilly, 1999b, p. 116) or escapism as a need of readers of mystery. Furthermore, Brewer has incorporated mystery in his structural-affect theory, but this approach does not take the resolution of the mystery into account when it comes to emotional effects. His concept closely corresponds to an initial part of Zillmann's considerations on mystery described in the following.

Zillmann (1991b) suggested a theory of mystery enjoyment in which he basically postulated three explanations. The first approach suggests that uncertainty about the finally revealed culprit influences the recipients' enjoyment to the effect that the higher their uncertainty, the higher their enjoyment. Uncertainty proper is instigated by (a) the introduction of suspects that are perceived equally likely to be guilty of the crime in question, and (b) the number of these suspects. Then again, the enjoyment cannot be increased by raising the number of suspects above the point where the recipients' capacity and motivation to process information is exceeded. The mystery novels covered by the content analysis mentioned earlier (Bryant et al., 2000) typically featured four suspects. In this regard the closed-world principle of detective stories matches with a limited number of suspects on whom the audience invests cognitive effort in the form of suspicion.

Zillmann queried this first idea with the assumption that it wasn't uncertainty during exposure that was enjoyed, but surprise resulting from an expected denouement (in the mystery ending). For this matter, the degree of enjoyment varies with surprise. For intense surprise, very low suspicion (down to zero) of the actual culprit and strong suspicion of alternative characters needs to be instigated and then thwarted in the very end. Again, surprise and, in consequence, enjoyment are higher the more fictional agents were suspected before the resolution. As Breen (1999) put it, "Readers enjoy finding guilt in unexpected places" (p. 259).

The third suggestion in Zillmann's theory of mystery enjoyment goes along with a common lay explanation that also can be found in literature on writing. Readers or viewers "take pleasure from guessing along" (Zillmann, 1991b, p. 298). But supposedly they not only ponder the puzzle but also enjoy having their expectation about the resolution confirmed—"guessing along and being right" (Zillmann, 1991b, p. 298). In this sense, exposure to mystery can provide self-affirmation, if the recipient anticipates the correct denouement. Then the resolution is crucial for the enjoyment, whereas the speculations along the fictional investigation are more means to an end.

These three possible origins of mystery enjoyment—uncertainty model, surprise model, and confirmation model—form alternatives that may apply to different recipients in different situations. Accordingly, psychological traits and states are critical determinants of the enjoyment respondents obtain from mystery. Zillmann (1991b) offered preconditions and mediators for the models of mystery enjoyment: (a) In order to experience surprise and not just uncertainty, the audience must develop expectations in the first place; (b) the acceptance for one's own erroneousness is an important mediator when it comes to the enjoyment of being surprised and, by the same token, misled or confirmed; and (c) confirmation of one's expectations will only be considered as self-affirming if the enigma was not too transparent or challenging enough.

Emotional Appeal of Mystery

Essentially the typical mystery plot plays on perceived probabilities of possible resolutions, represented by possible alternative perpetrators for the most part. The genre has often been characterized as cerebral animation lacking emotional appeal. Reproaches have been made that detective fiction is preoccupied with the investigation process and consequently trivializes through emotional neglect (Smyer, 1999). Then again, an emotional component has to be involved in any form of entertainment. The affects evoked by a mystery are essential for the motivation to expose oneself persistently to a whole mystery movie or to several hundred pages of a mystery story.

Various explanations of how fiction can induce emotion (for an overview see Frijda, 1994) seem to fail when it comes to mystery. Identification as an affect-conveying process has been generally defeated (e.g., Zillmann, 1994). Parasocial interaction (Horton & Wohl, 1956) is unlikely, because sleuths and/or culprits by rule never turn to the audience. Moreover, the recipient typically only learns about the incidents and the sleuths' reasoning via a narrator (e.g., Dr. Watson in the Sherlock Holmes mysteries by Arthur Conan Doyle). Hence, any form of parasocial interaction is not a compelling explanation for emotional involvement by mystery. Empathy (Zillmann, 1994), likewise, appears secondary when it comes to mystery, because the cast doesn't usually express much emotion. The victim certainly deserves sympathy, but in the case of murder, empathy is not appropriate. Emotions conveyed by suspects may not be what they appear, because every suspect may turn out to be a pretentious perpetrator. The sleuth is often detached from the goings-on and sober in terms of behavior and expression. The protagonist characteristically stands for high ethical standards but is very often described as an eccentric loner or an arrogant misfit. More emotional sleuths frequently act violently and thereby might not invite empathic involvement. In contrast to the suspense genre, good and evil are not clearly outlined due to obscure characters in mystery. Consequently, affective dispositions are not easily established. Generally speaking, the mystery often presents itself as dominated by analytical reasoning and pretense. Intense feeling with characters is unlikely.

Nonetheless, understanding social situations and actions depicted in mysteries requires at least cognitive perspective-taking (Steins & Wicklund, 1993) in order to follow the story. Although emotions are not forthrightly expressed by the cast, the audience presumably develops assumptions about the motivations of their fictional behavior. These motivations would then also relate to the supposed feelings of the characters. However, empathy involving "acute emotions" (Zillmann, 1991a; 1994, p. 40) does not seem to play an essential role, because feelings are usually only vaguely suggested.

An explanation for the appeal of mystery as entertainment may be inferred from the source of affective dispositions. According to Zillmann and his colleagues (Zillmann & Bryant, 1975; Zillmann & Cantor, 1977), moral considerations result in positive affective dispositions if the behavior of a character is deemed ethically favorable, and in negative dispositions, if the behavior is condemned. The importance of morality in mystery and story-space in general has also been discussed by others (Brewer & Ohtsuka, 1988; Carroll, 1996; Jose & Brewer, 1984; Sparks, 1992). Although ideosyncratic moral views may intermediate the development of affective dispositions in general, mysteries obviously refer to broadly accepted moral standards.

The very starting point of the typical mystery is a crime, the core of violation of social rules and morality. With murder being the most common crime investigated in mysteries, the instigation of the plot is a deed that is generally condemned—taking the life of another human being. "The story of criminal detection seems to be the product of anxiety about the danger of violation of the social contract by an unlawful appropriation of wealth or the destruction of life. Moreover, the genre invariably addresses the problem of crime by posing in opposition to it a character representing civilized values. The values may be ethical or moral" (Reilly, 1999c, p. 167). The unknown culprit is then pursued by the sleuth. Because the culprit is the villain, and the sleuth stands for the ethics of society, a very basic scheme applies that seems to suffice to interest the audience. The sense of justice motivates us to follow the efforts to clarify guilt and innocence in order to discover truth and attain (poetic) justice.

As Carroll (1996) pointed out, morality in fiction can bring up specific values inherent to the story. Ethics may be weighed by several factors. For instance, the sleuth may apply forbidden practices to access information, or the motivation for murder can be presented as understandable. Moral subtleties are, then, portrayed and discussed within fiction up to the point of the justifiable homicide (see mystery subcategory "who-gets-away-with-it," Rahn, 1999). The audience is put in the position of rating not only the possible outcomes by suspecting characters, but also moral values involved. Hence, the quest for justice is the central theme of mystery and ready made to evoke emotions based on ethical irritation that go beyond being right about the outcome.

MYSTERY: A NEAR RELATIVE TO SUSPENSE?

Suspense and mystery have been frequently compared (Brewer, 1996; Carroll, 1996; Zillmann, 1991b). Ironically, they have even been confused by experts; Carroll (1996) pointed out that Dove's (1989) book *Suspense in the Formula Story* should have been named "mystery in the formula story" (p. 75).

Both genres heavily rely on the development of expectations about the outcome. Suspense arises with the announcement of only two possible denouements, whereas mystery can in principle involve any number of outcomes represented by suspects. Moreover, suspense offers two opposite resolutions, in contrast to mystery, where the possible outcomes don't necessarily have any kind of logical relation. The arrangement of time concerning narration and narrated events differs fundamentally, resulting in apprehension in the case of suspense and in curiosity in the case of mystery.

From this perspective, one could argue that the two genres take up two basic approaches to general understanding, fostering a priori prediction in suspense narration and post-hoc explanation in mystery narration. Although suspense depicts good and evil clearly, mystery plays on personae perception by presenting opaque characters. This and the emphasis on action in suspense as a forceful plot and on reasoning in mystery as a fiddly puzzle typically leads to more arousal during exposure to suspense.

The moral is an important reference point in order to evoke emotions and thereby motivation for exposure to both entertainment forms. Both genres strongly refer to morality in order to create emotional interest, although suspense stories are concerned with the prevention of "wrong" outcomes, whereas mystery stories revolve around reestablishing justice after harm has already been done. Consequently, reactions at the outcome can be described as relief for suspense and as surprise or confirmation for mystery. Little is known about the emotional effects of the resolution of mysteries, yet it appears obvious that the ending has great importance, because the audience undergoes long tedious periods of piecing evidence together in order to get to the solution. Whether curiosity and bewilderment somehow become surprise similar to excitation-transfer in suspense is unknown. Zillmann's (1991b, p. 302) complaint that speculations on mystery enjoyment lack empirical substantiation still holds true 10 years later.

REFERENCES

Breen, J. L. (1999). Least likely suspect. In R. Herbert, C. Aird, J. M. Reilly, & S. Oleksiw (Eds.), *The Oxford companion to crime and mystery writing* (pp. 259–260). New York: Oxford University Press.

Brewer, W. F. (1996). The nature of narrative suspense and the problem of rereading. In P. Vorderer, H. J. Wulff, & M. Friedrichsen (Eds.), *Suspense: Conceptualizations, theoretical analyses, and empirical explorations* (pp. 107–127). Hillsdale, NJ: Lawrence Erlbaum Associates.

Brewer, W. F., & Lichtenstein, E. H. (1981). Event schemas, story schemas, and story grammars. In J. Long & A. Baddely (Eds.), *Attention and performance IX* (pp. 363–379). Hillsdale, NJ: Lawrence Erlbaum Associates.

Brewer, W. F., & Lichtenstein, E. H. (1982). Stories are to entertain: A structural-affect theory of stories. *Journal of Pragmatics, 6,* 473–486.

Brewer, W. F., & Ohtsuka, K. (1988). Story structure, characterization, just world organization, and reader affect in American and Hungarian short stories. *Poetics, 17,* 395–415.

Bryant, J., Mullikin Parcell, L., Bryant, J. A., & Kwon, J. C. (2000, August). *A systematic content analysis of eight decades of best-selling English-language mystery novels.* Presentation at the conference of the Internationale Gesellschaft fuer Empirische Literaturwissenschaft IGEL, Toronto, Canada.

Carroll, N. (1996). The paradox of suspense. In P. Vorderer, H. J. Wulff, & M. Friedrichsen (Eds.), *Suspense: Conceptualizations, theoretical analyses, and empirical explorations* (pp. 71–91). Mahwah, NJ: Lawrence Erlbaum Associates.

Conley Jones, L. (1999). Whydunit. In R. Herbert, C. Aird, J. M. Reilly, & S. Oleksiw (Eds.), *The Oxford companion to crime and mystery writing* (pp. 498–499). New York: Oxford University Press.

Dove, G. N. (1989). *Suspense in the formula story.* Bowling Green, OH: Bowling Green State University Popular Press.

Freier, M. P. (1999). Had-I-But-Known. In R. Herbert, C. Aird, J. M. Reilly, & S. Oleksiw (Eds.), *The Oxford companion to crime and mystery writing* (p. 197). New York: Oxford University Press.

Frijda, N. (1988). The laws of emotion. *American Psychologist, 43,* 349–358.

Frijda, N. (Ed.). (1994). Emotions and cultural products [special issue]. *Poetics, 23*(1–2).

Gärtner, S. (1999). *Zwischen Hoffen und Bangen: Eine experimentelle Studie der Motivation zur Rezeption spannender Unterhaltungsangebote* [Between hope and fear: An experimental study on the motivation of exposure to suspenseful entertainment]. Upublished master's thesis, Hanover University of Music and Drama, Germany.

Gerrig, R. J. (1996). The resiliency of suspense. In P. Vorderer, H. J. Wulff, & M. Friedrichsen (Eds.), *Suspense: Conceptualizations, theoretical analyses, and empirical explorations* (pp. 93–105). Mahwah, NJ: Lawrence Erlbaum Associates.

Gerrig, R. J., & Bernardo, A. B. (1994). Readers as problem-solvers in the experience of suspense. *Poetics, 22,* 459–472.

Hayne, B. (1999). Closed-world settings and open-world settings. In R. Herbert, C. Aird, J. M. Reilly, & S. Oleksiw (Eds.), *The Oxford companion to crime and mystery writing* (pp. 76–77). New York: Oxford University Press.

Herbert, R., Aird, C., Reilly, J. M., & Oleksiw, S. (Eds.). (1999). *The Oxford companion to crime and mystery writing*. New York: Oxford University Press.

Horton, D., & Wohl, R. R. (1956). Mass communication and para-social interaction. Observation on intimacy at a distance. *Psychiatry, 19,* 215–229.

Jose, P. E., & Brewer, W. F. (1984). Development of story liking: Character identification, suspense, and outcome resolution. *Developmental Psychology, 20,* 911–924.

Krasner, L. (1983). The psychology of mystery. *American Psychologist, 38,* 578–582.

Marx, M. (1940). *The enjoyment of drama*. New York: F. S. Crofts.

Rahn, B. J. (1999). Who-gets-away-with-it. In R. Herbert, C. Aird, J. M. Reilly, & S. Oleksiw (Eds.), *The Oxford companion to crime and mystery writing* (pp. 496–497). New York: Oxford University Press.

Reilly, J. M. (1999a). Clues. In R. Herbert, C. Aird, J. M. Reilly, & S. Oleksiw (Eds.), *The Oxford companion to crime and mystery writing* (pp. 78–79). New York: Oxford University Press.

Reilly, J. M. (1999b). Detective story. In R. Herbert, C. Aird, J. M. Reilly, & S. Oleksiw (Eds.), *The Oxford companion to crime and mystery writing* (pp. 116–117). New York, Oxford: Oxford University Press.

Reilly, J. M. (1999c). Formula. In R. Herbert, C. Aird, J. M. Reilly, & S. Oleksiw (Eds.), *The Oxford companion to crime and mystery writing* (pp. 165–167). New York: Oxford University Press.

Reilly, J. M. (1999d). Mystery story. In R. Herbert, C. Aird, J. M. Reilly, & S. Oleksiw (Eds.), *The Oxford companion to crime and mystery writing* (pp. 303–304). New York: Oxford University Press.

Rodell, M. (1952). *Mystery fiction: Theory and technique.* New York: Hermitage House.

Seeger, H. E. (1998). *Das erste zweite Mal. Informationsverarbeitung und Spannungserleben bei der wiederholten Rezeption narrativer Filme* [The first second time: Information processing and experience of suspense during repeated exposure to narrative films.] Unpublished master's thesis, Hanover University of Music and Drama, Germany:

Smyer, R. (1999). Escapism. In R. Herbert, C. Aird, J. M. Reilly, & S. Oleksiw (Eds.), *The Oxford companion to crime and mystery writing* (pp. 135–136). New York: Oxford University Press.

Sparks, R. (1992). *Television and the drama of crime. Moral tales and the place of crime in public life.* Buckingham: Open University Press.

Steins, G., & Wicklund, R. A. (1993). Zum Konzept der Perspektivenübernahme: Ein kritischer Überblick [On the concept of perspective-taking: A critical overview.] *Psychologische Rundschau, 44,* 226–239.

Tan, E., & Diteweg, G. (1996) Suspense, predictive inference, and emotion in film viewing. In P. Vorderer, H. J. Wulff, & M. Friedrichsen (Eds.), *Suspense: Conceptualizations, theoretical analyses, and empirical explorations* (pp. 149–188). Mahwah, NJ: Lawrence Erlbaum Associates.

Van Dine, S. S. (1928). Twenty rules for writing detective stories [Originally published in American Magazine]. Retrieved May, 27, 2001 from *http://www.mtroyal.ab.ca/gaslight/vandine.htm*

Vorderer, P., & Bube, H. (1996). Ende gut–alles gut? Eine empirische Studie über den Einfluß von empathischem Streß und Filmausgang auf die Befindlichkeit von Rezipienten und deren Bewertung des Films [All's well that ends well: An empirical study on the impact of empathic stress and film ending on the feeling state of recipients and their film evaluations]. *Medienpsychologie, 8*(2), 128–143.

Vorderer, P., & Knobloch, S. (1998). Ist interaktive Fernsehunterhaltung spannend? [Is interaactive TV entertainment thrilling?] *Siegener Periodicum zur Internationalen Empirischen Literaturwissenschaft SPIEL, 17*(1) [special issue on entertainment], 58–80.

Vorderer, P., & Knobloch, S. (2000). Drama, Suspense, and Conflict. In D. Zillmann & P. Vorderer (Eds.), *Media entertainment: The psychology of its appeal* (pp. 59–72). Mahwah, NJ: Lawrence Erlbaum Associates.

Vorderer, P., Knobloch, S., & Schramm, H. (2001). Does entertainment suffer from interactivity? The impact of watching an interactive TV movie on viewers' experience of entertainment. *Media Psychology, 3,* 343–363.

Vorderer, P., Wulff, H. J., & Friedrichsen, M. (Eds.). (1996). *Suspense: Conceptualizations, theoretical analyses, and empirical explorations.* Mahwah, NJ: Lawrence Erlbaum Associates.

Zillmann, D. (1971). Excitation transfer in communication-mediated aggressive behavior. *Journal of Experimental Social Psychology, 7,* 419–434.

Zillmann, D. (1980). Anatomy of suspense. In P. H. Tannenbaum (Ed.), *The entertainment functions of television* (pp. 133–163). Hillsdale, NJ: Lawrence Erlbaum Associates.

Zillmann, D. (1983). Transfer of excitation in emotional behavior. In J. T. Cacioppo & R. E. Petty (Eds.), *Social psychophysiology: A sourcebook* (pp. 215–240). New York: Guilford.

Zillmann, D. (1991a). Empathy: Affect from bearing witness to the emotions of others. In J. Bryant & D. Zillmann (Eds.), *Responding to the screen. Reception and reaction processes* (pp. 135–167). Hillsdale, NJ: Lawrence Erlbaum Associates.

Zillmann, D. (1991b). The logic of suspense and mystery. In J. Bryant & D. Zillmann (Eds.), *Responding to the screen. Reception and reaction processes* (pp. 281–303). Hillsdale, NJ: Lawrence Erlbaum Associates.

Zillmann, D. (1994). Mechanisms of emotional involvement with drama. *Poetics,* 23(1–2), 33–51.

Zillmann, D. (1996). The psychology of suspense in dramatic exposition. In P. Vorderer, H. J. Wulff, & M. Friedrichsen (Eds.), *Suspense: Conceptualizations, theoretical analyses, and empirical explorations* (pp. 199–231). Mahwah, NJ: Lawrence Erlbaum Associates.

Zillmann, D., & Bryant, J. (1975). Viewer's moral sanction of retribution in the appreciation of dramatic presentations. *Journal of Experimental Social Psychology, 11,* 572–582.

Zillmann, D., & Cantor, J. R. (1977). Affective responses to the emotions of a protagonist. *Journal of Experimental and Social Psychology, 13,* 155–165.

Zillmann, D., Hay, T., & Bryant, J. (1975). The effects of suspense and its resolution on the appreciation of dramatic presentations. *Journal of Research into Personality, 9,* 307–323.

17

Enjoyment of Sports Spectatorship

Arthur A. Raney
Florida State University

Whatever measure you use—the number of all-sports channels, television and radio ratings, advertising revenues, ticket or merchandising sales, frequency of tax referenda for new stadium construction, free-agent salaries, the variety of products endorsed by sports superstars—it is hard to deny the status of sports in our world today. Surely a key to this success is the pleasure that we experience from watching Tiger Woods effortlessly carve through the most difficult course, or from seeing the Los Angeles Lakers quickly dispose of all would-be challengers to their NBA crown, or from watching the U.S. women's soccer and softball teams conquer the world's best.

This chapter investigates the enjoyment that we derive from witnessing sporting events. Although attending a game or match is surely a thrilling experience, this text focuses on audience responses to mediated sports. To do so, the prevalence of sports spectatorship today is first discussed. Next, research findings are presented that detail how enjoyment is affected by various aspects of the sports contest, including the outcome, the drama within, and the various types of play displayed. The reader should note how the work of Dolf Zillmann and his colleagues has framed the study of sports spectatorship over the past three decades. Finally, several recent trends in sports spectatorship, as well as possibilities for future research, are explored.

THE STATE OF SPORTS SPECTATORSHIP

Media coverage of sports is huge business. If this were ever in doubt, consider that NBC paid $3.5 billion for the rights to the Sydney and four subsequent

Olympic Games. FOX recently plopped down $2.5 billion to show 6 years of Major League Baseball. In 2003, CBS will enter an 11-year, $6 billion extension of its existing contract to be the exclusive network of the NCAA Men's Basketball Tournament. The major reason for all of this money changing hands is, of course, the viewers that the contests bring to the advertising table. A quick glance at the history of sports spectatorship, in particular on television, might predict that the networks' money was well spent.

- Five of the all-time top 10 (11 of the top 20) rated U.S. television programs are sporting events: Super Bowl XVI, Super Bowl XVII, 1994 Winter Olympics, Super Bowl XX, and Super Bowl XII (Nielsen Media Research, 1998).

- Only the final episode of *M*A*S*H* had more viewers than the telecast of the ice-skating duel between Nancy Kerrigan and Tonya Harding at the 1994 Winter Olympics (Nielsen Media Research, 1998).

- For the week of June 14–20, 2001, the top seven—and eight of the top 12—highest-rated basic cable shows were sportscasts. The two highest rated shows were professional wrestling programs ("Top15 basic cable programs," 2001).

- The advertising rate for the 2001 Super Bowl between the New York Giants and the Baltimore Ravens was $2.3 million per 30-second ad, more than a 40% increase in just 2 years (Elliot, 2001).

However, household ratings for sports programming on the major networks, especially those for the traditional major sports, are actually on the decline. As Fig. 17.1 indicates, the primetime network ratings for sports programming has steadily declined since the 1994–1995 season. This decline is amplified in the network ratings for professional baseball (down more than 25% since 1997), basketball (down nearly 29%), and football (down 8.5%), as reported in Fig. 17.2. Although the Super Bowl—which, regardless of the teams competing, consistently garners a domestic audience of more than 40 million households—remains immune to this trend, many of the major championships have also fallen on hard times. For instance, the 2000 World Series between the New York Yankees and New York Mets was the lowest rated Fall Classic of all time, down 23% from 1999 (Ginn, 2001); NBC's prime-time coverage of the Sydney Olympic Games received the lowest rating of any Olympic (Winter or Summer) since 1968 (Bock, 2000); and the 2000 NCAA men's basketball tournament fell 6%, to its lowest mark in 18 years (Ginn, 2001). Hockey Night in Canada is even down 13% since 1999 (Zelkovich, 2000)!

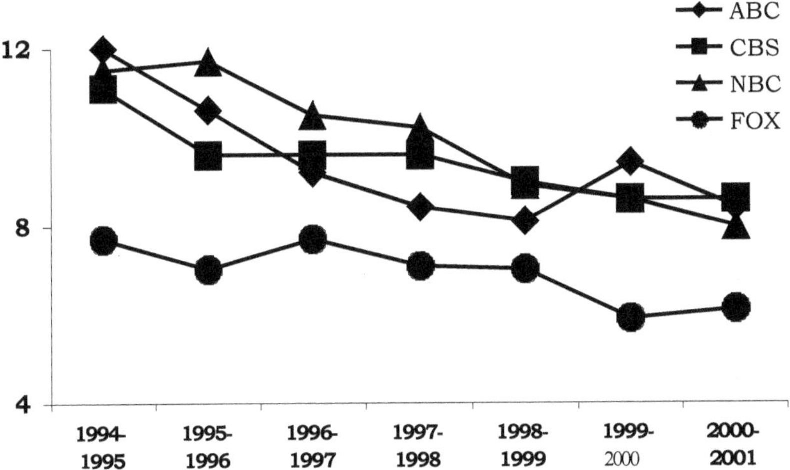

Fig. 17.1. Primetime sports ratings, 1994–2001. Source: Nielsen Media Research. Copyright © 2001, Nielsen Media Research.

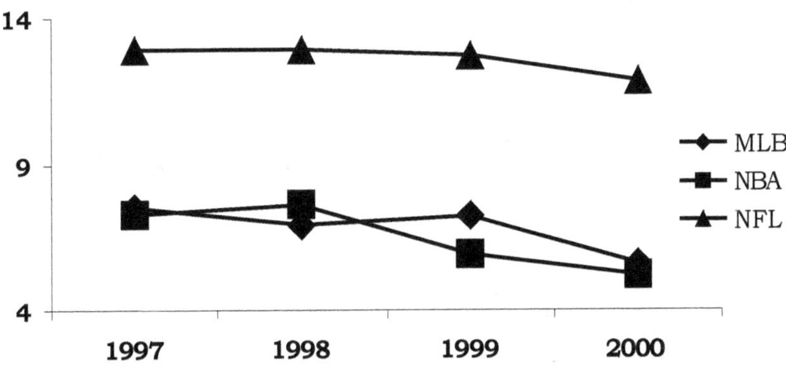

Fig. 17.2. Primetime sports ratings, 1994–2001. Source: Nielsen Television Index Sports Decks, Nielsen Galaxy Explorer. Copyright © 2001 Nielsen Media Research.

Although this decline might make a few broadcast executives a bit nervous, in reality, mediated sports spectatorship is still quite healthy. The audience loss on broadcast network sports programs mirrors the oft-cited loss in overall network viewing. Furthermore, the audiences for countless 24-hour-a-day national and regional cable sports networks, as well as an ever-increasing sports radio and Internet sports market, more than made up for the network decline. Whereas the traditional sports powerhouses of football, baseball, basketball, and hockey feel a slip in their popularity, a handful of other sports are experiencing a new ratings heyday.

Three sports in particular continue to attract viewers in record numbers: NASCAR racing, professional golf, and the so-called action sports (which, among others, include skateboarding, aggressive in-line skating, bicycle stunts, freestyle moto-X, street luge, snowboarding, snow mountain biking, and skysurfing). And the television industry is trying to capitalize on the current popularity of the three. For example, NBC and FOX recently teamed with Turner Sports in a $2.4 billion deal for six years of NASCAR coverage. The $400 million-a-year average is up from only $3 million for the same coverage in 1985 (Maynard, 2001). In July 2001, the PGA Tour agreed to a TV-rights deal worth $850 million, an increase of nearly 50% over the previous 4-year contract ("Deal puts Woods," 2001). ESPN's action sports centerpiece, the Olympic-style X Games, has spawned countless siblings, imitations, and cottage industries: the Winter X Games, Tony Hawk's Gigantic Skatepark Tour, the Gravity Games, and even the Action Sports and Music Awards.

For all of the money and investment, the three are delivering record-setting audiences. NBC's coverage of the July 2001 Pepsi 400 from the Daytona International Speedway drew nearly 25 million viewers, the largest prime-time audience in NASCAR's history (Ginn, 2001). During the first half of the 2001 season alone, NASCAR ratings were up 20% on FOX (Longman, 2001). The racing organization is seeking to further capitalize on its growing fandom. With merchandising revenues topping $1.2 billion in 1999—with miniature die-cast car sales accounting for $350 million alone! (Dunnavant & Muller, 1999)—NASCAR is preparing to launch its own cable network, as well as a children's show on FOX to star animated versions of their drivers (Longman, 2001). With these latest ventures, NASCAR officials are banking on the new generation of fans being as loyal as their predecessors: One report suggests that 72% of NASCAR fans consciously purchase products from manufacturers who back racing (Ford, 1998).

Several television networks are finding similar response to professional golf. CBS drew approximately 10 million viewers for its August 2000 final round coverage of the PGA Championship, a 30% increase from the previous year (Phillips, 2000). Much of the recent success of the PGA is due to the sport's top star, Tiger Woods. According to a June 2001 Gallup Poll, Woods is now seen as the "greatest athlete active in the world of sports today," mentioned six times more often than his nearest competition (Carlson, 2001). In fact, Woods' popularity now ranks him with Colin Powell, Michael Jordan, and John Glenn as second in all-time public favorability (at 83%), exceeded only by Pope John Paul II (who had a 86% favorable rating in 1998; Carlson, 2001). Based largely on these numbers, ABC has found so much success with its made-for-prime-time-TV, head-to-head, 18-hole events (e.g., The Battle at Bighorn) that it recently inked the bankable Woods to one such event annually through 2006.

Perhaps the greatest growth in sports spectatorship in the past few years, however, has come from the action sports. Promoted as much as a lifestyle as a competition, action sports have struck a variety of cords with, among others, the under-20 age demographic. Nickelodeon's *Rocket Power* is a top-rated cartoon based on four West Coast kids and their participation in the various sports. Mattel's Max Steel toy line, based on the WB's Saturday morning animated action sports series, was the number one selling action figure in 2000 (Prior, 2001). Although ABC received strong ratings (average of more than 1 million viewers per day) for its coverage of the 2000 X Games from San Francisco, the truly impressive audiences are in the international market. ESPN International, for instance, will distribute the 2001 Winter X Games to more than 20 million viewers in more than 140 countries. Not only are people watching the sports like never before, they are also participating in them: BMX has experienced a 70% growth rate among 12- to 24-year-olds since 1997 (Thomas, 2001), and nearly three times the number of people participated in in-line skating in 1999 as played baseball (Prior, 2001). But perhaps of utmost interest to network execs and Madison Avenuers alike, Heinz's Bagel Bites signed on as sponsor of the 2000 Winter X Games and increased their product consumption by 26% in the 8 weeks following the event (Cleland, 2001).

Overall, six in ten Americans consistently describe themselves as sports fans (Gallup poll: Sports, 2001). From fantasy baseball leagues to office pools on the big game, from Kentucky Derby parties to Super Bowl parties, from casual observers to rabid fans, sports is more thoroughly engrained in our social fabric than ever before. What, though, is the allure of athletic competition? What draws us to attend, view, discuss, debate, and videotape so that we can relive these events? What is so enjoyable about sports spectatorship? A rich tradition of communication scholarship offers some answers to these and similar questions.

ENJOYMENT AND THE OUTCOME OF SPORTS CONTESTS

Whether it is basketball, BMX, or the Belmont Stakes, every sports contest concludes in one of two ways: either one contestant is victorious or the participants play to a draw. The fact that sporting events end with a resolution of conflict or that they offer some finality or closure to an encounter alone helps us little in our understanding of sports enjoyment. Outcome-based theories of sports enjoyment are dependent on a lack of indifference about the contestants; in other words, they require that spectators have feelings toward the participants. This idea is, of course, not foreign to sports spectators. Virtually all of us have players and teams that we love and players and teams that we hate; this is the very nature of sports fanship. Because we tend to root for one team over another, outcomes matter. In fact, as the following theories will indicate, the sports cliché rings true for most fans: "Winning isn't everything; it's the only thing."

It has been observed that sports spectators find pleasure in seeing a liked team win or a disliked one lose. Many spectators are similarly disappointed when a liked team is defeated or a disliked one is victorious. However, great variance exists between sports fans when it comes to the emotional affiliation they have with these teams. For example, you probably know people that are casual, "wear the team colors on game day" observers of sports; likewise you probably know a few rabid, "wear the team uniform, hat, socks, and face paint to the office the day before the game" fans. The disposition theory of sports spectatorship (Bryant & Raney, 2000; Zillmann, Bryant, & Sapolsky, 1989; Zillmann & Paulus, 1993; chap. 3, this volume) identifies a fan's relative placement on a continuum of affect toward the participants (from intense liking to intense disliking) as a chief predictor of sports enjoyment.

More specifically, the disposition theory of sports spectatorship can be summarized in two major propositions. First, enjoyment from witnessing a team or player succeed increases with positive affective dispositions and decreases with negative affective dispositions toward that competitor. In other words, enjoyment increases the more we like the team that wins and decreases the more we dislike the team that wins. Secondly, enjoyment from witnessing a team or player fail increases with negative affective dispositions and decreases with positive affective dispositions toward that competitor. Or, enjoyment increases the more we dislike the losing team, but decreases the more we like the team that loses.

As a result of these two major proposals, we should expect that maximum enjoyment from sports spectatorship is derived from witnessing an intensely liked team defeat an intensely disliked team. Conversely, minimum enjoyment (as well as maximum disappointment or "negative enjoyment," Zillmann & Paulus, 1993, p. 605) comes from witnessing a loved team fall to a hated one. And finally, the outcome of a contest between similarly liked or disliked competitors will generate an intermediate level of enjoyment.

A wide variety of studies have supported the disposition theory of sports spectatorship for both individual and team contests. Zillmann, Bryant, and Sapolsky (1989) detailed the majority of these studies. What follows is an abbreviated reporting of those studies as well as summaries of subsequent investigations.

Zillmann et al. (1989) investigated the relationship between enjoyment of an NFL contest and viewers' dispositions toward the competing teams: the Minnesota Vikings and the St. Louis Cardinals. Affect toward the two teams was measured, with each participant falling into one of three levels of liking toward each team: positive, neutral, and negative. Participants were later exposed to a live-broadcast, regular-season contest between the two teams; the game was won by the Vikings. Enjoyment was measured for every play in the game, as well as the overall contest. The researchers predicted that those with a positive disposition toward the victorious Vikings would enjoy the game more than those who disliked the team and more than those who liked the Cardinals. In fact, it was predicted that enjoyment of the contest would be the greatest for those viewers who really liked the Vikings and really disliked the Cardinals. Conversely, it was predicted that enjoyment would be least (and disappointment greatest) for those viewers who were Cardinals fans and Viking haters. The findings of the study support each of these expectations based on disposition theory.

Additional support for the disposition theory of sports spectatorship was found in a study of Olympic basketball in which national pride served as a basis for disposition formation (Zillmann et al., 1989). Students at Indiana University viewed a portion of the 1976 men's gold medal contest between the United States and Yugoslavia and rated their enjoyment of each play. As expected, the American students reported increased enjoyment on plays resulting in a U.S. basket and decreased enjoyment when Yugoslavia scored. These findings lend support to the disposition theory of sports spectatorship. But the researchers found even more support for the theory when they isolated responses to scoring plays involving two U.S. team members (Scott May and Quinn Buckner) who also happened to be past members of the

Indiana University team. The increased positive dispositions that the participants held toward May and Buckner led to more intense enjoyment of baskets scored by the two players than for any other U.S. players. The study highlights the importance of dispositional intensity in determining enjoyment of various dimensions of a sports contest.

Sapolsky (1980) offered further support for the theory in a study of men's high school basketball. A videotape of a basketball game between an all-White and an all-Black team was manipulated to produce several versions in which either the all-White team or the all-Black team won the game. White and Black college students who were unfamiliar with the teams viewed one version and rated their enjoyment of the final series of plays and their pleasure (or disappointment) with the outcome. The Black students—89.6% of whom reported rooting for the Black team—reported significantly more enjoyment when Black players scored and, for those who saw a version in which the Black team won, significantly more enjoyment of the overall game. The same trends, although not as strong, were found among the White students as well.

One study suggests that the interaction of dispositions and outcomes may actually transcend simple enjoyment of sporting events (Hirt, Zillmann, Erickson, & Kennedy, 1992). The researchers found that the enjoyment derived from watching a favored team win can actually elevate a viewer's self-esteem, boosting their confidence in their own abilities and talents. Furthermore, the despair accompanying the loss of a favored team can be associated with opposite effects, with the viewer having diminished self-confidence and self-esteem. These and similar findings (Madrigal, 1995; Owens & Bryant, 1998) indicate that team affiliations, dispositions, and game outcomes potentially influence more than mere enjoyment, but also overall satisfaction and well-being.

A similar line of research also deals less with the actual enjoyment derived from watching sports and more with the utility of being (or being perceived as) a fan. Cialdini and his colleagues argued that a by-product of being aligned with a winning team is our ability to "bask in the reflected glory" (BIRG; Cialdini et al., 1976) of the team's success, and thereby improve our public image. In other words, you may be perceived more like a "winning person" if others can readily identify you with a winning team. In the same manner, it has been argued that you can minimize any damage to your public image arising from identification with a losing sports team by distancing yourself (or "cutting off reflected failure"; Snyder, Higgins, & Stucky, 1983) from that team. In this way, the researchers suggested that sports fanship can serve as a means of image management.

Cialdini and his associates found support for the existence of the BIRGing phenomenon in several studies of college football fans. In one study, the researchers found that a higher percentage of college students wore apparel identifying their university on Mondays following a football victory than on Mondays following a defeat. In another study, the researchers reported that students described the outcome of a game using the first-person pronoun "we" (e.g., "We won") significantly more after a victory than after a defeat. This phenomenon tended to be even more pronounced when researchers did not acknowledge their affiliation with the university (Cialdini et al., 1976). Therefore, it is possible that the need to bask in the glory of your team increases in the presence of individuals who you perceive to have less in common with you. This would be in line with other image-management theory (e.g., Heider's, 1958, balance theory). Further support for the BIRGing phenomenon can be found in Cialdini and Richardson (1980) and Snyder et al. (1983).

ENJOYMENT OF SPORTS DRAMA

The Battle for Bragging Rights. A Clash of Titans. The Rumble in the Jungle. The 50-Yard Indoor War. An Unstoppable Force Colliding with an Immovable Object. An Old Fashion Slobber-Knocker. The Grudge Match. From college basketball to professional boxing, from arena football to figure skating, images of war dominate the world of sports. Perhaps this is to be expected given that competition is at the heart of the activity. However, few would deny that today's sports coverage capitalizes on (and hypes) this feature, constructing the story of sport around conflict. Previous research has demonstrated that sports commentators often rely on dramatic statements and various televisual features to highlight actual and even potential "bitter conflict" (Bryant, Comisky, & Zillmann, 1977).

The purpose of this added drama is its apparent impact on viewer enjoyment. Several empirical studies have examined the relationship between the special features used in sports commentary and production to accentuate conflict, the viewer's perceived level of drama in the contest, and spectator enjoyment. An initial study sought to measure the effects of sports commentary on audience perceptions and enjoyment of violent hockey action (Comisky, Bryant, & Zillmann, 1977). The researchers presented either normal or unusually rough hockey action to groups of respondents. Additionally, the researchers presented the action either with or without color commentary. The participants then indicated certain perceptions about the play, as well as overall enjoyment. The findings demonstrate the power of sports commentary: Viewers of the normal play with accompanying conflict-centered commentary perceived it to be more intense and violent than those who saw the same action without commentary, as well as those who saw the rougher play with and without commentary. Furthermore, the viewers of the normal play with dramatic commentary had the highest ratings of enjoyment of the four conditions. Similar findings were reported in Sullivan's (1991) study of televised basketball game. Thus, the way that live sporting contests are described may play as potentially a powerful role in how we perceive and experience the game as the action itself.

Not only does the description of the play have an impact on a spectator's experience but also the description of the contestants. Bryant, Brown, Comisky, and Zillmann (1982) created three versions of a tennis match that varied only in the reported affective relationship between the players: The players were best friends, the players were bitter enemies, or the player's relationship was neither stated or implied. Participants viewing the players-as-enemies version described the action as significantly more enjoyable, exciting, involving, and interesting than participants viewing the other two versions. The participants also perceived the players themselves to be more hostile, tense, and competitive in the players-as-enemies condition. Remember, all three conditions viewed the exact same action; the only difference was the way in which the players were described. These finding are further suggestive of the potential of sports commentary to influence a spectator's experience.

Finally, as one might expect, a fan's attitudes toward the contestants might interact with the sports commentary to further impact enjoyment. Owens and Bryant (1998) studied the impact of hometown (or so-called "homer") announcers and commentators on audience perceptions and enjoyment of a televised high school football game. The commentary provided by some of these announcers, because of their ties with one of the teams, adds a one-sided melodramatic flare to the game that might truly enhance the experience for the hometown viewer (and thoroughly outrage one from the visiting team). The findings were consistent with previous results. As disposition theory would predict, the students from the home town school found the game more enjoyable than nonhometown viewers. Moreover, the commentary presented by the biased "homer" announcer also lead to an increase in fan involvement with the game and rooting for the home team.

Clearly, sports commentary has a great impact on audience perceptions and overall enjoyment of sporting events.

As was noted above, drama is inherent in sports; commentators for the most part only hype the drama that is already present. One key element of drama—suspense—has specifically been shown to impact the enjoyment of media sports, regardless of the commentary. Gan, Tuggle, Mitrook, Coussement, and Zillmann (1997) asked participants to rate their enjoyment of one of eight 1995 NCAA men's basketball tournament games. Based on the final score, the eight games were categorized as either minimally (15 or more point differential between the two teams), moderately (10–14 points), substantially (5–9 points), or extremely suspenseful (1–4 points). This categorization, of course, assumes an inverse relationship between point differential and suspense, where suspense is highest in the tightest games. The researchers predicted that suspense and enjoyment would be correlated; therefore, it was predicted that enjoyment would be highest for individuals that viewed the closest (and thus most suspenseful) game. This pattern was observed for the male participants: The higher the suspense, the greater the reported enjoyment. However, the findings indicate that enjoyment among female viewers increased through the substantially suspenseful category, but then decreased in the extremely suspenseful condition. The researchers suggested that the high level of suspense caused by the nip-and-tuck game may have lead to a certain amount of distress in the female viewers. As a result, the suspense became an irritant and thus hampered enjoyment. Regardless of the explanation, the findings lend further support to the claim that the dramatic elements of sporting contests—that is, those inherent in the games or those enhanced by the commentators—influence the way we experience and enjoy the action.

ENJOYMENT OF VARIOUS TYPES OF PLAY

Another aspect of sporting events that impacts enjoyment is the presence of unforgettable, unexpected, and unrepeatable plays. What football fan can forget Franco Harris' Immaculate Reception or Joe Thiesmann's broken leg? What basketball fan can forget Julius "Dr. J" Erving's miraculous out-of-bound, around-and-under-the-basket reverse scoop shot against the Los Angeles Lakers or any number of Michael Jordan's last-second, game-winning heroics? What about Kerri Strug's ability to withstand the pain in her ankle and stick the landing on her final vault, securing the first Gold Medal in the team competition for the U.S. Women's Gymnastics squad at the 1996 Olympics? Added to this sport's highlights Hall of Fame could be countless half-court shots, bone-crushing hits, and snatching-victory-from-the-jaws-of-defeat plays that crowd sports newscasts on a nightly basis. Although these plays range from the novel (e.g., the double steal in baseball) to the risky (e.g., the pass from the end zone in football) to the effective (e.g., the ferocious slam dunk in basketball) to the brutal (e.g., the bone-crushing cross check in hockey), their impact on our enjoyment of sports seems indisputable.

Television producers certainly understand the appeal of these odd, unusual, sometimes gory, sometimes graceful images. Most highlight packages feature not only the play or plays that led to one team's eventual triumph, but also (and often times more of) the novel and/or risky action that takes place along the way. The replay equipment and myriad cameras used to produce live telecasts can repeatedly show the action from countless vantage points and angles, while announcers "Ooo" and "Ahh" at the surprise and sometimes horrific qualities of the plays. Although it is generally agreed that these plays enhance our viewing experience, few investigations to date have sought to validate the effect of this type of action on overall spectator enjoyment.

One thing that all of these plays have in common is a lack of commonness; a large part of their appeal is the fact that they are decidedly uncommon, involving unparalleled risks and feats of athleticism. An initial study explored the relationship between various types of play and enjoyment in a study of professional football (Zillmann et al., 1989). As expected, more risky plays (e.g., very long pass) were enjoyed significantly more than less risky plays (e.g., quarterback sneak). Furthermore, participants found more effective plays (i.e., the more yardage gained) more enjoyable than less effective plays. As a result, the most appreciated plays were those that were successful, risky plays. Interestingly, the commonality of the play was not related to enjoyment. Thus, the researchers asserted that "the findings call into question the view that audiences applaud uncommon, rarely employed and hence surprising plays, and that they abhor plays that are used over and over again (p. 274).

More recent investigations have focused less on the various types of play within a single sport or contest in favor of evaluations of the differences in appreciation of various plays between sports. Sargent, Zillmann, and Weaver (1998) investigated differences in sports enjoyment between males and females based on the type of action in the games. The respondents evaluated 25 regularly televised sports for enjoyment, excitement, boredom, violence, activity, elegance, and danger. The researchers found that males tend to report greater enjoyment for combative sports (e.g., football, soccer, boxing), whereas females report greater enjoyment for stylistic sports (e.g., gymnastics, figure skating, and tennis). More specifically, enjoyment for men increased the more violent, active, and dangerous they perceived the sport to be. Women, however, tended to enjoy sports that they saw as elegant more than those that were seen as violent or dangerous. These findings are similar to those reported by Zillmann (1995) in which males tended to favor violent and risky sports, whereas females favored artistic ones. It is easy to understand, then, the appeal of auto racing and action sports to young men.

Although men do consistently report more enjoyment for violent sports action than women, it would be incorrect to think that women reject aggressive play altogether. Men are not alone in their liking of "rough-and-tumble play" (Bryant, Comisky, & Zillmann, 1981); females too report significant enjoyment of violent and aggressive action (see Bryant, Zillmann, & Raney, 1998, for a thorough discussion of the enjoyment of sports violence). We have already noted that play that is perceived as more aggressive—thanks to dramatic color commentary—leads to more overall enjoyment (Comisky et al., 1977; Sullivan, 1991). More specifically, commentary that stresses the violence inherent in the action makes the play appear even rougher than it actually is. Meanwhile, commentary that ignores the violence inherent in the action can make even rough play seem relatively innocuous (Bryant et al., 1998). With regard to the play itself, Sargent et al. (1998) found that men and women combined favored violent team sports significantly more than all other types. These findings echo those of Bryant et al. (1981) which reported that men and women alike enjoyed professional football plays containing a high level of aggression and roughness significantly more than those containing lesser amounts. Furthermore, DeNeui and Sachau (1996) found that enjoyment of intercollegiate hockey games for both men and women was not correlated with how competitive the game was or even with who won the contest. Rather, spectator enjoyment was correlated with how many penalty minutes were assessed! Clearly the type of action, in particular the presence or absence of sports violence, plays a tremendous role in our enjoyment of sporting events.

SPORTS SPECTATORSHIP: EXPLAINING THE PRESENT, EXAMINING THE FUTURE

Given the various explanations for the enjoyment of sports spectatorship, perhaps the current popularity of professional golf, action sports, and NASCAR racing should surprise no one. The latest iteration of each sport seems to capitalize on many of the essential elements of sports enjoyment today, as well as (perhaps) forecast what sports enjoyment will look like in the future.

Much has be en written about the growing cult of personality in professional sports (e.g., "Survey," 1998). Whether you blame free agency or personal endorsement and merchandising contracts or social trends toward individualism, most agree that athletes have solidified their places alongside film and music stars in the pantheon of pop-culture gods. Although there is still "no I in TEAM," individual athletes dominate sports headlines, drive ticket sales, and ensure television ratings. As a result, the entertainment experience that is sports spectatorship, in many ways, is more similar to traditional dramatic fiction than ever before, in that the performance of individual sports stars, much like the behaviors of protagonists within drama, drive our enjoyment (see chap. 3, this volume for a thorough treatment of drama appreciation). Historically, the disposition theory of sports spectatorship has relied on emotional involvement with both individuals and teams as a predictor of enjoyment. As individual personalities eclipse their teams—and at times even the sports that they play—we may find that team affiliation and fanship decrease in their importance.

Given this trend, one should not be surprised that the three sports flourishing in this environment are individual sports with larger-than-life personalities. As was noted earlier, Tiger Woods now ranks as the most popular athlete today; his closest competitor is the man who set new standards for sports stardom, Michael Jordan (Carlson, 2001). Woods' celebrity is so great that international tournaments consistently offer him a seven-figure sum just to show up and play; his merchandising contracts alone cost various companies more than $53 million in 2000 (Ferguson, 2000). However, when Tiger plays, people watch: His record 12-shot victory at the 1997 Masters gave CBS its highest two-day rating in its 45-year history of covering the event; his record 15-shot win at the 2000 U.S. Open led NBC to the highest two-day average for the championship ever (Shapiro, 2000).

Although Tiger Woods currently reigns as sports' leading celebrity, NASCAR's stars have similar cult-like followings. The Crown Prince of Winston Cup Racing, Jeff Gordon, draws thousands of adoring fans to the track each week; and with nearly 30,000 web hits, more than 13,000 newspaper hits, endorsement contracts with Pepsi and Ray-Ban, Gordon ranked in Forbes' Top 50 Highest Paid Celebrities and Top 10 Highest Paid Athletes for 2000 ("*Forbes* celebrity 100 2000," 2001). But perhaps the true impact of a driver's mythic status was seen in the outpouring of sadness after the death of Dale Earnhardt during the final lap of the 2001 Daytona 500. The tragedy involving Earnhardt, who was known and loved for his aggressive racing style and blue-collar appeal, set off a brushfire of activity in NASCAR circles: thousands gathered at various racing venues across the nation for memorial services; millions more watched the official service live and uninterrupted on Fox Sports Net and TBS; Sterling Marlin, a driver whose car had bumped Earnhardt's seconds before the fatal crash, was bombarded with hate mail and death threats; dozens of petition drives were launched to have Earnhardt's #3 retired by NASCAR and to have the Daytona 500 named in his honor; and the list goes on.

Though perhaps not household names for many, skateboarder Tony Hawk and BMXer Dave Mirra are adored by Generation Y-ers around the globe. With countless television specials, action figures available in toy stores and fast food kid's meals, apparel lines, and namesake video games, Hawk and Mirra are the Tiger Woods and Jeff Gordon of action sports. Furthermore, each of the individual action sports has its own superstars, worshipped by each sport's devoted fans (e.g., Mat Hoffman in freestyle bicycling, Travis Pastrana in freestyle moto-X, Barrett Christy in snowboarding).

It seems plausible given the focus on the individual athlete that enjoyment from sports spectatorship today may have less to do with winning—as is assumed in disposition theory and BIRGing research—and more to do with performance. Winning may not be everything anymore for the sports enthusiast, especially if "team" is secondary to "player." Therefore, it may be that enjoyment can still be high if our favorite player has a stellar effort in a losing cause. Such speculation requires and perhaps deserves inquiry.

Regardless, it is clear that networks and sports leagues have attempted to capitalize on the phenomenon: hyping games as personal battles between individuals (e.g., the 2001 NBA Finals were touted as the battle of David and Goliath, starring the diminutive Allen Iverson of the Phildelphia '76ers as David and the gigantic 7-foot 1-inch, 330-pound Shaquille O'Neal of the Los Angeles Lakers as Goliath) and creating competitions that highlight individual athleticism (e.g., MLB's Homerun Derby, NHL's SuperSkills competition). Golf, racing, and action sports have a certain advantage as individual sports in that each contest is a head-to-head competition (typically) involving all of the best players/athletes in the sport; every week is an all-star event.

Another trend in sports coverage is the use of new media technologies to enhance the entertainment experience of consumers. The amount of sports information on the World Wide Web is dizzying to even the most ardent sports fan; the Web does and will continue to meet the fan's need for up-to-the-minute information and in-depth analysis. Additionally, several networks provide "enhanced television services" over special Web sites during live sports broadcasts. So, while viewing some games, sports fans can access an Internet site through a personal computer and have simultaneous delivery of game statistics and information, updates, trivia, and games. The hope is that the increased interactivity offered through these new services will significantly improve and enrich the entertainment experience for their viewers. However, initial reactions to these services have been mixed. One network executive claimed that more than 80% of the users during regular season, professional football games were "enthusiastic" about the new web-delivered services; on average, between 50,000 and 100,000 homes utilized the services on any given Sunday or Monday night during the 1999–2000 NFL season (Schmuckler, 1999). However, although NBC offered an array of interactive Internet content during the 2000 Sydney Olympics "everything from biomedical analyses of gymnastic routines to Michael Johnson's heart-rate shifts in the 400-meter dash"—the overwhelming majority of individuals searched the site for the routine TV listings and athlete bios (Longman, 2001, p. C21).

One place where new technology and sports fandom have meshed well is in the area of action sports. Perhaps this is to be expected given the media-savvy target audience for the sports. Because action sports are marketed as much as a lifestyle as a competition, new media use fits nicely into the overall package (Cleland, 2001). Web sites highlighting the relationship between action sports, music, clothing, language, attitude, style, and expression are countless. Video streaming also offers what amounts to training videos for new bicycle and skateboarding moves/tricks across numerous sites. Also, online communities offer action-sports fanatics and lifestylers from around the globe a forum to exchange and create their subculture as they see fit.

Finally, as is the case in most areas, the globalization of sports looks to be opening new markets for leagues, athletes, and spectators. More than ever before, the major U.S. sports are welcoming athletes from other countries. For example, a major story during the 2001 Major League Baseball season was the success of Asian players: a no-hitter thrown by Hideo Nomo of the Boston Red Sox, the MVP-worthy hitting of Seattle's Ichiro Suzuki, and the unhittable pitching performances by former Mariner reliever Kazuhiro Sasaki. Furthermore, several U.S. leagues have started scheduling games on foreign soil: the NFL holds in the annual American Bowl in Mexico City, whereas MLB All-Stars hold an annual exhibition series against their Japanese counterparts in various cities in Japan. Along with the U.S. Olympic Committee's decision to loosen its prohibition on professional athletes competing in the Games, these developments have generated tremendous international interest in U.S. sports. In response, the NBA, whose televised games already reach 210 countries, will soon expand its Web site from 5 to 12 languages and will begin broadcasting games on the Internet using streaming video (Longman, 2001).

The action sports, professional golf, and even NASCAR may yet hold an edge in the international arena. European interest in and support for auto racing is well documented; it is only a matter of time before NASCAR capitalizes on its market. Professional golf continues to have a strong international flavor; many of the sport's top athletes (e.g., Sergio Garcia, Vijay Singh, Greg Norman, Jesper Parnevik, Colin Montgomerie) hail from countries other than the United States. Furthermore, many of the international tournaments and their prize money (e.g., the Honda Open in Thailand, the Dubai Desert Classic in the United Arab Emirates) are also gaining success and credibility with the major players. Of course, Tiger Woods' celebrity knows no boarders.

Action sports have long featured international stars, with 40% of the medals from the 1999 X Games going to non-U.S. competitors. The 2000 version of the Games featured athletes from 24 countries (Shallwani, 2000). The Asian X Games in Thailand and the European X Games in Barcelona are already scheduled, with ones in Latin America, Australia, and Japan in the works. ESPN Networks are also planning an X Games Global Challenge for 2002 in which athletes will compete for individual and national/regional honors (Cleland, 2001). The market for these innovative and death-defying challenges seems limitless.

The impact of player-over-team fanship, new technologies, and globalization all offer sports researchers interesting fodder for future study.

These developments, along with the continued emergence of women's sports, the unprecedented popularity of professional wrestling (or sports entertainment), and the unfathomable money battling for coverage contracts, will surely change the way that we use, think about, and enjoy sports in the future. One thing, though, is for sure: In our entertainment-laden society, sports spectatorship is now and will continue to be big business and big fun.

REFERENCES

Bock, H. (2000, November 5). Where have all the viewers gone? *Los Angeles Times,* p. D1.

Bryant, J., Brown, D., Comisky, P., & Zillmann, D. (1982). Sports and spectators: Commentary and appreciation. *Journal of Communication, 32*(1), 109–119.

Bryant, J., Comisky, P., & Zillmann, D. (1977). Drama in sports commentary. *Journal of Communication, 27*(3), 140–149.

Bryant, J., Comisky, P., & Zillmann, D. (1981). The appeal of rough-and-tumble play in televised professional football. *Communication Quarterly, 29,* 256–262.

Bryant, J., & Raney, A. A. (2000). Sports on the screen. In D. Zillmann & P. Vorderer (Eds.), *Media entertainment: The psychology of its appeal* (pp. 153–174). Mahwah, NJ: Lawrence Erlbaum Associates.

Bryant, J., Zillmann, D., & Raney, A. A. (1998). Violence and the enjoyment of media sports. In L. A. Wenner (Ed.), *MediaSport* (pp. 252–265). London: Routledge.

Carlson, D. K. (2001). Poll analysis: Public taps Tiger Woods as greatest active athlete. *Gallup News Service.* Retrieved January 10, 2002, from http://www.gallup.com/poll/releases/pr010614b.asp

Cialdini, R. B., Borden, R. J., Thorne, A., Walker, M. R., Freeman, S., & Sloan, L. R. (1976). Basking in reflected glory: Three (football) field studies. *Journal of Personality and Social Psychology, 34,* 366–375.

Cialdini, R. B., & Richardson, K. D. (1980). Two indirect tactics of image management: Basking and blasting. *Journal of Personality and Social Psychology, 39,* 406–415.

Cleland, K. (2001, April 16). Action sports form fabric of generation. *Advertising Age, 72,* pp. S22–S23.

Comisky, P., Bryant, J., & Zillmann, D. (1977). Commentary as a substitute for action. *Journal of Communication, 27*(3), 150–153.

Deal puts Woods in prime time for five years. (2001, July 30). *Associated Press.*

DeNeui, D. L., & Sachau, D. A. (1996). Spectator enjoyment of aggression in intercollegiate hockey games. *Journal of Sport & Social Issues, 21,* 69–77.

Dunnavant, K., & Muller, J. (1999, November 1). NASCAR: Unsafe at any speed. *Business Week,* 90–96.

Elliot, S. (2001, January 30). The Super Bowl XXXV commercials: From pleasant surprises to whose idea was this. *New York Times,* p. C1.

Ferguson, D. (2000, September 21). Tiger Woods' worth: $54 million without hitting a shot. *Associated Press.*

Forbes celebrity 100 2000. (2001). Retrieved January 10, 2002, from *http://www.forbes.com/lists/results.jhtml?passListId=53&passYear=2000&passListType=Person&searchParameter1=&searchParameter2=&resultsHowMany=25&resultsSortProperties=%2Bnumberfield1%2C%2Bstringfield1&resultsSortCategoryName=power+rank&fromColumnClick=&bktDisplayField=&bktDisplayFieldLength=&category1=&category2=&passKeyword=&resultsStart=26*

Ford, R. (1998, August 30). Hot wheels: What's America's fastest growing sport? *The Boston Globe,* p. 17.

Gallup poll: Sports. (2001). Gallup News Service. Retrieved January 10, 2002, from *http://www.gallup.com/poll/topics/sports.asp*

Gan, S., Tuggle, C. A., Mitrook, M. A., Coussement, S. H., & Zillmann, D. (1997). The thrill of the close game: Who enjoys it and who doesn't? *Journal of Sport & Social Issues, 21,* 53–64.

Ginn, S. (2001, January 5). Tiger's ratings great as other sports see decline. *St. Petersburg Times,* p. 5C.

Heider, F. (1958). *The psychology of interpersonal relations.* New York: Wiley.

Hirt, E. R., Zillmann, D., Erickson, G. A., & Kennedy, C. (1992). Costs and benefits of allegiance: Changes in fans' self-ascribed competencies after team victory versus defeat. *Journal of Personality and Social Psychology, 63,* 724–738.

Longman, J. (2001, July 31). Sports use technology and T.L.C. to hold onto fans. *New York Times,* pp. C19, C21.

Madrigal, R. (1995). Cognitive and affective determinants of fan satisfaction with sporting event attendance. *Journal of Leisure Research, 27,* 205–227.

Maynard, M. (2001, March 21). After Earnhardt's death: A rebound for NASCAR. *New York Times,* p. 3(9).

Nielsen Media Research (1998). *1998 report on television.* New York: Author.

Owens, J. B., & Bryant, J. (1998, July). *The effects of a hometeam ("homer") announcer and color commentator on audience perceptions and enjoyment of a sports contest.* Paper presented at the annual meeting of the International Communication Association, Jerusalem, Israel.

Phillips, R. (2000, August 24). PGA duel compelling for viewing. *The Montreal Gazette,* p. C14.

Prior, M. (2001). Extreme toys take market by storm. *DSN Retailing Today, 38,* 42.

Sapolsky, B. S. (1980). The effect of spectator disposition and suspense on the enjoyment of sports contests. *International Journal of Sports Psychology, 11*(1), 1–10.

Sargent, S. L., Zillmann, D., & Weaver, J. B. (1998). The gender gap in the enjoyment of televised sports. *Journal of Sports & Social Issues, 22,* 46–64.

Schmuckler, E. (1999, December 13). Making a play. *Adweek, 40,* 92–96.

Shallwani, P. (2000, August 17). ESPN will take X Games to global market in 2001. *San Francisco Chronicle,* p. E9.

Shapiro, L. (2000, June 20). Wood's historic run sets viewing record. *Washington Post,* p. D01.

Snyder, C. R., Higgins, R. L., & Stucky, R. J. (1983). *Excuses: Masquerades in search of grace.* New York: Wiley-Interscience.

Sullivan, D. B. (1991). Commentary and viewer perception of player hostility: Adding punch to televised sport. *Journal of Broadcasting & Electronic Media, 35,* 487–504.

Survey: The World of Sports: The cult of personality (1998, June 6). *The Economist,* p. S7.

Thomas, P. (2001, June 8). Hermosa Beach is place to catch the action. *Los Angeles Times,* p. 4(8).

Top 15 basic cable programs, (2001). Retrieved January 20, 2002, from *http://tv.zap2it.com/ news/ratings/cable/010520cable.html*

Zelkovich, C. (2000, November 7). The ratings crunch. *The Toronto Star,* Edition 1, Sportspage.

Zillmann, D. (1995). Sports and the media. In J. Mester (Ed.), *Images of sport in the world* (pp. 423–444). Cologne: German Sports University.

Zillmann, D., Bryant, J., & Sapolsky B. S. (1989). Enjoyment from sports spectatorship. In J. H. Goldstein (Ed.), *Sports, games, and play: Social and psychological viewpoints* (2nd ed., pp. 241–278). Hillsdale, NJ: Lawrence Erlbaum Associates.

Zillmann, D., & Paulus, P. B. (1993). Spectators: Reactions to sports events and effects on athletic performance. In R. N. Singer, M. Murphey, & L. K. Tennant (Eds.), *Handbook of research on sport psychology* (pp. 600–619). New York: Macmillan.

18

Enjoyment and Social Functions of Horror

Ron Tamborini
Michigan State University

When I was a graduate student at Indiana University, I went home over break to visit my family. My nephew Brian, who was 10 years old at the time, begged his mom to let me take him to a scary movie. My sister was hesitant, warning of nightmares that often accompanied these movies. Still, Brian persisted and confidently declared that he was no longer a little boy, that these things didn't scare him anymore, and that his mom was being ridiculous. Knowing that I studied this type of thing, my sister felt secure enough to let me take Brian to see *Alien*. Brian was thrilled not only to be going, but also to be going with his big uncle. With popcorn, M&Ms, and soda in hand we sat near the back of the large theater in anticipation of the thrills to come.

When the theater went dark, Brian sat erect with eyes wide open and an ear-to-ear grin to match. But as the film progressed, I noticed him starting to slouch into the seat and draw closer to my side. On screen, the astronauts started closely inspecting some kind of spider like organisms contained in specimen jars. The embalmed alien embryos were floating eerily in the large glass containers when—Bang! With one shocking thrust toward the viewer, the disgusting embryo exploded out of the jar and onto the startled face of the defenseless astronaut. At the same instant, as if matching the embryo's thrust off the screen, my nephew's arms jerked forward, sending popcorn and M&Ms sailing high into the air, showering everyone around us. As Brian dove for cover under my arms I listened to scores of M&Ms bouncing loudly down the concrete floors and smiled sheepishly at those around. For the rest of the movie, Brian's face was buried against my arm as he alternately watched and hid his eyes from the terrors on screen. At its end, he gleefully proclaimed that this was the best film he had ever seen and asked if we could do it again.

At home that night, I couldn't help but think of how many factors played a part in governing our very different experiences: developmental stage, social setting, relational ties, frightening themes, special effects, M&Ms, and popcorn—all playing their part leading to our enjoyment. I was excited by these thoughts, and when I returned from break, I shared the event with my advisor. I told him in some detail my views on how all these things influence our experiences. He paused briefly and said "Hmmmm, well, yes, of course, all this may be plausible, but to be sure we need to first put it to the test." I guess the only sure thing to come from this at that time was my sister's understanding of how foolish it was to trust me with her children. Since then, however, I have tried to look more closely at issues related to the enjoyment and social functions of horror. Why do we watch? How do we experience it? What is the aftermath of our emotions? Surprisingly few scientific studies have asked these questions and "put it to the test." Yet the enormous popularity and consumption of the genre make it important for us to do this.

WHY DO WE WATCH?

Think of those times when you put yourself in a situation knowing that it will be upsetting: a film, the news, a personal or public event. On a Memorial Day visit to Washington DC, I accompanied a friend to the Vietnam Veterans Memorial. Unlike many other monuments, the Vietnam Memorial is a simple, austere, almost hauntingly beautiful place that evokes powerful emotions. While walking away my companion turned and asked, "Why do I do this to myself?" The question didn't surprise me, but it was still difficult to answer.

Explaining selective exposure to some distressing events is a challenge for media entertainment research. The appeal of barbarous slaughter seems counterintuitive at first. Although research in this area helps us explain some of the forces at work, much remains to be learned. Exposure to tragic and horrifying events seems the most difficult to grasp. When choosing horror we intentionally place ourselves in peril of great emotional anguish. Excluding those motivated by sadistic or masochistic needs, why do millions seek this? Some scholars suggest that horrific violence has limited appeal and its apparent popularity is overestimated due to the high profile of media violence (American Psychological Association, 1993; Centers for Disease Control, 1991; "The killing screens," 1994; National Academy of Science, 1993). Even if this is true, horror's appeal to millions of hard-core fans remains to be explained. Extreme violence in many forms sells (Carey, 1994; Gerbner, 1988; Medved, 1992; Weinraub, 1993). Explanations for this behavior tend to fall into one of three categories: for pleasure derived from horrific content, for protective surveillance, or for concomitants of exposure to horror.

Pleasure From Horrific Content

Some scholars claim that people often enjoy being disgusted and frightened by the types of images we find in horror (Brosnan, 1976). For example, Sparks and Sparks (2000) suggested that horror frequently contains properties associated with sensory delight, novelty, or dispositional alignment that are inherently attractive and enjoyable. However, close inspection of these properties suggests that their appeal is best understood based on rewards from other things confounded with exposure. A better example of this is the position of McCauley (1998), who began with the position that emotional reactions to fiction are distinct from those we experience in response to real events. He claimed that horror's appeal comes directly from watching it, not from some other associated benefit. Zillmann (1998) dismissed these claims as "simply untenable," a position that he defended based on empirical evidence.

For Protective Surveillance

Another possibility is that the attraction to horrific media has evolutionary origins associated with protective vigilance and curiosity. According to this belief, we do not enjoy these experiences. In fact, quite the opposite is true. Witnessing these events is distressing. Nevertheless, innate cognitive processes focus our attention on images that contain cues of danger, cues often associated with horrific violence. This position is based on the notion that structures in the brain's limbic system that control emotion have remained essentially unchanged over thousands of years. Zillmann (1998) posited that continuous monitoring of the environment for danger was adaptive in early humans, and much of this endures today. Even though this behavior has lost most of its utility (Zillmann, 1979), our impulse to watch violent events remains.

Of course, in acknowledging that phylogenic assertions of this nature are by and large impossible to test, we are eventually left looking for other explanations. Perhaps most widespread among other accounts are those attributing attention to a learned association between exposure to horror and gratifications confounded with the experience. Several explanations fall into this category and can be understood best by considering how people experience exposure.

HOW DO WE EXPERIENCE EXPOSURE?

Accounts of viewing experience can be distinguished along several lines. At the most rudimentary level, accounts vary in terms of those positing the positive versus negative experiences of witnessing extreme violence. Some scholars claim that people enjoy horrifying images (Brosnan, 1976; McCauley, 1998), whereas others maintain that we do not (Denny, 1991; Gray, 1971; Rachman, 1990; Tamborini, 1991, 1996; Zillmann, 1998). The simple difference between assertions of delight or distress is less illuminating, however, than the logic associated with various claims and the factors said to determine the nature of experience.

Aesthetic Emotions

McCauley (1998) claimed that emotional reactions to fiction can be qualitatively different from their everyday emotional counterparts. In fact, he suggested that we blunder when we use the same names to represent dramatic emotions, as they are a parallel but different reality. Counter to everyday emotions, dramatic emotions are always positively valenced. This perspective helps explain the perplexing difference in audience reactions to fictional versus real-life events. In contrast to those asserting that feelings elicited by fictional media are irrational (Rorty, 1978), incoherent (Radford, 1975), or not real emotions (Binkley, 1977; Gombrich, 1962), this position simply states that aesthetic emotions are distinct from emotional reactions to real events (Bell, 1914; Danto, 1964, 1981; Fry, 1920).

Frijda (1989) explained that the distinct character of aesthetic emotions comes from audience perceptions of witnessed events as actual occurrences in an imaginary world. When watching a film, viewers do not suspend disbelief, but observe "real" events occurring in a fantasy world. Belief is the observant baseline, and it is maintained unless film cues force the viewer to think about its fictional nature. According to Frijda, fiction simply allows viewers to inhibit certain emotions because they know some parts are unreal. This realization gives aesthetic emotions their distinct character. Our awareness that witnessed fictional events are irrelevant to our welfare and that actions cannot intervene leads to "complementing emotions." Although we identify with characters and sense their imminent fates, we are free of any consequences. Yet we can still experience a deep "responding emotion" to films that make us aware of a meaningful real-world experience or the possibility of its tangible consequences for us.

McCauley's (1998) position on "dramatic" emotions is similar to the notions of Frijda. In his claim that dramatic emotions are always appealing in spite of their content, McCauley asserted that the pleasure experienced from viewing horrifying images comes only when the violence is framed as fiction. As such, the initial experience of a horror film is not determined by the horror's negative tone but is determined instead by its ability to mark and qualify the viewer's humanity, a quality that is always experienced positively. This requires that the film allow the person to achieve dramatic distance by presenting certain cues that signal its fictional nature. These cues provide a "protective frame" that allows the viewer to experience a dramatic emotion rather than the "everyday" emotion expected from violent stimuli. The pleasure in the human "transcendence" produced by this experience is likened to that experienced with tragedy. Fictional tragedy is said to induce grief that goes beyond the viewer's individual problems, making those problems seem less significant. In a similar vein, the experience of horror in reaction to a film can be enjoyed because it is "purified" of personal consequence and makes us appreciate our humanity.

Although seemingly untestable, the proposition that dramatic distance qualitatively changes our initial experience of horrifying images is at least internally consistent with the contention that reactions to fictional horror are positive from the onset. However, when further noting that the pleasure in dramatic emotions is akin to that of catharsis, the logic seems to be called into question. If catharsis is the basis for the experience of pleasure, perhaps we should look there for our understanding of factors that determine the hedonic nature of the experience that McCauley tried to distinguish.

Catharsis

One of the most widely debated schemes for explaining our experience of horror and other violent media is the catharsis doctrine. Broadly interpreted, this principle suggests that violent media have therapeutic properties. It holds that exposure to certain content can purge us of various fears, phobias, negative emotions, and antisocial behavioral impulses (Alloway; 1972; Evans, 1984; Harrington, 1972; Thomas, 1972). Initial research suggested the possibility that angered individuals were cleansed of their hostilities (Feshbach, 1955, 1976; Feshbach & Singer, 1971). It was held, presumably, that watching others performing violent behaviors allowed viewers to fantasize about acting out their violent impulses. This vicarious experience substituted for the need to actually perform the aggressive behavior, thus the impulse to aggress was reduced. Subsequent investigations, however, not only demonstrated the dubious nature of data originally thought supportive of catharsis (Chaffee & McLeod, 1971; Liebert, Sobol, & Davidson, 1972), but offered substantial evidence refuting the notion that exposure rids us of hostile or harmful negative emotions (Baron & Richardson, 1994; Geen & Quanty, 1977; Zillmann, 1979). In light of this, a prudent treatment of the issue might simply state that media-induced catharsis is unsupported by evidence. Nevertheless, the continued attention it receives suggests that there are questions remaining to be answered.

Why does support for the catharsis position continue in spite of evidence to the contrary found in the study of media violence? McCauley (1998) reasoned that failure to find support for catharsis results from flaws in research. He noted, for example, that media research tended to show short excerpts of violence that omit the plot and character development necessary to instigate the types of emotions required for catharsis to occur. He faulted research for using measures that fail to differentiate aggressive behavior motivated by impulse versus instrumentality and submitted that perhaps fictional violence rids us only of impulsive aggression. He concluded that work in this area does not provide a good test of catharsis, and that the concept deserves more attention.

Certainly, many film scholars treat symbolic catharsis as a credible principle. Some see it as a form of human transcendence that can result from our watching man's brutality to man and the terror it begets (Moeran, 1986; Rockett, 1988). Most talk simply of purging (Carroll, 1990; Denne, 1972; King, 1981). In fact, it seems that many observers accept as a given the notion that film violence can and does cleanse viewers of all types of unpleasant emotions. Although little detail is given to explicate the underlying mechanisms at work, fictional scholars often talk of identification, vicarious experience, and other similarly vague processes.

Zillmann (1998) took issue with such conjecture by questioning how this "miraculous cleansing" of our emotions could occur, and he expressed surprise over psychologists' neglect in the construction of theories that explain phenomena associated with violent media exposure. Although little theoretical development directly addresses this issue, perhaps some insight can be gained from work in emotion theory. Lazarus provided one approach that might prove useful in this regard.

Lazarus (1991) claimed that aesthetic emotions in response to films are governed by the same mechanisms that control the generation of all emotions. His cognitive-motivational-relational theory contends that environmental and personality factors influence event appraisal. Appraisal governs all that follows, including coping strategies and the specific emotional state. The same process occurs with emotional response to film. The exposure experience is determined by relevant personality traits and situational cues both internal and external to the film. The traits and cues impact appraisal of the film experience in terms of its relevance for the individual's well being. Resulting coping processes regulate both the type and the strength of the emotion experienced. Central to this theory is knowledge of the emotions under consideration. Understanding the core relational themes (the essence, or defining features of an emotion) and coping tendencies associated with the emotion can inform us of the manner in which exposure should be related to the unfolding of emotional experience, whether that be one of relief (e.g., catharsis) or intensification.

From this perspective, we might propose that a catharsis should occur in response to film exposure only under circumstances in which appraisal and coping processes function in a manner allowing essential relief. If so, the central issue becomes identifying the circumstances where film cues are appraised in a manner generating relief from the experience of negative emotions. At first, this might seem no more demonstrable than speculations about inaccessible emotional processes offered by many critical film scholars. However, Lazarus's detailed explication of emotions along with their associated action and coping strategies offer the promise of testable hypotheses specifying when relief from negative affect should occur.

Central to predictions of experiential relief is the distinction between cognitive and action coping strategies designed to deal with specific threats. People attempt to manage environmental demands (the person–environment relationship) through coping responses designed to maximize their welfare. In efforts to deal with threats and dangers, people can either attempt to change the environment through actions (e.g., attack, flight, or other modifying behaviors) or cognitive adaptation (e.g., avoidance, denial, ridicule, or other forms of reappraisal). For example, anger occurs when appraisal reveals a demeaning offense or threat to one's ego. If appraisal indicates that the offense can be rectified by attack, the coping action will occur. However, if the likely outcome of physical action is appraised as dysfunctional, cognitive coping ensues. Cognitive coping strategies that change the appraised meaning of the offense or stop its deliberation can benefit well-being by inhibiting the experience of anger completely or by preventing its escalation to dangerous levels.

From a functional perspective, catharsis should occur only in conditions where dysfunctional emotions exist and a means for diminishing the emotion can be found. With regard to media, we might expect that the type of passive activity associated with viewing is suitable only for advancing behavior associated with cognitive coping mechanisms. In this regard, it reasons that cathartic reactions through media can occur only for emotional states requiring cognitive coping, and only in circumstances where the media content and exposure setting provide the coping benefits required by the specific emotion in question. To the extent that the experience of, and reaction to, these content and exposure conditions is universal, we should expect anybody experiencing the relevant emotional state to experience the cathartic effect. However, if individual differences moderate the experience of the content and setting, we should expect related differences in resultant relief.

If we compare the different core relational themes and coping tendencies for negative emotions that might require purging (e.g., anger, sorrow), it reasons that, in order for media to relieve the emotion, the exposure experience must embody the action tendency required by the specific emotion considered. For example, if the emotion was sorrow, defined as a somewhat transient feeling of helplessness over an irrevocable loss, Lazarus submitted that the action tendency is withdrawal (inaction), to pull away from others. In this sense, instead of problem-focused coping, sorrow leads to coping that is emotion focused—the type of cognitive response called for when the person believes that nothing they can do will change the problem. One can easily see how viewing a sad film offers opportunity to withdraw and serves the necessary emotion-focused function. As such, the experience of sadness should be relieved by the exposure encounter. Notably, the process leading to relief here might be considered simple intervention by some, and not a purging of the emotion. Then again, the notion of "purging" is itself indistinct, and because the function and outcome here is analogous to catharsis, it might be considered comparable in all practical senses.

If we consider anger, however, it is harder to see how a media experience would advance behavior associated with the action tendency for this emotion. Anger is experienced when we perceive demeaning offense, a threat of harm to self-esteem. The immediate action tendency is to stop the offense by attacking the person responsible. Of course, the attack will not occur if it seems unlikely to succeed. Concern for reprisal could delay an attack or prevent it altogether. In this case, more deliberate cognitive coping strategies take place to maximize long-term benefits. If cognitive coping can prevent thinking about the offense or change its appraised meaning, it can function to eliminate anger completely or prevent it from reaching hazardous levels. Considered in this regard, film exposure appears dysfunctional in relation to both prevention and reappraisal. Clearly we should not expect violent film to prevent thinking about the offense. In fact, just the opposite should be true. The intervention potential of violent film content on angered individuals should be decidedly low. Instead, its affinity with this emotional state should facilitate rehearsal of hostility and perpetuate anger. Similarly, we should not expect violent film to bring about change in appraised meaning. Instead of reappraisal, the film's hostile images should help preserve appraisal of behavior as demeaning and should discourage the type of "positive thinking" sometimes associated with successful reappraisal (Hart, 1991).

We gain added understanding by considering the experiences of fright and anxiety. Fright is regarded as a reaction to concrete threats of imminent physical harm. We are scared about the immediate prospect of death or injury, a condition that calls for escape. No additional appraisal or coping behaviors are pertinent to its instigation. The most useful response is physical avoidance or escape, which would quickly terminate the fright. Because the action tendency for fright is physical avoidance or escape, it is difficult to see how exposure to horror films would prove advantageous. A similar situation is seen for anxiety: the experience of uncertain existential threats to self or important others that we might think of as a threat to one's ego-identity.

Although anger results from our holding someone responsible for a threat to our self-esteem, anxiety occurs when the threat is to our existential welfare and we have no target for blame. It is the type of dread experienced when we contemplate terrible possibilities that we are incapable of controlling. Because no action can deter the threat, anxiety can only be dealt with through emotion-focused coping. In fact, beyond the type of reappraisal found in cognitive coping, we have few options for managing anxiety other than learning to endure it. Given that watching film promotes imaginative deliberation of fictional and real-life events, exposure to horror seems likely to breed dysfunctional thoughts, generating anxiety instead of those thoughts that relieve it. Research that shows apprehensive participants avoiding exposure to victimizing violence is consistent with the notion that this content is unlikely to function as a cathartic relief (Wakshlag, Vial, & Tamborini, 1983). At that same time, because the thematic focus of most horror films tends to deal with just the types of existential threats considered to cause anxiety, we might posit that habituation of anxious tendencies could result from repeated exposure to the genre. Of course, this process is clearly distinguishable from anything resembling catharsis. Instead, it touches on learning mastery of fears, which is, in essence, learning to tolerate them.

So what do we conclude from this? Zillmann (1998) has argued convincingly against popular notions of catharsis, certainly more convincingly than those holding to its existence based on any empirical evidence. Even so, theoretical work on emotion offers further insight into these popularly held beliefs. Application of cognitive-motivational-relational theory (Lazarus, 1991) illustrates that catharsis seems obtainable from film exposure given the right antecedent conditions. Then again, the conditions required do not favor catharsis occurring from exposure to violent film. Instead, we suggest that if catharsis occurs, it should take place in viewers watching tragedy. These arguments seem inconsistent with most popular notions of catharsis that suggest that it can occur in angered men watching violent and horrifying images on screen. We hold that these conditions favor further hostility. Similarly with fright, conditions do not warrant the expectation of media induced relief. Perhaps reduced affect can be found over time for those prone to experiencing anxiety; however, it is difficult to interpret this form of relief as an example of catharsis. By contrast, the conditions produced by watching tragedy seem capable of promoting catharsis in those experiencing sorrow and other emotions susceptible to cognitive coping processes.

Dispositional Determinants

Certainly events in the film are central in shaping the experience of horror. Zillmann (1998) described viewers as mere witnesses whose emotional reactions are determined by events they observe on screen in much the same way that witnessed events shape emotions in real life. Yet, reactions commonly experienced while viewing horror seem most uncommon in everyday life. In contrast to what might be expected, horror film fans seem to take great pleasure from scenes of agonizing suffering and death. Though rare in real life, we expect this type of devastating violence to repulse and dismay an observer. What then explains these joyous reactions to the infliction of pain in horror? Understanding the witness perspective in terms of the dispositional alignments viewers bring to watching horror offers insight.

Disposition theory (Zillmann, 1980) holds that our likes and dislikes for characters play a critical role in determining reactions to events witnessed in all parts of life. Simply put, we take great pleasure in witnessing good things happen to liked others and bad things to those we dislike. Similarly, we loath witnessing bad things happen to liked others or good things to those we dislike. This widely applied and methodically tested theory explains emotional reactions to sports, humor, suspense and other genres (Zillmann, 1980, 1983, 1991b; Zillmann & Cantor, 1976; Zillmann & Paulus, 1993). Applied to horror, it helps explain the surprisingly festive reactions found in viewers who watch scenes of pain and suffering by considering the development of character dispositions.

Zillmann (1998) submitted that character development plays a pivotal role in the creation of dispositions and their subsequent impact on reactions to film events. We are constantly monitoring the behavior of characters to judge their actions as right or wrong against our own moral standards. The outcome of this scrutiny cultivates character-related dispositions that promote morality-based viewer expectations. These expectations govern our experience of and reactions to anticipated and witnessed events. The confirmation of expectations generates great pleasure, whereas their disconfirmation causes anguish. Even the mere expectation of these outcomes promotes affect. We expect the evil villain to be punished severely and await it with joyous anticipation. We celebrate when it happens, and disparage its failure to occur. A crucial element controlling enjoyment of violence is perceived justification for its performance. We are more than happy to see increasingly brutal treatment of villains, but only if they first commit acts vile enough to warrant severe retribution. Vicious acts against rogues perceived as unjustified lead to viewer displeasure. Applied to horror this supports the need for atrocities in plot development to justify enjoyment of horrific violence taken in revenge. This storyline has been a successful formula for horror film since the early 1930s (Sontag, 1966), and for horror in other media forms since late 18th century (Hallie, 1969).

The extent of violence in horror is great (Sapolsky & Molitor, 1996), with villains and heroes alike who slaughter to achieve their noble or ignoble goals (Hoberman, 1998). Ferocious injury is inflicted on victims throughout the story's development, and in the end the debt must be paid. The graphic annihilation of the villain serves to restore justice and create euphoria in the viewer, the payback often more violent than the original offense. Negative dispositions override norms dictating that we take no pleasure in witnessing others' pain and misfortune. When the villain represents evil incarnate, the social bounds to expressing hate and enjoying retaliatory violence wane. Zillmann (1998) argued that although a villain might profit temporarily for dramatic purposes, the plot resolution in drama very rarely shows benefaction for evil characters. Notably, however, this discussion focused on dramatic violence. It remains less clear that the same processes govern similar reactions to horror. Some critics question disposition logic as an explanation for horror's appeal, arguing that many recent films end in the triumph of evil (Rickey, 1982; Rosenbaum, 1979). Box office hits like *Halloween, Friday the 13th, The Blair Witch Project,* and lists of others end with the menace vanished but not vanquished, while the hero is left weak and frightened instead of triumphant. The enormous popularity of these movies suggests that horror film devotees are attending for other reasons.

Some explanations combine features of film content and viewer attributes. For example, Zuckerman (1996) argued that biologically determined trait differences nurture the desire for fright and shock. Other scholars consider individual differences important determinants of how we experience horror itself. Research shows psychoticism a strong predictor of preference for film horror and graphic violence (Aluja-Fabregat, 2000; Weaver, 1991). Similar work shows dimensions of Machiavellian personality a predictor of exposure and appeal (Tamborini, Stiff, & Zillmann, 1987). As such, we might expect that experiences with horror vary as a function of personality. Tamborini (1996) proposed that trait empathy can alter viewer experiences with horror. Differences in empathy associated with well-learned cognitive coping mechanisms are said to short-circuit negative affect and shape emotional experience. Though some work has been done in this area, considerable effort is needed before personality's enjoyment-modifying effect is understood.

Social Determinants

Several scholars attempted to explain horror's appeal using evolutionary conceptions. Sparks and Sparks (2000) argued that violent stimuli in horror films have acquired an inherent attraction. They based their claim on evidence that over millennia a gender-biased interest in violence evolved as an adaptive response to basic human needs (Buss & Shackelford, 1997) and pointed to repeat findings that gender predicts horror film's appeal as congruent with this logic (Cantor, 1998; Fenigstein, 1979; Sparks, 1991; Tamborini & Stiff, 1987). In a related manner, Zillmann and Gibson (1996) traced the evolution of horror's appeal to gender-socialization practice. They explained the functions of today's horror film as a forum for adolescent rites of passage that date back to preliterate societies.

Most cultures socialize children in a gender-specific fashion (Barry, Bacon, & Child, 1957). Boys are trained to hide their fear, and girls are encouraged to exhibit it (Brody, 1985; Saarni, 1989; Shennum & Bugental, 1982). However, the manner in which these customs are learned has changed considerably over time. Peers now impose norms once conveyed by parents, and the cinema has become the classroom for adolescent education. This should be particularly important for young men wanting to master their fears. Horror films facilitate socialization processes by providing conditions for routine confrontation of fears (Dickstein, 1980). They offer a safe forum for testing one's courage. In fact, frequent exposure to these films should facilitate insensitivity to their graphic violence and render them no longer disturbing. The desire to master these fears is a powerful force governing the appeal of horror.

An important part in the process is the comfort of protectors. It can help explain the initial ability for young boys to confront fears they have not begun to master. For the boy who has not learned to cope with this fear, the images in the film may be so upsetting that initial exposure should be avoided at all costs. Under these conditions an adult companion provides the comfort and feelings of security necessary for exposure to commence. For a young woman, the same comforting can come from the adult or the presence of a desirable companion.

Several scholars consider the social gratifications associated with expressing fear as central to horror films' appeal (Mundorf, Weaver, & Zillmann, 1989; Zillmann, Weaver, Mundorf, & Aust, 1986). A functional understanding of these gratifications is offered in the gender-socialization theory of affect (Zillmann & Weaver, 1996). The theory holds that exposure to horror offers an opportunity for young viewers to profit from enacting gender-specific behaviors prohibited in most other settings. In this setting, adolescent males can demonstrate their manhood by acting fearless when confronted by atrocities on screen. In contrast, young women can demonstrate their vulnerability by showing suitably high levels of fear, seeking protection from their young male companions, and admiring them for their bravery (Mundorf et al., 1989). In line with this reasoning, research shows that young men enjoy watching horror films more when viewing with frightened females. In contrast, young women take more pleasure from the film when they watch with young men displaying mastery. Moreover, performance of gender-appropriate behavior can increase attraction to opposite-gender companions (Zillmann et al., 1986). The theory explains this behavior as resulting from the powerful impact of gender-role norms on the way young viewers perceive and govern their own behaviors as well as the behaviors of others (Bem, 1976, 1985). Reward comes from performing gender-appropriate behaviors, one of these being the expression of affect. The degree to which viewers follow prescribed norms determines the level of enjoyment. However, the source of reward is misattributed to pleasure derived from attributes of film content.

Several factors, then, appear capable of turning the inherently distressing experience of horror into a rewarding viewing encounter. Dispositional alignment within the film content as well as external social determinants can generate pleasure from what would otherwise be a distressing experience. Nevertheless, though these factors can override the natural response to gruesome images in film, horror still plays a critical role in shaping viewer experience.

Intensity of Experience

Media's ability to generate powerful emotional response to entertainment is well documented. Drama, humor, erotica and other media forms can create intense arousal (cf. Zillmann, 1982). Critical here is reasoning that arousal from extreme violence can intensify emotional reactions given direction by other means, and that stimulation expected can be particularly high in empathically distressed individuals (Tamborini, Stiff, & Heidel, 1990). Zillmann (1991a) classified arousal from empathic distress as a response energizer that bolsters affect without giving it emotional direction. Excitation-transfer logic (Zillmann, 1982) suggests that arousal from any prior activity remains after activities end and heightens reactions to subsequent experiences, making them more intense than they would otherwise be. Applied to horror films this reasoning indicates that arousal from distress experienced throughout exposure is capable of heightening reactions to later events. Although these excitatory mechanisms control response strength, other factors dictate its emotional tenor.

If we accept that arousal energizes subsequent behavior, strong reactions are expected from horror. The content and form of today's super-violent horror have great excitatory capacity. Both the images and the media's ability to present them in startling form are intrinsically arousing. Dark rooms, sharp objects, poison, pits, and killers; most horror films confront viewers with repeated aversive stimuli. When you add shrieking sounds, eerie music, and disquieting visual effects, elevated levels of arousal are inescapable. Consequently, viewers exposed to horror undergo an exhilarating emotional experience. Empirical evidence offers strong support for excitation transfer's impact on exposure to media in general (Cantor, Zillmann, & Bryant, 1975; de Wied, Zillmann, & Ordman, 1994; Zillmann, Hay, & Bryant, 1975; Zillmann, Mody, & Cantor, 1974) and exposure to horror in particular (Sparks, 1991). Though innate reactions to this preposterous violence are great emotional anguish, appraisal processes can modify these initial responses (Tamborini, 1991). The disparity in these two contrasting reactions has lead to other accounts of arousal mechanisms' relationship to the appeal of graphic horror.

Some maintain that the jolt of horror is exhilarating, and this stimulation is enjoyable (Rickey, 1982). Consistent with theories on arousal asserting that "reinforcement, and in particular reward, can result in some circumstances from an increase in arousal" (Berlyne, 1967, p. 30), this logic supports claims that a horror film's ability to evoke increased arousal is a source of pleasure for certain viewers (cf. Tannenbaum, 1980). As such, these viewers should seek out horror for the gratifications expected. Research showing that arousal in high sensation seekers increases dramatically during exposure to horror (Tamborini, Miller, Stiff, & Heidel, 1988) is consistent with the revised arousal-jag explanation of the appeal of thrilling fears (Berlyne, 1967). Though some denounce revised arousal-jag notions as logically inconsistent (Zillmann, 1980), evidence that sensation seeking predicts graphic horror's appeal corresponds with this account (Aluja-Fabregat, 2000; Edwards, 1984; Sparks, 1986; Tamborini & Stiff, 1987; Zuckerman & Litle, 1986).

Debate continues between scholars who contend that pleasure comes from the jolt of horror and those who insist that horrific violence evokes only negative affect. Zillmann (1998) argued that empathic distress from harm to liked protagonists is just a way to strengthen later experienced joy. Eventually, he claimed, these protagonists overcome danger. They destroy the threat, or at least escape its pending doom. Both the protagonist's victory and relief from escape are a source of dispositional pleasure, and an arousal residue from prior distress intensifies viewer enjoyment. As such, gruesome violence is an essential prelude to joy from emotional override. Moreover, if critics contend that horror films today often fail to provide even minimal forms of dispositional reward, other factors, like social gratification, can be used to explain obtained pleasure.

WHAT IS THE AFTERMATH OF EMOTION?

Although research provides insight on some aspects of horror's emotional aftermath, other areas go largely unexamined. Our previous discussion of viewing experience shows considerable insight concerning the short-term reactions to watching extreme violence. In contrast, we know much less about the lasting effects of exposure.

The Immediate Aftermath of Horror

The most apparent aftermath resulting from exposure to horror is the remnant of the emotion from the extreme-violence experience. Most of our prior discussion addresses this issue directly, yet clearly debate persists over some of these issues confronted. Do we experience pleasure from the aesthetic emotion, a form of cathartic relief, or even gratification of some biologically controlled need for sensation? If not, do we maintain that only negative affect comes from viewing horrific violence, dismiss catharsis as pseudo explanation inconsistent with empirical evidence, and contest speculation that witnessing horror in safety could satisfy sensation needs (Zillmann, 1998). Some debate on these issues is likely to remain. Still, agreement exists on several immediate outcomes. Support for the fact that distress from graphic violence can amplify the emotional aftermath of exposure is not in doubt. Nor is belief that dispositional alignment with characters can influence joy following exposure. Similar agreement exists for claims that social factors associated with distress mastery and gender norms can turn exposure to intrinsically unpleasant images into a pleasurable experience.

Beyond these immediate experiential effects, horror's short-term influence on social perception and behavior is an issue of some concern. The application of priming principles plays a key role in this discussion. Priming can influence judgments by bringing to mind thoughts of connected events and semantically related matter (Forgas, 1991). When considering horror's focus on negative events, priming logic leads us to expect harsh judgments and behavior following exposure. Though some empirical evidence directly addresses horror in this regard, work in other areas applies as well. Social judgment research concentrating on person perception, as well as behavioral work focusing on aggression and social support, is relevant to these concerns.

As indicated earlier, evidence shows that the social environment created by film exposure plays a strong role in interpersonal attraction. Viewers perceive opposite-gender companions as more attractive when gender-role norms are displayed during exposure to horror (Zillmann, Weaver, Mundorf, & Aust, 1986). On the other hand, horror's impact isn't always beneficial. Social judgments of victims and punishment for criminals are disturbingly impacted by horror. Though scholars disagree on erotica's role in these judgmental effects, evidence clearly indicates that some forms of horror promote callousness toward females. Exposure facilitates perceptions that violence against women is justifiable (Malamuth & Check, 1981), that rape victims are worthless and their injuries less serious (Donnerstein & Linz, 1984; Linz, Donnerstein, & Penrod, 1984), and that lighter sentences are appropriate for convicted rapists (Weaver, 1987).

Beyond social judgment outcomes, research examines horror's impact on specific social behavior. Investigations on aggression and social support show horror's relation to critical processes of attention, learning, and sensitization. Aggression research indicates that exposure to violent images like those in horror produces short-term activation of cognitive structures semantically related to hostile action. Though research here generally focuses on other violent genres, similarities to horrific violence make this work seem directly applicable to horror. Meta-analysis of both field (Wood, Wong, & Chachere, 1991) and laboratory studies (Andison, 1977) offers compelling evidence that violent media act as powerful aggressive primes. At the same time, similar primes are found in prosocial contexts (cf. Liebert & Sprafkin, 1988). Recent work on social support generally indicates that insensitive portrayals like those in horror reduce comforting behaviors (Borkgrevink & Tamborini, 1994, Tamborini, Bahk, & Salomonson, 1993; Tamborini, Salomonson, & Bahk, 1993a, 1993b).

Horror's Chronic Aftermath

In general, research on short-lived priming effects of horror is limited but supports arguments for its impact. Predictably, its lasting influence is harder to demonstrate. Few seem to question the claims that repeated exposure to horror acts as a socializing agent, assisting young men in mastering empathic distress (Zillmann & Gibson, 1996), but there is no direct evidence of this effect. When considering evidence of other long-term effects on adolescent development, ethical issues limit the ability to study these questions under controlled conditions. Survey evidence suggests mild fright reactions in adolescents that are short lived (Cantor, 1992). In contrast, evidence from other sources shows stronger and more lasting effects. Anecdotal reports of extreme enduring adolescent fears are reported in psychiatric literature (Buzzuto, 1975; Mathai, 1983). Retrospective reports of adults (Johnson, 1980) and college students (Cantor & Oliver, 1996) also suggest more lasting influence. Although evidence in this area is speculative at best, it provides reason for future concern.

Debate persists concerning other outcomes due to learning, extinction, and desensitization processes, but the considerable research on long-term effects of other violent media forms is informative. According to Geen (1994), evidence clearly supports assertions that observing violence can increase aggressive behavior under certain conditions. Several of the conditions typically found in horror should work toward this lasting impact. For example, because all major characters perform violent acts, horror fosters identification with aggressors and makes identification with suffering victims difficult (Tamborini & Salomonson, 1996). Moreover, the convention in horror to show protagonist violence going unpunished and justifiable is thought to inhibit learning of internal regulators that govern aggressive behavior (Pearl, Bouthilet, Lazar, 1982; Tan, 1981). Likewise, repeated images of horrific violence can lead to desensitization and render viewers indifferent to aggression (Cline, Croft, & Courrier, 1973; Linz, Donnerstein, & Adams, 1989; Linz, Donnerstein, & Penrod, 1988; Thomas, 1982). Reactions of this type encourage the performance of aggressive behavior (Berkowitz, 1993).

WHAT OF HORROR'S FUTURE?

Although horror has existed in literature for years, most research on modern entertainment horror concentrates on film. No doubt much of this attention is due, once again, to its high media profile. Earlier in this century, scholars looking at media of their time focused on horror in fictional writing (Tamborini, 1991), and it seems logical that scholars in the not too distant future will focus on the next generation of horror technology. Perhaps we have seen the start of horror's future in the video-game genre called *survival horror*. These games feature a morbid story line, where the player must find clues, solve puzzles, and fight something dark and evil ("The survival horror genre," 1999). Whereas early games like Resident Evil offered third-person perspectives and failed to provide sound or character development on a par with modern horror films, today successful horror-film makers like Clive Barker are producing immersive video games that put players in the first-person perspective as they enter the horrific media environment (Smith, 2001).

A central issue in research on this technology concerns how its active user role and first-person point of view will change the user's experience. If critical processes of empathic distress result from film viewer's being mere witnesses (Zillmann, 1998), these processes will change in the game's interactive environment, and perhaps the expected outcomes will vary in response. Grodal (2000) asserted that video games differ as a result from change in appraised coping. Whereas the appraised coping potential of a film character determines emotional experience for the viewer, appraisal of the player's own coping potentials controls emotional experience in video games, a process closer to real life. In contrast to those who caution of users developing aggressive behavioral scripts, Grodal envisioned video games as tools for emotional control that would function much like other past media. Conceivably the more active and realistic experience of horror in a virtual reality environment could facilitate both cognitive and action coping strategies to eradicate negative emotions by means unavailable through film exposure today. Perhaps interacting with avatars chosen to personify targets of anger will foster reappraisal of behaviors initially taken as a demeaning offense, or physically prevailing over a world of survival horror will offer forms of reassurance needed to rid anxiety. Certainly, at least, one could reason that if film has become the modern day forum for young men to master distress, interactive horror is better suited for practicing these gender-role behaviors.

The active user issue has received great attention from those concerned with information technology, but entertainment scholars have been slow to address its impact on user experience. Vorderer (2000) questioned whether audience members want to labor as much as interactivity demands, and observed that games allow users to alternate between witness and player perspectives. He called for new theory to account for the increasingly complex experience of users who are now ensnared in these dual roles. Understanding this multifaceted experience becomes even more challenging with the complex emotions from horror. The processes leading to emotional override and misattributed joy will be no simpler to understand when experienced in immersive media worlds.

In the end, then, what does all this tell us about the enjoyment and social functions of horror? We can be confident that there are multiple sources of pleasure, some internal to the narrative form and others with social functions at their root. We are learning more about the processes at work, but know quite little about others. And when considering the likely horror in store, we see more complex questions to come. What happens when taking my nephew to see a scary film is replaced by going with him into a world of survival horror? Perhaps it means that I will hold him with one arm and kill the monster with the other as I help him fight his demons more literally then ever before.

REFERENCES

Alloway, L. (1972). Monster films. In R. Huss & T. J. Ross (Eds.), *Focus on the horror film* (pp. 121–124). Englewood Cliffs, NJ: Prentice-Hall.

Aluja-Fabregat, A. (2000). Personality and curiosity about TV and films violence in adolescents. *Personality and Individual Differences, 29,* 379–392.

American Psychological Association. (1993). *Violence and youth: Psychology's response.* Washington, DC: Author.

Andison, F. S. (1977). TV violence and viewer aggression: A cumulation of study results. *Public Opinion Quarterly, 41,* 314–331.

Baron, R. A., & Richardson, D. R. (1994). *Human aggression* (2nd ed.). New York: Plenum.

Barry, H., Bacon, M. K., & Child, L. L. (1957). A cross-cultural survey of some sex differences in socialization. *Journal of Abnormal and Social Psychology, 55,* 327–332.

Bell, C. (1914). *Art.* London: Chatto & Windus.

Bem, S. L. (1976). Probing the promise of androgyny. In A. G. Kaplan & J. P. Bean (Eds.), *Beyond sex-role stereotypes: Readings toward a psychology of androgyny* (pp. 48–62). Boston: Little, Brown.

Bem, S. L. (1985). Androgyny and gender schema theory: A conceptual and empirical investigation. In T. B. Sonderegger (Ed.), *Nebraska symposium on motivation: Psychology and gender* (pp. 176–226). Lincoln: University of Nebraska Press.

Berkowitz, L. (1993). *Aggression: Its causes, consequences, and control.* New York: McGraw-Hill.

Berlyne, D. E. (1967). Arousal and reinforcement. In D. Levine (Ed.), *Nebraska symposium on motivation* (pp. 1–111). Lincoln: University of Nebraska Press.

Binkley, T. (1977). Piece: Contra aesthetics. *Journal of Aesthetics and Art Criticism, 35,* 265–277.

Borkgrevink, C., & Tamborini, R. (1994, November). *Empathy and the verbal immediacy of messages in face-to-face comforting.* Paper presented at the annual conference of the Speech Communication Association, New Orleans, LA.

Brody, L. R. (1985). Gender differences in emotional development: A review of theories and research. *Journal of Personality, 53,* 102–149.

Brosnan, J. (1976). *The horror people.* New York: St. Martin's Press.

Buss, D. M., & Shackelford, T. K. (1997). Human aggression in evolutionary psychological perspective. *Clinical Psychology Review, 17,* 605–619.

Buzzuto, J. C. (1975). Cinematic neurosis following "The Exorcist." *Journal of Nervous and Mental Disease, 161,* 43–48.

Cantor, J. (1992). Children's emotional responses to technological disasters conveyed by the mass media. In J. M. Wober (Ed.), *Television and nuclear power: Making the public mind* (pp. 31–53). Norwood, NJ: Ablex.

Cantor, J. (1998). Children's attraction to television programming. In J. H. Goldstein, (Ed.), *Why we watch: The attractions of violent entertainment* (pp. 88–115). New York: Oxford University Press.

Cantor, J., & Oliver, M. B. (1996). Developmental differences in responses to horror. In J. Weaver & R. Tamborini (Eds.), *Horror films: Current research on audience preferences and reactions* (pp. 63–80). Mahwah, NJ: Lawrence Erlbaum Associates.

Cantor, J., Zillmann, D., & Bryant, J. (1975). Enhancement of experienced sexual arousal in response to erotic stimuli through misattribution of unrelated residual excitation. *Journal of Personality and Social Psychology, 32,* 69–75.

Carey, P. M. (1994, May 9–15). NY firms feed Asia's entertainment appetite. *Crain's New York Business,* International section, p. 19.

Carroll, N. (1990). *The philosophy of horror, or paradoxes of the heart.* New York: Routledge.

Centers for Disease Control. (1991). *Position papers from the Third National Injury Conference: Setting the National Agenda for Injury Control in the 1990s.* Washington, DC: Department of Health and Human Services.

Chaffee, S. H., & McLeod, J. M. (1971, September). *Adolescents, parents, and television violence.* Paper presented at the meeting of the American Psychological Association, Washington, DC.

Cline, V. B., Croft, R. G., & Courrier, S. (1973). Desensitization of children to television violence. *Journal of Personality & Social Psychology, 27,* 360–365.

Danto, A. (1964). The art world. *Journal of Philosophy, 61,* 571–584.

Danto, A. (1981). *The transfiguration of the commonplace.* Cambridge, MA: Harvard University Press.

Denne, J. D. (1972). Society and the monster. In R. Huss & T. J. Ross (Eds.), *Focus on the horror film* (pp. 125–131). Englewood Cliffs, NJ: Prentice-Hall.

Denny, M. R. (1991). *Fear, avoidance, and phobias.* Hillsdale, NJ: Lawrence Erlbaum Associates.

De Wied, M., Zillmann, D., & Ordman, V. (1994). The role of empathic distress in the enjoyment of cinematic tragedy. *Poetics, 23,* 91–106.

Dickstein, M. (1980, September). The aesthetics of fright. *American Film,* 32–41.

Donnerstein, E., & Linz, D. (1984, January). Sexual violence in the media: A warning. *Psychology Today,* 14–15.

Edwards, E. (1984). *The relationship between sensation-seeking and horror movie interest and attendance.* Unpublished doctoral dissertation, University of Tennessee, Knoxville.

Evans, W. (1984). Monster movies: A sexual theory. In B. K. Grant (Ed.), *Planks of reasons: Essays on the horror film* (pp. 53–64). Metuchen, NJ: Scarecrow Press.

Fenigstein, A. (1979). Does aggression cause a preference for viewing media violence? *Journal of Personality and Social Psychology, 37,* 2307–2317.

Feshbach, S. (1955). The drive-reducing function of fantasy behavior. *Journal of Abnormal and Social Psychology, 50,* 3–11.

Feshbach, S. (1976). The role of fantasy in the response to television. *Journal of Social Issues, 32,* 71–85.

Feshbach, S., & Singer, R. D. (1971). *Television and aggression.* San Francisco: Jossey-Bass.

Forgas, J. P. (1991). *Emotion & social judgments.* Oxford: Pergamon.

Frijda, N. H. (1989). Aesthetic emotions and reality. *American Psychologist, 44,* 1546–1547.

Fry, R. (1920). *Vision and design.* London: Chatto & Windus.

Geen, R. G. (1994). Television and aggression: Recent developments in research and theory. In D. Zillmann, J. Bryant, & A. Huston (Eds.), *Media, children, and the family* (pp. 151–165). Hillsdale, New Jersey: Lawrence Erlbaum Associates.

Geen, R. G., & Quanty, M. B. (1977). The catharsis of aggression: An evaluation of a hypothesis. In L. Berkowitz (Ed.), *Advances in experimental social psychology* (Vol. 10, pp. 1–37). New York: Academic.

Gerbner, G. (1988). Violence and terror in the mass media. In *Reports and papers in mass communication,* No. 102. Paris: UNESCO.

Gombrich, E. H. (1962). *Art and illusion.* London: Phaidon.

Gray, J. A. (1971). *The psychology of fear and stress.* New York: McGraw-Hill.

Grodal, T. (2000). Video games and the pleasures of control. In D. Zillmann & P. Vorderer (Eds.), *Media entertainment: The psychology of its appeal* (pp. 197–214). Mahwah, NJ: Lawrence Erlbaum Associates.

Hallie, P. P. (1969). *The paradox of cruelty.* Middletown, CT: Wesleyan University Press.

Harrington, C. (1972). Ghoulies and ghosties. In R. Huss & T. J. Ross (Eds.), *Focus on the horror film* (pp. 14–23). Englewood Cliffs, NJ: Prentice-Hall.

Hart, K. E. (1991). Coping with anger-provoking situations: Adolescent coping in relation to anger-reactivity. *Journal of Adolescent Research, 6,* 357–370.

Hoberman, J. (1998). "A test for the individual viewer": Bonnie and Clyde's Violent Reception. In J. H. Goldstein (Ed.), *Why we watch: The attractions of violent entertainment* (pp. 116–143). New York: Oxford University Press.

Johnson, B. R. (1980). General occurrence of stressful reactions to commercial motion pictures and elements in films subjectively identified as stressors. *Psychological Reports, 47,* 775–786.

The killing screens: Media and the culture of violence [video]. (1994). Northampton, MA: Media Education Foundation.

King, S. (1981). *Danse macabre.* New York: Everest House.

Lazarus, R. S. (1991). *Emotion and adaptation.* New York: Oxford University Press.

Liebert, R. M., Sobol, M. P., & Davidson, E. S. (1972). Catharsis of aggression among institutionalized boys: Fact or artifact? In G. A. Comstock, E. A. Rubinstein, & J. P. Murray (Eds.), *Television and social behavior, Vol. V: Television effects: Further explorations* (pp. 351–358). Washington, DC: U.S. Government Printing Office.

Liebert, R. M., & Sprafkin, J. (1988). *The early window.* New York: Pergamon.

Linz, D., Donnerstein, E., & Adams, S. M. (1989). Physiological desensitization and judgments about female victims of violence. *Human Communication Research, 15,* 509–522.

Linz, D., Donnerstein, E., & Penrod, S. (1984). The effects of multiple exposures to filmed violence against women. *Journal of Communication, 34*(3), 130–147.

Linz, D. G., Donnerstein, E., & Penrod, S. (1988). Effects of long-term exposure to violent and sexually degrading depictions of women. *Journal of Personality & Social Psychology, 55,* 758–768.

Malamuth, N. M., & Check, J. V. P. (1981). The effects of mass media exposure on acceptance of violence against women: A field experiment. *Journal of Research in Personality, 15,* 436–446.

Mathai, J. (1983). An acute anxiety state in an adolescent precipitated by viewing a horror movie. *Journal of Adolescence, 6,* 197–200.

McCauley, C. (1998). When screen violence is not attractive. In J. H. Goldstein (Ed.), *Why we watch: The attractions of violent entertainment* (pp. 144–162). New York: Oxford University Press.

Medved, M. (1992). *Hollywood vs. America: Popular culture and the war on traditional values.* New York: Harper Collins.

Moeran, B. (1986). The beauty of violence: Jidaigeki, yakuza, and "eroduction" films in Japanese cinema. In D. Riches (Ed.), *The anthropology of violence* (pp. 103–117). Oxford: Blackwell.

Mundorf, N., Weaver, J., & Zillmann, D. (1989). Effects of gender roles and self perceptions on affective reactions to horror films. *Sex Roles, 20,* 655–673.

National Academy of Science. (1993). *Understanding and preventing violence.* Washington, DC: National Academy Press.

Pearl, D., Bouthilet, L., & Lazar, J. (Eds.). (1982). *Television and behavior: Ten years of scientific progress and implications for the eighties. Vol. 2.* Washington, DC: U.S. Government Printing Office.

Rachman, S. J. (1990). *Fear and courage* (2nd ed.). New York: W. H. Freeman.

Radford, C. (1975). How can we be moved by the fate of Anna Karenina? *Proceedings of the Aristotelian Society, 49,* 67–93.

Rickey, C. (1982, November). Hooked on horror: Why we like scary movies. *Mademoiselle,* 168–170.

Rockett, W. H. (1988). *Devouring whirlwind: Terror and transcendence in the cinema of cruelty.* New York: Greenwood.

Rorty, A. (1978). Explaining emotions. *Journal of Philosophy, 75,* 139–161.

Rosenbaum, R. (1979, September). Gooseflesh. *Harpers Magazine,* 86–92.

Saarni, C. (1989). Children's understanding of strategic control of emotional expression in social transactions. In C. Saarni & P. L. Harris (Eds.), *Children's understanding of emotion* (pp. 181–208). New York: Cambridge University Press.

Sapolsky, B. S., & Molitor, F. (1996). Content trends in contemporary horror films. In J. B. Weaver, III & R. Tamborini (Eds.), *Horror films: Current research on audience preferences and reactions* (pp. 33–48). Mahwah, NJ: Lawrence Erlbaum Associates.

Shennum, W. A., & Bugental, D. B. (1982). The development of control over affective expression in nonverbal behavior. In R. Feldman (Ed.), *Development of nonverbal behavior in children* (pp. 101–122). New York: Springer-Verlag.

Smith, P. (2001, April 19). Clive Baker's undying, PC. *Computer Weekly, 87.* Retrieved May 5, 2001, from http://www.computerweekly.co.uk

Sontag, S. (1966). *Against interpretation.* New York: Farrar, Straus & Giroux.

Sparks, G. (1986). Developing a scale to assess cognitive responses to frightening films. *Journal of Broadcasting and Electronic Media, 30,* 65–73.

Sparks, G. G. (1991). The relationship between distress and delight in males' and females' reactions to frightening films. *Human Communication Research, 17*, 625–637.

Sparks, G. G., & Sparks, C. W. (2000). Violence, mayhem and horror. In D. Zillmann & P. Vorderer (Eds.), *Media entertainment: The psychology of its appeal* (pp. 73–92). Mahwah, NJ: Lawrence Erlbaum Associates.

The survival horror genre. (1999, October 29). techtv. Retrieved May 14, 20 01, from http://www.techtv.com/extendedplay/videofeatures/story/0,23008,2381223,00.html

Tamborini, R. (1991). Responding to horror: Determinants of exposure and appeal. In J. Bryant & D. Zillmann (Eds.), *Responding to the screen: Reception and reaction processes* (pp. 305–329). Hillsdale, New Jersey: Lawrence Erlbaum Associates.

Tamborini, R. (1996). A model of empathy and emotional reactions to horror. In J. Weaver & R. Tamborini (Eds.), *Horror films: Current research on audience preferences and reactions* (pp. 103–124). Mahwah, NJ: Lawrence Erlbaum Associates.

Tamborini, R., Bahk, C., & Salomonson, K. (1993, May). *The moderating impact of film exposure on the relationship between empathy and comforting.* Paper presented at the annual conference of the International Communication Association, Washington, DC.

Tamborini, R., Miller, K., Stiff, J., & Heidel, C. (1988, May). *Predictors of emotional reactions to audio and visual elements in graphic horror: A time series analysis.* Paper presented at the annual con-ference of the Speech Communication Association, New Orleans, LA.

Tamborini, R., & Salomonson, K. (1996). Horror's effect on social perceptions and behaviors. In J. Weaver & R. Tamborini (Eds.), *Horror films: Current research on audience preferences and reactions* (pp. 179–198). Mahwah, NJ: Lawrence Erlbaum Associates.

Tamborini, R., Salomonson, K., & Bahk, C. (1993a). The relationship of empathy to comforting behavior following film exposure. *Communication Research, 20*, 723–738.

Tamborini, R., Salomonson, K., & Bahk, C. (1993b, November). *Situational determinants of comforting: The impact of messages differing in hedonic quality.* Paper presented at the annual conference of the Speech Communication Association, Miami, FL.

Tamborini, R., & Stiff, J. (1987). Predictors of horror film attendance and appeal: An analysis of the audience for frightening films. *Communication Research, 14*, 415–436.

Tamborini, R., Stiff, J., & Heidel, C. (1990). Reacting to graphic horror: A Model of empathy and emotional behavior. *Communication Research, 17*, 616–640.

Tamborini, R., Stiff, J., & Zillmann, D. (1987). Preference for graphic horror featuring male versus female victimization: Personality and past film viewing experiences. *Human Communication Research, 13*, 529–552.

Tan, A. S. (1981). *Mass communication theories and research.* Columbus, OH: Grid Publishing.

Tannenbaum, P. H. (1980). Entertainment as vicarious emotional experience. In P. H. Tannenbaum (Ed.), *The entertainment functions of television* (pp. 107–131). Hillsdale, NJ: Lawrence Erlbaum Associates.

Thomas, J. (1972). Gobble, gobble . . . one of us! In R. Huss & T. J. Ross (Eds.), *Focus on the horror film* (pp. 135–138). Englewood Cliffs, NJ: Prentice-Hall.

Thomas, M. H. (1982). Physiological arousal, exposure to a relatively lengthy aggressive film, and aggressive behavior. *Journal of Research in Personality, 16,* 72–81.

Vorderer, P. (2000). Interactive entertainment and beyond. In D. Zillmann & P. Vorderer (Eds.), *Media entertainment: The psychology of its appeal* (pp. 21–36). Mahwah, NJ: Lawrence Erlbaum Associates.

Wakshlag, J., Vial, V., & Tamborini, R. (1983). Selecting crime drama and apprehension about crime. *Human Communication Research, 10,* 227–242.

Weaver, J. (1987). Effects of portrayals of female sexuality and violence against women on perceptions of women. *Dissertation Abstracts International, 48,* 2482-A.

Weaver, J. (1991). Are slasher horror films sexually violent? A content analysis. *Journal of Broadcasting and Electronic Media, 35,* 385–392.

Weinraub, B. (1993). Despite Clinton, Hollywood is still trading in violence. *New York Times,* December 28, p. A1.

Wood, W., Wong, F. Y., & Chachere, J. G. (1991). Effects of media violence on viewers' aggression in unconstrained social interaction. *Psychological Bulletin, 109,* 371–383.

Zillmann, D. (1979). *Hostility and aggression.* Hillsdale, NJ: Lawrence Erlbaum Associates.

Zillmann, D. (1980). Anatomy of suspense. In P. H. Tannenbaum (Ed.), *The entertainment functions of television* (pp. 133–163). Hillsdale, NJ: Lawrence Erlbaum Associates.

Zillmann, D. (1982). Television viewing and arousal. In D. Pearl, L. Bouthilet, & J. Lazar (Eds.), *Television and behavior: Ten years of scientific progress and implications for the eighties* (Vol. 2, pp. 53–67). DHHS Publication No. ADM 82-1196. Washington, DC: U.S. Government Printing Office.

Zillmann, D. (1983). Transfer of excitation in emotional behavior. In J. T. Cacioppo, & R. E. Petty (Eds.), *Social psychology: A source book* (pp. 215–240). New York: Gilford.

Zillmann, D. (1991a). Empathy: Affect from bearing witness to the emotions of others. In J. Bryant & D. Zillmann (Eds.), *Responding to the screen: Reception and reaction processes* (pp. 135–164). Hillsdale, NJ: Lawrence Erlbaum Associates.

Zillmann, D. (1991b). The logic of suspense and mystery. In J. Bryant & D. Zillmann (Eds.), *Responding to the screen: Reception and reaction processes* (pp. 281–304). Hillsdale, NJ: Lawrence Erlbaum Associates.

Zillmann, D. (1998). The psychology of the appeal of portrayals of violence. In J. H. Goldstein (Ed.), *Why we watch: The attractions of violent entertainment* (pp. 179–211). New York: Oxford University Press.

Zillmann, D., & Cantor, J. R. (1976). A disposition theory of humor and mirth. In A. J. Chapman & H. C. Foot (Eds.), *Humour and laughter: Theory, research, and applications* (pp. 93–115). London: Wiley.

Zillmann, D., & Gibson, R. (1996). Evolution of the horror genre. In J. Weaver & R. Tamborini (Eds.), *Horror films: Current research on audience preferences and reactions* (pp. 15–32). Mahwah, NJ: Lawrence Erlbaum Associates.

Zillmann, D., Hay, T. A., & Bryant, J. (1975). The effect of suspense and its resolution on the appreciation of dramatic presentations. *Journal of Research in Personality, 9,* 307–323.

Zillmann, D., Mody, B., & Cantor, J. (1974). Empathetic perception of emotional displays in films as a function of hedonic and excitatory state prior to exposure. *Journal of Research in Personality, 8,* 335–349.

Zillmann, D., & Paulus, P. B. (1993). Spectators: Reactions to sports events and effects on athletic performance. In R. N. Singer, M. Murphey, & L. K. Tennant (Eds.), *Handbook of research on sport psychology* (pp. 600–619). New York: Macmillan.

Zillmann, D., & Weaver, J. B., III. (1996). Gender-socialization theory of reactions to horror. In J. B. Weaver, III & R. Tamborini (Eds.), *Horror films: Current research on audience preferences and reactions* (pp. 81–101). Mahwah, NJ: Lawrence Erlbaum Associates.

Zillmann, D., Weaver, J. B., Mundorf, N., & Aust, C. F. (1986). Effects of an opposite-gender companion's affect to horror on distress, delight, and attraction. *Journal of Personality and Social Psychology, 51,* 586–594.

Zuckerman, M. (1996). Sensation seeking and the taste for vicarious horror. In J. B. Weaver, III & R. Tamborini (Eds.), *Horror films: Current research on audience preferences and reactions* (pp. 147–160). Mahwah, NJ: Lawrence Erlbaum Associates.

Zuckerman, M., & Litle, P. (1986). Personality and curiosity about morbid sexual events. *Personality and Individual Differences, 2,* 49–56.

19

Enjoyment of Violence

Dorina Miron
University of Alabama

> *The socially more relevant question must be what our fascination with barbarous violence in entertainment efforts does to us and ultimately to society.*
>
> –Zillmann (1998b, p. 210)

PHILOSOPHERS: GOING OVER THE EDGE

The first thinkers to tackle the issue of human pleasure were barehanded. Their instrument was their own mind, scrutinizing the painful but also enjoyable stream of life events and also relying on introspection. What did they see and think?

The Social Perspective

Circus and Acculturation

In the ancient Mediterranean world, warfare was a major occupation that engaged a large part of the male population. Some exhilaration intrinsic to the process seems to have kept warriors involved in mutual and self-destruction: the pleasure of extreme physical exercise and eventually the enjoyment of winning, that is, killing and robbing others, appropriating goods and pleasures that used to belong to their enemies. Physical abilities and weapon handling (killing skills) came to be associated with wealth, status, and sexual desirability. Their value expanded into peacetime activities.

When not engaged in war, the ancient Greek and Roman males would enjoy physical training and competitions (e.g., the Olympic Games, which started in Greece in 776 B.C., and three other famous sporting festivals held at Delphy, Nemea, and Corinth) as well as gladiatorial games (circus spectacles). The popularity of games in ancient times is hard to imagine. Suffice it to say that Circus Maximus in Rome was rebuilt in the time of Julius Caesar (1st century B.C.) to seat 150,000 spectators. In the middle of the fourth century A.D., the Roman Empire had 175 days a year dedicated to state-supported entertainment (Zillmann, 2000b), mostly games, and Circus Maximus reached a seating capacity of 250,000 under Constantine I.

Satirist Juvenal (60–140 A.D.), in his famous *panem et circenses*[1] statement (see Juvenal, 1991, *Satirae,* X.78), intuitively aligned the pleasure provided by the circus with the most basic of needs, which is food. But the fact that individual life in antiquity did not have much value—because of the frequent wars and the pervasive human killing for entertainment[2] outside the battlefield—biased early thinkers toward a social rather than individual consideration of the prevailing form of violent[3] pleasures.

The stoics (5th century B.C.), and later Cicero (106-43 B.C.), appreciated circus spectacles as visual apprenticeship of pain and death, as a means to develop in the audience endurance to those widespread and unpleasant realities (Frau-Meigs & Jehel, 1997). Their view reflects a schema shared by rites of passage across societies and time, which also underlies the current use of cinematic horror by adolescents (Zillmann, 1998b; Zillmann & Gibson, 1996; Zillmann & Weaver, 1996). Bok (1998) went even further, contending that in ancient Rome circus was an official policy: "Violent spectacles kept the citizenry distracted, engaged, and entertained" and "provided the continuing acculturation to violence needed by a warrior state" (p. 16). Bok's speculation is consistent with Zillmann's (1979, 1983) excitation–transfer theory, which posits arousal lag and transfer from one emotional state to the next, irrespective of hedonic valence, leading to emotional buildup.

---

[1]"The people that once bestowed commands, consulships, legions, and all else, now concerns itself no more, and longs eagerly for just two things–bread and circuses!" (Juvenal, Satirae, X.78).

[2]In the Roman Empire, in the middle of the 4th century, almost every other day, that is 175 days a year, was dedicated to state-supported entertainments (Kraus, 1971, cited by Zillmann, 2000b), mostly circus spectacles.

[3]Violence was defined as "intentional physical harm to another individual" (Harris, 1994, p. 186) or, more elaborately, "the overt expression of physical force (with or without a weapon, against self or other) compelling action against one's will on pain of being hurt and/or killed or threatened to be so victimized" (Gerbner, Gross, Morgan, & Signorielli, 1980, p. 11). For a discussion of hostile and aggressive behavior, see Zillmann (1979).

Tragedy, Catharsis, and... Ethics

Another form of violent entertainment in the classical Mediterranean world was tragedy. Early philosophers expressed concern about people's willingness to expose themselves to theatrical events that would naturally elicit strong negative feelings.

Plato[4] (427–347 B.C.) was mostly concerned about the effects of tragedy on the audience. He believed that "empathic[5] distress would render respondents vulnerable to self-pity upon encountering misfortunes of their own. He deemed such sensitivity inappropriate—that is, antagonistic to his notion of virtue—and favored the banishment of the genre altogether" (Zillmann, 1998a, p. 5). Obviously, such feelings were deemed undesirable in warrior states because they tended to inhibit the aggressiveness needed for waging wars.

Plato's view would translate in modern terms as repeated exposure, rehearsal of empathic distress, and chronic accessibility of fear and pity schemata—therefore, we may regard it as a proto-exemplification[6] theory.

Aristotle[7] (384–322 B.C.) disagreed with Plato and proposed the catharsis hypothesis. He presumed that a tragedy could get the audience to experience fear and pity, which would thus be consumed (purged, eliminated). The notion of catharsis challenged thinkers for more than 2,000 years before the development of psychology allowed for empirical testing.

Catharsis Disconfirmed

Zillmann's research on excitation caused by exposure to the media (e.g., Zillmann, 1971; Zillmann & Bryant, 1974) revealed emotional buildup, which was the very opposite of the purging of negative emotions predicted by the catharsis theory. Thus Zillmann's excitation-transfer theory (e.g., Zillmann, 1979, 1983) practically falsified the hypothesis that exposure to extremely violent spectacles generates relief pleasure. But the question of what made violent spectacles so liked, so popular, remained unanswered.

---

[4]Cited by Zillmann (1998a, p. 5).

[5]For the role of empathy in the processing of drama, see Zillmann (1991).

[6]For the exemplification theory, see Zillmann (1999).

[7]Cited by Zillmann (1998a, p. 5).

The Mystery Resolved: The Ethical Theory of Violence Enjoyment

Zillmann tenaciously persevered in his efforts to account for the enjoyment of drama. He pointed out that the concept of witness identification with actors, running from Aristotle's catharsis theory to Freud's ego confusion theory, failed to account for a spectator's enjoyment of someone else's distress (Zillmann, 1998b). What Zillmann suggested instead was that we witness drama as third parties (1991) and voluntarily rather than automatically "identify" with characters (Zillmann, 1998b): We pick the characters we want to "identify" with, and we choose the degree and duration of "identification" in such a way as to maximize our personal pleasure. Zillmann's disposition theory (e.g., Zillmann, 1980, 1985, 1994; Zillmann & Cantor, 1977) or theory of dispositional alignments (Zillmann, 1998b) posited that disposition toward characters (liking or disliking) mediates moral judgment and renders enjoyable the harms suffered by enemies, deemed deserved punishments, that is, punitive violence (Zillmann & Bryant, 1975). Although refuting catharsis, Zillmann's dispositional alignment theory confirmed Aristotle's intuition that humans derive pleasures not only from sensorial stimulation but also from exercising moral judgment (Zillmann, 2000a).

Zillmann's disposition theory accounted for enjoyment of spectacle violence based on endorsement of social norms. To round out the picture, Zillmann also proposed a norm violation theory of violence enjoyment hinged on some people's "desire to violate the norms of socially acceptable behavior, or to see them violated by others" (Tamborini, Stiff, & Zillmann, 1987, p. 584). Zillmann's norm violation theory is tangent to Nietzsche's (1887/1956, 1886/1966) celebration of cruelty as "liberating and exhilarating" (Bok, 1998, p. 27). Nietzsche's and Zillmann's joy of transgression makes perfect sense under a system of norms perceived by individuals as oppressive. It provides an appealing alternative to Freud's (1933) mysterious death instinct that allegedly drives people toward the destruction of self and others. Zillmann's norm violation theory can be applied to explain the enormous popularity in the United States of hard rock, heavy metal, gangsta, and other similarly violent music, whose lyrics create a coherent universe of "satanism, drug abuse, sexual assaults and murder" (Jipping, 2001, p. 65). The American youth may experience a power crisis and may use such music as a vehicle for power trips of violence, sexism, and greed (Davis, 1990). The norm violation theory would also help account for the .39 correlation coefficient between preference for horror films and the deceit measure for the Machiavellianism personality trait cited by Sparks and Sparks (2000).

A legitimate question is whether Zillmann's modern explanations can be retrospectively applied to account for the enjoyment of violence in ancient history. Zillmann (2000a) demonstrated the congruence between his disposition theory and Aristotle's normative theory of dramatic situations and emotions, which required that bad characters be presented as undergoing misfortune (deserved punishment), not good fortune. On the other hand, the massive acculturation to violence in the ancient Mediterranean world (Bok, 1998) involved a great risk: the contagion of violence, because those rudimentary societies did not have judicial institutions (Girard, 1972). Examples of game-related social disorder and political unrest abound.[8]

Faced with political emergencies such as the violence spillover from an entertainment environment into real life, ancient philosophers developed ethics as a system of norms for mutual/social adjustment of individual pleasure seekers who tended to harm others in their pursuit of self-gratification. In Athens, the imperious need to impose the rule of law made Socrates (469?–399 B.C.) sacrifice his own life (Plato, 1984) in a high-profile trial in order to give an extreme-violence (thus memorable) example that an individual's rights and pleasures must be curtailed in order to prevent escalation of violence and community destruction. So, moral judgment was indeed a component of ancient societies at the time when circus and tragedies became popular.

Although Aristotle's catharsis has been repeatedly invalidated (e.g., Geen & Quanty, 1977; Zillmann, 1998a), the concept has nevertheless endured as a "legend" (Harris & Scott, 2002). We may choose to regard it as an illegitimate member of the desensitization theory club. Sparks and Sparks (2000), for example, talked about a "catharsis-type process" underlying the treatment of phobias (little enjoyment involved, the same as in viewing ancient tragedies). We may also consider for membership in the same club the rite-of-passage use of violence, horror, and mayhem (VHM) entertainment (enjoyed probably as much as the ancient circus).

---

[8]"After a victory by Porphyrius in 507 in the circus at Antioch, the jubilant Greens ran wild and, in the course of the riot, burned the local synagogue (Guttmann, 1998, p. 14). In 532, In Constantinople, "supporters of the Blues and Greens joined forces. Prisoners about to be executed were rescued by the mob," which also "proclaimed a new emperor [to replace Justinian], to whom a number of senators paid hasty homage.... General Belisarius arrived in time to save the day–at the cost of an estimated thirty thousand lives" (Guttmann, 1988, p. 14).

Aristotle's catharsis (and its modern desensitization interpretation) and Plato's "sensitization" (and its modern schema-accessibility interpretation) established a dual perspective on response to violence that has focused research and theorizing on emotional and memory processes.

The Individual Perspective

The predominantly social (macro) approach to violence enjoyment in the ancient world was due not only to political priority and the low value attached at that time to individual human life. Another major factor that shaped the beginnings of pleasure theory was the embryonic stage of the methods of scientific inquiry in general. Dialectic and logic were rather clumsy and insufficient instruments for examining human emotions at the individual level. Therefore, it is not surprising that the domain of aesthetics (defined by the ancients as the study of the nature of sensations) was initially inhabited mostly by the arts, which described rather than explicated emotional phenomena.

The Arts: Rape and the Life of Pleasure

Ancient literature recorded sequential patterns of emotions, thoughts, and behaviors related to the enjoyment of violence. Such documents are inaccurate representations of genuine experiences because artists were competing for people's attention with real life events (e.g., wars) and other artificial events (e.g., games, as alternative forms of entertainment). It was a race of pleasure intensity. The art genres and the individual works that won the race and endured were those that abridged/condensed and exaggerated realities in order to enhance tension and pleasure—which makes them rather unreliable sources of knowledge about real life.

Unfortunately, art served as a very effective disseminator of the inaccurate information it contained. The artistic simplification of reality and superior vividness made representations of enjoyment of violence more comprehensible and memorable than reality itself. Whatever art managed to add to reality constituted the attraction of art. Yet, a basic match (isomorphism) between art schemata and reality schemata ensured comprehension, and that match made possible schema transfer, that is, learning from art, having one's behavior modeled by the arts available in the environment.

A famous example of what was available in ancient arts in terms of depictions of violence enjoyment at the individual level is Ovid's (43

B.C.–17/18? A.D.) story of Philomela (Ovid, 2001, *Metamorphoses* 6.424–674), mutilated and raped by her brother-in-law, Tereus. The story combines sex, violence, and violation of social order (a barbarous and tyrannical man confronts two women from the civilized Athenian democracy). Tereus' sadism breaks down the family structure, and humiliates, brutalizes, enrages, and maddens the women, whose lives are consumed in revenge. Violence is represented as a gradual dehumanization, inhibition of reason and restraint, and unleashed emotion and physical force effecting destruction. As observed by Segal (1993), the depiction is masterful, but the very popularity of the piece justifies "the charge of perpetuating a cultural pattern of subjugating and exploiting women and of demonizing their rage at such subjugation" (p. 276).

From a theoretical viewpoint, Ovid's Philomela story captured the basic schema of pleasure escalation: inclusion of violence in pleasure practices, aggravation of violence, and increasingly violent response from the aggressed parties—which absorb the lives of the individuals involved, dissolve the original social structure that supported the pleasure, and ultimately terminate pleasure. Such escalation of pleasure activities by individual pleasure seekers is, in the long run, destructive for both individuals and society, which may come to be "consumed" by pleasure/violence.

Aristotle on Pleasure

Aristotle was among the first to provide a conceptualization of pleasure, which he considered to be an activity (process), with enjoyment occurring at peak performance (Urmson, 1968). Aristotle, in his *Poetics* (1999), distinguished between bodily pleasures and pleasures of the soul (e.g., righteousness or justice). The former were conceived as enjoyment of sense perceptions (sight, hearing, and smell in the sphere of temperance; smell and touch, associated with food, drink, and sex, in the sphere of intemperance; Urmson, 1968). Aristotle believed that an activity was promoted by its enjoyment, which also inhibited alternative activities (Urmson, 1968). This observation is a precursor of the modern displacement concept, popular especially in the literature of media effects on children. But it may also be considered a precursor of the addiction concept.

One striking thing in Aristotle's classification is the diversity of sensorial pleasures as compared to a single soul/intellectual pleasure, which seems to indicate that in terms of pleasure, he expected more from the senses than from intelligence. The criterion of temperance points to the critical issue of pleasure control. Within the Aristotelian framework, two-way control was theoretically possible, either inhibiting or enhancing pleasure, but inhibition was problematic for the intemperate senses.

Epicurus' Philosophy of Pleasure

One of the most popular ancient philosophers was Epicurus (341 B.C.?–270 B.C.; 1993), simply because he advocated a lifetime of pleasure leading to happiness (*ataraxia,* undisturbed satisfaction; Anderson, 2001). That was a very agreeable normative system—Epicurus must have hit the right key. As we go into detail, the glaze cracks and the glitter fades. Epicurean pleasure is defined as the opposite or complete absence of pain or discomfort (Anderson, 2001), as an end-state toward which we can work by removing troubles or sources of pain (e.g., hunger, thirst, sexual pressure). Epicurus warned that if the pursuits (such as eating, drinking, sexual activities) diverted attention from the end-state (pleasure/happiness), anxieties and addictions would develop (Anderson, 2001).

Epicurus' concept of end state was rendered obsolete by psychological science, which demonstrated the simultaneity of sensorial stimulation and pleasure. Nevertheless, Epicurus remains interesting for two things: his classification of pleasures and his massive popularity. Epicurus' treatise *On Choice and Avoidance* was lost, but in *Principal Doctrines* (Epicurus, 1993) he emphasized the wise choice of pleasures, which he grouped into three categories, to be dealt with differently: the natural and necessary needs—roughly corresponding to Maslow's (1943) physiological and safety needs—which were to be satisfied in the most economical way possible; the natural and unnecessary needs (e.g., sexual gratification and entertainments such as sports, arts, travel)—relatively close to Maslow's affiliation and self-actualization needs—whose variety could be explored if the natural and necessary needs were efficiently satisfied; and the unnatural and unnecessary needs—equivalent to Maslow's ego-esteem needs and associated with social competition—which were to be avoided because they involved long-range costs/pains/discomforts, in excess of the pleasure they could bring. Epicurus, as an early pleasure expert, was thus stewarding individuals away from the high-risk-high-cost enjoyment of exercising power over others in the public sphere. The Epicurean philosophy practically cultivated hedonic autonomy, making pleasure affordable for everybody in solitude or within a small social circle. In this sense, Epicurean pleasure was as "democratic" as the Roman circus[9] and games, which accounts for their joint popularity until the "dark" Middle Ages, when the Church drastically censored sensuous excesses in order to elevate the population to spiritual life and pleasures.

But the "addiction" to pleasures (as predicted by Epicurus), especially to those intense pleasures associated with violence, proved intractable. The story goes that Pope Innocent II, appalled by the violence of early tournaments where the distinction between mock and real warfare was minimal, banned that activity at the Council of Clermont in 1130. Alas, the attraction of the forbidden entertainment increased: Priests continued to flock to watch and, in 1471, a tournament was held in St. Peter's Square (Guttmann, 1998). Moreover, throughout the Middle Ages, the stories about the lives of saints contained graphic descriptions of suffering and misery (Cohen, 1982) that rivaled the grotesque brutality of popular art and paved the way for the 18th century gothic novels (Oliver, 1992). The 18th century was the time when the issue of violence enjoyment reemerged in full force in arts, philosophy, and politics.

The Enlightenment: The Sublime Outrage… Ad Libitum, Ad Nauseam

When Kant (1724–1804) reassessed the domain of aesthetics, he distinguished between an aesthetic of beauty (a pleasure of conformity between the stimulus and human capacities) and an aesthetic of the sublime (an anxious pleasure of conformity disruption, "an outrage of the imagination"[10]; Kant, 1790/1952, p. 91). The fact that the supreme authority on reason acknowledged/legitimated anxious and disruptive pleasures had a tremendous impact. The sublime as liberation from/defeat of reason became the hallmark of the Romantic and Baroque movements in art, and served as a mold for modern sensibility.

Kant remained a staunch classical rationalist, in spite of the sweeping cultural change he witnessed. In terms of pleasure theory, the major ideologist and propagandist of the change was Marquis de Sade (1740–1814), who practiced, literaturized, and "philosophized" (see *La Philosophie dans le boudoir,* 1795/1995) about the exclusive pursuit and maximization of sensuous pleasure. The

---

[9]For a discussion of the democratization of pleasure, see Zillmann, 2000b.

[10]The original meaning of *sublime* in Latin was "beyond the threshold," or "going over the edge" (Connor, 1992, p. 214). In the 19th century, the sublimis root put forth a new word, *subliminal,* meaning "beyond the threshold of conscious experience" (p. 214).

ingredients of Sade's recipe were sex, violence, and violation of social norms—nothing new under the sun after Ovid's Philomela story. Sade's innovations were of nuance rather than content: the programatic systematicity of his approach, the rationalization (rational enhancement) of sensuality, his propagandizing, and his overtly political/antiestablishment discourse. He attacked both traditional Christian checks on sensuous pleasure and the political concept of natural law en vogue at that time (Edmiston, 1995, p. 123, 133). Sade's goal was to empower individuals and get them to promote their personal interests (pleasure) against public interests (restrictions to pleasure).

Sade's personal implementation of his theory can be retrospectively regarded as an attempted natural experiment by a participant observer, as historic as Lenin's communism later on, but on a smaller and less disastrous scale. Sade's political stance was extreme, pushing toward complete eradication of social life. Once that objective/pleasure was achieved, the individuals would inevitably be left with the lesser pleasure (violation of social order removed) of consuming ad libitum and ad nauseam just bodies (of others and their own).

Although Sade has been regarded as an inconsequential philosopher, his work did make a strong and lasting impression and contribution to the repertoire of pleasure enhancement techniques. The "magic"/power of his prose comes from the complex orchestration of violent sex, iconoclastic philosophical thinking, aggressive political and educational strategies, and virulent rhetoric into a pleasure methodology and practice. In terms of effectiveness, Sade seems to have reached the uppermost limit afforded by the technology of his time. A more explosive combination could only have been achieved by adding to the mix the modern audiovisual media.

Our Blissful Time of Stress, Crises, Despair, and Dissolution

Have contemporary thinkers contributed anything really new? Lacan (1979) contested Freud's (1920/1989) conservative, homeostatic, pleasure principle and proposed a different concept of jouissance or desire, an insatiable drive toward unattainable limits (self-constructed stress). Barthes (1990) argued that the conservative homeostatic pleasure dwells on culture, and he endorsed bliss or jouissance, which he believed to be a self-generated crisis associated with unsettling historical, cultural, and psychological assumptions. According to Barthes, "the extreme *guarantees* [emphasis added] bliss: an average perversion quickly loads itself up with a play of subordinate finalities: prestige, ostentation, rivalry…." (pp. 51–52). Beside intervening subordinate finalities that tended to extend pleasure, Barthes' bliss involved a seemingly paradoxical feature of evanescent momentariness: *Bliss* was defined as the final and most intense stage of pleasure, the state between pleasure and its transcendence in anxiety and death, between the consolidation of the ego and its dissolution, "the site of loss, the seam, the cut, the deflation..., an edge" (p. 7). The intensity of the moment was due to experiencing pleasure *with* the enhancing/arousing anticipation of its imminent loss. The loss/termination of pleasure became t h emost important ingredient for maximizing pleasure. Thus we got to the point of knowingly, willingly, deliberately pleasuring ourselves with death. Barthes' theory of bliss can finally account for the gladiator's and the matador's "romance with death" (Guttmann, 1998, p. 24) and the macabre thrills of snuff pornography.[11]

This theoretical trend dislodged any relics of the Epicurean concept of end-state pleasure that might have endured in modern times and resurrected Aristotle's notion of process. But the present context is a more precipitous life, in which fleeting plumes of bliss brush past peaks of disaster. This is probably the most democratic of all environments of pleasure, the most affordable, with catastrophies at the tip of your fingers: live war newscasts to relish, the lunch-hour-car-crash thrill, the mall or school shooting extravaganza, which make up the nonstop fun of "cool" western life.

In another development, Lyotard (1988), in his post-modern aesthetic, redefined the sublime as the melancholy and despair "of never being able to present something within reality on the scale of the Idea" that "overrides the joy of being nonetheless called upon to do so" (p. 179). Prior to him, from antiquity to the present, pleasure has been a challenge for intelligence, which had to harness and exploit the senses in order to beat the level of natural, spontaneous, pleasure. The new spin Lyotard put on hedonism—designing one's pleasure(s), assuming leadership and authorship—brought with it a new problem: the gap between experience and ideation. Lyotard's grand Idea is, metaphorically speaking, spurring for a pleasure ride a beaten up plough horse, and feeding it fire to make it fly. Certainly, the pleasure achieved will be inferior to the pleasure imagined. As the enactment of pleasure in real life is bound to be disappointing, we are left mostly with our minds and "virtual" reality to enjoy.

Now that Barthes more or less prescribed the killing of pleasures (for better enjoyment), and Lyotard has shifted the responsibility (leadership) of

---

[11]"Snuff" pornography is a category of pornography that depicts the killing of women through sexual torture" (Jacob, 2000, p. 110).

pleasure making to cortical activities, the questions are, can the cortex fulfill these tasks, and are these tasks realistic?

SCIENTISTS: DEFYING THE GENETIC TYRANNY

"To Be an Animal Is to Be a Pleasure Seeker"[12]

The early brain scientists mapped the pleasure areas, "a variety of brain regions that cluster around the hub, or the brain stem" and form the limbic system, which functions as a "regulator of emotion" (Greenfield, 2000, p. 4). The fact that the limbic system is an older part of the brain indicates that the pleasure seeking function it performs has been important for survival (Campbell, 1973). Neuroscientists discovered quite early that the nerve fibers serving pleasure seeking are inextricably interwoven with fibers that control physiological functions that are indispensable for individual and species survival, such as heart beating, breathing, blood pressure, and sexual excitation (Campbell, 1973). Those functions activate pleasure networks and are in turn activated by neural constellations in the pleasure areas. Thus the limbic system (pleasure headquarters) emerged as a coordinator of the basic survival functions.

The fact that the limbic system is the highest part of the brain in the earliest vertebrates suggests that "it evolved as a more efficient organizer of pleasure seeking than our closest invertebrate ancestor possessed" (Campbell, 1973, p. 67). Efficiency comes from centralized control: "Other parts of the brain exist and carry out their tasks solely to contribute to the proper activation of the limbic system" (p. 67). Even the neocortex, the brain structure that supports advanced operations such as logic or time-and-space referencing, "survived and evolved because its intricate neuronal organization is superlatively efficient at keeping the limbic system active" (p. 68).

Hardwired for a Life of Pleasure

Besides anatomy, neuroscientists also addressed the physiology of pleasure in terms of electrical and chemical processes[13] (e.g., Greenfield,

---

[12]Campbell (1973, p. 67).

[13]Greenfield (2000) criticized the "gene for" and the "brain region for" (p. 13) fallacies, arguing that the pleasure-seeking behavior involves holistic functioning.

2000; Kahneman, Diener, & Schwarz, 1999). Campbell (1973) redefined pleasure in technical terms as "activation of the limbic areas." (p. 70). "In normal animals, including man, the pleasure areas deep inside the brain are activated when the sense organs on the periphery of the body are stimulated" (pp. 40–41). It is no coincidence that we speak of "*feeling* pleasure" (p. 65). Neurophysiological science thus confirms Aristotle's bodily pleasures.

The five senses are the interface between the environment and an individual's autonomic system, which is the part of the human brain that looks after basic survival and reproduction processes and ensures that these functions are performed "automatically" (unconsciously). The pleasure provided by the autonomic activity in general and sensorial activity in particular (i.e., the stimulation of neurons located in the pleasure areas) has survival value because it motivates us to stay connected to the world and adjust (respond in ways that minimize discomfort and maximize pleasure; Greenfield, 2000).

The autonomic system energizes and monitors two types of functions: routine maintenance processes, for which resource deployment is minimized, and processes that support emergency activities, for which resource deployment needs to be maximized (fight-or-flight response, sexual intercourse).

Autonomic activities surface in consciousness typically in relation to deprivation (pain in case of deficiency, and pleasure in case of remedied deficiency—for example, pleasure of movement after immobility, pleasure of breathing fresh air after stifling in a crowded room). But it is also possible to experience pleasure during energy-intensive activities. Examples mentioned in literature are, among others, "the ebullience of Battle of Britain pilots and of members of the German Luftwaffe" (Campbell, 1973, p. 198) and the "runner's high" (Kahneman, Diener, & Schwarz, 1999, p. xi). The role of pleasure in such situations is to supplement resource investment beyond the "automatic" deployment encoded for the base level of that function.

The pleasure seeker's advantages in using autonomic sources of stimulation are the "sure fire" (automatically generated response/pleasure) and the simple strategy for heightening such stimulations to the level of consciousness. Autonomic pleasure (associated with the five senses and basic activities such as eating, drinking, physical activity, sexual activity) can be enhanced by sequencing deprivation and excess, repeating the sequence, simultaneously applying the schema to several autonomic processes, and further synergizing by means of combinations with other nonautonomic activities/stimulations.

The additional pleasure does not come without costs, though: Both deprivation and excesses throw the neatly coordinated autonomic system out of balance and reduce its functional efficiency and/or effectiveness (cause resource dissipation/waste). If practiced long term, they may lead to physical exhaustion and illnesses. Fortunately, some natural protection mechanisms have evolved to balance human greed for pleasure and to promote homeostasis (system stability).

The most basic safety mechanism is adaptation, the decay of excitation at the level of peripheral receptors (Campbell, 1973). The pleasure seeker's strategies for circumventing adaptation are changing the sources of stimulation and searching for new sources. Each novel stimulus triggers fewer associations and is more readily displaced. The turnover rate of processing novel stimuli is faster, and that keeps a pleasure seeker bombarded by his or her senses, experiencing intense pleasure (Greenfield, 2000).

A second natural protection against stimulation excesses is hedonic reversal. At too high speed of change and excessive stimulus density, the processing capacity is overwhelmed and the hedonic quality of the experience is spontaneously reversed from pleasure to displeasure. "Pleasure shades into fear when the stimulation is just *too* fast and *too* novel" (Greenfield, 2000, p. 113).

One strategy for dealing with this problem is choosing sources of stimulation in such a way as to optimize arousal and thus maximize the hedonic balance. Zillmann's (1988; Bryant & Zillmann, 1984) mood-management theory and Apter's (1994) reversal theory of enjoyment of violence endorse the notion that pleasure is a curvilinear function of arousal, with displeasure occurring at too high or too low levels of stimulation.

Another strategy for avoiding hedonic reversal is sustaining pure pleasure (Greenfield, 2000) by adding a "protective frame" (Apter, 1994, p. 9) so that the pleasure seeker does not feel in immediate unavoidable personal danger. Examples of "protected" experiences are sports, which exploit environmental dangers and control risk primarily through equipment (e.g., skydiving with a parachute); games, which exploit dangers associated with personal interactions and control risk primarily through rules and equipment; and spectacles, which exploit all possible dangers and limit risk through environment artificiality (controllability) and the indirect (vicarious) nature of the experience that gives the spectator a choice between empathy and detachment.

A third natural protection against excessive stimulation is habituation, a "safety cognition" that develops through repeated stimulation experiences. If an unpleasant (potentially dangerous) stimulus has not involved aggravation (in terms of harmful effects) in prior experiences, then the brain will decide "not to pay attention" simply "because there is nothing to worry about" (Campbell, 1973, p. 73).

The pleasure seeker's strategy to overcome this natural protection is beating memory on its own ground by increasing stimulus intensity (which heightens arousal and strengthens the memory trace) and by repetition (which develops chronic accessibility). A typical example is that of a teenager playing the same music over and over again, and turning up the volume higher and higher: This keeps giving him or her pleasure, but it also prevents the neighbors from habituating. Escalation distinguishes this stimulation from the whistling of trains that cross the neighborhood, which nobody either enjoys or suffers from.

Your Self Is There to Pleasure You

A human being has about 10^6 genes that contain the "programmed" survival activity of the species. For activities that are not autonomic, a mechanism of choice (individual latitude) has developed in philogenesis to handle the increasing richness of pleasure opportunities historically produced by social life. Our choices are instrumented by a system of 10^{11} neurons with possibilities of connecting through 10^{15} synapses (Greenfield, 2000)—which gives us 10^{26} choice power.

The problem is that we can exercise choice (respond in nonautomatic ways) only in situations that we are conscious of. The more arousing a situation and the more frequently repeated, the more extensive is the constellation of neurons it activates in our brains, and the deeper our consciousness of it (Greenfield, 2000).

Consciousness as a *Readout.* Greenfield (2000) argued that consciousness is the necessary "means for synchronizing the appropriate readout from brain to body" (p. 177). She hypothesized that the elusive phenomenon of consciousness is served by peptides, the "molecules of emotion" that act as "intermediaries between net brain states (net neuron assembly size and turnover rate), the endocrine and immune systems, and the vital organs" (p. 179). According to Grossmann (1988), peptides "have evolved to antagonize excessive activity in the stress hormone axes" (p. 380). Based on neurophysiological advances in peptide research, Zillmann (1998a) speculated that during exposure to tragedy (a prolonged acutely stressful experience) we can expect that "pleasure-mediating peptides will be liberated, and that pleasure shall be the reward for empathic torment" (p. 8). But what is the purpose of this peptide-instrumented mechanism of high-stimulation screening?

Consciousness As the Forum of Choice. One value of brains is considered to be their ability to generate "appropriate and fast reactions to a fast-moving, ever-changing environment" (Greenfield, 2000, p. 48). "The less at the mercy of genes you are, the greater the repertoire of behavior, and thus the more choice at your disposal" (Greenfield, 2000, p. 49). Whereas some animals adapted to the changing environment by changing color, growing fur, developing wings, or strengthening jaws, humans evolved from primates by dramatically expanding their brain in the process of choosing the most appropriate behavioral responses.

The common denominator in the default hedonic choice is pleasure. Each activity has a hedonic component,[14] which means that the neural constellation activated during the experience of that activity includes neurons located in the pleasure areas. Neurons have the property of being irreversibly changed by any single activation. Their plasticity serves to store patterns of activation corresponding to an individual's successive experiences. Repeated activation through similar experiences builds meaning into our experience of the world by means of quasi-permanent connections among neurons (preferred pathways) that personalize our brain (Greenfield, 2000). This cell circuitry configured by personal experiences "is constantly updated as we live out each moment" (p. 13).

The most sophisticated part of memory is supported by the prefrontal cortex that individualizes a brain by means of time and space referencing, which is essential for an individual's history. The human prefrontal cortex is twice as large as that of a primate of our weight, although our "DNA is only 1 percent different" from a chimpanzee's (Greenfield, 2000, p. 45)—which points to the heavy use and importance of this part of the human brain. The contextualization of experiences makes possible the recognition and choice of situations (rather than isolated stimuli) that provide similar pleasures. Theoretically, this can serve both hedonic optimization and homeostasis. Practically, this linkage makes us prisoners of our gradually stabilizing (closing) universe of pleasures. Responsible for this unfortunate tendency is the natural decay of our memory (i.e., deactivation of unused links), which

---

[14]Zajonc (1980, 1997) and Bargh (1997) described strong experimental evidence that every stimulus evokes an effective evaluation, and that this evaluation can occur outside of awareness.

is an efficiency bias that pushes us toward extreme and easy (sensorial) sources of pleasure and makes us disregard other activities that have either lower hedonic potential or have higher hedonic potential but are more difficult to derive pleasure from.[15] Once a child has developed the habit of listening to heavy metal, he/she will have less desire to learn how to play the flute, and once a teenager has become interested in hard porn, he/she will find gender psychology books less attractive.

Yes, Pleasure Seeking Is Compulsive

In ordinary life, "when activation [of the pleasure areas] decreases, nerve impulses are sent to the motor centers that control the muscles involved in exploratory behavior, until the animal finds a new source of sensory stimulation and a new source of temporary pleasure. This scheme is to be regarded as the most fundamental and basic neural mechanism of behavior" (Campbell, 1973, pp. 76–77).

What happens when pleasure more intense than that naturally provided by ordinary life experiences becomes available? Experiments with intracranial self-stimulation revealed compulsive pleasure seeking behavior that preempts other activity. The findings led brain scientists to the conclusion that everything animals (including humans) do in their normal life, their entire behavior "is directed at evoking electrical activity in the pleasure areas of the brain" (Campbell, 1973, p. 66). It is preposterous, then, not only to blame people for making pleasures their main occupation in life, but also to decry their natural tendency to pursue more and more intense pleasures.

How Does Hedonic Escalation Happen?

A perennial sore point in aesthetics and in hedonic science has been the relation between pleasure and displeasure, positive and negative affect: Is this a single bipolar dimension, where factors that produce one kind of affect cancel the effects of factors that operate in the opposite direction? Or should we understand positive and negative affect as separate attributes of experience (Kahneman, Diener, & Schwarz, 1999)?

[15]"Difficult" pleasures are those that involve little pleasure and/or some pain in the early stages of building the neural constellations that would support those pleasures.

The Paradoxical Enjoyment of Violence: Tension, Pain, and Pleasure

Bousfield (1926/1999) proposed that pain is not a true antithesis of pleasure. "Pleasure appears to be in some measure proportional to the rate of fall of tension" (p. 28) and is therefore "a factor of time, as well as of tension" (p. 29)—which supports Freud's (1920/1989) theory that pain and pleasure depend on the quantity of excitation present in the psychic life and the amount of diminution or increase of tension in a given time. Bousfield (1926/1999) concurred that "the degree of unpleasant affect is relatively proportional to the degree of tension present" (p. 26) and further observed that "there is no loss of tension without tension having first being produced, and so there can be no pleasure without pain or potential pain having first being present, so finally, it may be there can be no love unless hate or potential hate has first existed" (pp. 88–89). Such convoluted elaborations do not essentially contradict Epicurus' belief that pleasure was the elimination of pain, although they support Aristotle's intuition that pleasure was not a result but a process. The Freud-Bousfield line of argument would justify us to make peace with arts and entertainments in general, admitting that they have to include pain and build up tension in order to provide pleasure.

Other contemporary theorists question the concept of pleasure as tension reduction based on findings that pleasure and pain appear to be mediated by different neurotransmitters, and approach and avoidance tendencies can occur simultaneously or in rapid alternation, generating internal conflict (Kahneman, Diener, & Schwarz, 1999). The model proposed as an alternative posits that affective evaluation is bivalent rather than bipolar (Cacioppo & Berntson, 1994; Ito & Cacioppo, 1999). In an effort at reconciliation, Lang (1995) argued that the two models are not necessarily exclusive, and a bivalent system can yield a bipolar structure if the separate mechanisms that mediate Good and Bad are reciprocally innervated and mutually inhibitory, or if the relevant output of the system is the difference between the levels of activity of the two mechanisms. Davidson (1992) suggested that the brain may compute both the sum and the difference of the levels of activity in the separate systems that mediate positive and negative affect, and proposed that the GB (good/bad) value corresponds to the difference, and the emotional arousal corresponds to the summed activity in the two systems—which would account for forms of entertainment that are felt to be exciting without being perceived as "good."

A Nonparadoxical View of Violence Enjoyment

The analytic practice in empirical research (i.e., the habit of looking for factors and decomposing them into variables) is consistent with the older cognitive-neoassociationistic model of semantic memory (spreading activation; Collins & Loftus, 1975), the more recent connectionist notion of parallel processing (e.g., McClelland, Rumelhart, & the PDP Research Group, 1986), and the newer notion of neural constellations (Greenfield, 2000). This convergence between theory and research methodology comes from a general assumption that neural networks are activated by different sensorial inputs that mobilize different transmitters. The constellation approach pictures activated neural networks criss-crossing simultaneously and/or successively in the same pleasure "areas" but having different configurations and different ramifications beyond those pleasure areas. The nonoverlapping parts of such constellations make them "feel" (show in our consciousness as) qualitatively different, although they share/use some pleasure (and/or pain) neurons that make them all feel good (and/or bad). The constellation model can accommodate findings of paradoxical feelings of pain-and-pleasure and may even account for the associate feeling of "tension" as concomitant activation through different transmitters that connect (pull/push) the neurons in the pleasure areas in different directions, which burdens/stresses their functioning.

Basic Models of Enjoyment Escalation

Under the assumption of parallel activation of neural constellations that cross in the pain/pleasure areas, let us now consider an isolated experience of simultaneous feelings of pain and pleasure. A trivial pain will attenuate and, if not completely eliminated from consciousness, will tend to be habituated. If the pain is nontrivial, it will trigger what has traditionally been called the instinct for self-preservation—which Bousfield (1926/1999) claimed to be fear and avoidance of pain inculcated by "social heredity" (p. 10). The outcome will be avoidance behavior that will momentarily prevail over our general tendency to pursue pleasure. Thus the activity that caused simultaneous pleasure and nontrivial pain will be discontinued.

I. Repetition: Habituation. If the same activity is repeated, though, even nontrivial pain will tend to be habituated if it does not aggravate or develop alarming effects. The brain will cease to pay attention to those components of the stimulation that cause stable pain. The neural constellation corresponding to the experience of that activity will lose pain connections, which will shift the individual's behavioral priority away from self-preservation toward pleasure maximization ("liberating" him/her for enjoyment). This model would cover experiences such as football players' insensitivity to severe bodily injuries while happily engaged in their games, or regular moviegoers' enjoyment of at least the aesthetic qualities of violent or otherwise unpleasant movies.

One problem associated with this type of practices is the amount of harm (body damage and loss or establishment of certain neural pathways) incurred by the individual without being aware (i.e., eliminated from his/her consciousness through habituation). Another problem is the projection of the individual's personal harm (incurred for pleasure) onto the social structure he/she belongs to, through modified perception, values, and ultimately behavior. The media effects literature is replete with examples of harms produced at both the individual and the social levels by consumption of VHM (e.g., Berkowitz, 1964, 1974; Berkowitz & Rawlings, 1963; Tamborini, Zillmann, & Bryant, 1984; Weaver & Wakshlag, 1986) and pornography (e.g., Bryant & Zillmann, 2001; Donnerstein, 1980a, 1980b, 1983, 1984; Donnerstein & Linz, 1986; Donnerstein, Linz, & Penrod, 1987; Donnerstein & Malamuth, 1983; Zillmann, 1989; Zillmann & Bryant, 1982, 1984; Zillmann & Weaver, 1989).

II. Repetition: Imagination. A more sophisticated exploitation of habituation for the purpose of pleasure maximization is that in which pleasure is not copresent in reality but merely imagined, or evoked from memory. Such imagination may naturally develop through repetition of specific sequences of painful and pleasurable activities: During the unpleasant activity, the brain may anticipate the subsequent pleasure expected to follow. This "fore-pleasure" (Bousfield, 1926/1999, p. 84) is enjoyed, and the pain of the current activity is habituated. This model would cover pleasures associated with "perverse" practices such as sadomasochism.

The problems associated with these practices are more serious. At the individual level, the activation of neural pathways through imagination mobilizes top–down control (Hobson, 1994) by the cortex. Cortical control is hedonically more efficient than the haphazard trial-and-error pattern underlying Type I practices because it achieves coordination among brain and body activities and tends to produce a coherent and stable set of hedonic behaviors at the individual level.

On the other hand, Type II includes stable patterns of behavior activities that are naturally avoided and socially discouraged because they consistently cause nontrivial harm (and no pleasure). The adopters tend to put pressure on the social system to accept such behaviors (remove restrictions and sanctions).

III. Socialization: Learning. A different pattern of hedonic behaviors, originally described for drug consumption, covers a class of activities that combine initial lack of pleasure with subsequent copresence of pain and pleasure. Even repeated experiences of such activities by individuals in isolation would have a negative hedonic balance that would discourage adoption. But the problem is, individuals do not live in isolation.

Hirsch, Conforti, and Graney (1998) recently revamped Becker's (1953) three-stage process theory of drug consumption, applicable to the whole class. The theory posits that in order for individuals to experience pleasure, they need to develop a conception of the means (drug, sexual practice, etc.) as a source of pleasure. The construction of that concept (the means–pleasure neural linkage in memory) involves learning the technique (in the case of drugs, quantities, administration procedures), experiencing and recognizing the effects, and learning to enjoy the effects (i.e., habituating to initially unpleasant feelings and anticipating subsequent pleasures). This learning process requires initiation by other, more "advanced," practitioners and encouragement to overcome the pain during the habituation process.

This type of practice is the most aggressive. At the individual level, it may be very harmful physically to the extent it involves addictive noxious stimuli. As learning is conducted in a social context, abundant opportunities for interpersonal pressure and social norm pressure occur. If the practice is successful and very intense sensorial stimulation is achieved, consciousness is flooded with fleeting "pure pleasures" (Greenfield, 2000, p. 116), and the high turnover of small neural constellations precludes the development of links to higher levels of the brain that support contextualization and control functions. The very simple and standard neural activation will make group members feel more "alike" and "together," which will tend to materialize in uncontrolled herd behavior. The fact that your pals are there to pleasure you is likely to prove even more pernicious than the fact that your self is there to pleasure you.

At the social level, cohesive groups of pleasure seekers develop that tend to proselytize and to propagandize for their preferences. Large groups come to develop market and political power and begin to shape social life from values to consumption patterns and distribution of wealth. This is far more serious than having a beer and shaking to the beating of drums under flashing lights.

A WINDOW OF OPPORTUNITY

We are faced with synergistic effects of the current hedonic practices. These effects have started to cross the traditional divide between the individual and the social levels of effects: Teenagers listen to Marilyn Manson singing "no time to discriminate, hate every motherf**er that's in your way" (Jipping, 2001, p. 62), then play Mortal Combat, then go out in the street and shoot others, and people blame this new pattern of behaviors on the media. We may choose to deal with the telepresence revolution in entertainment (see Tamborini, 2000) in the same old way, making it another insular and obsessive concern, to succeed VHM and hardcore porn. But we have an alternative: conducting research on aggregate hedonic behaviors. This would be an opportunity to shape research for socially strategic pleasure seeking. We may start by posing research questions in Professor Zillmann's (1998b) sociopsychological terms: What does our fascination with violence do to us and to our society?

REFERENCES

Anderson, E. (2001). *Hedonism and the happy life: The Epicurean theory of pleasure.* Retrieved March 13, 2001, from http://www.epicureans.org/intro.htm

Apter, M. J. (1994, October). *Why we enjoy media violence: A reversal theory approach.* Paper presented at the International Conference on Violence in the Media, St. John's University, New York, NY.

Aristotle. (1999). *Poetics.* Cambridge, MA: Harvard University Press.

Bargh, J. A. (1997). The automaticity of everyday life. In R. S. Wyer, Jr. (Ed.), *Advances in social cognition* (Vol. 10). Mahwah, NJ: Lawrence Erlbaum Associates.

Barthes, R. (1990). *The pleasures of the text* (R. Miller, Trans.). Oxford, UK: Blackwell.

Becker, H. S. (1953). Becoming a marijuana user. *American Journal of Sociology, 59,* 235–242.

Berkowitz, L. (1964). The effects of observing violence. *Scientific American, 210*(2), 35–41.

Berkowitz, L. (1974). Some determinants of impulsive aggression: The role of mediated associations with reinforcements for aggression. *Psychological Review, 81,* 165–176.

Berkowitz, L., & Rawlings, E. (1963). Effects of film violence on inhibitions against subsequent aggression. *Journal of Abnormal and Social Psychology, 66,* 405–412.

Bok, S. (1998). *Mayhem: Violence as public entertainment.* Reading, MA: Merloyd Lawrence & Addison-Wesley.

Bousfield, P. (1999). *Pleasure and pain: A theory of the energic foundation of feeling.* London: Routledge. (Original work published 1926)

Bryant, J., & Zillmann, D. (1984). Using television to alleviate boredom and stress: Selective exposure as a function of induced excitational states. *Journal of Broadcasting, 28,* 1–20.

Bryant, J., & Zillmann, D. (2001). Pornography, models of (effects on sexual deviancy). In C. D. Bryant (Ed.), *Encyclopedia of criminology and deviant behavior* (Vol. 3, pp. 241–244). Oxford, UK: Brunner/ Routledge.

Cacioppo, J. T., & Berntson, G. G. (1994). Relationships between attitudes and evaluative space: A critical review with emphasis on the separability of positive and negative substrates. *Psychological Bulletin, 115,* 401–423.

Campbell, H. J. (1973). *The pleasure areas: A new theory of behavior.* New York: Delacorte.

Cohen, D. (1982). *Horror in the movies.* New York: Clarion Books.

Collins, A. M., & Loftus, E. F. (1975). A spreading-activation theory of semantic processing. *Psychological Review, 82,* 407–428.

Connor, S. (1992). Aesthetics, pleasure and value. In S. Reagan (Ed.), *The politics of pleasure: Aesthetics and cultural theory* (pp. 203–220). Buckingham, UK: Open University Press.

Davidson, R. J. (1992). Anterior cerebral asymmetry and the nature of emotion. *Brain and Cognition, 6,* 245–268.

Davis, M. (1990). *City of quartz: Excavating the future of Los Angeles.* New York: Verso.

Donnerstein, E. (1980a). Aggressive erotica and violence against women. *Journal of Personality and Social Psychology, 39,* 269–277.

Donnerstein, E. (1980b). Pornography and violence against women: Experimental studies. *Annals of the New York Academy of Sciences, 347,* 277–288.

Donnerstein, E. (1983). Erotica and human aggression. In R. G. Geen & E. Donnerstein (Eds.), *Aggression: Theoretical and empirical reviews* (Vol. 2, pp. 127–154). New York: Academic.

Donnerstein, E. (1984). Pornography: Its effect on violence against women. In N. M. Malamuth & E. Donnerstein (Eds.), *Pornography and sexual aggression* (pp. 53–81). Orlando, FL: Academic.

Donnerstein, E., & Linz, D. G. (1986). Mass media sexual violence and male viewers: Current theory and research. *American Behavioral Scientist, 29,* 601–618.

Donnerstein, E., Linz, D., & Penrod, S. (1987). *The question of pornography: Research findings and policy implications*. New York: Free Press.

Donnerstein, E., & Malamuth, N. (1983). Pornography: Its consequences on the observer. In L. Schlesinger & E. Revitch (Eds.), *Sexual dynamics of anti-social behavior* (pp. 31–50). Springfield, IL: C. C. Thomas.

Edmiston, W. F. (1995). Nature, sodomy, and semantics in Sade's *La Philosophie dans le boudoir.* In C. H. Hay & S. M. Conger (Eds.), *Studies in eighteenth-century culture* (Vol. 24, pp. 121–136). Baltimore, MD: John Hopkins University Press.

Epicurus. (1993). *The essential Epicurus: Letters, principal doctrines, Vatican sayings, and fragments* (E. O'Connor, Trans.). Buffalo, NY: Prometheus.

Frau-Meigs, D., & Jehel, S. (1997). *Les ecrans de la violence: Enjeux economiques et responsabilites sociales* [Screens of violence: Economic interests and social responsibilities]. Paris: Economica.

Freud, S. (1933). *New introductory lectures on psycho-analysis.* New York: Norton.

Freud, S. (1989). *Beyond the pleasure principle.* New York: Norton. (Original work published 1920)

Geen, R. G., & Quanty, M. B. (1977). The catharsis of aggression: En evaluation of a hypothesis. In L. Berkowitz (Ed.), *Advances in experimental social psychology* (Vol. 10, pp. 1–37). New York: Academic.

Gerbner, G., Gross, L., Morgan, M., & Signorielli, N. (1980). The "mainstreaming" of America: Violence profile no. 11. *Journal of Communication, 30,* 10–29.

Girard, R. (1972). *La violence et le sacre* [Violence and the sacred]. Paris: Grasset.

Greenfield, S. (2000). *The private life of the brain: Emotions, consciousness, and the secret of the self.* New York: Wiley.

Grossman, A. (1988). Opioids and stress in man. *Journal of Endocrinology, 119,* 377–381.

Guttmann, A. (1998). The appeal of violent sports. In J. Goldstein (Ed.), *Why we watch: The attractions of violent entertainment* (pp. 179–211). New York: Oxford University Press.

Harris, R. J. (1994). The impact of sexually explicit media. In J. Bryant & D. Zillmann (Eds.), *Media effects: Advances in theory and research* (pp. 247–272). Hillsdale, NJ: Lawrence Erlbaum Associates.

Harris, R. J., & Scott, C. L. (2002). Effects of sex in the media. In J. Bryant & D. Zillmann (Eds.), *Media effects: Advances in theory and research* (2nd ed., pp. 307–333). Hillsdale, NJ: Lawrence Erlbaum Associates.

Hirsch, M. L., Conforti, R. W. & Graney, C. J. (1998). The use of marijuana for pleasure: A replication of Howard S. Becker's study of marijuana use. In J. A Inciardi & K. McElrath (Eds.), *The American drug scene: An anthology* (2nd ed., pp. 27–35). Los Angeles, CA: Roxbury.

Hobson, J. A. (1994). *The chemistry of conscious states: How the brain changes its mind.* New York: Little, Brown & Co.

Ito, T. A., & Cacioppo, J. T. (1999). The psychophysiology of utility appraisals. In D. Kahneman, E. Diener, & H. Schwarz (Eds.), *Well-being: The foundations of hedonic psychology* (pp. 470–488). New York: Sage.

Jacob, K. K. (2000). Crime without punishment: Pornography in a rape culture. In J. Gold & S. Villari (Eds.), *Just sex: Students rewrite the rules on sex, violence, activism, and equality* (pp. 105–120). Lanham, MD: Rowman & Littlefield.

Jipping, T. L. (2001). Popular music contributes to teenage violence. In J. D. Torr (Ed.), *Violence in the media* (Current Controversies Series; pp. 61–66). San Diego, CA: Greenhaven.

Juvenal, D. J. (1991). *The satires* (N. Rudd, Trans.). Oxford, England: Clarendon.

Kahneman, D., Diener, E., & Schwarz, H. (Eds.). (1999). *Well-being: The foundations of hedonic psychology* (pp. 355–373). New York: Sage.

Kant, I. (1952). *The critique of judgment* (J. C. Meredith, Trans.). Oxford, England: Clarendon. (Original work published 1790)

Kraus, R. (1971). *Recreation and leisure in modern society.* New York: Appleton-Century-Crofts.

Lacan, J. (1979). *The four fundamental concepts of psycho-analysis* (A. Sheridan, Trans.). Harmondsworth, UK: Penguin.

Lang, P. (1995). The emotion probe: Studies of motivation and attention. *American Psychologist, 50,* 372–385.

Lyotard, J.-F. (1984). *The postmodern condition: A report on knowledge* (G. Bennington & B. Massumi, Trans.). Manchester, UK: Manchester University Press.

Lyotard, J.-F. (1988). *Jean-Francois Lyotard: Réécrire la modernité* [Rewriting modernity]. Lille: Les Cahiers de Philosophie.

Maslow, A. (1943). A theory of human motivation. *Psychological Review, 50,* 370–396.

McClelland, J. L., Rumelhart, D. E., & the PDP Research Group. (Eds.). (1986). *Parallel distributed processing: Explorations in the microstructure of cognition: Vol. 2. Psychological and biological models.* Cambridge, MA: MIT.

Nietzsche, F. (1956). *The birth of tragedy: The genealogy of morals* (F. Golffing, Trans.). Garden City, NY: Doubleday. (Original work published 1887)

Nietzsche, F. (1966). *Beyond good and evil: Prelude to a philosophy of the future* (W. Kaufmann, Trans.). New York: Vintage. (Original work published 1886)

Oliver, M. B. (1992). Adolescents' enjoyment of graphic horror: Effects of viewers' attitudes and portrayals of victim. *Dissertation Abstracts International, 53,* 10A.

Ovid. (2001). *The metamorphoses of Ovid* (M. Simpson, Trans.). Amherst, MA: University of Massachusetts.

Plato. (1984). Plato's Apology of Socrates. In T. G. West & G. S. West (Eds.), *Plato and Aristophanes: Four texts on Socrates: Plato's Euthyphro, Apology, and Crito and Aristophanes' Clouds* (pp. 63–97). Ithaca, NY: Cornell University Press.

Sade, D. A. F., Marquis de (1995). *La philosophie dans le boudoir, ou les instituteurs immoraux* [Philosophy in the bedroom, or the immoral teacher]. Paris: Gallimard. (Original work published 1795)

Segal, C. (1993). Philomela's web and the pleasures of the text: Reader and violence in the Metamorphoses of Ovid. In I. J. F. DeJong & J. P. Sullivan (Eds.), *Modern critical theory and classical literature* (pp. 257–280). Leiden, The Netherlands: Brill.

Sparks, G. G., & Sparks, C. W. (2000). Violence, mayhem, and horror. In D. Zillmann & P. Vorderer (Eds.), *Media entertainment: The psychology of its appeal* (pp. 73–91). Mahwah, NJ: Lawrence Erlbaum Associates.

Tamborini, R. (2000, November). *The experience of telepresence in violent video games.* Paper presented at the 8th annual convention of the National Communication Association, Seattle, WA.

Tamborini, R., Stiff, J., & Zillmann, D. (1987). Preference for graphic horror featuring male versus female victimization: Personality and past film viewing experiences. *Human Communication Research, 13,* 529–552.

Tamborini, R., Zillmann, D., & Bryant, J. (1984). Fear and victimization: Exposure to television and perceptions of crime and fear. In R. N. Bostrum (Ed.), *Communication Yearbook 8* (pp. 492–513). Beverly Hills, CA: Sage.

Urmson, J. O. (1968). Aristotle on pleasure. In J. M. E. Moravcsik (Ed.), *Aristotle: A collection of critical essays* (pp. 323–333). Notre Dame, IN: University of Notre Dame Press.

Weaver, J., & Wakshlag, J. (1986). Perceived vulnerability to crime, criminal victimization experience, and television viewing. *Journal of Broadcasting & Electronic Media, 30,* 141–158.

Zajonc, R. B. (1980). Feeling and thinking: Preferences need no inferences. *American Psychologist, 35,* 151–175.

Zajonc, R. B. (1997). Emotions. In D. T. Gilbert, S. T. Fiske, & G. Lindzey (Eds.), *Handbook of social psychology* (4th ed., pp. 591–632). New York: Oxford University Press.

Zillmann, D. (1971). Excitation transfer in communication-mediated aggressive behavior. *Journal of Experimental Social Psychology, 7,* 419–434.

Zillmann, D. (1979). *Hostility and aggression.* Hillsdale, NJ: Lawrence Erlbaum Associates.

Zillmann, D. (1980). Anatomy of suspense. In P. Tannenbaum (Ed.), *The entertainment functions of television* (pp. 133–163). Hillsdale, NJ: Lawrence Erlbaum Associates.

Zillmann, D. (1983). Transfer of excitation in emotional behavior. In J. T. Cacioppo & R. E. Petty (Eds.), *Social psychophysiology: A sourcebook* (pp. 215–240). New York: Guilford.

Zillmann, D. (1985). The experimental exploration of gratifications from media entertainment. In K. E. Rosengren, L. A. Wenner, & P. Palmgreen (Eds.), *Media gratifications research: Current perspectives* (pp. 225–239). Beverly Hills, CA: Sage.

Zillmann, D. (1988). Mood management: Using entertainment to full advantage. In L. Donohew, H. E. Sypher, & E. T. Higgins (Eds.), *Communication, social cognition, and affect* (pp. 147–171). Hillsdale, NJ: Lawrence Erlbaum Associates.

Zillmann, D. (1989). Effects of prolonged consumption of pornography. In D. Zillmann & J. Bryant (Eds.), *Pornography: Research advances and policy considerations* (pp. 127–157). Hillsdale, NJ: Lawrence Erlbaum Associates.

Zillmann, D. (1991). Empathy: Affect from bearing witness to the emotions of others. In J. Bryant & D. Zillmann (Eds.) *Responding to the screen: Reception and reaction processes* (pp. 135–167). Hillsdale, NJ: Lawrence Erlbaum Associates.

Zillmann, D. (1994). Mechanisms of emotional involvement with drama. *Poetics, 23,* 33–51.

Zillmann, D. (1998a). Does the tragic drama have redeeming value? *Spiel, 17*(1), 4–14.

Zillmann, D. (1998b). The psychology of the appeal of portrayals of violence. In J. Goldstein (Ed.), *Why we watch: The attractions of violent entertainment* (pp. 179–211). New York: Oxford University Press.

Zillmann, D. (1999). Exemplification theory: Judging the whole by some of its parts. *Media Psychology, 1,* 69–94.

Zillmann, D. (2000a). Basal morality in drama appreciation. In I. Bondebjerg (Ed.), *Moving images, culture and the mind* (pp. 53–63). Luton, UK: University of Luton Press.

Zillmann, D. (2000b). The coming of media entertainment. In D. Zillmann & P. Vorderer (Eds.), *Media entertainment: The psychology of its appeal* (pp. 1–20). Mahwah, NJ: Lawrence Erlbaum Associates.

Zillmann, D., & Bryant, J. (1974). Effect of residual excitation on the emotional response to provocation and delayed aggressive behavior. *Journal of Personality and Social Psychology, 30,* 782–791.

Zillmann, D., & Bryant, J. (1975). Viewer's moral sanction of retribution in the appreciation of dramatic representations. *Journal of Experimental Social Psychology, 11,* 572–582.

Zillmann, D., & Bryant, J. (1982). Pornography, sexual callousness, and the trivialization of rape. *Journal of Communication, 32*(4), 10–21.

Zillmann, D., & Bryant, J. (1984). Effects of massive exposure to pornography. In N. M. Malamuth & E. Donnerstein (Eds.), *Pornography and sexual aggression* (pp. 115–138). Orlando, FL: Academic.

Zillmann, D., & Cantor, J. R. (1977). Affective responses to the emotions of a protagonist. *Journal of Experimental Social Psychology, 13,* 155–165.

Zillmann, D., & Gibson, R. (1996). Evolution of the horror genre. In J. Weaver & R. Tamborini (Eds.), *Horror films: Current research in audience preferences and reactions* (pp. 15–31). Mahwah, NJ: Lawrence Erlbaum Associates.

Zillmann, D., & Weaver, J. B. (1989). Pornography and men's sexual callousness toward women. In D. Zillmann & J. Bryant (Eds.), *Pornography: Research advances and policy considerations* (pp. 95–125). Hillsdale, NJ: Lawrence Erlbaum Associates.

Zillmann, D., & Weaver, J. B. (1996). Gender socialization theory of horror. In J. B. Weaver & R. Tamborini (Eds.), *Horror films: Current research in audience preferences and reactions* (pp. 81–101). Mahwah, NJ: Lawrence Erlbaum Associates.

20

Fitness and Excitation

Kristen Harrison
University of Michigan

> Paul, age 52, retired military officer, sits behind the wheel of his car in stop-and-go traffic. He checks his watch every few minutes; each minute that passes adds to his frustration. He will be late again, thanks to his doctor and her inefficient waiting room. His belly pushes uncomfortably against the steering wheel as he pops one of the blood pressure control pills his doctor prescribed. He has no water and nearly chokes getting the pill down, which sends him into a panic. He will surely lose his mind if he cannot get out of this traffic jam. Finally, the cars ahead begin to move; relieved, Paul creeps forward behind them. A few minutes later, a truck, blaring irritating pop music, pulls by on the shoulder and cuts ahead of Paul, stopping his progress. Paul's heart rate leaps up again. This is the last straw. Paul reaches into the backseat and grabs the heaviest thing he can find, an iron jack. Stepping out of his car, veins pulsating in his head, Paul can think of nothing but teaching the truck's driver a lesson…

In an age marked by long commutes, suburban overcrowding, and road rage, this scene is all too familiar. It does not take a psychic to predict that Paul's actions will create more problems than they solve, yet "road ragers" like Paul rarely seem to think about the outcome of their actions, so consumed are they with what they are feeling at the moment. Popular explanations of the causes of road rage seem to center on one factor, layered again and again upon itself: stress, stress, and more stress. In Paul's case, the stress of being forced to wait at his doctor's office is followed by the stress of learning he must take medicine for his high blood pressure. Added to this are the stressors of being forced to wait in traffic, the clock's continuous reminder of his lateness, his discomfort of being too plump for his car seat, and the trauma of nearly choking. By the time the truck appears on the scene, Paul has decided he has been provoked enough.

The propositions of excitation transfer (Zillmann, 1996) neatly explain why Paul's stress continues to build. His arousal is not permitted to return to baseline before another provocation increases it. Moreover, each provocation is annoying enough in its own right that misattribution is likely to occur. In other words, Paul is probably not thinking that his extreme excitatory response to the other driver's rudeness is actually the sum of his excitatory responses to checking his watch, choking, hearing the irritating music, and being cut off by the other driver; all he can think about at this point is being cut off, and the extremity of his excitatory response seems, to Paul, to warrant extreme measures of retribution.

Yet this description of Paul's arousal trajectory does little to explain why Paul eventually resorts to violence, or whether another person in Paul's place would have reacted the same way. Indeed, individual differences in patterns of road rage suggest that certain people are at higher risk than others for giving in to this destructive pattern of behavior. Harding, Morgan, Indermaur, Ferrante, and Blagg (1998) examined the characteristics of Western Australian road ragers between 1991 and 1995 and reported that the groups at high risk of committing street violence (e.g., young men and Aboriginals) against strangers were actually at reduced risk of committing road rage violence. In contrast, groups at low risk of committing street violence (older men) were more likely to commit road rage violence. The authors reasoned that this pattern derived from older men's tendency to spend more time on the road. Yet there is another reason, unexplored in that study, why older men may be at greater risk for aggressive behavior linked to built-up, undecayed aggravation: Their poorer fitness impedes their ability to recover from it before another provocation drives them over the edge.

Zillmann (1978, 1983; 1996, p. 250) advanced the following propositions to describe the conditions under which transfer of excitation would occur, how it would occur, and, most importantly for the purposes of this essay, how it would differ between individuals based on their fitness level:

> Proposition 1. Given a situation in which (a) individuals respond to emotion-inducing stimuli and assess their responses, (b) levels of sympathetic excitation are still elevated from prior, potentially unrelated stimulation, and (c) individuals are not provided with obtrusive inter- and/or exteroceptive cues that unambiguously link their excitatory state to prior stimulation, residues of excitation from prior stimulation will inseparably combine with the excitatory reaction to the present stimuli and thereby intensify both emotional behavior and emotional experience.

Proposition 2. Emotional behavior and/or emotional experience will be enhanced in proportion to the magnitude of transferred residual excitation.

Proposition 3. Both the period of time during which transfer can occur and the magnitude of residues for transfer are a function of (a) the magnitude of the preceding excitatory reaction and/or (b) the rate of recovery from the associated excitatory state.

Proposition 4. Individuals' potential for transfer is (a) proportional to their excitatory responsiveness and (b) inversely proportional to their proficiency to recover from excitatory states.

Our sample case of Paul illustrates the first three propositions well. Paul's arousal level continues to climb because he experiences one unrelated provocation after another and fails to acknowledge that his extreme irritation at the other driver's carelessness is all out of proportion to the other driver's crime. So many minor provocations have occurred, moreover, that by the time Paul is cut off by the truck, he is extremely agitated; his arousal has been building since his visit to the doctor's office, over an hour ago. Clearly, the few minutes of relief Paul experienced once the traffic started moving again was not enough time for him to recover before the truck's driver cut him off, but why was this time span insufficient? Proposition 4 provides the answer: Paul's potential for transfer is not only a function of his excitatory responsiveness but also an inverse function of his proficiency to recover. In other words, Paul appears to be more easily agitated and slower to recover than others. Could Paul's poor cardiorespiratory fitness have anything to do with his easy-to-agitate, slow-to-recover demeanor? Might a fitter man have experienced less excitation and recovered from it more quickly, thus possibly avoiding a violent altercation at the end? According to Zillmann and colleagues, the answer is yes.

Figure 20.1 (adapted from Zillmann, 1979, p. 345) shows the excitation and time of recovery trajectories for three hypothetical individuals, one of high fitness, one of intermediate fitness, and one of low fitness. For the sake of illustration, let us pretend that the innermost diagonal line represents the trajectory of a highly fit individual, say, Michael. The middle diagonal line represents a moderately fit individual, say, Dolf. The outermost diagonal line represents our sample case, Paul. When all three of these men are aroused by some environmental provocation at Time 0, we expect to observe the greatest increase in cardiorespiratory excitation in Paul, a moderate increase in Dolf, and a minor increase in Michael. If all three men are allowed to relax so that their excitation has sufficient time to decay, we find that Michael's time of recovery is the shortest. At Time 1 (represented by the vertical line marked 1 in the illustration), all three men are still experiencing some residual excitation. At Time 2, though, Michael has returned to baseline, whereas Dolf and Paul are still measurably aroused. At Time 3, Dolf has returned to baseline, and Paul is the only one left with residual arousal. The least fit man experiences the greatest increase in arousal and the slowest recovery time.

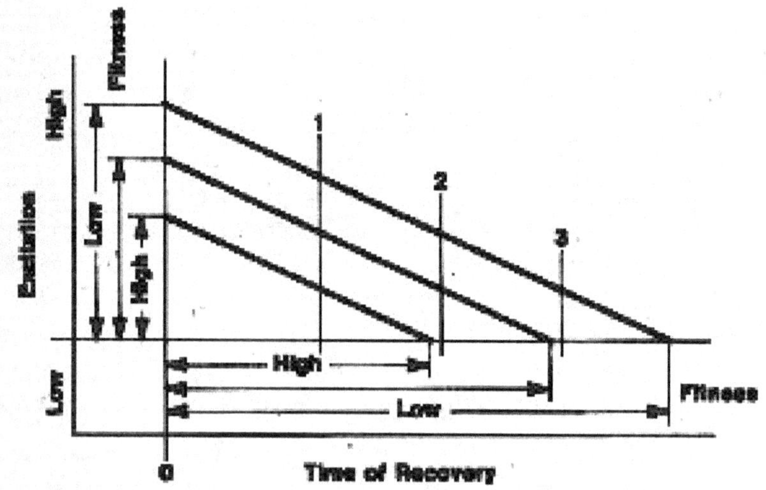

Fig. 20.1. Illustration of the hypothesized inverse relationship between cardiovascular fitness and the propensity for excitation transfer. *Note.* As shown in the simplified decay gradients, the excitatory reaction to a particular stimulus (Time 0) and the time of recovery from that reaction decrease as cardiovascular fitness increases. At Time 1, residual excitation for transfer exists in all fitness conditions in differing amounts. At Time 2, recovery to basal levels of excitation is complete for high fitness, but the propensity for transfer is maintained, to different degrees, for intermediate and low fitness. At Time 3, the propensity for transfer is maintained only for low fitness. From Zillmann (1979). Copyright © 1979 by Lawrence Erlbaum Associates. Reprinted with permission.

LOOKING BACK

Figure 20.1 nicely illustrates Zillmann's (1978, 1983, 1996) theoretical Proposition 4, but is there any empirical research in support of this proposition? Again, the answer is yes. In 1974, Zillmann, Johnson, and Day (1974a, 1974b) conducted two experiments to test whether individual differences in proficiency to recover from arousal would moderate the effects of excitation transfer on aggressive behavior. In the first experiment (Zillmann et al., 1974a), the authors asked a sample of 60 male undergraduates to pedal strenuously on a stationary bicycle for one and a half minutes while viewing various (nonaggressive) slides. After they had finished pedaling, participants rested for another 8 minutes while continuing to view slides. The students' proficiency to recover from sympathetic arousal was assessed by measuring their systolic blood pressure 6 minutes after exertion. At this point, the authors reasoned, between-subjects variability in residual arousal should be at its greatest, and the students should no longer be thinking about the bicycle-riding (rather than the content of the slides) as the source of their residual arousal. Based on the students' residual arousal levels at the 6-minute mark, the authors then placed them in one of three fitness categories created by blocking the sample into thirds, representing high, medium, and low recovery proficiency.

One to two weeks later, the students went on to participate in the main experiment, where they were placed in a teaching situation in which they had to administer shocks to a (bogus) learner each time the learner made an error. Participants were then aggressively provoked by the learner, who administered painful shocks back to them during an opinion-exchange session. Immediately afterward, half of the research participants were assigned to sit still for 6 minutes, then to ride a stationary bicycle for one and a half minutes (the "no decay" condition); the other half were assigned to ride the stationary bicycle first, then sit still for 6 minutes (the "partial decay" condition). Both groups viewed a series of slides while riding and sitting. Afterward, the students engaged in a rematch with their learners, in which they were once again afforded the opportunity to shock the learners for errors. Zillmann and colleagues expected that participants in the no-decay condition could easily attribute their residual arousal to their recent physical exertion, and thus would not display significant excitation-transfer effects in the form of increased aggressive behavior (i.e., more intense shocks) toward their research partners. Moreover, because all participants in the no-decay condition would still have yet to recover from their exertion, the authors expected little difference in excitation-transfer effects between high-, medium-, and low-fitness participants. This is, indeed, what they found: In the no-decay condition, the increase in intensity of shocks given to learners during the second teaching situation (after provocation) was negligible for all three groups: On a scale of 1 to 10, the change for high-fitness participants was 0.69, for medium-fitness participants, 0.62, and for low-fitness participants, 0.43. These means did not differ significantly from one another.

In the partial-decay condition, however, participants were expected to display marked excitation-transfer effects, as the young men in this condition should have had fewer cues linking their residual arousal to their previous exertion. Moreover, because they would have had 6 minutes to recover from that exertion, there should have been marked differences in excitation-transfer effects between high-, medium-, and low-fitness participants. Again, the authors' expectations were met: The increase in shock intensity for high-fitness participants was negligible, at 0.01, whereas the increase for intermediate-fitness participants was 1.70, and for low-fitness participants, 1.98. The change for high-fitness participants was significantly lower than that for the other two recovery proficiency groups, which did not differ from each other.

In summary, Zillmann et al. (1974a) were able to show that the classic excitation transfer effect on aggressive behavior was moderated by cardiorespiratory fitness. Those who were fit enough to recover in the 6 minutes following provocation and exertion did not demonstrate a subsequent increase in aggressive retaliatory behavior. Those who were less fit, in contrast, displayed the classic excitation transfer effect of increased aggression after—even several minutes after—provocation. Does this mean that Paul, our low-fitness sample case, could have avoided a violent altercation if he had been more fit? The answer would seem to be yes. But is there anything else about Paul's history that might have led him to use violence anyway, in spite of his fitness?

The second Zillmann et al. (1974b) study pointed to an affirmative answer, one having to do with Paul's former occupation. For this study, the authors recruited 60 male undergraduates: 20 varsity contact-sport (football and wrestling) athletes, 20 varsity noncontact-sport (swimming, tennis, track, gymnastics, baseball, and basketball) athletes, and 20 nonathletes. Participants played three rounds of Battleship, an electronic game requiring each player to strategically deceive a (bogus) opponent by providing pleasant or noxious auditory feedback to the opponent after each guess made by the opponent about the location of the player's battleships. After the first game, in the no-provocation condition, the bogus opponent was heard to ask the experimenter, "How many trials did it take for me?" In the provocation condition, the bogus opponent's comment was decidedly more inflammatory: "Jesus Christ, who needs strategy for him? The dumb ass led me right to it!" (p. 144). After a short waiting period (one minute), all participants then played two more games. The feedback they gave to the opponent—both the use of noxious noise and the failure to use pleasant noise—constituted measures of aggressive behavior.

As they had expected, Zillmann and associates failed to find any difference in aggressive responses of athletes and nonathletes who were not provoked. Among those who received the provocation, however, there was an interesting effect by athletic status. First, when lumped together, those in the provocation condition understandably provided significantly more negative feedback to their opponents than those in the no-provocation condition; that is, the provocation was indeed provocative. Within the provocation condition, though, the greatest aggressive response was displayed by the nonathletes. This finding is consistent with those of Zillmann et al. (1974a), in that the least physically fit young men (the nonathletes) displayed the most aggression after provocation. The findings for contact-sport and noncontact-sport athletes differed, however. The noncontact sport athletes displayed the least aggressive behavior, significantly less than the nonathletes. The contact sport athletes, in contrast, displayed a moderate level of aggression, right in between (and not significantly different from) that of the nonathletes and that of the noncontact sport athletes. In other words, although the contact sport athletes should have been just as fit as the noncontact sport athletes—and heart rate data reported in this study suggested that they were even more fit—they still behaved more aggressively. How could this be?

Zillmann and colleagues explained these findings in terms of coping skills learned by players of contact sports. In the provoked condition, both the noncontact sport athletes and the contact sport athletes were angered, but the contact sport athletes had to contend with their learned habit of meeting the provocation of an opponent with aggressive behavior. Moreover, the authors reasoned, contact sport athletes would likely have received aggression-disinhibition training. Thus, although the contact sport athletes' recovery time was as good as or better than that of the noncontact sport athletes, the aggressive coping skills learned in conjunction with the contact sport athletes' training counteracted the aggression-dampening effects of their superior recovery capability. In other words, even if Paul had been a fitter man and recovered from most of his agitation in the few minutes prior to the young truck driver's appearance, his Army training might still have disinhibited an aggressive coping response against a youthful "opponent" he most likely perceived as an obnoxious subordinate.

At this point, it would appear that the interactive relationship between cardiorespiratory fitness and the effects of residual excitation occurs only for men. Not so. Four years after the publication of the two Zillmann et al. (1974a, 1974b) studies, Cantor, Zillmann, and Day (1978) published a study on the role of fitness in the excitation-transfer effect induced by arousing films, for which they used a sample of both males and females. The key question Cantor and associates wanted to answer was, "Do differences in cardiorespiratory fitness have implications for emotional responses which do not follow exercise and which do not involve the performance of motor activities?" (p. 1124). To a media effects researcher, this is a compelling question indeed. Cantor and associates followed up this question with another: "If less fit individuals do experience greater physiological responses to the films, will they report their *emotional* responses to be more intense than those of subjects in better physical condition?" (p. 1124–1125). Plainly stated, do less fit individuals perceive themselves to be more physiologically or emotionally affected by arousing films than do fitter individuals?

To answer these questions, Cantor and her collaborators recruited 36 male and 36 female undergraduates at Indiana University to participate in an experiment in which they viewed two short film clips, both of which were potentially arousing, in random order. One clip was taken from a medical film depicting eye surgery; the other featured an erotic sequence in a dimly lit room. Before viewing the first clip and after viewing both clips, participants' physiological responses (systolic blood pressure, heart rate, and skin temperature) were recorded. After viewing each clip, respondents also indicated on a questionnaire how intense they felt their physiological and emotional responses to be. Finally, participants rode a stationary bicycle for 30 seconds to provide the researchers with data to split the sample into high and low fitness groups.

Cantor and her collaborators found that high-fitness respondents were better able to withstand the film clips, physiologically speaking. Compared to low-fitness participants, high-fitness participants displayed less arousal all around: They had significantly lower blood pressure, a marginally lower heart rate, and a significantly higher skin temperature. Moreover, there were no sex differences in these effects. Thus it seems that a person's fitness can act as a protective factor against the potentially agitating effects of arousing media. But do people recognize this fact when they find themselves in a state of excitation? Cantor and associates' second question, about individuals' ability to recognize changes in their own physiological and emotional responses, was answered with analyses of respondents' ratings of the intensity of their responses to the films. Here, an interesting finding emerged: Respondents' ratings of their physiological and emotional responses were uncorrelated with their actual physiological responses. Moreover, when the authors split their sample into fitness-level quadrants, they found a curvilinear relationship between fitness and perception of physiological response. The average intensity of perceived physiological response, on a scale of 1 to 100, increased from 47.8 for the fittest quarter of the sample to 60.5 for the second fittest quarter. The mean for the third fittest quarter dropped slightly to 58.8, and the mean for the least fit quarter, to 53.1. In other words, those respondents who were least fit were also the most inaccurate in reporting their own physiological responses!

Thus, when we look at the three studies together, we conclude that not only are the least fit men and women most susceptible to the potentially dangerous effects of overexcitation, but also that they are relatively unaware that these effects are happening to them. If we flash forward to Paul's inevitable postviolence interaction with the police, we can almost hear his heartfelt pleas: "I was NOT overreacting! I was angry, yes, but in complete control, and besides, that kid deserved it. You should have seen how he swerved right in front of me!" After he grabs the police officer's shoulders and shakes her to make his point, Paul will undoubtedly be thoroughly bewildered to find himself in a holding cell. How could all of this have happened when he was in complete control?

LOOKING FORWARD

Zillmann's 1970s studies with Johnson, Day, and Cantor on the role of fitness in moderating the excitation transfer effect constitute one of the smallest segments of Zillmann's vast publication list. Yet the number of studies in a body of work is not the best indicator of the importance of the findings therein. In this author's opinion, at least two other outcomes more accurately illustrate the importance of a body of work: first, its impact on succeeding work, and second, the implications of its findings and the profundity of the questions raised thereby.

The impact of the studies covered in this essay on succeeding work (conducted by investigators other than the original authors, of course) can be gauged both by the diversity of the publications inspired by them, and by how many years they have served to inspire. On both of these counts the 1970s work on fitness and excitation by Zillmann and colleagues has proven highly successful. The findings of the Zillmann et al. (1974a, 1974b) studies have inspired original research on a variety of topics, most but not all in the realm of sports, including leadership behavior in youth sports (Smoll & Smith, 1989), emotional responsivity in athletes and nonathletes (Collins, Hale, & Loomis, 1995), how the "will to win" is positively correlated with athletic performance (Pezer & Brown, 1980), how depression is negatively correlated with sports participation (Ramirez, Poveda de Agustin, & Cajal, 1978), and even characteristics of selling-related anxiety among salespeople (Verbeke & Bagozzi, 2000). As can be seen, the publication dates of these studies span more than two decades.

Two very recent publications on aggression and sports extended the findings of the 1974 Zillmann et al. studies to adolescent boys (Huang, Cherek, & Lane, 1999) and to the belief in catharsis (Wann, Carlson, Holland, Jacob, Owens, & Wells, 1999). Huang et al. (1999) observed high school male athletes' aggressive behavior in a series of laboratory sessions, and discovered that the contact-sport (e.g., basketball and football) athletes were significantly more aggressive than the noncontact sport (e.g., baseball and track) athletes, both in the laboratory sessions and in self-reports of aggressive behavior outside the laboratory. This finding nicely corroborates those of Zillmann et al. (1974b), who studied college athletes. Moreover, Wann et al. (1999) measured participation in aggressive and nonaggressive sports and the belief in "symbolic sport catharsis," that is, the mythic conviction that watching violent sports on television or in person will reduce aggression in the spectator. These authors found that involvement in aggressive sports positively predicted the belief in symbolic sport catharsis from both television and live sports; there was no such correlation for involvement in nonaggressive sports. Thus, those who practiced aggression regularly through sports participation were also most likely to believe (erroneously) that viewing sports relieved them of this aggression, a finding that disturbs this author almost as much as Cantor and colleagues' (1978) finding that the least fit (and therefore most excitable) individuals were the least aware of their own excitation!

Like Zillmann, Johnson, and Day's 1974 studies, the simple experiment by Cantor et al. (1978) has inspired a surprisingly wide variety of successive studies whose publication dates also span two decades. The most frequently addressed topic in these studies has been the relationship between fitness and tolerance of both physiological and psychological stress (Crews & Landers, 1987; Czajkowski, Hindelang, Dembroski, & Mayerson, et al., 1990; Duda, Sedlock, Melby, & Thaman, 1988; Folkins & Sime, 1981; Holmes & Roth, 1985; Hull, Young, & Ziegler, 1984; Light, Obrist, James, & Strogatz, 1987; McGilley & Holmes, 1988; Plante & Karpowitz, 1987; Roth & Holmes, 1987; Sedlock & Duda, 1994; Shulhan, Scher, & Furedy, 1986; Szabo, Peronnet, Frenkl, Farkas, Petrekanits, Meszaros, Hetenyi, & Szabo, 1994; Tucker, 1990; Vandoornen & Degeus, 1993); followed by the impact on stress tolerance of experimentally induced exercise in both "normals" (Fillingim, Roth, & Cook, 1992; Holmes & McGilley, 1987; Keller & Seraganian, 1984; Roth, 1989; Sinyor, Golden, Steinert, & Seraganian, 1986) and middle-aged "type A's" like our sample case, Paul (Blumenthal, Emery, Walsh, & Cox, et al., 1988; Sherwood, Light, & Blumenthal, 1989). In keeping with the work of Zillmann and his collaborators, these studies generally show that aerobic (cardiorespiratory) fitness, whether preexisting or experimentally induced, improves tolerance to stress. Rounding out the diverse list of study topics inspired by the Cantor et al. (1978) research are publications on subjective perceptions of both physiological states and emotions (Myrtek & Brugner, 1996) and physical fitness (Abadie, 1988); fitness as a predictor of military success (Burke, Sauser, Kemery, & Dyer, 1989); the development of a wellness program for dealing with headaches (Simons, Solbach, Sargent, & Malone, 1986); personality traits rather than fitness as moderators of the excitation-transfer effect (Bunce, Larsen, & Cruz, 1993); and even the effects of an exercise program (swimming) on *rats'* ability to withstand stress induced by foot shock (Cox, 1991).[1]

One of the most valuable aspects of the Cantor et al. (1978) study is its contribution to our understanding of media stimuli as arousal inducers. At least two groups of researchers have drawn on Cantor et al. (1978) in their efforts to continue exploring this issue. Unlike most of the other studies on fitness and stress tolerance, which involved the inducement of stress through forced completion of some difficult nonmedia task, Czajkowski et al. (1990) chose to induce stress in their sample of 62 middle-aged men by having them play a video game. As expected, these researchers found that the fitter

---

[1]This may be one of the few known cases where research on humans has guided research on rats, not the other way around!

men handled the stress of the video game better than the less fit men: The fitter men experienced a smaller rise in heart rate and diastolic blood pressure, and also reported themselves to be less angry and anxious. Further, Myrtek, Scharff, Brugner, and Muller (1996) conducted a survey with fifty 11-year-old boys, measuring physiological, psychological, and behavioral data over the course of a normal school day, which included, on average, over 2 hours of television viewing. When they split the sample into lighter and heavier television viewers, the authors found that the heavier viewers experienced a lower heart rate and lower emotional arousal during television viewing than did the lighter viewers, a finding that seems to suggest some degree of desensitization occurring with greater television use.

LOOKING TO THE FUTURE

The impact of a body of work on succeeding research is only one indicator of that work's importance; the second indicator lies in its findings and the questions raised thereby. There is no doubt that Dolf Zillmann and colleagues' work on fitness and excitation has greatly influenced the work of successive researchers. This is especially impressive given the small number of studies in this segment of Zillmann's research career. Just as impressive, though, is the fact that the findings of these studies raise critical questions about the interaction between television viewing, fitness, and arousal in the real world, outside of the laboratory.

At least two questions—simple on the surface but profound when one stops to think about them—immediately present themselves. The first is the question of how to untangle the relationships between real-world television viewing, fitness, and desensitization. Fitness is not only a moderator of television's effects, it is an effect itself. Work in the 1980s by Larry Tucker (Tucker, 1986, 1987) and a recent study in the *Journal of the American Medical Association* (Robinson, 1999) both suggest that heavy television viewing impedes cardiovascular fitness and encourages obesity. Television viewing is, after all, a sedentary activity. Thus, heavy exposure to television in one's day-to-day life should decrease one's fitness, which in turn should make one more vulnerable to the arousal potential of exciting television content like violence and sex. Yet a large collection of work on the desensitization capability of arousing television shows just the opposite: The more one is exposed to arousing content, the less arousing it becomes (for a recent review, see Smith & Donnerstein, 1998). The previously cited study by Myrtek et al. (1996), which showed that heavier viewers experienced a lower heart rate and lower emotional arousal during viewing than did lighter viewers, supports the desensitization effect. How, then, are we to untangle the seemingly opposite yet simultaneous possibilities that television viewing, in the real world, increases arousal (by decreasing fitness) and decreases arousal (by increasing desensitization)? Clearly, more work needs to be done in this area, and it is hoped that some fearless and enterprising researcher will pick up where Zillmann and his associates left off.

The second question that presents itself in the wake of Zillmann and colleagues' work on fitness and excitation is more controversial. Simply stated, if we can reduce the negative effects of arousing television on ourselves by improving our own cardiorespiratory fitness, are we not obliged to do so? Public sentiment regarding the negative effects of violence and erotica on children and teenagers generally supports action on the media's part or on parents' part: Problematic programs should be rewritten or banned; concerned parents should censor their children's television viewing. Would it offend parents to suggest that another way to arm their children against "trash TV" is to fortify them with fitness? Maybe so. Such an argument, taken to the extreme, would take the onus off media professionals for producing gratuitous garbage and instead put it on the children most affected by such content for not having been "fit enough" viewers. But when children, and adults for that matter, a e affected by what they view, when they do act out aggressively following a provocation, we as a society force them to bear some of the blame anyway. They (or their parents) are still responsible for their behavior. Paul, our sample case, finds himself behind bars because of the way he behaved, regardless of what caused him to behave that way.

In closing, this author once witnessed Dolf Zillmann in a public forum answering questions about his research career. One of his comments, paraphrased here, was that social science is about elucidating processes and revealing effects one did not expect to find. In other words, what good is there in predicting and finding the obvious? Taking this wisdom a bit further, we might ask the same sort of question when faced with research findings and implications that do not support our pre-existing political or social views: What good is there in ignoring research findings that implicate us as viewers, and only accepting those findings that blame the media and absolve us of personal responsibility? To that end, we have Dolf Zillmann and his colleagues to thank for gently reminding us, with their clear and straightforward research, that the discovery of individual differences in effects sometimes implies the need for individual responsibility in solutions.

REFERENCES

Abadie, B. R. (1988). Construction and validation of a perceived physical fitness scale. *Perceptual and Motor Skills, 67,* 887–892.

Blumenthal, J. A., Emery, C. F., Walsh, M. A., Cox, D. R., et al. (1988). Exercise training in healthy Type A middle-aged men: Effects on behavioral and cardiovascular responses. *Psychosomatic Medicine, 50,* 418–433.

Bunce, S. C., Larsen, R. J., & Cruz, M. (1993). Individual-differences in the excitation transfer effect. *Personality and Individual Differences, 15,* 507–514.

Burke, B. G., Sauser, W. T., Kemery, E. R., & Dyer, F. N. (1989). Intelligence and physical fitness as predictors of success in early infantry training. *Perceptual and Motor Skills, 69,* 263–271.

Cantor, J. R., Zillmann, D., & Day, K. D. (1978). Relationship between cardiorespiratory fitness and physiological responses to films. *Perceptual and Motor Skills, 46,* 1123–1130.

Collins, D., Hale, B., & Loomis, J. (1995). Differences in emotional responsivity and anger in athletes and nonathletes: Startle reflex modulation and attributional response. *Journal of Sport and Exercise Physiology, 17*(2), 171–184.

Cox, R. H. (1991). Exercise training and response to stress: Insights from an animal-model. *Medicine and Science in Sports and Exercise, 23,* 853–859.

Crews, D. J., & Landers, D. M. (1987). A meta-analytic review of aerobic fitness and reactivity to psychosocial stressors. *Medicine and Science in Sports and Exercise, 19*(5), 114–120.

Czajkowski, S. M., Hindelang, R. D., Dembroski, T. M., & Mayerson, S. E., et al. (1990). Aerobic fitness, psychological characteristics, and cardiovascular reactivity to stress. *Health Psychology, 9,* 676–692.

Duda, J. L., Sedlock, D. A., Melby, C. L., & Thaman, C. (1988). The effects of physical activity level and acute exercise on heart rate and subjective response to a psychological stressor. *International Journal of Sport Psychology, 19*(2), 119–133.

Fillingim, R. B., Roth, D. L., & Cook, E. W. (1992). The effects of aerobic exercise on cardiovascular, facial EMG, and self-report responses to emotional imagery. *Psychosomatic Medicine, 54*(1), 109–120.

Folkins, C. H., & Sime, W. E. (1981). Physical fitness training and mental health. *American Psychologist, 36,* 373–389.

Harding, R. W., Morgan, F. H., Indermaur, D., Ferrante, A. M., & Blagg, H. (1998). Road rage and the epidemiology of violence: Something old, something new. *Studies on Crime and Crime Prevention, 7,* 221–238.

Holmes, D. S., & McGilley, B. M. (1987). Influence of a brief aerobic training program on heart rate and subjective response to a psychologic stressor. *Psychosomatic Medicine, 49,* 366–374.

Holmes, D. S., & Roth, D. (1985). Association of aerobic fitness with pulse rate and subjective responses to psychological stress. *Psychophysiology, 22,* 525–529.

Huang, D. B., Cherek, D. R., & Lane, S. D. (1999). Laboratory measurement of aggression in high school age athletes: Provocation in a nonsporting context. *Psychological Reports, 85,* 1251–1262.

Hull, E. M., Young, S. H., & Ziegler, M. G. (1984). Aerobic fitness affects cardiovascular and catecholamine responses to stressors. *Psychophysiology, 21,* 353–360.

Keller, S., & Seraganian, P. (1984). Physical fitness level and autonomic reactivity to psychosocial stress. *Journal of Psychosomatic Research, 28,* 279–287.

Light, K. C., Obrist, P. A., James, S. A., & Strogatz, D. S. (1987). Cardiovascular responses to stress: II. Relationships to aerobic exercise patterns. *Psychophysiology, 24*(1), 79–86.

McGilley, B. M., & Holmes, D. S. (1988). Aerobic fitness and response to psychological stress. *Journal of Research in Personality, 22*(2), 129–139.

Myrtek, M., & Brugner, G. (1996). Perception of emotions in everyday life: Studies with patients and normals. *Biological Psychology, 42*(1–2), 147–164.

Myrtek, M., Scharff, C., Brugner, G., & Muller, W. (1996). Physiological, behavioral, and psychological effects associated with television viewing in schoolboys: An exploratory study. *Journal of Early Adolescence, 16,* 301–323.

Pezer, V., & Brown, M. (1980). Will to win and athletic performance. International *Journal of Sport Psychology, 11*(2), 121–131.

Plante, T. G., & Karpowitz, D. (1987). The influence of aerobic exercise on physiological stress responsivity. *Psychophysiology, 24,* 670–677.

Ramirez, J. M., Poveda de Agustin, J. M., & Cajal, J. G. (1978). Depression and sport. *International Journal of Sport Psychology, 9*(3), 199–204.

Robinson, T. N. (1999). Reducing children's television viewing to prevent obesity: A randomized controlled trial. *JAMA: Journal of the American Medical Association, 282,* 1561–1567.

Roth, D. L. (1989). Acute emotional and psychophysiological effects of aerobic exercise. *Psychophysiology, 26,* 593–602.

Roth, D. L., & Holmes, D. S. (1987). Influence of aerobic exercise training and relaxation training on physical and psychologic health following stressful life events. *Psychosomatic Medicine, 49,* 355–365.

Sedlock, D. A., & Duda, J. L. (1994). The effect of trait anxiety and fitness level on heart-rate and state anxiety responses to a mental arithmetic stressor among college-age women. *International Journal of Sport Psychology, 25,* 218–229.

Sherwood, A., Light, K. C., & Blumenthal, J. A. (1989). Effects of aerobic exercise training on hemodynamic responses during psychosocial stress in normotensive and borderline hypertensive Type A men: A preliminary report. *Psychosomatic Medicine, 51*(2), 123–136.

Shulhan, D. L., Scher, H., & Furedy, J. J. (1986). Phasic cardiac reactivity to psychological stress as a function of aerobic fitness level. *Psychophysiology, 23,* 562–566.

Simons, A., Solbach, P., Sargent, J., & Malone, L. (1986). A wellness program in the treatment of headache. *Headache, 26,* 343–352.

Sinyor, D., Golden, M., Steinert, Y., & Seraganian, P. (1986). Experimental manipulation of aerobic fitness and the response to psychosocial stress: Heart rate and self-report measures. *Psychosomatic Medicine, 48,* 334–337.

Smith, S. L., & Donnerstein, E. (1998). Harmful effects of exposure to media violence: Learning of aggression, emotional desensitization, and fear. *Human aggression: Theories, research, and implications for social policy* (pp. 167–202). San Diego, CA: Academic.

Smoll, F. L., & Smith, R. E. (1989). Leadership behaviors in sport: A theoretical model and research paradigm. *Journal of Applied Social Psychology, 19,* 1522–1551.

Szabo, A., Peronnet, F., Frenkl, R., Farkas, A., Petrekanits, M., Meszaros, J., Hetenyi, A., & Szabo, T. (1994). Blood-pressure and heart-rate reactivity to mental strain in adolescent judo athletes. *Physiology and Behavior, 56,* 219–224.

Tucker, L. A. (1986). The relationship of television viewing to physical fitness and obesity. *Adolescence, 21*(84), 797–806.

Tucker, L. A. (1987). Television, teenagers, and health. *Journal of Youth and Adolescence, 16,* 415–425.

Tucker, L. A. (1990). Physical fitness and psychological distress. International *Journal of Sport Psychology, 21*(3), 185–201.

Vandoornen, L. J. P., & Degeus, E. J. C. (1993). Stress, physical-activity and coronary heart-disease. *Work and Stress, 7*(2), 121–139.

Verbeke, W., & Bagozzi, R. P. (2000). Sales call anxiety: Exploring what it means when fear rules a sales encounter. *Journal of Marketing, 64*(3), 88–101.

Wann, D. L., Carlson, J. D., Holland, L. C., Jacob, B. E., Owens, D. A., & Wells, D. D. (1999). Beliefs in symbolic catharsis: The importance of involvement with aggressive sports. *Social Behavior and Personality, 27*(2), 155–163.

Zillmann, D. (1978). Attribution and misattribution of excitatory reactions. In J. H. Harvey, W. J. Ickes, & R. F. Kidd (Eds.), *New directions in attribution research* (Vol. 2, pp. 335–368). Hillsdale, NJ: Lawrence Erlbaum Associates.

Zillmann, D. (1979). *Hostility and aggression.* Hillsdale, NJ: Lawrence Erlbaum Associates.

Zillmann, D. (1983). Transfer of excitation in emotional behavior. In J. T. Cacioppo & R. E. Petty (Eds.), *Social psychophysiology: A sourcebook* (pp. 215–240). New York: Guilford.

Zillmann, D. (1996). Sequential dependencies in emotional experience and behavior. In R. D. Kavanaugh, B. Zimmerberg, & S. Fein (Eds.), *Emotion: Interdisciplinary perspectives* (pp. 243–272). Mahwah, NJ: Lawrence Erlbaum Associates.

Zillmann, D., Johnson, R. C., & Day, K. D. (1974a). Attribution of apparent arousal and proficiency of recovery from sympathetic activation affecting excitation transfer to aggressive behavior. *Journal of Experimental Social Psychology, 10,* 503–515.

Zillmann, D., Johnson, R. C., & Day, K. D. (1974b). Provoked and unprovoked aggressiveness in athletes. *Journal of Research in Personality, 8,* 139–152.

21

Communication and Emotion in the Context of Music and Music Television

Silvia Knobloch
Dresden University of Technology

Norbert Mundorf
University of Rhode Island

Music is the least expensive and most easily available form of electronic entertainment. Because of its "packaging" in small 3- to 4-minute units, popular music in particular lends itself to being consumed in numerous situations without great time investment or effort. The combination with video has created the opportunity for music to carry additional levels of meaning. Due to the radio, record player, audio tape, CD, and current digital technologies such as MP3, Napster, and its successors, thousands, even millions of listeners can enjoy to the same song by the same performer at the same or different time in widely dispersed locations. The media create a musical culture that is at the same time highly individualized, and also tremendously standardized.

This chapter explores music as entertainment and as a phenomenon in social communication. In spite of a long-standing tradition of music psychology and philosophical speculation about music, its aesthetics, and therapeutic effects (e.g., Horden, 2000), rigorous research on the affective and social processes involved in the consumption of popular music is limited. Dolf Zillmann has conducted and inspired a significant line of research. As such, this area of exploration provides another piece of the puzzle that ultimately will be a comprehensive theory of entertainment.

We focus on the music consumption of adolescents and young adults, which is the key demographic both for Top 40-type pop music and for a range of "alternative" music styles, such as rap, heavy metal, and "shock rock." As children grow into adolescence, TV is gradually replaced by listening to music as the favorite media consumption activity. Musical preferences established during adolescence are often maintained into early adulthood and beyond (Behne, 1997). In fact, much of the playlists of current classic rock and oldies radio stations originally hit the charts when the baby boomer generation was in its teenage years. Music consumption also "converges" with other media: TV provides music video, teenage magazines focus on music topics from 'Nsync to heavy metal. Teenage fashion and hair styles are heavily influenced through modeling after rock idols. Online activities involve music and music video downloads via Napster and its successors. Even the ever more popular online chat is accompanied by transfer of music files and discussion of music preferences.

This chapter briefly addresses the psychological functions of music and music videos. However, we do not emphasize differences between music and music videos. We initially discuss studies on habitual music preferences and their relationships with personality traits. Sociopsychological aspects of music being a tool to communicate one's identity will be outlined. Among the emotional effects of music, we discuss arousal in particular. Finally, we address the selection of music.

POPULAR MUSIC CONSUMPTION AND PERSONALITY

Although situational factors and music itself play a key role in determining effects and enjoyment of music consumption, in order to fully appreciate such responses, understanding the role that individual differences play in consumption and response to music is of critical importance. Exploration of such individual differences during the past two decades has led to important insights in factors mediating responses to media content such as violence, horror, and erotica (see chaps. 10 and 7, this volume). The investigation of personality with regard to music started even earlier. Personality traits and their connections with music preferences have frequently been studied with special regard to rebellion and aggression.

Early on Cattell (a psychologist well known for his contribution of fundamental importance in the field of individual differences) and Saunders (1954) worked on "musical preferences and personality diagnosis" (p. 3). Later research has repeatedly established connections between excitement, sensation seeking, and liking of rock, but also between openness to experience and multifaceted music preferences. In a study by Litle and Zuckerman (1986), sensation seeking was linked to enjoyment of rock and disliking soundtracks. Dollinger (1993) found empirical associations between openness to experience and liking of new age, classical, jazz, folk-ethnic, soul, and reggae music, whereas excitement seekers liked hard rock. Rawlings and Ciancarelli (1997) conducted a study on personality and music in which they established three factors of music preferences: liking of rock music, general breadth of musical preference, and liking for pop music such as easy listening. The breadth dimension was, not surprisingly, correlated with the trait openness to experience. Extraverts particularly liked pop music. Similarly, Rawlings, Barrantes i Vidal, and Furnham (2000) surveyed English and Spanish students and found intercorrelations between sensation seeking, including experience seeking, openness to experience, and liking of hard rock versus easy-listening music.

The preference for rock music has not only been studied with regard to sensation-seeking, but also to rebelliousness (see also Hansen & Hansen, 2000). As Bleich, Zillmann, and Weaver (1991) pointed out, adolescent defiance in the face of limitations imposed by adults and their institutions is pervasive throughout popular, and in particular rock music. It serves as a useful tool for self-expression in particular for male hard rock and heavy metal fans and has considerable influence on social perception (see also section on this topic). Such defiance is even more pronounced in music videos because visual symbols of defiance can easily be added to the music and lyrics of rebellious songs. Defiance has been a pervasive part of popular music ever since Elvis Presley sang "You Ain't Nothing but a Hound Dog" accompanied by his equally rebellious nonverbal cues. It not only expresses teenage refusal to conform with societal limitations, but it also resonates with deep-seated adolescent emotions. Although such songs often gained immense popularity across broad population segments (e.g., Don McLean's "American Pie" or Jimi Hendrix's distorted rendition of the National Anthem to protest the Vietnam War), Zillmann and his colleagues have explored the question of whether and to what extent rebellious personality traits affect enjoyment of and exposure to rebellious and nonrebellious music and music videos.

Bleich, Zillmann, and Weaver (1991) exposed high school students to rebellious and nonrebellious videos. Their level of rebelliousness had been previously determined. As expected, rebellious adolescents preferred defiant music. However, an unexpected interaction effect revealed that both rebellious and nonrebellious respondents enjoyed defiant rock music.

Enjoyment of nondefiant videos was yet nondefiant videos was significantly higher for nonrebellious compared to rebellious participants. In other words, nonrebellious adolescents enjoy music videos along a wide spectrum of defiance, whereas their rebellious peers are clearly biased toward the defiant variety. In terms of enjoyment of particular aspects of the video, judgments of singing, lyrics, and performers in defiant videos were most clearly polarized between rebellious and nonrebellious youths. In terms of ownership of recordings, the two groups did not differ significantly for defiant music, although rebellious teens owned significantly fewer nondefiant than defiant recordings. Rebelliousness, according to this study, expresses itself as avoidance of mainstream videos and recordings, rather than exposure to extreme materials. A reason for this surprising outcome may be that defiant music has become a *de facto* standard among adolescents.

Robinson, Weaver, and Zillmann (1996) addressed methodological shortcomings related to the assessment of rebelliousness in the earlier research. McDermott (1988) differentiated proactive and reactive rebelliousness, the former referring to pleasure seeking that pushes the limits imposed by parents and society, whereas the latter addresses negativity, frustration, and vengeful behavior addressed to parents, peers, romantic interests, and society at large. Robinson et al. (1996) related rebelliousness to subscales of Eysenck's (Esyenck & Eysenck, 1985) Psychoticism Inventory, a group of personality characteristics that were found to be reliable predictors of other media preferences and responses. Proactive rebelliousness was related to extraversion, whereas reactive rebelliousness corresponded to psychoticism. (For another study relating Eysenck's personality dimension to music genre preferences see Weaver, 2000.)

Robinson et al. (1996) found an interaction between gender and rebellion in the music video: Men enjoyed rebellious music videos considerably more than women did. Psychoticism and reactive rebelliousness both differentiated enjoyment of rebellious and nonrebellious rock videos in a parallel fashion: Those high on either showed greater appreciation of hard/rebellious rock videos and lesser appreciation of the soft or nonrebellious, whereas those low on these scales preferred soft or nonrebellious videos to hard/rebellious videos. Interestingly, these effects materialized for reactive rebelliousness and not proactive rebelliousness, which constitutes an important clarification versus the earlier Bleich et al. (1991) study.

Arnett (1991) investigated liking of heavy metal with reckless behavior such as reckless driving, sexual casualness, and drug use among adolescents. According to his results, respondents who stated a preference for heavy metal were more likely, for example, to drink and drive, to drive without a seatbelt, and to have sex with someone only casually known or without contraception. Nonetheless, Arnett pointed out that the preference for heavy metal music is probably more an indication of attitude, but not the cause of reckless behavior. Similar findings were reported by Hansen and Hansen (1991). They found, for instance, that heavy metal fans have lower respect for women and score higher on machiavellianism and lower on need for cognition. Fans of punk rock showed less acceptance of authority.

In closing, when reflecting on aggression conveyed by music, more recent research on rap, obviously the "Black" rebellious music, has to be discussed, although it has to be more focused on effects versus correlations with traits. Rap is commonly evaluated as offensive and dangerous (Fried, 1999) and suspected to widen ethnic gaps (Johnson, Trawalter, & Dovidio, 2000). But Zillmann et al. (1995) found that the political message of radical rap was of little importance for its enjoyment. Moreover, according to their findings, radical rap turned out to foster more ethnic tolerance of White students. A less delightful finding was reported by Gan, Zillmann, and Mitrook (1997). Exposure to rap laden with sexual imagery resulted in unfavorable evaluations of Black women. Similar stereotyping effects of music and music videos, for example, on sex roles, have been shown repeatedly (Hansen & Hansen, 2000), which leads to our next topic.

MUSIC AND SOCIAL PERCEPTION

The fact that musical tastes are correlated with personality traits means that information on music can be used in part as a valid indicator for the social environment. This knowledge, although it may only exist subliminally, can influence social reality in two ways. First, individuals may use the expression of musical taste as a social signal to communicate, though only implicitly, with others and to associate themselves with certain social groups. This idea has been widely discussed, mostly with respect to adolescents (e.g., Bennett, 2000; Denisoff & Levine, 1972; Dollase, 1997; Epstein; 1994; Finnäs, 1989; Frith, 1981; Hansen & Hansen, 1991; Johnstone & Katz, 1957; Lull, 1985, 1992; Müller, 1994; Russell, 1997; Zillmann & Gan, 1997). An extensive body of literature exists on music sociology (for recent editions of early works see Adorno, 1996; Silbermann, 1998) regarding various countries (France: Green, 2000; Germany: Inhetveen, 1997; Great Britain: Martin, 1995; Scott, 2000; the United States: Bryson, 1996).

Second, individuals could use information on musical taste as an indicator of the personality of others. Efficient impression formation is in the interest of the individual in order to predict others' behavior and possibly act accordingly. Social cognition, influenced by musical taste information, thus impacts interactions with the person by "what the perceiver brings to the interaction" (Jones, 1990, p. 5). In this case, stereotypes (Lippmann, 1922) of fans of various music genres are used for impression formation. Information related to music could be considered particularly valuable because music is commonly associated with emotions and emotional viewpoints that are usually not publicly expressed. Consequently, musical taste may be used as a source for further insight into the emotional traits of acquaintances. These private traits may not otherwise be accessible, and they are of great interpersonal interest nonetheless. Knowledge of musical preferences, supposedly permits learning about rather intimate characteristics. Fischoff's (1999) research shows that social information related to music can have a strong impact. In his study, being a writer of "gangsta" rap music lyrics affected social perception more negatively than being accused of murder. Empirical investigations by Zillmann and Bhatia (1989) and Knobloch, Vorderer, and Zillmann (2000) studied the formation of impressions based on musical taste as social information. Both studies focused on specific social constellation, because the social setting and the possible social relationship were considered important for the influence that musical taste might have on impression formation.

Zillmann and Bhatia (1989) were interested in the impact on perception of potential heterosexual partners for a romantic relationship. They exposed undergraduates (average age 19.8 years) to video dating tapes on which target individuals introduced themselves and mentioned they liked a certain music style. Musical bias was experimentally manipulated for four categories: country, classical, heavy metal rock, soft rock, or no music for a control condition. Respondents rated the target individual for attractiveness and on various trait dimensions. Expressed musical bias significantly influenced the perception of the potential date. A preference for country music generally diminished attractiveness, whereas classical music worked favorably for potential female partners, but was disadvantageous for the prospective male date. For heavy metal rock, a reverse effect could be demonstrated: It was detrimental for the female date and beneficial for the male. Furthermore, consequences of taste compatibility between target individual and participants were investigated. Sharing musical preferences proved to be considerably more important for male respondents. Hence, formation of opposite-gender relationship can be influenced by musical tastes, because the revelation of taste results in inferences regarding the personality and it affects perceived attractiveness.

Knobloch, Vorderer, and Zillmann (2000) also investigated the impact of music on person perception, but they focused on friendship instead of a romantic heterosexual relationship. Their sample consisted of German high-school students (average age 14.9 years). The respondents were exposed to videos in which a prospective schoolmate introduced himself or herself. According to experimental variation, the target individual talked about liking various music styles: Pop/Love-Songs, Alternative Rock/Punk, HipHop/Rap, Dance/Techno. In a control condition, no specific music was mentioned. Respondents reported their impressions of the person depicted and their interest in the person as a potential friend. Furthermore, desired features of an ideal friend and ratings of respondents' own music preferences were collected. The results show that the perception of shared musical taste fosters positive character appraisals and enhances friendship aspirations. However, close correspondence between the concept of an ideal friend and the overall impression made by peers was found to be a factor of at least equal strength in the formation of friendship dispositions. Taste-based stereotypes were in evidence: It was observed, for instance, that boys, irrespective of their own musical preference, favored boys who appeared to be tough because of their preference for Rock and Punk "hard" music, as well as their disdain for Soft Pop and Love Songs.

Although the sociological and sociopsychological importance of music has been widely recognized and empirically substantiated, factors influencing actual music selection in social situations have rarely been investigated thus far. Only Konecni (1979, 1982) conducted studies regarding social factors in music selection, focusing on aggression. However, his experiments featured overly complicated designs and used computer-generated tone sequences instead of ordinary music.

EFFECTS OF MUSIC CONSUMPTION

Music effects have been studied extensively, but research has been biased toward elite classic music and socially desirable effects such as better learning due to music or complex cognitive processing of music. Our interest here will be popular music and its emotional effects, which tend to have broad appeal.

Arousal plays a critical role in explaining the consumption, perception, and enjoyment of music—as it does with other media fare such as horror, suspense, and sexually explicit media (see Brown, chap. 10; Knobloch, chap. 16; Mundorf & Mundorf, chap. 7, this volume). Although other types of music may obviously be arousing to various listener groups, Zillmann's excitation-transfer theory (see chap. 2, this volume) applies in particular to the teenage response to popular music. Much rock music is designed to be arousing—with strong rhythms, loud, sometimes extreme sounds, and intense vocalization.

This arousal serves to facilitate the dynamics of group listening at concerts, clubs, and parties, but it can also serve considerable adaptive functionality in solitary listening. Not only will it enhance the enjoyment of concurrent experiences, it can also achieve a level of arousal that corresponds to a situational goal (North & Hargreaves, 1997). This goal may be an average level of arousal (excitatory homeostasis), but it could also be heightened arousal to counteract boredom or fatigue. Music in this sense can be considered one of the most popular mood-management tools (see also the section on selection).

Konecni (1979) explored the use of music by listeners to control their own arousal levels. His studies showed that participants who were provoked by an experimental confederate and as a result were aroused listened to simple nonarousing music 70% of the time. Konecni also demonstrated that arousal-optimizing music reduced aggression compared to music that polarizes arousal. Finally, another study showed that participants chose simpler music while engaged in complex tasks. These findings fit in with Zillmann's mood-management theory (see chap. 4, this volume).

North and Hargreaves (1997) pointed to other variables that influence music choice, notably situational appropriateness or typicality. In their 1996 study North and Hargreaves assessed music choice of participants while exercising or relaxing, and found that their preferences were determined by typicality (i.e, arousing music during exercise, relaxing music while relaxing), rather than by arousal moderating (mood management) processes. The authors interpreted these choices as associated with specific situational preferences and goals.

Cantor and Zillmann (1973) investigated the effect of prior arousal on music enjoyment in the context of the excitation-transfer paradigm. Respondents were aroused prior to exposure to rock music. Prior arousal was achieved by exposure to pleasant or unpleasant drama. Appreciation of the music selection was greater for respondents who were prearoused compared to respondents who were not aroused. Excitation-transfer theory assumes that individuals are typically not aware of the simultaneous contribution of varied sources of arousal. As a result, prior arousal from varied sources can serve to enhance the enjoyment of rock music. Thus, the process compares with other media content, such as suspense, horror, humor, and erotica, where the intensity of the emotional experience is largely determined by the prevailing level of sympathetic arousal (Zillmann, 1978). Violent and erotic depictions as sources of arousal are obviously also used in music videos, but also in lyrics, as the following study shows (see also Moore, Skipper, & Willis, 1979).

Zillmann and Mundorf (1987) tested the impact of arousal generated by visuals in music video on music enjoyment. Respondents were exposed to five experimental conditions, a 2 × 2 factorial design with violence (absent, present) and sex (absent, present) as independent variables, as well as a no-video condition. The video used was a concept video, that is, a video that tells a rudimentary story (rather than focusing on the performers). The same music video with identical music was used in all conditions. However, the visuals were varied such that in the sex-present condition a short R-rated erotic clip replaced a section of the video; in the violence-present condition, a violent clip of the same length was inserted, and in the combined version both erotic and violent clips were inserted. Male and female respondents combined enjoyed the music the most when sex was added to the video. Music enjoyment was also heightened to a lesser extent when violence was added. Surprisingly, the combined version failed to generate the expected increase in music enjoyment.

Apparently, in this study, arousal from the erotic video added to the overall level of arousal generated by the music and the original video. Participants misattributed arousal from the visuals to the music and interpreted their heightened arousal level to the music per se. Hansen and Hansen (1990) also founder greater enjoyment of rock music resulting from sexual, but not from aggressive images. This finding might provide insight regarding the success of music video in giving new momentum to the music industry in the 1980s (along with introduction of the CD). Music that otherwise may be bland or uninteresting can gain considerable appeal resulting from the added arousal generated by stimulating visuals. It comes as little surprise that the 1980s witnessed the tremendous success of stars such as Madonna and Michael Jackson, who relied heavily on video to promote their music.

Another interesting finding of this study pertains to the perception of what is romantic with regard to music video. Participants were asked how romantic they found the music. An interesting interaction emerged: Males considered the sex-only condition most romantic, whereas females considered music alone most romantic. This effect may be caused by differing definitions of *romantic*, where males are more focused on the sexual aspect, and females lean toward phantasizing and daydreaming, which is encouraged by music alone. It could also result from the greater visual orientation of males versus the verbal orientation of females (cf. chaps. 11 & 15, this volume).

In the light of the enlisted demonstrations of music effects and the permanent exposure to (background) music in everyday situations like shopping or driving, the question arises whether music is constantly setting our "frame of mind" (Morris, 1990). Interestingly, Behne (2001) reported a meta-analysis on 153 investigations of music effects and found that since the 1960s, the effect of music listening, notably background music, has gradually declined over time. The percentage of significant effects found in the studies reviewed dropped, and the number of studies with nonsignificant findings increased. Behne pointed out that these findings appear robust because methodologies have become more sophisticated over time and outcomes are presumably more conservative. He interpreted this trend as the result of the constant background music to which teenagers (and others) are currently exposed and the ensuing habituation. He spoke of a "cornea in the ear that has made us emotionally deaf" (Behne, 2001, p. 147, translated). Yet he expected that conscious self-exposure to music may still allow unspoiled hearing and its emotional impact.

However, the studies reflected in Behne's analyses primarily address background music. To better understand realistic listening situations it is important to consider situational and individual difference variables. Behne (2001) himself pointed out various listening styles that differ with situation and motivation: regulative listening in the sense of mood management, concentrated listening, and superficial listening to background music. Although we can observe an overall habituation effect, it might be mitigated by individual listener dispositions. Also, it might be of interest to compare music consumption to the consumption of other media content to understand if and how listeners counteract the effects of habituation. For instance, research on sexually explicit media (chap. 10, this volume) showed that participants habituated to common pornography will no longer experience increased arousal level during exposure to the same type of fare. However, more extreme, XXX-rated fare will lead to recovery of arousal levels and moderate arousal of this more extreme fare. Interestingly, habituated participants still enjoy common pornography more than nonhabituated participants, even though the latter would seem to benefit from considerable increase in arousal levels. Apparently, respondents also counteract habituation through increased quantity of consumption.

The analogy for music (which still needs empirical verification) would be both a move toward greater quantity of music exposure, but more importantly toward more extreme types of music. Although it is fairly easy to simulate habituation to erotica in an experimental setting (cf. Zillmann & Bryant, 1984), most participants are continually exposed to musical stimuli, and have probably habituated. Habituation to violence may be more similar to music, because most TV viewers are constantly surrounded by it. Here again, greater frequency, explicitness, and realism seem to entice viewers to repeat exposure. It appears that in music consumption a number of external stimuli serve to counteract habituation effect. Notably it might be of interest to explore different consumption situations to address how they are used to optimize arousal conditions.

MUSIC SELECTION

Music research concerned with lay listeners has emphasized effects of music or focused on favorite music styles. Both aspects are comparatively easy to study. For the former interest, participants are exposed to music, and dependent measures are collected; for the latter, respondents report their general musical tastes in a survey. These approaches to data collection are simple but do not take into account that individuals typically choose the music they are exposed to. As postulated in the selective-exposure paradigm (Zillmann & Bryant, 1985), media messages can only develop impact if the audience decides to turn to them in the first place. The same logic applies to music, where the "captive audience" is an exception to the rule. The old-fashioned music jukebox illustrates people's selectivity pertaining to popular music. Furthermore, popular music is commonly considered entertainment. From a media-psychological perspective, entertainment can be conceptualized as mood management (see Vorderer, chap. 6, this volume). Hence, because mood-management is closely connected to the selective-exposure paradigm it lends itself to the study of music and its uses. However, investigating musical choices in the past entailed technical problems. Prior to widespread digitization it was difficult to provide song selections in a manageable number without rebuilding a jukebox or presenting participants with a confusing apparatus of tapes and buttons.

Consequently, besides the studies by Konecni (1979, 1982, described previously), situational music preferences have been primarily studied based on hypothetical scenarios (e.g., Behne, 1984, 1986; Gembris, 1985, 1990; Lehmann, 1993, 1994; North & Hargreaves, 1996, 1997). Typically, respondents were asked to imagine a specific situation and describe the kind of music they supposedly would listen to in this imaginary situation. These descriptions, then, were collected via rating scales for adjectives. Evidently, this technique is questionable, because the respondent's situation was only envisioned and the choice of music was indicated by self-report data instead of behavioral measures. Describing preferred music by rating adjectives also deviates from normal music selection. In the worst case, results primarily reflect naive lay theories of music selection, but not actual patterns of music choice (for a more detailed critique see Behne, 1984). Other investigations connected reported genre preferences with recollected moods or feelings while listening (Hakanen, 1995; Stratton & Zalanowski, 1991, 1997; Wells & Hakanen, 1991) and are subject to similar shortcomings.

Gibson, Aust, and Zillmann (2000) took a somewhat different approach to studying choice and appeal of love-celebrating and love-lamenting music. Their interest was to gain insight into the attraction of love music, particularly of sad love songs. In the context of mood-management theory, self-exposure to sad media content is paradoxical at first glimpse and needs complementary explanation, for example, referring to social-comparison processes (Mares & Cantor, 1992; Zillmann, 2000). Gibson et al. also asked respondents to envision a situation of great romantic happiness (e.g., learning about reciprocated love) or of romantic despair (being abandoned by lover) and to indicate the music they would probably listen to in this situation. To improve ecological validity, respondents did not abstractly describe their likely music choice on scales (as in other studies), but simply named the title and the performer. These songs were categorized *post-hoc* as positive, negative, or neutral with regard to love by music experts unaware of the given love-related scenario. The authors concluded that respondents chose music compatible to their situation: sad love music in lovelorn and happy love music in romantic delight. However, this approach to study music selection still can be questioned for the lack of actual behavioral measures—both the scenarios and the selections were imaginary.

With the advent of the information technology era, interfaces to music selections have altered. Every up-to-date personal computer features sound devices and playback software for music files. An overwhelming amount of music is now accessible by mouse click due to the compression format MP3 for sound files and internet swapping communities (the first well-known community being Napster). New information technology also allows very innovative approaches to social research, because data collection via multimedia can be used in innumerous ways (e.g., Müller, 1995). A multimedia interface—a digital jukebox—was used by Knobloch and Zillmann (in press) to study mood management via music choices.

The purpose of this study was to test whether the preference for energetic-joyful music over alternatives is higher for persons in a bad mood than for persons in a neutral mood and, in turn, higher for persons in a neutral mood than for persons in a good mood. Current Top-40 chart songs were rated for energy and joyfulness as musical qualities. Based on this pretest, sets of songs were created that were either low or high in these qualities. In the main experiment, respondents were placed in bad, neutral, or good moods and then, in an allegedly unrelated study, asked to listen to musical selections as they desired. The selections were offered by computer software that unobtrusively recorded individual exposure times by selection. Each song was accessible by clicking a button labeled with the song title and the performer—resembling the classic jukebox interface. Exposure time as a whole was limited to about one third of the total run time of all available songs in order to establish a selection situation. As hypothesized, results showed that respondents in bad moods preferred highly energetic-joyful music for longer periods compared to respondents in good moods. Moreover, respondents in bad moods proved to be more determined in choosing music and switched less often between songs.

CONCLUSION

The research discussed has demonstrated a number of promising trends in the understanding of consumption and effects of music and music video. It has pointed to the importance of personality, both as a predictor of music choice and a correlate that is revealed by the musical "badge" worn by adolescents and young adults. Also, it has discussed a number of other factors that are crucial in determining music choice and preferences. In particular arousal was shown to be of critical importance. Zillmann's excitation-transfer paradigm and mood-management theory have considerable explanatory power in the response to music.

However, this discussion has also shown that much work is still needed. Recent use of digital technology in determining selective exposure promises a more differentiated picture of who chooses what music under which circumstances. Also, more developmental research is still needed in understanding how adolescents develop their musical preferences.

OUTLOOK

Access to music is easier than ever. Interfaces to music choices are changing, because listeners can store, categorize, and assort music on computers in any imaginable way. Moreover, music video downloads have also become common. In fact, the traditional music industry fears this new form of distribution badly. Furthermore, the music fan can easily style the look of the interface proper via download of interface styles or simple programming (see, for instance, www.winamp.com). Music as a tool to express identity (Hargreaves & North, 1999) clearly develops with society and modern living circumstances.

Although we seem to be subjected to almost permanent background music and have learned to more or less close our ears nonetheless, self-selected exposure may become a precondition for intense effects of music on emotions. New technologies not only support selective music use via convenient access, Internet music sites offer highly sophisticated selection criteria. For instance, at www.launch.com, users can design their "own" streaming music station by rating songs, albums, artists and sampling other community members' stations. The software adapts to what the individual member likes to listen to. Moreover, members can connect with other members with similar music interests through chat and instant messaging. Another music website, www.hifind.com, allows individualized music selections via a comprehensive catalog of criteria, for example, about 60 mood descriptors (e.g., suspenseful, harmonic, or erotic) and 80 situations (e.g., adventure, farewell, or candlelight dinner) to which the selected music is to fit. Modern technology, it seems, will even make mood management easier for us, if the software in question is capable of matching music with the user's need. The acceptance of such services is still uncertain. A cynical speculation of future developments is the vision of a next generation of interfaces that will probably decode the user's mood and the corresponding music need from information such as heart rate, body heat, and pupil width.

REFERENCES

Adorno, T. W. (1996). *Einleitung in die Musiksoziologe: 12 theoretische Vorlesungen* [Introduction to the sociology of music: 12 theoretical lectures](9th ed.). Frankfurt/Main, Germany: Suhrkamp.

Arnett, J. (1991). Heavy metal music and reckless behavior among adolescents. *Journal of Youth and Adolescence, 20,* 573–592.

Behne, K.-E. (1984). Befindlichkeit und Zufriedenheit als Determinanten situativer Musikpräferenzen [Feeling state and contentment as determinants of situational musical preferences]. *Jahrbuch Musikpsychologie, 1,* 7–21.

Behne, K.-E. (1986). Die Benutzung von Musik [The usage of music]. *Jahrbuch Musikpsychologie, 3,* 11–31.

Behne, K.-E. (1997). The development of "Musikerleben" in adolescence: How and why young people listen to music. In I. Deliege & J. Sloboda (Eds.), *Perception and cognition of music* (pp. 143–159). East Sussex: Psychology Press.

Behne, K.-E. (2001). Musik-Erleben: Abnutzung durch Überangebot? [Musical experience: Wearout by oversupply?]. *Media Perspektiven, 3,* 142–148.

Bennett, A. (2000). *Popular music and youth culture: Music, identity, and place.* Basingstoke: Macmillan.

Bleich, S., Zillmann, D., & Weaver, J. (1991). Enjoyment and consumption of defiant rock music as a function of adolescent rebelliousness. *Journal of Broadcasting and Electronic Media, 35,* 351–366.

Bryson, B. (1996). "Anything but heavy metal": Symbolic exclusion and musical dislikes. *American Sociological Review, 61,* 884–899.

Cantor, J. R., & Zillmann, D. (1973). The effect of affective state and emotional arousal on music appreciation. *Journal of General Psychology, 89,* 97–108.

Cattell, R. B., & Saunders, D. R. (1954). Musical preferences and personality diagnosis: A factorization of one hundred and twenty themes. *Journal of Social Psychology, 39,* 3–24.

Denisoff, R. S., & Levine, M. (1972). Youth and popular music: A test of the taste culture hypothesis. *Youth & Society, 4,* 237–256.

Dollase, R. (1997). Musikpräferenzen und Musikgeschmack Jugendlicher [Musical preferences and musical taste of adolescents]. In D. Baacke (Ed.), *Handbuch Jugend und Musik* (pp. 341–368). Opladen: Leske + Budrich.

Dollinger, S. J. (1993). Personality and music preference: Extraversion and excitement seeking or openness to experience? *Psychology of Music, 21*(1), 73–77.

Epstein, J. S. (Ed.). (1994). *Adolescents and their music: If it's too loud, you're too old.* New York: Garland.

Eysenck, H. J., & Eysenck, M. (1985). *Personality and individual differences: A natural science approach.* New York: Plenum.

Finnäs, L. (1989). A comparison between young people's privately and publicly expressed musical preferences. *Psychology of Music, 17,* 132–145.

Fischoff, S. P. (1999). Gangsta' rap and a murder in Bakersfield. *Journal of Applied Social Psychology, 29,* 795–805.

Fried, C. B. (1999). Who's afraid of rap. Differential reactions to music lyrics. *Journal of Applied Social Psychology, 29,* 705–721.

Frith, S. (1981). *Sound effects: Youth, leisure, and the politics of rock.* New York: Pantheon.

Gan, S., Zillmann, D., & Mitrook, M. (1997). Stereotyping effect of black women's sexual rap on white audiences. *Basic and Applied Social Psychology, 19,* 381–399.

Gembris, H. (1985). *Musikhören und Entspannung: theoretische und experimentelle Untersuchungen über den Zusammenhang zwischen situativen Bedingungen und Effekten des Musikhörens* [Music listening and relaxation: Theoretical and experimental examination of the relationship between situational conditions and effects of music listening]. Hamburg, Germany: Wagner.

Gembris, H. (1990). Situationsbezogene Präferenzen und erwünschte Wirkungen von Musik [Situational preferences and desired effects of music]. *Jahrbuch Musikpsychologie, 7,* 73–95.

Gibson, R., Aust, C. F., & Zillmann, D. (2000). Loneliness of adolescents and their choice and enjoyment of love-celebrating versus love-lamenting popular music. *Empirical Studies of the Arts, 18*(1), 43–48.

Green, A.-M. (Ed.). (2000). *Musique et sociologie: Enjeux méthodologiques et approches empiriques* [Music and sociology: Methodological concepts and empirical approaches]. Paris: L'Harmattan.

Hakanen, E. A. (1995). Emotional use of music by African American adolescents. *The Howard Journal of Communication, 5,* 214–222.

Hansen, C. H., & Hansen, R. D. (1990). The influence of sex and violence on the appeal of rock music videos. *Communication Research, 17,* 212–234.

Hansen, C. H., & Hansen, R. D. (1991). Constructing personality and social reality through music: Individual differences among fans of punk and heavy metal music. *Journal of Broadcasting & Electronic Media, 35,* 335–350.

Hansen, C. H., & Hansen, R. D. (2000). Music and music videos. In D. Zillmann & P. Vorderer (Eds.), *Media entertainment. The psychology of its appeal* (pp. 175–196). Mahwah, NJ: Lawrence Erlbaum Associates.

Hargreaves, D. J., & North, A. C. (1999). The functions of music in everyday life: Redefining the social in music psychology. *Psychology of Music, 27*(1) 71–83.

Horden, P. (Ed.). (2000). *Music as medicine: The history of music therapy since antiquity.* Aldershot: Ashgate.

Inhetveen, K. (1997). *Musiksoziologie in der Bundesrepublik Deutschland* [Music sociology in Germany]. Opladen, Germany: Westdeutscher Verlag.

Johnson, J. D., Trawalter, S., & Dovidio, J. F. (2000). Converging interracial consequence of exposure to violent rap music on stereotypical attributions of blacks. *Journal of Experimental Social Psychology, 36,* 233–251.

Johnstone, J., & Katz, E. (1957). Youth and popular music: A study in the sociology of taste. *The American Journal of Sociology, 62,* 563–568.

Jones, J. E. (1990). *Interpersonal perception.* New York: Freeman.

Knobloch, S., Vorderer, P., & Zillmann, D. (2000). Musikgeschmack und Freundschaft unter Jugendlichen [Musical taste and friendship among adolescents]. *Zeitschrift für Sozialpsycho-logie, 31*(1), 18–30.

Knobloch, S., & Zillmann, D. (in press). Mood management via the digital jukebox. *Journal of Communication.*

Konecni, V. (1979). Determinants of aesthetic preference and effects of exposure to aesthetic stimuli: Social, emotional, and cognitive factors. In B. A. Maher (Ed.), *Progress in experimental personality research* (Vol. 9, pp. 149–197). New York: Academic.

Konecni, V. (1982). Social interaction and musical preference. In D. Deutsch (Ed.), *The psychology of music* (pp. 497–516). New York: Academic.

Lehmann, A. C. (1993). Habituelle und situative Rezeptionsweisen beim Musikhören im interkulturellen Vergleich [Habitual and situational patterns of music listening in cross-cultural comparison]. *Jahrbuch Musikpsychologie, 10,* 38–55.

Lehmann, A. C. (1994). *Habituelle und situative Rezeptionsweisen beim Musikhören: Eine einstellungstheoretische Untersuchung* [Habitual and situational patterns of music listening: An attitude-theoretical study]. Frankfurt/Main, Germany: Lang.

Lippmann, W. (1922). *Public opinion.* New York: Harcourt, Brace.

Litle, P., & Zuckerman, M. (1986). Sensation seeking and music preferences. *Personality and individual differences, 7,* 575–578.

Lull, J. (1985). On the communicative properties of music. *Communication Research, 12,* 363–372.

Lull, J. (Ed). (1992). *Popular music and communication.* Beverly Hills, CA: Sage.

Mares, M.-L., & Cantor, J. (1992). Elderly viewers' responses to televised portrayals of old age. *Communication Research, 19,* 459–478.

Martin, P. J. (1995). *Sounds and society: Themes in the sociology of music.* Manchester: Manchester University Press.

McDermott, M. (1988). Measuring rebelliousness: The development of the negativism dominance scale. In M. Apter, J. Kerr, & M. Cowles (Eds.), *Progress in reversal theory* (pp. 297–311). Amsterdam: Elsevier Science.

Moore, M. C., Skipper, J. K., & Willis, C. L. (1979). Rock and roll: Arousal music or a reflection of changing sexual moral? In M. Cook & G. Wilson (Eds.), *Love and attraction: An international conference* (pp. 481–486). Oxford: Pergamon.

Morris, W. N. (1990). *Mood: The frame of mind*. New York: Springer.

Müller, R. (1994). Selbstsozialisation: Eine Theorie lebenslangen musikalischen Lernens [Self-socialization: A theory of life-long musical learning]. *Jahrbuch Musikpsychologie, 11,* 63–75.

Müller, R. (1995). Neue Forschungstechnologien: Der Multimedia-Fragebogen in der musiksoziologischen und musikpädagogischen Forschung [New research technologies: The multimedia-questionnaire in research within music sociology and music education]. *Rundfunk und Fernsehen, 43,* 205–216.

North, A. C., & Hargreaves, D. J. (1996). Situational influences on reported musical preference. *Psychomusicology, 15,* 30–45.

North, A. C., & Hargreaves, D. J. (1997). Experimental aesthetics and everyday music listening. In D. J. Hargreaves & A. C. North (Eds.), *The social psychology of music* (pp. 84–103). Oxford: Oxford University Press.

Rawlings, D., Barrantes i Vidal, N., & Furnham, A. (2000). Personality and aesthetic preference in Spain and England: Two studies relating sensation seeking and openness to experience to liking for paintings and music. *European Journal of Personality, 14,* 553–576.

Rawlings, D., & Ciancarelli, V. (1997). Music preference and the five-factor model of the NEO Personality Inventory. *Psychology of Music, 25*(2), 120–132.

Robinson, T. O., Weaver, J. B., & Zillmann, D. (1996). Exploring the relation between personality and the appreciation of rock music. *Psychological Reports, 78,* 259–269.

Russell, P. A. (1997). Musical tastes and society. In D. J. Hargreaves & A. C. North (Eds.), *The social psychology of music* (pp. 141–158). New York: Oxford University Press.

Scott, D. B. (Ed.). (2000). *Music, culture, and society: A reader.* Oxford: Oxford University Press.

Silbermann, A. (1998). *The sociology of music* (C. Stewart, Trans.). London: Routledge. (Original work published 1963)

Stratton, V. N., & Zalanowski, A. H. (1991). The effects of music and cognition on mood. *Psychology of Music, 19,* 121–127.

Stratton, V. N., & Zalanowski, A. H. (1997). The relationship between characteristic moods and most commonly listened to types of music. *Journal of Music Therapy, 34*(2), 129–140.

Weaver, J. B. (2000). Personality and entertainment preferences. In D. Zillmann & P. Vorderer (Eds.), *Media entertainment: The psychology of its appeal* (pp. 235–248). Mahwah, NJ: Lawrence Erlbaum Associates.

Wells, A., & Hakanen, E. A. (1991). The emotional use of popular music by adolescents. *Journalism Quarterly, 68,* 445–454.

Zillmann, D. (1978). Attribution and misattribution of excitatory reactions. In J. H. Harvey, W. J. Ickes, & R. F. Kidd (Eds.), *New directions in attribution research* (Vol. 2, pp. 335–368). Hillsdale, NJ: Lawrence Erlbaum Associates.

Zillmann, D. (2000). Mood management in the context of selective exposure theory. In M. E. Roloff (Ed.), *Communication Yearbook 23* (pp. 103–123). Thousand Oaks, CA: Sage.

Zillmann, D., Aust, C. F., Hoffman, K. D., Love, C. C., Ordman, V. L., Pope, J. T., & Seigler, P. D. (1995). Radical rap: Does it further ethnic division? *Basic and Applied Social Psychology, 16* (1&2), 1–25

Zillmann, D., & Bhatia, A. (1989). Effects of associating with musical genres on heterosexual attraction. *Communication Research,* 263–288.

Zillmann, D., & Bryant, J. (1984). Effects of massive exposure to pornography. In N. M. Malamuth & E. Donnerstein (Eds.), *Pornography and sexual aggression* (pp. 115–141). Orlando: Academic.

Zillmann, D., & Bryant, J. (Eds.). (1985). *Selective exposure to communication.* Hillsdale, NJ: Lawrence Erlbaum Associates.

Zillmann, D., & Gan, S. (1997). Musical taste in adolescence. In D. J. Hargreaves & A. C. North (Eds.), *The social psychology of music* (pp. 161–187). New York: Oxford University Press.

Zillmann, D., & Mundorf, N. (1987). Image effects in the appreciation of video rock. *Communication Research, 14,* 316–334.

22

Factors in the Appeal of News

Charles F. Aust
Kennesaw State University

> *Yet if the news is so deadening, why does it feel like a resuscitation, a thump on the chest to get the day on beat? Merely the expectation of the morning bulletins seems to place the body on alert. No, it is not beauty, wisdom or deep knowledge,* but it is the news, *a million panicked animals bounding up the stairs. The blood, the senses, everything races. . . .*
>
> –Rosenblatt (1983, p. 93)

The attraction to hard news seems like a contradiction. Content thought to be unappealing, if not completely repulsive appeals to large audiences—violent crime, disasters, accidental and intentional death and injury, acrimonious disputes, deceit and cruel exploitation of innocents. This has caused media scholars to wonder about the motives for exposure to such content. Dolf Zillmann has led efforts to address this puzzlement. Among other reasons for the appeal of news of suffering and misfortune, Zillmann and various collaborators have established that the dramatic nature of news and audience reactions to that drama offer much insight about this matter. This chapter reviews evidence that establishes the abundance of so-called bad news, its widespread appeal, and the variety of motives for that appeal, the most ubiquitous being interest in and enjoyment of drama. Zillmann has led the way in demonstrating the keys to understanding this—dispositional and empathy-mediated reactions the news consumers have toward the happy and successful as well as the suffering and defeated parties featured in news.

NEWS ABOUT MISFORTUNE IS ABUNDANT

There is a lot of what is commonly labeled *bad news,* filled with unpleasant, unfortunate, conflict-laden, and otherwise aversive events, circumstances, and conditions. And its frequency far exceeds the frequency of accounts of good fortune (e.g., R. L. Carroll, 1985; Haskins, 1984; Stone & Grusin, 1984; Stone, Hartung, & Jensen, 1987).

News providers appear to be partial to covering mishaps, setbacks, tragedies, and disasters suffered by people from all walks of life, whether or not such reports are of consequence to news consumers. This partiality to unfortunate and aversive happenings is apparent to the public. According to a survey, 64% of news consumers believe that the news media focus too much on negative themes (Shaw, 1993). Moreover, news professionals are aware of this dominance of negative stories about misfortune (Galician & Pasternack, 1987) and justify the disproportional selection of bad news, contending it is more newsworthy than good news. The surveillance function practiced by journalists advocates that the greatest attention be given to the coverage area's problems because of their impact on the audience and the potential benefit that awareness of the occurrence of such problems could have on amelioration of their causes (Burroughs, 1999; Galtung & Ruge, 1981; Head, Sterling, Schofield, 1994; Lasswell, 1948; Severin & Tankard, 1997).

News that dwells on misfortune has been criticized because of the concern that it desensitizes and depresses news consumers (e.g., Cowdy, 1993; Galician, 1986; Gerbner & Gross, 1976; Jaehnig, Weaver, & Fico, 1981; Levine, 1986; Veitch & Griffitt, 1976). In fact, the expectation that the preponderance of negative news evokes depressive and cynical reactions is said to have motivated TV news programs to close with one or two stories about upbeat, good news (Scott & Gobetz, 1992; Zillmann, Gibson, Ordman, & Aust, 1994). Such placement of enlightening or amusing reports is thought to provide "a release from the deathwatch" that, in the judgment of some, defines much of the news (Marc, 1989, p. 1). Bennett (1983) similarly suggested that the purpose of upbeat closing stories is to "send people off to bed reassured that, despite its problems, the world is still a safe and positive place" (p. 5). The fact remains, however, that the preponderance of news content is negative, the so-called bad news, and thus is seen as triggering apprehensions, depressive states, lingering anxieties, and bad moods.

One might expect that such accounts of dangers and victimization would likely evoke uncomfortable emotional reactions. In fact, this expectation is supported by research about the effects of news reports that feature victimization of others by dangers that also threaten the news recipients. For example, an investigation about carjacking (Gibson & Zillmann, 1994) shows a clear correspondence between aversive emotional reactions to various versions of a news report that detailed incidents of carjacking, on the one hand, and the perception of the threat of carjacking to the motorists, on the other. Specifically, the reported carjackings varied from minimally injurious, through violent and crippling, to fatal. Ratings of being emotionally upset about the report increased progressively with the brutality of the carjackings. The respondents' assessment of the general and, perhaps more importantly, the threat to self of carjackings varied analogously.

A similar investigation established that when TV news featured testimonials by highly emotional victims, viewers perceived themselves to be at greater risk of similar victimization (Aust & Zillmann, 1996).

Yet such negative mass media content attracts large audiences (Donsbach, 1991; Eilders, 1997; Haskins, 1984). There is a significant demand for news. The news media by and large are for-profit businesses. They operate in ways that will attract the largest audience in order to justify the maximum prices they charge advertisers. If negative-laden news content did not attract, if audience interest was scant or infrequent, commercial news media would likely offer less or none of it. In fact, news providers admit to the entertainment value of news (e.g., Jacobs, 1990). A quite sizable audience regularly seeks out the news. November 2000 measurements by Nielsen Media Research indicated that NBC's *Nightly News* attracted more than 11 million households (8.4 rating). ABC's *World News* was viewed by more than 10 million households (7.9 rating). The CBS *Evening News* attracted about 9.5 million households (7.1 rating). Although not the top attractions on commercial TV (compare them to *ER* with 26 million households, a 19 rating), network news shows garner significant viewership comparable to almost all but the top 10 network entertainment programs (Bauder, 2000).

Almost two thirds of adults read the newspaper regularly (Lester, 2000b). Circulation for national news magazines is considerable: *Time* at 4.1 million, *Newsweek* at 3.2 million, and *U.S. News & World Report* at 2.2 million (Campbell, 1998). Another indication of widespread demand for news is the effort by traditional print and broadcast news operations to expand news distribution via the Internet (Gay, 2000). At least one third of the public now goes online for news at least once a week (Lester, 2000a).

APPEAL OF NEWS FOR SELF-PRESERVATION

Given that most news is about misfortune, the fact that many people are drawn to it seems counterintuitive. What makes this so? Motives serving self-preservation (Frijda, 1988; Zillmann, 1998) are one reason. The inclination to continually monitor one's environment for threats and dangers is thought to be defined in evolutionary terms and thus be deep rooted. The news media service this inclination by means of their surveillance function (Lasswell 1948; Shoemaker, 1996). They bring to the public's attention tragic and otherwise adverse conditions and events considered newsworthy because they inform about risks and dangers. Attention by news consumers to such information is thought to provide utility as a measure of protection through precautionary action (Iyengar & Kinder, 1987; Lasswell, 1948; Severin & Tankard, 1997).

The media have, of course, greatly extended the "immediate environment" beyond that which had to be monitored in earlier times. News consumers are now apprised of a multitude of dangers that threaten in virtually all regions of the globe. Many of these dangers are inconsequential to news consumers. News of a catastrophic earthquake in India, for example, is not a threat to Midwesterners in the United States. Yet news coverage in the Midwest is likely to attract large audiences and stir pathos about the plight of earthquake victims. Therefore, such news, although about distant dangers, remains interesting, if not enthralling, even to consumers not directly threatened by the conditions reported in the news.

The point to be made is that the large majority of threats and dangers that are more-or-less continually featured in news are of little, if any, consequence for most news consumers. Utility as a compelling reason for news consumption, then, is inadequate as the only or even the most important reason (Zillmann & Knobloch, 2001). However, extraordinary curiosity about the events in question is obtrusively evident. Such curiosity about threats and dangers, along with the human suffering that is associated with them, is better understood as an exploitable residue of agonistic vigilance that had, but no longer has, general utility (Zillmann, 1998). This interpretation is preferable to the term morbid curiosity (Haskins, 1984), which deems a natural inclination to be aberrant.

APPEAL OF NEWS FOR ACTIVISM

Humanitarian impulses also motivate some people to pay attention to news, particularly news of catastrophes and other disturbances wrought against innocents by nature or human acts. Some news consumers utilize news coverage to gauge the severity of catastrophic events and respond accordingly with material or financial contributions. In some cases they get physically involved in the plight of victims, assisting in disaster clean-up, donating blood, and even rescuing endangered persons seen in live TV coverage (Standish, 1992).

Another interest in news is motivated by the social and political activism of group members working for particular causes. However, not all news consumers are actively involved in groups or parties, even though they may be linked to one cause or another. In all probability, these news consumers will be strongly involved with only a limited number of causes addressed in daily reports, and they will qualify as interested bystanders for the remaining vast majority of reports that cover the success or failure of social agendas and initiatives (Zillmann & Knobloch, 2001).

APPEAL OF NEWS AS NONFICTION THEATER

The motive of self-preservation does not completely explain the appeal of news. The large majority of threats and dangers that are continually featured are of little if any immediate consequence for most news consumers. Yet even news that has no obvious utility to news consumers can generate interest levels ranging from mild curiosity to enthralling captivation and elicit emotional reactions (Zillmann & Brosius, 2000). The motive of activism does not completely explain the appeal of news. Most news consumers, even though they may be linked to one cause or another, qualify as interested bystanders for the vast majority of reports that cover the success or failure of social agendas and initiatives.

A motive, likely a ubiquitous one, that makes news appealing involves the appreciation of drama. News is full of drama. Drama relies on conflict and endangerment (Zillmann, 1980; Zillmann, 1996; Zillmann & Bryant, 1986). As in drama, conflict is one of the essential and enduring themes of journalism (Bird & Dardenne, 1990; Cohen, Adoni, & Bantz, 1990; Fedler, Bender, Davenport, & Kostyu, 1997). It adds interest because it engages the emotions, particularly empathy (Aust & Zillmann, 1996; Bird & Dardenne, 1990; Zillmann, 1991). News producers intentionally look for stories that contain dramatic elements (Brooks, Kennedy, Moen, & Ranly, 1996; Lule, 2001). News has been characterized as a form of storytelling (Bird & Dardenne, 1990; Darnton, 1975; Fowles, 1992; Schudson, 1982; Sperry, 1981).

Virtually all news consumers are likely to be interested in the news in part for its dramatic appeal. Because news is laden with drama, and therefore also abounding in emotions, it is important to address the role of affective reactions. Disposition theory is most helpful in this regard. This theory has aided in the understanding of reactions to fictional narratives (Zillmann, 1994) as well as to some nonfiction situations, such as athletic competitions (Zillmann & Paulus, 1993). Disposition theory holds that witnessing characters or persons doing agreeable, good things, in the moral judgment of the observer, will foster liking, caring, and friend-like feelings in that observer. Witnessing them doing disagreeable, bad things, in the moral judgment of the observer, in contrast, will foster disliking, resentment, and enemy-like feelings in the observer (Zillmann, 1996). Once dispositions toward people in the news have been formed in this manner, drama-appreciation theory (Zillmann, 1991, 1996, 2000) may be applied to contribute to an understanding of the appeal of news as nonfiction theater.

One might wonder if the mechanisms of disposition formation apply to all communication experiences, whether mediated or nonmediated, fictional or factual, and so on. Recent theorizing about emotional reactions to drama (cf. N. Carroll, 1996; Tan, 1996; Zillmann, 1996) holds that disposition formation is governed by the same processes during both theatrical presentation and actual social exchanges. Furthermore, the governing processes are thought to be the same for immediate and mediated observations. Therefore, whether in fiction, the news, or immediate interaction, witnessing characters or persons doing agreeable, good things will foster liking and friend-like treatment. Witnessing them doing disagreeable, bad things, in contrast, will foster disliking and enemy-like treatment.

Because it also can be applied to understanding of reactions in immediate (nonmediated) social interactions (Zillmann, 1991; Zillmann & Bryant, 1980), its application to understanding reactions to news reports is logical and useful.

A DISPOSITION CONTINUUM

Character development is essential in fictional drama in order to develop dispositions of liking or disliking, caring or uncaring, toward vital characters, and to engage the audience's emotions. In drama-theoretical terms, those who are liked become protagonists and those who are disliked become antagonists. Regarding the news, however, affective dispositions need not be created for each individual featured in every story. This phenomenon of character development in news accounts about real people can be conceptualized as a continuum that illustrates wide variation in the amount of knowledge on which an immediately felt disposition could be based. The knowledge base might be sparse or extensive, yet disposition is immediately established on comprehension of the details in the news account. At one extreme of this continuum, the news consumer's readily felt disposition might be based on no particular knowledge about a distressed victim in a news report except a shared fundamental experience of the human condition. In the instance of negative news, the news consumer's knowledge about the suffering person might be as basic as knowing what it feels like to bleed, to suffer burns, to fear for one's safety, or to be bereft of a precious loved one or vital possession. For example, news consumers might know nothing about a car crash victim (e.g., gender, age, occupation) except that the victim is trapped in a burning vehicle. Very little is known about this person, yet because of a shared experience of the human condition—knowing the intense pain of burn injuries—a disposition is likely to be generated immediately in the news consumer, to be felt only mildly in low-empathy observers, but intensely by high-empathy observers.

At the other extreme of this continuum, a readily felt disposition toward a person in the news could be based on in-depth knowledge of that person based on a long-existing interest. Examples include one's favorite political or religious leader, musical performer, or movie star. For example, the President of the United States and his entourage, along with their current political foes, are well-developed "players." So are the leaders of other prominent nations and the promoters of popular and unpopular causes. The same can be said for entertainment and sports celebrities. Because these persons are well-established entities, most news consumers possess knowledge about them, in some cases extensive, and will hold specific and readily felt dispositions toward them (Zillmann, Taylor, & Lewis, 1998).

In between these extremes of sparse and extensive knowledge, amounts of knowledge may vary yet are available to generate a readily felt disposition toward persons featured in the news. The continuum structure is useful also because some persons appear recurrently in the news. As news consumers build their knowledge about these persons and their actions, dispositions of liking and caring or hatred and resentment toward them, and the intensity of such feelings, could shift on the continuum. Emotional experiences about people in the news can build in intensity over time. The news media do provide accounts and displays of events and people that are likely to evoke emotions capable of fostering indelible, memory-vivid, salient accounts and imagery that become accessible both in the short term as well as the long term (Zillmann & Brosius, 2000).

News of massacres, disease outbreaks, or disasters in far away places might be expected to leave large segments of the news audience indifferent. In drama-theoretical terms, the "characters" suffering these misfortunes would seem to be insufficiently developed. Insufficient character development is known to result in drama that feels emotionally flat because it fails to engender caring or resentful feelings of appreciable intensity in the respondents. Applied to news, however, with only a sparse amount of information about the suffering parties or their circumstances, audience reactions can be quite strong. For example, a favorable disposition and intense caring by audience members about suffering persons in the news was observed during the famine in Somalia in 1993 ("SOS in Somalia," 1993). Repeated coverage of the suffering children and their circumstances resulted in the rapid formation of affective dispositions, dispositions sufficiently strong and widespread to be acknowledged by the government and to motivate a policy shift and humanitarian relief efforts. Subsequently, unfavorable dispositions were formed in news consumers when their attention was drawn to villains in the story. Based only on reports of brutalizing actions by locals against U.S. Marines, news consumers became emotionally involved, and their strong emotional reactions quickly evoked a switch from support to anger about U.S. military involvement in Somalia, resulting in yet another foreign policy shift (Sharkey, 1993; Zillmann, Taylor, & Lewis, 1998).

The point to be made is that people in the news are, as a rule, sufficiently developed characters so that dispositions toward them in the news consumers are readily felt to varying degrees and can change when persons appear recurrently in the news (Zillmann, Taylor, & Lewis, 1998, 1999; Zillmann & Knobloch, 2001).

PARASOCIAL RELATIONSHIPS IN DISPOSITION FORMATION

A related phenomenon to disposition formation, the so-called parasocial relationship, also is thought to be at work in evoking dispositional reactions to people in the news. Horton and his collaborators (Horton & Strauss, 1957; Horton & Wohl, 1956) proposed that media consumers develop a quasisocial relationship with media characters to whom they are repeatedly exposed and about whom they often learn more than about persons in their immediate social environment. Such relationships are not restricted to characters in the news but readily extend to fictional characters. "Relationships built up and the understanding that sustains them, seem no different in kind from those characteristics of normal social life" (Horton & Strauss, 1957, p. 587). Stable affective dispositions are thought to develop. Fictional television characters could become "friends," much like actual friends. A large volume of research has explored the validity of this proposal and has generated empirical support for it (Fabian, 1993; Isotalus, 1995; Levy, 1979; Perse & Rubin, 1989; Rubin & McHugh, 1987). It is widely accepted that respondents do develop quasisocial relationships with media characters, and that affective dispositions toward the targeted individuals are an integral part of these relationships.

Oddly, the research on parasocial relations has very much neglected that media characters may also become enemy-like; that is, they may become disliked, resented, and even hated. However, because the disposition-generating mechanisms outlined by Horton and collaborators apply to negative dispositions as well as to positive ones, it must be assumed that the media develop "parasocial enemies" as easily as they develop "parasocial friends" (Zillmann & Knobloch, 2001). The research on parasocial relations, moreover, has been limited to such relations with individual media characters. The concept readily extends, however, to relations with coherent groups in the media.

THE ROLE OF EMPATHY

Affective reactions are a function of affective dispositions toward the persons to whom good or bad things are happening and who express positive or negative emotions in response to those happenings. Empathy research provides compelling evidence for this (e.g., Aronfreed, 1970; Berger, 1962; Eisenberg & Strayer, 1987; Hoffman, 1978; Stotland, 1969; Zillmann, 1991). When observers hold favorable dispositions toward those they observe; they respond in a hedonically compatible fashion to the good or bad fortunes of those observed. In other words, they will be pleased and joyous when learning about good fortunes for liked others, and they will be displeased and disturbed when learning about bad fortunes of liked others. When the dispositions in the observer are unfavorable, however, the observer responds in a counterempathic or hedonically incompatible way: The experience of good fortunes by disliked others is distressing to the observer, and the experience of bad fortunes by them is enjoyable to the observer. Empathic reactivity may be expected, then, wherever and whenever dispositions of liking exist.

In contrast, dispositions of disliking, contempt, resentment, or open hatred must be expected to foster counterempathic reactions. In such situations, the negative disposition virtually overrides empathic concerns, mostly because of moral considerations (cf. N. Carroll, 1996; Wilson, Cantor, Gordon, & Zillmann, 1986; Zillmann, 1991). Resented others are deemed undeserving of good fortunes and deserving of bad fortunes. Observing those resented others experiencing such good fortune thus irritates and distresses. Observing those resented others experiencing bad fortunes does not call for any form of cosuffering but, in fact, may spark satisfaction and joy.

ONE'S BAD NEWS MIGHT BE ANOTHER'S GOOD NEWS

Regarding the news, it cannot be assumed that the affective dispositions toward all featured persons are uniform. They are likely to vary substantially, and empathic reactivity also must be expected to vary. Any report of good or bad fortunes for particular individuals must therefore be expected to foster empathic reactions in favorably disposed audience members and counterempathic reactions in audience members who are unfavorably disposed. Because research about empathic reactivity in a dramatic context indicates that dispositionally indifferent persons tend to be somewhat empathic (Zillmann & Cantor, 1977), one can expect that the affective reactions will be rather subdued in audience members who are neither favorably nor unfavorably disposed toward the featured individuals or groups.

Applied to news, then, empathy theory projects that news accounts of mishaps, setbacks, endangerments, victimizations, or tragic losses for specific individuals or groups will evoke distress and sadness in some, amusement and delight in others, and leave yet others only mildly moved, if at all.

Therefore, affective reactions to the news are not simply a function of the stimulus-defined nature of the content. That is, they are not a function of the normative goodness or badness of events. Instead they are mediated by dispositions toward the recipients of good or bad fortunes. Thus, affective dispositions in news consumers influence their subjective perception of the news as good or bad, depending on affective dispositions the news consumers hold toward persons in the reports. Dispositions of news consumers vary, so the emotional reactions to identical news reports are diverse. The goodness or badness of the news, then, can be said to be "in the eye of the beholder" (Zillmann et al., 1998; Zillmann & Knobloch, 2001).

In any event, to the extent that news consumers possess a disposition toward persons in the news, or to the extent that pertinent details about such persons are provided as the news story is presented, to that extent will the news consumer's disposition toward those persons influence the perceived goodness or badness of news accounts and their enjoyment of the reported outcomes in news.

EVIDENCE FOR NEWS AS NONFICTION THEATER

These empathic and counterempathic response dynamics have been demonstrated, mostly in dramatic contexts (e.g., N. Carroll, 1996; Tan, 1996; Zillmann, 1994, 1996; Zillmann & Cantor, 1976; Zillmann & Paulus, 1993). They also have been shown to apply to news reception (Zillmann et al., 1998, 1999; Zillmann & Knobloch, 2001).

In the same way persons respond to fictional dramatic presentations, respondents to the news react affectively to persons whose actions they applaud or despise and whose fortunes they enjoy or deplore (Zillmann et al., 1998). The less news consumers care, one way or another, about persons in the news, the less they are distressed by negative happenings endured by those featured persons, and likewise, the less the news consumers are joyful in response to positive happenings enjoyed by those persons (Zillmann et al., 1998). Indifference or apathy toward persons and groups, along with their striving, successes, and failures, thus emerges as the condition that accounts for nonempathic, insensitive reactions to reports of the plight as well as the triumph of people in the news (Zillmann et al., 1998).

In a demonstration of the role of disposition theory in reactions to news, the report of a leading politician's contracting of a venereal disease was applauded by those who hated him and deplored by those who loved him. The same set of responses was observed for the mishaps or setbacks befalling famous entertainers (i.e., actors and singers) and athletes. The hedonic response pattern reversed for reports of good fortune being experienced by these public characters. That is, the news of good fortune evoked applause in admirers and dejection in haters. Regardless of the hedonic quality of the reaction, however, emotional intensity proved to be a function of the magnitude of affective disposition. Additionally, these findings lend support to the claim that emotions appear to be readily engaged even by news revelations that are of no consequence for the personal welfare of the audience (Zillmann et al., 1998, 1999).

In an experiment about recurring public characters in the news, Zillmann and Knobloch (2001) demonstrated that the more a person was liked, the less enjoyable it was to learn of his or her misfortune. Conversely, the more a person was disliked, the stronger was the enjoyment reaction to disclosed misfortune. As predicted by empathy theory, the misfortunes of disliked persons was good news for those not bothered by empathic concerns; and the joyful reactions were stronger, the more intense the resentment. In contrast, the more a person was liked, the more enjoyable it was to witness his or her benefaction. Conversely, the less a person was liked, the less enjoyment was elicited. These findings established that news consumers develop and maintain affective dispositions toward public persons who are frequently featured in the news, and that these dispositions determine the recipients' emotional reactions to the revelation of fortunes as predicted by drama-appreciation theory (Zillmann & Knobloch, 2001).

In drama, punitive violence can generate intense satisfaction, if not euphoria, when it is meted out to the villains by the heroes (Zillmann, 1998). Likewise, for example, news reports of vigilantism or accounts of targeted crime victims who are able to turn on and vanquish their attackers could be expected to trigger intense satisfaction in news consumers.

Live news coverage presents a special possibility for intensifying the appeal of news accounts. During live news coverage, excitation transfer (see chap. 2, this volume) can intensify celebratory and joyful reactions if a sudden turn of events occurs. When a person is emotionally aroused, the endocrine glands release chemicals that elevate sympathetic excitation, which decays slowly in the bloodstream. Combining this residual excitation with the excitatory activity generated by an immediately occurring subsequent stimulus can intensify the emotional reaction to that stimulus (Zillmann, 1980). An unfolding live news feed in which an initially highly distressing situation quickly gets resolved to the satisfaction of the viewer could intensify such satisfaction because of the excitation-transfer mechanism. A state of suspense in the news consumer about an impending and likely noxious outcome would be an instance in which great intensity of distress is evoked. When the noxious, suspenseful emotional state is suddenly followed by a pleasing resolution of the suspense, excitation-transfer theory suggests the hedonically positive emotional reaction would be intensified by the residual excitation from the suspenseful state, making the outcome feel all the more gratifying.

This could account for the enthralling captivation and intense emotions many TV viewers and radio listeners seem to experience during and immediately after the satisfactory resolution of a police chase of a known, criminally dangerous person (see chap. 16, this volume, on suspense and mystery).

In addition, a sequence in which a pleasing situation suddenly becomes even more pleasing because of new developments would also elicit more intense reactions of joy and satisfaction.

These considerations regarding punitive violence and excitation transfer, as they apply to reactions to news, await experimental investigation.

APPLICATION OF DISPOSITION THEORY TO NEWS ABOUT GROUPS, ISSUES

Dispositional differentiation can be applied to groups also. The so-called mass media audience is actually composed of a multitude of interest groups in pursuit of goals they deem essential. News revelations are bound to touch on the objectives of at least some groups in the audience, on occasion, or those concerning nearly the entire audience. News revelations will mean progress to some, setback to others. Accordingly, they will elicit joy in some, dejection in others. News revelations, if not entirely irrelevant, will touch the emotions of at least a good portion of the audience (Zillmann & Brosius, 2000).

News consumers will have interest in and emotional reactions to the successes and setbacks of groups whose goals and concerns are shared and actively supported by those news consumers. It has been demonstrated that the more resentment news consumers held toward a group, the greater their enjoyment response to news of misfortune of that resented group. For example, regarding the abortion issue, the two diametrically opposed action groups were shown to inflict damage on the political agenda of their countergroup in an experiment by Zillmann and Knobloch (2001). Specifically, the pro-choice agenda was set back by a pro-life activist, or vice versa. Those resenting the agenda that suffered the setback reported greater enjoyment of such a report. Additionally, it was shown that misfortunes that were deplored by news consumers when their liked and supported group was victimized were enjoyable to the news consumers when their disliked opponent group was victimized. The findings showed consistently greater enjoyment after news revelations of detrimental happenings to action groups toward whom negative affective dispositions were held than to such groups when met with favorable dispositions (Zillmann & Knobloch, 2001).

One can apply this classification scheme to all conceivable social groupings. Groups will be seen as protagonists when their goals correspond with those embraced by the audience members, antagonists when their goals are opposite to those embraced by the audience members, or insignificant if their goals are deemed immaterial by the audience members. Such categorizations are useful to audience members as they attend to news content about the vast array of possible social groupings, often defined by the vital interests of those groups. Dispositions toward groups apply to demographic-style groupings, such as by nationality, race, ethnicity, age, education, religion, political affiliation, sexual orientation, and so on. Disposition also applies to tacitly defined groups such as sports fans, movie buffs, music devotees, and cult followers. For example, Trekkies, Punks, and Skinheads are groups of well-developed characters, as are feminists, environmentalists, fundamentalists, and innumerable others (Zillmann et al., 1998).

These dispositional effects also extend to reports of setbacks and advancements of supported or opposed public issues. Reports of the advancement of supported causes enhanced joyful reactions. In contrast, reports of the setback of supported causes enhance reactions of disappointment and dejection. In addition, reports of the setback of opposed causes enhanced joyful reactions, and in contrast, reports of the advancement of opposed causes enhanced reactions of disappointment and dejection. Strength of reactions also consistently increased with the strength of the associated dispositions (Zillmann et al., 1999).

These findings thus extend the established dispositional effects found for reports of bad or good fortunes experienced by liked or disliked persons to news accounts of setbacks and advancements of supported or opposed public issues (Zillmann et al., 1998).

CONCLUSION

Dispositional emotion-mediating mechanisms are essentially the same for fictional and nonfiction representations of events of consequence to the observers of those events. Whether in theatrical presentations or in news reports about actual persons, groups, and issues, dispositions of the observers toward the good or bad fortunes experienced by those recipients and causes influence the affective reactions of the observers of those eventualities. That is, news consumers enjoy news reports of good fortune of liked and cared-for persons, groups, and issues. News consumers enjoy news reports of bad fortunes for disliked and resented persons, groups, and issues.

Thus it can be argued that, in addition to the utility of news for self-preservation and social activism, the dramatic nature of news is an appealing feature that compels news consumers to attend to accounts about the striving and triumphs as well as the suffering and defeat of real people, the groups to which they belong, and the causes they pursue.

From the empirical investigations reviewed, it has been established that affective reactions to the news, and to bad news in particular, vary greatly and are determined largely by dispositions of news consumers toward the persons featured in the news, rather than by the stimulus-defined goodness or badness of the content. That is, whether a news story is deemed to be good or bad is in the disposition-based "eye of the beholder."

Furthermore, the empathic dynamics are the same in audience reactions to news accounts as to theatrical presentations. Audience members will find joy and satisfaction when persons in the news whom they like and care about experience good fortune and when persons they dislike and resent suffer misfortune. Conversely, audience members will feel dejected and dissatisfied when persons they like and care about suffer misfortune and when persons they dislike and resent experience good fortune.

Contrary to the long-held belief in the hedonic congruence of news—that bad news is always deemed bad and good news is invariably deemed to be good—it is rather the case that diverse affective reactions occur, depending on dispositions toward impacted persons, groups, and issues in those news reports. Put another way, these studies establish that affective reactions to the news are not uniform, but rather will vary based on the news consumers' dispositions toward persons, groups, and causes witnessed as recipients of good or bad fortune in news reports.

REFERENCES

Aronfreed, J. (1970). The socialization of altruistic and sympathetic behavior: Some theoretical and experimental analyses. In J. Macaulay & L. Berkowitz (Eds.), *Altruism and helping behavior* (pp. 103–126). New York: Academic.

Aust, C. F., & Zillmann, D. (1996). Effects of victim exemplification in television news on viewer perception of social issues. *Journalism & Mass Communication Quarterly, 73,* 787–803.

Bauder, D. (2000, December, 15). Network news gains big jump from election story. *Detroit News,* p. 2.

Bennett, W. L. (1983). *News: The politics of illusion*. New York: Longman.

Berger, S. M. (1962). Conditioning through vicarious instigation. *Psychological Review, 29,* 450–466.

Bird, S. E., & Dardenne, R. W. (1990). News and storytelling in American culture: Reevaluating the sensational dimension. *Journal of American Culture, 12*(2), 33–37.

Brooks, B. S., Kennedy, G., Moen, D. R., & Ranly, D. (1996). *News reporting and writing.* New York: St. Martin's Press.

Burroughs, P. (1999, February 20). At local papers, news touches nerves. *Editor & Publisher,* 78.

Campbell, R. (1998). *Media and culture* (2nd ed.). New York: St. Martin's Press.

Carroll, N. (1996). The paradox of suspense. In P. Vorderer, H. J. Wulff, & M. Friedrichsen (Eds.), *Suspense: Conceptualizations, theoretical analyses, and empirical explorations* (pp. 71–91). Mahwah, NJ: Lawrence Erlbaum Associates.

Carroll, R. L. (1985). Content values in TV news programs in small and large markets. *Journalism Quarterly, 62,* 877–938.

Cohen, A. A., Adoni, H., & Bantz, C. R. (1990). *Social conflict and television news.* Newbury Park, CA: Sage.

Cowdy, A. (1993). Can "good" news make good TV? *Media Ethics, 6*(1), 11.

Darnton, R. (1975, September). Writing news and telling stories. *Daedalus, 104,* 175–194.

Donsbach, W. (1991). *Medienwirkung trotz Selektion: Einflußfactoren auf die Zuwendung zu Zeitungsinhalten* [Media effects despite selectivity: Factors influencing exposure to newspaper content]. Köln: Böhlau.

Eilders, C. (1997). *Nachrichtenfaktoren und Rezeption: Eine empirische Analyse zur Auswahl und Verarbeitung politischer Information* [News factors and reception: An empirical analysis of selection and processing of political information]. Opladen: Westdeutscher Verlag.

Eisenberg, N., & Strayer, J. (Eds.). (1987). *Empathy and its development.* Cambridge, NY: Cambridge University Press.

Fabian, T. (1993). *Fernsehen und Einsamkeit im Alter: Eine empirische Untersuchung zu parasozialer Interaktion* [Television and loneliness among the elderly: An empirical investigation of parasocial interaction]. Münster: LIT.

Fedler, F., Bender, J. R., Davenport, L., & Kostyu, P. E. (1997). *Reporting for the media.* Fort Worth, TX: Harcourt Brace.

Fowles, J. (1992). *Why viewers watch: A reappraisal of television's effects.* Newbury Park, CA: Sage.

Frijda, N. (1988). The law of emotion. *American Psychologist, 43,* 349–358.

Galician, M. L. (1986). Perceptions of good news and bad news on television. *Journalism Quarterly, 63,* 611–616.

Galician, M. L., & Pasternack, S. (1987) Balancing good news and bad news: An ethical obligation? *Journal of Mass Media Ethics, 2*(2), 82–92.

Galtung, J., & Ruge, M. (1981). Structuring and selecting news. In S. Cohen & J. Young (Eds.), *The manufacture of news: Deviance, social problems, and the mass media* (pp. 52–63). Beverly Hills: Sage.

Gay, V. (2000, September 4). All the news that fits. *Adweek,* IQ30–IQ34.

Gerbner, G., & Gross, L. (1976, April). The scary world of TV's heavy viewer. *Psychology Today,* 41–45, 89.

Gibson, R., & Zillmann, D. (1994). Exaggerated versus representative exemplification in news reports: Perception of issues and personal consequences. *Communication Research, 21,* 603–624.

Haskins, J. B. (1984). Morbid curiosity and the mass media: A synergistic relationship. In J. A. Crook, J. B. Haskins, & P. G. Ashdown (Eds.), *Morbid curiosity and the mass media: Proceedings of a symposium* (pp. 1–44). Knoxville, TN: University of Tennessee & the Gannett Foundation.

Head, S. W., Sterling, C. H., & Schofield, L. B. (1994). *Broadcasting in America* (7th ed.). Boston: Houghton Mifflin.

Hoffman, M. L. (1978). Toward a theory of empathetic arousal and development. In M. Lewis & L. A. Rosenblum (Eds.), *The development of affect* (pp. 227–256). New York: Plenum.

Horton, D., & Strauss, A. (1957). Interaction in audience-participation shows. *American Journal of Sociology, 62,* 579–587.

Horton, D., & Wohl, R. R. (1956). Mass communication and para-social interaction: Observations on intimacy at a distance. *Psychiatry, 19,* 215–229.

Isotalus, P. (1995). Friendship through screen. *The Nordicom Review of Nordic Research on Media and Communication, 1,* 59–64.

Iyengar, S., & Kinder, D. R. (1987). *News that matters.* Chicago: University of Chicago Press.

Jacobs, J. (1990). *Changing channels: Issues and realities in television news.* Mountain View, CA: Mayfield Publishing.

Jaehnig, W., Weaver, D., & Fico, F. (1981). Reporting crime and fearing crime in three communities. *Journal of Communication, 3*(Winter), 88–96.

Lasswell, H. D. (1948). The structure and function of communication in society. In L. Bryson (Ed.), *The communication of ideas: A series of addresses* (pp. 37–51). New York: Harper & Brothers.

Lester, W. (2000a, June 12). Internet gaining as news source. *Denver Post,* A6.

Lester, W. (2000b, June 12). More people turning to Internet for news. *Detroit News,* 2.

Levine, G. F. (1986). Learned helplessness in local TV news. *Journalism Quarterly, 63,* 12–18.

Levy, M. R. (1979). Watching TV news as para-social interaction. *Journal of Broadcasting, 23,* 69–80.

Lule, J. (2001). *Daily news, eternal stories*. New York: Guilford.

Marc, D. (1989). *Comic visions: Television comedy and American culture.* Boston: Unwin Hyman.

Perse, E. M., & Rubin, A. M. (1989). Attribution in social and parasocial relationships. *Communication Research, 16,* 59–77.

Rosenblatt, R. (1983, December 12). The news: Living in the present tense. *Time,* 93.

Rubin, R. B., & McHugh, M. P. (1987). Development of parasocial interaction relationships. *Journal of Broadcasting & Electronic Media, 31,* 279–292.

Schudson. M. (1982). The politics of narrative form: The emergence of news conventions in print and television. *Daedalus, 3,* 97–112.

Scott, D. K., & Gobetz, R. H. (1992). Hard news/soft news content of the national broadcast network, 1972–1987. *Journalism Quarterly, 69,* 406–412.

Severin, W. J., & Tankard, J. W. (1997). *Communication theories: Origins, methods, and uses in the mass media* (4th ed.). New York: Longman.

Sharkey, J. (1993, December). When pictures drive foreign policy: Somalia raises serious questions about media influence. *American Journalism Review,* pp. 14–19.

Shaw, D. (1993, March 31). *Trust in media is on decline.* Los Angeles Times, A1.

Shoemaker, P. J. (1996). Hardwired for news: Using biological and cultural evolution to explain the surveillance function. *Journal of Communication, 46,* 32–47.

"SOS in Somalia," (1993, Nov. 8). *Newsweek,* p. 8.

Sperry, S. (1981). Television news as narrative. In R. P. Adler (Ed.), *Understanding television* (pp. 295–312). New York: Praeger.

Standish, K. (1992, June). Hell in the City of Angels. *Communicator* (Radio and Television News Directors' Association magazine), 14–15.

Stone, G. C., & Grusin, E. (1984). Network TV as the bad news bearer. *Journalism Quarterly, 61,* 517–523.

Stone, G. C., Hartung, B., & Jensen, D. (1987). Local TV news and the good-bad dyad. *Journalism Quarterly, 64,* 37–44.

Stotland, E. (1969). Exploratory investigations of empathy. In L. Berkowitz (Ed.), *Advances in experimental social psychology* (Vol. 4, pp. 271–314). New York: Academic.

Tan, D. S. (1996). *Emotion and the structure of narrative film: Film as an emotion machine.* Mahwah, NJ: Lawrence Erlbaum Associates.

Veitch, R., & Griffitt, W. (1976). Good news–bad news: Affective and interpersonal effects. *Journal of Applied Social Psychology, 6,* 69–75.

Wilson, B. J., Cantor, J., Gordon, L., & Zillmann, D. (1986). Affective response of nonretarded and retarded children to the emotions of a protagonist. *Child Study Journal, 16*(2), 77–93.

Zillmann, D. (1980). Anatomy of suspense. In P. Tannenbaum (Ed.), *The entertainment functions of television* (pp. 133–163). Hillsdale, NJ: Lawrence Erlbaum Associates.

Zillmann, D. (1991). Empathy: Affect from bearing witness to the emotions of others. In J. Bryant & D. Zillmann (Eds.), *Responding to the screen: Reception and reaction processes* (pp. 135–167). Hillsdale, NJ: Lawrence Erlbaum Associates.

Zillmann, D. (1994). Mechanisms of emotional involvement with drama. *Poetics, 23,* 33–51.

Zillmann, D. (1996). The psychology of suspense in dramatic exposition. In P. Vorderer, H. J. Wulff & M. Friedrichsen (Eds.), *Suspense: Conceptualizations, theoretical analyses, and empirical explorations* (pp. 199–231). Hillsdale, NJ: Lawrence Erlbaum Associates.

Zillmann, D. (1998). The psychology of the appeal of portrayals of violence. In J. H. Goldstein (Ed.), *Why we watch: The attractions of violent entertainment* (pp. 179–211). New York: Oxford University Press.

Zillmann, D. (2000). Basal morality in drama appreciation. In I. Bondebjerg (Ed.), *Moving images, culture and the mind* (pp. 53–63). Luton, England: University of Luton Press.

Zillmann, D., & Brosius, H-B. (2000). *Exemplification in communication.* Mahwah, NJ: Lawrence Erlbaum Associates.

Zillmann, D., & Bryant, J. (1980). Misattribution theory of tendentious humor. *Journal of Experimental Social Psychology, 16,* 146–160.

Zillmann, D., & Bryant, J. (1986). Exploring the entertainment experience. In J. Bryant & D. Zillmann (Eds.), *Perspectives on media effects* (pp. 303–324). Hillsdale, NJ: Lawrence Erlbaum Associates.

Zillmann, D., & Cantor, J. R. (1976). A disposition theory of humour and mirth. In A. J. Chapman & H. C. Foot (Eds.), *Humour and laughter: Theory, research, and applications* (pp. 93–115). London: Wiley.

Zillmann, D., & Cantor, J. R. (1977). Affective responses to the emotions of a protagonist. *Journal of Experimental Social Psychology, 13,* 155–165.

Zillmann, D., Gibson, R., Ordman, V. L., & Aust, C. F. (1994). Effects of upbeat stories in broadcast news. *Journal of Broadcasting & Electronic Media, 38*(1), 65–78.

Zillmann, D., & Knobloch, S. (2001). Emotional reactions to narratives about the fortunes of personae in the news theater. *Poetics, 29,* 189–206.

Zillmann, D., & Paulus, P. B. (1993). Spectators: Reactions to sports events and effects on athletic performance. In R. N. Singer, M. Murphey, & L. K. Tennant (Eds.), *Handbook on research in sports psychology* (pp. 600–619). New York: Macmillan.

Zillmann, D., Taylor, K., & Lewis, K. (1998). News as nonfiction theater: How dispositions toward the public cast of characters affect reactions. *Journal of Broadcasting & Electronic Media, 42,* 153–169.

Zillmann, D., Taylor, K. & Lewis, K. (1999). Dispositions toward public issues as determinants of reactions to bad and good news. *Medienpsychologie, 11,* 231–243, 287.

SECTION V:

Theoretical Advances and Emerging Perspectives

23

Theory of Affective Dynamics: Emotions and Moods

Dolf Zillmann
University of Alabama

> *Lacking sound and fury, emotions as cognitions signify nothing, or at least nothing very emotional.*
>
> –LeDoux (1996, p. 42)

I stand in awe of my academic progeny and some less immediate relations for finding common ground for this Festschrift in the contestable concept of emotion. Might I have had a hand in their choice of such focus? In paraphrasing a media-influence cliché, I suspect that with my teachings I probably failed to convince this group of scholars of the merits of my particular theoretical stand on emotion, but I apparently managed to make everybody think about emotion as a key to productive analyses. Be this as it may, I was delighted to learn of their embrace of emotion as an entity that provides a unifying perspective on media influence. Moreover, it took little prodding by the editors to get me to contribute a "keystone statement" on the affections. In fact, I greatly appreciated being given the opportunity to clarify my theorizing on emotion as a principal force in life at large—and in media influence as well.

In my exposition of affective dynamics, I concentrate on emotions and moods. Initially, I detail various conceptualizations of emotions, moods, sentiments, and temperaments. I then discuss the basic theoretical approaches to the affections. After indicating the discipline-specific, limiting circumstances of most of these theories, I develop my own position as integrative theory that cuts across various disciplines and, in fact, brings together many of the theoretical and empirical contributions from different, usually segregated fields of inquiry. In particular, I make an effort to support my theoretical proposals with recent discoveries in neurophysiology and endocrinology. Following the outline of general principles of emotion and mood dynamics, I briefly present the excitation-transfer paradigm and discuss, in some detail, the empathic mediation of affections.

The final section is dedicated to exploring the affective dynamics of media influence and alternative media effects. I examine the capacity of both the informative and entertaining media for evoking immediate, basic emotions. I give special attention to the instigation of emotions and moods by way of empathy. Moreover, I elaborate the uniqueness of formative features of media presentations and use this uniqueness to show the ubiquity of excitation transfer for the media. Last, but not least, I consider the media manipulation of emotions and moods and offer a choice paradigm for emotion and mood management.

AFFECTIVE BEHAVIORS AND EXPERIENCES

In contrast to the relaxed contemplation of phenomena, affective experiences entail preferences and behavioral inclinations, along with a preparedness for action in the service of these partialities. The preparedness for action is usually associated with some degree of excitedness. Excitedness varies greatly across affections, however, and this circumstance, among others, has prompted the conceptualization of numerous forms of affective behaviors and experiences. Specifically, differences have been articulated between emotions and moods, and additional affective conditions, such as sentiment and temperament, have been proposed.

It is generally held that emotions, compared to moods, are characterized by greater excitatory intensity, shorter duration, and stronger focus on both causal circumstances and motivational implications (Damasio, 1997; Frijda, 1993, 1994; Morris, 1989, 1992; Nowlis & Nowlis, 1956; Thayer, 1989, 1996). Acute emotions are associated with intense sympathetic excitation that serves to energize a comparatively short behavioral episode. Moods, in contrast, are associated with low levels of such excitation, but are so for substantial periods of time. This episodic versus tonic energization of emotions and moods, respectively, is mediated by different endocrine mechanisms (Zillmann & Zillmann, 1996). High emotional intensity is primarily a function of activity in the sympathetic adrenomedullary system with its release of catecholamines. Low mood intensity is primarily mediated by activity in the pituitary adrenocortical system with its release of cortical steroids. Activity in the pituitary gonadal axis with its release of gonadal steroids is likely to assist the excitatory function of both these systems. The intensity and duration differences between emotion and mood are by no means clear-cut, however. Emotions may be repeatedly instigated and then amount to prolonged agitated behaviors and experiences. On the other hand, moods may give way to emotions or fatigue and thus terminate after brief manifestation.

More compelling criteria for differentiation may be found in the causal and motivational circumstances of affections. The evocation of emotions tends to be obtrusive, resulting in the mostly correct attribution of reactions to causes. In case of moods, causal connections are less apparent. People may feel good, for instance, without being able to pinpoint the causal conditions of their feelings. It has been suggested that such ambiguity results from the fact that moods often manifest themselves in the wake of emotions, and that the greater temporal remoteness between cause and effect compromises the causal attribution of moods (Isen, 1984; Morris, 1989, 1992; Schwarz, 1990). It would seem likely, however, that moods that immediately follow emotions, as both experiential states tend to be hedonically compatible, will be attributed, often correctly so, to the causal conditions of the precipitating emotions. Nonetheless, the fact remains that, as a rule, emotions have apparent causes, whereas the evocation of moods may be transparent at times and opaque at others.

The clearest distinction between emotions and moods appears to be the strong focus on action that typifies the former and the motivational diffuseness that is characteristic of the latter (Frijda, 1993). This distinction has been elaborated by Stumpf (1899; see also Reisenzein & Schönpflug, 1992), who pointed to the invariable existence of definitive goals for actions during emotions, on the one hand, and the diffuseness and globality of motives during moods, on the other.

Emotions, then, not only have rather obvious causes, they also are characterized by motivational specificity. In particular the so-called emergency emotions fear and anger are associated with courses of action—escape or attack, respectively—that are designed to resolve the emotion-evoking emergencies. In contrast, moods not only can be causally diffuse, they are, in addition, unconnected to behavioral emergencies and social or environmental happenings that might call for specific actions. If there is motivational specificity in moods, it is restricted to the maintenance of the state when agreeable, as well as to the abandonment of the state when noxious (Zillmann, 1988, 2000b). These related objectives can be served, however, by a broad range of activities. It might be argued that there also exists a range of activities for the resolution of emergency emotions, even for the perpetuation of desirable emotions. Surely, this is so. But in comparison to moods, the options for emergency-resolving action during emotions are severely limited. The motivational specificity of emotions versus the motivational diffuseness of moods may therefore be considered an acceptable criterion for the conceptual separation of emotions and moods.

In order to account for persisting affective consequences of emotional experiences and possibly of mood states, consequences capable of outlasting emotions and moods for substantial periods of time, the concept of sentiment has been introduced (Frijda, 1994). Sentiments are emotional attitudes that have well-defined objects. They are manifest in the attraction to, or the repulsion by, particular entities. Likes and dislikes, or love and hate, are sentiments that influence thoughts about, and actions toward, the sentiments' objects. It is assumed that these sentiments are formed on the basis of emotional experiences with their objects. Such sentiments may become dormant for extended periods, but they can be readily revived by the ideational or actual reconfrontation with their objects (Davidson & Ekman, 1994). Because of the potential longevity of sentiments, they have been treated, on occasion, as an individual-difference variable akin to a trait.

Sentiments relate to the concept of affective disposition. Dispositions of this kind are also thought to be formed on grounds of affective experience in the interaction with the dispositional objects (Zillmann, 1991a, 1994). In stark contrast to the persistence and presumed stability of sentiments, however, affective dispositions are considered to be highly flexible and to undergo continual adjustment. Specifically, it is assumed that they are formed and altered, at times drastically so, in accordance with the affective valuation of incoming information about the dispositional objects. This dynamic conception of affective dispositions has been productively applied to the understanding of communication phenomena that necessitate the quasi-instantaneous formation and adjustment to the flow of compressed disclosures about dispositional objects (Zillmann, 1994, 2000a). The indicated dispositional dynamics do not preclude, however, that exposure to narration can form comparatively stable dispositions that become dormant and are later reinstated by the confrontation with the dispositional object (Zillmann & Knobloch, 2001; Zillmann, Taylor, & Lewis, 1998).

Finally, distinctions have been drawn between affective traits and temperament as individual-difference variables (Campos, Barrett, Lamb,

Goldsmith, & Stenberg, 1983; Goldsmith, 1993; Goldsmith & Campos, 1990; Watson & Clark, 1992, 1994).

Affective traits are manifest in the longitudinal propensity for affective experiences and behaviors. The traits need not express themselves at all times but persist in a readiness for affective experiences of particular kinds. Affective traits, then, may be understood as defining an enduring undercurrent for specific moods and emotions, lowering the elicitation threshold for these experiences and behaviors (Ekman, 1994).

Temperament manifests itself in much the same way. In contrast to the essentially descriptive ascertainment of affective traits, however, temperament is thought to be genetically determined, with individual differences expressing themselves neuroendocrinologically. In other words, whereas affective traits may mostly, if not entirely, be based on pertinent experiences, temperament is considered to be largely predetermined by the physiological endowment of individuals. Temperament is also seen to be broader in range and to control interrelated sets of affective traits. Neuroticism, for instance, may be viewed as an aspect of temperament that fosters the propensity for negative affectivity as a general trait. This affectivity, in turn, would foster a readiness for the frequent experience of a range of negative moods and emotions, including bouts of anxiety, depression, and aggressiveness (Watson & Clark, 1994).

Emotions

One might expect that emotions, especially the so-called basic emotions, are characterized by discernible features that make them readily distinguishable from one another, and that as a result a set of primary human emotions has been reliably identified and is consensually accepted. Surprisingly, this is not at all the case.

A systematic comparison of the classification of emotions by the more prominent scholars in this field shows that consensus exists for the emotions of fear and anger only (Turner, 2000). Experiences of happiness (alternatively labelled *joy, pleasure,* or *satisfaction*) and sadness (alternatively labelled *sorrow, grief,* or *depression*) are mostly agreed on also. There is little agreement, however, in the classification of other emotions. For instance, some scholars deem guilt a basic emotion (e.g., Emde, 1980; Izard, 1992), whereas most others do not; and on occasion, scholars stand alone in granting experiences such as appetite (Arieti, 1970) or pain (Malatesta & Haviland, 1982) emotion status.

Moreover, secondary and even tertiary emotions have been constructed by combining basic emotions. A well-known system of this sort was developed by Plutchik (1962, 1980). This theorist arranged eight basic emotions as pairs of polar opposites and placed them along a circle, such that, in clockwise order, acceptance is followed by surprise, fear, sorrow, disgust, expectancy, anger, and joy. In a primary dyad of mixed emotions, adjacent emotions are combined. This procedure yields, for instance, cynicism as an admixture of disgust and expectancy, or pride as an amalgamate of anger and joy. In a secondary dyad, emotions once removed are combined. The combination of anger and acceptance, for instance, yields dominance. Finally, emotions twice removed form the tertiary dyads. The admixture of joy and fear, for instance, is said to define guilt. The combination of trice removed emotions form, of course, the initial polar opposites, like joy and sorrow or anger and fear. With two admixtures left unlabeled, this system yields 30 emotions. In order to account for intensity differences in his polar-opposite wheel of emotions, Plutchik (1970) added a third dimension. Terror, for instance, is conceived of as intensified fear, loathing as intensified disgust. Analogously, low-level fear is considered apprehension, and low-level disgust boredom. This incorporation of high- and low-intensity basic emotions brings the number of affective states to 46.

Numerous less mechanistically created and more empirically derived emotion taxonomies have been suggested (e.g., Izard, 1992; Johnson-Laird & Oatley, 1992; Ortony, Clore, & Collins, 1988; Roseman, 1984). Many are based on consensually held linguistic sensitivities. Specifically, differences in emotional experience are inferred from sufficient linguistic agreement in differentiating the experiences in question. Such agreement is often elusive, however, as different linguistic communities have different expressive sensitivities and, on occasion, make excessive, unmanageable use of these sensitivities. Speakers of English, for instance, are known to distinguish more than 200 emotional states (Fehr & Russell, 1984). Adequate commonality in referring to these states was limited to happiness, anger, sadness, love, fear, hate, and joy, however. Such commonality was nonexistent for the multitude of declared states, among them experiences such as meditation and stubbornness.

Taxonomies based on extralinguistic and physical manifestations yield markedly fewer distinctions between emotions and hence more fundamental classifications. Focus on facial expression (Ekman, 1982, 1984) led to six basic states: fear and anger, happiness and sadness, and surprise and disgust. The analysis of social interaction yielded comparable distinctions. Kemper (1987,

1993), for instance, arrived at four basic states: fear and anger, and satisfaction and depression. Turner (1999, 2000) started similarly on grounds of these four emotions. However, in recognition of intensity differences, he treated them as dimensions: aversion-fear and assertion-anger, and satisfaction-happiness and disappointment-sadness. Along these dimensions, affective experiences are considered to manifest themselves at three intensity levels: low, moderate, and high. Turner then listed up to 78 affective nuances for the 12 emotion classes. High-intensity happiness, for instance, included joy, bliss, rapture, jubilation, gaiety, elation, delight, thrill, and exhilaration as variants; low-intensity anger included annoyance, agitation, irritation, among other variants. This enumeration of affective states within basic emotion categories can be considered a parsimonious way of accounting for considerable variation in emotional experiences and their labeling. The parsimony of the enumeration is compromised, however, by Turner's (2000) extension of his scheme to emotion admixtures. Much like Plutchik (1970), Turner systematically combined each of his four dimensions with the remaining others, even with seemingly opposite ones. Combining assertion-anger with disappointment-sadness, for instance, is thought to produce bitterness, depression, and betrayal; and combining satisfaction-happiness with disappointment-sadness is said to produce nostalgia, yearning, and hope.

The systematic derivation of secondary affections as admixtures of basic emotions invariably entails elements that are not part of the combined emotions. How, for instance, can assertion plus disappointment produce betrayal? Only if moral considerations such as deceit are applied to disappointment. But such considerations are alien to the initial, more broadly conceived constructs. Or similarly, how can the combination of happiness and sadness produce nostalgia without implying that sadness is acute and linked to reveling in memories of happiness experienced in the distant past? Any plausibility of constructions of this kind can only be the result of benevolent hermeneutics. As a rule, the derivation of affective states by combination of more basic states leaves the derived states incompletely defined and open to arbitrary interpretation, a circumstance that renders these nomenclatures highly ambiguous.

Deriving the categorization of basic emotions not so much from the analysis of behavioral contexts, but from aspects of bodily expression or covert physiological processes, does not have the indicated semantic ambiguities but suffers from other complicating conditions.

The aforementioned use of facial expressions as indicators of emotional experiences produced a set of clearly distinguishable emotions. However, as facial expression is subject to voluntary control and can readily be used to camouflage acute emotions or to simulate emotions not presently experienced, such expression does not provide secure grounds for state inferences.

The search for neurophysiological, endocrine, and autonomic indicators, although productive in many ways, has also failed to disclose circuits or patterns that uniquely identify and separate all basic emotions. Progress in the delineation of the central control of aspects of emotion (LeDeaux, 1996; Panksepp, 1998) shows that opposite emotions, such as fear and anger, derive from activity in the same structures, primarily the amygdala. Endocrine analyses (Henry, 1986; Zillmann & Zillmann, 1996) revealed that the catecholamines play a central role in all active emotions. Studies of autonomic activity have, on occasion, suggested some patterned cardiovascular reactions specific to emotion (Ekman, Levenson, & Friesen, 1983). But again, there exists a high degree of cardiovascular commonality across the basic states, such that emotions cannot be reliably inferred on grounds of autonomic activity. Even investigators who initially pursued the search for emotion-specific patterns have come to conclude that there is no single condition that would reliably distinguish the basic emotions from one another (Ekman, 1999).

It would seem prudent, then, to conceive of emotional behaviors and experiences in terms of the environmental context that places demands on the individual, as well as of the response to these demands in all their overt and covert manifestations. This multifaceted approach holds promise of eventually identifying any complex patterns that may be associated with at least the basic emotions (Damasio, 1994).

Considering the basics, it is surprising that general theories of emotion have invariably ignored a domain of behavior, namely sexuality, that would seem to meet the definition of emotion in every regard. Libido, like other primary emotions, has an apparent object and consummatory response, and in acute form it is connected with intense arousal. In addition, libido, along with the actual sexual activities it motivates, is characterized by excitatory patterns that are much the same as those of fear and anger (Zillmann, 1998a). Granted that the central control differs markedly, libido—especially in view of the significant role it plays in social relations—has all the markings of an emotion and should be treated as such (Zillmann, 1986).

Although the conceptualization of discrete affective states as distinguishable behavioral episodes is vital for human affairs (and to the extent that the various manifestations of these states are reliably ascertained, for scientific inquiry also), this conceptualization has been severely challenged. Frijda (1994) considers the adherence to the classification of states an indication that many scholars are still "in the grips of Aristotelian or medieval science" (p. 63), and he urges conceptualization in terms of processes. Others have called for a paradigm shift that centers on recognition of the lack of synchrony between neural, endocrine, autonomic, and cognitive manifestations of emotions and embraces so-called nonlinear, dynamic approaches (Mayne & Ramsey, 2001; Ochsner & Feldman Barrett, 2001; Scherer, 2000).

In this context, attention to the time course of autonomic and cognitive processes during emotion fostered the reconceptualization of states as potentially fleeting moments (Zillmann, 1983, 1996b). Whereas cognitive adjustment to environmental changes is rapid, autonomic reactions, once elicited, run their course and generally outlast cognitive adaptation. Autonomic activity thus may come to energize and intensify behaviors and experiences other than those responsible for its elicitation. For instance, as the autonomic activity during acute fear and anger is highly compatible, a person learning that his stocks have lost much of their value may alternate between fear and anger as he considers the consequences of his losses or attributes them to a consultant's bad advice, respectively. He might also fluctuate between anger and sadness, or between fear and hopes for a prompt recovery of the market. The point is that pure, prolonged affective states of a particular kind may rarely exist, and that the conceptualization of states is now in terms of sequences of momentary conditions whose emotional classification is determined by the flow of changing cognitions. In other words, the stream of consciousness dictates affective experience, and the categorization of emotional episodes is meaningful only to the extent that cognition within a particular category is dominant throughout the episode (Zillmann, 1996b). Moreover, mixed emotions are no longer considered a fusion of more basic constituent emotions, but the result of variation in cognitive focus. Betrayal, for instance, may be manifest in the fluctuation between recognition of deceit, its moral condemnation, surprise about its perpetration, anger about its hurtful consequence, and thoughts of retaliation. As an emotional state, betrayal would be a composite of brief cognition-determined affective experiences whose intensity derives from essentially the same autonomic undercurrent.

Moods

As indicated earlier, moods are affective experiences of low to moderate excitatory intensity and comparatively long duration. Their important distinguishing characteristic is the absence of consummatory targets. As no particular goal has to be reached, cognition is not engaged and preoccupied with the attainment of goals. Similarly, the cause for moods, if known, is usually not an issue that would call for great cognitive investment. The search for agreeable moods would be the only object that might require cognitive assistance. Cognition during moods thus is comparatively free to be arbitrarily engaged.

There is some disagreement, however, concerning awareness of the mood-experience itself. Morris (1989), for instance, argued that moods may be consciously experienced or manifest themselves without awareness. Nonconsciously experienced moods are nonetheless considered capable of influencing cognitions and behaviors (cf. Martin & Clore, 2001). Thayer (1989), on the other hand, insisted that mood experiences necessitate awareness. He argued that this awareness is vital in that it informs individuals about their state of wellness. Thayer highlighted the hedonic distinctness of moods, a feature that moods share with emotions. Specifically, he distinguished between moods marked by energetic arousal (i.e., moods linked with sensations of energy, vigor, and peppiness) and tense arousal (i.e., moods associated with feelings of tension, anxiety, and fearfulness). These arousal types are consistent with the hedonic classification of moods as unpleasant versus pleasant or as bad versus good, respectively. Thayer suggested that all moods can be mapped along a continuum ranging from depression to elation, and he emphasized the consequences for individual wellness that accrue to all these moods.

Morris (1992), in a biopsychological theory of mood functions, similarly stressed consequences for wellness. Specifically, he proposed that good moods express the organism's effective coping with environmental challenges, whereas bad moods are manifestations of deficient coping and failure in meeting ecological demands. Individuals in pursuit of wellness thus should be motivated to alter, to the extent possible, depressive states toward experiences of elation, and to seek courses of action that hold promise of accomplishing this objective.

THEORETICAL APPROACHES TO EMOTIONS AND MOODS

Psychological theories of emotions and moods differ considerably in their focus. This selective diversity is very much the result of specialization in the disciplines from which the theories originate. It is easy to understand why neurophysiologists concentrate on the brain, endocrinologists on the viscera, cognitive psychologists on thought, social psychologists and sociologists on interactivity, biopsychologists on individual wellness, developmental psychologists on affective ontogenesis, and evolutionary psychologists on the phylogenesis of emotion-mediating structures. It is the rare exception that different approaches are combined and integrated. The result is that many approaches stand in isolation, with at times obvious limitations in their explanatory capacity.

The present discussion of affect theories cannot possibly be exhaustive. Instead, it is to provide a brief overview of distinct approaches.

Central Theories

Central theories aim at delineating the central-nervous-system structures that mediate emotional behaviors and experiences (e.g., Damasio, 1994; Davidson, 1992; LeDoux, 1987, 1996; MacLean, 1964; Ochsner & Feldman Barrett, 2001; Panksepp, 1998; Rolls, 1999). Essentially, perceptual input is considered to be processed by the sensory thalamus, the amygdala, the sensory cortex, the transition cortex, the hippocampus, the prefrontal cortex, along with immediately related structures, and give impetus to unconditional or acquired affective behaviors and the excitatory activity that energizes them. These reactions are mostly automatic, but allowances are made for some degree of volitional control. Such control is provided by the lateral prefrontal and association cortices and by the orbital and ventromedial frontal cortex that mediate reflection for the conception and evaluation of courses of action (Fuster, 1989; Weinberger, Berman, Gold, & Goldberg, 1994). At least in the context of acute basic emotions, then, cognitive deliberation is a secondary consideration.

The demonstration that perceptual input is screened for vital implications in the amygdala prior to reaching the cortex (LeDoux, 1996) is significant in this connection. The amygdala apparently ascertains the magnitude of threats to individual welfare, as well as of opportunities for its enhancement, and then signals its estimate to the cortex for further consideration. A significant aspect of this sequence of events is that excitatory reactions are initiated before the perceptual input reaches awareness and is comprehended.

As endocrine processes, especially the systemic release of catecholamines, mediate the indicated excitatory activity, approaches that focus on mostly automatic, centrally instigated autonomic aspects of emotion (e.g., Cannon,

1932; Fredrikson, 1989; Henry, 1986; Levi, 1967; Smith, 1973) may be considered central theories. The momentous finding in the associated research is that affective behaviors and experiences are invariably accompanied by elevated activity in the sympathetic nervous system. The elevation is, per definition, more pronounced in emotions than in moods, the latter being linked to release of cortical corticoids more than to that of catecholamines.

Central theories of emotion, as they emphasize the function of archaic brain structures, the function of the amygdala in particular, are understandably part and parcel of evolutionary theories of emotion. Moreover, as the archaic structures control vital behaviors that stand in the service of the preservation and welfare of individuals and the species (including aggressive, cooperative, and reproductive objectives), they also permeate biopsychological analyses (e.g., Thayer, 1996; Williams, 1985).

Cognitive Theories

Appraisal processes define the core of cognitive theories of emotion (e.g., Averill, 1980; Frijda, 1986; Izard, 1993; Lazarus, 1991; Oatley & Jenkins, 1996; Stein, Trabasso, & Liwag, 1994). Lazarus (1991) distinguished between primary and secondary appraisals. Primary appraisals are thought to serve the discernment of the meaning of conditions capable of affecting the welfare of individuals. This discernment entails the comprehension of specific emotional reactions to these conditions. The differentiation of emotional states is thus part of this initial appraisal (Roseman, 1984). Secondary appraisals are thought to serve coping with the circumstances, including the construction of action strategies. Action readiness and its preparation are also emphasized in the theories of Frijda (1986) and of Oatley and Jenkins (1996). Moreover, Scherer (2000) suggested that appraisals take the form of a hierarchically organized evaluation system that progresses from condition screening to action preparation. Appraisal theories that focus on the preparation of interactive schemas (e.g., Averill, 1980; Oatley & Jenkins, 1996) are also known as constructivist theories of emotion.

These appraisal theories place the burden of emotion instigation and emotion differentiation squarely on the neocortex, irrespective of the fact that the existence of archaic brain structures may be acknowledged on occasion. All relevant aspects of emotional behavior are considered governed by mostly deliberate and rather detailed contemplation and evaluation. The elicitation of excitatory reactions, as well as the function of these reactions, is given little if any attention (cf. LeDoux, 1996; Rolls, 1999;

Zillmann, 1978), and the independence from volitional control of many such reactions is simply ignored. Cognitive theories, then, may be considered incomplete theories of emotion because they fail to give an adequate account of the most basic emotional behaviors—behaviors that are invariably characterized by spontaneity and automaticity of activation.

Peripheral Theories

Peripheral theories of emotion derive from James' (1884) famous reversal of the common sense sequence that, as we encounter danger, we experience fear and then decide to run. He argued that we run first, and that then, while running, we become aware of bodily changes and experience fear. Technically speaking, behavior is triggered by whatever means, and the extero- and interoceptive feedback of our behavior is what makes us aware of our emotions. It is an appraisal of peripheral cues from elicited actions, then, that creates cognizance of feelings, which James declared to be the emotions.

In his two-factor theory of emotion, Schachter (1964) conceptualized the peripheral component primarily in what he called *physiological arousal;* and he argued that such arousal, once instigated, would impose itself in awareness and give impetus to an epistemic search for its cause. The detection of a cause then would provide a label for the emotion. For instance, a person noticing his heart pounding and his palms sweating is expected to screen his immediate environment and, if finding himself confronted with a snarling dog, should attribute his reaction to the dog's behavior and thus infer being in a state of acute fear.

Damasio (1994), in a somatic-marker theory of emotion, essentially postulated the same sequence of events, but focused on somatic feedback's effect on action decisions rather than on the mere labeling of experiential states. In terms of Lazarus' (1991) nomenclature, Schachter's epistemic search is within primary appraisal, whereas Damasio addressed decision-making within secondary appraisal.

Facial efference (actually feedback thereof; that is, feedback from facial expressions) has also been considered a form of peripheral cue that informs individuals about their own emotions and helps them to decide what they feel (Adelman & Zajonc, 1989; Ekman, 1999; Izard, 1971; Laird, 1974).

Peripheral approaches also have been pronounced incomplete theories of emotion because, except for Damasio's (1994) theorizing, they fail to account for the initial bodily reaction—its overt as well as its covert manifestations—that gives rise to the labeling of experiential states (cf.

LeDoux, 1996; Zillmann, 1978). Rolls (1999) additionally deemed the evidence concerning emotion differentiation on grounds of any such inner and outer body cues wanting.

Reinforcement Theories

Reinforcement theories treat emotion as a variant of motivation in that both conditions are considered subject to acquisition and modification by prevailing contingencies of reinforcement (cf. Cofer & Appley, 1966; Nevin, 1973). Specifically, much like motivations, emotions are thought to be instigated, intensified, diminished, and terminated by the presence, omission, and removal of rewards and punishers (e.g., Gray, 1981; Millenson, 1967; Strongman, 1996; Weiskrantz, 1968). Rewards are operationalized as conditions that individuals will work to attain and retain, punishers as conditions that they will work to avoid and escape from. The acquisition and alteration of emotional responding, brought about by such external stimuli, thus constitutes the central object of reinforcement theories. However, motivation from changes in internal milieu, such as during hunger and thirst, tends to be excluded from consideration as emotion (Leeper, 1970).

Rolls (1999) consequently understands emotions such as pleasure, elation, and ecstasy to result from exposure to rewarding conditions of different strength. Apprehension, fear, and terror arise analogously from exposure to punishers of different strength. Relief and related affective experiences are thought to result from the omission or removal of punishers. Analogously, frustrations, anger, and rage, as well as experiences of sadness and grief, are expected to result from various ways of omitting or removing rewards. Rolls, who traced the proposed mechanisms in neurophysiological analyses, contended that the indicated reinforcement contingencies permeate, although only implicitly, the conception of emotions by alternative theories, in particular by appraisal theories.

INTEGRATIVE THEORY

Approaches to emotion and mood tend to reflect scholarship and research in particular domains of inquiry. Such scholarship and research is all too often isolated, and integrations of complementary approaches are rare. They do exist, however. One such interdisciplinary integration is manifest in the three-factor theory of emotion proposed by Zillmann (1978, 1983, 1996b, 1998a). This theory brings together various aspects of the discussed approaches (among them the proposals concerning neural, endocrine, and autonomic processes, cognitive appraisals, extero- and interoception, and reinforcement contingencies) and arranges them in a way that provides a more complete account of emotions and moods.

Three-Factor Theory of Emotion

The three-factor theory of emotion projects emotional experience and emotional behavior as the result of the interaction of three principal components of emotional state: the dispositional, the excitatory, and the experiential component.

1. The dispositional component is conceived of as a response-guiding mechanism.

The skeletal-motor manifestations of emotional behavior are unconditionally or conditionally linked to eliciting conditions. Conditional linkages are acquired through learning in accordance with the various known mechanisms. Emotional memory, which may, but need not, involve conscious deliberation, is part and parcel of acquired response dispositions. Essentially, then, the incipient skeletal-motor reaction to the presentation of emotion-inducing stimuli is viewed as a direct response that is made without appreciable latency because it does not require explicit cognitive assessment, judgment, and strategy construction.

This conceptualization is in full agreement with recent developments in neurophysiological research (cf. Damasio, 1994; LeDoux, 1993, 1996; Rolls, 1999). Specifically, it is known that so-called natural triggers (i.e., pre-existing connections) and learned triggers (i.e., established connections) are capable of initiating adaptive overt reactions—along with response potentiation through activation of the pituitary-adrenal system and its effect on autonomic excitation—without involving the neocortex proper. The amygdala has emerged as the pivotal structure for the operation of triggers. A direct path to this structure is via the sensory thalamus. An alternative route is from the sensory thalamus through the sensory cortex to the amygdala. The direct path takes about half the processing time, allowing responses to be made prior to full awareness and contemplation of the circumstances.

The amygdala not only triggers a coordinated set of emotional responses, it also helps build the memory systems needed to give learned triggers their power. In this regard, this structure projects to the sensory cortex in registering perceptions for short-term storage and to the hippocampus and related areas for long-term storage of explicit memories.

The amygdala further projects to the prefrontal cortex to facilitate attention and operations in working memory. It is this projection that enables awareness of the goings-on and that invites conscious information processing. The consequences of this function are addressed in the experiential component of three-factor theory. Suffice it here to underscore that in their incipient stages emotional reactions are devoid of contemplation and deliberation. As LeDoux (1996, p. 161) put it, "The fact that emotional learning can be mediated by pathways that bypass the neocortex is intriguing, for it suggests that emotional responses can occur without the involvement of the higher processing systems of the brain, systems believed to be involved in thinking, reasoning, and consciousness."

2. The excitatory component is conceived of as the response-energizing mechanism.

Analogous to skeletal-motor reactions, excitatory reactions are also unconditionally or conditionally linked to eliciting conditions. Conditional linkages are again thought to be acquired through learning. The natural and learned emotional triggers function as already detailed. Emotional stimuli may take the fast-track via the sensory thalamus to the amygdala, or they may take the detour via sensory thalamus and cortex. The immediate route will trigger autonomic excitation, which will manifest itself systemically after a short delay. The detoured triggering will do the same somewhat more slowly, but then allow awareness of the reactivity (cf. LeDoux, 1993, 1996).

In accordance with Cannon's (1932) proposal of the emergency nature of emotional behavior, the excitatory reaction associated with emotional states is primarily conceived of as heightened activity in the sympathetic adrenomedullary axis that expresses itself in, among other things, transitory peripheral hyperglycemia and increased activity in the sympathetic nervous system. More specifically, Cannon suggested that the release of catecholamines, of epinephrine in particular, eventuates a comparatively fast-acting but short-lived increase of blood glucose, thereby readying the body for muscular exertion. The excitatory reaction is thus seen as providing the organism with the energy needed for the performance of vigorous action such as needed for fight or flight, but also for the engagement in energy-demanding gratifying behaviors, such as sexual intercourse (cf. Zillmann, 1998a).

Cannon's conceptualization requires some adjustment, however. Recent research (cf. Landsberg & Young, 1992) has made it clear that in behavioral emergencies epinephrine mobilizes free fatty acids and glucose, while inhibiting insulin secretion. The metabolic pattern of high fatty acid and low insulin concentration actually restricts glucose entry into skeletal muscles and tends to conserve glucose for the central nervous system. This shifts the burden of energy provision for muscular exertion from glucose to free fatty acids (cf. Cryer, 1992). Notwithstanding such modification, Cannon's biological emergency model has remained the central paradigm for the involvement and function of excitation in acute emotions. Endangerment and threats to well-being generally, along with the prospect of essential but contested gratifications, are conditions that continue to instigate heightened activity in the sympathetic adrenomedullary system with its partiality to prepare the organism for vigorous action—whether or not such action has immediate utility in warding off threats or in assisting the attainment of gratifications.

In considering the mediation of the excitatory component of emotions, it must be recognized that sympathetic adrenocortical activity interacts with activity in other neuroendocrine systems, foremost the pituitary adrenocortical system and the gonadal system. Heightened activity in the adrenocortical axis is known to increase sympathetic excitation through the confounded release of cortisone and catecholamines (cf. Frankenhaeuser, 1986). Similarly, testosterone release is associated with increased sympathetic activity (cf. Henry, 1986). To the extent that activity in these and yet other systems augments sympathetic excitation, they enhance emotional behavior; and to the extent that these systems impair sympathetic excitation, they diminish emotionality.

3. The experiential component is conceived of as a response-monitoring and response-adjusting mechanism. It entails consciousness of the emotional behavior.

Both interoception and exteroception of the skeletal-motor and/or excitatory manifestations of incipient or persistent emotional actions force awareness of the emotionality of the behavior on the individual. Cognizance of this emotionality defines emotional experience. Such experience is expected to instigate scrutiny of the utility of the action. Cognition now comes to serve the appraisal of emotional reactions and action in the context of circumstances. Behavior monitoring of this kind may sanction incipient reactions and foster continued action. It may, at times, give added impetus to the action and enhance emotionality. Additionally and more characteristically, however, monitoring may lead to disapproval and censure of emotional action; and such censure may, in turn, foster diminished emotionality by curbing the motor and/or excitatory manifestations of the incipient or persistent emotional behavior.

The experiential component of emotions, then, is viewed as a modifier or a corrective that, within limits, controls spontaneous emotional responsiveness that is governed by more fundamental, if not archaic, unlearned and learned stimulus–response connections. The function of this component may thus be viewed as the exercise of cognitive control over emotional responding. However, as the corrective intervention in incipient or persistent emotional behavior is also subject to response acquisition by the mechanics of learning, the modified response, if repeatedly performed, may come to dominate the original one. The elicitation of emotion thus can be postcognitive—yet controlled by subcontemplative mechanisms.

These considerations are again in accord with recent discoveries in neurophysiology (cf. LeDoux, 1993, 1996). Projections from the amygdala and the hippocampus, in particular, to the prefrontal cortex provide awareness-fostering somatic feedback and instigate attention to, and evaluation of, emotional actions. Actions deemed inopportune may then be deliberately inhibited or modified. Cognitive appraisals assert their influence in these modifications of behavior. Such neocortex-mediated appraisal was not involved in the triggering of the initial emotional reaction, however. This point is drastically made by LeDoux (1996, p. 165): "The cortex's job is to prevent the inappropriate response rather than to produce the appropriate one."

The interdependencies between the three specified components of emotions are detailed elsewhere. Suffice it here to summarize some of their implications.

Generally speaking, three-factor theory emphasizes the automaticity of emotional reactivity. It is recognized that some reactions, such as startle, are precoded. Most reactions, however, are thought to be formed by prevailing contingencies of reinforcement. Such reactions do not depend on prior contemplation. Nor are they necessarily subject to volitional control. Excitatory reactions, in particular, largely elude such control.

At the same time, the theory makes allowances for the elicitation of emotional reactions to nonimmediate elicitors. The activation of neural representations of specific elicitors is considered capable of triggering emotional reactions comparable to those of the actual elicitors. This means that emotions can be instigated by exposure to any kind of iconic or symbolic, especially linguistic, representation of emotion elicitors. Moreover, emotions can be instigated by reflection during which elicitor representations (i.e., representations stored in memory) are incidentally or deliberately encountered.

By emphasizing the automaticity of emotional reactivity, three-factor theory denies the need for explicit cognitive deliberations prior to reacting. The theory stipulates, however, that all activities, including emotional reactions, are continually subjected to cognitive monitoring. This monitoring fosters the immediate alteration of reactions deemed inappropriate and redirects behavior into the service of accepted objectives. In addition, the evaluative, judgmental function of monitoring fosters appraisals that become part of the neural representation of emotion elicitors and thus may alter affective preparedness for future encounters of the elicitors. This aspect of monitoring ensures adjustments and even dramatic changes in affective dispositions toward emotion-evoking entities. Monitoring thus leads to the conception of emotion-controlling affective dispositions as the key elements of a dynamic, continually fine-tuning and up-dating system of response preparation.

Finally, the focus on sympathetic activity as the principal determinant and indicator of emotional intensity serves as a distinguishing characteristic, making sympathetic excitation a necessary condition for emotion.

Three-Factor Theory of Mood

In keeping with the conceptualization of mood as an experience characterized by the absence of targeted, consummatory behavior, the dispositional, behavior-directing component of emotions loses much of its significance. As stated earlier, the dispositional component can be considered limited to altering or maintaining the mood states themselves. The remaining functions, excitatory and experiential, fully apply, however.

Although excitation associated with moods is held to comparatively low levels by definition, the excitatory component is nonetheless considered to determine the experiential intensity of moods. Sympathetic excitation, mediated by systemic catecholamines, is essential. Mood intensity, especially the intensity of energetic positive moods, is further associated with the release of central catecholamines—mostly norepinephrine, but also dopamine (Friedhoff & Silva, 1998).

The experiential component focuses on the hedonic quality of experienced moods. Monitoring this quality ultimately motivates the maintenance of agreeable moods, as well as the abandonment of disagreeable ones (cf. Zillmann, 2000b). It further controls mood setting, that is, the deliberate creation of moods for particular leisure or labor situations.

EXCITATION-TRANSFER THEORY

Excitation-transfer theory is the application of three-factor theory to contiguous emotional behaviors and experiences (Zillmann, 1978, 1983, 1996b). The theory is based on the time discrepancy between neurally mediated, comparatively quick cognition and hormonally mediated, sluggish sympathetic excitation. More specifically, this theory projects that, as a rule, slow excitatory regulation (i.e., the return of excitation to basal levels) outlasts the quasi-instantaneous adjustment to environmental changes by minutes, at times by hours. Because sympathetic dominance in the autonomic nervous system—through somatic efference and intero- and exteroception—determines the intensity of emotional behavior and experience, and moreover, because behavioral direction and its experience as emotion are determined by obtrusive events prevailing in changing environmental conditions, the excitatory response to a particular condition may come to intensify related or unrelated emotional behaviors that are experienced at a later time. In technical terms, sympathetic excitation, once elicited, dissipates rather slowly, leaving behind a tail of residual excitation. This residual excitation combines inseparably with excitation in response to subsequent elicitors. The amount of excitation available during the response to the subsequent elicitor is thus "artificially" increased and fosters "artificially" enhanced emotional reactivity and experience.

The dissynchrony between cognition and excitation in emotion sequences is likely to be influenced by the fact that amygdaloid activity, once instigated by strong affective stimulation, tends to persist for minutes after cessation of the stimulation (Joseph, 1998). The amygdala thus continues to signal severe challenges when these challenges have ceased to exist and have been superseded by alternative conditions.

The transfer paradigm extends to the accumulation of excitation from several elicitors. If, for instance, excitation is elicited by four consecutive emotion-arousing conditions, the undecayed excitation from all four conditions is compounded in the response to a fifth contiguous condition and determines its intensity. Excitation associated with moods may also contribute to the excitation and thus to the intensity of emotions that are triggered during the mood states.

Excitation-transfer effects are to be expected between all affective and emotional actions and experiences associated with appreciable excitatory reactions. Excitatory residues from anger, for instance, will intensify subsequent anger, fear, libido, elation, or despair. Residues from sexual excitedness will have the same capacity (cf. Zillmann, 1998a).

EMPATHIC MEDIATION OF EMOTIONS AND MOODS

Theories of emotion focus on reactions and their experience that are brought about by conditions directly affecting the welfare of those responding. The fact that emotions are also evoked by witnessing others' affective experiences and bad or good fortunes, although these happenings are of no immediate consequence to the onlooker, tends to be neglected and left unexplained. Supplementary explanations exist, however, and are elaborated in theories of empathy (e.g., Hoffman, 1978; Stotland, 1969; Zillmann, 1991a).

The empathic mediation of emotion and mood has been characterized as reflexive (Lipps, 1907; McDougall, 1908), acquired (Aronfreed, 1970; Humphrey, 1922), and cognitive (Feshbach, 1978; Stotland, 1969). The three modes of operation have also been considered to function in concert (Zillmann, 1991a).

Reflexive mediation is apparent in motor mimicry, as well as in involuntary vocal and facial expressions that parallel the emotional expressions of observed others. The automaticity of "expression copying" is thought to serve the creation of emotional synchrony in groups. During the course of evolution, such synchrony had obvious survival value—in particular, by coordinating fight and flight (cf. Ekman, 1999; Plutchik, 1987). This function is not lost in contemporary society, as emotional contagion may motivate the rendering of assistance to persons in pain or other distress. Moreover, such contagion may spread emotions and moods through groups and thereby deepen experiences of joy or grief, among others.

Acquired mediation focuses on the formation and modification of affective dispositions. Essentially, the hedonic valence of affective experiences from encounters with specific social agents is considered stored and aggregated. This aggregation is solidified in affective dispositions that, when positive, foster liking, approach, and acceptance and, when negative, disliking, avoidance, and rejection. Given these dispositions, witnessing others' emotional experiences is likely to evoke concerns that invite a "sharing" of emotions in case of favorable dispositions.

Cognitive mediation refers to efforts at putting oneself into another's place, specifically for the purpose of comprehending and appreciating the other's emotional experience. In contrast to the automatic and semi-automatic nature of reflexive and acquired mediation, cognitive mediation can be viewed as deliberate role-playing that depends on epistemic motivation and that is limited by emotional maturity (i.e., experience with the emotions to be appreciated).

Disposition Theory

In the three-factor theory of empathy (Zillmann, 1991a), the formation and continual updating of affective dispositions assume a central function in determining when empathetic reactions will occur, when they will not, and most significantly, when reactions opposite to empathic ones will occur.

The formation of such dispositions is considered to progress through stages: (1) Agents are observed and (2) their behavior as well as their apparent intentions are judged to be good or bad. (3) If behaviors and intentions are approved and deemed laudatory, positive affective dispositions toward the agents are formed, manifest in liking and caring. (4) Implicit in liking and caring is that good fortunes are hoped for and bad fortunes are feared. (5) As good or bad fortunes materialize and reactions to them are witnessed, the agents' affective experiences foster concordant affect. In other words, observers will empathize, feeling good when the agents do, and feeling bad when the agents do. (6) If agents toward whom positive dispositions are held experience the fortunes that were hoped for and that are judged to be deserved and justified, appreciable dispositional changes are not expected. However, if such agents experience the fortunes that were feared and that are judged to be undeserved and unjust, affective dispositions are adjusted. Specifically, the greater the perceived injustice of bad fortunes, the more favorable the dispositional adjustment. This dispositional enhancement is recursive.

The discussed conception of the formation and modification of affective dispositions assigns a primary role to moral judgment and, in fact, treats observers as untiring moral monitors of the actions and intentions of others (cf. Zillmann, 2000a).

Dispositional Override

Not all responses to others' emotions are concordant, however, and moral judgment turns out to hold the key to understanding when they are not and, especially, when they reverse to hedonically opposite reactions.

The sequence of events is as detailed through stages 1 and 2. Asymmetry of the scheme becomes apparent thereafter. (3) If observed behaviors and their apparent intentions cannot be condoned and are condemned, negative affective dispositions toward the agents are formed, manifest in disliking and resenting. (4) Implicit in disliking and resenting is that bad fortunes are hoped for and good fortunes are feared. (5) As bad or good fortunes materialize and reactions to them are witnessed, the agents' affective experiences foster discordant affect. This means that observers will rejoice over the bad fortunes of those they resent, and that they will suffer irritation, if not infuriation, if those they resent are gratified by unwarranted benefaction. (6) If agents toward whom negative dispositions are held experience the fortunes that were hoped for and that are judged to be deserved and justified, appreciable dispositional changes are not expected. However, if such agents experience the fortunes that were feared and that are judged to be undeserved and unjust, affective dispositions are adjusted. Specifically, the greater the perceived injustice of good fortunes, the more unfavorable the dispositional adjustment. This dispositional enhancement is also recursive.

EMOTIONS AND MOODS VIA THE MEDIA

The media, no doubt, have an enormous capacity to engage our emotions. This capacity differs greatly, however, across various formats of information conveyance.

Affect From Informative Presentations

Media contents are traditionally divided into informational and entertaining presentations. The former category entails the news and, along with educational efforts, is to serve the public by apprising the citizenry of relevant goings-on. There is a commitment to veridical representation in this surveying of the physical and social environment for threats and opportunities. As a rule, attempts to incite action are not made. On occasion, however, the news may aim at the instigation and coordination of civic action, provided that such action is consensually thought to serve public welfare. Of interest here is that the news does not have any official or unofficial mandate to incite emotions or to create agreeable moods in the citizenry (cf. Zillmann, 2002; Zillmann & Brosius, 2000). In stark contrast, it is the declared mission of entertainment to touch our emotions and to place us into agreeable moods, if only to "re-create" us by restoring our energies for the upcoming demands of everyday life (cf. Mendelsohn, 1966; Schwab, 2001; Zillmann & Vorderer, 2000).

The fact that the news is without mandate to engage our emotions does not mean that news revelations do not evoke them. On the contrary, such revelations, to the extent that they disclose threats and dangers of immediate concern to the news recipients themselves, must be expected to instigate emotions of the utmost intensity. Learning of terrorist attacks that caused the crash of several commercial planes, for instance, is bound to activate strong apprehensions and anxieties in anyone who flies with regularity. In fact, the news, along with related informational programming, must be considered the very format that conveys threats to personal welfare—in abundance at that (Zillmann, 1998b). The anthrax-by-mail scare in the United States (September and October of 2001), which escalated to the creation of anxieties about smallpox and any number of additional highly contagious diseases, is a telling recent example of the dominance of fear-arousing messages in the news. As all such dangers concern personal welfare, the emotions that their disclosure elicits are unmitigated reactions to genuine endangerment and thus should accord with expectations derived from theories of basic emotions.

Fortunately, however, most reported dangers are not directed at the news recipients themselves but at fellow humans. Disclosure of a hurricane threatening the Carolinas, for instance, will stir emotions in those living in the threatened coastal regions but leave all others without immediate concern for their own welfare. Similarly, associated reports about the victimization of families who suffered the loss of loved ones do not convey threats to people living elsewhere. Reports of this kind evoke emotions nonetheless, even emotions of considerable intensity. Theories of basic emotions are at a loss in explaining these emotions, and the mechanisms of empathy need to be called upon to provide a more complete account of them.

The elicitation of emotional reactions to reports about others' victimization tends to confound, however, elements of responding to depictions of endangerment with elements of empathic responding to others' reactions to their endangerment or victimization. A report on salmonella poisoning in a fast-food restaurant, for instance, may foster much empathy with the plight of victims but also create fear of contracting such an ailment on future visits to such restaurants (Aust & Zillmann, 1996). Similarly, news about melanoma skin cancer from extensive sun exposure may motivate much empathy with depicted victims but also give rise to anxieties of being victimized by sun bathing (Zillmann & Gan, 1996).

There is reason to believe that the imagery of the news is particularly powerful in eliciting empathy as well as in promoting empathy-based action. For instance, the public's inundation with images of starving children in Somalia is thought to have sparked an outcry that led to U.S. military intervention in the region. Images of the abuse of mutilated bodies of soldiers promptly reversed this course of action. Imagery, then, appears to have fostered empathic emotions that led to remedial action and its abandonment despite the fact that those in an uproar were never immediately threatened by the events in question (Sharkey, 1993; Zillmann & Brosius, 2000).

Affect from Entertaining Presentations

One might be inclined to believe that entertainment is incapable of creating such extensions from empathic reactions to the suffering of "mere fictional characters" to anxieties about conditions in the so-called real world. Such beliefs seem unwarranted, however, as illustrations of extensions abound. Seeing swimmers dismembered by sharks, fictional though it is, apparently has many moviegoers foregoing swimming in the sea (Cantor, 1998); and watching people burn to death in a "towering inferno" has them reluctant to enter tall buildings (even prior to the September 11, 2001, terrorist attack on the World Trade Center towers in New York). However, whereas the fictional creation of fear of actual dangers may be considered the exception, the confounding of emotional responding to representations of manifestations of danger with empathic responding to the portrayal of others' victimization by the danger permeates fiction as much as it does the news. In order to fully empathize with persons who express emotions it is simply necessary to know to what these persons respond (cf. Zillmann, 1991a). The display of the causal circumstances—infernos, earthquakes, raging floods, snarling tigers, hatchet-wielding monsters, and the like—also evokes affective reactions. The indicated confounding, therefore, should be considered to be the rule.

Irrespective of this fiction-to-life extension of emotions, however, one of the foremost objectives of entertainment is to provide "emotional roller-coaster rides," and there can be little doubt that the entertainment media manage to manipulate and toy with our emotions, often creating affective intensities that rival and often equal those of distress during actual personal challenges or elation from meeting them successfully (e.g., Carruthers & Taggart, 1973; Grimm, 1997; Janschek, Vitouch, & Tinchon, 1997; Levi, 1965; Zillmann, 1991b; Zuckerman, 1996).

Ubiquity of Excitation Transfer

Excitation-transfer theory uniquely applies to media-elicited emotions. In real life, emotions are often, but by no means always, allowed to take their course. Frightened persons will be frightened for some time, and happy persons will even resist getting "short-changed" on their experience. For media presentations, especially for presentations via audio-visual media, no such allowances are made. As a matter of principle, elements of narrative are condensed and compacted into sequences that do not permit any emotional reaction to a singular element to run its course. Any element that evokes an affective reaction is immediately followed by other elements that may or may not elicit affect themselves. Excitatory reactions are bound to outlast the episodes that triggered them. Their residues thus will enter into subsequent episodes and influence affect experiences during their presentation.

In both nonfictional and fictional formats, then, transfer will assert itself and foster potential misreactions. The news, for instance, may feature a report about the territory expansion of encephalitis-spreading ticks immediately after a report of a plane crash. Residual excitation from the initial report thus should "artificially" enhance the affective reaction to the second report, even creating unnecessarily intense fear of the ticks. In fiction, a scene of danger might be followed by clownery and foster an "artificially" intense amusement reaction in this comic-relief arrangement.

The latter illustration shows that transfer, although capable of creating undesirable "misreactions," may also be used strategically to good advantage. The theory has been employed, in fact, to suggest ways of maximizing reactions of enjoyment (cf. Tan, 1996; Vorderer & Knobloch, 2000; Zillmann, 1996a). An entire transfer dramaturgy serving the intensification of emotions of any kind, ultimately the enjoyment of drama, has also been developed (Zillmann, in press).

Mood Manipulation and Management

Notwithstanding the media's indisputable capacity to touch and manipulate our emotions, their influence on the less rousing, somewhat subdued variety of affect, on moods in particular, appears to be paramount (cf. Kubey & Csikszentmihalyi, 1990). Being well entertained may require the engagement of our emotions—along with our intellect, to be sure. However, as acute emotions, largely for physiological reasons, cannot be maintained for hours on end without becoming counterproductive (i.e., creating exhaustion rather than enterprising mood states), the comings and goings of intense affective experiences appear to define a superior entertainment formula. Having been well entertained must mean having been placed into a lingering, highly desirable mood state. The creation of such lingering moods might, in fact, be considered the very object of entertainment. But there is no contradiction in the contention that "getting there" may necessitate "going through" even more desirable and more intensive affective states and emotional experiences.

Whether desirable mood is experienced during or following exposure to entertainments or to related presentational formats, such stimulation, by engaging intellect and emotions, offers ways out of pre-existing undesirable or at least less desirable moods. This consideration is the focal point of mood-management theory (Zillmann, 1988, 2000b). This theory implicates a mechanism that allows people to choose—instantaneously, quasi-automatically, and without much agonizing deliberation—what holds promise of improving their moods. No comprehension of the causal connection between stimulation and its effect is required, although it may exist on occasion. In view of these choice dynamics on the one hand, and the ever increasing wealth of media offerings capable of affecting emotions and moods on the other hand, allusions to "affective self-medication" by entertainment choices have lost much of their incredulity.

REFERENCES

Adelmann, P. K., & Zajonc, R. B. (1989). Facial efference and the experience of emotion. *Annual Review of Psychology, 40,* 249–280.

Arieti, S. (1970). Cognition and feeling. In M. B. Arnold (Ed.), *Feelings and emotions: The Loyola Symposium* (pp. 135–143). New York: Academic.

Aronfreed, J. (1970). The socialization of altruistic and sympathetic behavior: Some theoretical and experimental analyses. In J. Macaulay & L. Berkowitz (Eds.), *Altruism and helping behavior* (pp. 103–126). New York: Academic.

Aust, C .F., & Zillmann, D. (1996). Effects of victim exemplification in television news on viewer perception of social issues. *Journalism & Mass Communication Quarterly, 73*(4), 787–803.

Averill, J. R. (1980). A constructivist view of emotion. In R. Plutchik & H. Kellerman (Eds.), *Emotion: Theory, research, and experience: Vol. 1. Theories of emotion* (pp. 305–339). New York: Academic.

Campos, J. J., Barrett, K. C., Lamb, M. E., Goldsmith, H. H., & Stenberg, C. (1983). Socioemotional development. In P. H. Mussen (Series Ed.), M. M. Haith, & J. J. Campos (Vol. Eds.), *Handbook of child psychology: Vol. 2. Infancy and developmental psychobiology* (4th ed., pp. 783–915). New York: Wiley.

Cannon, W. B. (1932). *The wisdom of the body*. New York: Norton.

Cantor, J. (1998). *"Mommy, I'm scared:" How TV and movies frighten children and what we can do to protect them*. San Diego: Harcourt Brace.

Carruthers, M., & Taggart, P. (1973). Vagotonicity of violence: Biochemical and cardiac responses to violent films and television programmes. *British Medical Journal, 3,* 384–389.

Cofer, C. N., & Appley, M. H. (1966). *Motivation: Theory and research.* New York: Wiley.

Cryer, P. E. (1992). Glucose homeostasis and hypoglycemia. In J. D. Wilson & D. W. Foster (Eds.), *Williams textbook of endocrinology* (8th ed., pp. 1223–1253). Philadelphia: Saunders.

Damasio, A. R. (1994). *Descartes' error.* New York: Putnam.

Damasio, A. R. (1997). Towards a neuropathology of emotion and mood. *Nature, 386,* 769–770.

Davidson, R. J. (1992). Emotion and affective style: Hemispheric substrates. *Psychological Science, 3,* 39–43.

Davidson, R. J., & Ekman, P. (1994). Afterword: How are emotions distinguished from moods, temperament, and other related affective constructs? In P. Ekman & R. J. Davidson (Eds.), *The nature of emotion: Fundamental questions* (pp. 94–96). New York: Oxford University Press.

Ekman, P. (1982). *Emotions and the human face.* Cambridge, UK: Cambridge University Press.

Ekman, P. (1984). Expression and the nature of emotion. In K. Scherer & P. Ekman (Eds.), *Approaches to emotion* (pp. 319–344). Hillsdale, NJ: Lawrence Erlbaum Associates.

Ekman, P. (1994). Moods, emotions, and traits. In P. Ekman & R. J. Davidson (Eds.), *The nature of emotion: Fundamental questions* (pp. 56–58). New York: Oxford University Press.

Ekman, P. (1999). Basic emotions. In T. Dalgleish & M. J. Power (Eds.), *Handbook of cognition and emotion* (pp. 45–60). Chichester, UK: Wiley.

Ekman, P., Levenson, R. W., & Friesen, W. V. (1983). Autonomic nervous system activity distinguishes among emotions. *Science, 221,* 1208–1210.

Emde, R. N. (1980). Levels of meaning for infant emotions: A biosocial view. In W. A. Collins (Ed.), *Development of cognition, affect, and social relations: The Minnesota Symposium on Child Psychology* (Vol. 13, pp. 1–37). Hillsdale, NJ: Lawrence Erlbaum Associates.

Fehr, B., & Russell, J. A. (1984). Concept of emotion viewed from a prototype perspective. *Journal of Experimental Psychology, 11,* 464–486.

Feshbach, N. D. (1978). Studies of empathetic behavior in children. In B. A. Maher (Ed.), *Progress in experimental personality research* (Vol. 8, pp. 1–47). New York: Academic.

Frankenhaeuser, M. (1986). A psychobiological framework for research on human stress and coping. In M. H. Appley & R. Trumbull (Eds.), *Dynamics of stress: Physiological, psychological, and social perspectives* (pp. 101–116). New York: Plenum.

Fredrikson, M. (1989). Psychophysiological and biochemical indices in "stress" research: Applications to psychopathology and pathophysiology. In G. Turpin (Ed.), *Handbook of clinical psychophysiology* (pp. 241–279). Chichester: Wiley.

Friedhoff, A. J., & Silva, R. (1998). Catecholamines and behavior. In H. S. Friedman (Ed.) *Encyclopedia of mental health* (Vol. 1, pp. 379–385). San Diego, CA: Academic.

Frijda, N. H. (1986). *The emotions.* Cambridge: Cambridge University Press.

Frijda, N. H. (1993). Moods, emotion episodes, and emotions. In M. Lewis & J. M. Haviland (Eds.), *Handbook of emotions* (pp. 381–403). New York: Guilford.

Frijda, N. H. (1994). Varieties of affect: Emotions and episodes, moods, and sentiments. In P. Ekman & R. J. Davidson (Eds.), *The nature of emotion: Fundamental questions* (pp. 59–67). New York: Oxford University Press.

Fuster, J. M. (1989). *The prefrontal cortex: Anatomy, physiology, and neuropsychology of the frontal lobe* (2nd ed.). New York: Raven.

Goldsmith, H. H. (1993). Temperament: Variability in developing emotion systems. In M. Lewis & J. M. Haviland (Eds.), *Handbook of emotions* (pp. 353–364). New York: Guilford.

Goldsmith, H. H., & Campos, J. J. (1990). The structure of infant temperamental dispositions to experience fear and pleasure: A psychometric perspective. *Child Development, 61,* 1944–1964.

Gray, J. A. (1981). Anxiety as a paradigm case of emotion. *British Medical Bulletin, 37,* 193–197.

Grimm, J. (1997). Physiologische und psychosoziale Aspekte der Fernsehgewalt-Rezeption: TV-Gefühlsmanagement zwischen Angst und Aggressionen. [Physiological and psychosocial aspects of television-violence reception: Mood management between anxiety and aggressiveness.] *Medienpsychologie, 9*(2), 127–166, 177.

Henry, J. P. (1986). Neuroendocrine patterns of emotional response. In R. Plutchik & H. Kellerman (Eds.), *Emotion: Theory, research, and experience: Vol. 3. Biological foundations of emotion* (pp. 37–60). Orlando, FL: Academic.

Hoffman, M. L. (1978). Toward a theory of empathetic arousal and development. In M. Lewis & L. A. Rosenblum (Eds.), *The development of affect* (pp. 227–256). New York: Plenum.

Humphrey, G. (1922). The conditioned reflex and the elementary social reaction. *Journal of Abnormal and Social Psychology, 17,* 113–119.

Isen, A. M. (1984). Toward understanding the role of affect in cognition. In R. S. Wyer & T. K. Srull (Eds.), *Handbook of social cognition* (pp. 179–236). Hillsdale, NJ: Lawrence Erlbaum Associates.

Izard, C. E. (1971). *The face of emotion*. New York: Appleton-Century-Crofts.

Izard, C. E. (1992). Basic emotions, relations among emotions, and emotion-cognition relations. *Psychological Review, 99,* 561–565.

Izard, C. E. (1993). Four systems for emotion activation: Cognitive and non-cognitive processes. *Psychological Review, 100,* 68–90.

James, W. (1884). What is an emotion? *Mind, 9,* 188–205.

Janschek, E., Vitouch, P., & Tinchon, H.-J. (1997). Wer reagiert wie auf Actionfilme?: Versuch einer mehrdimensionalen Typenbildung unter besonderer Berücksichtigung der Medienkompetenz. [Who reacts how to action films?: Attempt at a multidimensional type construction with special consideration of media competency.] *Medienpsychologie, 9*(3), 209–234, 248.

Johnson-Laird, P. N., & Oatley, K. (1992). Basic emotions, rationality, and folk theory. *Cognition and Emotion, 6,* 201–223.

Joseph, R. (1998). Limbic system. In H. S. Friedman (Ed.) *Encyclopedia of mental* health (Vol. 2, pp. 555–569). San Diego, CA: Academic.

Kemper, T. D. (1987). How many emotions are there? Wedding the social and autonomic components. *American Journal of Sociology, 93,* 263–289.

Kemper, T. D. (1993). Sociological models in the explanation of emotions. In M. Lewis & J. M. Haviland (Eds.), *Handbook of emotions* (pp. 41–51). New York: Guilford.

Kubey, R., & Csikszentmihalyi, M. (1990). *Television and the quality of life: How viewing shapes everyday experience.* Hillsdale, NJ: Lawrence Erlbaum Associates.

Laird, J. D. (1974). Self-attribution of emotion: The effects of expressive behavior on the quality of emotional experience. *Journal of Personality and Social Psychology, 29,* 475–486.

Landsberg, L., & Young, J. B. (1992). Catecholamines and the adrenal medulla. In J. D. Wilson & D. W. Foster (Eds.), *Williams textbook of endocrinology* (8th ed., pp. 621–703). Philadelphia: Saunders.

Lazarus, R. S. (1991). *Emotion and adaptation.* New York: Oxford University Press.

LeDoux, J. E. (1987). *Emotion.* In V. B. Mountcastle (Section Ed.) & F. Plum (Vol. Ed.), *Handbook of physiology: A critical, comprehensive presentation of physiological knowledge and concepts, Section 1: The nervous system: Vol. 5. Higher functions of the brain, Part 1* (pp. 419–459). Bethesda, MD: American Physiological Society.

LeDoux, J. E. (1993). Emotional networks in the brain. In M. Lewis & J. M. Haviland (Eds.), *Handbook of emotions* (pp. 109–118). New York: Guilford.

LeDoux, J. E. (1996). *The emotional brain: The mysterious underpinnings of emotional life.* New York: Simon & Schuster.

Leeper, R. W. (1970). The motivational and perceptual properties of emotions as indicating their fundamental character and role. In M. B. Arnold (Ed.), *Feelings and emotions: The Loyola Symposium* (pp. 151–168). New York: Academic.

Levi, L. (1965). The urinary output of adrenalin and noradrenalin during pleasant and unpleasant emotional states: A preliminary report. *Psychosomatic Medicine, 27,* 80–85.

Levi, L. (1967). Sympatho-adrenomedullary responses to emotional stimuli: Methodologic, physiologic and pathologic considerations. In E. Bajusz (Ed.), *An introduction to clinical neuroendocrinology* (pp. 78–105). Basel, Switzerland: Karger.

Lipps, T. (1907). Das Wissen von fremden Ichen. [Knowledge of foreign I-s.] *Psychologische Untersuchungen, 1*(4), 694–722.

MacLean, P. D. (1964). Man and his animal brains. *Modern Medicine, 32,* 95–106.

Malatesta, C. Z., & Haviland, J. M. (1982). Learning display rules: The socialization of emotion expression in infancy. *Child Development, 53,* 991–1003.

Martin, L. L., & Clore, G. L. (Eds.). (2001). *Theories of mood and cognition: A users handbook.* Mahwah, NJ: Lawrence Erlbaum Associates.

Mayne, T. J., & Ramsey, J. (2001). The structure of emotion: A nonlinear dynamic systems approach. In T. J. Mayne & G. A. Bonanno (Eds.), *Emotions: Current issues and future directions* (pp. 1–37). New York: Guilford.

McDougall, W. (1908). *An introduction to social psychology.* London: Methuen.

Mendelsohn, H. (1966). *Mass entertainment.* New Haven, CT: College & University Press.

Millenson, J. R. (1967). *Principles of behavioral analysis.* New York: MacMillan.

Morris, W. N. (with Schnurr, P. P.). (1989). *Mood: The frame of mind.* New York: Springer–Verlag.

Morris, W. N. (1992). A functional analysis of the role of mood in affective systems. In M. S. Clark (Ed.), *Review of personality and social psychology, Vol. 13, Emotion.* Newbury Park, CA: Sage.

Nevin, J. A. (Ed.). (1973). *The study of human behavior: Learning, motivation, emotion, and instinct.* Glenview, IL: Scott, Foresman.

Nowlis, V., & Nowlis, H. H. (1956). The description and analysis of mood. *Annals of the New York Academy of Sciences, 65,* 345–355.

Oatley, K., & Jenkins, J. M. (1996). *Understanding emotions.* Oxford: Blackwell.

Ochsner, K. N., & Feldman Barrett, L. (2001). A multiprocess perspective on the neuroscience of emotion. In T. J. Mayne & G. A. Bonanno (Eds.), *Emotions: Current issues and future directions* (pp. 38–81). New York: Guilford.

Ortony, A., Clore, G. L., & Collins, A. (1988). *The cognitive structure of emotions.* New York: Cambridge University Press.

Panksepp, J. (1998). *Affective neuroscience: The foundations of human and animal emotions.* New York: Oxford University Press.

Plutchik, R. (1962). *The emotions: Facts, theories, and a new model.* New York: Random House.

Plutchik, R. (1970). Emotions, evolution, and adaptive processes. In M. B. Arnold (Ed.), *Feelings and emotions: The Loyola Symposium* (pp. 3–24). New York: Academic.

Plutchik, R. (1980). *Emotion: A psychoevolutionary synthesis.* New York: Harper & Row.

Plutchik, R. (1987). Evolutionary bases of empathy. In N. Eisenberg & J. Strayer (Eds.), *Empathy and its development* (pp. 38–46). Cambridge: Cambridge University Press.

Reisenzein, R., & Schönpflug, W. (1992). Stumpf's cognitive-evaluative theory of emotion. *American Psychologist, 47,* 34–45.

Rolls, E. T. (1999). *The brain and emotion.* Oxford: Oxford University Press.

Roseman, I. (1984). Cognitive determinants of emotion: A structural theory. In P. Shaver (Ed.), *Review of personality and social psychology: Vol. 5. Emotions, relationships, and health* (pp. 11–36). Beverly Hills, CA: Sage.

Schachter, S. (1964). The interaction of cognitive and physiological determinants of emotional state. In L. Berkowitz (Ed.), *Advances in experimental social psychology* (Vol. 1, pp. 49–80). New York: Academic.

Scherer, K. R. (2000). Emotions as episodes of subsystem synchronization driven by nonlinear appraisal processes. In M. D. Lewis & I. Granic (Eds.) *Emotion, development, and self-organization: Dynamic systems approaches to emotional development* (pp. 70–99). New York: Cambridge University Press.

Schwab, F. (2001). Unterhaltungsrezeption als Gegenstand medienpsychologischer Emotionsforschung [Entertainment reception as object of emotion research in media psychology]. *Zeitschrift für Medienpsychologie, 13*(2), 62–72.

Schwarz, N. (1990). Feelings as information: Informational and motivational functions of affective states. In E. T. Higgins & R. Sorrentino (Eds.), *Handbook of motivation and cognition* (pp. 527–559). New York: Guilford.

Sharkey, J. (1993, December). When pictures drive foreign policy: Somalia raises serious questions about media influence. *American Journalism Review,* pp. 14–19.

Smith, G. P. (1973). Adrenal hormones and emotional behavior. In E. Stellar & J. M. Sprague (Eds.), *Progress in physiological psychology* (pp. 299–351). New York: Academic.

Stein, N. L., Trabasso, T., & Liwag, M. (1994). The Rashomon phenomenon: Personal frames and future-oriented appraisals in memory for emotional events. In M. M. Haith, J. B. Benson, R. J. Roberts, & B. F. Pennington (Eds.), Future *oriented processes* (pp. 409–435). Chicago: University of Chicago Press.

Stotland, E. (1969). Exploratory investigations of empathy. In L. Berkowitz (Ed.), *Advances in experimental social psychology* (Vol. 4, pp. 271–314). New York: Academic.

Strongman, K. T. (1996). *The psychology of emotion* (4th ed.). New York: Wiley.

Stumpf, C. (1899). Über den Begriff der Gemühtsbewegung [On the concept of feeling]. *Zeitschrift für Psychologie und Physiologie der Sinnesorgane, 21,* 47–99.

Tan, E. S. (1996). *Emotion and the structure of narrative film: Film as an emotion machine.* Mahwah, NJ: Lawrence Erlbaum Associates.

Thayer, R. E. (1989). *The biopsychology of mood and arousal.* New York: Oxford University Press.

Thayer, R. E. (1996). *The origin of everyday moods: Managing energy, tension, and stress.* New York: Oxford University Press.

Turner, J. H. (1999). Toward a general sociological theory of emotions. *Journal for the Theory of Social Behavior, 29,* 133–162.

Turner, J. H. (2000). *On the origins of human emotions: A sociological inquiry into the evolution of human affect.* Stanford: Stanford University Press.

Vorderer, P., & Knobloch, S. (2000). Conflict and suspense in drama. In D. Zillmann & P. Vorderer (Eds.), *Media entertainment: The psychology of its appeal* (pp. 59–72). Mahwah, NJ: Lawrence Erlbaum Associates.

Watson, D., & Clark, L. A. (1992). On traits and temperament: General and specific factors of emotional experience and their relation to the five-factor model. *Journal of Personality, 60,* 441–476.

Watson, D., & Clark, L. A. (1994). Emotions, moods, traits, and temperaments: Conceptual distinctions and empirical findings. In P. Ekman & R. J. Davidson (Eds.), *The nature of emotion: Fundamental questions* (pp. 89–93). New York: Oxford University Press.

Weinberger, D. R., Berman, K. F., Gold, J., & Goldberg, T. (1994). Neural mechanisms of future-oriented processes: In vivo physiological studies of humans. In M. M. Haith, J. B. Benson, R. J. Roberts, Jr., & B. F. Pennington (Eds.), *The development of future-oriented processes* (pp. 221–242). Chicago: University of Chicago Press.

Weiskrantz, L. (1968). Emotion. In L. Weiskrantz (Ed.), *Analysis of behavioral change* (pp. 50–90). New York: Harper & Row.

Williams, R. B. (1985). Neuroendocrine response patterns and stress: Biobehavioral mechanisms of disease. In R. B. Williams (Ed.), *Perspectives on behavioral medicine: Vol. 2. Neuroendocrine control and behavior* (pp. 71–101). Orlando: Academic.

Zillmann, D. (1978). Attribution and misattribution of excitatory reactions. In J. H. Harvey, W. J. Ickes, & R. F. Kidd (Eds.), *New directions in attribution research* (Vol. 2, pp. 335–368). Hillsdale, NJ: Lawrence Erlbaum Associates.

Zillmann, D. (1983). Transfer of excitation in emotional behavior. In J. T. Cacioppo & R. E. Petty (Eds.), *Social psychophysiology: A sourcebook* (pp. 215–240). New York: Guilford.

Zillmann, D. (1986). Coition as emotion. In D. Byrne & K. Kelley (Eds.), *Alternative approaches to the study of sexual behavior* (pp. 173–199). Hillsdale, NJ: Lawrence Erlbaum Associates.

Zillmann, D. (1988). Mood management: Using entertainment to full advantage. In L. Donohew, H. E. Sypher, & E. T. Higgins (Eds.), *Communication, social cognition, and affect* (pp. 147–171). Hillsdale, NJ: Lawrence Erlbaum Associates.

Zillmann, D. (1991a). Empathy: Affect from bearing witness to the emotions of others. In J. Bryant & D. Zillmann (Eds.), *Responding to the screen: Reception and reaction processes* (pp. 135–167). Hillsdale, NJ: Lawrence Erlbaum Associates.

Zillmann, D. (1991b). Television viewing and physiological arousal. In J. Bryant & D. Zillmann (Eds.), *Responding to the screen: Reception and reaction processes* (pp. 103–133). Hillsdale, NJ: Lawrence Erlbaum Associates.

Zillmann, D. (1994). Mechanisms of emotional involvement with drama. *Poetics, 23,* 33–51.

Zillmann, D. (1996a). The psychology of suspense in dramatic exposition. In P. Vorderer, H. J. Wulff, & M. Friedrichsen (Eds.), *Suspense: Conceptualizations, theoretical analyses, and empirical explorations* (pp. 199–231). Mahwah, NJ: Lawrence Erlbaum Associates.

Zillmann, D. (1996b). Sequential dependencies in emotional experience and behavior. In R. D. Kavanaugh, B. Zimmerberg, & S. Fein (Eds.), *Emotion: Interdisciplinary perspectives* (pp. 243–272). Mahwah, NJ: Lawrence Erlbaum Associates.

Zillmann, D. (1998a). *Connections between sexuality and aggression: Second edition.* Mahwah, NJ: Lawrence Erlbaum Associates.

Zillmann, D. (1998b). The psychology of the appeal of portrayals of violence. In J. H. Goldstein (Ed.), *Why we watch: The attractions of violent entertainment* (pp. 179–211). New York: Oxford University Press.

Zillmann, D. (2000a). Basal morality in drama appreciation. In I. Bondebjerg (Ed.), *Moving images, culture and the mind* (pp. 53–63). Luton, England: University of Luton Press.

Zillmann, D. (2000b). Mood management in the context of selective exposure theory. In M. E. Roloff (Ed.), *Communication yearbook 23* (pp. 103–123). Thousand Oaks, CA: Sage.

Zillmann, D., (2002). News effects. In J. R. Schement (Ed.), *Encyclopedia of communication and information* (pp. 645–651). New York: Macmillan.

Zillmann, D. (in press). Cinematic creation of emotion. In J. D. Anderson & B. Fisher Anderson (Eds.), *Moving image theory: Ecological considerations*. Carbondale, IL: University of Southern Illinois Press.

Zillmann, D., & Brosius, H.-B. (2000). *Exemplification in communication: The influence of case reports on the perception of issues*. Mahwah, NJ: Lawrence Erlbaum Associates.

Zillmann, D., & Gan, S. (1996). Effects of threatening images in news programs on the perception of risk to others and self. *Medienpsychologie: Zeitschrift für Individual- und Massenkommunikation, 8*(4), 288–305, 317–318.

Zillmann, D., & Knobloch, S. (2001). Emotional reactions to narratives about the fortunes of personae in the news theater. *Poetics, 29,* 189–206.

Zillmann, D., Taylor, K., & Lewis, K. (1998). News as nonfiction theater: How dispositions toward the public cast of characters affect reactions. *Journal of Broadcasting & Electronic Media, 42*(2), 153–169.

Zillmann, D., & Vorderer, P. (Eds.). (2000). *Media entertainment: The psychology of its appeal.* Mahwah, NJ: Lawrence Erlbaum Associates.

Zillmann, D., & Zillmann, M. (1996). Psychoneuroendocrinology of social behavior. In E. T. Higgins & A. W. Kruglanski (Eds.), *Social psychology: Handbook of basic principles* (pp. 39–71). New York: Guilford.

Zuckerman, M. (1996). Sensation seeking and the taste for vicarious horror. In J. B. Weaver & R. Tamborini (Eds.), *Horror films: Current research on audience preferences and reactions* (pp. 147–160). Mahwah, NJ: Lawrence Erlbaum Associates.

Author Index

A

B

C

D

E

F

G

H

I

J

K

L

M

N

O

P

Q

R

S

T

U

V

W

Y

Z

Subject Index

A

I

J

K

L

M

N

O

P

Q

R

S

T

U

V

W